Learning Japanese Made Simple

Complete Series Workbook Edition
(4-in-1 Book)

Learn how to Read, Write, and Speak Japanese with Hiragana, Katakana, & Kanji

Beginner's Guide & Integrated Workbook

Dan Akiyama

JAPANESE
FOR BEGINNERS

MADE SIMPLE®

BEGINNER'S GUIDE + INTEGRATED WORKBOOK

LEARN
HIRAGANA
KATAKANA
+ KANJI

JLPT N5 KANJI

ひらがな
カタカナ
漢字

LEARN HOW TO READ, WRITE AND SPEAK JAPANESE

- Comprehensive Grammar, Verb and Particle Guidance
- Culture, Honorifics, Politeness and Formality Explained
- Practice Reading, Writing, and Pronouncing Japanese
- Additional Study Tools, Quiz Revision and Mnemonics
- Hundreds of DIY paper Fashcard templates to cut out.

DAN AKIYAMA

Learning Japanese Made Simple
Complete Series Workbook Edition (4-in-1 Book)

Learn how to Read, Write, and Speak Japanese with Hiragana, Katakana, and Kanji

Beginner's Guide & Integrated Workbook
by Dan Akiyama

ISBN: Print 978-1-7392387-0-4 (Paperback)
First Edition

**Copyright © 2022 by Dan Akiyama.
All Rights Reserved.**

No part of the content within this publication may be reproduced, duplicated, stored in a retrieval system, or transmitted in any form or by any means, electronic, mechanical, photocopying, recording, scanning, or otherwise, except as provided by United States of America copyright law and fair use, without the prior written permission of the Publisher and author. You are not permitted to amend, distribute, sell, use, paraphrase, or quote any part of this publication without the author and Publisher's consent.

Limit of Liability/Disclaimer of Warranty:
The author and Publisher make no representations or warranties with respect to the accuracy or completeness of the contents of this work and expressly disclaim all warranties, including, without limitation, warranties of fitness for a particular purpose. No warranty may be created or extended by sales or promotional materials.

The advice and strategies contained herein may not be suitable for every situation. This work is published and sold with the understanding that the Publisher is not engaged in rendering medical, legal, or other professional advice or services. If professional assistance is required, the services of a competent professional should be sought. Neither the Publisher nor the author shall be liable for any damages arising from the information contained within this publication.

The fact that an individual, organization, or website is referred to in this work as either a citation and/or potential source of further information does not mean that the author or Publisher endorses the information from the individual, organization, or website that may provide, or recommendations that they/it may make.

Furthermore, readers should be aware that any websites listed in this work may have changed or disappeared between when this publication was written and when it is read.

Contents

1 Introduction — 007
- Learning Japanese — 009
- Japanese 'Alphabets' — 011
- Writing Japanese — 013
- About Mnemonics — 016
- Syllables & 'Mora' — 017

2 Hiragana — 019
- Hiragana Chart — 021
- Learning Hiragana — 022

3 Katakana — 095
- Katakana Chart — 097
- Learning Katakana — 098

4 Additional Sounds — 161

5 Japanese Kanji — 169
- The Origins of Kanji — 170
- Why Learn Kanji? — 172
- Kanji & Radicals — 174
- Where to Start — 176
- Identifying Kanji — 180
- Stroke Order — 182
- Kanji Essentials — 184
- About Readings — 186
- Japanese Punctuation — 191

6 JLPT & N5 Kanji — 196
- About the JLPT — 197
- The N5 Kanji — 201
- Quick Reference Charts — 207
- Kanji Numbers — 208
- Time & Date — 226
- People and Things — 246
- Direction & Place — 280
- Common Verbs — 297
- Adjectives & Color — 314

7 Using Japanese — 329
- About Respect & Titles — 330
- Honorific Speech — 332
- Basics of Grammar — 334
- Masu & Desu (Politeness) — 336
- About Uchi/Soto — 338
- Verb Categorization — 339
- Common Conjugations — 340
- Useful Grammar Patterns — 345
- About Particles — 348
- More Particles — 356

8 Extra Study Tools — 357
- Writing Templates — 358
- Mini Flashcard Deck — 379
- Answer Key — 418

Note of Thanks — 421

///////////////////////////////// **PART 1**

Introduction

Welcome to this 4-in-1 edition of the *Learning Japanese Made Simple* workbook. Having an understanding of how the whole writing system works will help you learn how to read, write, and pronounce Japanese logically and systematically. This book is aimed at beginners and starts by covering the elementary **Hiragana** and **Katakana** scripts before studying **Kanji** and how all the pieces come together with **grammar**.

It's a fascinating language that will be enjoyable and satisfying to learn but also presents a challenge compared to other foreign languages. We will start with the basics, as with all of my workbooks, and only introduce extra detail when it is valuable or practical. The guided self-study materials in this workbook will help you reach your goals quickly and efficiently.

By the end, you will have memorized the kana scripts and learned how all the sounds in Japanese are pronounced. You will also learn about lots of useful, everyday kanji - the knowledge typically required for taking the first *Japanese Language Proficiency Test* exam *(JLPT)* at the N5 level.

You will learn how to read, write, and pronounce hundreds of individual characters and understand lots of essential subjects, such as the role of formality, common grammar patterns, particles, hundreds of vocabulary words, and more. In other words, you will be well-equipped to take your Japanese to the next level!

About this Book

This book emphasizes writing practice to learn and remember characters. Most would probably concede that manual handwriting is not required much in any language since most communication has moved into digital and online spaces. Writing skills are not a high priority when learning other foreign languages, such as French or Spanish, but they play a different role when studying one with an entirely new set of characters or letters.

Writing and spaced repetition remain one of the most effective tools for memorization, so this workbook provides space to practice your penmanship. This technique helps to build muscle memory and make information stick, helping you recognize and recall characters' shapes later. Neat written Japanese is an essential skill that you will achieve naturally.

It will help to practice pronouncing each character out loud as you learn to write them in the correct stroke order. The process of repeatedly writing out characters and pronouncing the terminology will help attach sounds to shapes. Mnemonics are valuable tools for learning kanji, so use the space provided on the kana pages to practice - any connection you can make with a sound, shape, or meaning will make characters much easier to remember.

It is always good to begin immersing yourself in the language as soon as possible. Find ways to read, watch, or listen to Japanese language materials, even though you may not understand them. Hearing the sounds will make saying things aloud in Japanese feel less awkward and help improve pronunciation to become more natural-sounding.

How hard is it?

When you learn the right way, *Japanese is not that difficult*. Many of the common problems and frustrations that learners face are caused by simply starting with the wrong strategy. They often choose a difficult study route without knowing that there are other, better ways. *By buying this book, you have already taken a step in the right direction.*

Anybody beginning with a path that involves learning random words or spoken phrases at the start will find themselves confused sooner or later. Without understanding how all the pieces go together, they are likely to waste a lot of time or become discouraged when the difficulty ramps up - *and it will.*

Every aspect of the language works relatively logically, so it makes sense to also take a systematic approach to your studies. This book will help you understand how the whole language works making your study more efficient and saving you lots of time and effort at every stage.

Learning Japanese

Learning Japanese will seem incredibly difficult to do right now, which is why this workbook will start with the basics, introducing more information only when it will be helpful. This chapter will begin with a quick assessment of what lies ahead.

At an elementary level, there are three stages to learning Japanese. Each subsequent level will be more demanding than the previous, relying on the knowledge you gain in the last stage - there is no practical way to skip ahead. That said, there are more and less effective ways to learn about some topics.

1. Learning Kana

What: The kana *'alphabets'* enable you to read and pronounce all Japanese as they effectively spell everything out in a way that's easy to understand.

How: Memorizing the shapes and pronunciations through repetition. There are two sets of 46 basic symbols, plus a few extras to learn afterward. It could take just a day or two but should not be rushed. Practice them frequently, as they are the foundation on which you will build everything else.

2. Acquiring Kanji

What: More complex symbols representing whole words, making up a large part of Japanese - are often pronounced multiple ways and have multiple meanings. *A command of the kana scripts is a pre-requisite for kanji study.*

How: Due to the sheer number of unique characters, they inevitably take longer than learning kana. There are a variety of routes and methods, and, with the right strategy, they do not have to be as tricky as they seem.

3. Adding Grammar

What: Equipped with kanji knowledge *(or a dictionary)*, you can understand lots of Japanese when you learn about sentence structure, how to make other word forms, can recognize particles, and appreciate respectful speech.

How: We will examine different types of words and how to use them; learn about verb conjugations, and explore some of the most useful grammatical patterns that you can start using in everyday Japanese language.

The book is divided into sections to help structure your learning effectively:

Part 1

A brief overview of the Japanese writing system, explaining the different *alphabets* or scripts, and how text is written and read. It's the sort of language that becomes easier as soon as you make a start - this first chapter is short so you can make a start, sooner.

Parts 2, 3 & 4

The second and third chapters will teach you about the two Japanese phonetic *'alphabets,'* **Hiragana** and **Katakana.** Divided into groups of similar-sounding 'letters', to make things a little quicker, you will learn how to write each symbol step by step and how it should sound when spoken. Each group ends with exercises designed to help you memorize the shapes and pronunciations.

Part 5

Beginning with an introduction to the characters that make up most of the Japanese language, you will learn how the **Kanji** writing system originated, how it functions, what makes a kanji, and how to identify any given symbol. This section also details the different ways we can read them, why there are different types of readings, and, later, explore how you might save time and effort when studying kanji.

Part 6

After a brief look at the kanji characters that this book will teach you about, the work begins. Over 100 N5-level kanji have been grouped by theme or word type and have a page dedicated to learning their stroke order, readings, vocabulary words, and more. Some bonus vocabulary has been added between relevant groups, with revision questions to test your knowledge and see where you may need to spend more time.

Part 7

The following section takes things a step further and explains how to bring all of your kanji knowledge together to form real Japanese. You will learn how to assemble characters to make sentences, recognize different types of words, and conjugate verbs so that they show alternate meanings. Whether you have acquired kanji knowledge or not by this stage, a broader appreciation of how the language works can only help.

Part 8

The final section of the book features additional study tools, including some double-sided pages of *flashcards*. These are designed to be cut out and turned into a deck of helpful memory prompts. Feel free to make copies if you prefer not to remove pages. They might not be as large or durable as cards, but they are still handy and save any further cost.

You will also find a small section of extra blank writing grids. I recommend using a separate notepad for practicing Japanese, but these sheets may be handy for repeating characters that you found particularly tricky. My companion writing pads are ideal for this, and they work well with flashcards to check whether you remember stroke orders or just for writing out essential vocabulary.

The 'Alphabets'

You will use **four different types of characters** while learning the language, although *one isn't strictly Japanese*. We will refer to each set as an *'alphabet'* for ease since that is a more familiar concept that will simplify your initial studies. The *main* alphabets are **Hiragana, Katakana, and Kanji,** and they are frequently used together:

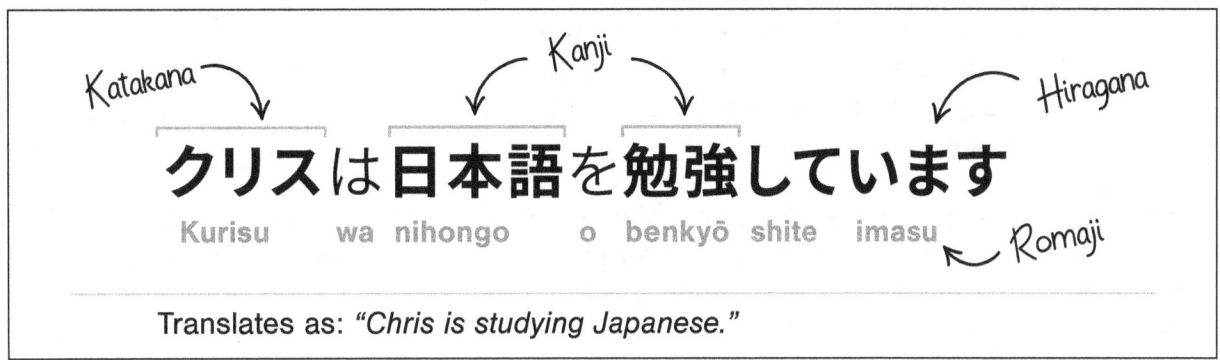

Translates as: *"Chris is studying Japanese."*

Romaji

Romaji is the **English lettering** used to transcribe Japanese symbols into a format that beginners can read and understand. It illustrates the sounds that make up the language when first starting, but it's not truly compatible with Japanese sounds, so often inaccurate. You will find that romaji transcriptions may also vary from one learning resource to another and inconsistencies like that inevitably lead to confusion later.

With very few practical uses beyond learning pronunciations, you should aim to reduce your reliance on romaji and eliminate it from your studies as soon as you can memorize the kana scripts. *After all, you aim to learn Japanese!*

Hiragana & Katakana

The subsequent two alphabets are known collectively as the **Kana scripts**, and they are distinctly *Japanese-looking* by comparison. Each consists of 46 basic characters (or *'letters'*) and they are used frequently throughout the language, often together.

Kana characters are very different from other alphabets. Technically, **Hiragana and Katakana** are **'phonetic syllabaries,'** meaning individual symbols represent a sound instead of a letter. It also means that each character is pronounced as a separate, distinct *'syllable'* when speaking Japanese. They are essential for kanji study *(the fourth character system)*.

Japanese writing typically contains characters from each of the hiragana, katakana, and kanji scripts, although we never mix hiragana and katakana within a single word. You will soon recognize which is which, but they are easy to tell apart when you look at the general shapes:

Hiragana tend to have more rounded shapes and are drawn or written with curved, sometimes sweeping, lines *(a little like cursive handwriting)*. Katakana generally have more angular or pointy shapes, by comparison:

The two sets of kana represent the same sounds, but each script has different uses within the language. Very briefly, hiragana is used to show how to pronounce kanji *(effectively spelling them out)* and also to show grammatical information. On the other hand, Katakana is used to spell words from outside Japan - *foreign vocabulary, such as names, objects, brands, etc., from overseas* - and for spelling your name. Later in the book, you will learn more about the different ways in which you can use both of the kana scripts.

Kanji

Japanese Kanji characters are *extremely numerous* compared to the kana, and there are tens of thousands in existence, with more created over time. To be considered literate in Japan, one must memorize over two thousand, but you can start reading lots of everyday Japanese with a knowledge of *just a few hundred*.

The kanji writing system is very different from the kana scripts, as the characters represent large blocks of meaning and vocabulary - for the most part, verbs and nouns. Essentially, they are the types of words that make up most of any language. Some of the characters are simple in appearance, even resembling the kana in some instances, but lots of kanji are far more complex-looking. Kanji are also combined to make additional words with new, often related meanings.

Initially adopted from the Chinese language, Japanese kanji often have more than one meaning, and most will usually have several different pronunciations. It's easy to see why Japanese is considered one of the most challenging languages to learn. The writing system works relatively logically, making it easier to study than you may think.

Writing in Japanese

In addition to helping with memorization, the careful writing of characters or texts is a part of learning Japanese. Both the way and order in which we draw lines can affect the shape and legibility of your writing. Before you begin learning about hiragana, the following pages provide some practical information about Japanese text and writing.

Text Direction

When Japan first imported the kanji writing system from China, it adopted the vertical writing configuration, show to the right *(A)*. Vertical text is written and read in columns, starting in the upper right, from top to bottom, and from right to left. The spine of all books, magazines, and newspapers with vertical text is positioned on the right side. *They are, effectively, read back to front compared to books written in English.*

Modern Japanese uses the more familiar horizontal writing direction *(B)*. Text is read and written in rows, from *left to right*, and top to bottom, as in European languages that use the Roman lettering system.

The text direction tends to be apparent from the line spacing, creating a gap for certain types of notation. *You can read more about this in a later chapter on kanji.*

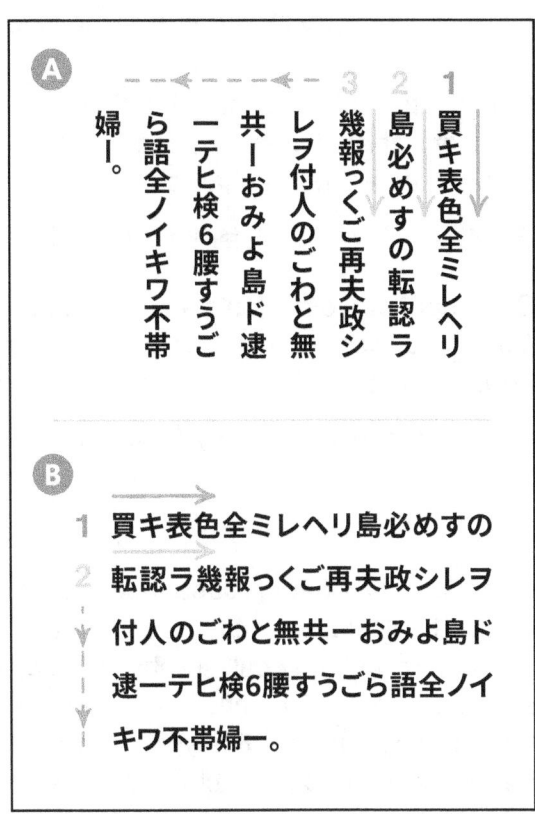

Above: the same dummy text in (A) vertical and (B) horizontal writing directions.

Stroke Order

The lines that make up Japanese characters are all drawn in a set order. You will learn the correct way to write individual kana and develop muscle memory through practice.

In most cases, two rules apply: we start in the upper left of a symbol, and make strokes from left to right, top to bottom until reaching the lower right.

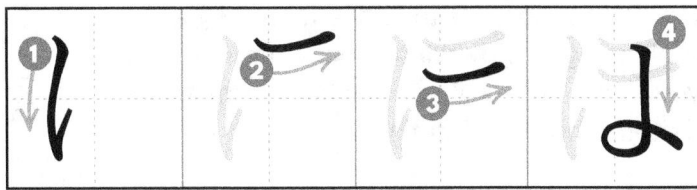

Some slightly extended rules apply to kanji, but the same general steps still apply.

Text Styles

Japanese characters can be presented in a wide variety of styles, from ornate, brushed calligraphy, to the contemporary, bold typefaces featured on packaging designs. While words and characters may have a completely different appearance from one place to another, they always mean the same thing.

Just as there is a wide range of fonts or typefaces available for *Roman* lettering, the style of Japanese symbols can be altered to suit different styles, tones, and designs. There are two types of system font at a basic level with slight but notable differences:

Serif fonts feature decorative flourishes and lines of varied thickness, replicating details found in handwritten characters:

- Similar style to: [**Times New Roman**]

Sans-serif or *Gothic* fonts are more uniform or *'plain,'* with consistent line thicknesses and no added decoration:

- Similar style to [**Century Gothic**]

Above: kanji 日本語 means "Japanese (language)"

Like any language, Japanese handwriting comes in all shapes and sizes, both tidy and... *less so.* As with any calligraphy, you can often see *how* characters have been written, and the more writing practice you do, the easier it becomes to recognize characters written by other people:

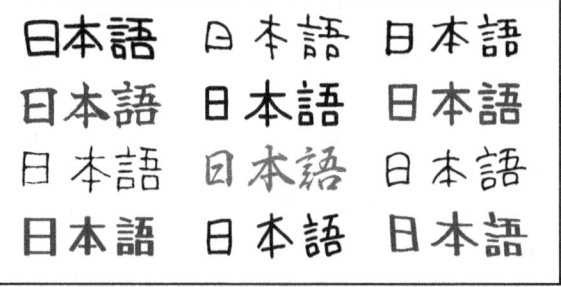

Bold and modern fonts provide lots of options for contemporary designs. Some can be pretty abstract, but most make for effective display typography. Decorative flourishes tend to be more for the style than they are for replicating handwriting. The characters that you know are easily understood, with shapes that are more well-defined:

Kana and kanji can look significantly different without losing their meaning, as long as their overall *proportion and shapes remain the same* relative to the other characters.

Stroke Types

There are three distinctly different types of mark that you can make with your pen. It may be tricky to emulate these shapes unless using a a brush-tipped pen and, in some ways, this style of writing is comparable with cursive handwriting, so not *essential*.

Referred to as a *'tome'* or *'stop stroke'*, from 止める (とめる), or *Tomeru*, which means "to stop", these lines have clearly defined start and end points. Your pen or pencil is brought to a hard stop before lifting from the page:

The second type of mark, known as a *'sweep'* or *'harai'*, comes from the Japanese 払う (はらう), or *Harau*, meaning "to sweep". It also features a well-defined start point but as you approach the end of the stroke, you would flick your pen from the paper. The line should continue in the same direction, slowly trailing off before lifting completely from the page:

Typically referred to as a *'hane'*, from the Japanese 跳ねる (はねる), or *Haneru*, which means "to jump". These strokes are confident lines where your pen or pencil is flicked from the paper, usually in the opposite direction:

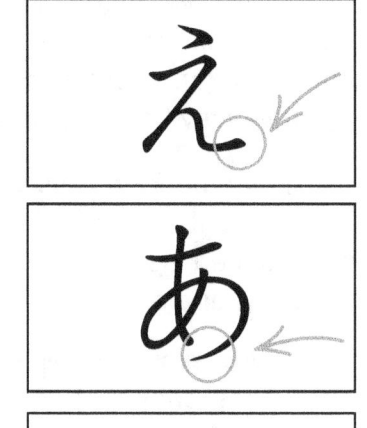

Most people use a ballpoint pen or pencil to write, making it difficult to achieve this level of accuracy. Unless you intend to practice more traditional styles of calligraphy, concentrate on the shape of your kana characters before addressing these details.

Writing in this Book

This workbook is for writing in, and while the paper is relatively good quality, you should try to avoid using any markers or pens with especially wet ink that is prone to bleeding. The pages are better suited to ballpoint pens, pencils, or even gel-based stationery, which should not transfer to the pages beneath. *You can test your writing tools in the spaces below, checking how they affect the following pages:*

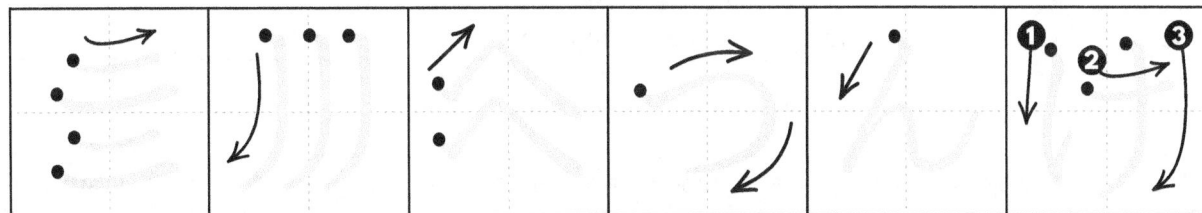

Once you have learned and practiced the kana, it could be worth investing in a notebook with a high-quality paper for advanced studies. A traditional brush-style pen can make your Japanese writing more natural-looking but require more specialist types of paper.

About Mnemonics

Mnemonics are simply tools that can aid with memorization. They are particularly effective for those learning Japanese, and we use them to remember what each of the characters represents.

Essentially, we can either associate new information with something we already know or develop a mechanism to prompt our brain to recall what we are learning. The kana scripts are visual representations of sounds, so we create mnemonics based on their shapes. An example may help to illustrate the point:

The hiragana あ represents an *'a-'* or *'ah'* sound. We transcribe it as equivalent to the letter 'a' in romaji, pronounced as a short *'ah,'* similar to the *'a'* in car, father, or apple.

It may be easier to remember if you visualize あ as having the shape of an apple *(also starting with the letter 'a')*. The shapes of the letters *'A'* and *'a'* also hide within the character あ. It doesn't matter how vague or obvious the connection, so long as it will remind you that あ = a / or an 'a- sound.'

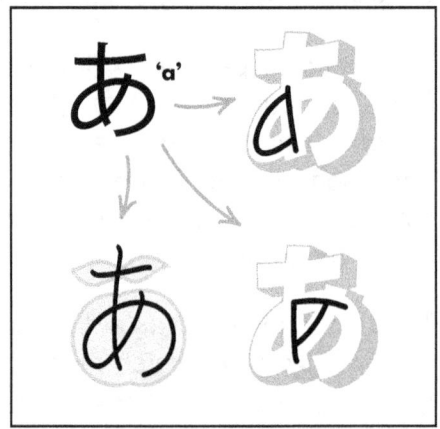

Examine the shape of each new symbol and the sound it represents. Look for any sort of immediate connections that can be made between the romaji version, the pronunciation, and its general appearance. You may need to think outside the box for some shapes, but even the most abstract ideas, once visualized a certain way, are not forgotten as quickly, and *that's the whole idea!*

Another example *(right)* shows a mnemonic created for the hiragana け *(or 'ke')*, pronounced in a similar way to the *"ke-"* in the word *"keg."* The character has a shape that looks a little like a barrel or *keg of beer*:

One of the more *obvious* mnemonics now, this time for the hiragana character の *(or 'no')*, which sounds and looks similar to the *"no-"* in the word *"nose."* This shape could be compared to a *'no smoking'* sign too:

Mnemonics may not work for everybody and can hamper progress for some learners. Some of the examples you find elsewhere will seem inaccurate or silly, putting people off their use. Try to come up with personal visualizations before dismissing them altogether. Even if you only recall a character from an especially bad mnemonic, it will have served its purpose and helped you to remember.

About 'Syllables'

Japanese is one of the few languages where pronunciation is based on timing and rhythm. We structure sounds around a system of **'mora,'** which are simply timing units in the context of language and speech. For ease, you can think of **'morae'** *(the plural of 'mora')* as *beats.* A *'moraic system'* organizes sound units differently to languages based on syllables, such as English.

Each kana character represents one syllable sound, and they all take one *mora*, or one *beat*, to pronounce. Words written with two kana take twice as much time to pronounce as one kana*, and those with three or four kana are three or four beats long. The actual amount of time is unimportant and will vary from one person to another, depending on how fast they talk.

Above: 3 Syllable Word, 3 Mora.

If you're wondering the difference between a syllable and a mora, **syllables** are broad chunks of sound that can be of different lengths. Each syllable has a vowel in the middle, with consonants on one or both sides. **Morae** are smaller, timed units of sound that set an underlying rhythm by which we pronounce all Japanese sounds.

In the example (*right*), the kana have separate sounds that we say over two distinct beats in the Japanese pronunciation. The English pronunciation has just one syllable because the 'n,' without a vowel, attaches to the 'ka-' sound. Syllables in Japanese can contain multiple morae, but mora can have only one syllable sound:

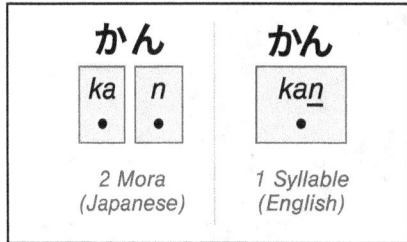

To further illustrate the difference: the Japanese word for *'teacher'* is 先生, *or 'Sensei.'* This is a word that's also used in the English language to describe martial arts teachers. There are two units of sound *(two syllables)* in the English pronunciation, *"sen-say."* We spell the kanji *'reading'* (pronunciation) using four hiragana, so it's four morae long and said in 4 equal beats. *Morae are the way that we differentiate between long and short syllables:*

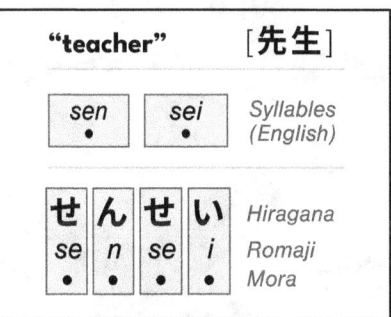

We still speak Japanese in syllables, but morae dictate the timing with which each sound is made. We pronounce individual sounds at a fixed rate (at regular intervals), all roughly equal length. Hopefully, that should make some sense, but it may take some time and practice with the language to fully understand how mora work.

* Two characters are not *always* pronounced as two morae, but you will learn more about special *'combination kana'* and their sounds in a later chapter.

/////////////////////////////// **PART 2**

Hiragana

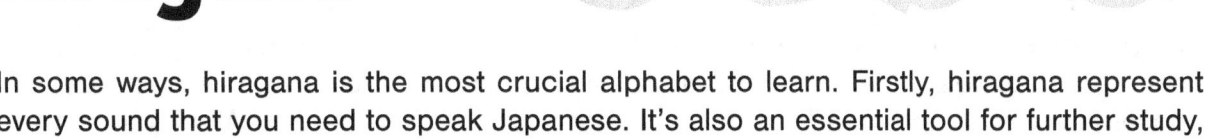

In some ways, hiragana is the most crucial alphabet to learn. Firstly, hiragana represent every sound that you need to speak Japanese. It's also an essential tool for further study, as we use it to read all of the kanji, effectively *'spelling'* kanji words out with sounds.

Eventually, you will use hiragana across the whole writing system as they are suffixed to kanji (Japanese words), like verbs and adjectives, to provide extra information. Later still, you will use hiragana as particles to add structure to sentences and implement grammar. Before looking at any of those topics, the most important thing you can do is learn the alphabet.

As you work your way through this chapter, pay particular attention to how characters are pronounced. The *'alphabet'* in the following chapter represents the same sounds. Doing a thorough job here could save lots of time later.

The chart to the right shows all of the **46 basic hiragana symbols** you are about to learn. You should see that romaji vowels are written to one side, with consonant letters above, and most symbols follow a consistent pattern where two sounds are combined - we take a consonant (top row) and add a vowel sound afterward (right column), with just one exception.

This pattern will become your key to mastering the pronunciation of most hiragana. The basic vowel sounds in the right column are carried across the chart, with subsequent consonant sounds added in front to pronounce the others characters. All characters in the 'A-row' will sound similar, *e.g. ka, sa, ta, etc.*

Traditional Japanese texts are written and read from top to bottom, and from right to left, column by column. This chart should be read the same way but, in reality, you will find everyday modern Japanese texts are written from left to right - just like in English and other European languages.

Over the following pages, you will learn the alphabet in groups, roughly column by column. Learning the letters in chunks will make it more manageable. Each block of letters ends with a revision section to test your memory and determine where you might need more practice.

Notes:

* ん iis the only character in this table that we pronounce as a syllable without adding any of the vowel sounds.

** を is a *"particle"* and is used for grammar. We write it as *"wo"*, but it is transcribed in romaji as either *"o"* or *"wo"*.

Hiragana

	a	i	u	e	o	
	あ a	い i	う u	え e	お o	p. 022
k	か ka	き ki	く ku	け ke	こ ko	p. 030
s	さ sa	し shi	す su	せ se	そ so	p. 038
t	た ta	ち chi	つ tsu	て te	と to	p. 046
n	な na	に ni	ぬ nu	ね ne	の no	p. 055
h	は ha	ひ hi	ふ fu	へ he	ほ ho	p. 061
m	ま ma	み mi	む mu	め me	も mo	p. 069
y	や ya		ゆ yu		よ yo	p. 075
r	ら ra	り ri	る ru	れ re	ろ ro	p. 081
w	わ wa		ん *n		を **wo	p. 087

H1. The Vowel Column

The first column of the basic hiragana chart is arguably the most important. Learning how to pronounce all five characters in this group properly is going to make the rest much easier. They set you up with sounds that are used across the whole alphabet so it is worth spending time to practice these well.

Symbols in this learning block.

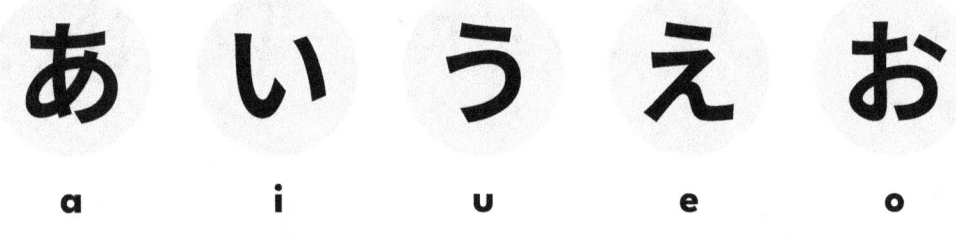

Pronunciation

Each of the vowel characters have a short, sharp pronunciation and these sounds should not drawn out or elongated. For example, the first symbol あ is pronounced as a short *'ah'* sound (like the *'a'* in *'apple'*) and not as *'ahh'*.

The second symbol い is shown in romaji as *'i'* but never pronounced like *'I' (or, eye)*. It always has a shortened 'ee' sound, similar to the *'i'* in *'igloo'*.

When you pronounce the 'oo' sound for the third character, 'u' or う, your lips make a round shape and move forwards - try saying the word 'pool' once or twice. This is less pronounced with the Japanese *'u'* sound, and the *'oo'* sound is shorter.

The sound for the character え or *'e'* is similar to normal pronunciation in the middle of a word. It is a short *'eh'* sound, *like the 'e' in bed, tell, send, and so on.*

Lastly, お is the Japanese vowel sound for *'o'* and it is pronounced as *'oh'*, *like the 'o' in 'no' or 'original'.*

Similar to the 'a' sound in car, like 'ah'.

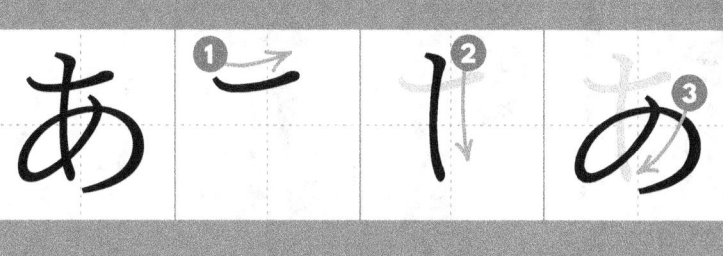

Practice writing あ by tracing these characters, using **three** strokes.

Try to maintain accurate shapes while writing あ on a smaller scale.

Mnemonic.

Examples.
- Shape of an <u>a</u>pple
- Contains letter 'a'

い

i — Sounds like 'i' in king, or 'ee' in cheek.

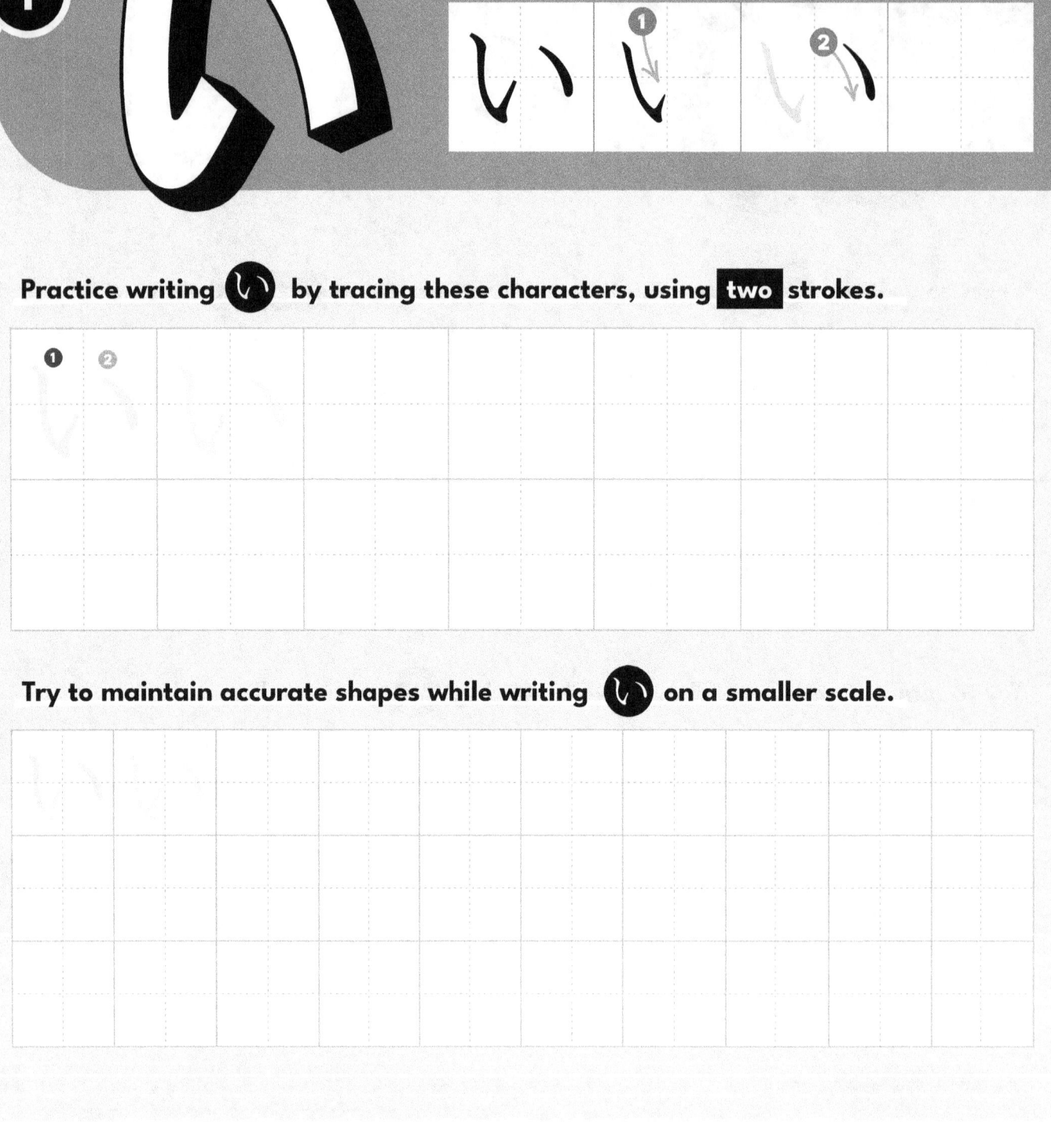

Practice writing い by tracing these characters, using two strokes.

Try to maintain accurate shapes while writing い on a smaller scale.

Mnemonic.

Examples.
- Letter 'i' x 2
- Picture two <u>fee</u>t
- Pair of <u>ee</u>ls

u / う

Similar to 'oo' but like the 'ue' in true.

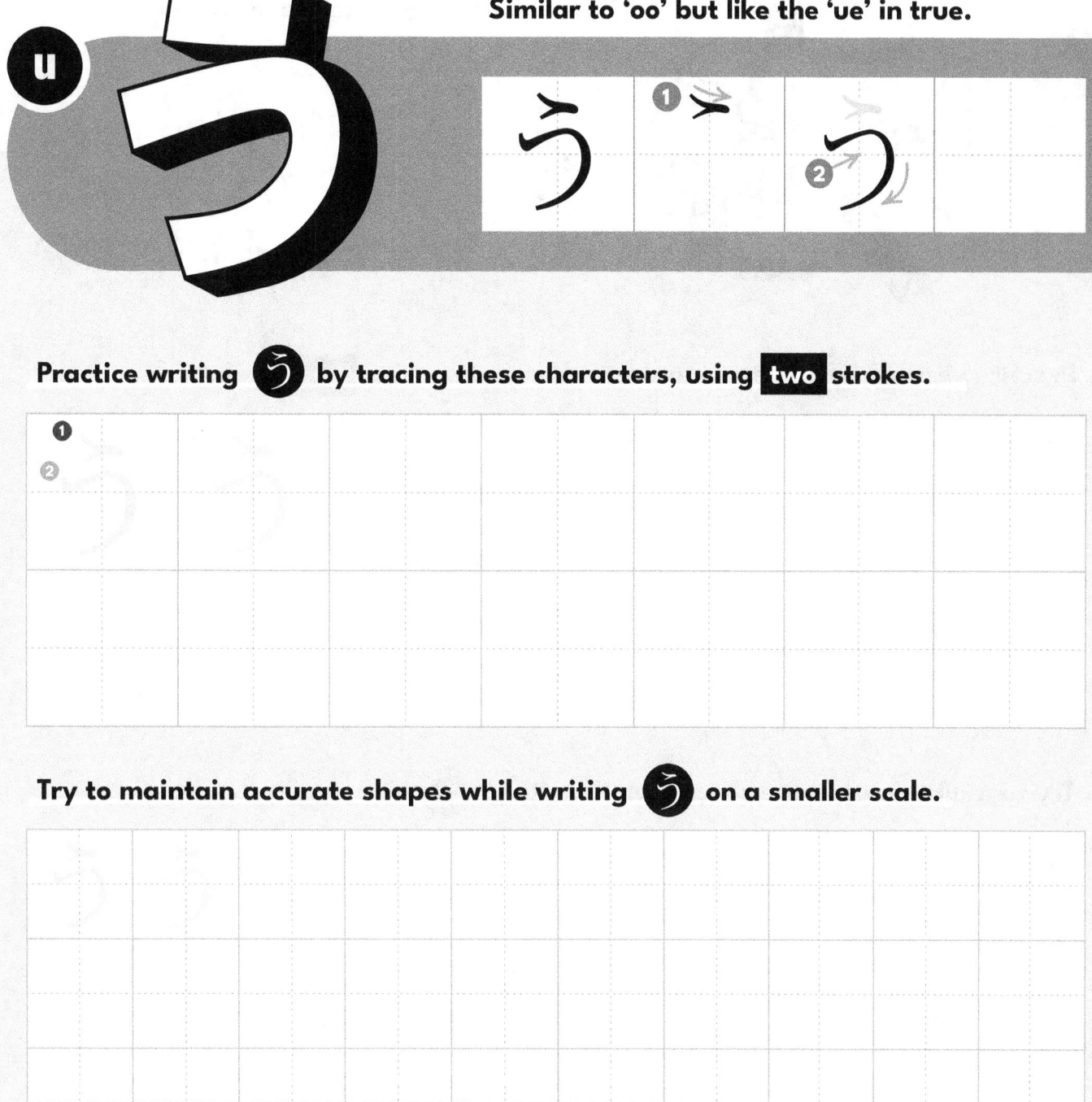

Practice writing う by tracing these characters, using two strokes.

Try to maintain accurate shapes while writing う on a smaller scale.

Mnemonic.

Examples.

- Sideways letter 'u'
- Imagine an open mouth eating f<u>oo</u>d

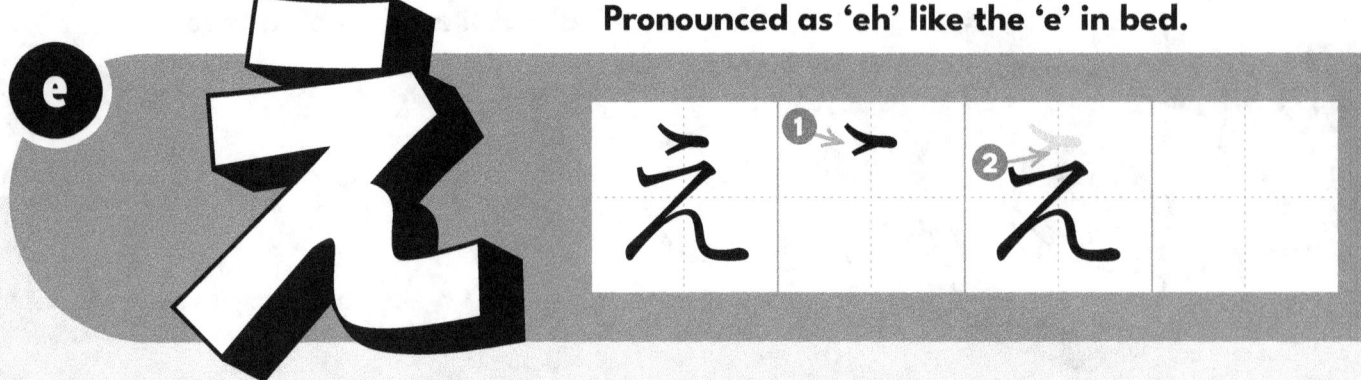

Pronounced as 'eh' like the 'e' in bed.

Practice writing え by tracing these characters, using two strokes.

Try to maintain accurate shapes while writing え on a smaller scale.

Mnemonic.

Examples & ideas.
- Looks energetic, like a running man
- Shape of exotic bird

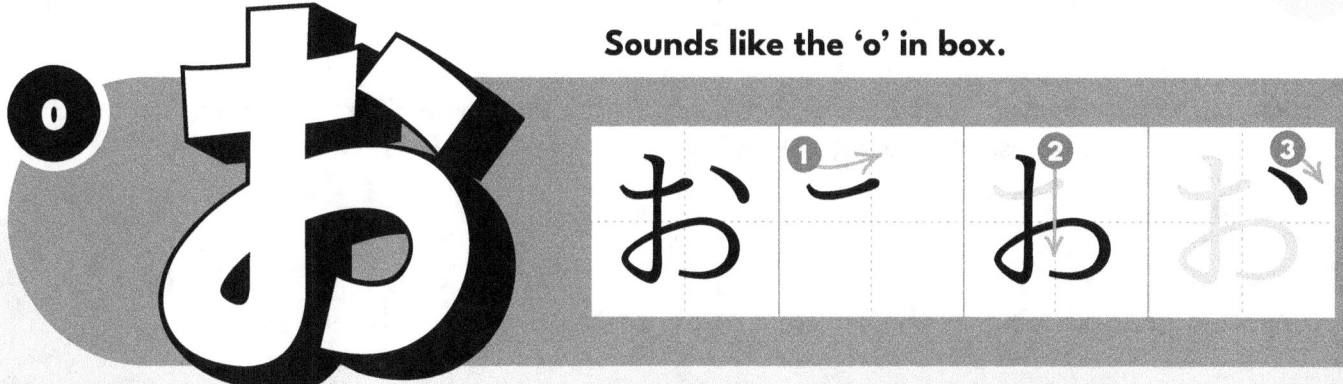

Sounds like the 'o' in box.

Practice writing お by tracing these characters, using three strokes.

Try to maintain accurate shapes while writing お on a smaller scale.

Mnemonic.

Examples.
- Picture an <u>O</u>live <u>o</u>n a stick
- Contains letter 'o'

How good is your memory? This exercise should be easy but try to write the romaji for each of these hiragana in the boxes below - without looking back at the previous pages.

Practice pronouncing each symbol as you write the romaji beneath.

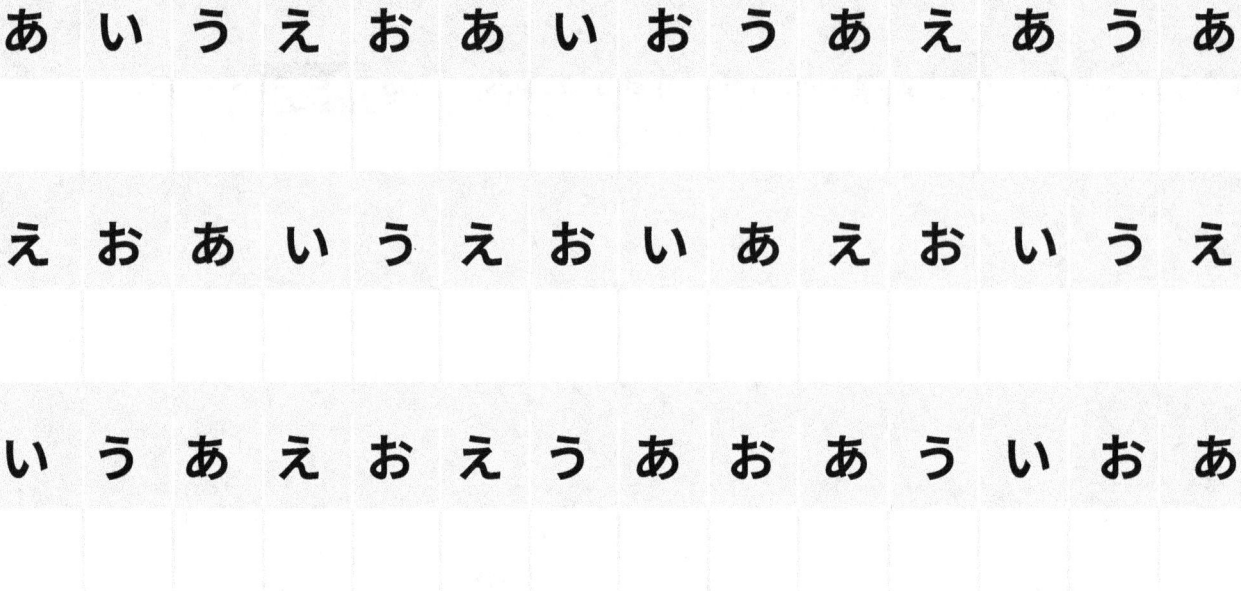

Take a break for 5 minutes, and then do the same for these symbols too.

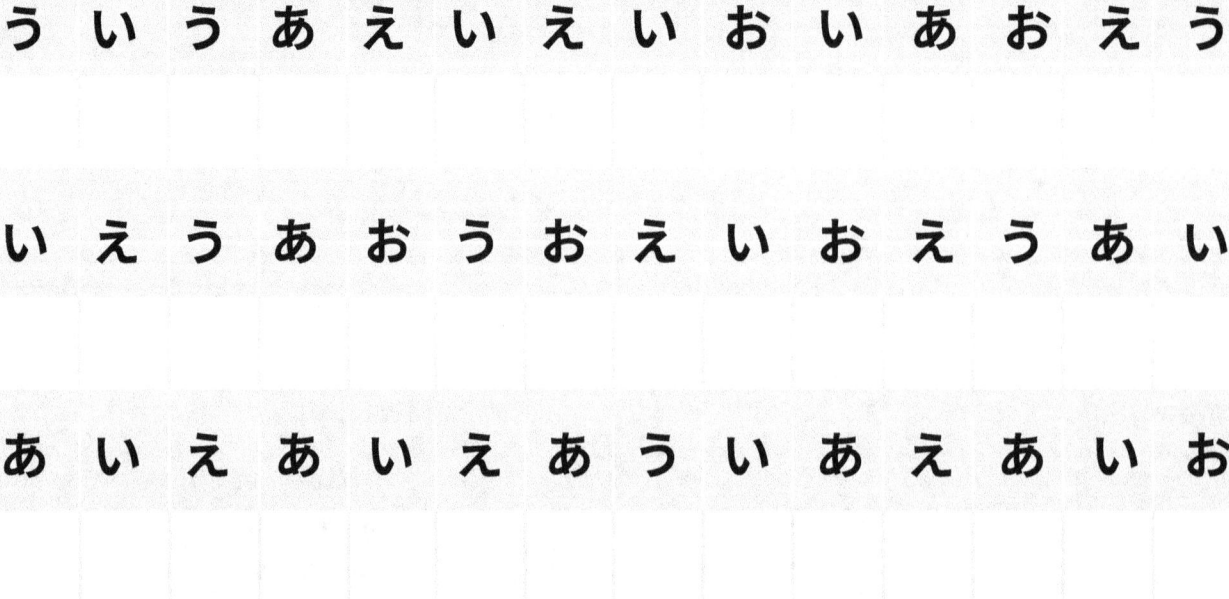

Reading Practice

With the ability to recognize the sounds that each character represents, you can start to read Japanese words. Reading is a great way to practice the language and simultaneously collect new vocabulary. You should try to practice your pronunciation at the same time by reading aloud.

When we read Japanese words, each *'syllable sound'* should take the same length of time to say. When we write characters together to form words, we pronounce each character one after the other - the sounds are not usually* merged. For example, the term **あい** *(meaning love)* is pronounced as *'a-i'* so that both sounds can be heard *("ah-ee")*.

The pronunciation of vowels like *'a'* and *'i'* often changes when they are joined together in English words. Compare how you pronounce the word *"man"* to the word *"main"* or how the vowels sound when you say *"bit," "bat,"* and *"bait."* Some describe Japanese as more straightforward to learn as a foreign language than English because what you see is often what you say.

We can write several words using just those five hiragana you have learned so far. Some examples are shown below, with space to write the romaji for each:

あう		to meet	あい		love/ indigo
いえ		house	あお		blue
おい		nephew	ああ		ah! / oh!
うえ		up/above	いい		good
いう		to say	おう		chase/King

* Certain letter combinations can be written and pronounced differently. You will learn more about these later in this book.

H2. The K Column

The second column of the chart has similar pronunciation to the vowel column. All that is needed to pronounce these characters is a *'k-'* sound in front of the vowel sounds. In other words, the *'eh'* sound of え becomes a *'keh'* sound, and so on.

Symbols in this learning block.

Pronunciation

The *'k-'* sound that you add to each of the vowel sounds is made in much the same way as in English. Your tongue is pressed up into the upper part of the mouth, towards the back of your mouth.

This is a *'voiceless'* consonant sound, meaning that your vocal chords are not used when you say it out loud. The sound is made as you push air through them and out of your mouth. These types of sounds have relatively high levels of aspiration when pronounced by an English speaker.

Aspiration is just the name for the force that is applied to air being pushed out of your mouth. You can feel the level of aspiration your normal *'k-'* sound has by holding your hand in front of your mouth and saying words like *'key'* or *'kelp'*. The real Japanese *'k-'* sound is not as strong, so try to hold back some of that force as you pronounce the sounds.

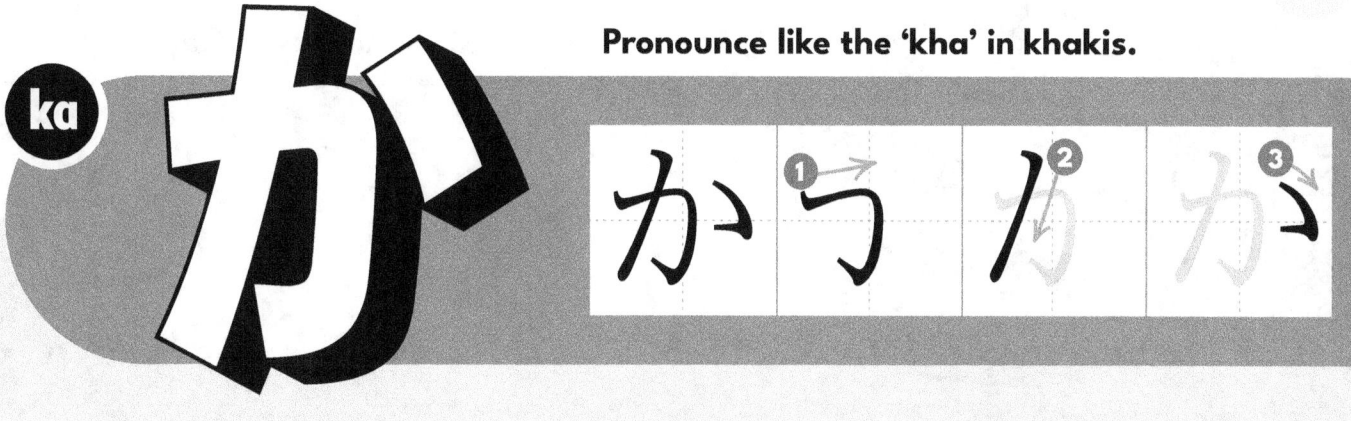

ka — Pronounce like the 'kha' in khakis.

Practice writing か by tracing these characters, using three strokes.

Try to maintain accurate shapes while writing か on a smaller scale.

Mnemonic.

Examples.
- Letter 'k' shape with piece broken off
- Picture kicking a <u>can</u> up in the air.

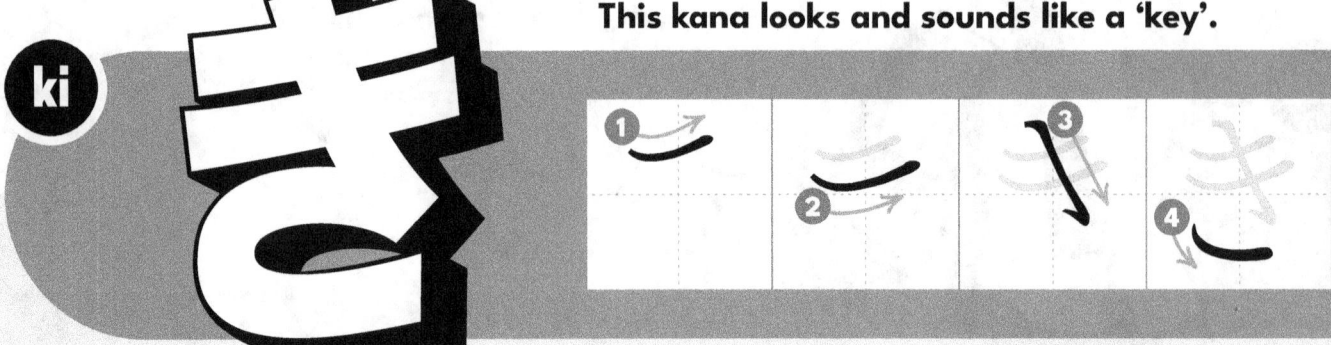

This kana looks and sounds like a 'key'.

Practice writing ぎ the correct way, with four* strokes (not three).

Try to maintain accurate shapes while writing ぎ on a smaller scale.

Mnemonic.

Examples.

- Looks like a key, for the '<u>ki</u>' sound

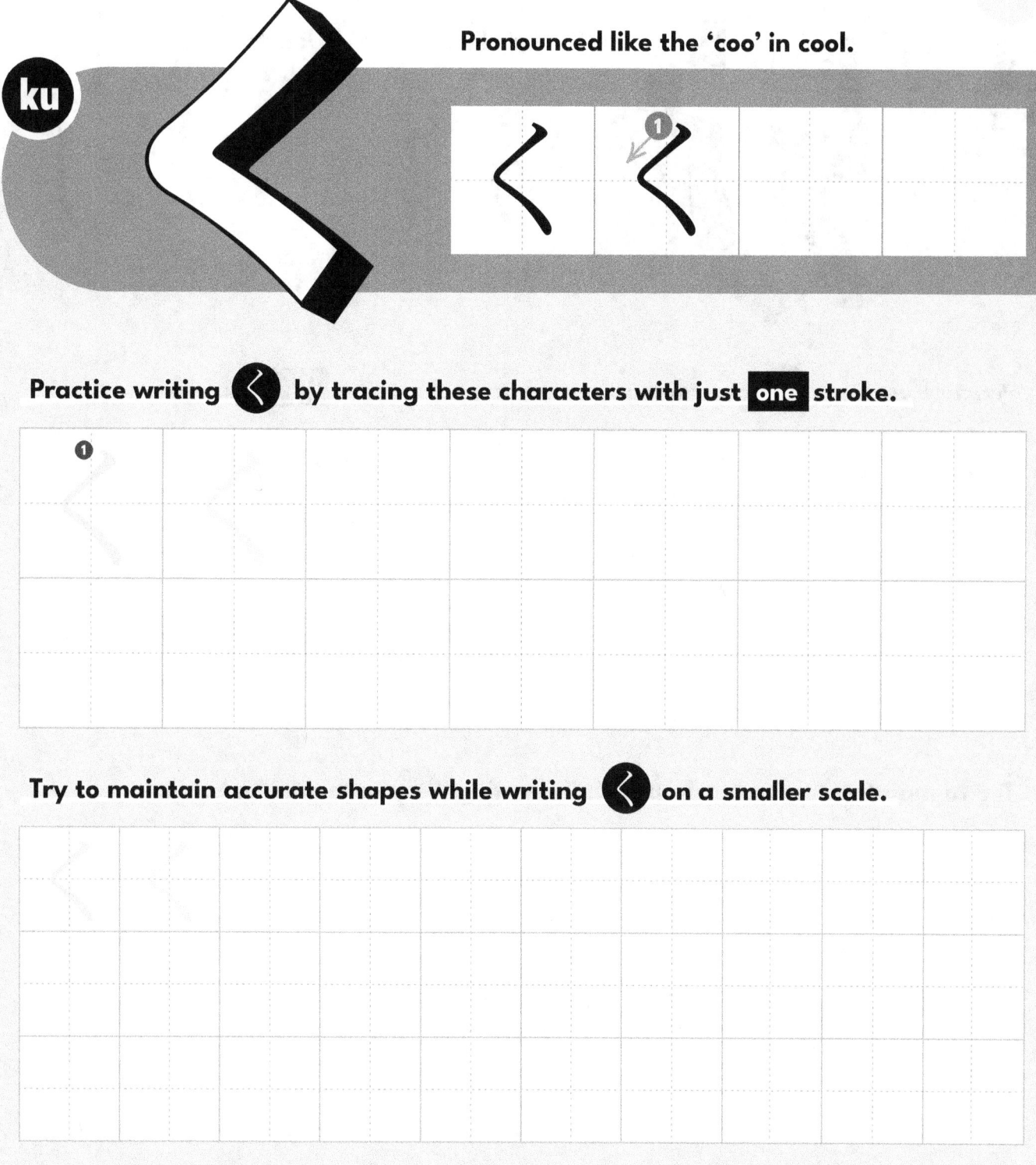

ku

Pronounced like the 'coo' in cool.

Practice writing く by tracing these characters with just **one** stroke.

Try to maintain accurate shapes while writing く on a smaller scale.

Mnemonic.

Examples.
- Picture the beak of a cuckoo bird.
- Or any <u>coo</u>-ing bird

ke け

Sounds like the 'ke' in kettle.

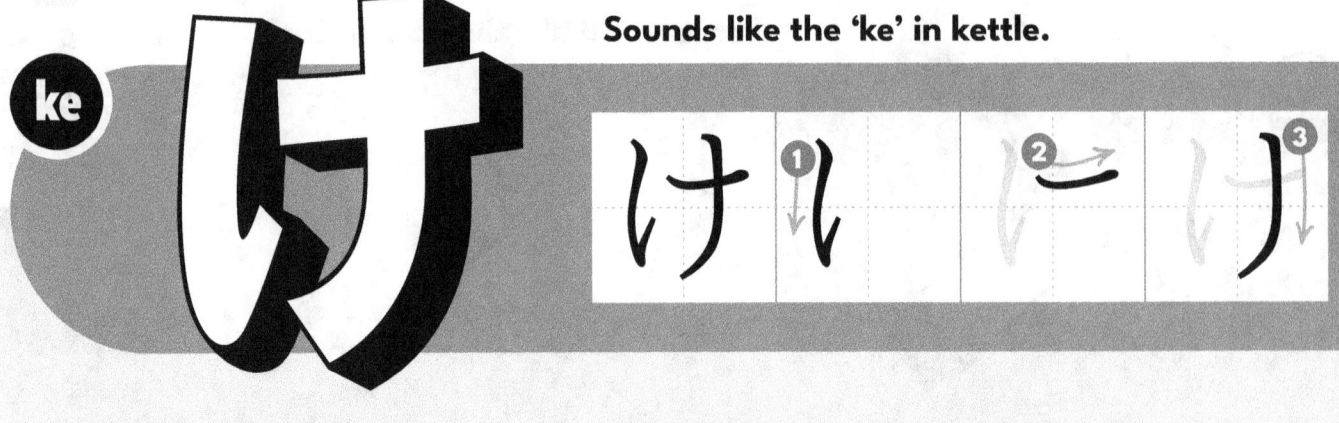

Practice writing け by tracing these characters, using three strokes.

Try to maintain accurate shapes while writing け on a smaller scale.

Mnemonic.

Examples.
- Picture as a barrel shape, or <u>keg</u>
- Could be a broken <u>kettle</u>

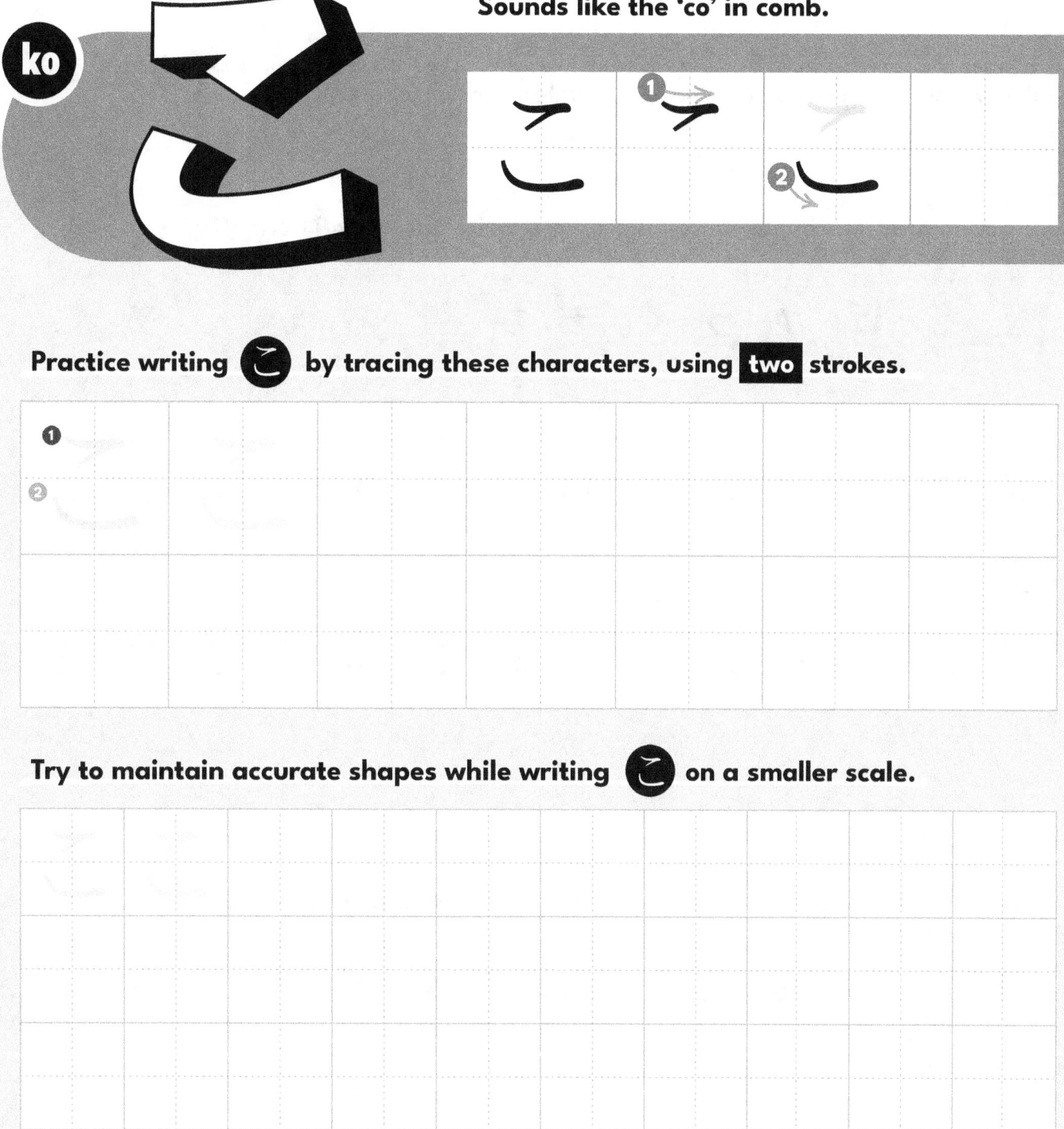

ko

Sounds like the 'co' in comb.

Practice writing こ by tracing these characters, using two strokes.

Try to maintain accurate shapes while writing こ on a smaller scale.

Mnemonic.

Examples.
- Could resemble a round coin shape
- Maybe a corner?
- Rolling can of cola?

This set of exercises should be more challenging than the previous set, as it includes all ten of the hiragana you have learned. Once again, write the romaji for the characters below.

Practice pronouncing each symbol as you write the romaji beneath.

え う け か う く き か け お い く あ こ

え こ か お け こ お え く か け あ こ お

く き い お か く こ あ き い け き け き

Take a 5-minute break, and then do the same for this set of symbols too.

き か け お え こ け い か く き い え く

く け お か こ お く か お あ き お く う

い こ う こ け お え き く か き あ こ け

Practice reading and writing words with characters from all group so far.

あい — love		あう — meet	
うえ — above / top		こえ — voice	
お — hill		かく — write	
きく — hear / ask		おけ — wooden bucket	
こけ — moss		かお — face / honor	
いけ — pond		あき — autumn	
かう — buy		いう — say	
えき — station		あかい — red	
いく — go		あおい — blue	
ここ — here		きおく — memory	

H3. The S Column

The *[consonant + vowel]* pattern applies to most groups of symbols, but not all. This third group contains the first of a few exceptions you will meet along the way. Fortunately, they are not any more difficult to pronounce.

Symbols in this learning block.

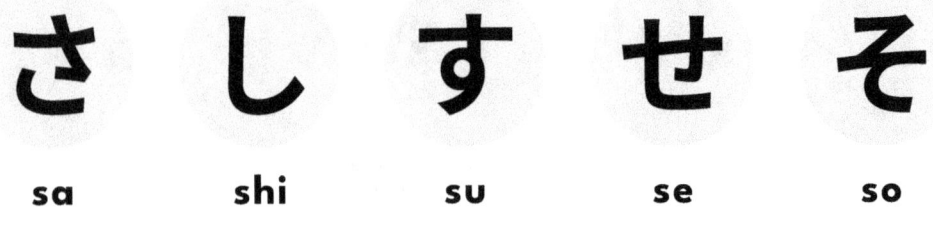

Pronunciation

With the exception of the second character, the symbols in this column follow the usual pattern. Simply add a normal *'s-'* sound to the vowels you have learned.

The exception here is し or *'shi'* which is pronounced slightly differently. Instead of saying *'si' (like 'see')* this character is *'shi'* and sounds like the English word *'she'*.

Accurate pronunciation of a Japanese 'sh-' is not far from the English 'sh' and it is unlikely to cause problems. If you want to achieve a more accurate sound, the tongue would need to make a slightly different shape. You may be able to feel the difference by saying the words *'he'* and *'she'* alternately a few times. The tongue tends to be pushed upwards with a bend in the middle when you say 'he'. Introduce more of this tongue shape into your pronunciation of *'shi'*.

sa

Sounds like the 'sa-' in sarcasm.

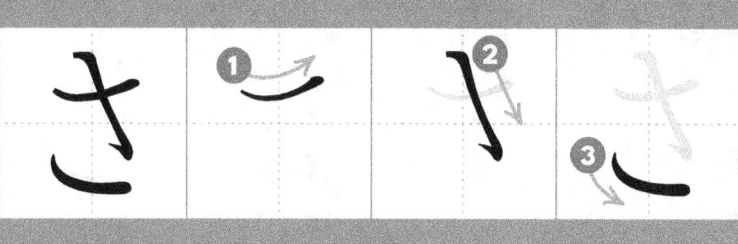

Practice writing さ the proper way, with three* strokes (not two).

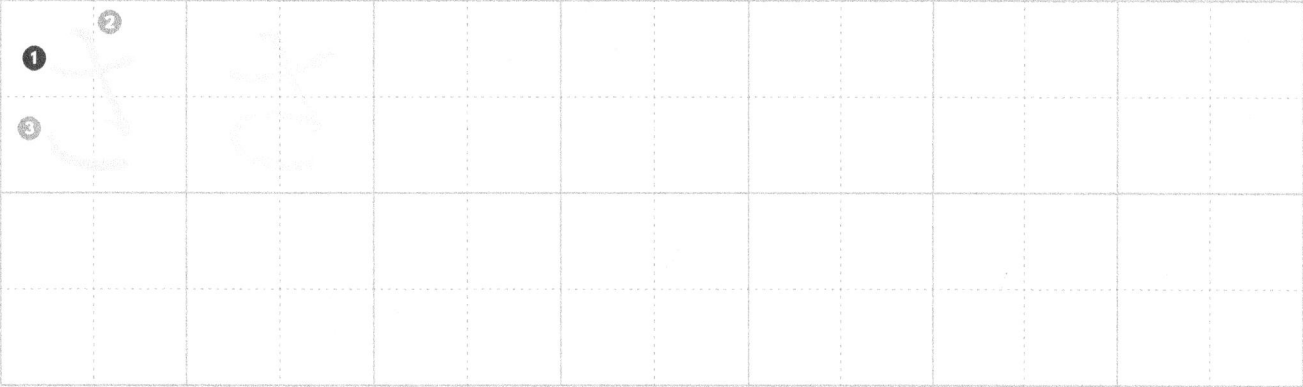

Try to maintain accurate shapes while writing さ on a smaller scale.

Mnemonic.

Examples.
- Imagine the shapes as a <u>sa</u>d face?
- Similar to KI, but not the <u>same</u>

shi

Sounds exactly like the 'shi' in sashimi.

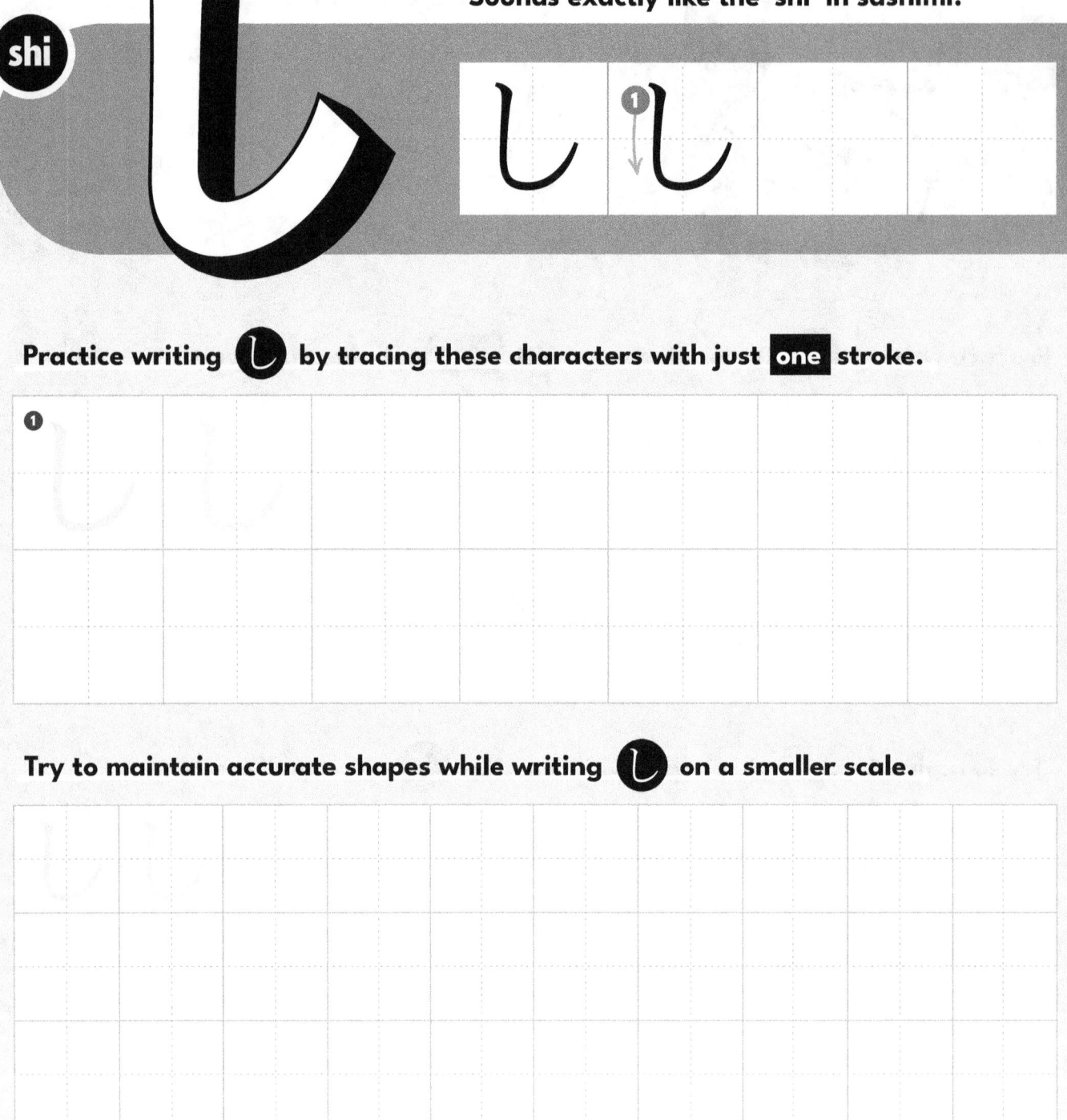

Practice writing し by tracing these characters with just one stroke.

Try to maintain accurate shapes while writing し on a smaller scale.

Mnemonic.

Examples.

- A fi<u>shi</u>ng hook
- <u>She</u> has long hair

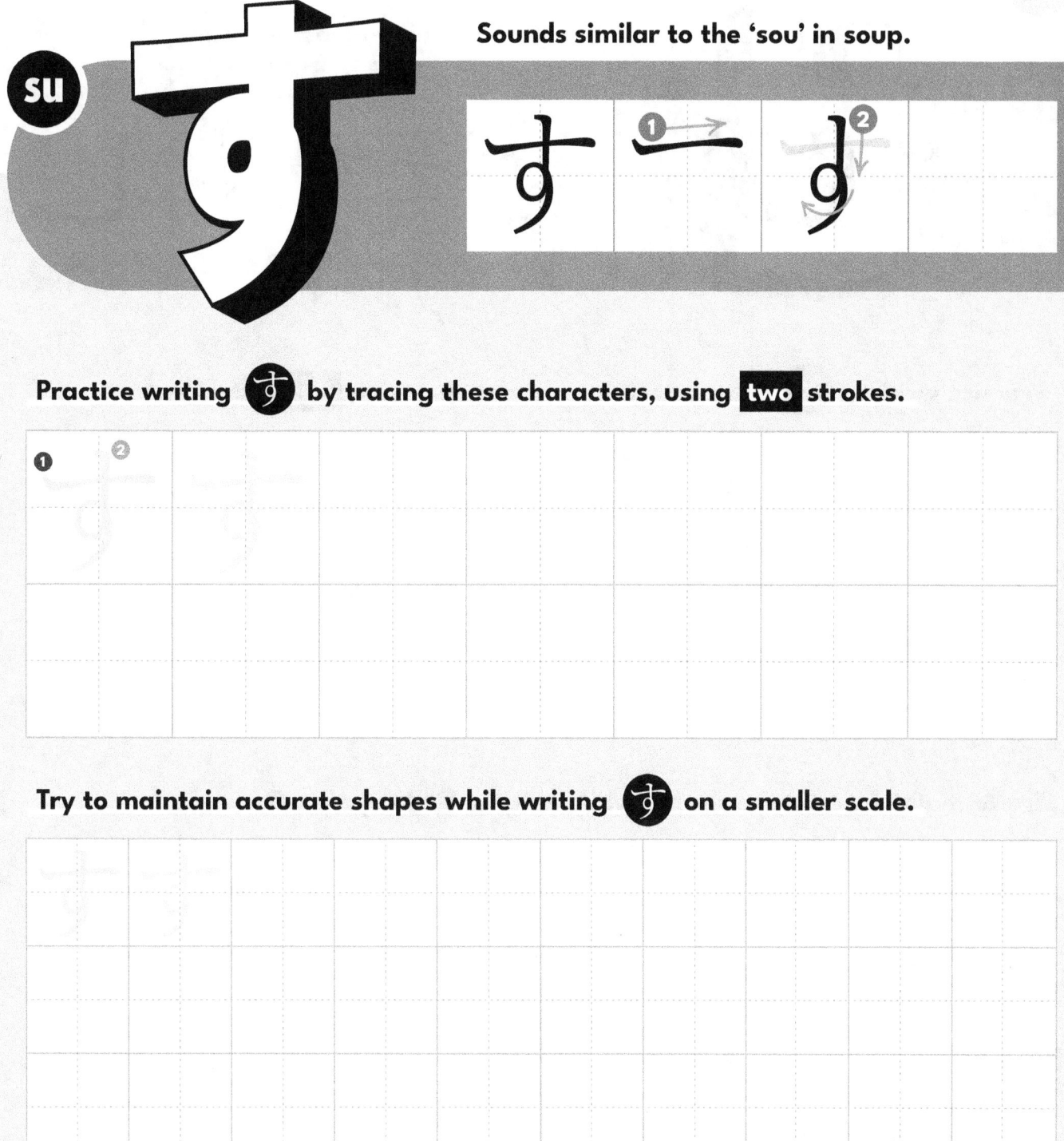

su — す

Sounds similar to the 'sou' in soup.

Practice writing す by tracing these characters, using two strokes.

Try to maintain accurate shapes while writing す on a smaller scale.

Mnemonic.

Examples.
- Picture a pig with a curly tail, called <u>Sue</u>
- Somebody wearing a hat, oh it's <u>Sue</u>

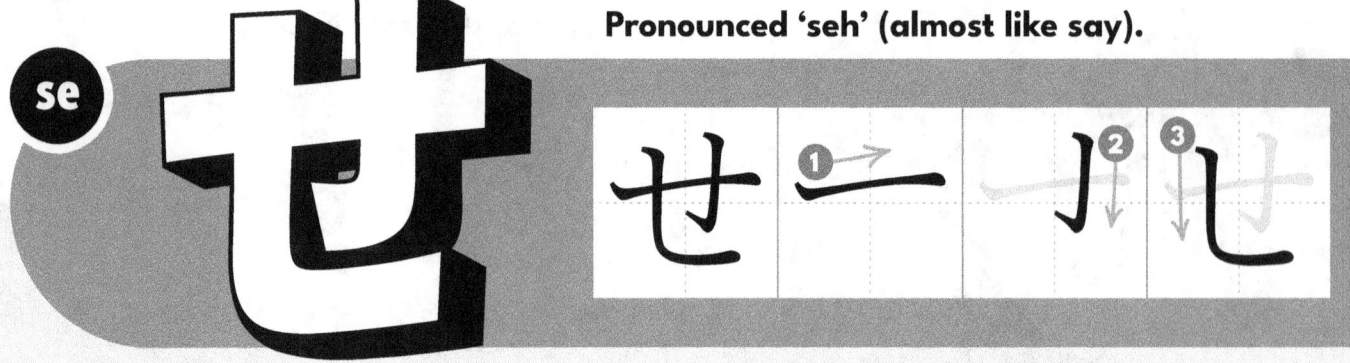

Pronounced 'seh' (almost like say).

Practice writing せ by tracing these characters, using three strokes.

Try to maintain accurate shapes while writing せ on a smaller scale.

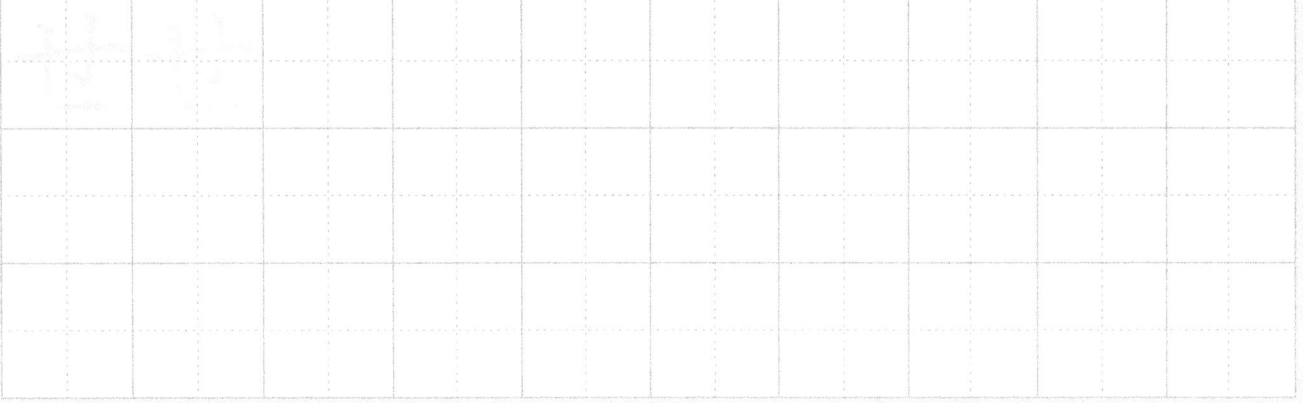

Mnemonic.

Examples.
- imagine its a mouth <u>seh</u>-ing something
- Upside down <u>sevens</u>

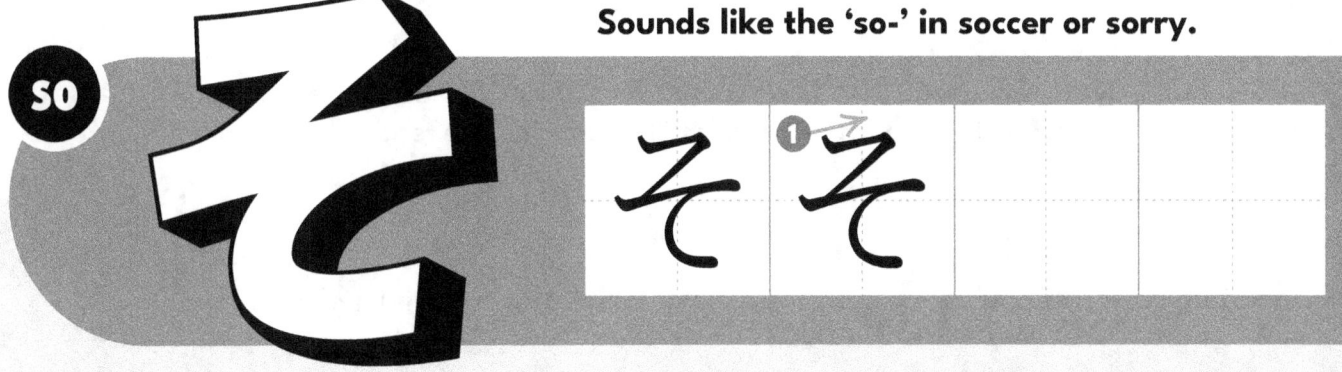

SO

Sounds like the 'so-' in soccer or sorry.

Practice writing そ by tracing these characters with just **one** stroke.

Try to maintain accurate shapes while writing そ on a smaller scale.

Mnemonic.

Examples.

- It's <u>so</u> abstract
- Picture a <u>sewing</u> needle and thread

Now that the five new hiragana have been added to the others, repeat this memorization exercise. Take a break between each set, as this will help to improve recall.

Practice pronouncing each symbol as you write the romaji beneath.

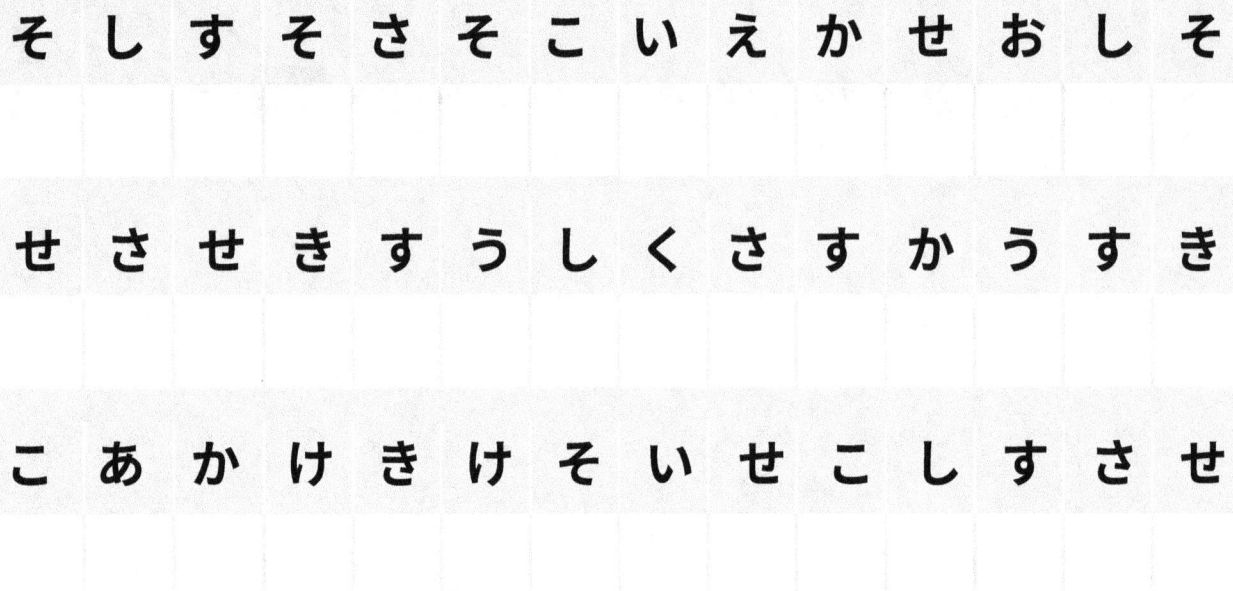

Take a 5-minute break, and then do the same for these symbols too.

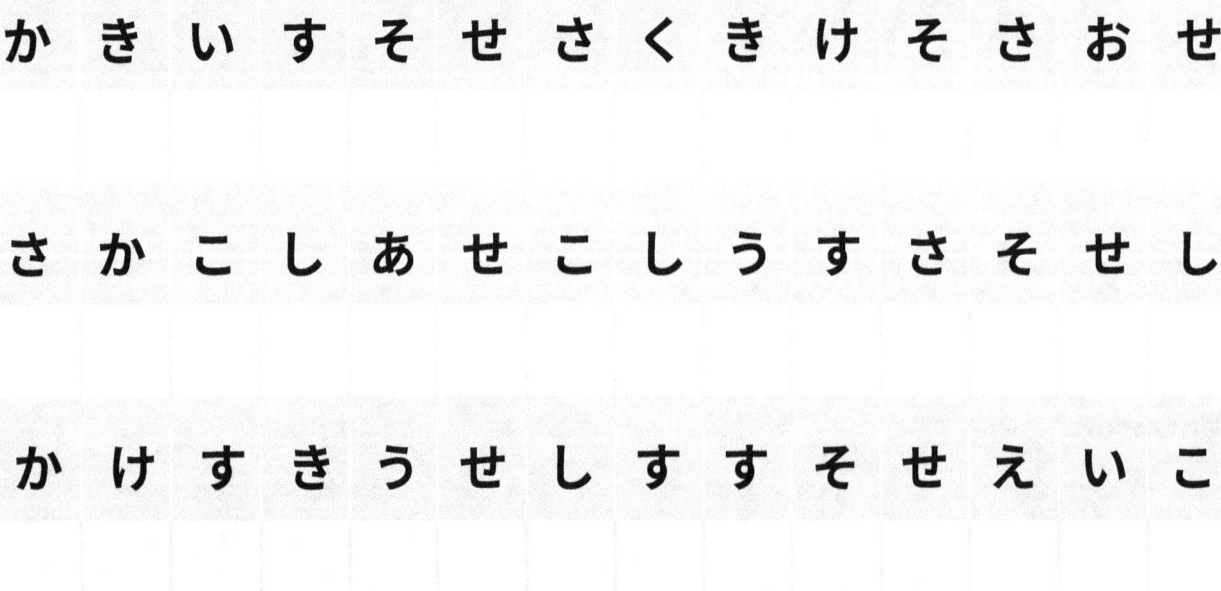

This time, take a 10-minute break and come back to complete these.

き す く し す さ か そ せ か う せ そ さ

す し か せ こ そ さ お き き す せ え い

あ さ け い う こ こ け し そ そ せ し す

After a much longer break, add the romaji for each symbol below.

せ そ あ す お く き そ さ し か こ け う

き う す せ け そ さ え す こ そ こ か お

く し そ す か い き せ さ す せ い し そ

H4. The T-Column

The fourth column contains two characters that fall outside the usual pattern but, once again, they are not difficult to say and simply need to be remembered. They only really seem like exceptions because of the romaji beneath and, before long, you will simply recognize the character as the sound that it represents.

Symbols in this learning block.

Pronunciation

Characters with the pure *'t-'* sound are simple enough to pronounce. The tip of your tongue touches the top of your mouth, just behind your upper teeth, and air is released with some aspiration. Try to reduce the amount of force and air that is released.

The second character in the T column is simply pronounced as *'chi'* or a short *'chee-'*. While not exactly the same as the *'ch-'* in English pronunciation, this will be close enough. To achieve a more accurate pronunciation, the tip of your tongue would make contact with the roof of your mouth still, but further back from the position for a pure *'t-'* sound. It would be located on the area that feels slightly ribbed, at the end of the ridge that runs across the roof of your mouth, from front to back.

Finally, the character つ represents a *'tsu'* sound. The *'u'* part of the sound is the same as the basic vowel character う but the *'t-'* sound is now a *'ts-'*. Try not to view this as a silent *'t'*, as it should certainly be heard. Instead, try to isolate the sound of *'-ts'* from words like *'boats'* or *'knots'* and add the short *'oo'* sound to that. This almost sounds like the word *'zoo'* but shorter and with the *'t'*. Remember that this syllable is no longer than the others and is pronounced in the same length of time.

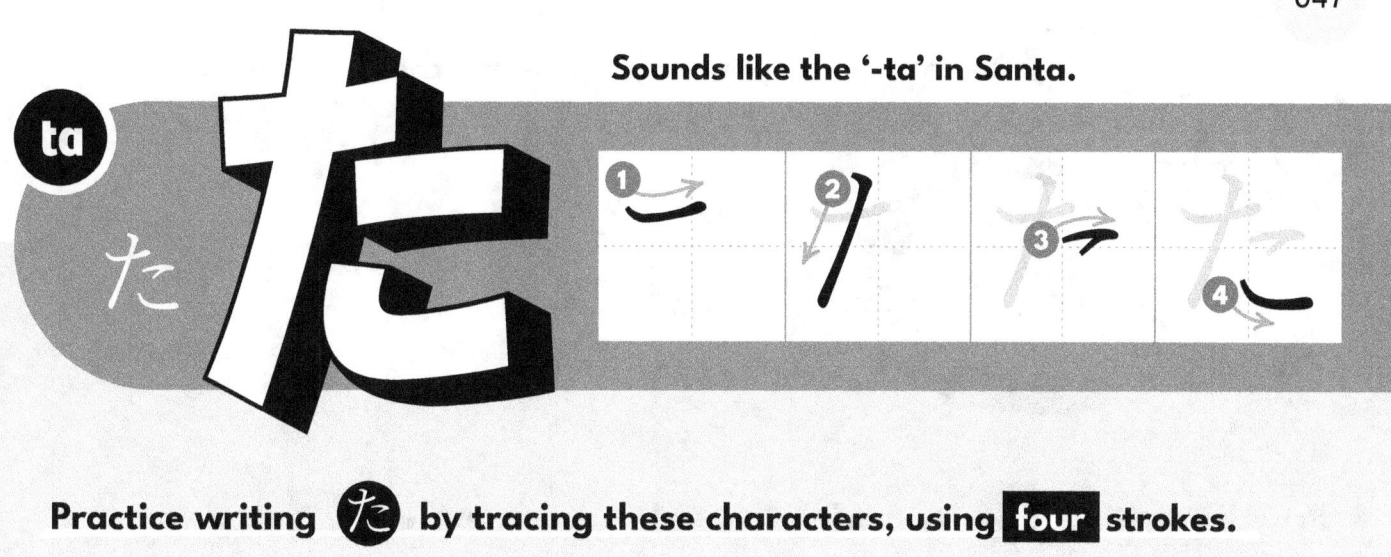

Sounds like the '-ta' in Santa.

Practice writing た by tracing these characters, using four strokes.

Try to maintain accurate shapes while writing た on a smaller scale.

Mnemonic.

Examples.
- Looks like letters 'ta'
- Tackling a ball

Sounds just like the 'chee' in cheeks.

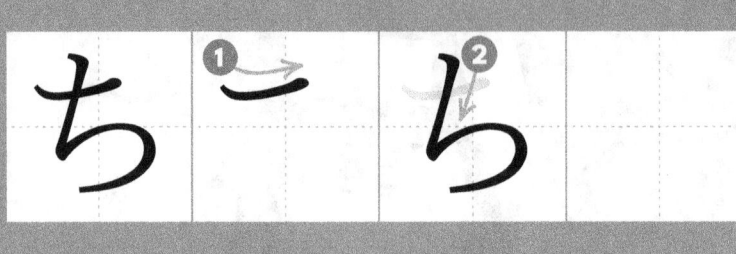

Practice writing ち by tracing these characters, using two strokes.

Try to maintain accurate shapes while writing ち on a smaller scale.

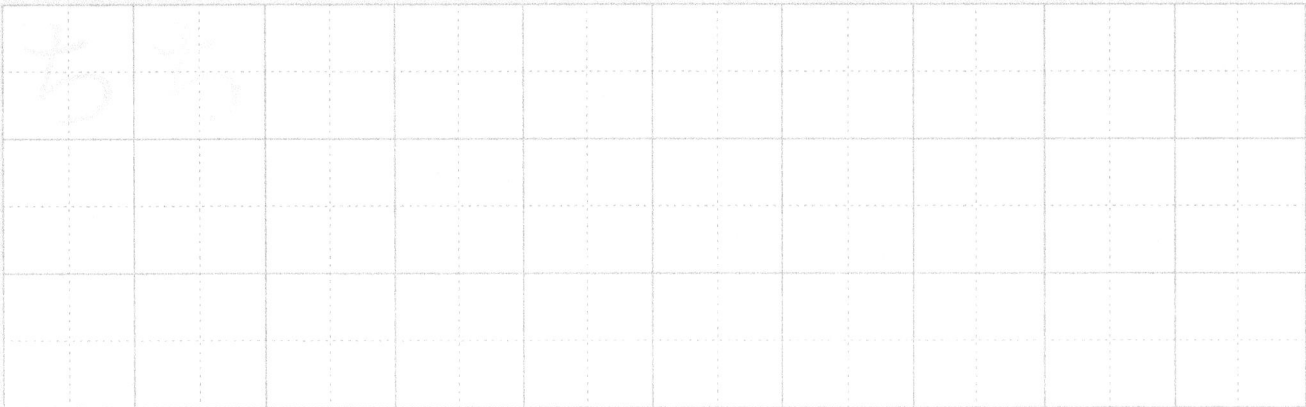

Mnemonic.

Examples.

- A face, from the side with no <u>chi</u>n
- It sneezes, Aa<u>chi</u>oo!
- A <u>che</u>ap number 5?

tsu つ

Sounds just like the name 'Sue'.

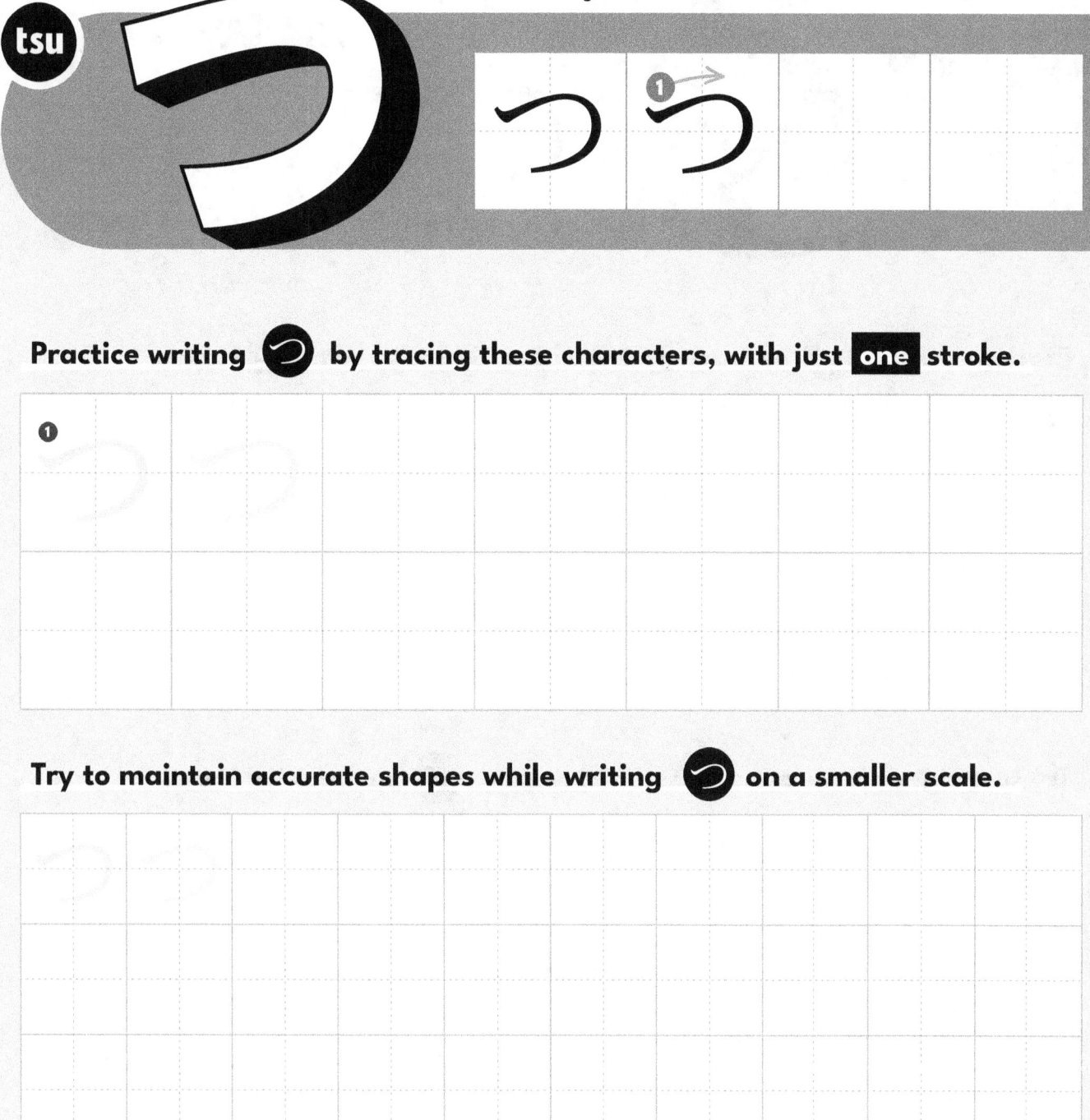

Practice writing つ by tracing these characters, with just one stroke.

Try to maintain accurate shapes while writing つ on a smaller scale.

Mnemonic.

Examples.

- A tsunami wave

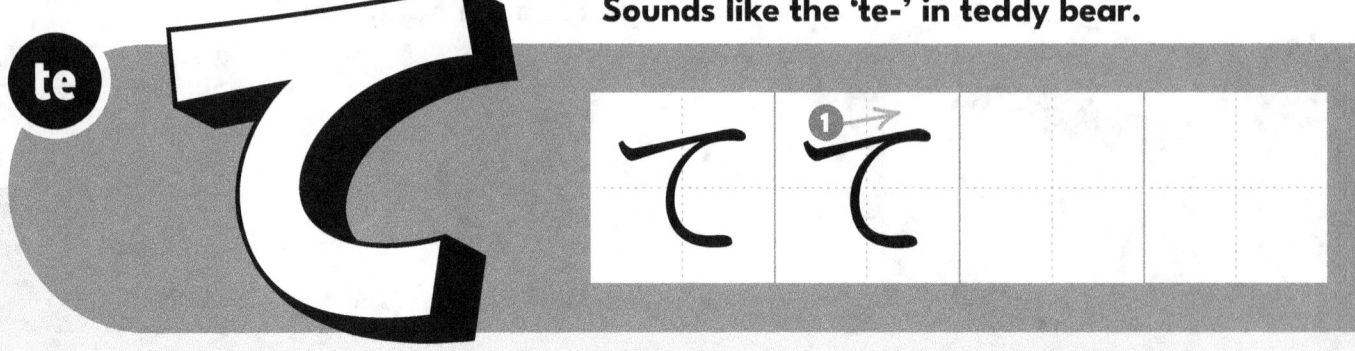

Sounds like the 'te-' in teddy bear.

Practice writing て by tracing these characters with just one stroke.

Try to maintain accurate shapes while writing て on a smaller scale.

Mnemonic.

Examples.

- Letter T for <u>te</u>n.
- <u>Te</u>rrible number 7

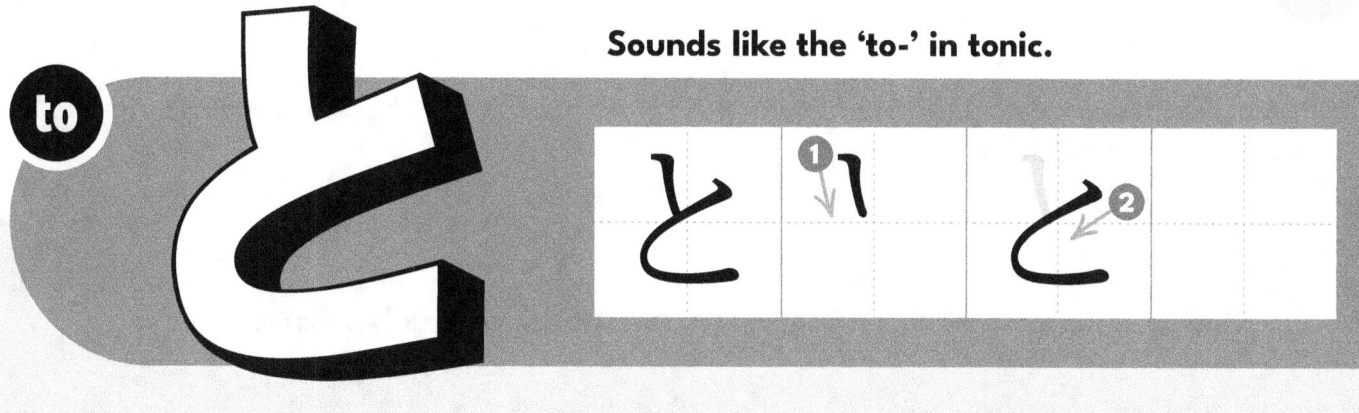

Sounds like the 'to-' in tonic.

Practice writing と by tracing these characters, using two strokes.

Try to maintain accurate shapes while writing と on a smaller scale.

Mnemonic.

Examples.
- Picture a big <u>to</u>e with a splinter
- Imagine a thorn in your <u>to</u>ngue

These exercises will test your memorization of all twenty hiragana you have encountered. Take a break and continue.

Practice pronouncing each symbol as you write the romaji beneath.

す と く そ と つ さ う た と ち あ つ ち

そ せ え て た き け こ と ち つ こ か て

し た せ お ち さ あ す た せ い て し つ

Take a 5-minute break, and then do the same for these symbols too.

う た そ せ さ い き そ お ち か け す う

ち か て そ あ て え た け し こ と す お

せ さ う き つ え こ す と あ つ せ と し

Your brain should be saving earlier symbols to your longer-term memory, making them easier to recognize and recall.

This time, take a 10-minute break and come back to complete these.

し	ち	た	つ	あ	て	す	か	さ	ち	け	い	う	え

け	え	さ	て	そ	せ	こ	お	す	き	と	う	そ	し

お	す	き	そ	せ	ち	あ	し	つ	と	か	せ	た	こ

After a much longer break, add the romaji for each symbol below.

お	き	こ	す	せ	こ	あ	う	け	ち	そ	て	ち	す

と	つ	た	せ	け	さ	そ	さ	と	お	し	か	え	し

せ	ち	と	つ	か	う	あ	た	い	そ	す	き	え	た

Practice reading and writing words with characters from all group so far.

すし
sushi

つち
soil

そと
outside

さけ
sake

こと
thing

くつ
shoes

かこ
past

てつ
iron/steel

せき
cough

たつ
to stand/leave

とち
land

うた
song

かた
shoulder

しち
seven

さす
to point

あした
tomorrow

とおい
far

きせつ
season

さとい
clever

ちかてつ
subway

H5. The N & H Columns

This group is a little larger than the previous few and, largely, follows the *[consonant + vowel]* pattern. One symbol will immediately stand out as different. Instead of having a *'h-'* sound added, like the others in this column, it is shown with *'f-'* and it is pronounced with a sort of mixture of sounds - generally, this should almost sound like *'hfu-'* when you pronounce it.

Symbols in this learning block.

Pronunciation

Most of this group will sound exactly how it reads. Add a regular *'n-'* and *'h-'* sound like those used when saying words like *'north'* and *'house'* to the basic vowel sounds. Both are voiced consonants, and the *'n-'* sounds are nasal sounding.

The pronunciation of ふ is a little odd and may be sound like *'fu'* and *'hu'* depending on use. Generally, this has a *'hfu'* sound that is made by trying to say *'foo'* without your teeth making contact with your lip. You still need to bring your lips closer together but the huff of air is expelled through open lips, instead of the puff of air generated by touching your lip against the upper teeth.

Sounds just like the '-na's in banana

Practice writing な **by tracing these characters, using** four **strokes.**

Try to maintain accurate shapes while writing な **on a smaller scale.**

Mnemonic.

Examples.

- A <u>na</u>ughty person, praying at a cross.

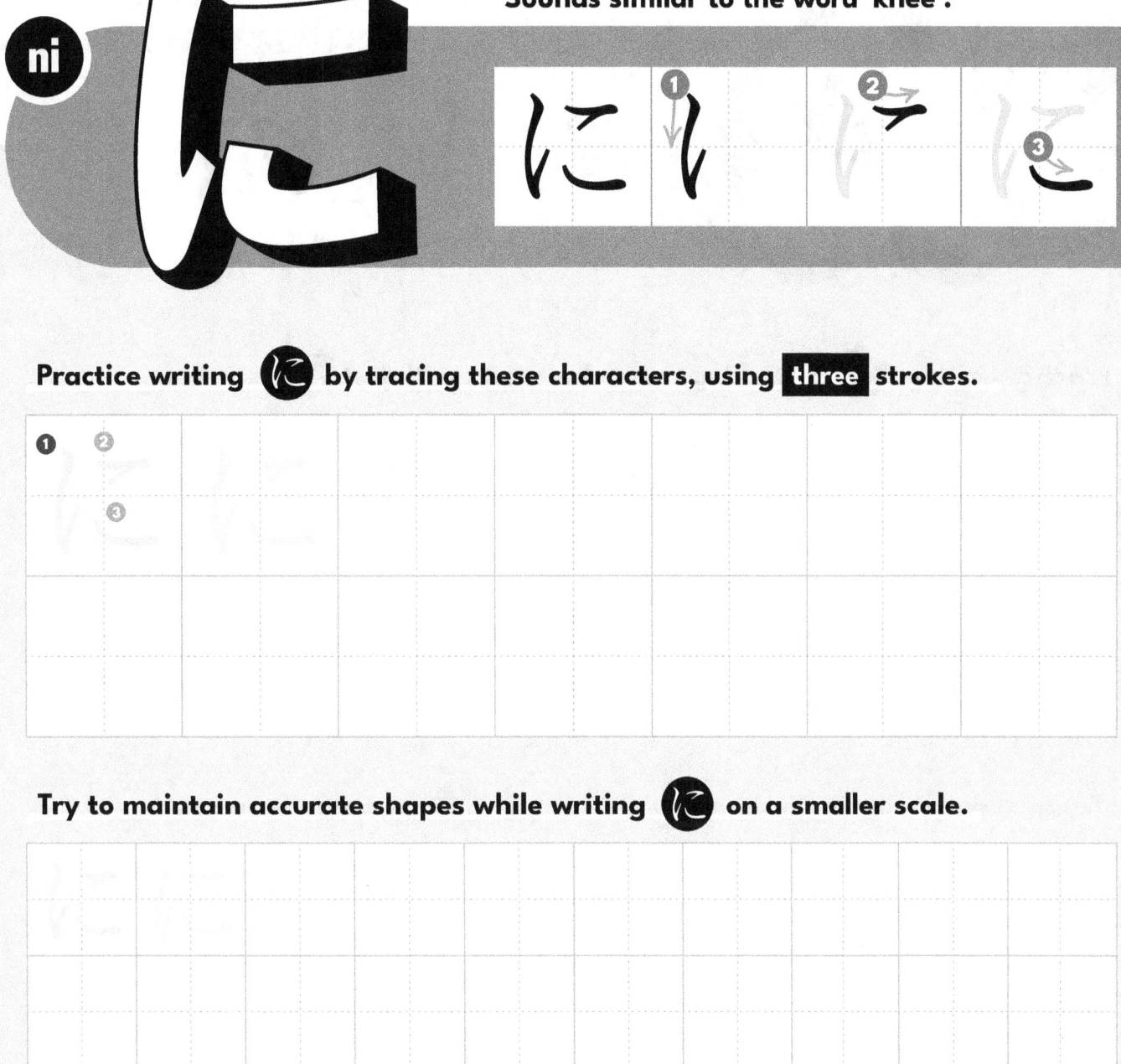

Practice writing に **by tracing these characters, using** three **strokes.**

Try to maintain accurate shapes while writing に **on a smaller scale.**

Mnemonic.

Examples.
- Picture as a <u>knee</u>
- <u>Nearly</u> a square?

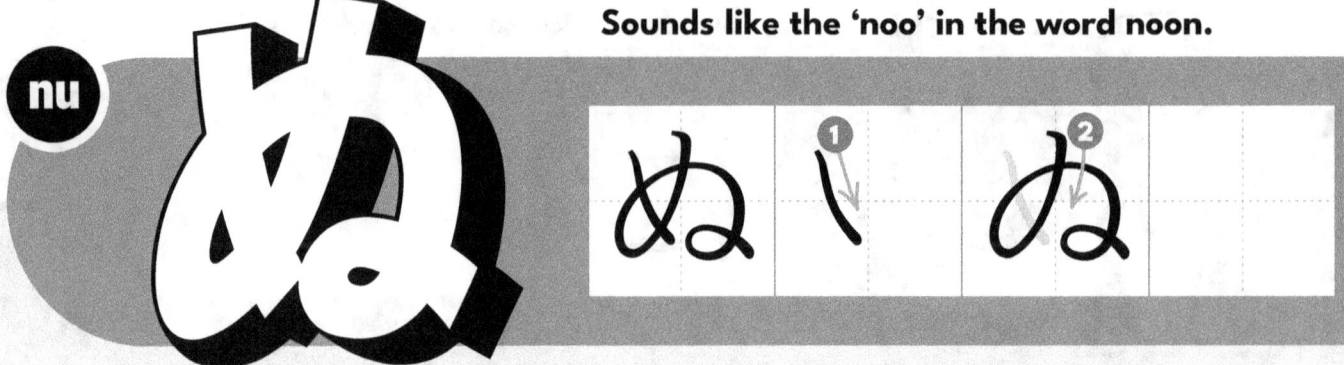

Sounds like the 'noo' in the word noon.

Practice writing ぬ by tracing these characters with just two strokes.

Try to maintain accurate shapes while writing ぬ on a smaller scale.

Mnemonic.

Examples.
- A bowl of <u>noo</u>dles with chopsticks
- A clockface, and it's almost <u>noon</u>

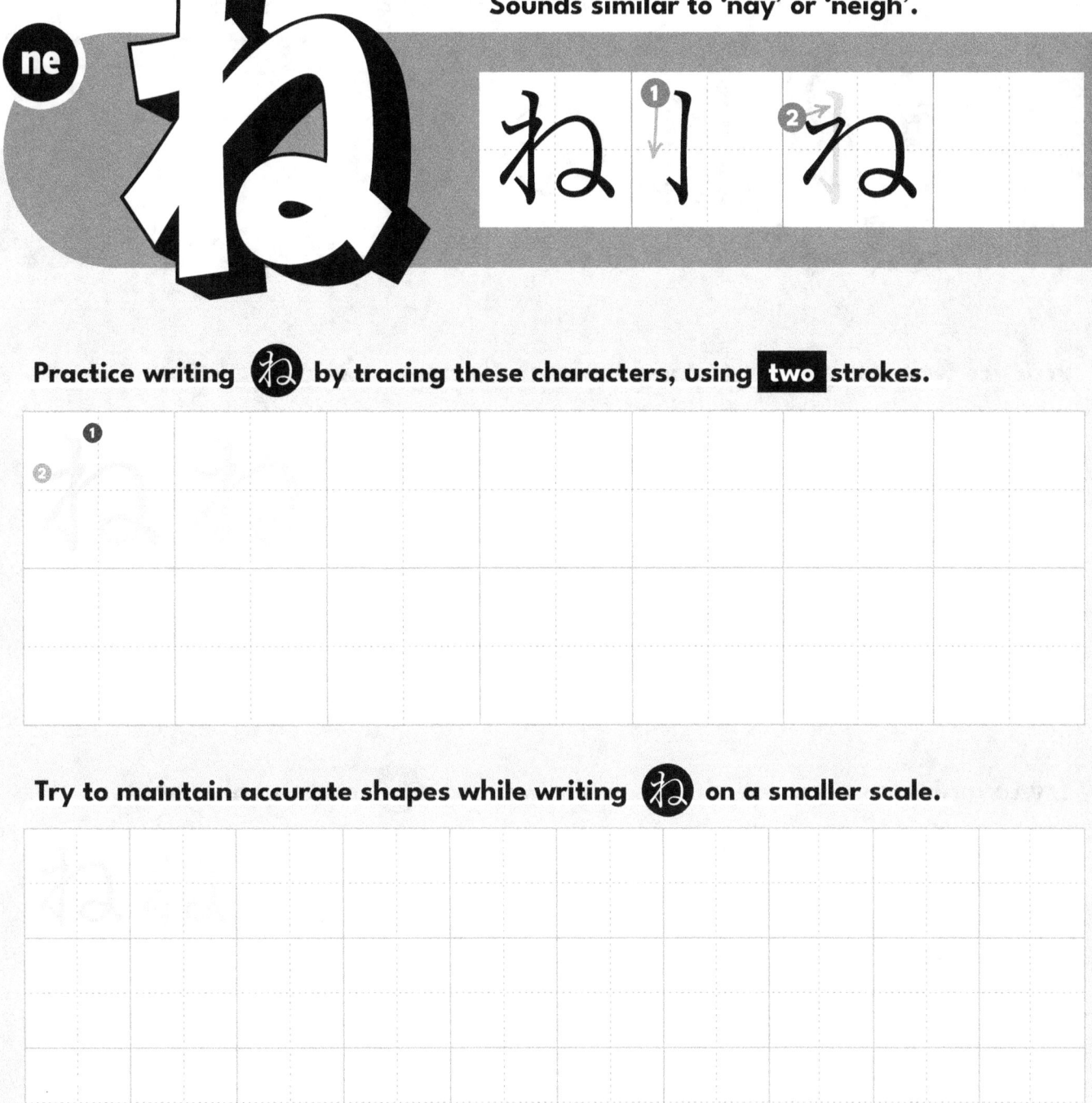

Sounds similar to 'nay' or 'neigh'.

Practice writing ね by tracing these characters, using two strokes.

Try to maintain accurate shapes while writing ね on a smaller scale.

Mnemonic.

Examples.
- <u>N</u>elly the elephant, with a curly trunk
- A cat, curled up, or '<u>n</u>eko' in Japanese

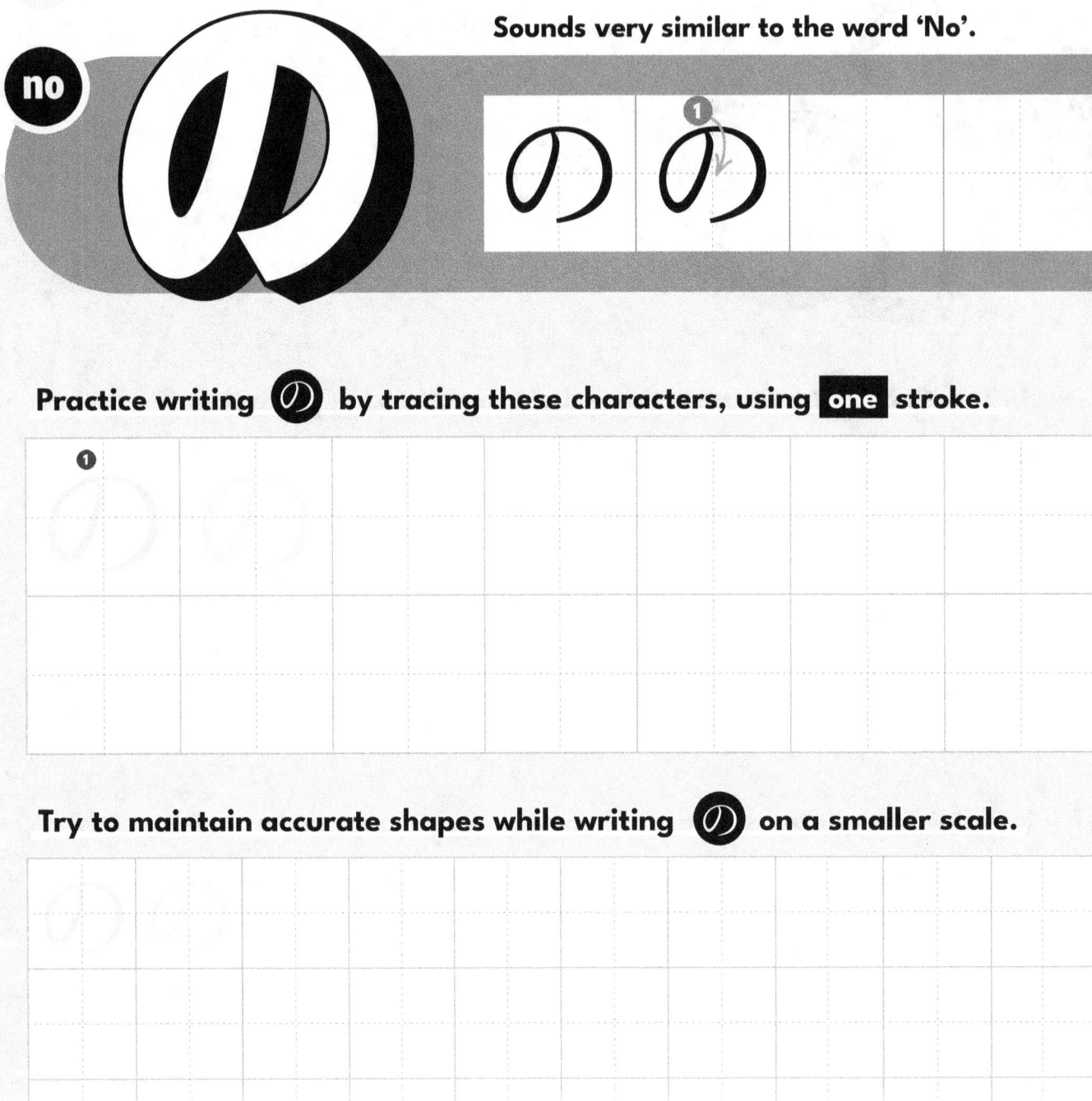

Sounds very similar to the word 'No'.

Practice writing の by tracing these characters, using one stroke.

Try to maintain accurate shapes while writing の on a smaller scale.

Mnemonic.

Examples.
- A pigs <u>no</u>se
- A sign that says <u>NO</u> Smoking

Pronounce as 'ha' like in hand.

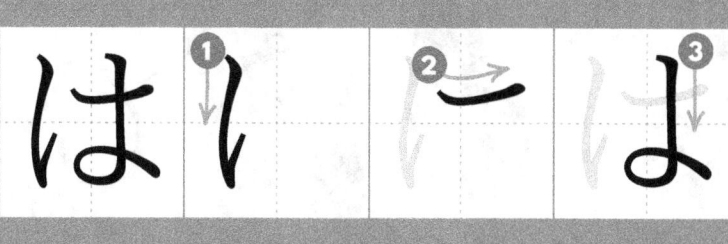

Practice writing は **by tracing these characters, using** three **strokes.**

Try to maintain accurate shapes while writing は **on a smaller scale.**

Mnemonic.

Examples.

- Looks like letters 'h' and 'a', for '<u>ha</u>'

Practice writing ひ **by tracing these characters with just** one **stroke.**

Try to maintain accurate shapes while writing ひ **on a smaller scale.**

Mnemonic.

Examples.
- Big smile, laughing mouth, "<u>hee</u> hee!"
- Like a mans nose, <u>H</u>e has a big nose

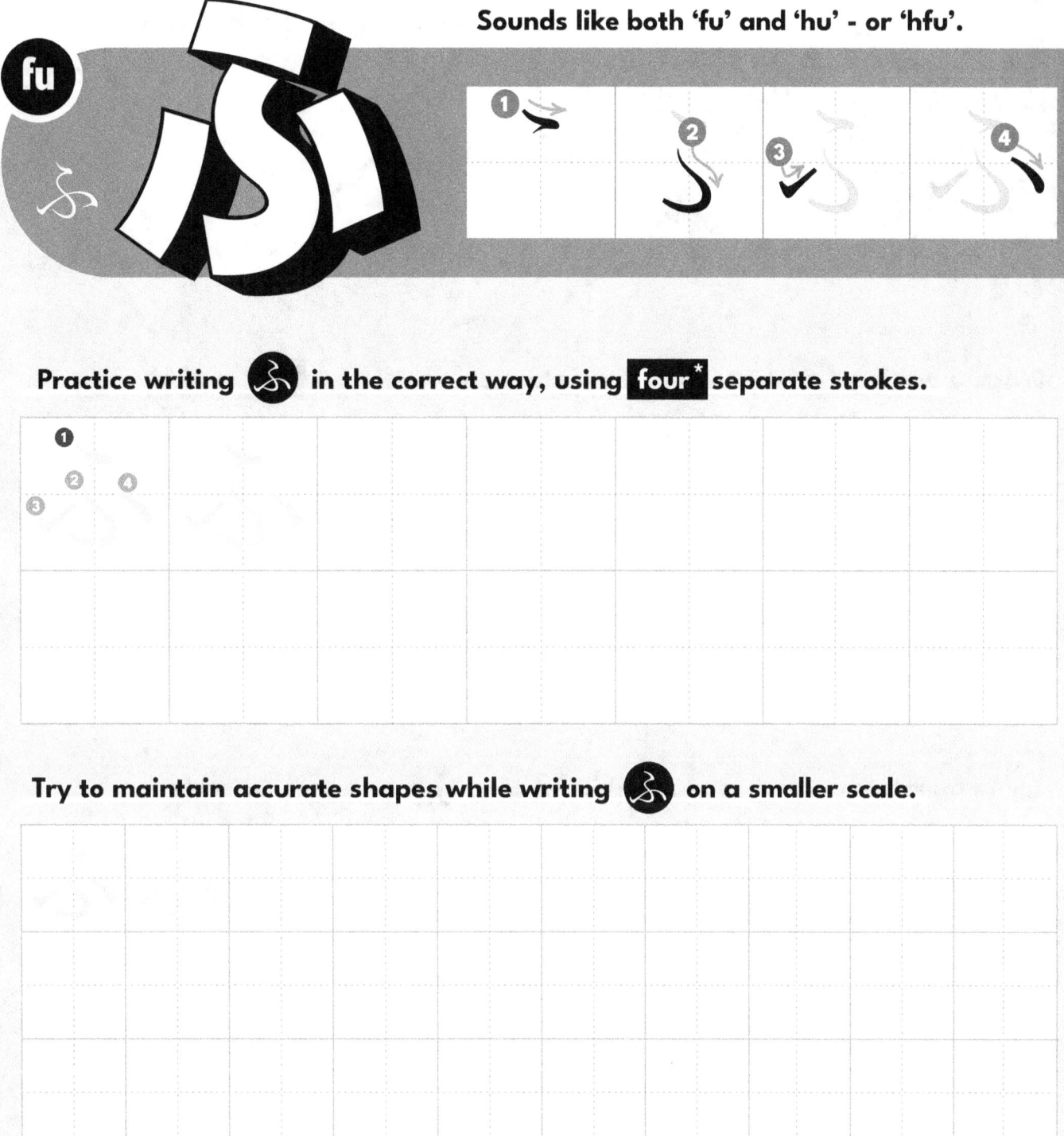

fu

Sounds like both 'fu' and 'hu' - or 'hfu'.

Practice writing ふ in the correct way, using four* separate strokes.

Try to maintain accurate shapes while writing ふ on a smaller scale.

Mnemonic.

Examples.
- Imagine Mount <u>Fu</u>ji
- Can you picture a <u>hu</u>la dancer?
- Upside-down, <u>wh</u>o?

064

he

Pronounce as 'heh', like the 'he-' in hey!

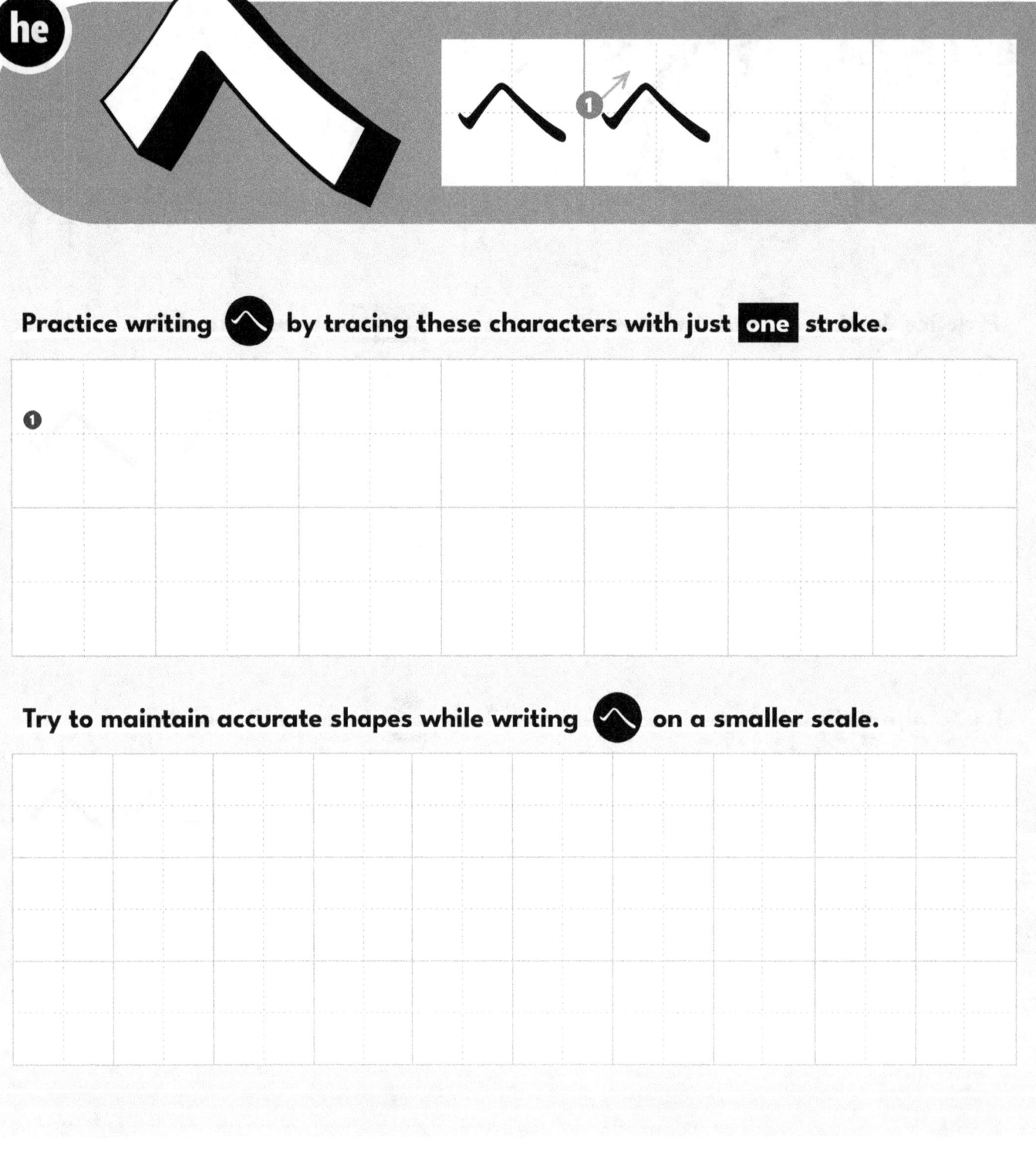

Practice writing ∧ by tracing these characters with just one stroke.

❶

Try to maintain accurate shapes while writing ∧ on a smaller scale.

Mnemonic.

Examples.
- Points to heaven
- Hey, that's easy to write

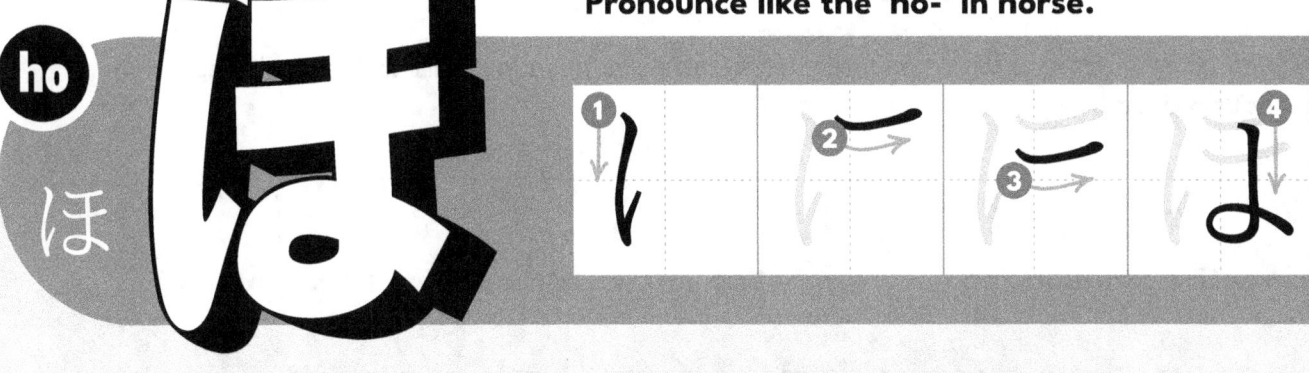

Pronounce like the 'ho-' in horse.

Practice writing ほ **by tracing these characters, using** four **strokes.**

Try to maintain accurate shapes while writing ほ **on a smaller scale.**

Mnemonic.

Examples.

- 'ha' with a hat = Santa! Ho ho <u>ho</u>!
- A <u>who</u>le lot of lines.

Even after learning a large group of new characters, this may start to feel easier each time. That's a good thing!

Practice pronouncing each symbol as you write the romaji beneath.

に な ほ は ち そ へ は そ す ひ の と せ

へ く つ ひ ね あ て こ な ふ し ほ へ は

ぬ ふ の す ち ふ ほ つ き お ひ に た さ

Take a 5-minute break, and then do the same for these symbols too.

せ つ う へ き え さ こ あ し す そ の い

な か け ひ ね た は す ぬ く け せ ふ ほ

に と お い の ほ そ く し あ え こ き て

You could make this more challenging by introducing a time limit for each group and reducing it for each set. Try to improve from one group to the next.

This time, take a 10-minute break and come back to complete these.

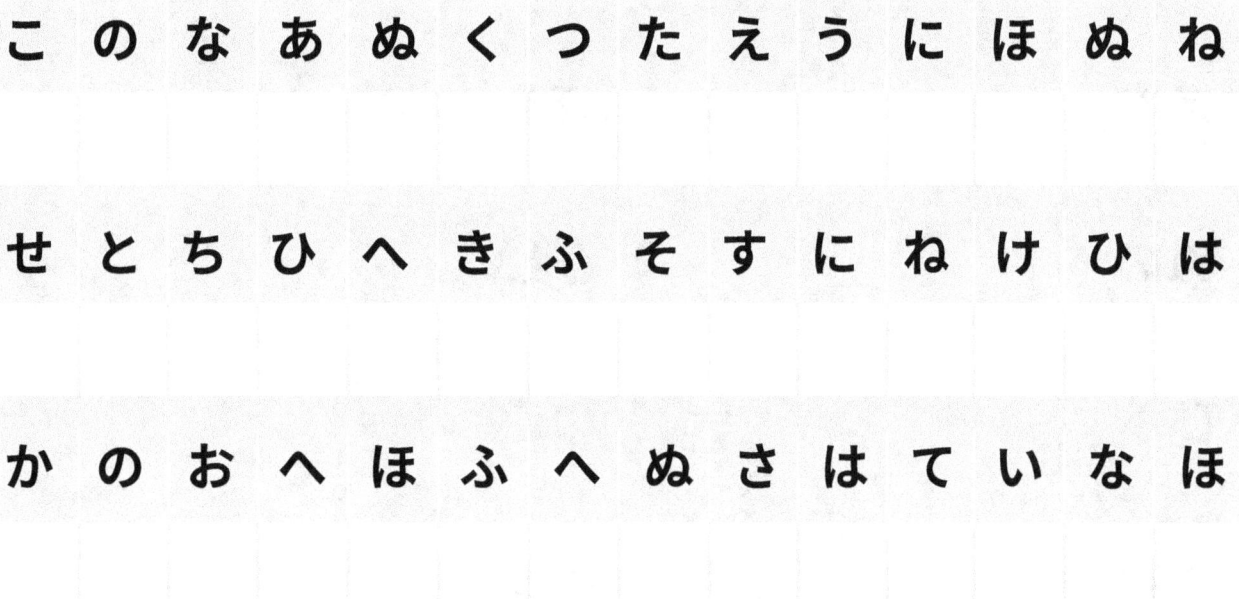

After a much longer break, add the romaji for each symbol below.

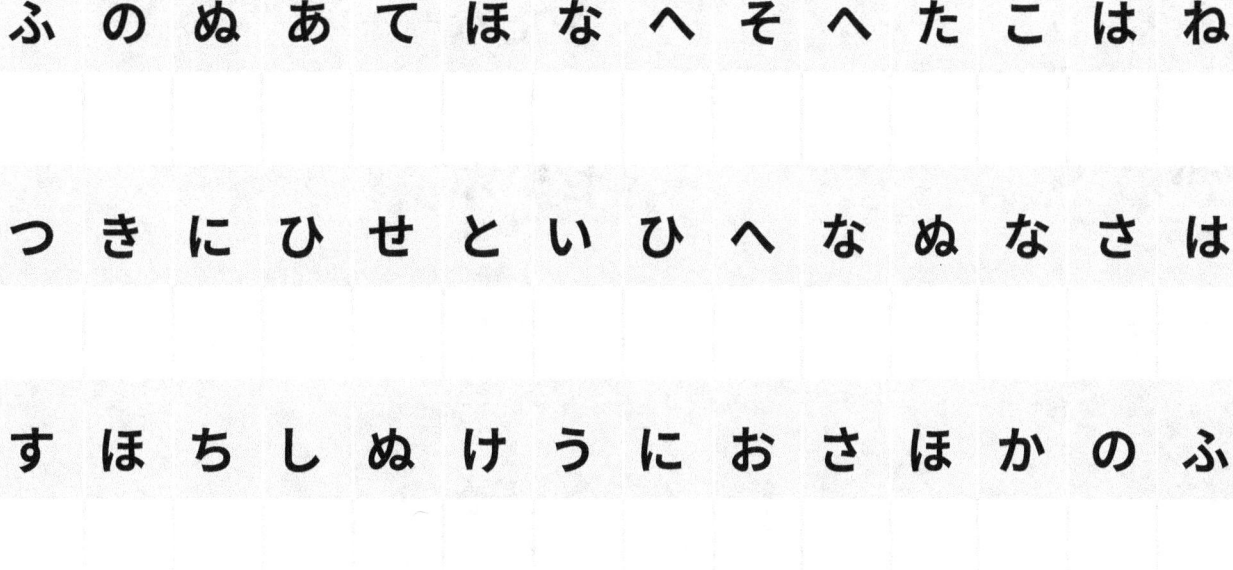

Practice reading and writing words with all the characters so far.

なに — what

ほね — bone

ぬの — cloth

ひふ — skin

へた — unskillful

はな — nose/flower

ふね — ship

かに — crab

ひな — doll/fledgling

はし — chopsticks/bridge

きぬ — silk

ほし — star

ひと — person

のき — eaves

にし — west

はいく — Haiku

かたな — Katana

せいふ — government

いのしし — boar

へいそつ — soldier

H6. The M & Y Columns

Two more columns coming up in this section. The two symbols that seem to be 'missing' from the Y column *(YE and YI)* sounded similar enough to the vowel-only column that the Japanese dropped them altogether (い & え). This just simplified the alphabet, meaning fewer symbols to learn!

Symbols in this learning block.

Pronunciation

The *'m-'* sounds are pronounced in virtually the same way as in English, bringing your lips together, voiced *(your vocal chords are used)*, and nasal like *'n-'* sounds.

The *'y-'* sound characters are very much like the English pronunciation and you will notice that there are only three to learn. It is possible to hear the occasional *'ye'* but this is usually limited to foreign words and so isn't a sound that you need to learn for the Japanese language.

070

ma

Sounds like 'ma-' in the word man.

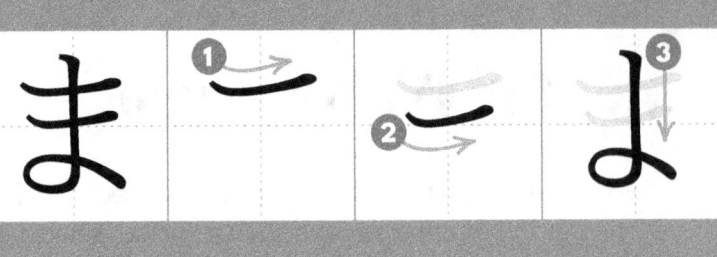

Practice writing ま by tracing these characters, using three strokes.

Try to maintain accurate shapes while writing ま on a smaller scale.

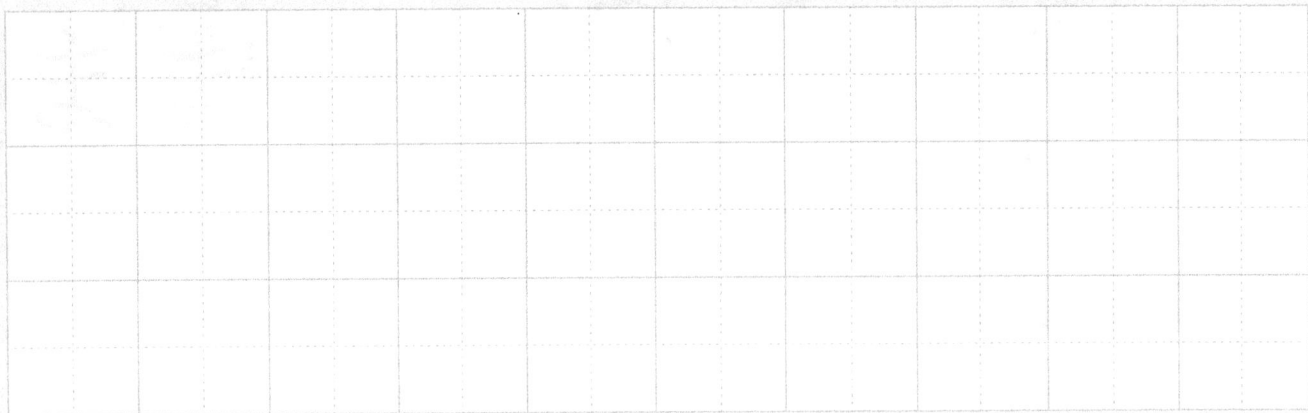

Mnemonic.

Examples.
- <u>Ma</u>gma, exploding from a volcano
- Looks <u>ma</u>thematical

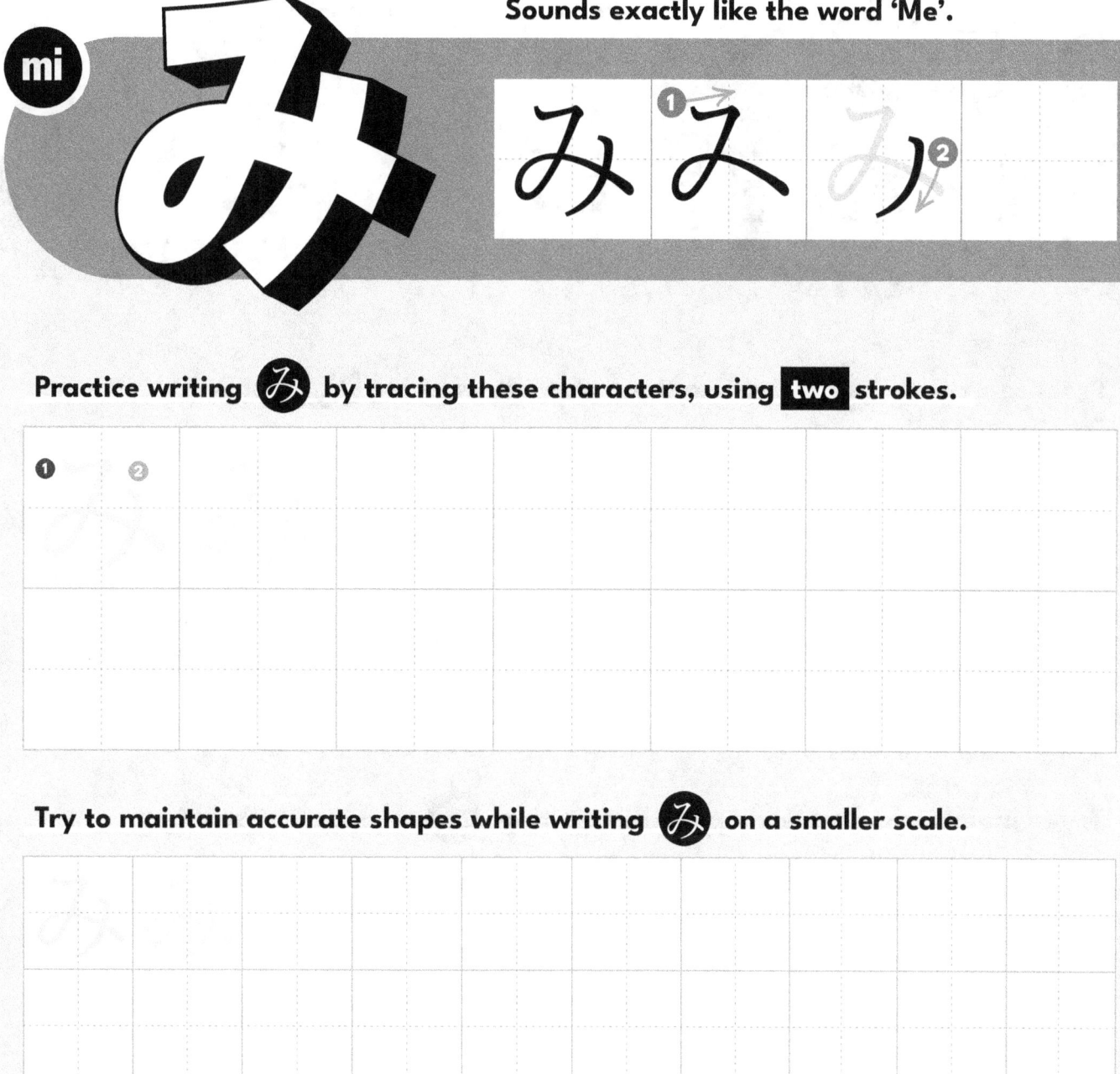

mi み — Sounds exactly like the word 'Me'.

Practice writing み by tracing these characters, using **two** strokes.

Try to maintain accurate shapes while writing み on a smaller scale.

Mnemonic.

Examples.
- Looks like 21 to <u>me</u>.
- Who wishes to be aged 21 again? <u>Me</u>!

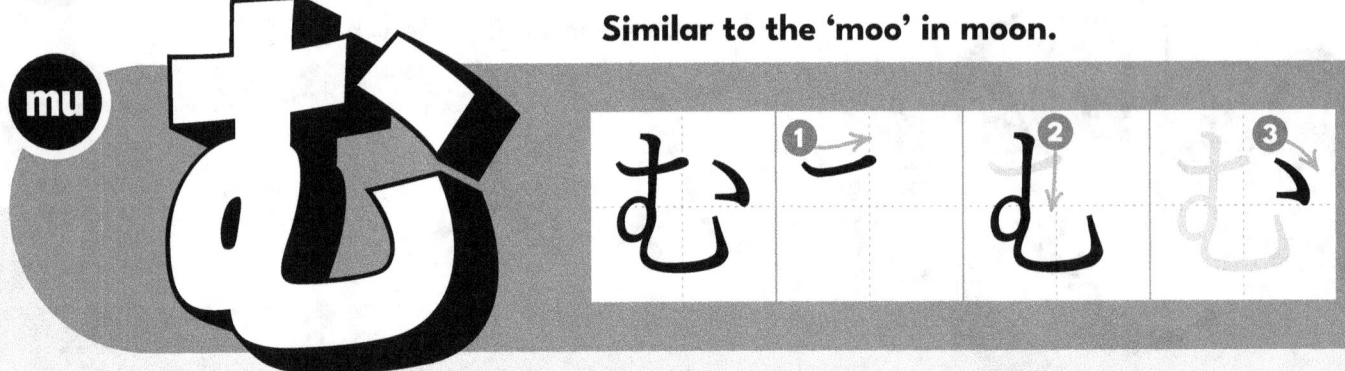

Similar to the 'moo' in moon.

Practice writing む by tracing these characters, using three strokes.

Try to maintain accurate shapes while writing む on a smaller scale.

Mnemonic.

Examples.
- Picture the shape of a cow... <u>Moo</u>!
- A projector, showing a <u>mo</u>vie?

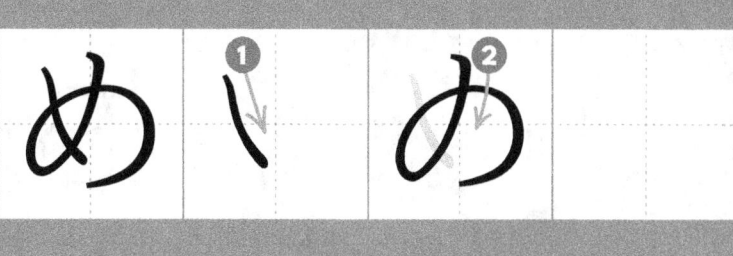

Sounds like the 'me-' in men.

Practice writing め **by tracing these characters, using** two **strokes.**

Try to maintain accurate shapes while writing め **on a smaller scale.**

Mnemonic.

Examples.

- Like an eye, which is '<u>me</u>' in Japanese
- Like 'nu' for noodles, but not as <u>me</u>ssy.

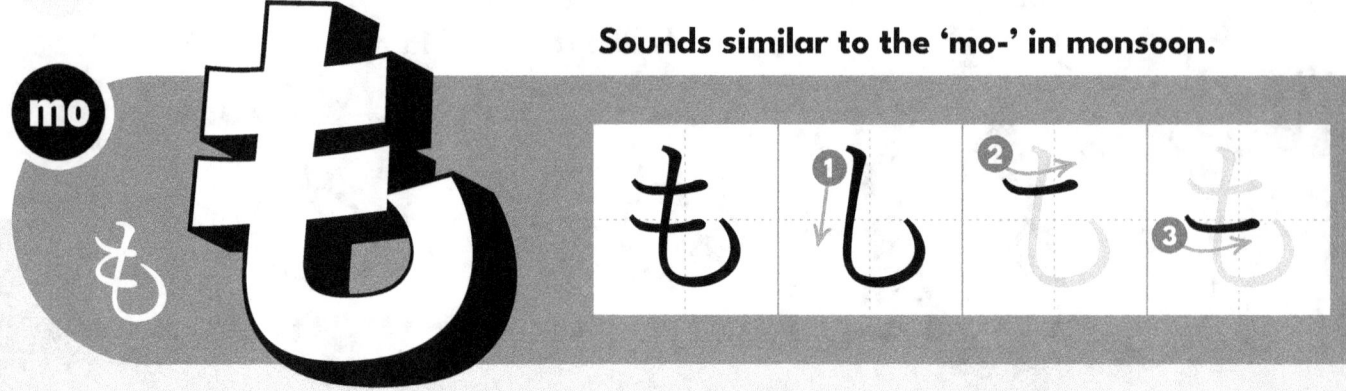

Sounds similar to the 'mo-' in monsoon.

Practice writing も **by tracing these characters, using** **three** **strokes.**

Try to maintain accurate shapes while writing も **on a smaller scale.**

Mnemonic.

Examples.

- A fishing hook with <u>more</u> worms.
- You will catch <u>more</u> fish with this hook.

Sounds much like the 'ya-' in yak.

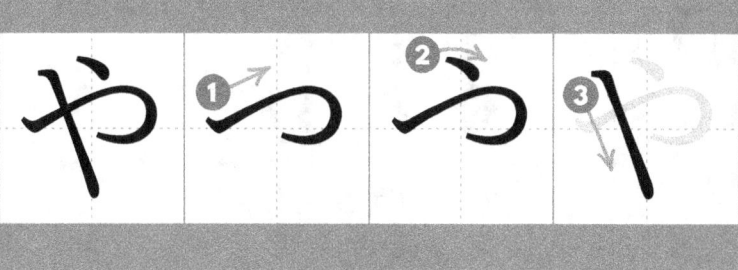

Practice writing や by tracing these characters, using three strokes.

Try to maintain accurate shapes while writing や on a smaller scale.

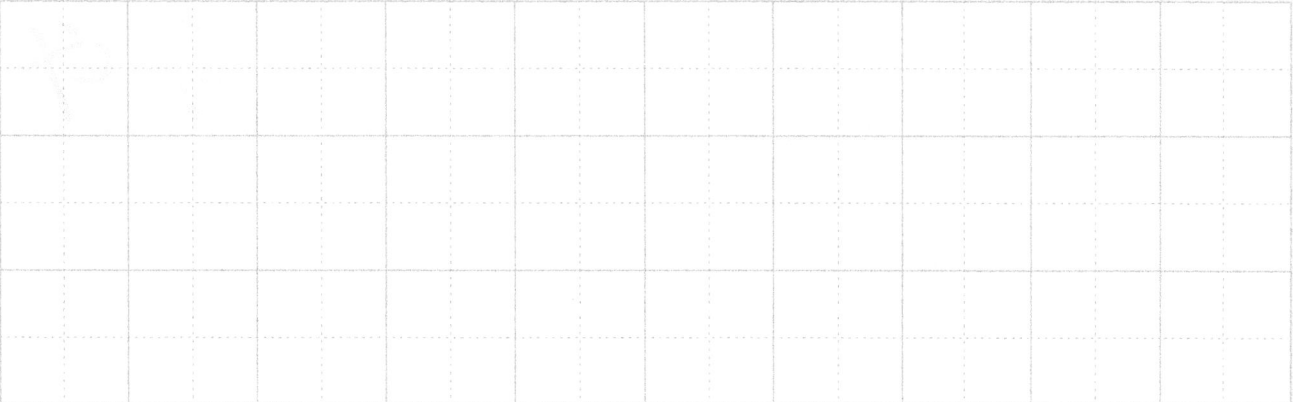

Mnemonic.

Examples.
- Picture the shape of a <u>ya</u>k's head
- Maybe the sail from a <u>ya</u>cht?

Sounds just like the word 'You'.

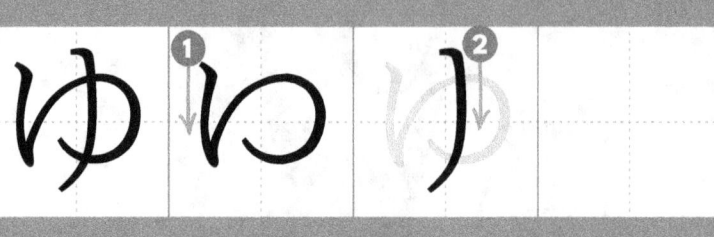

Practice writing ゆ by tracing these characters, using two strokes.

Try to maintain accurate shapes while writing ゆ on a smaller scale.

Mnemonic.

Examples.

- Combines letters that spell '<u>yo</u><u>u</u>'
- Picture a new and <u>u</u>nique fish

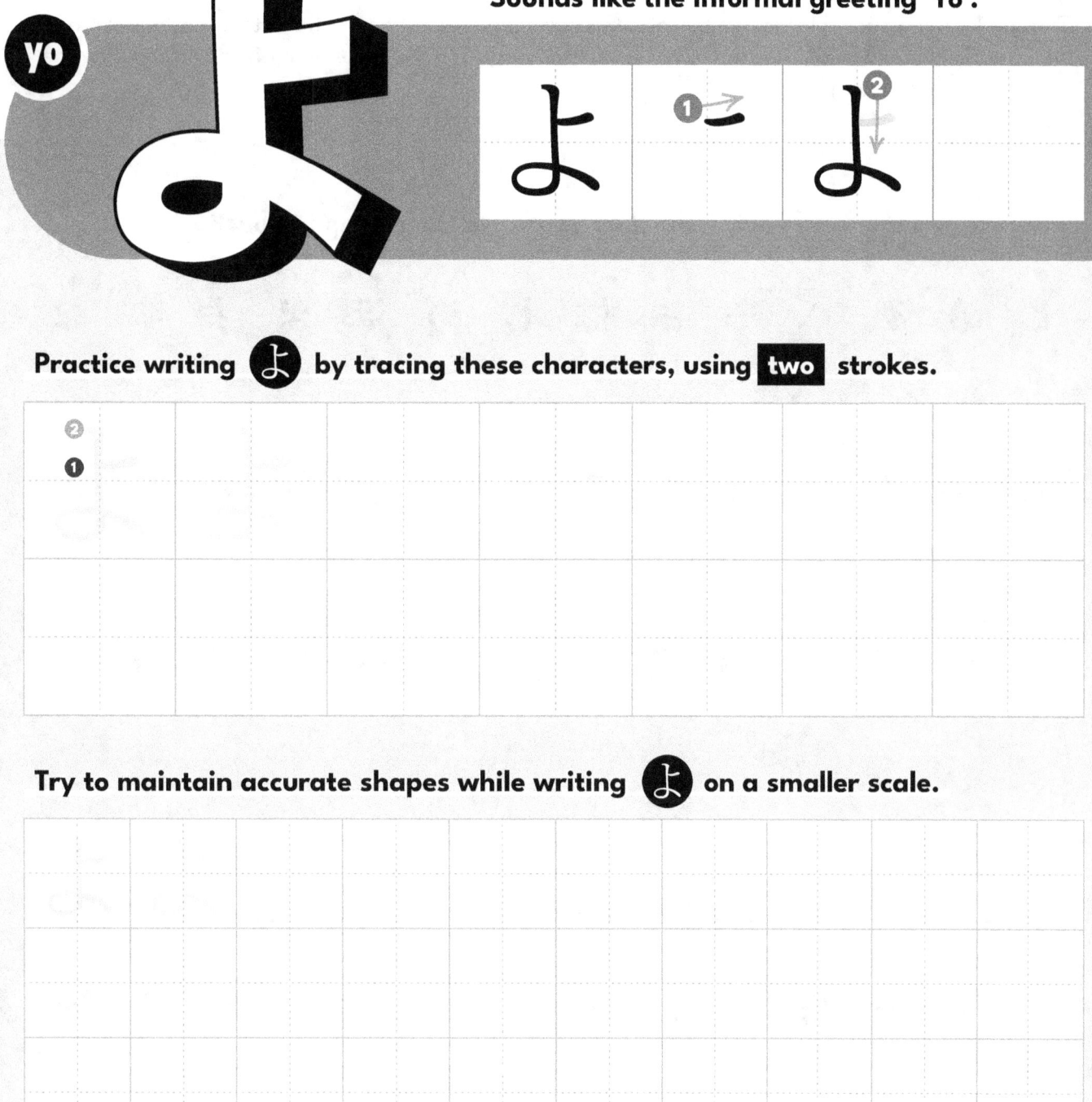

yo — Sounds like the informal greeting 'Yo'.

Practice writing よ by tracing these characters, using two strokes.

Try to maintain accurate shapes while writing よ on a smaller scale.

Mnemonic.

Examples.
- A new <u>yo</u>-yo trick?
- A hitch-hiker needs a ride, he yells "<u>yo!</u>"

Despite learning such a large number of new characters, repetition of characters that you learned much earlier should mean they are firmly in your memory. You can focus your efforts on ensuring the newer ones are sinking in too.

Practice pronouncing each symbol as you write the romaji beneath.

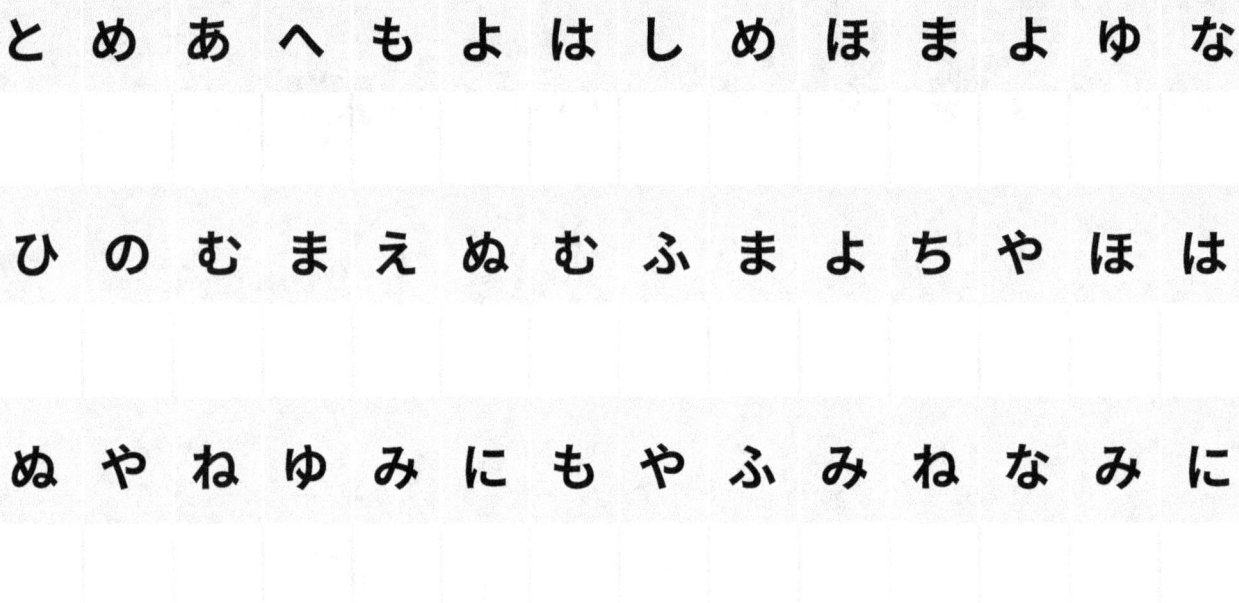

Take a 5-minute break, and then do the same for these symbols too.

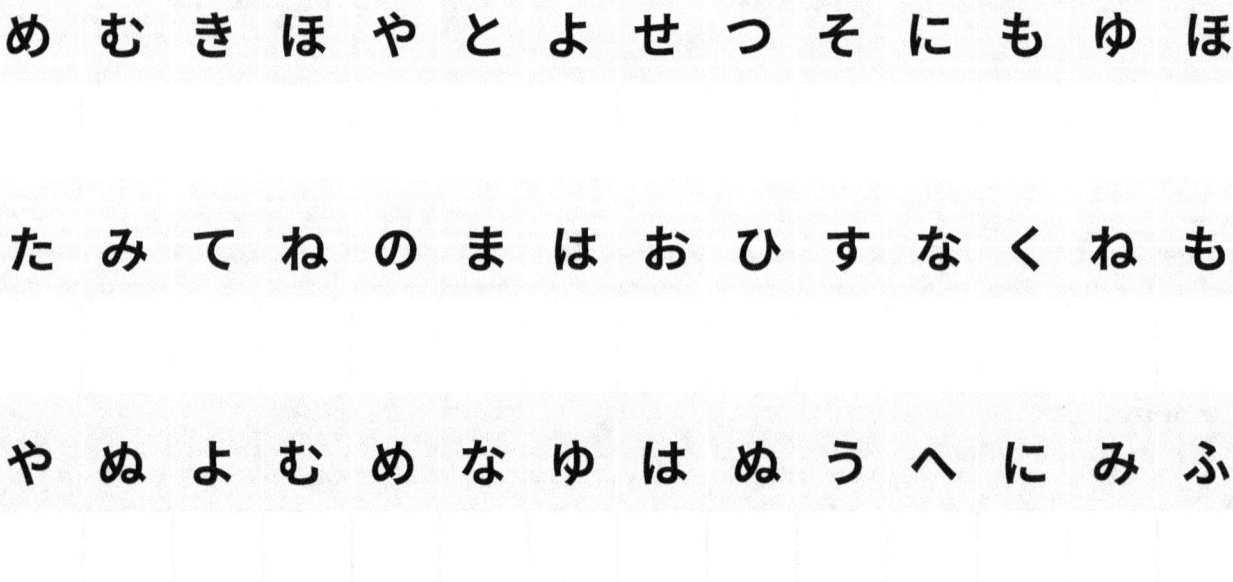

This time, take a 10-minute break and come back to complete these.

し	ね	か	や	と	い	ぬ	す	へ	つ	ゆ	た	そ	さ

ま	ひ	く	せ	え	な	て	め	に	こ	せ	こ	の	よ

み	あ	も	か	し	ち	き	お	う	く	ふ	む	お	い

After a much longer break, add the romaji for each symbol below.

け	め	て	ち	え	ゆ	け	す	お	き	い	か	や	さ

ひ	ぬ	む	も	へ	ふ	せ	の	く	こ	せ	た	み	と

し	は	う	ほ	つ	そ	ま	そ	な	よ	お	に	ね	い

The words below are all written with syllables you have now studied.

やま — mountain

ゆめ — to dream

よむ — to read

もも — peach

みや — shrine

こめ — uncooked rice

つゆ — dew

むし — insect

まつ — to wait/pine tree

うめ — plum

むね — chest, breast

きもの — kimono

さしみ — sashimi

ゆかた — cotton kimono

えまき — picture scroll

みこし — portable shrine

うきよえ — woodblock print

せともの — porcelain

すきやき — sukiyaki

H7. The R Column

The romaji letter *'r'* is a poor substitute for the Japanese *'r-'* sound and pronunciation of characters in this column can be difficult to master. It is a mixture of romaji letter sounds that is only two thirds *'r'*. A quarter of the sound feels like a lower case *'l' (as in 'learn')*, and the remainder almost a lower case *'d'* sound *(like in 'dark')*.

Symbols in this learning block.

Pronunciation

Combining the sounds of three letters in one is tricky. We found the exercise below can help English speakers to understand and produce an accurate Japanese *'r-'* sound:

Begin with a regular *'l'* sound, saying *'La'* out loud a few times. Your tongue will point upwards a little so that the bottom of it makes contact with the roof of your mouth. Say *'La'* a few more times, paying attention to the position of your tongue and location that it makes contacts with the top of your mouth. *"La. La. La"*.

Now do the same with a *'d'* sound, saying *'Da'* until you can feel exactly where your tongue is touching the inside of your mouth. Your tongue will have a much flatter shape and forward position, touching the back of your upper front teeth. *"Da. Da. Da"*.

Finally, alternate between saying *'La'* and *'Da'*, paying attention to the placement of your tongue. Both positions should be the same as in the steps above. As your tongue moves back and forth, you may begin to notice that your it skips over the same spot each time. *"La. Da. La. Da"*.

The Japanese *'r'* sound is made by positioning the tongue in that space between *'La'* and *'Da'*. It takes some getting used to but with enough practice, muscle memory will take over. Simply follow these same steps for the other vowel sounds, swapping out the *'a'* sound each time. *"Li, Di"... "Lu, Du"... and so on.*

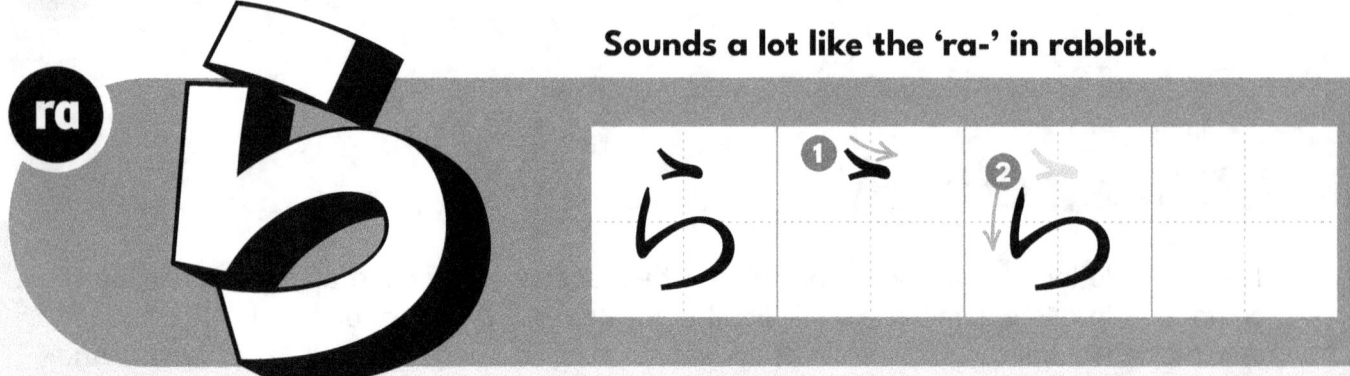

Sounds a lot like the 'ra-' in rabbit.

Practice writing ら by tracing these characters, using two strokes.

Try to maintain accurate shapes while writing ら on a smaller scale.

Mnemonic.

Examples.
- Imagine the shape of a <u>ra</u>bbit
- Maybe the number 5 but it's a bit <u>ra</u>ttled

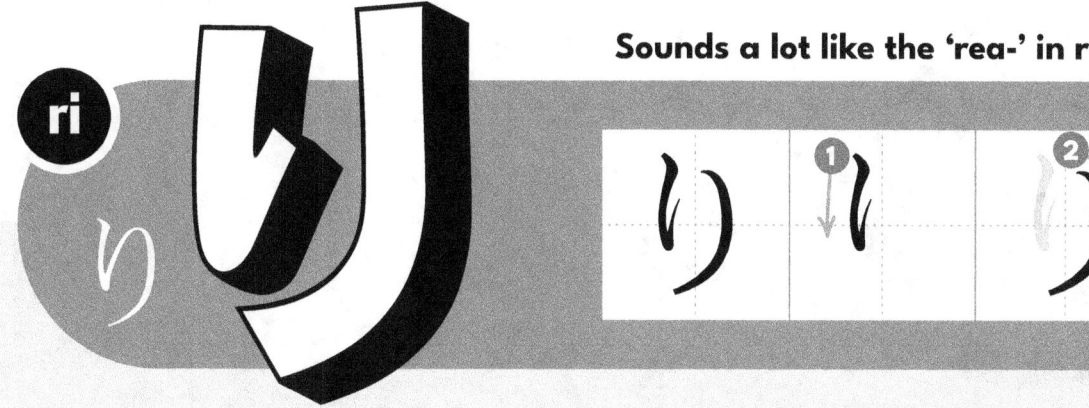

Sounds a lot like the 'rea-' in reach.

Practice writing り **by tracing these characters, using** **two** **strokes.**

Try to maintain accurate shapes while writing り **on a smaller scale.**

Mnemonic.

Examples.

- Two <u>rea</u>ching arms
- Maybe two <u>ree</u>ds

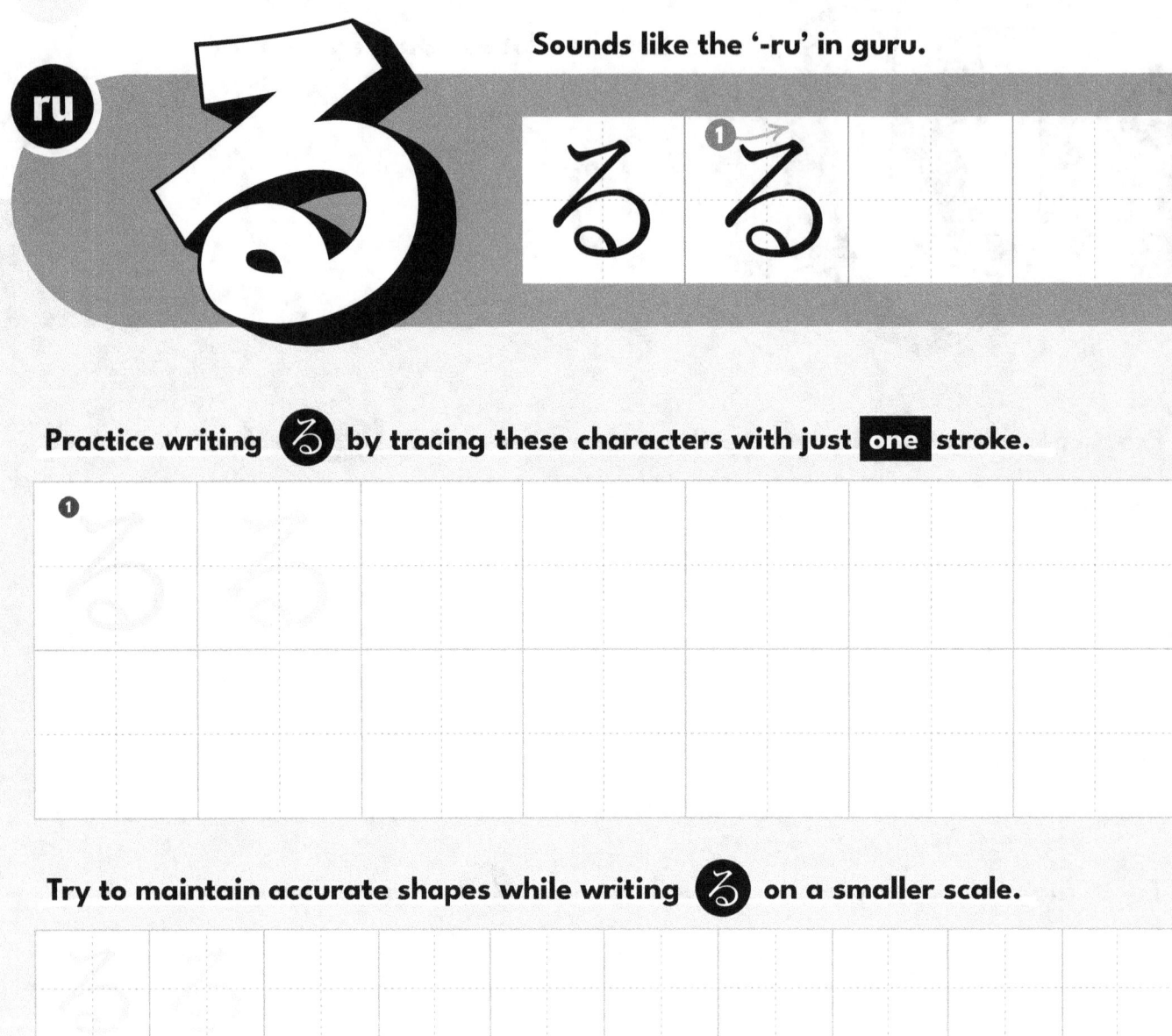

ru

Sounds like the '-ru' in guru.

Practice writing る by tracing these characters with just one stroke.

Try to maintain accurate shapes while writing る on a smaller scale.

Mnemonic.

Examples.
- Rope, with a <u>loop</u>
- As roads go, this is the scenic <u>route</u>.

Sounds like the 'ra-' in race, like 'ray'.

Practice writing れ by tracing these characters, using two strokes.

Try to maintain accurate shapes while writing れ on a smaller scale.

Mnemonic.

Examples.

- A <u>race</u> across the finish line
- Picture a snake, <u>res</u>ting on a branch

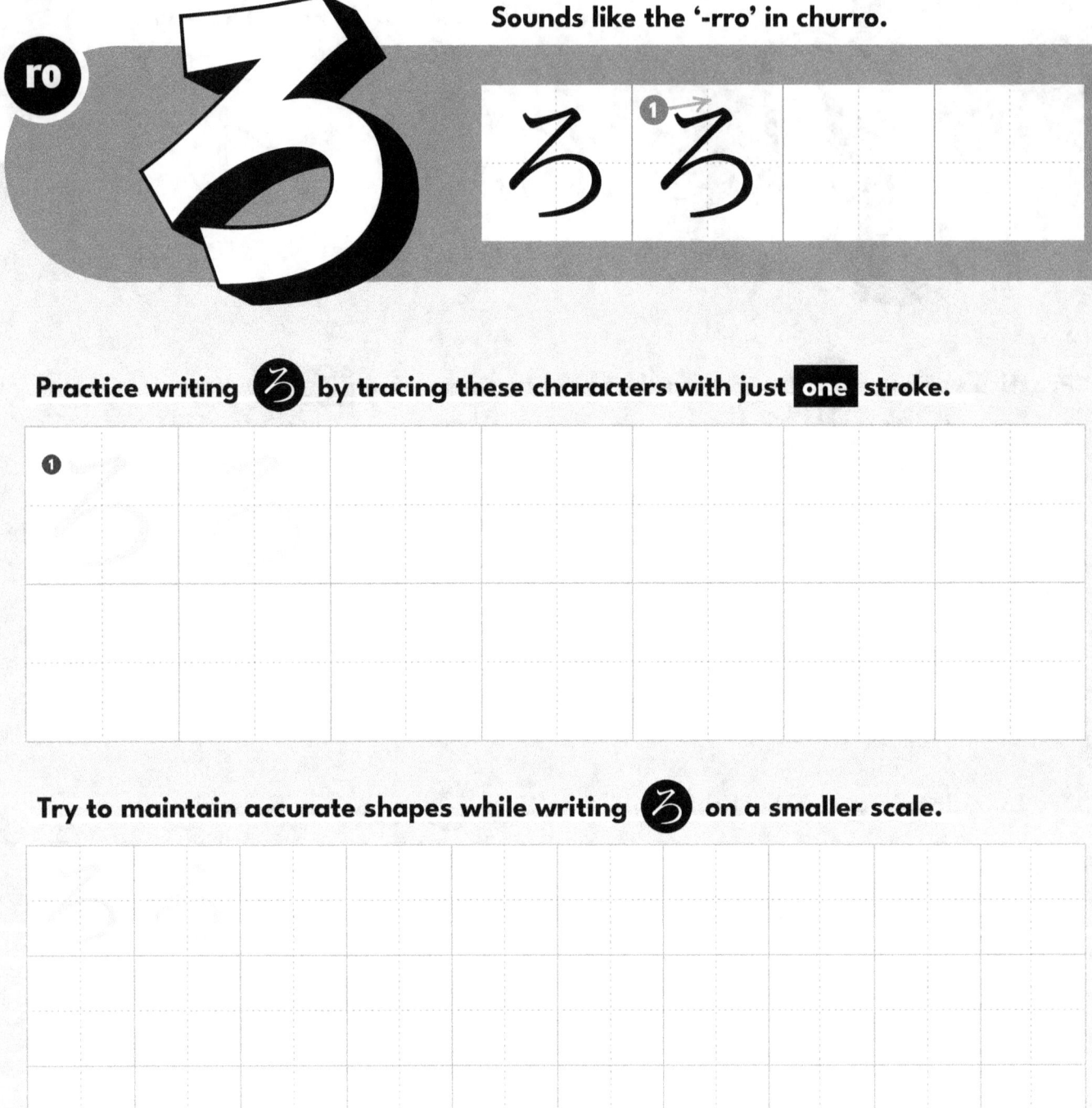

Practice writing ろ by tracing these characters with just one stroke.

Try to maintain accurate shapes while writing ろ on a smaller scale.

Mnemonic.

Examples.
- This <u>ro</u>ad is less bendy than in 'ru'
- <u>Ro</u>pe, but no loop

H8. The W Column + N

This last block of hiragana has just three characters to learn. The first is relatively normal but the second and third are a little different. The 'w-' is quite close to the 'u', and should be pronounced this way. The last symbol doesn't actually have any vowel sound but needed to be placed in a group:

Symbols in this learning block:

Pronunciation

As mentioned above, the 'w-' characters are pronounced in a similar way to the vowel sounds for 'u' and less like the letter 'w' in English. Your lips should not be pushed out as they would if saying 'oo' but they do need to be compressed. When pronouncing 'wa', it should almost sound like 'oo-wah' and taking the same length of time to say as any other symbol.

The sound of 'wo' is similar, sounding like 'oo-woh'. This character is mainly found in use as a particle.

Unlike all the other kana you have learned, the Japanese 'n' character ん has no vowel sound attached to it. Pronounce this as 'nnn', as it sounds in ten or rain.

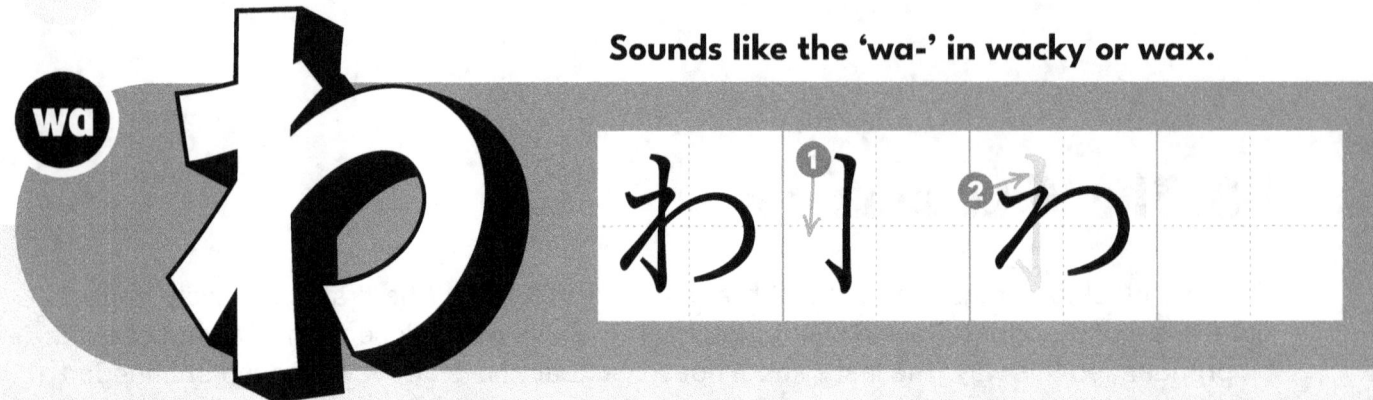

Sounds like the 'wa-' in wacky or wax.

Practice writing わ by tracing these characters, using **two** strokes.

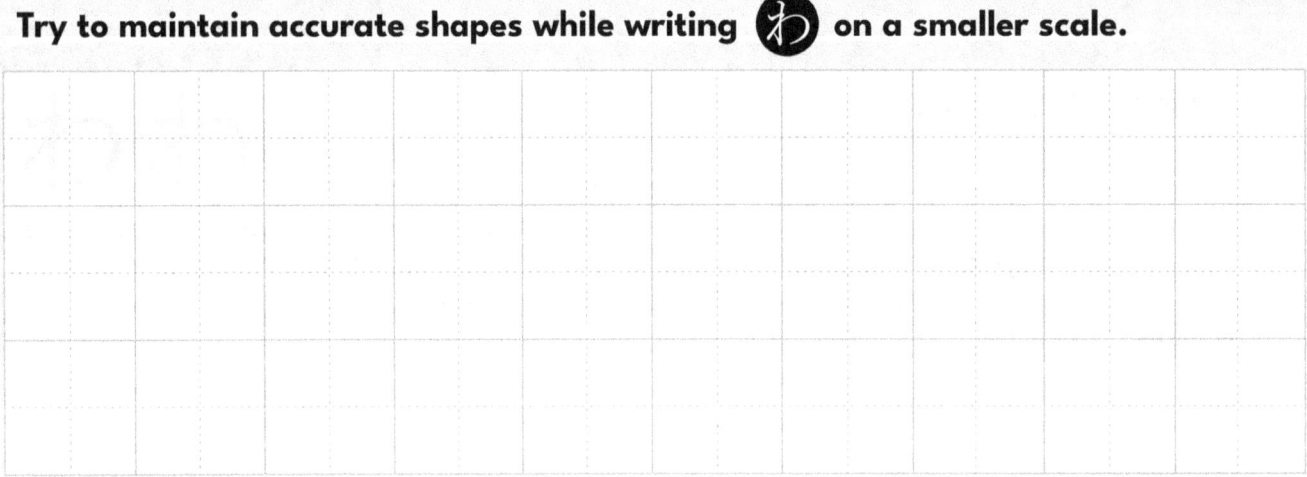

Try to maintain accurate shapes while writing わ on a smaller scale.

Mnemonic.

Examples.

- Picture a <u>wa</u>sp, crawling up a tree
- Maybe a <u>wa</u>iter, and their big, round tray

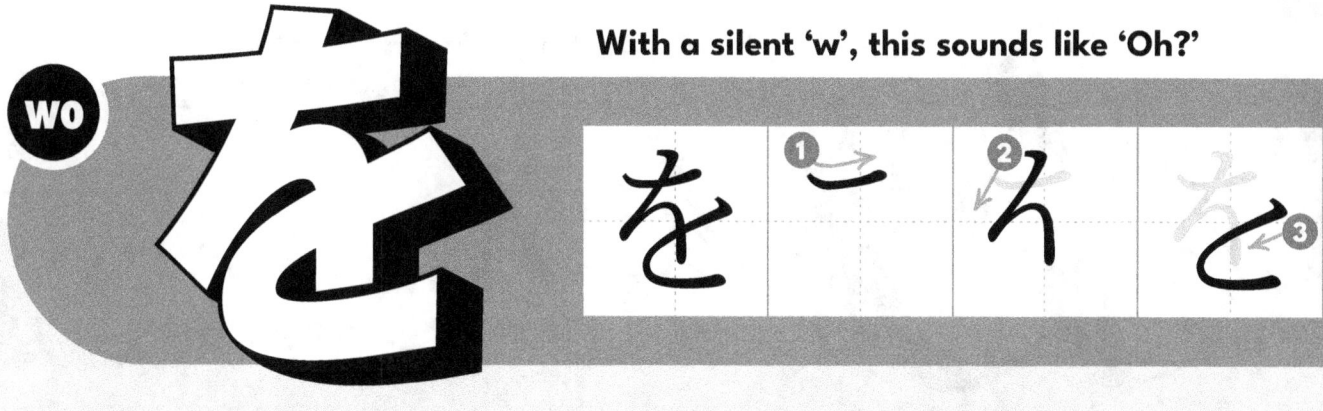

WO

With a silent 'w', this sounds like 'Oh?'

Practice writing を by tracing these characters, using three strokes.

Try to maintain accurate shapes while writing を on a smaller scale.

Mnemonic.

Examples.

- Dipping a toe in a cold pond... "w<u>oah</u>"
- Picture a cowboy on a horse... "w<u>oah</u>"

n ん

Similar to the '-n' in plane, or 'nnn'.

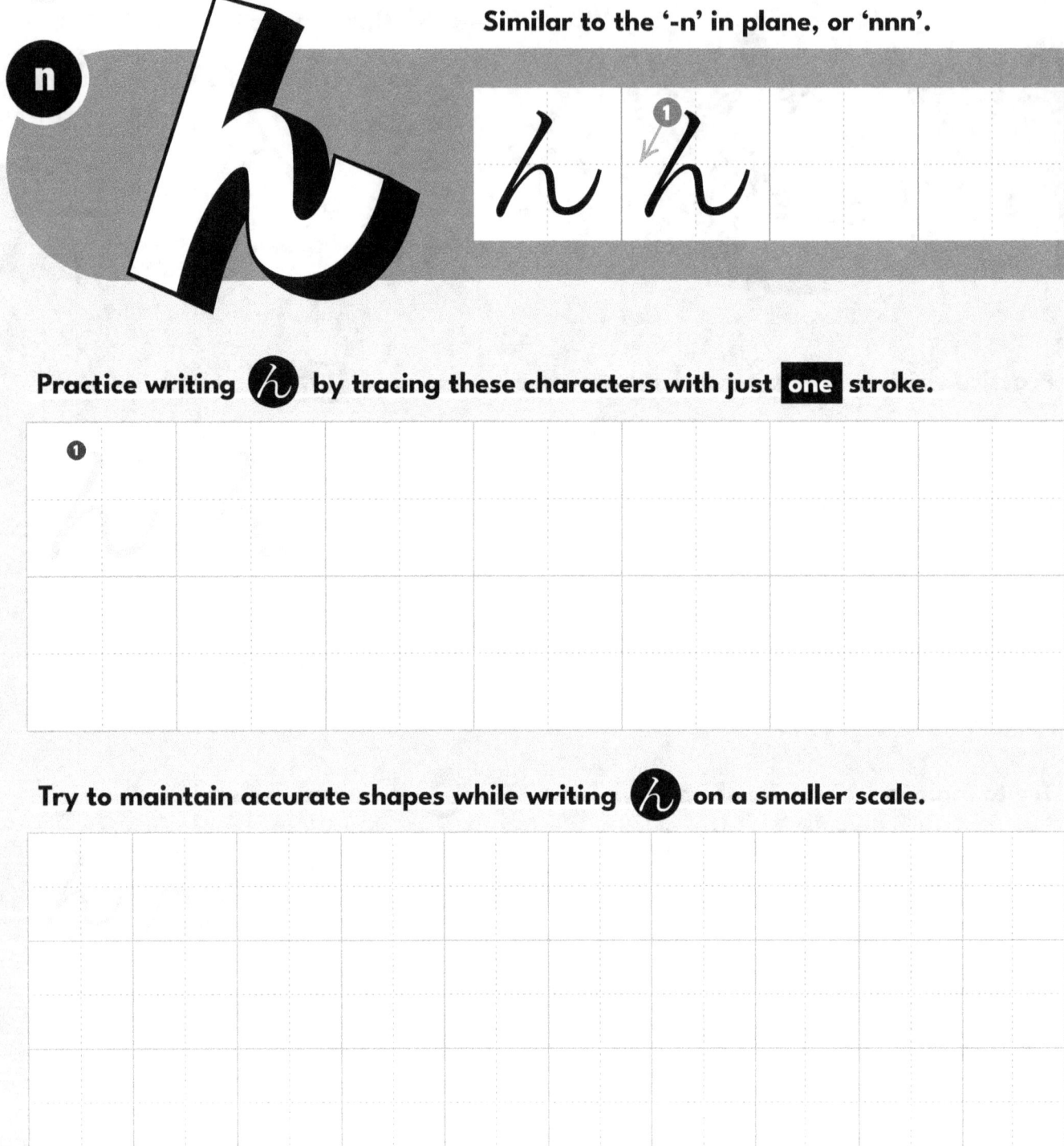

Practice writing ん by tracing these characters with just one stroke.

Try to maintain accurate shapes while writing ん on a smaller scale.

Mnemonic.

Examples.
- Lower case letter 'n'
- The last hiragana, at the end.

That last group completes the set, meaning this exercise may contain any of the 46 hiragana. Most should be familiar by now; write the romaji below characters from all groups below.

Practice pronouncing each symbol as you write the romaji beneath.

り む を ろ ほ み ん さ ま ゆ ち ら ろ よ

わ ろ も よ れ む ん と ん り る く み る

れ る ら り も や ま め を け れ わ め や

Take a 5-minute break, and then do the same for these symbols too.

て ゆ ら ほ へ む け は す う ろ く ね や

る い の き お か あ を に ち も し つ こ

そ ひ ら わ を ふ れ み な り ま え さ め

This time, take a 10-minute break and come back to complete these.

ひ ら ん そ り ぬ た む わ る れ ろ に ら

み め ゆ る や へ え も よ す く む ま ん

ろ を め も ま ほ つ の み は ふ あ れ わ

After a much longer break, add the romaji for each symbol below.

ゆ よ や を ね た ん せ と ゆ ら わ あ を

ほ よ に む も る り み つ ら れ ろ を す

は を ひ ん や ね わ の る ゆ く め も ふ

These final word lists may contain characters from all hiragana study blocks.

わん
bay/bowl

てら
temple

つる
crane / to fish

これ
this

ふろ
bath

のり
seaweed/glue

はる
to stretch

れい
example/soul

しろ
castle/white

にほん
Japan

さくら
cherry blossom

うちわ
round fan

まつり
festival

ほたる
firefly

ふとん
futon

れきし
history

わふく
Japanese clothing

りろん
theory

ひのまる
Rising Sun flag

さむらい
Samurai

//////////////////////////////// **PART 3**

Katakana

The *letters* in this alphabet **represent the same sounds as hiragana,** and we pronounce them the same way. While it might seem strange to have two alphabets for the same syllable sounds, we use them differently. You could almost think of katakana as having a similar role to a Japanese speaker, as romaji has for you.

Katakana is mainly for reading and writing foreign *'loanwords,'* though. The terms to describe ideas or objects originating from outside of Japan. Pronunciations transcribed in katakana often sound similar *(but with a Japanese twist)*, and these spellings become the Japanese word for that *'thing.'* Some of the most common examples are the names for certain foodstuffs from abroad, such as chocolate, hamburger, or pizza. In written Japanese, this script also represents sound effects (onomatopoeia). Essentially, it spells words for which there is not already a Japanese equivalent. The English language also has loanwords, such as 'karaoke' imported from Japan, funnily enough.

It's important to mention that loanwords originate from non-English-speaking countries too. The Japanese word for bread derives from the Portuguese word *'pão,'* written in katakana as **パン** *(pan)*, for example. This everyday food item was entirely new to the Japanese people when it was first introduced, shipped over by traders from Portugal in the 1500s. Katakana loanwords are a sort of placeholder for words that don't exist.

Foreign loanwords can often sound quite similar to the original word in Japanese. The easiest way to understand this concept is to look at an example or two. Here are some loanwords in katakana, shown with romaji and the original English word:

アメリカ	タクシー	クリスマス
A-me-ri-ka	*ta-ku-shii*	*Ku-ri-su-ma-su*
America	Taxi	Christmas
カメラ	ホテル	フライドポテト
Ka-me-ra	*Ho-te-ru*	*fu-ra-i-do-po-te-to*
Camera	Hotel	French fries

Certain English syllable sounds are difficult to reproduce in kana, much like how romaji cannot transcribe Japanese accurately. You can see in the examples above that there is no 'X' sound in the word 'taxi'. Instead, a relatively close equivalent must be used, further illustrating how the two languages don't share all of the same syllable sounds.

The following chart displays the **46 primary katakana characters** you are about to learn. They are organized similarly to the hiragana, with romaji transcriptions below. The vowel sounds are on the right side, shown with romaji vowels, and each consonant sound shown across the top row. Pronunciations follow the pattern where both sounds are combined - a vowel sound is added to the end of a consonant sound - and the same exception applies to 'n' sounds.

Notes:

* ン iis the only character in this table that we pronounce as a syllable without adding any of the vowel sounds.

** ヲ is a *"particle"* and is used for grammar. We write it as *"wo"*, but it is transcribed in romaji as either *"o"* or *"wo"*.

Katakana

	a	i	u	e	o	
	ア a	イ i	ウ u	エ e	オ o	p. 098
k	カ ka	キ ki	ク ku	ケ ke	コ ko	p. 104
s	サ sa	シ shi	ス su	セ se	ソ so	p. 111
t	タ ta	チ chi	ツ tsu	テ te	ト to	p. 117
n	ナ na	ニ ni	ヌ nu	ネ ne	ノ no	p. 125
h	ハ ha	ヒ hi	フ fu	ヘ he	ホ ho	p. 131
m	マ ma	ミ mi	ム mu	メ me	モ mo	p. 138
y	ヤ ya		ユ yu		ヨ yo	p. 144
r	ラ ra	リ ri	ル ru	レ re	ロ ro	p. 149
w	ワ wa		ン n*		ヲ wo**	p. 155

K1. The Vowel & K Columns

As the symbols in katakana represent the same syllable sounds as hiragana, they will be learned in the same order. The first column contains the characters that represent the basic vowel sounds, followed by the K column with exactly the same *[consonant + vowel]* pattern of pronunciation.

Symbols in this learning block.

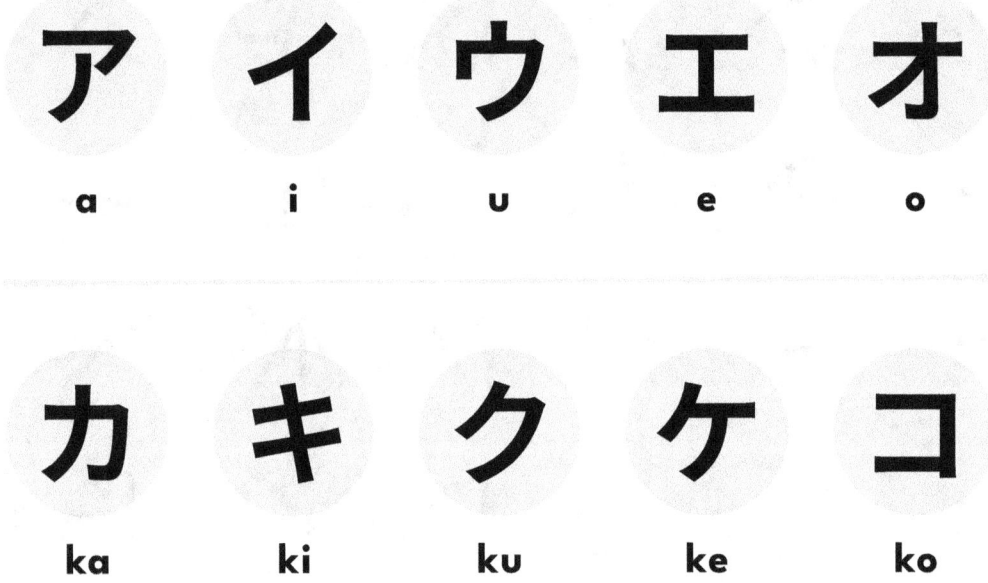

Pronunciation

There are no differences in sound between the first ten hiragana that you learned and the way in which you should pronounce these characters.

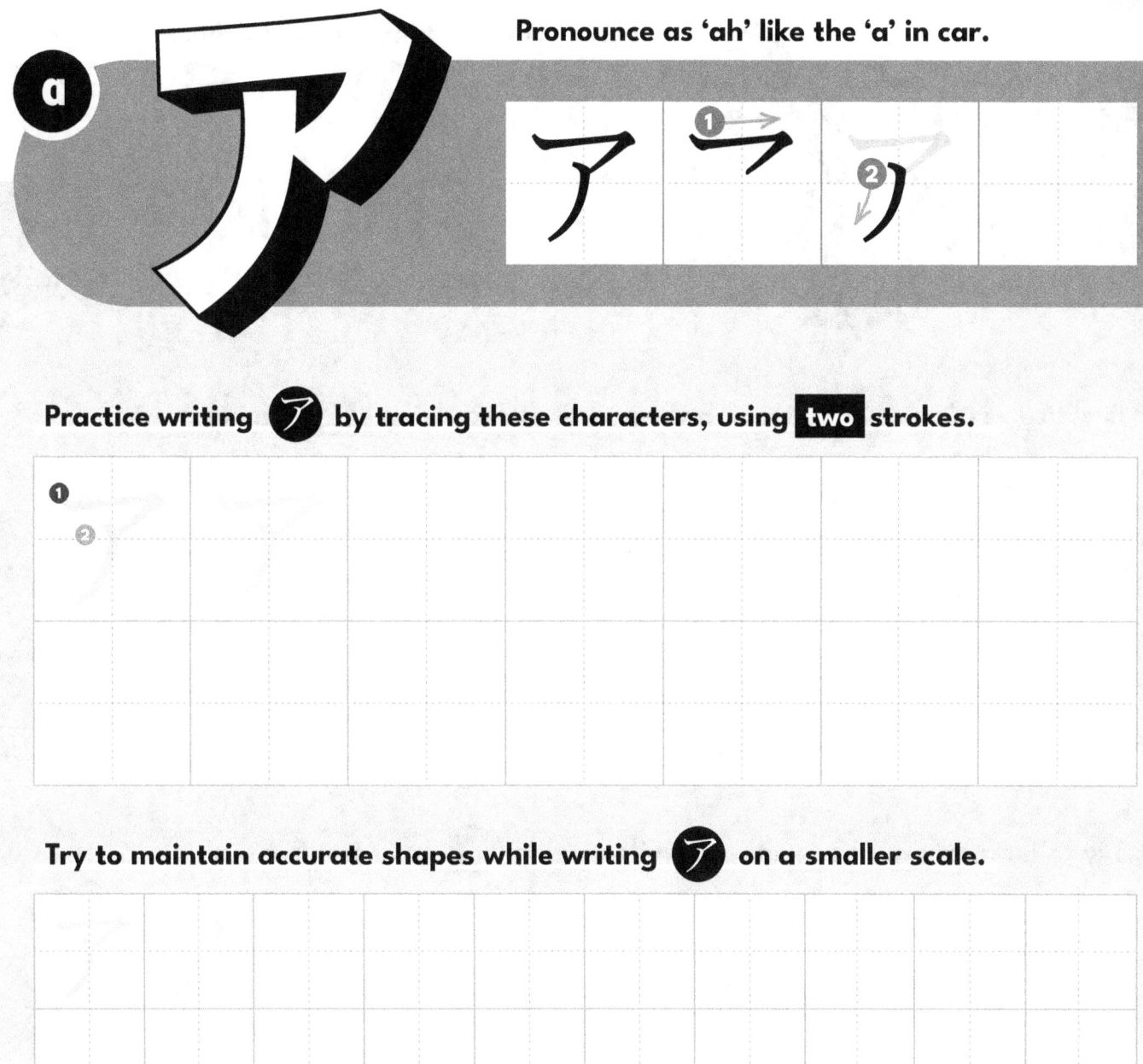

Pronounce as 'ah' like the 'a' in car.

Practice writing ア by tracing these characters, using **two** strokes.

Try to maintain accurate shapes while writing ア on a smaller scale.

Mnemonic.

Examples.
- The letter 'A' rotated to the right.

i

Sounds like 'i' in king, or 'ee' in cheek.

Practice writing イ by tracing these characters, using two strokes.

Try to maintain accurate shapes while writing イ on a smaller scale.

Mnemonic.

Examples.
- An artist would paint on their <u>ea</u>sel
- Letter 'i' with a hat

u ウ

Similar to 'oo' but like the 'ue' in true.

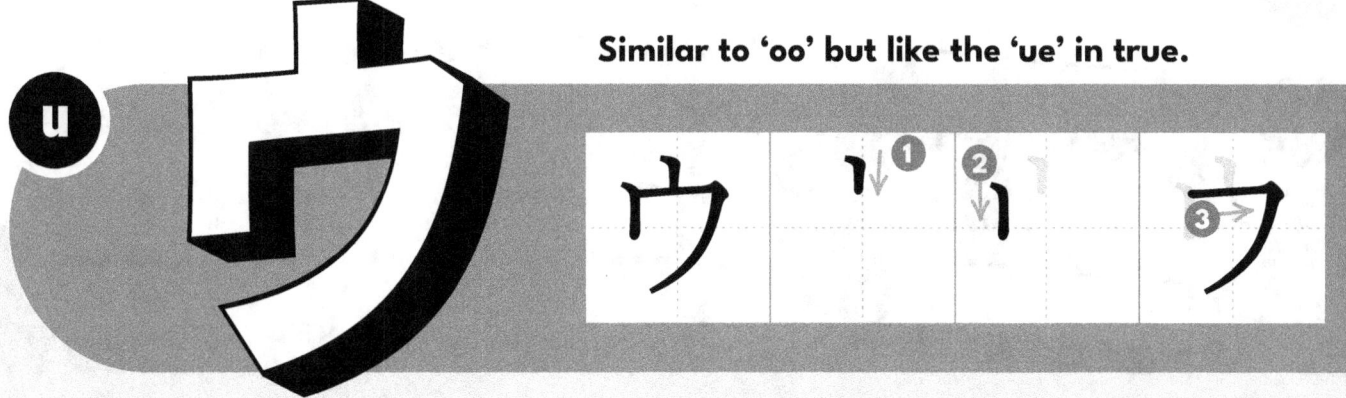

Practice writing ウ by tracing these characters, using three strokes.

Try to maintain accurate shapes while writing ウ on a smaller scale.

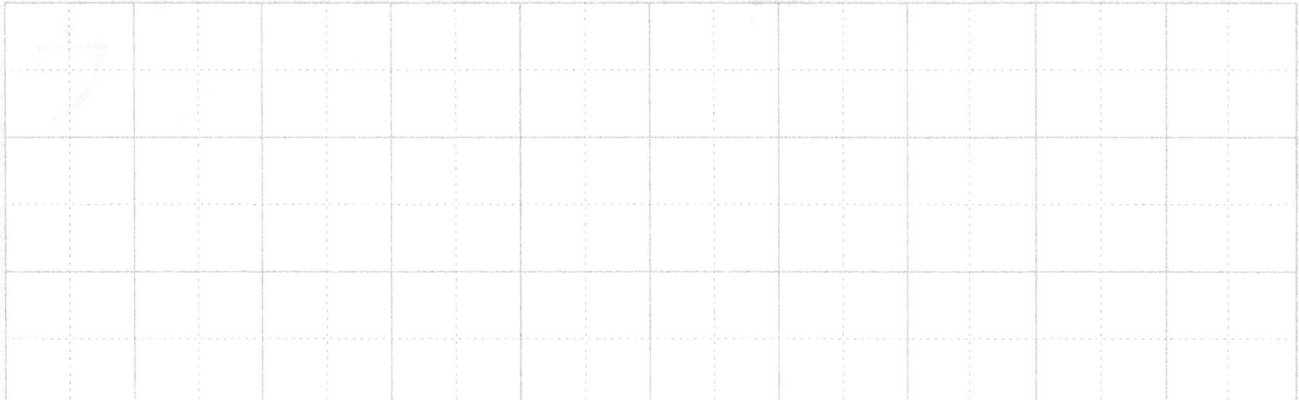

Mnemonic.

Examples.

- Similar to hiragana
- Upside down 'u'

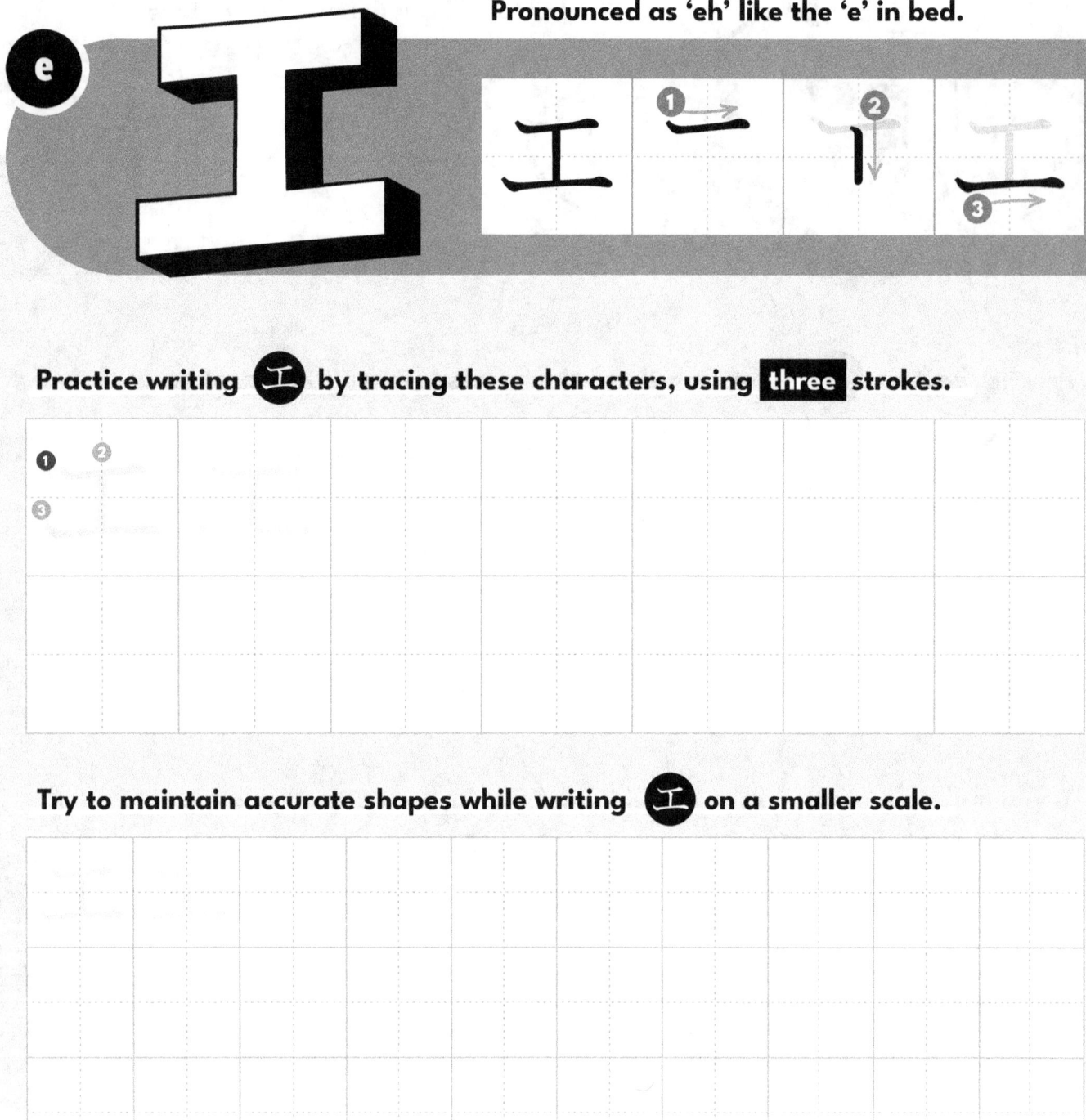

Pronounced as 'eh' like the 'e' in bed.

Practice writing 工 by tracing these characters, using three strokes.

Try to maintain accurate shapes while writing 工 on a smaller scale.

Mnemonic.

Examples.

- Picture a set of <u>e</u>levator doors
- <u>En</u>gineers use steel girders to build

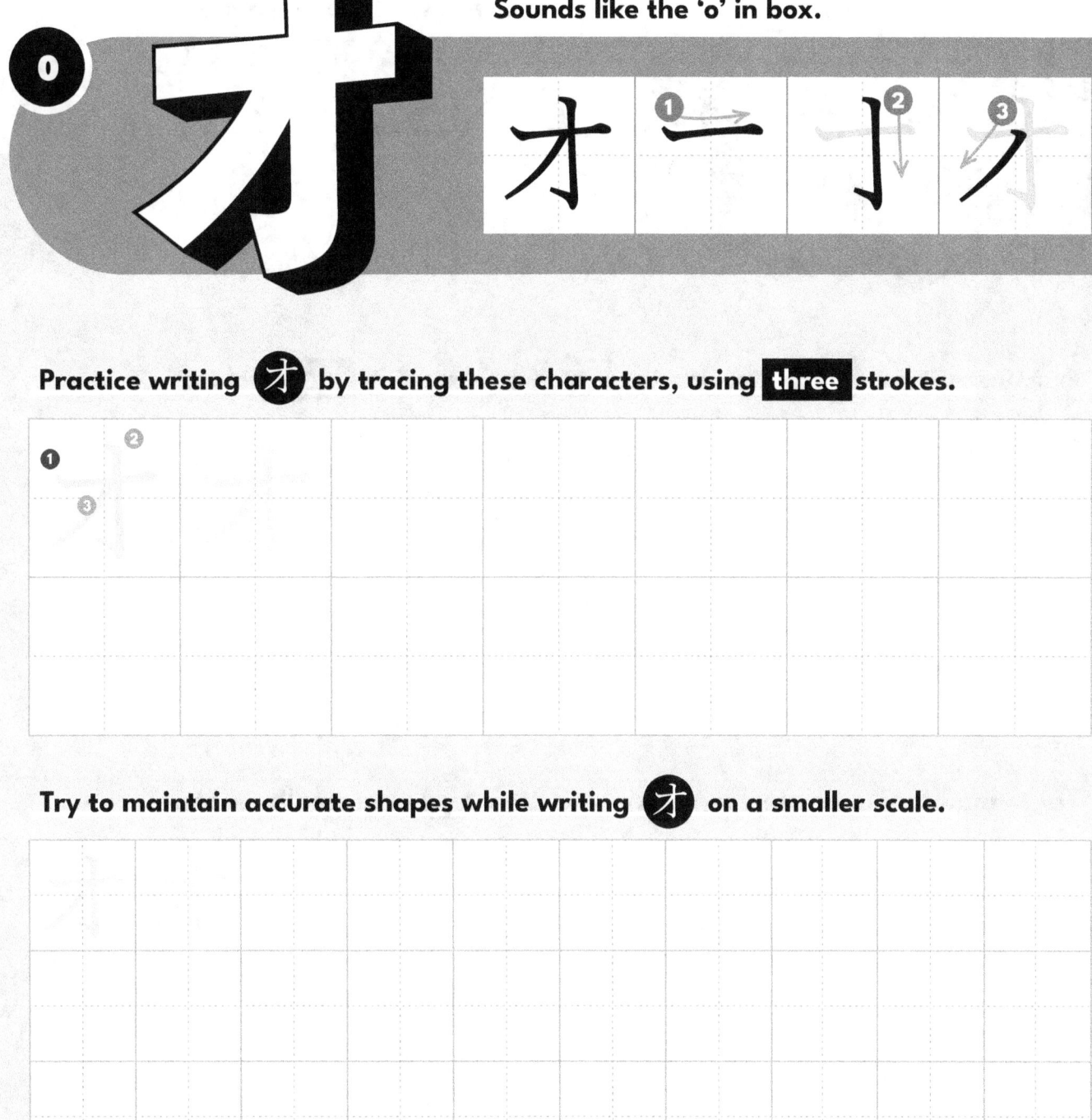

オ

Sounds like the 'o' in box.

Practice writing オ by tracing these characters, using three strokes.

Try to maintain accurate shapes while writing オ on a smaller scale.

Mnemonic.

Examples.
- A person falling backwards, "oh no!"
- Superhero with a cape, "oh wow!"

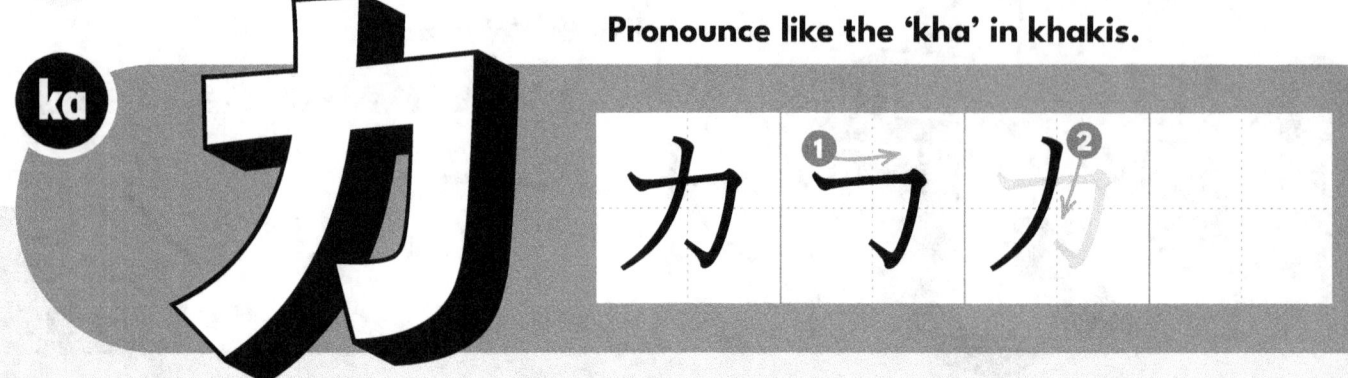

Pronounce like the 'kha' in khakis.

Practice writing 力 by tracing these characters, using two strokes.

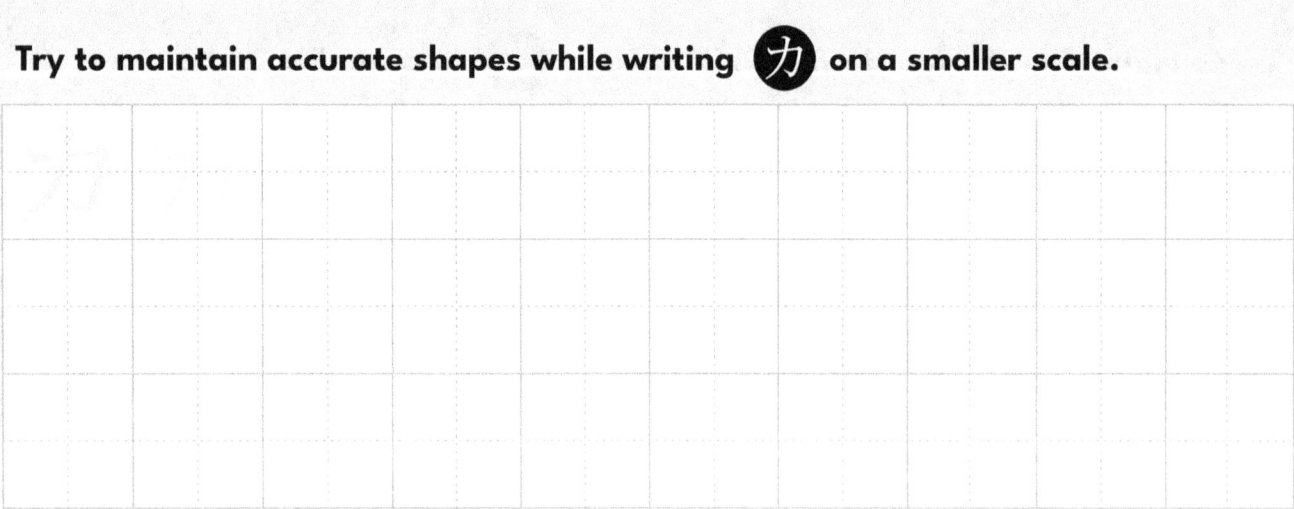

Try to maintain accurate shapes while writing 力 on a smaller scale.

Mnemonic.

Examples.
- Very similar to the hiragana

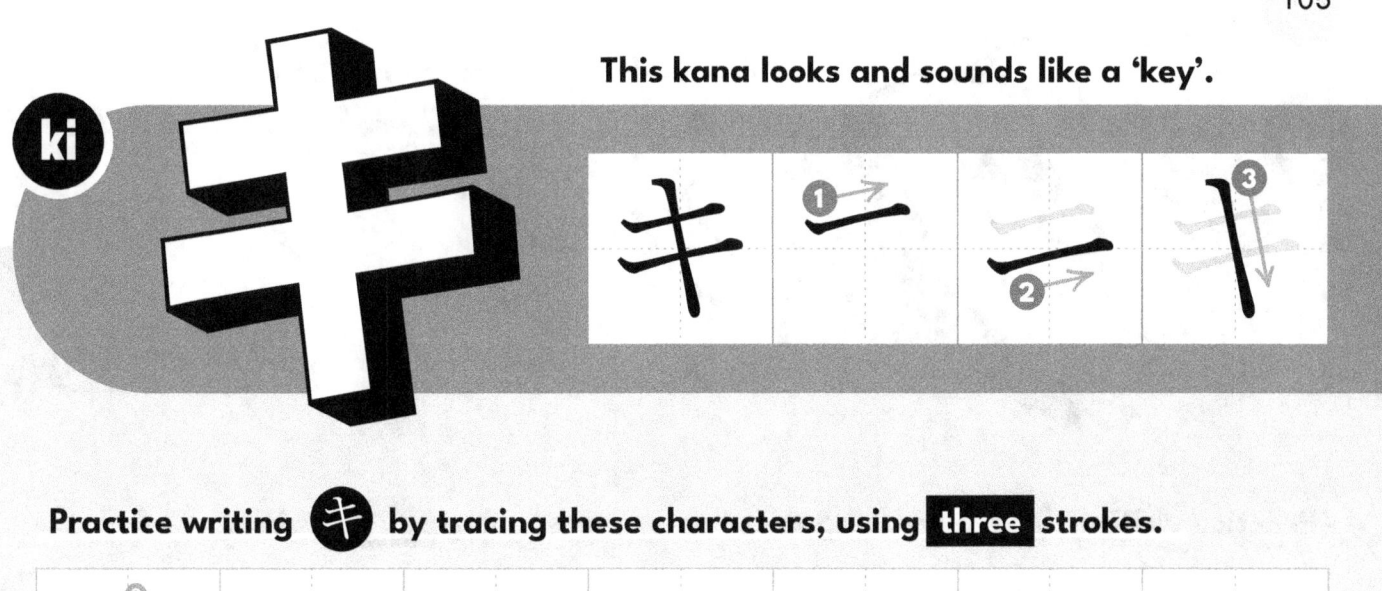

This kana looks and sounds like a 'key'.

Practice writing キ **by tracing these characters, using** three **strokes.**

Try to maintain accurate shapes while writing キ **on a smaller scale.**

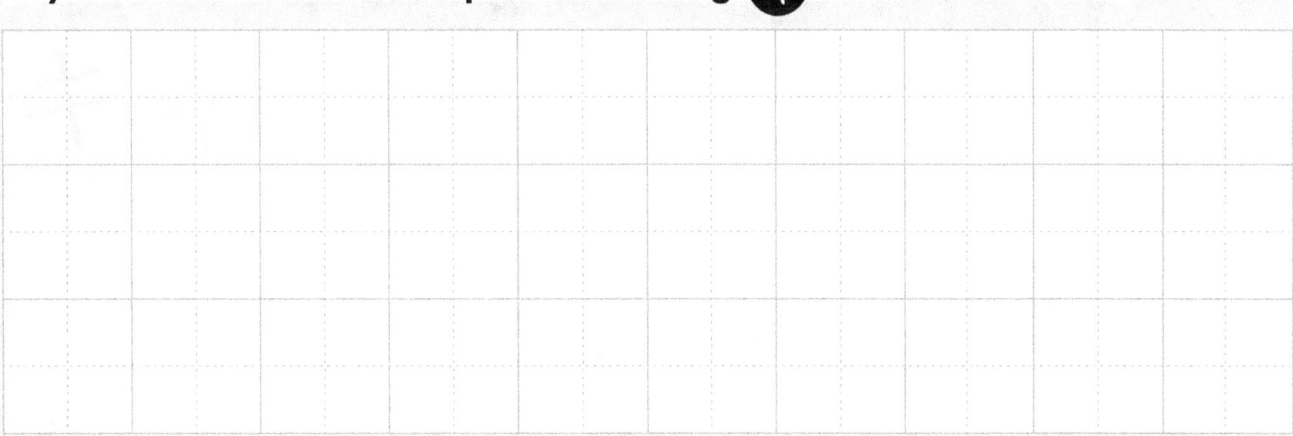

Mnemonic.

Examples.

- Similar to hiragana
- A slightly different <u>k</u>ey this time.

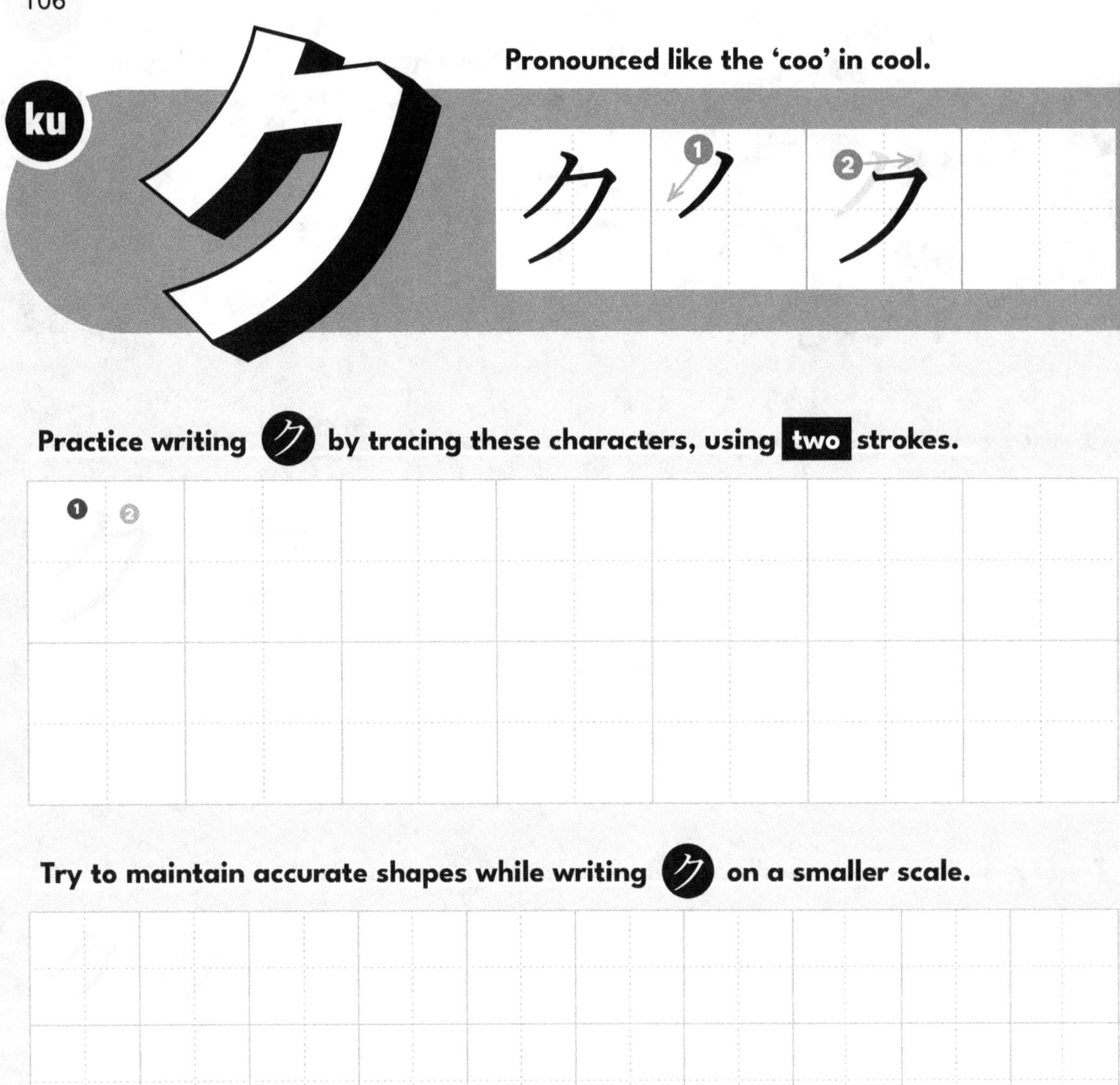

ku — Pronounced like the 'coo' in cool.

Practice writing ク by tracing these characters, using **two** strokes.

Try to maintain accurate shapes while writing ク on a smaller scale.

Mnemonic.

Examples.
- Picture a <u>coo</u>k's hat
- Number 7, with a <u>cool</u> hat

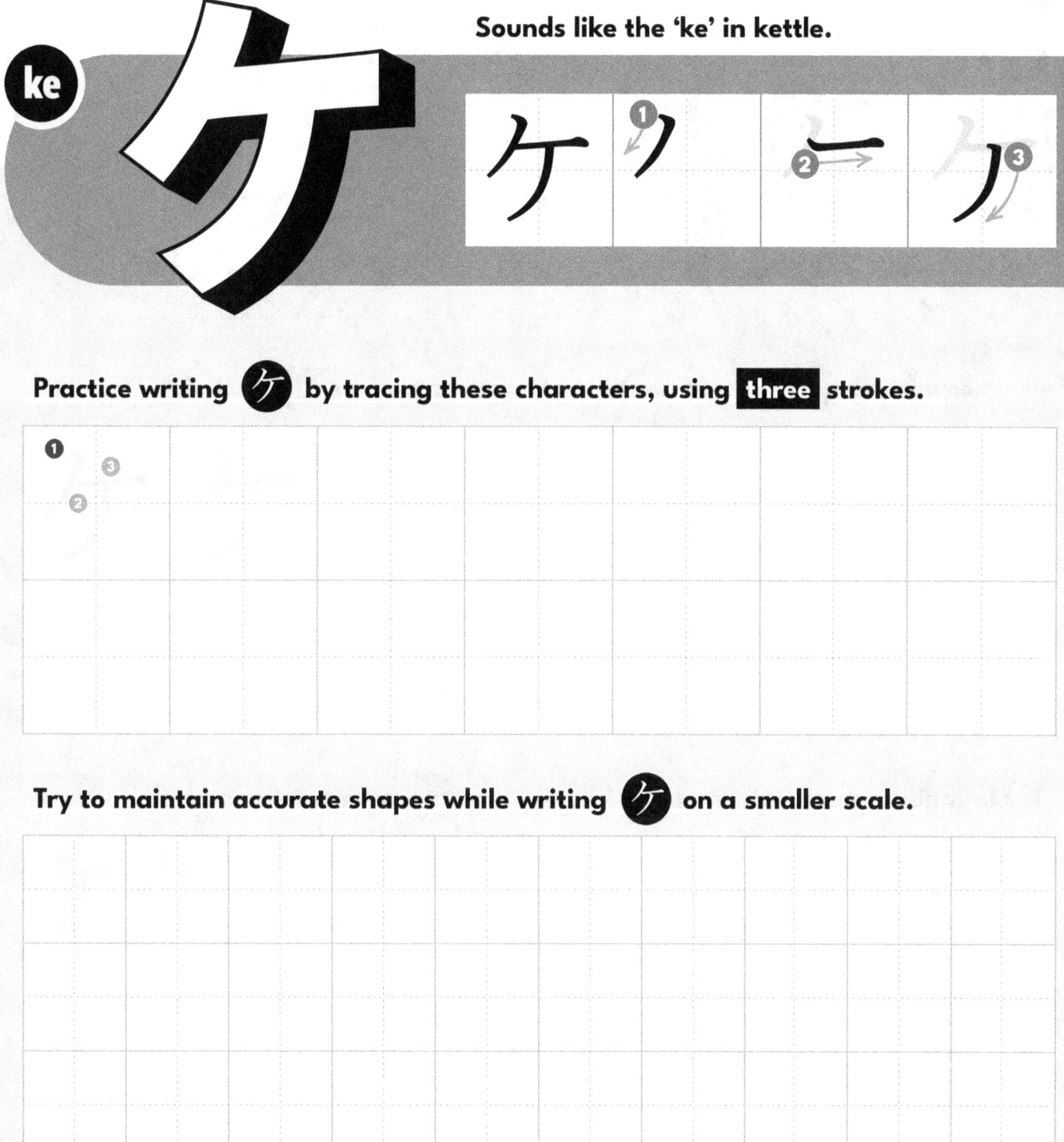

ke

Sounds like the 'ke' in kettle.

Practice writing ケ by tracing these characters, using three strokes.

Try to maintain accurate shapes while writing ケ on a smaller scale.

Mnemonic.

Examples.
- Letter 'k' tilting to the right

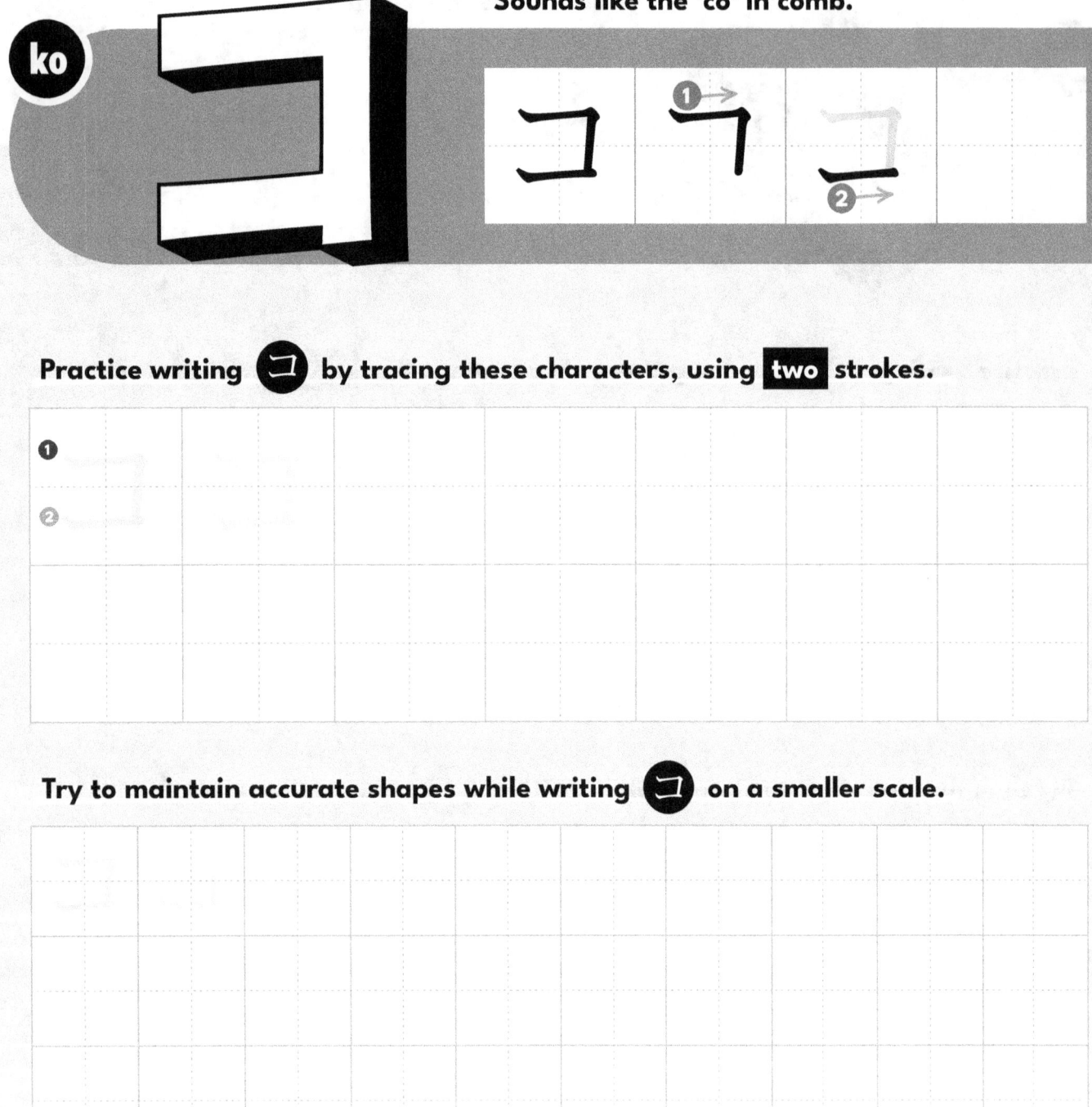

ko

Sounds like the 'co' in comb.

Practice writing コ **by tracing these characters, using two strokes.**

Try to maintain accurate shapes while writing コ **on a smaller scale.**

Mnemonic.

Examples.
- This katakana has two <u>corners</u>

This first set of exercises will test how well you can attach the shape of the new katakana symbol to the same sound as its hiragana counterpart.

Practice pronouncing each symbol as you write the romaji beneath.

ア ウ ア イ オ エ オ イ ア エ オ エ オ ア

ウ イ オ ウ イ エ イ オ ア ウ ア エ ウ ア

ウ イ オ ア エ ウ オ ア エ イ ウ ア エ イ

Take a break for 5 minutes, and then do the same for these symbols too.

ア オ カ オ キ ケ ク ウ エ イ ア ク ウ ア

ク イ オ エ イ カ エ ウ ケ カ オ カ イ ウ

キ ウ カ ク オ イ エ キ カ ケ ア キ オ カ

It may feel easy, but the difficulty is going to ramp up as you learn larger groups of characters.

This time, take a 10-minute break and come back to complete these.

コ ウ ク カ イ キ ケ ク エ キ ア イ オ ク

ウ カ エ イ コ イ ウ ケ ア キ オ コ キ カ

ア ウ オ ク エ ク カ ケ コ オ ア ウ ケ エ

After a much longer break, add the romaji for each symbol below.

キ ケ オ イ コ ク キ ウ コ イ エ ア オ ク

ク コ ウ カ オ ア ケ エ キ ク ア ケ カ イ

カ エ ウ ケ カ ア ウ キ ク コ オ イ ウ エ

K2. The S & T Columns

Once more, pronunciation of this set mirrors the hiragana. The characters in this section are taken from both the S and T columns in the basic katakana table.

Symbols in this learning block.

Pronunciation

The same pronunciation rules apply to the exceptions for *'shi'*, *'chi'*, and *'tsu'*.

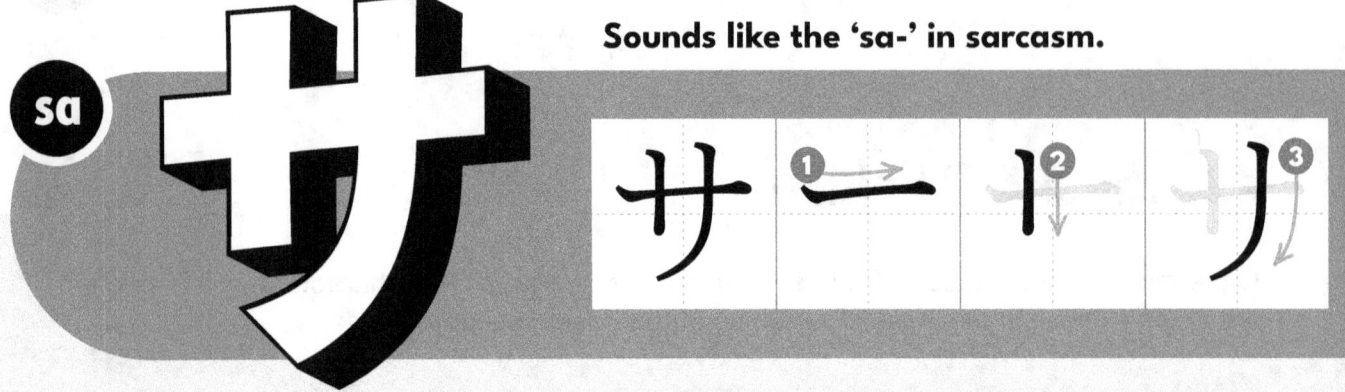

Sounds like the 'sa-' in sarcasm.

Practice writing サ **by tracing these characters, using three strokes.**

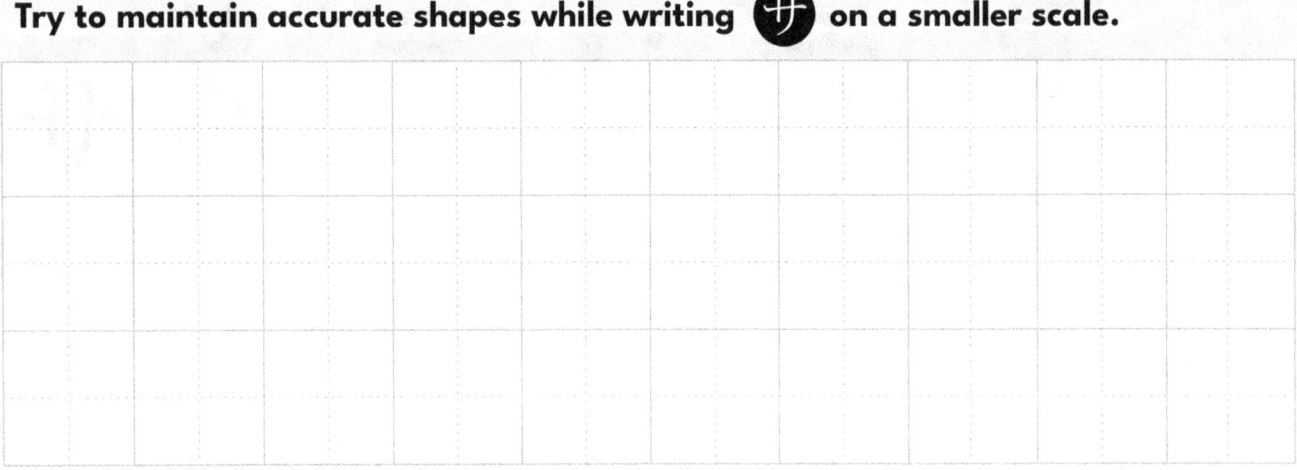

Try to maintain accurate shapes while writing サ **on a smaller scale.**

Mnemonic.

Examples.
- Imagine the shape of a <u>sa</u>ddle

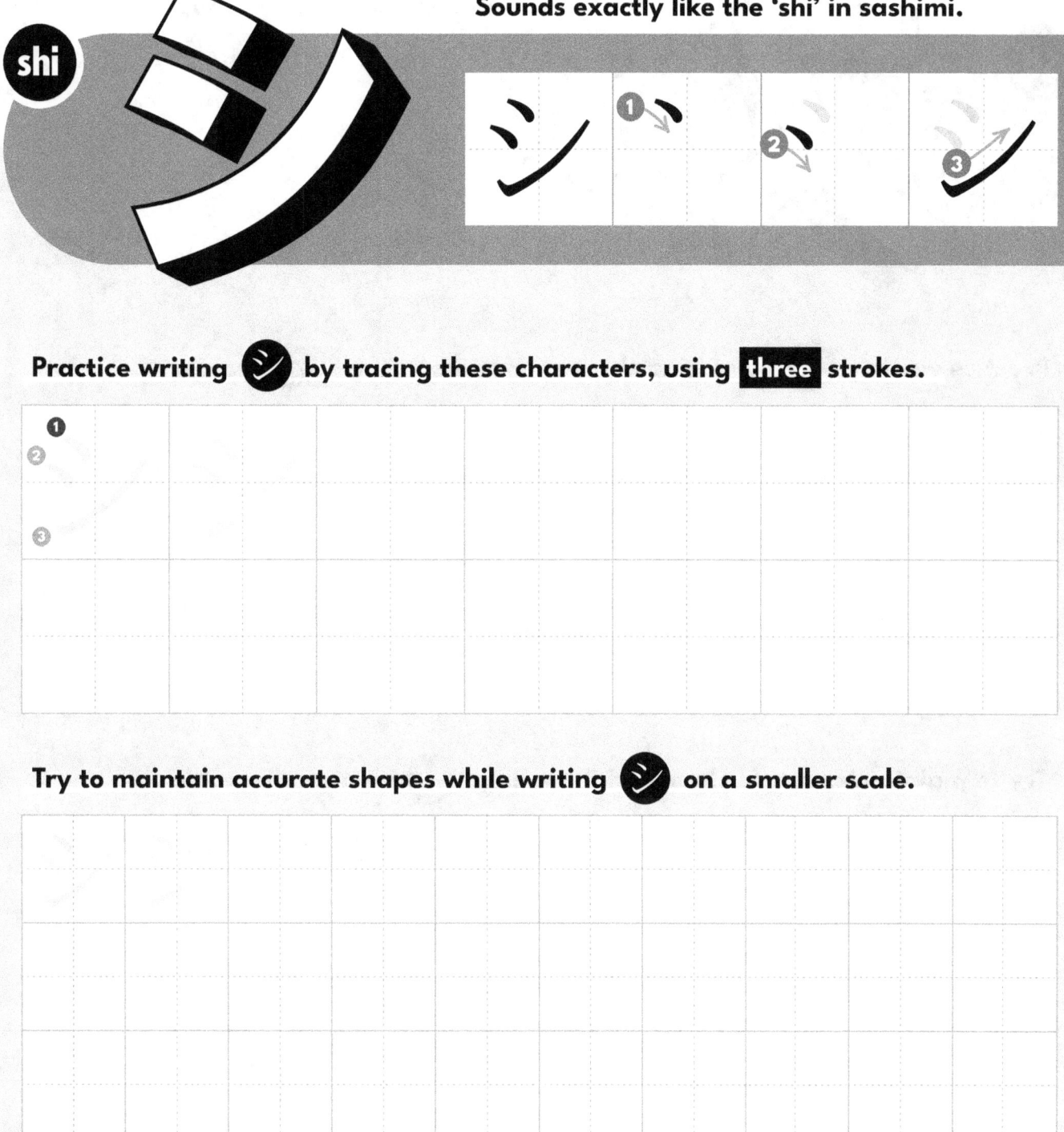

Sounds exactly like the 'shi' in sashimi.

Practice writing ツ **by tracing these characters, using** three **strokes.**

Try to maintain accurate shapes while writing ツ **on a smaller scale.**

Mnemonic.

Examples.

- <u>She</u> has a crooked smile

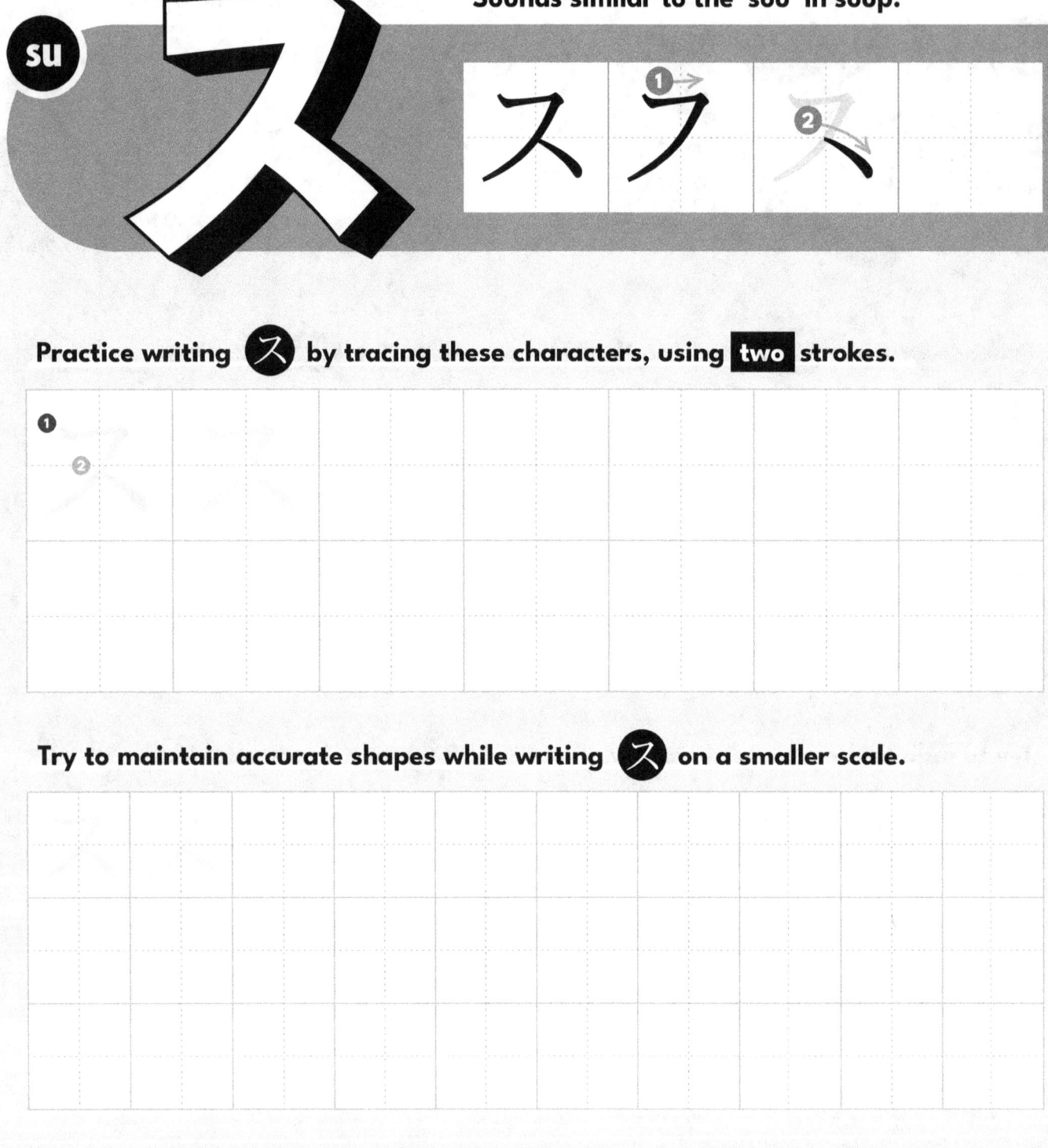

su — Sounds similar to the 'sou' in soup.

Practice writing ス by tracing these characters, using two strokes.

Try to maintain accurate shapes while writing ス on a smaller scale.

Mnemonic.

Examples.
- You hang <u>su</u>its on a coathanger

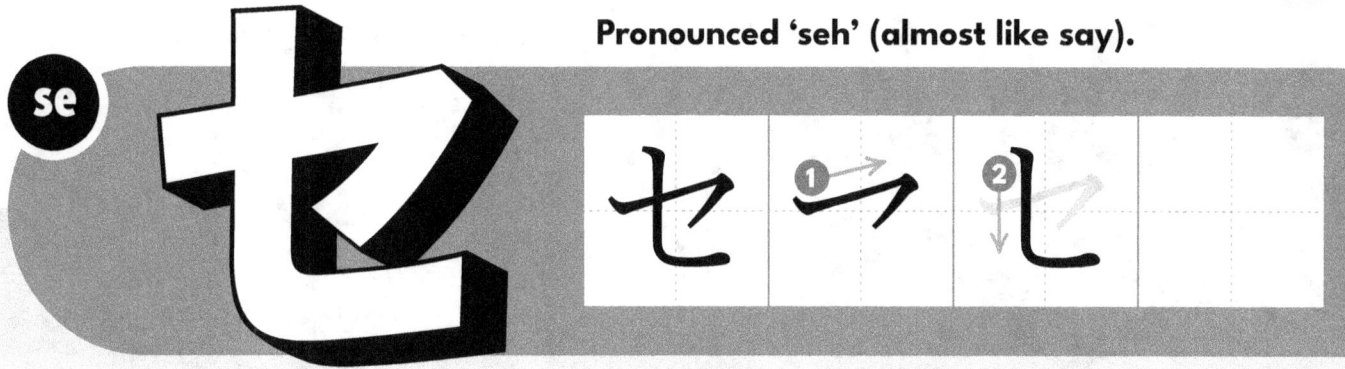

Pronounced 'seh' (almost like say).

Practice writing セ by tracing these characters, using two strokes.

Try to maintain accurate shapes while writing セ on a smaller scale.

Mnemonic.

Examples.
- Picture a big mouth, <u>say</u>ing something
- Similar to hiragana

SO ツ

Sounds like the 'so-' in soccer or sorry.

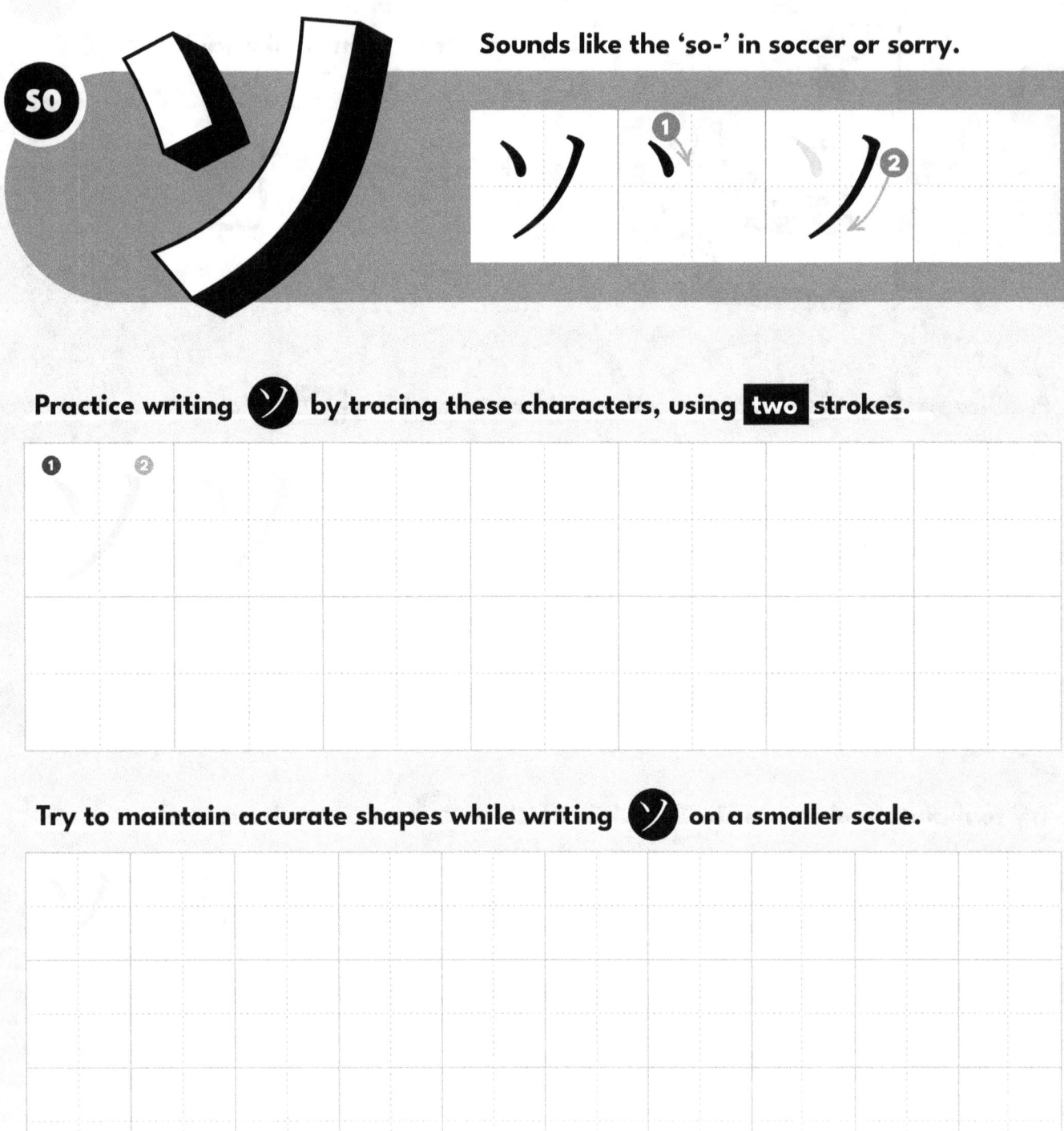

Practice writing ツ **by tracing these characters, using** **two** **strokes.**

Try to maintain accurate shapes while writing ツ **on a smaller scale.**

Mnemonic.

Examples.

- One <u>sew</u>-ing needle, pulling a thread (notice the small line is vertical)

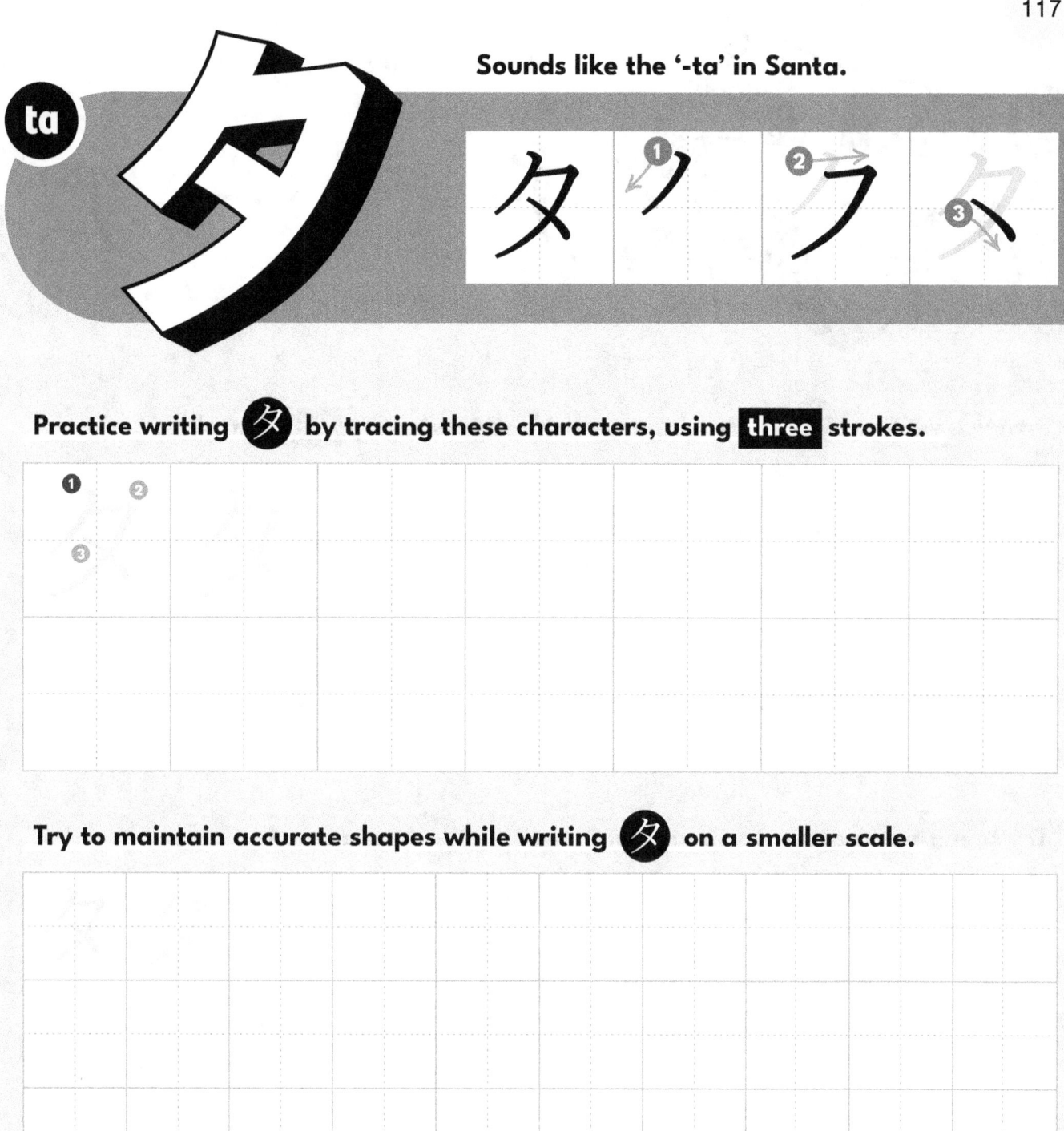

Sounds like the '-ta' in Santa.

Practice writing タ **by tracing these characters, using three strokes.**

Try to maintain accurate shapes while writing タ **on a smaller scale.**

Mnemonic.

Examples.
- The letters 't' and 'A' are hidden inside
- A <u>t</u>idal wave

Sounds just like the 'chee' in cheeks.

Practice writing チ by tracing these characters, using three strokes.

Try to maintain accurate shapes while writing チ on a smaller scale.

Mnemonic.

Examples.
- The same shape as a <u>chee</u>rleader

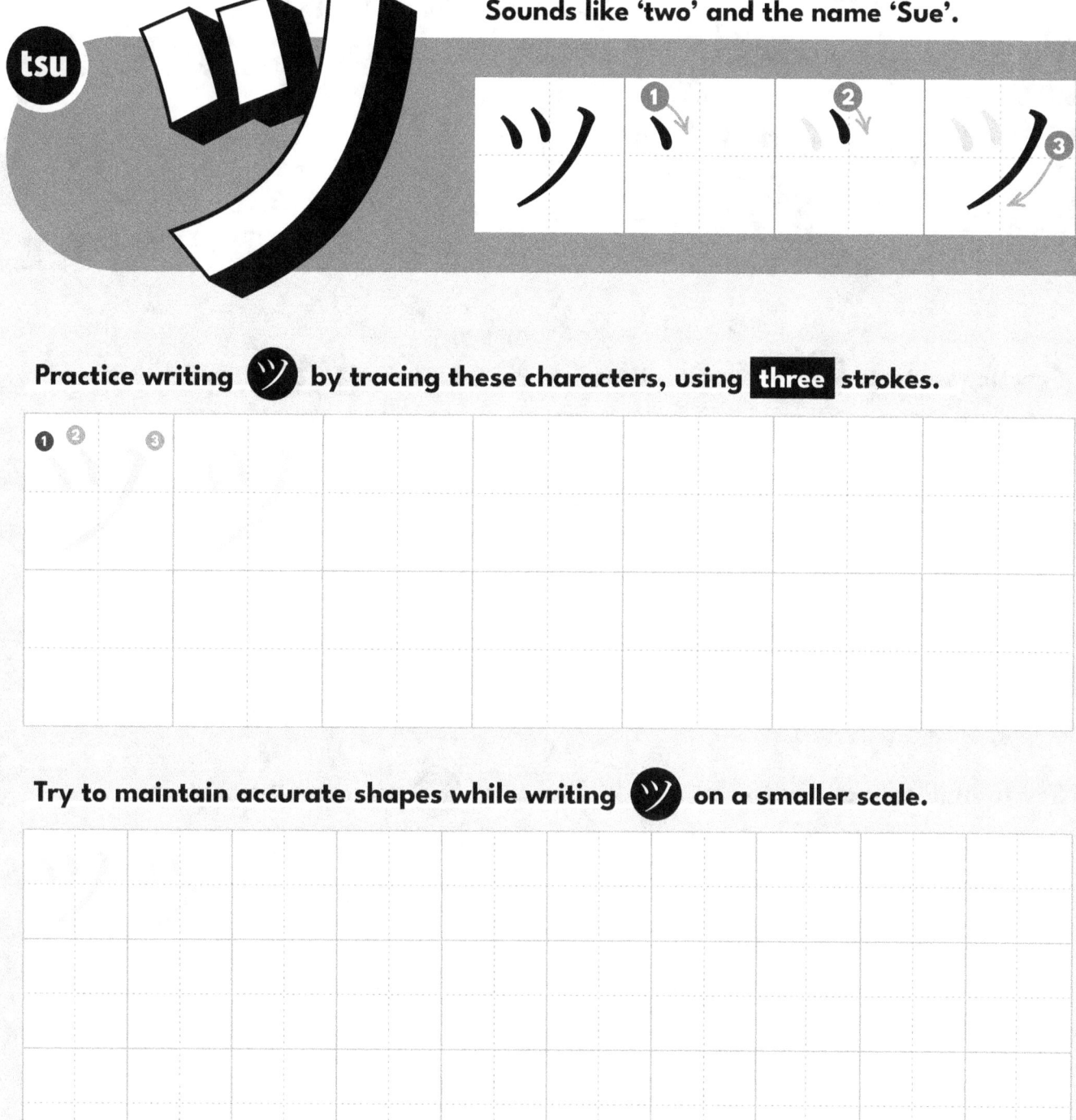

tsu ツ

Sounds like 'two' and the name 'Sue'.

Practice writing ツ **by tracing these characters, using three strokes.**

Try to maintain accurate shapes while writing ツ **on a smaller scale.**

Mnemonic.

Examples.

- <u>Two</u> needles pulling the same thread (vertical lines just like in kana 'so')

te

Sounds like the 'te-' in teddy bear.

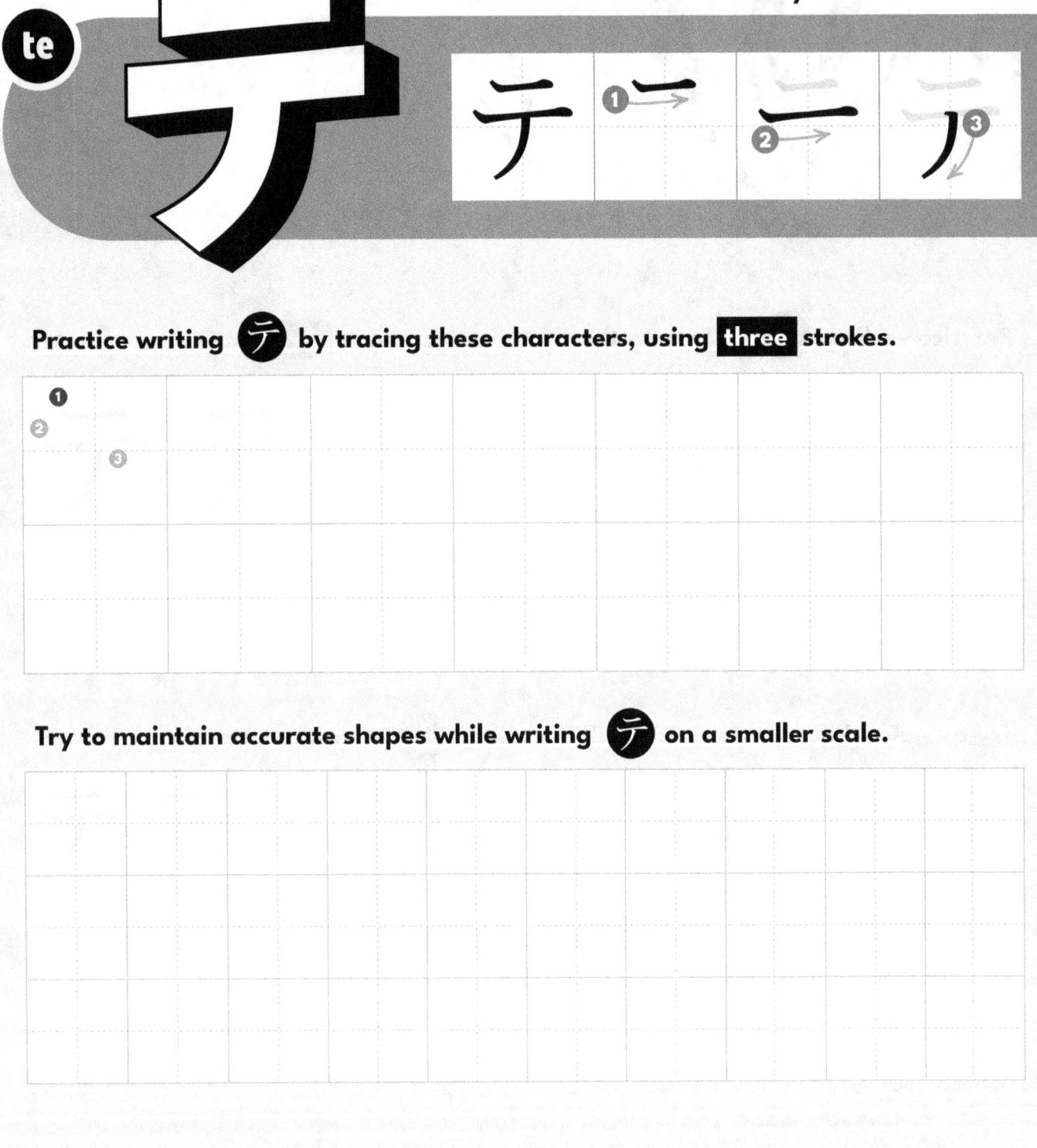

Practice writing テ **by tracing these characters, using three strokes.**

Try to maintain accurate shapes while writing テ **on a smaller scale.**

Mnemonic.

Examples.
- Picture the shape of <u>te</u>legraph poles

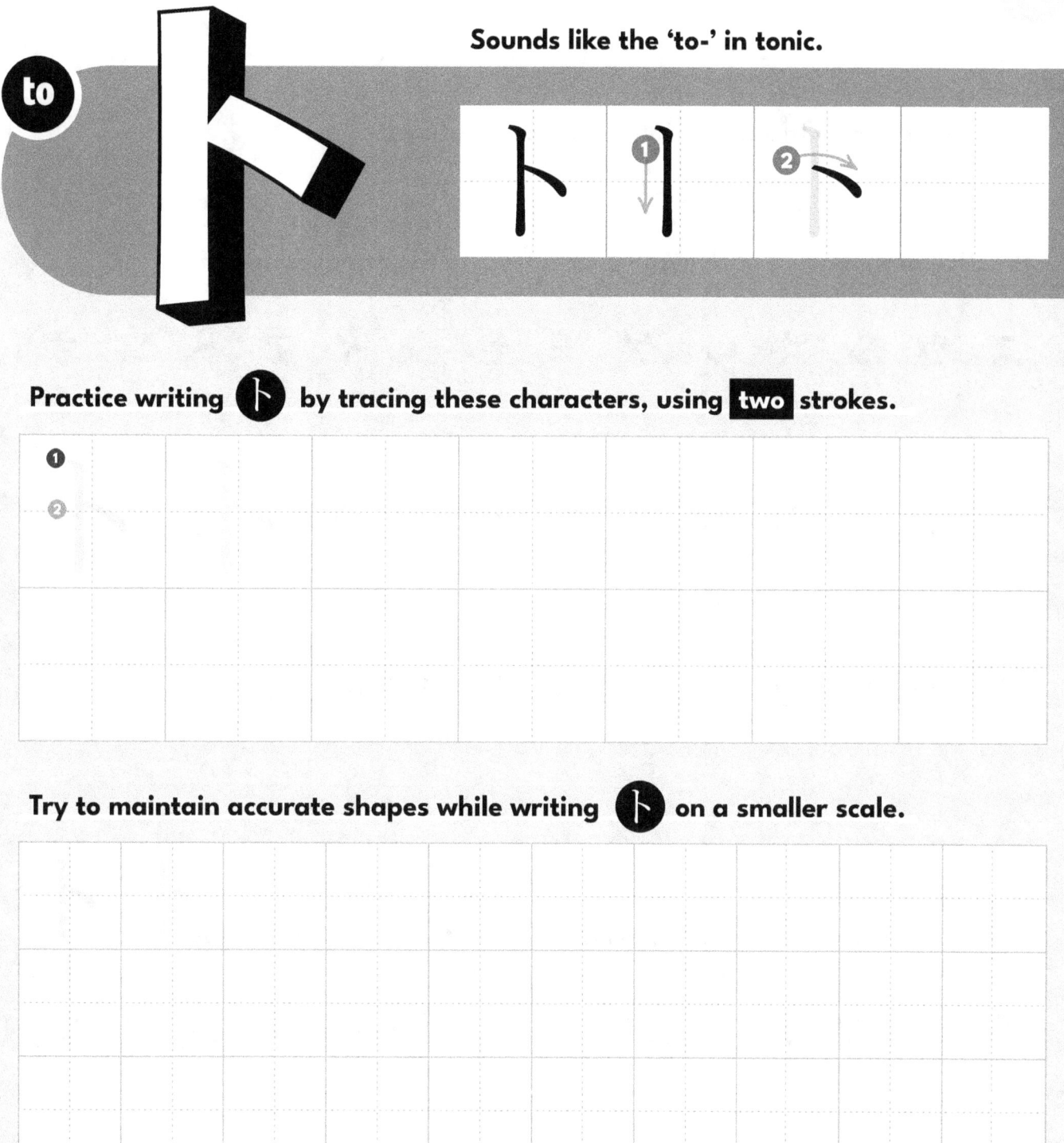

Practice writing ㅏ **by tracing these characters, using** **two** **strokes.**

Try to maintain accurate shapes while writing ㅏ **on a smaller scale.**

Mnemonic.

Examples.
- Lower case 't'
- Imagine this as a totem pole

Ten more symbols, and a total of twenty to recall on these pages.

Practice pronouncing each symbol as you write the romaji beneath.

ス ツ シ キ ソ ケ チ セ タ イ ア ト ソ オ

テ エ サ ス タ エ ウ セ コ テ イ カ ト ク

タ テ ツ サ キ ト コ ウ チ オ ス カ シ エ

Take a 5-minute break, and then do the same for these symbols too.

シ チ セ テ ソ タ ツ ス テ ス サ ツ タ セ

サ カ タ ト キ テ ケ サ チ ソ エ セ シ ソ

タ ス ツ ト イ セ ウ ソ コ サ テ ス オ ト

This time, take a 10-minute break and come back to complete these.

エ タ チ セ サ コ チ オ エ ウ イ ツ セ サ

ソ シ テ ス イ ト シ イ サ セ オ ア ク チ

テ ス ウ ア ト タ ソ ツ タ オ キ ウ エ シ

After a much longer break, add the romaji for each symbol below.

ソ チ タ サ エ サ チ ア テ セ ツ セ ソ オ

イ セ ス ト オ ク シ ス シ エ ア ウ タ ト

エ シ イ オ コ キ テ ツ サ チ タ ウ イ ウ

Practice reading the katakana you have learned so far with these examples.

Note: It is common for words in katakana to have horizontal lines. They show that the vowel sound from the previous character should be doubled in length. For example: カ *= ka , and* カー *= ka-a. (You will learn more about this later)*

カツ cutlet

アイス ice

ケーキ cake

アウト out

サーチ search

コート coat

ツアー tour

テスト test

シーツ sheet

コーチ coach

ソース sauce

スキー skiing

タクシー taxi

ステーキ steak

セーター sweater

サーカス circus

オーケー ok

エーカー acre

K3. The N & H Columns

Another block of ten symbols to learn. This time, we are looking at katakana from both the N and H columns. One exception to the usual pattern is again *'fu'* in place of *'hu'*. The sound is somewhere between *'hu'* and *'fu'*, like *'hfu'*.

Symbols in this learning block.

Pronunciation

There are no differences in sound between the first ten hiragana that you learned and the way in which you should pronounce these characters. Remember to pay attention to your pronunciation of *'fu'*.

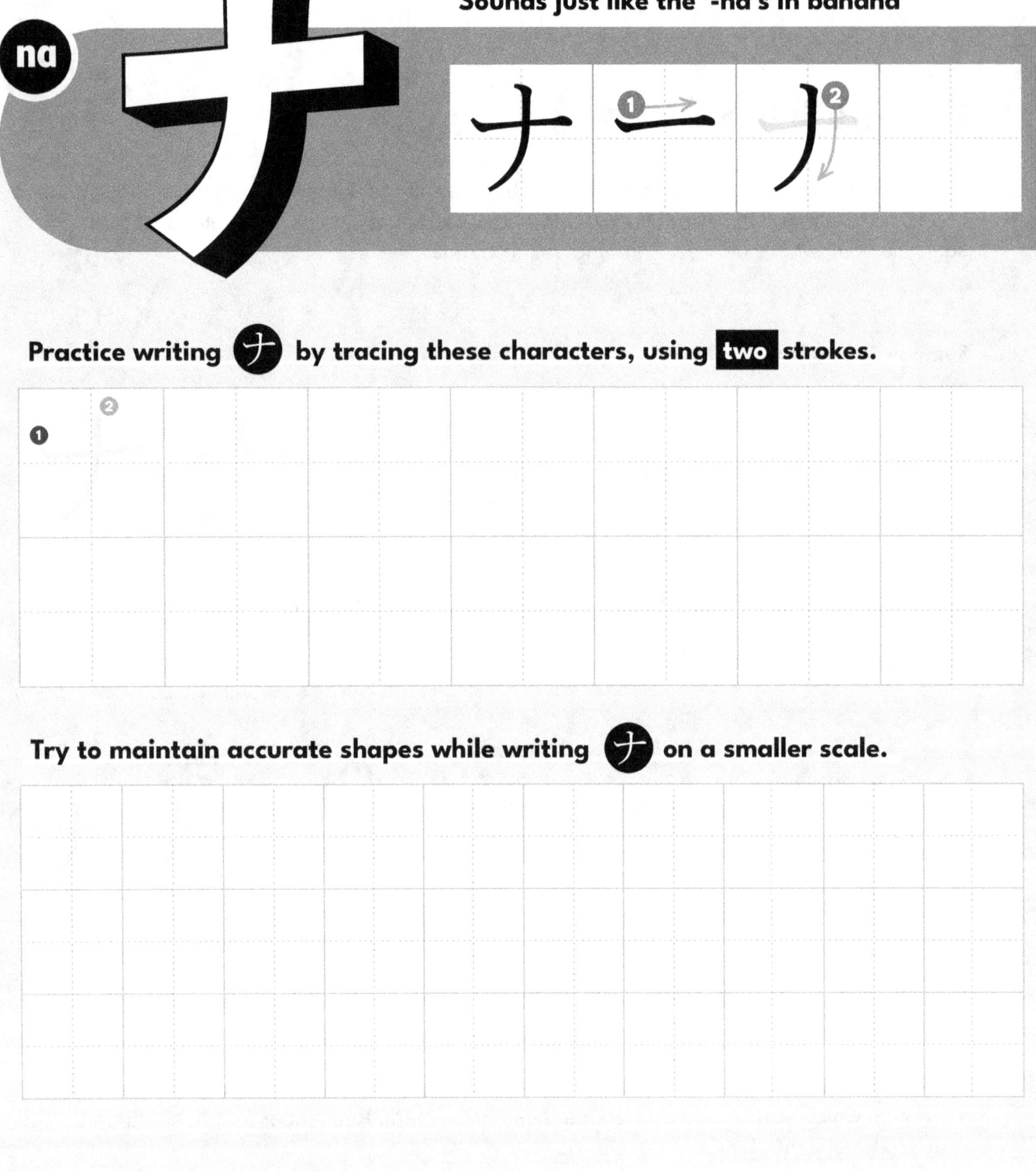

na — **ナ** — Sounds just like the '-na's in banana

Practice writing ナ by tracing these characters, using two strokes.

Try to maintain accurate shapes while writing ナ on a smaller scale.

Mnemonic.

Examples.
- The shape of a knife
- A peeled banana
- Narwhal with horn

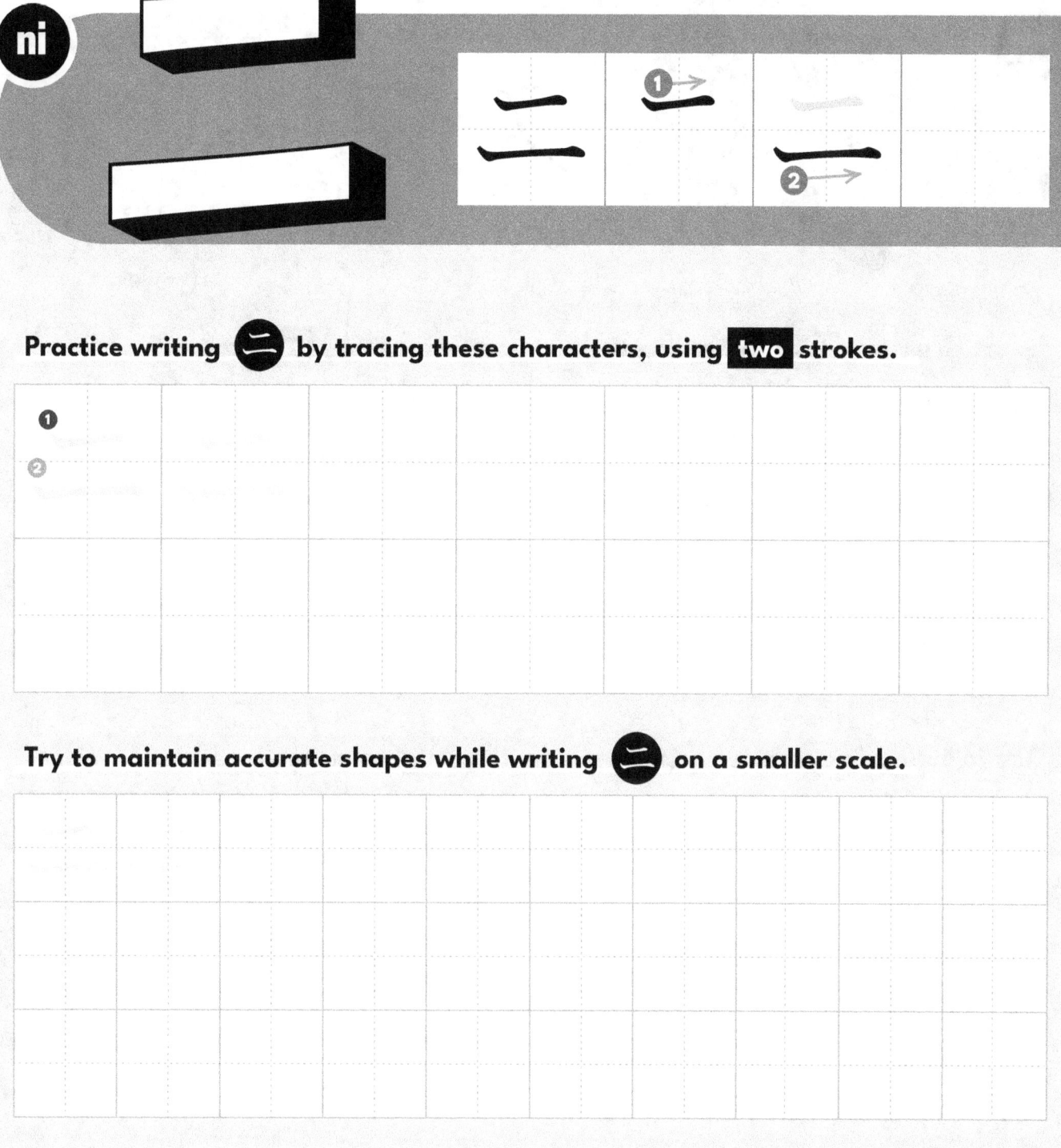

ni

Sounds similar to the word 'knee'.

Practice writing 二 by tracing these characters, using two strokes.

Try to maintain accurate shapes while writing 二 on a smaller scale.

Mnemonic.

Examples.

- Two <u>nee</u>dles

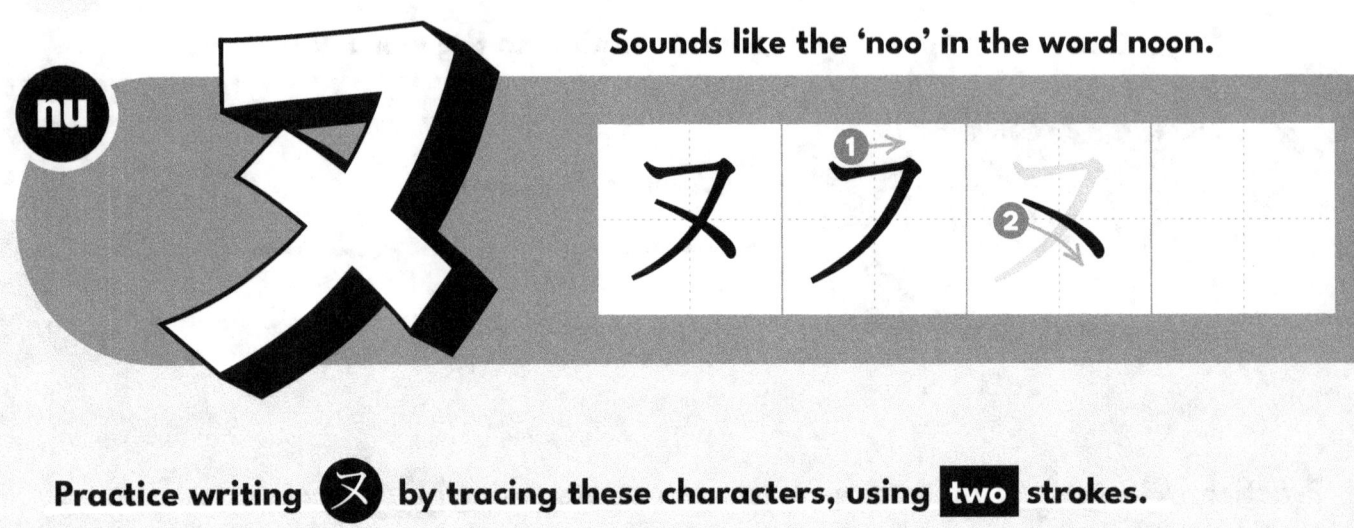

Sounds like the 'noo' in the word noon.

Practice writing ヌ by tracing these characters, using two strokes.

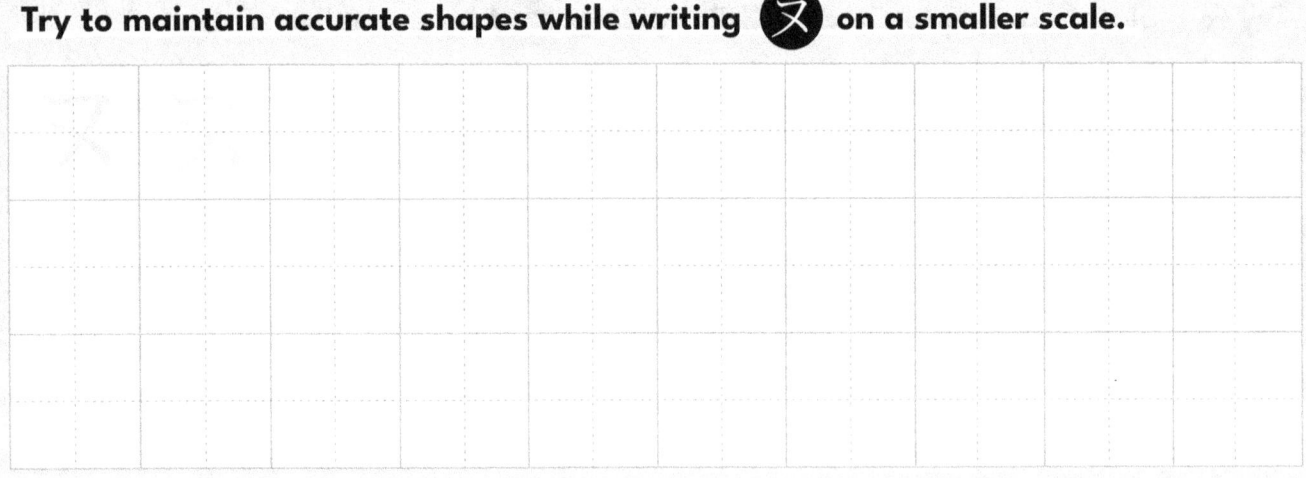

Try to maintain accurate shapes while writing ヌ on a smaller scale.

Mnemonic.

Examples.

- Chopsticks, picking up one <u>noo</u>dle
- A <u>new</u> type of scythe

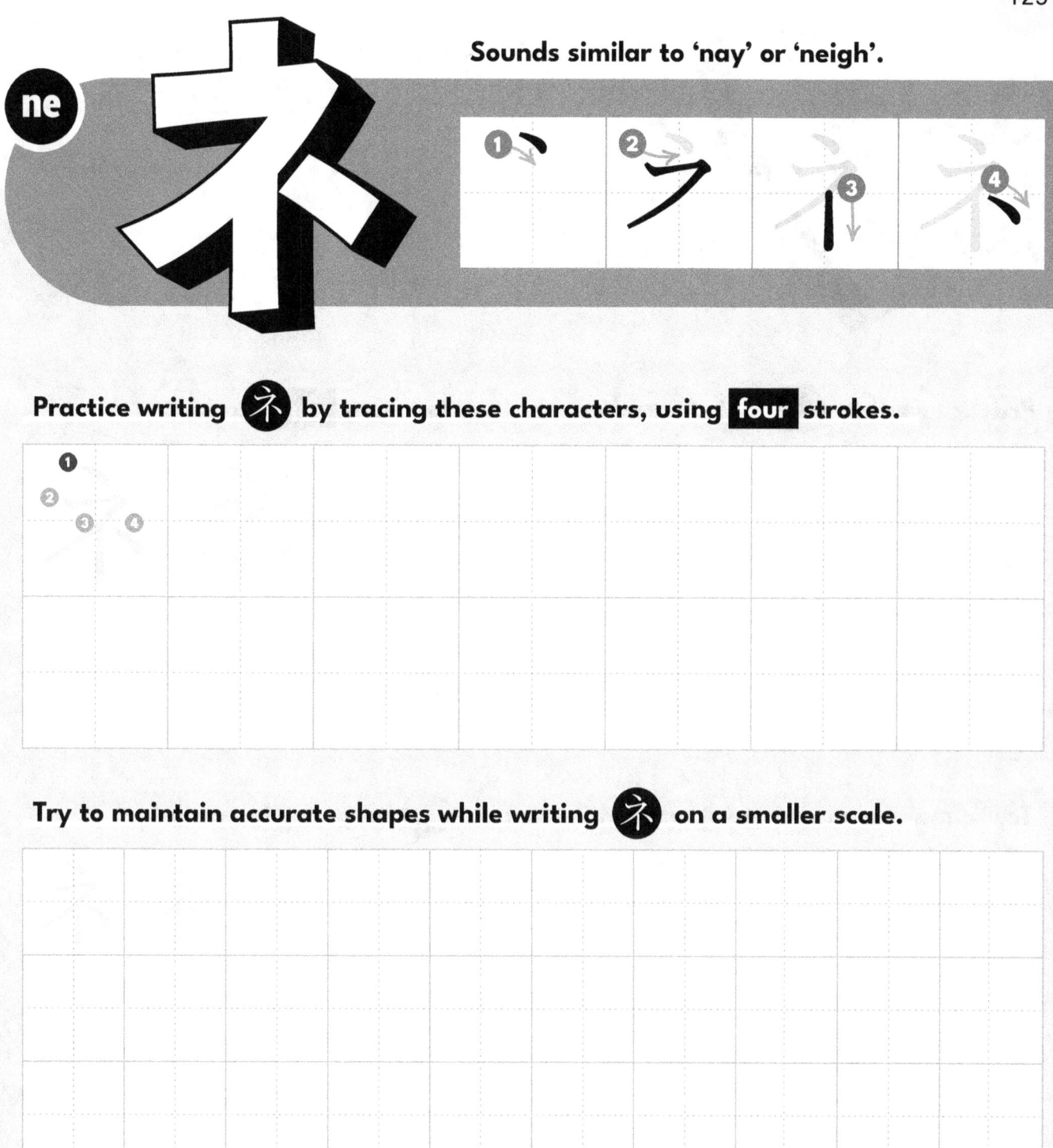

ne — ネ

Sounds similar to 'nay' or 'neigh'.

Practice writing ネ by tracing these characters, using four strokes.

Try to maintain accurate shapes while writing ネ on a smaller scale.

Mnemonic.

Examples.

- <u>Ne</u>lly has grown tusks and charges towards you!

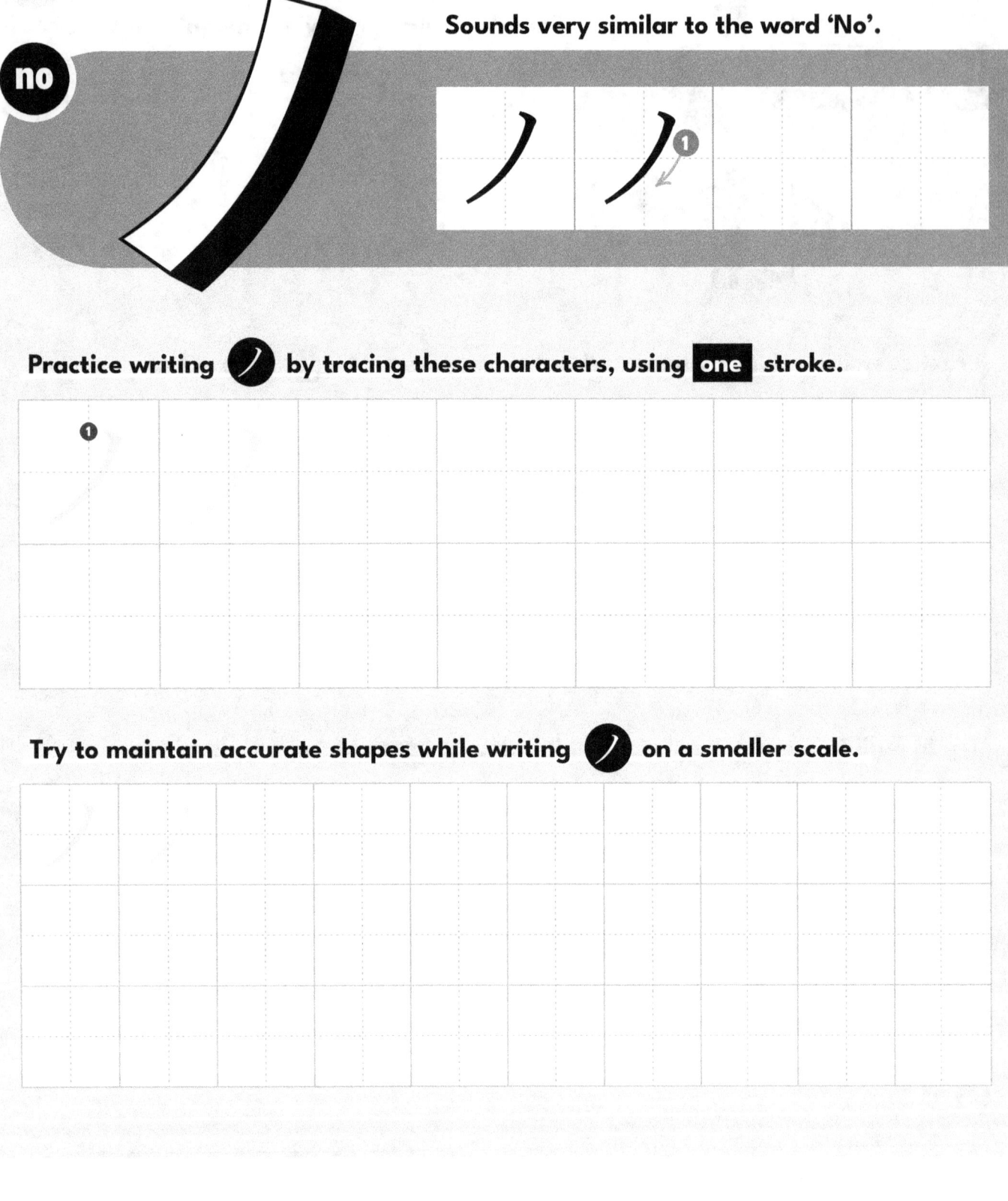

no

ノ

Sounds very similar to the word 'No'.

Practice writing ノ **by tracing these characters, using** **one** **stroke.**

Try to maintain accurate shapes while writing ノ **on a smaller scale.**

Mnemonic.

Examples.
- The first part of the 'No Smoking sign' in hiragana.
- A very long nose.

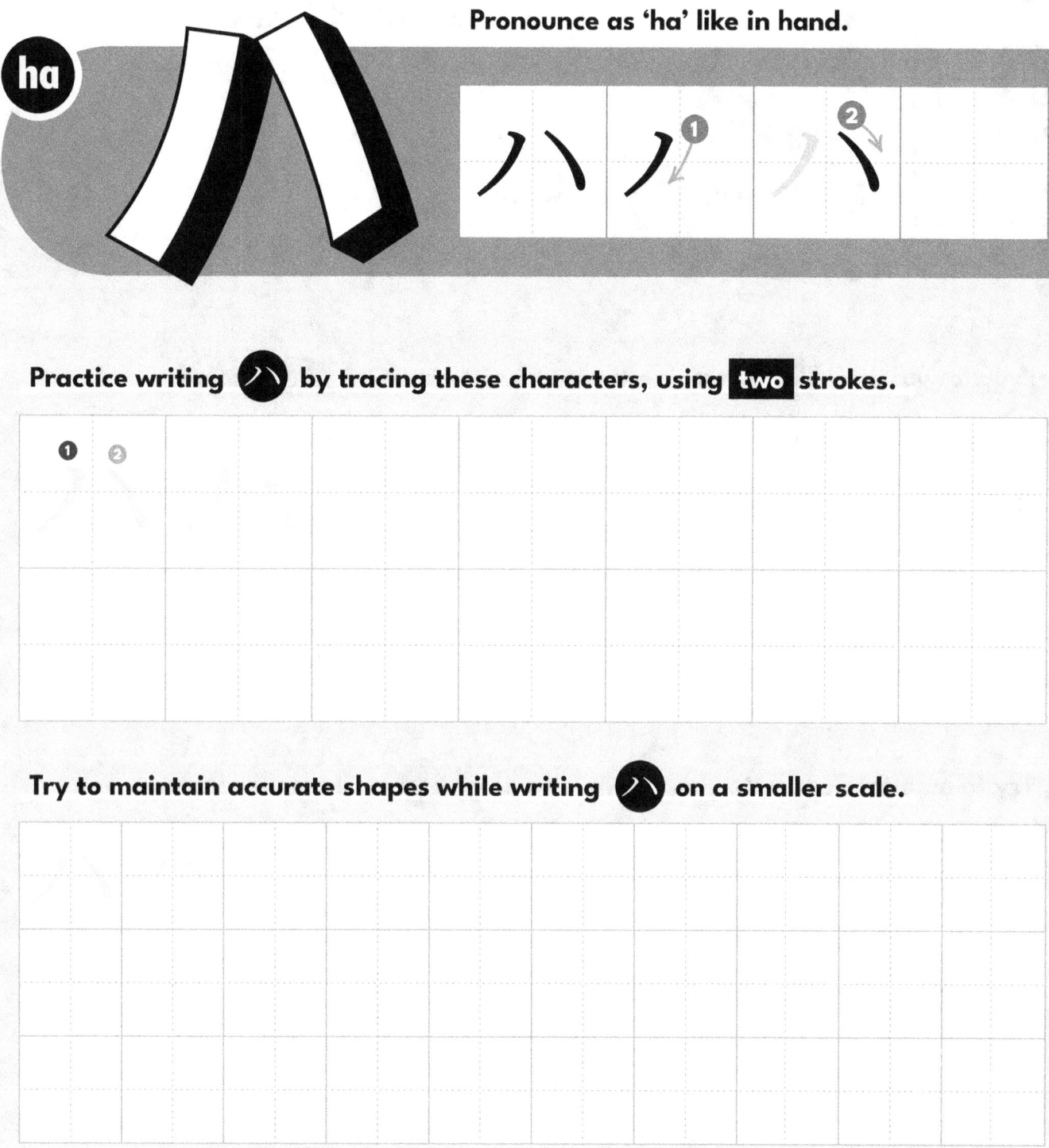

ha

Pronounce as 'ha' like in hand.

Practice writing ハ by tracing these characters, using two strokes.

Try to maintain accurate shapes while writing ハ on a smaller scale.

Mnemonic.

Examples.

- The shape of a hat

Pronounced like the 'hee' in heel.

Practice writing ヒ by tracing these characters, using two strokes.

Try to maintain accurate shapes while writing ヒ on a smaller scale.

Mnemonic.

Examples.

- <u>He</u> is sitting down at the table.
- A grinning mouth, "<u>hee</u> <u>hee</u>!"

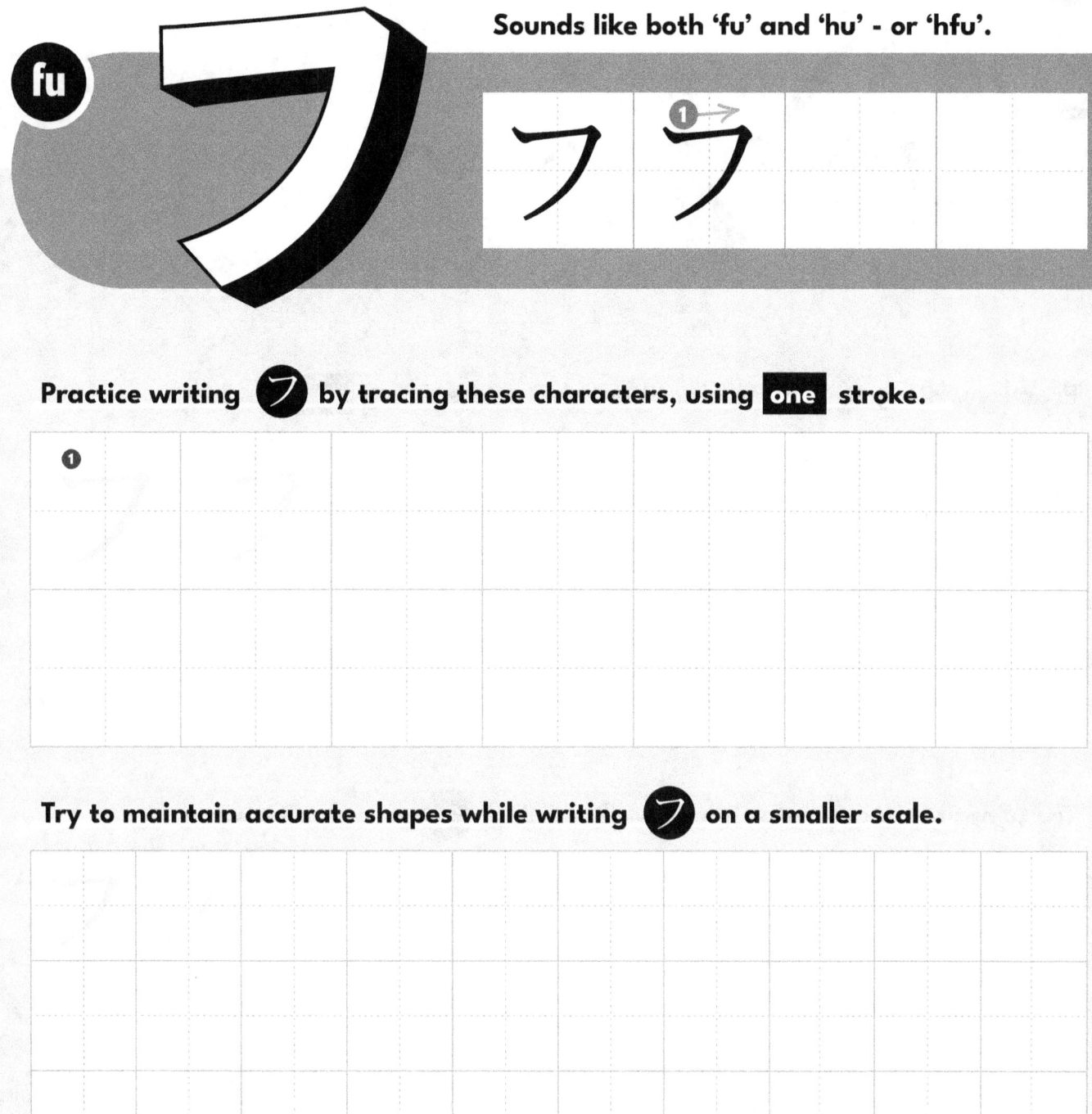

fu

Sounds like both 'fu' and 'hu' - or 'hfu'.

Practice writing フ by tracing these characters, using one stroke.

Try to maintain accurate shapes while writing フ on a smaller scale.

Mnemonic.

Examples.

- <u>Wh</u>o said 7 is lucky?
- A huge beak. Maybe an owl... "<u>hu hu</u>!" (or "<u>fu fu</u>!")

he

Pronounce as 'heh', almost like 'hey'.

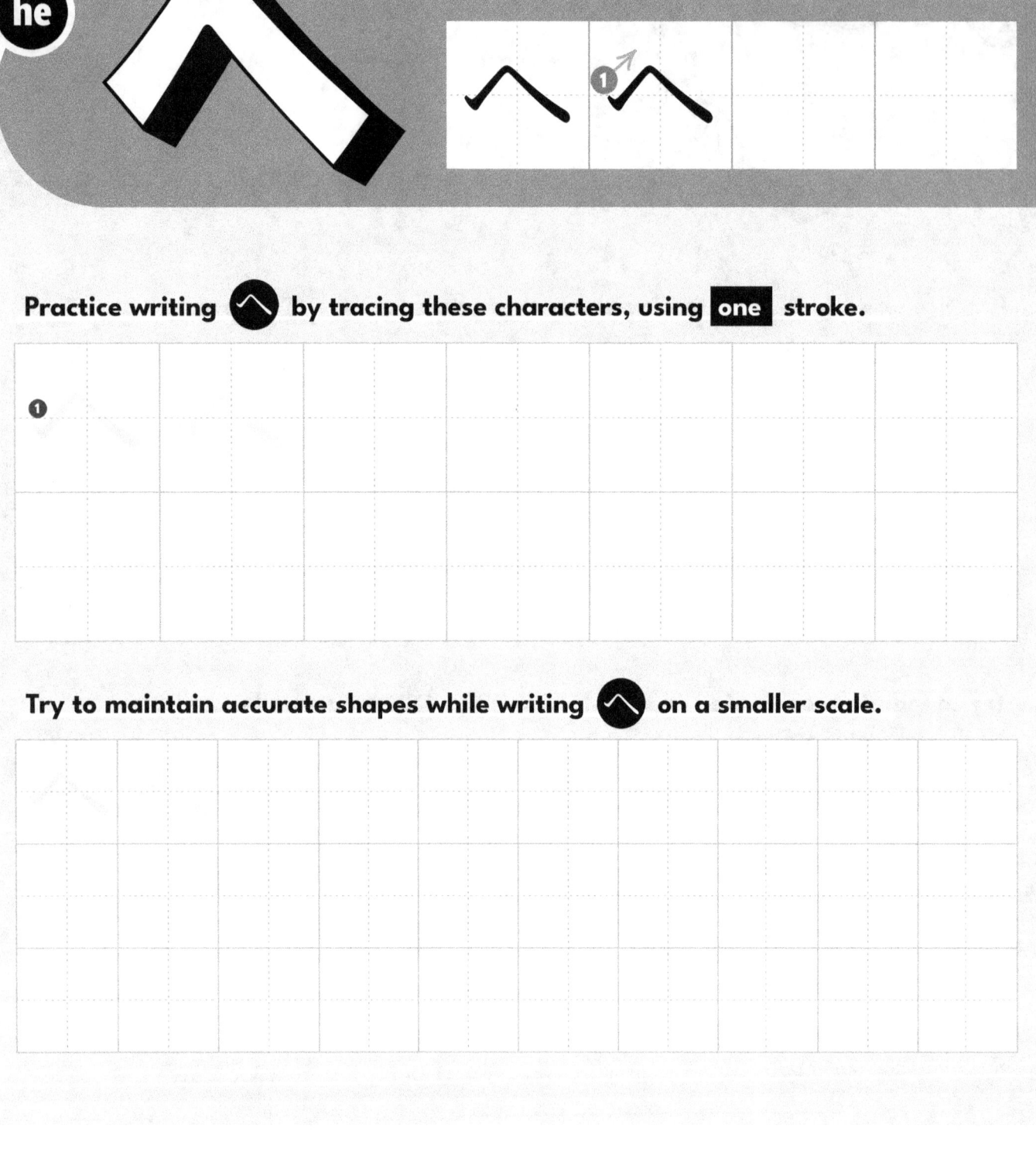

Practice writing ヘ by tracing these characters, using **one** stroke.

Try to maintain accurate shapes while writing ヘ on a smaller scale.

Mnemonic.

Examples.
- Same as hiragana

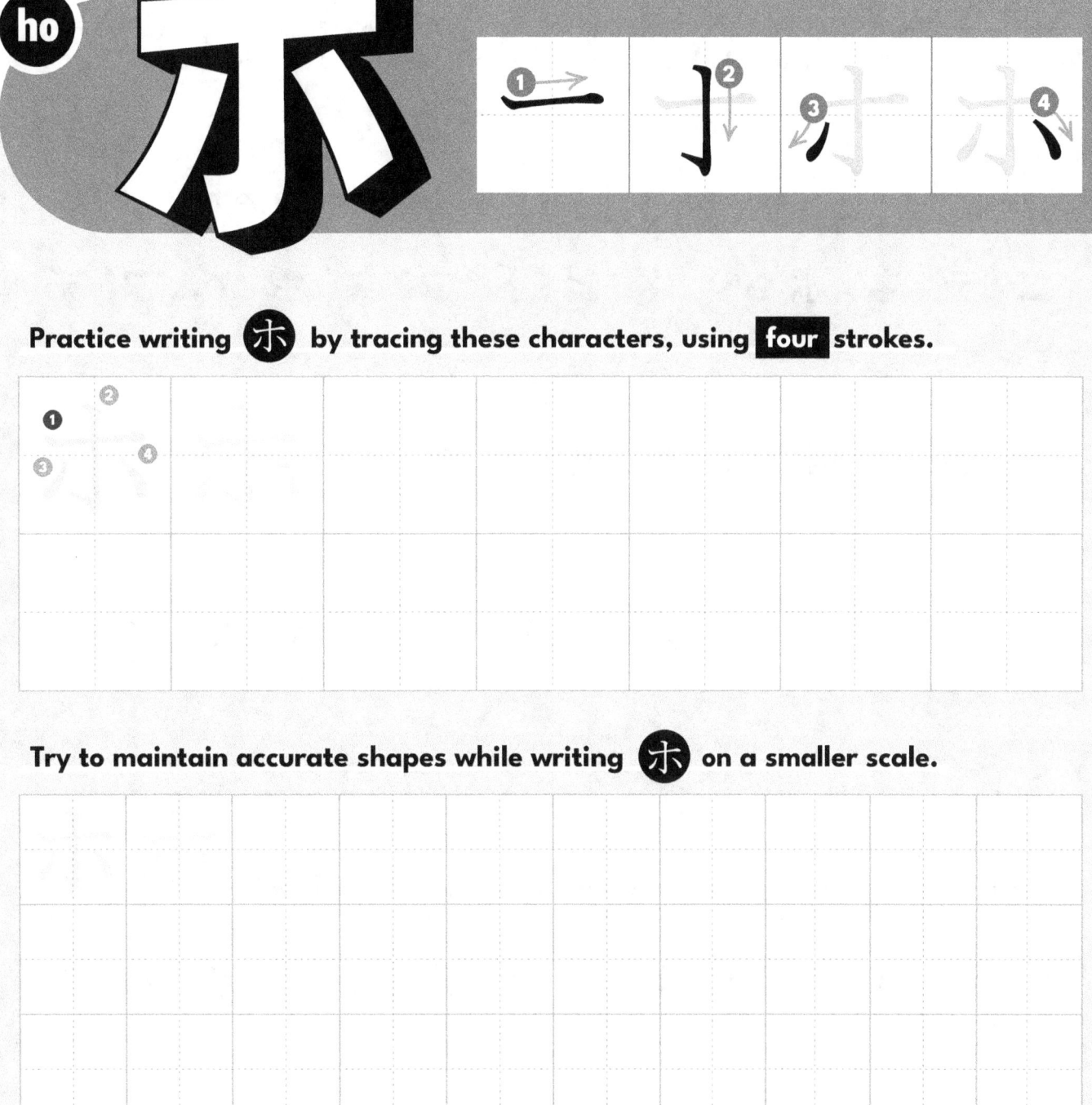

ho

Pronounce like the 'ho-' in horse.

Practice writing ホ by tracing these characters, using four strokes.

Try to maintain accurate shapes while writing ホ on a smaller scale.

Mnemonic.

Examples.
- A <u>ho</u>ly cross
- Outstretch arms, <u>ho</u>lding a cross.

With several similar shapes amongst the characters in the groups, this should start pushing your memorization skills. When this task becomes too easy, time yourself and try to improve.

Practice pronouncing each symbol as you write the romaji beneath.

ニ テ ネ ホ ヘ ネ ヒ ト フ ヌ ホ ヘ ヌ チ

ヘ ホ ヌ ネ ス ニ ヒ コ フ ニ ヌ ハ ナ ソ

フ ハ ノ ハ オ ノ ナ ヒ ハ ヒ ホ ネ タ ナ

Take a 5-minute break, and then do the same for these symbols too.

セ ノ オ コ オ ツ キ ナ ス フ シ チ ヒ ク

ア ケ テ ツ エ ハ カ ニ サ ヌ ケ シ ソ タ

セ ソ キ ホ ト コ ウ ネ イ ク ウ チ サ ア

This time, take a 10-minute break and come back to complete these.

ツ テ チ ト キ エ ホ ノ サ イ ヒ フ ニ シ

セ ソ ス テ コ ニ ハ ネ ヌ ヘ ツ ネ ヌ ウ

ナ シ サ タ セ タ ヘ ナ チ ス ノ ホ ア ハ

After a much longer break, add the romaji for each symbol below.

エ ハ ヒ チ テ ホ ヘ ツ セ イ ト ヌ ソ ウ

ナ ヘ タ サ ツ ス テ タ ノ ネ ヌ ス セ ニ

ニ コ ホ ノ シ ネ ア ハ ナ サ チ フ シ キ

K4. The M & Y Columns

This group of eight katakana symbols represent the sounds in both the M and Y columns of the basic katakana table. Pronunciations will be familiar but with characters that look completely different.

Symbols in this learning block.

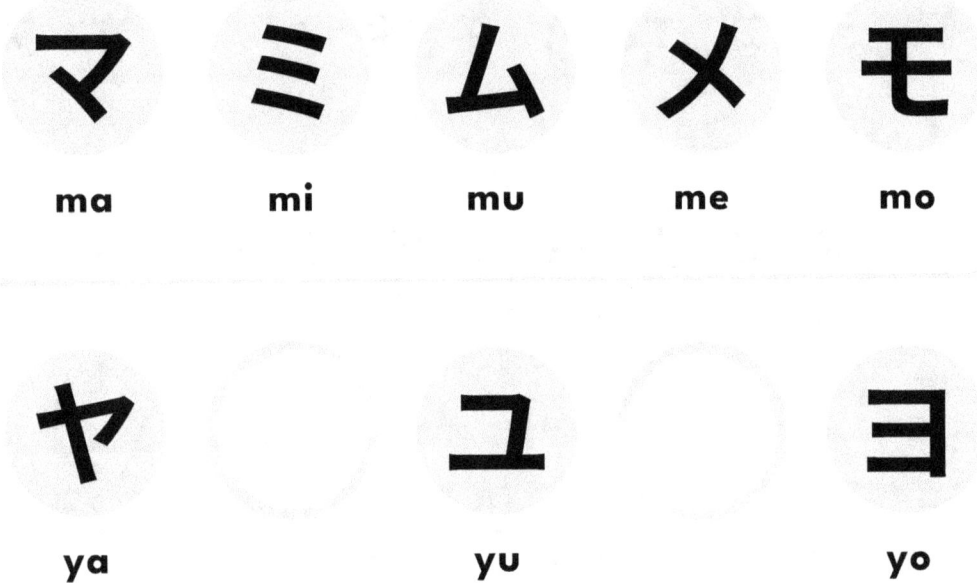

Pronunciation

There are no new exceptions to the pronunciation of these characters.

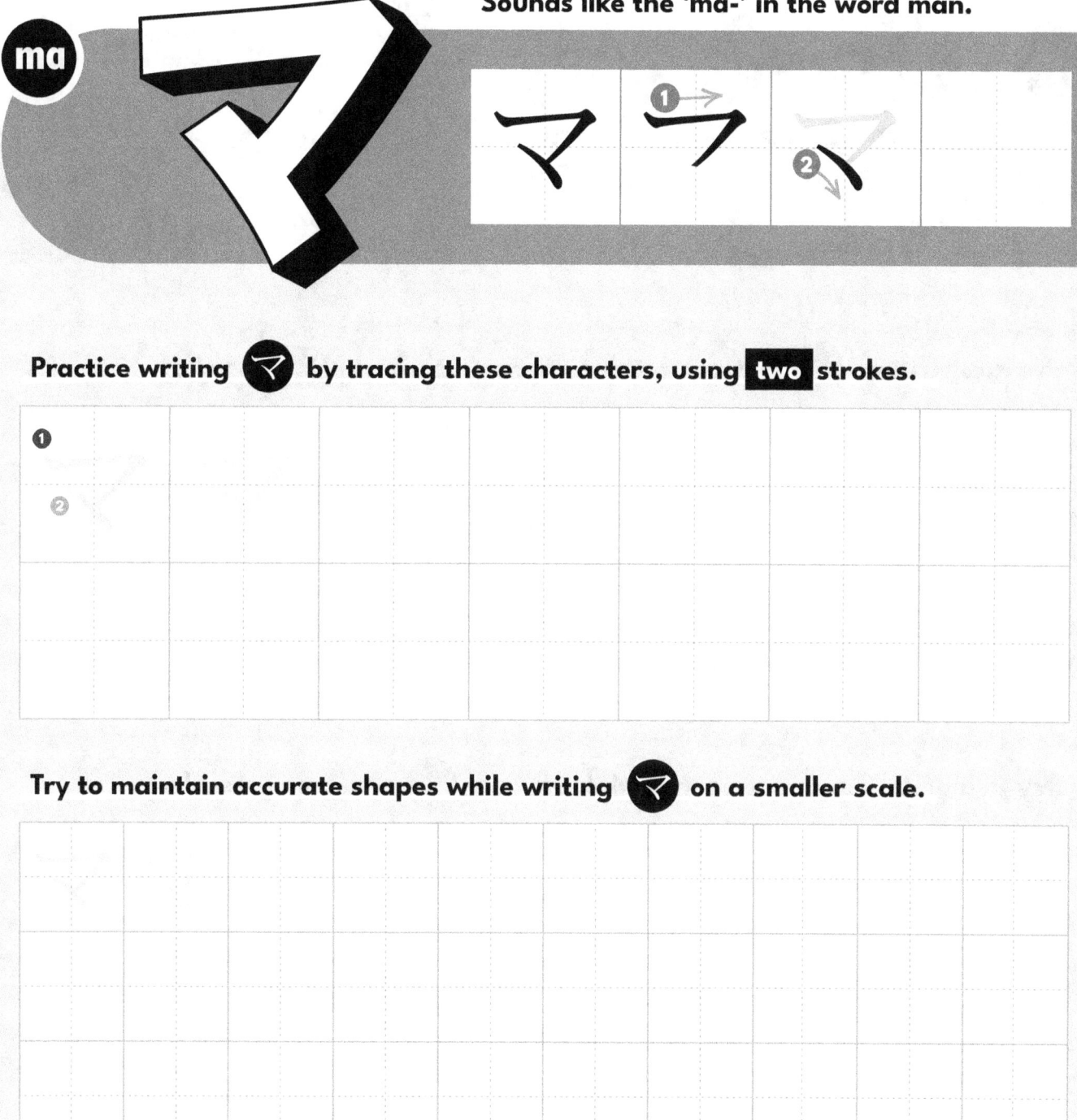

ma — マ

Sounds like the 'ma-' in the word man.

Practice writing マ by tracing these characters, using **two** strokes.

Try to maintain accurate shapes while writing マ on a smaller scale.

Mnemonic.

Examples.
- Imagine a <u>m</u>artini cocktail glass
- <u>M</u>aths, angles et.
- <u>M</u>arathon medal

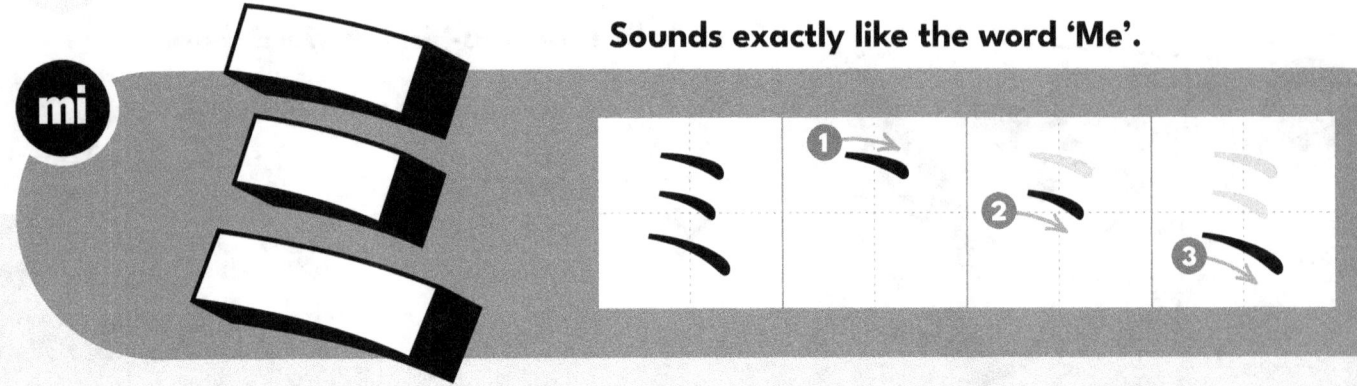

Sounds exactly like the word 'Me'.

Practice writing 三 **by tracing these characters, using** **three** **strokes.**

Try to maintain accurate shapes while writing 三 **on a smaller scale.**

Mnemonic.

Examples.

- The letter 'm' on its side, now 'E'... "me!"
- Three <u>mi</u>ssiles

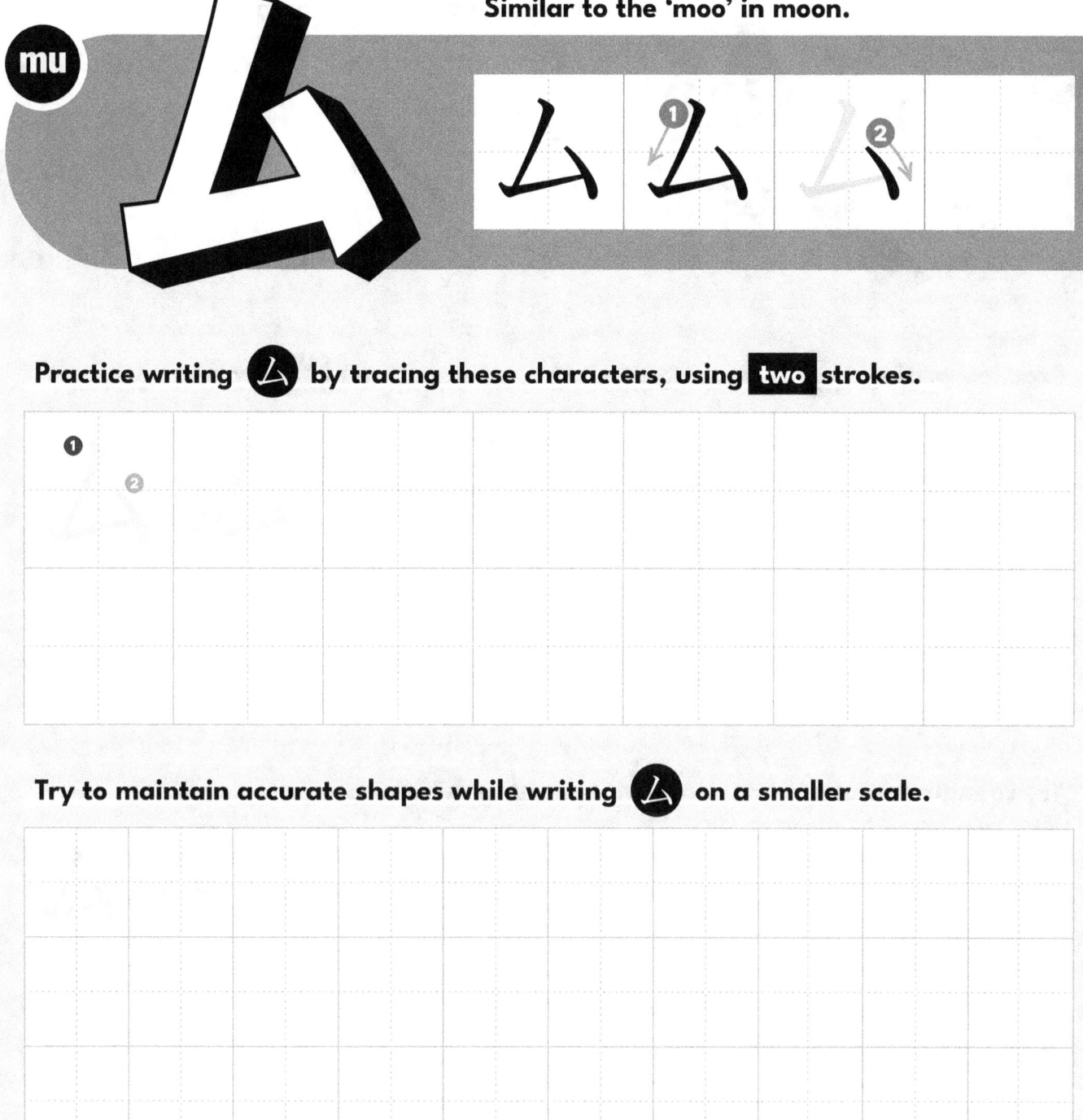

mu

Similar to the 'moo' in moon.

Practice writing ム **by tracing these characters, using two strokes.**

Try to maintain accurate shapes while writing ム **on a smaller scale.**

Mnemonic.

Examples.

- An arm, flexing to show off <u>mu</u>scles

me

Sounds like the 'me-' in men.

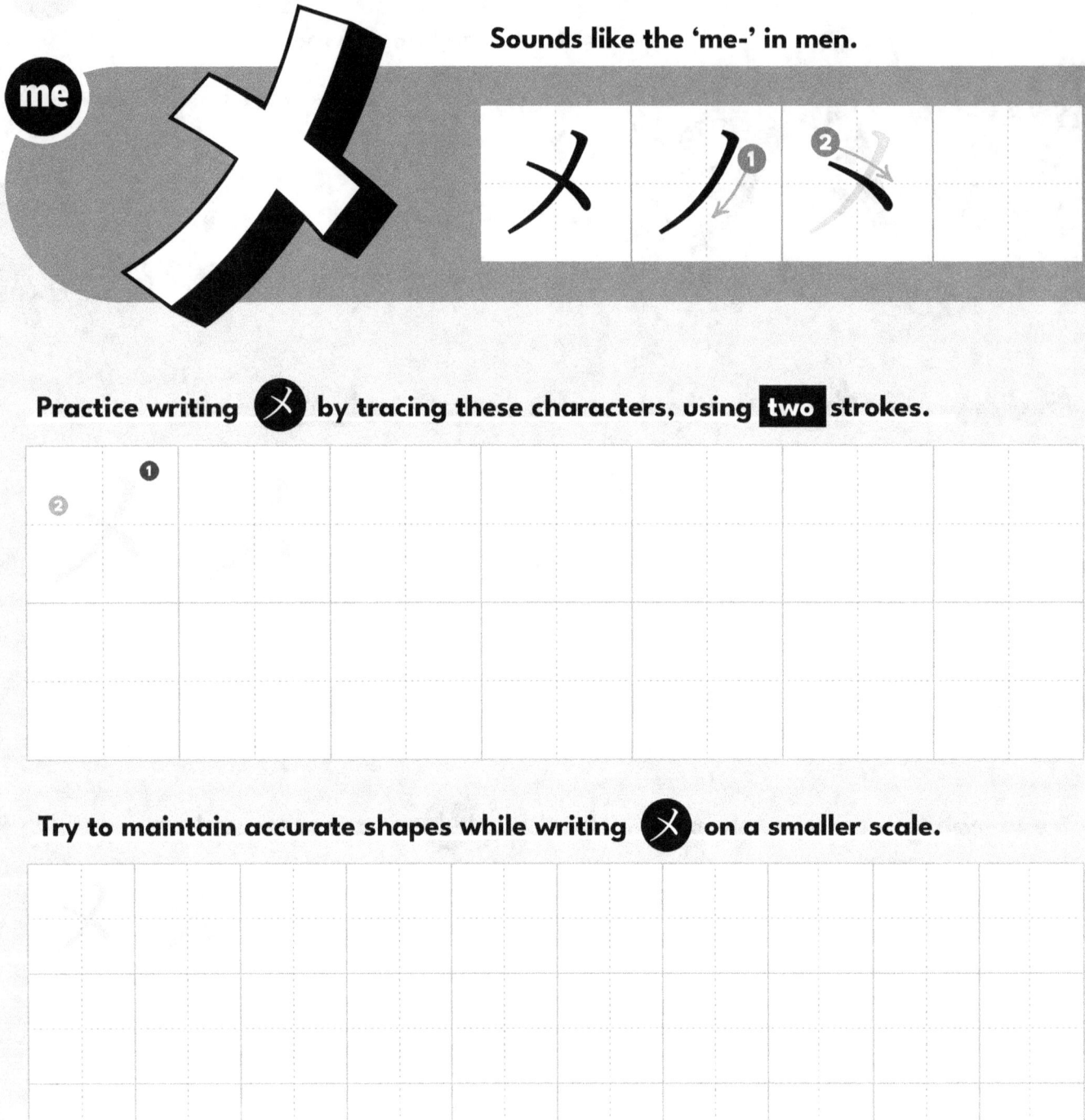

Practice writing メ **by tracing these characters, using** **two** **strokes.**

Try to maintain accurate shapes while writing メ **on a smaller scale.**

Mnemonic.

Examples.
- Simplified version of hiragana 'Me', the Japanese for eye. Picture X on an eye

mo モ

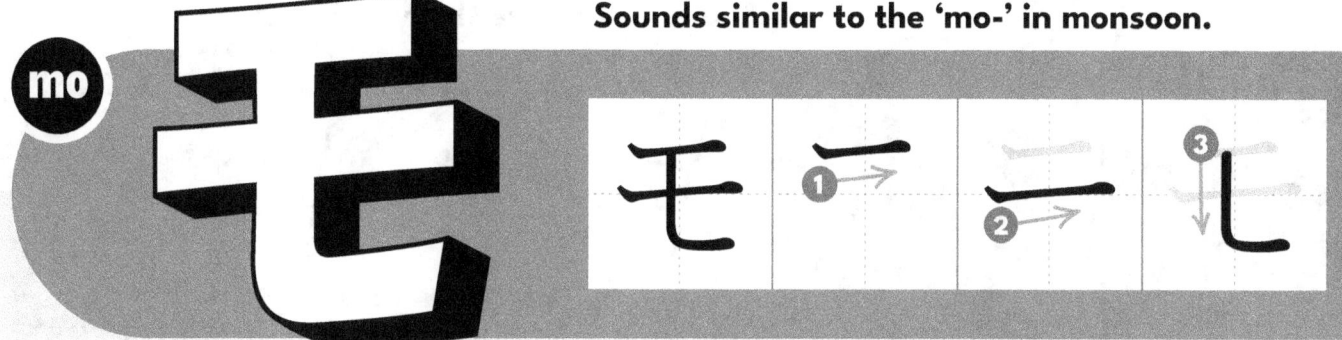

Sounds similar to the 'mo-' in monsoon.

Practice writing モ **by tracing these characters, using** three **strokes.**

Try to maintain accurate shapes while writing モ **on a smaller scale.**

Mnemonic.

Examples.

- Similar to hiragana
- <u>M</u>ore worms on a hook shape.

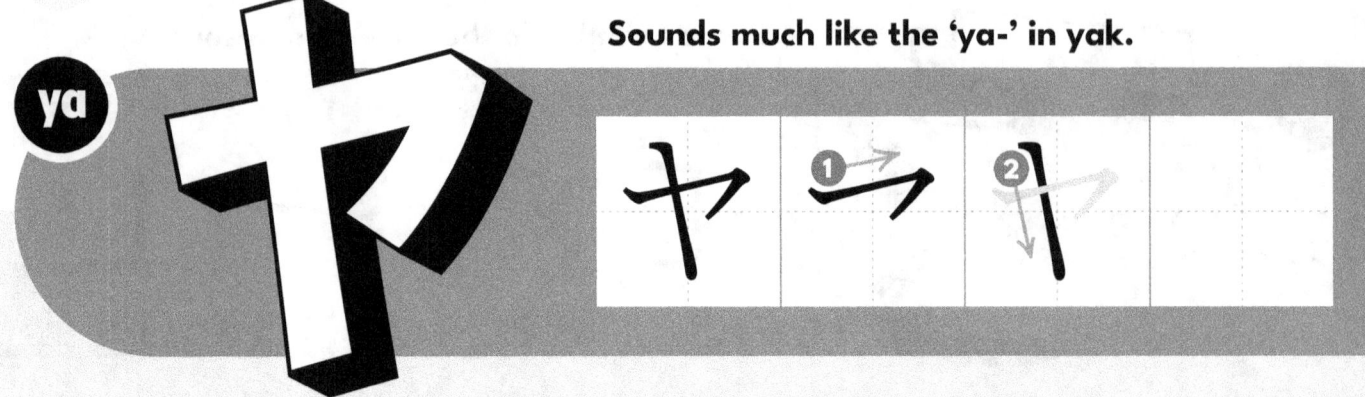

ya — Sounds much like the 'ya-' in yak.

Practice writing ヤ by tracing these characters, using two strokes.

Try to maintain accurate shapes while writing ヤ on a smaller scale.

Mnemonic.

Examples.
- Similar to hiragana
- <u>Y</u>ak with one horn

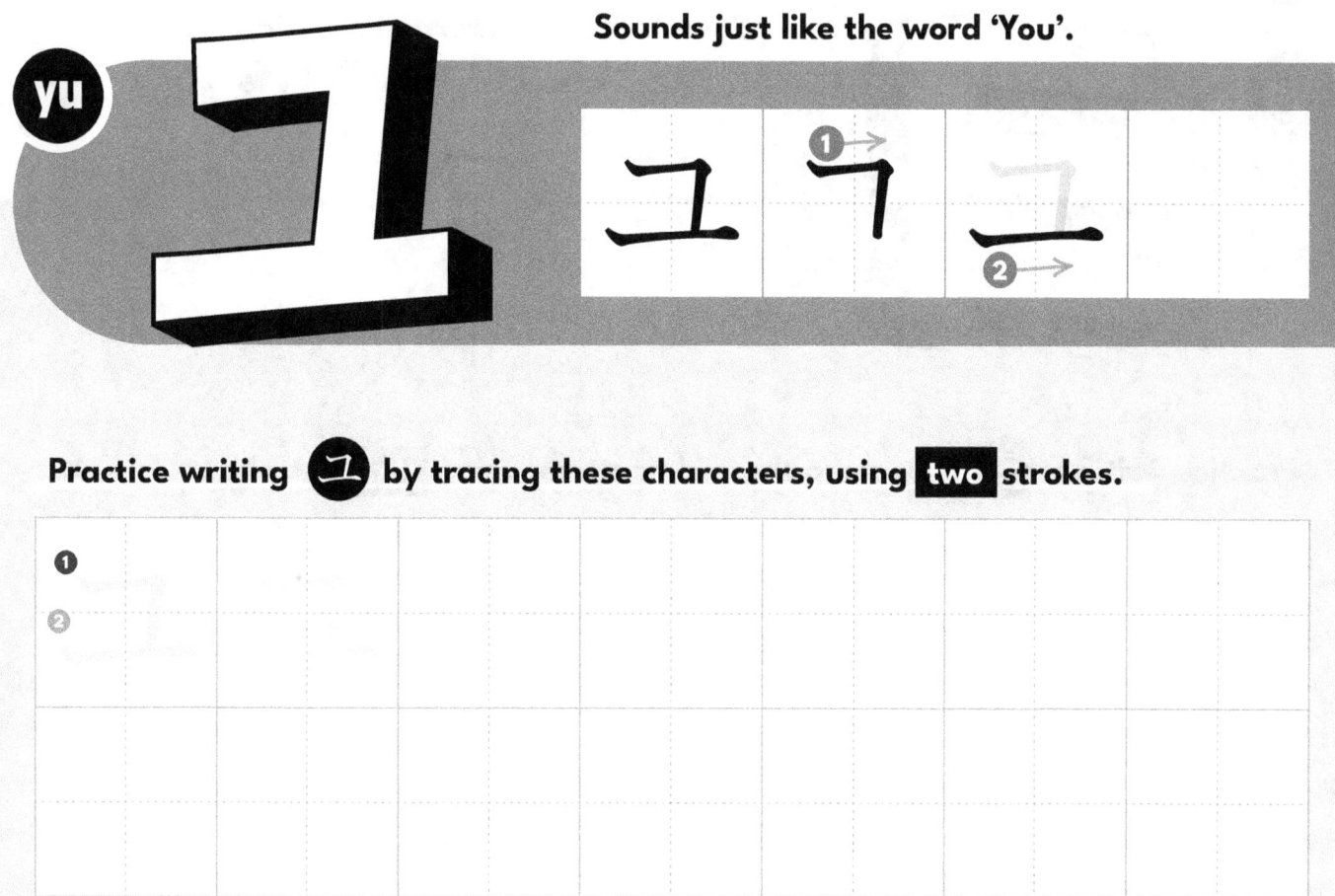

Practice writing ユ **by tracing these characters, using** **two** **strokes.**

Try to maintain accurate shapes while writing ユ **on a smaller scale.**

Mnemonic.

Examples.

- Like a submarine, or <u>YU</u>-boat (u-boat)

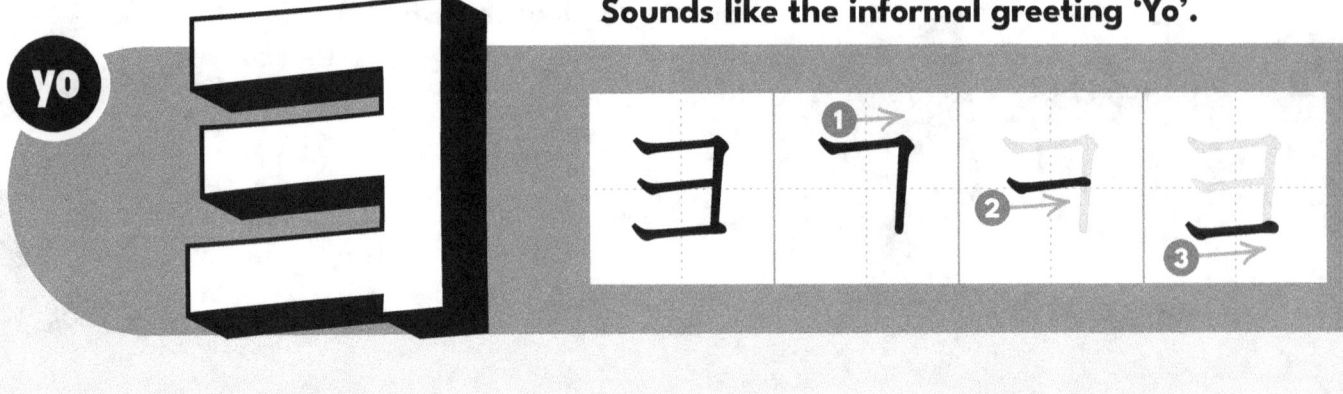

Sounds like the informal greeting 'Yo'.

Practice writing ㅋ **by tracing these characters, using** three **strokes.**

Try to maintain accurate shapes while writing ㅋ **on a smaller scale.**

Mnemonic.

Examples.

- Backwards 'E'...
  "Yo, what happened?"
- Awkward yoga pose.

The gaps between each group are helping to teach your brain that you will need to recall this new information again in the future - and that it should store it in your longer-term memory.

Practice pronouncing each symbol as you write the romaji beneath.

ナ マ ヌ ニ ミ モ ヘ ハ ス フ モ メ ヨ ノ

ネ ム ヘ ツ メ ノ ヒ ナ ハ ユ ヤ ユ ム シ

ホ ミ マ ク メ ホ モ ヌ マ ヨ ユ ム ヒ ネ

Take a 5-minute break, and then do the same for these symbols too.

ホ コ カ ネ メ ト ノ モ ユ ハ ク イ サ フ

ヌ ナ ヘ ス ム フ オ ヤ ヨ ツ ヒ ミ ソ シ

モ ニ エ ケ マ ア テ メ タ キ チ ム ウ セ

Regular breaks are a vital part of the memorization process!

This time, take a 10-minute break and come back to complete these.

ミ ユ ツ ア ナ コ サ ユ カ ヒ オ ハ ネ ヌ

ノ モ タ ウ ス イ ム チ メ ヨ ミ ト ヤ ヘ

ク キ ム ホ ケ ハ ヤ フ セ エ マ シ テ ニ

After a much longer break, add the romaji for each symbol below.

タ セ ヤ ス ヌ メ ケ モ ツ ト ム フ ヤ イ

ハ オ ネ ニ ナ テ ウ ハ ヒ ノ コ ク マ サ

シ ム ア ユ ユ カ ホ ミ キ チ ヨ ミ エ ヘ

K5. The R & W Columns + N

This is your final group of basic katakana to learn. After these few pages, you will have learned all of the basic kana symbols. The section that follows will cover additional sounds that kana are used to represent. Fortunately, there are no new symbols to learn.

Symbols in this learning block.

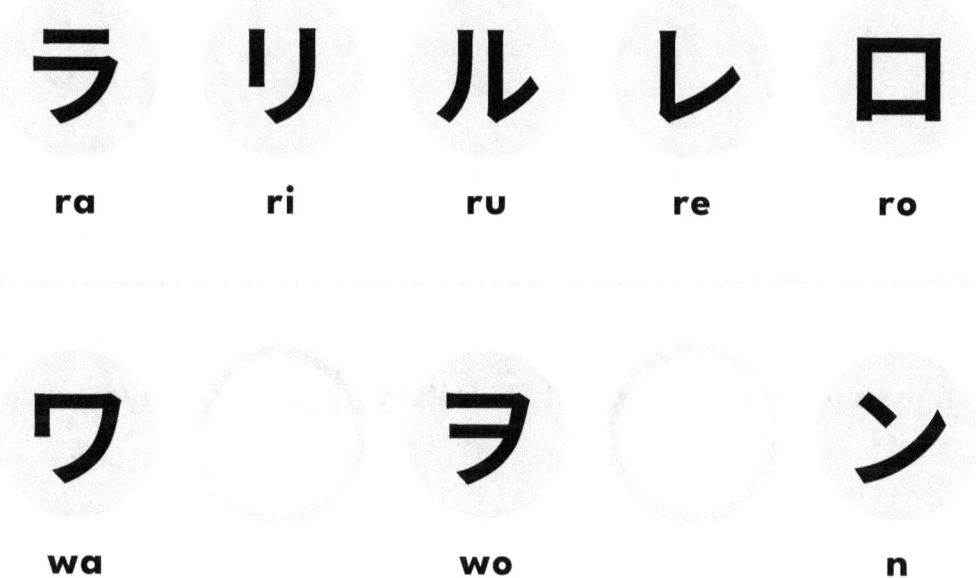

Pronunciation

Refer to the exercises in the hiragana section to assist with pronunciation 'r-' sounds.

ra ラ

Sounds a lot like the 'ra-' in rabbit.

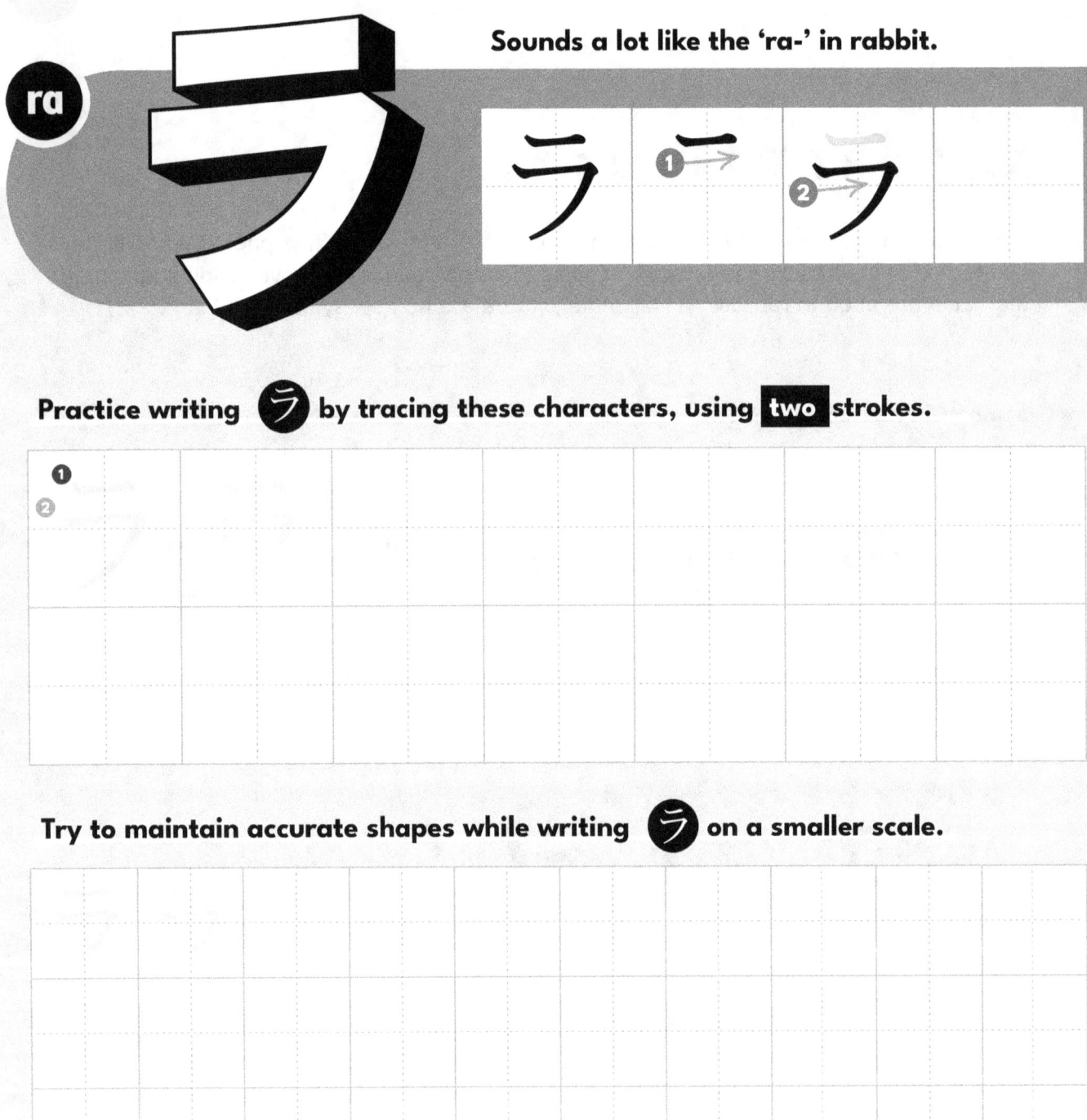

Practice writing ラ by tracing these characters, using two strokes.

Try to maintain accurate shapes while writing ラ on a smaller scale.

Mnemonic.

Examples.
- Similar to hiragana, long-eared <u>ra</u>bbit
- Umbrellas simply stop the <u>ra</u>in.

ri リ

Sounds a lot like the 'rea-' in reach.

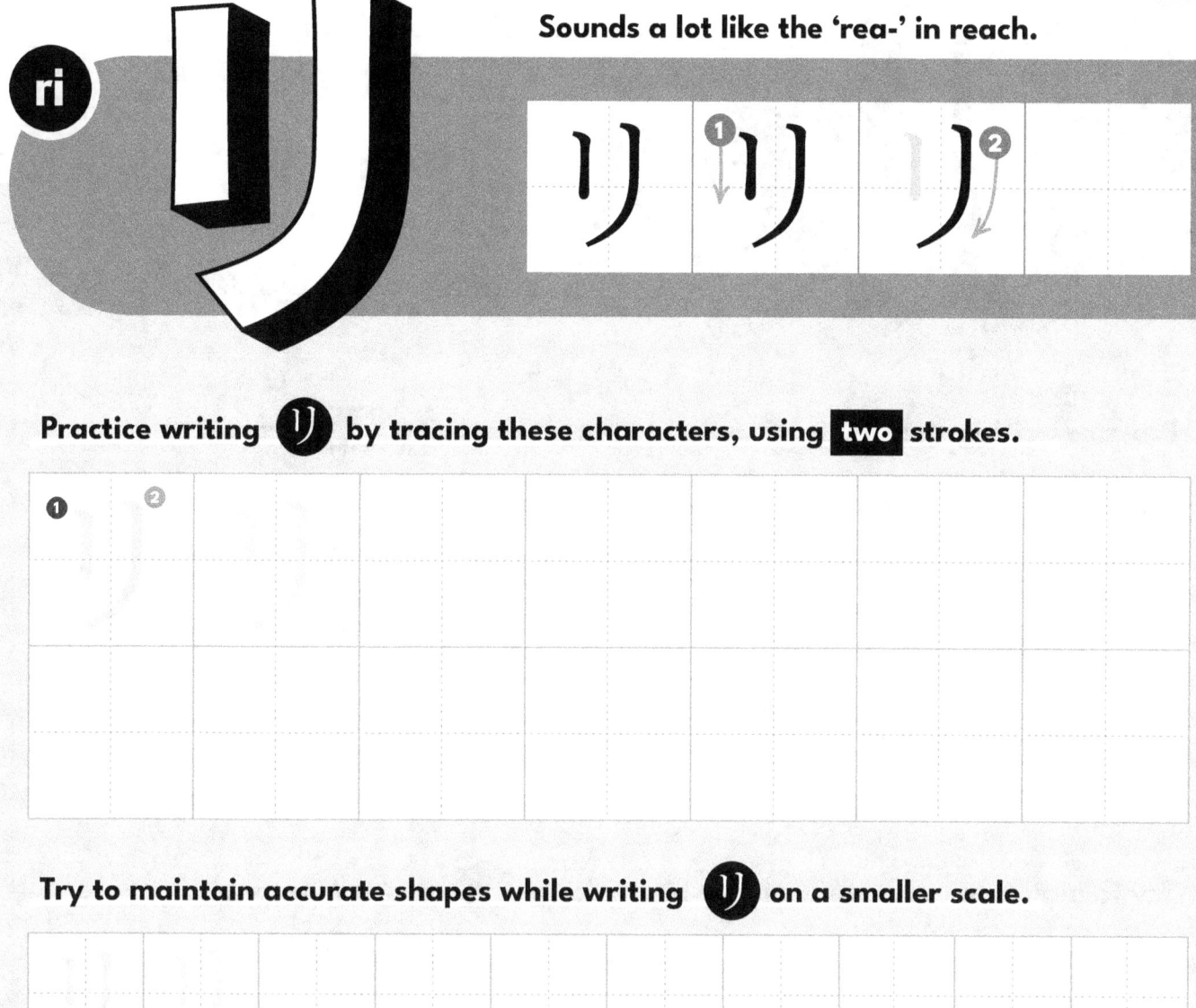

Practice writing リ **by tracing these characters, using** **two** **strokes.**

Try to maintain accurate shapes while writing リ **on a smaller scale.**

Mnemonic.

Examples.
- Same as hiragana
- Two <u>reed</u>s
- <u>Reach</u>ing arms

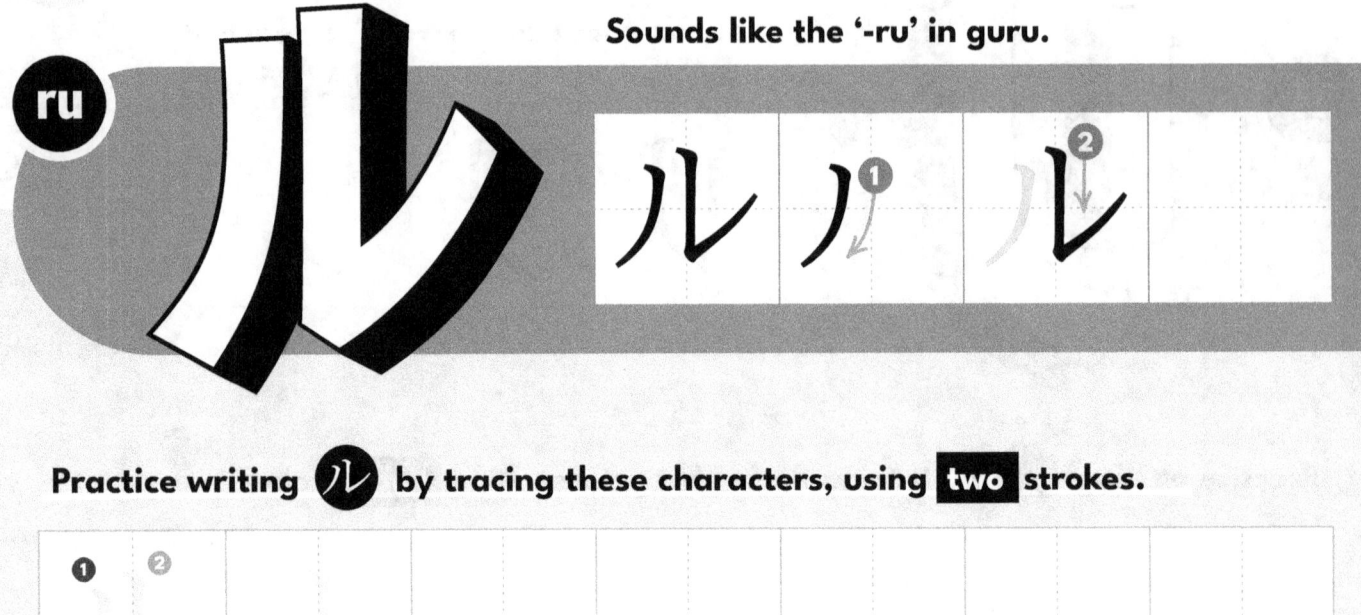

Sounds like the '-ru' in guru.

Practice writing ル by tracing these characters, using two strokes.

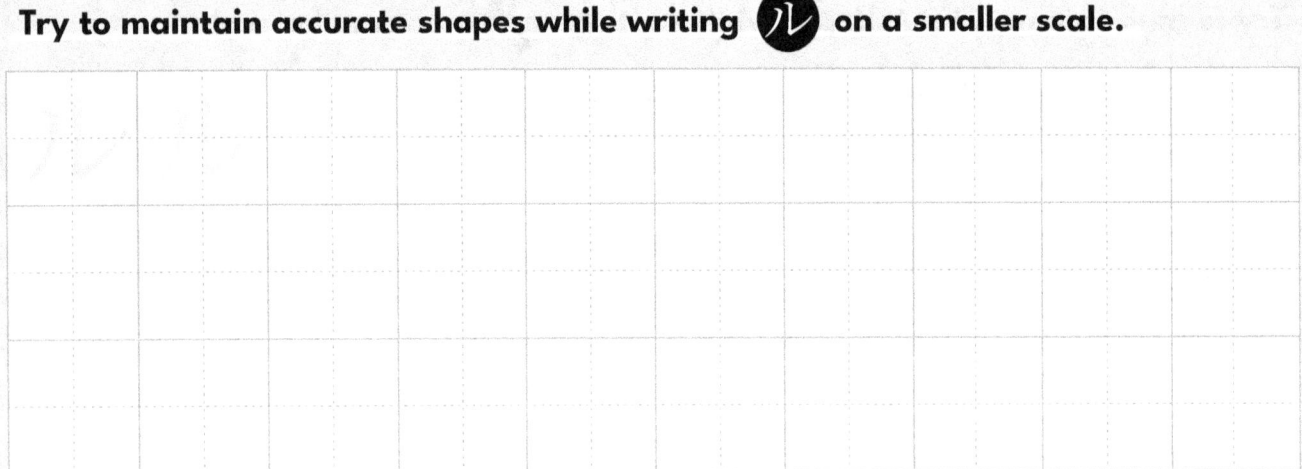

Try to maintain accurate shapes while writing ル on a smaller scale.

Mnemonic.

Examples.
- Routes one and two
- A tree's roots

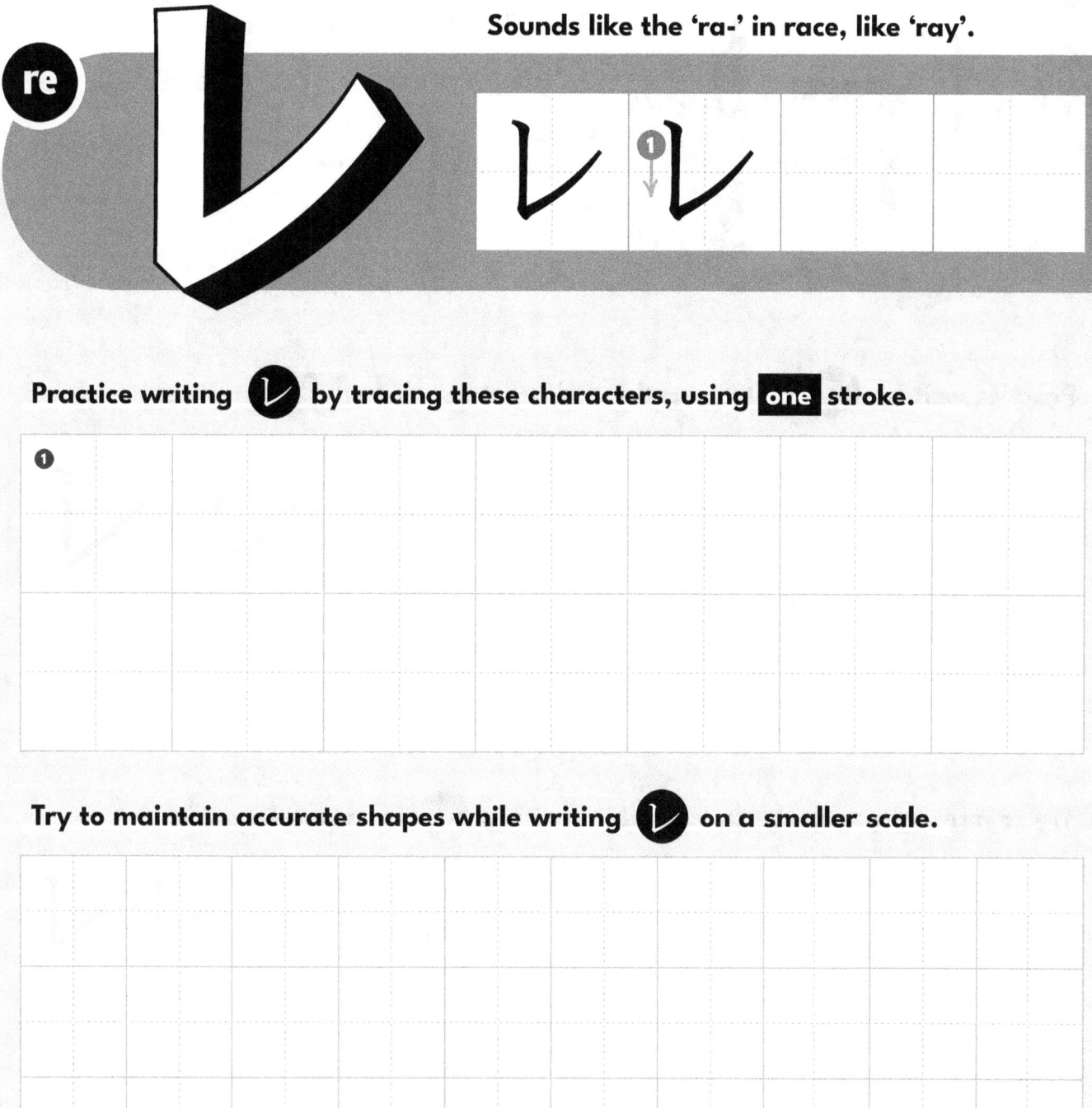

re レ

Sounds like the 'ra-' in race, like 'ray'.

Practice writing レ **by tracing these characters, using one stroke.**

Try to maintain accurate shapes while writing レ **on a smaller scale.**

Mnemonic.

Examples.
- Like hiragana 'shi' but she has long <u>re</u>d hair.
- <u>Le</u>mon wedge, which is '<u>re</u>mon' in Japanese

ro

Sounds like the '-rro' in churro.

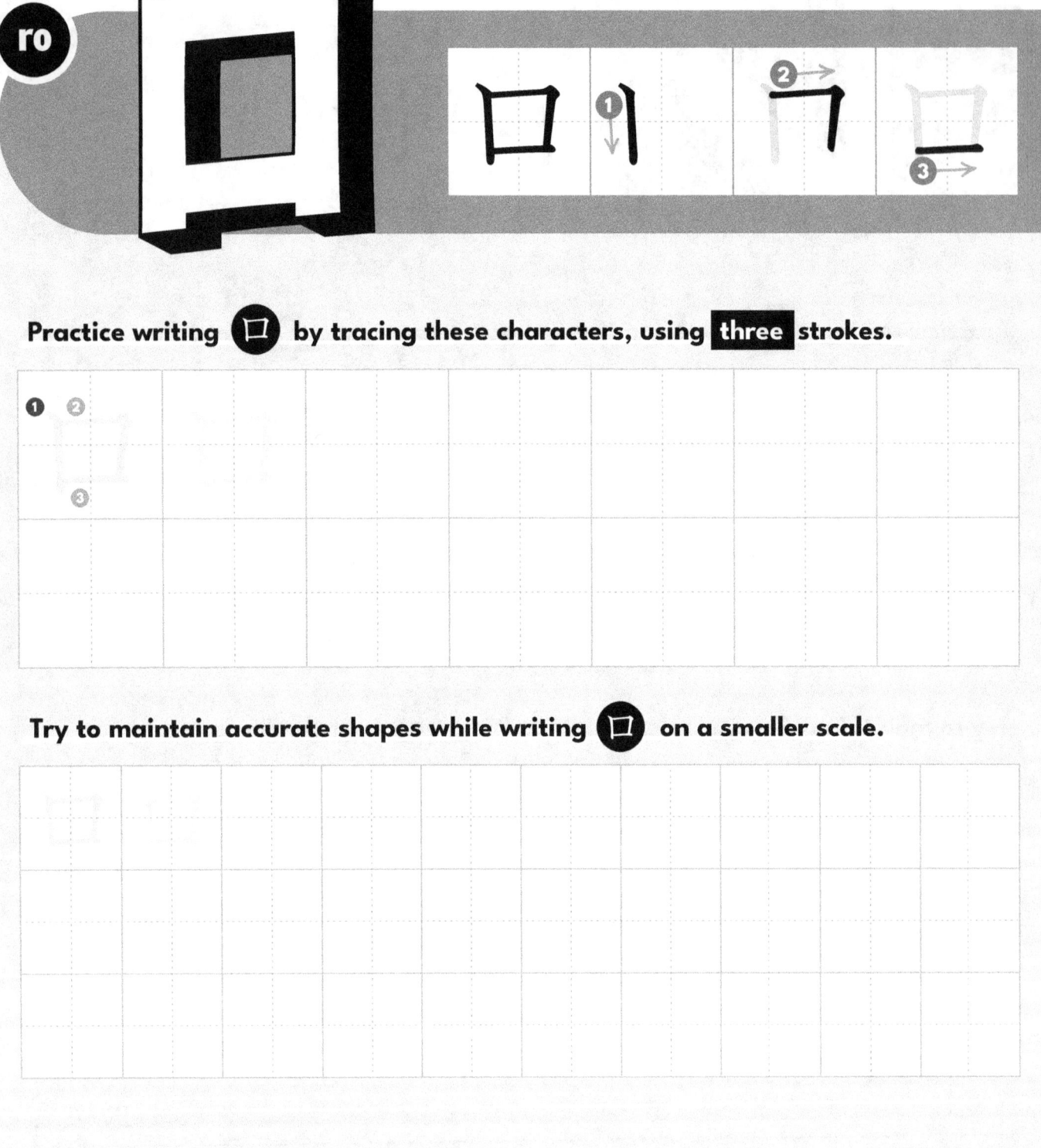

Practice writing ロ by tracing these characters, using **three** strokes.

Try to maintain accurate shapes while writing ロ on a smaller scale.

Mnemonic.

Examples.
- <u>Ro</u>bot head shape
- A sign that says "<u>ro</u>ad tunnel ahead"

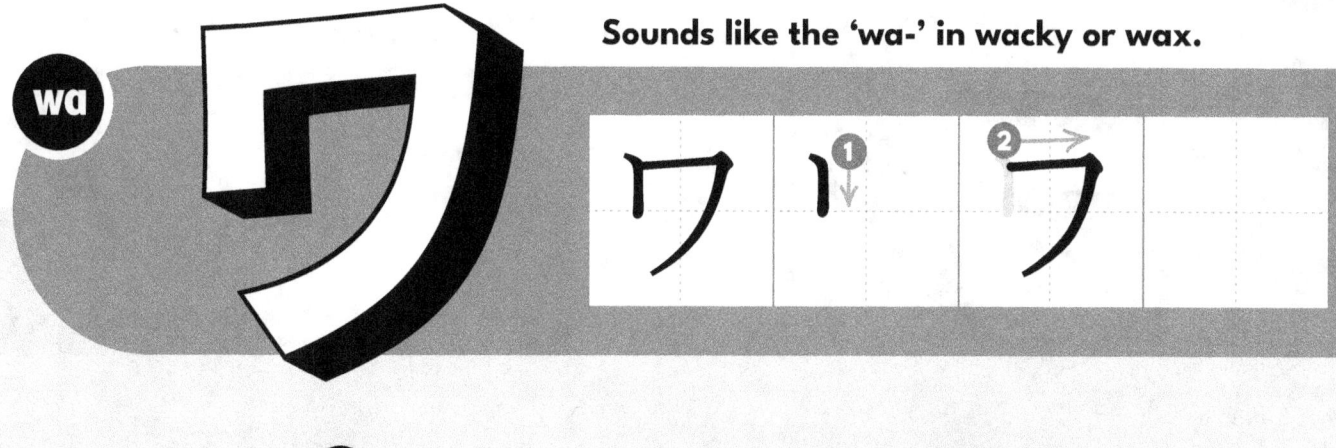

wa — Sounds like the 'wa-' in wacky or wax.

Practice writing ワ by tracing these characters, using two strokes.

Try to maintain accurate shapes while writing ワ on a smaller scale.

Mnemonic.

Examples.
- Shape of question marks... "What?"
- Picture a wine glass

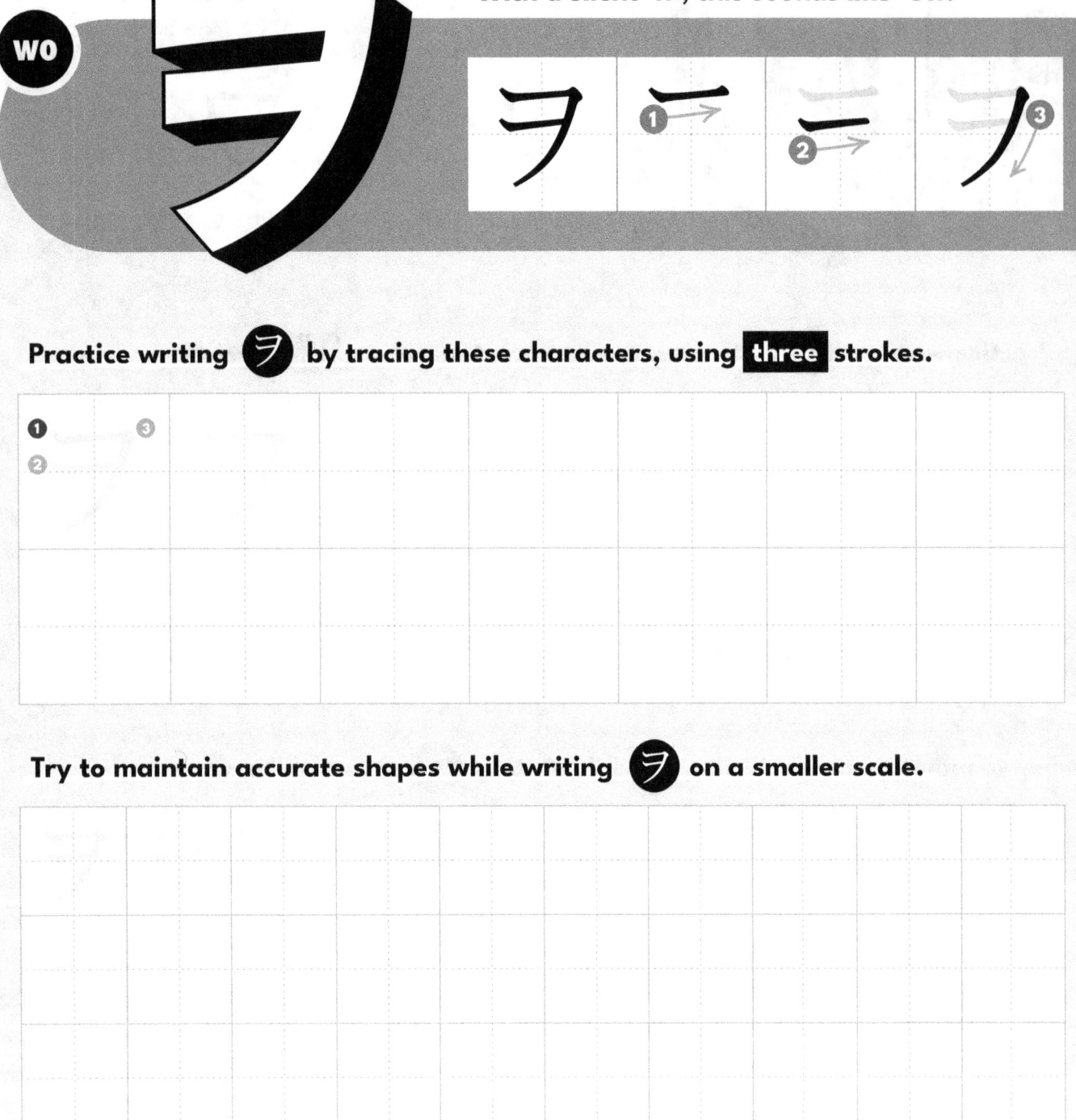

WO

With a silent 'w', this sounds like 'Oh?'

Practice writing ヲ by tracing these characters, using **three** strokes.

Try to maintain accurate shapes while writing ヲ on a smaller scale.

Mnemonic.

Examples.

- "Woah, a double-7!"
- 7 sticking a tongue out... "woah!"

n

Similar to the '-n' in plane, or 'nnn'.

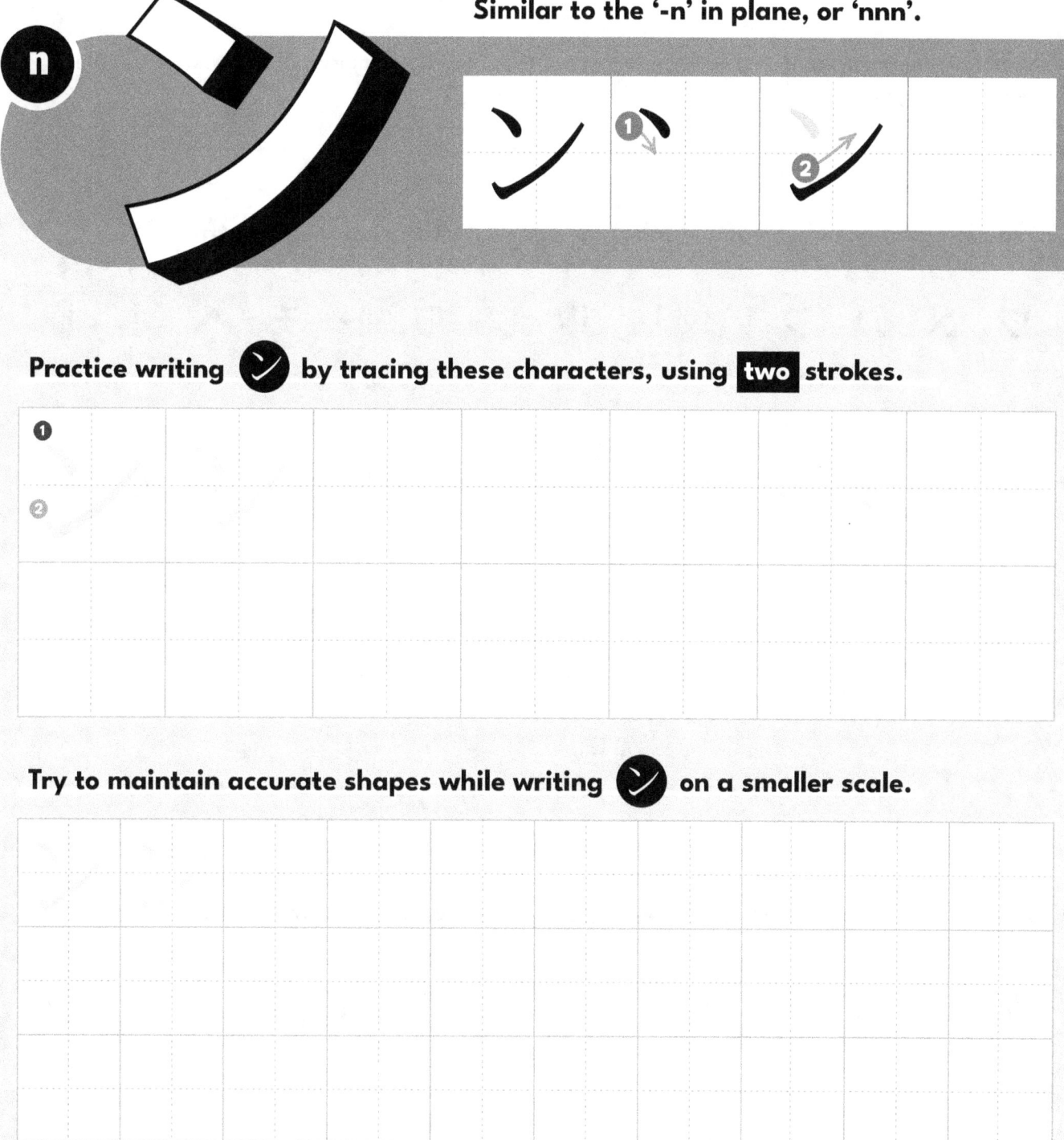

Practice writing ン by tracing these characters, using **two** strokes.

Try to maintain accurate shapes while writing ン on a smaller scale.

Mnemonic.

Examples.

- First, a crooked smile... now, 'shi' is wi<u>n</u>king (small horizontal lines compared to tsu & ni)

Now that you have learned all 46 basic katakana, the following memory exercises may be a little more challenging.

Practice pronouncing each symbol as you write the romaji beneath.

ワ メ ハ フ ヤ リ ル ツ ワ ト チ ヘ ホ レ

ラ ヌ ソ ン ワ リ テ タ ユ リ ン ム ル ナ

ミ ロ レ ネ マ ヲ ル レ ン ニ モ ラ ロ ヨ

Take a 5-minute break, and then do the same for these symbols too.

ヲ ノ ヒ ヲ ロ ノ ヒ ラ エ カ タ キ ヤ ソ

チ ラ オ ス テ ウ ネ シ ン ニ ヌ フ ホ ミ

ワ レ モ ナ イ リ ヲ セ ヘ コ ケ ワ マ ヨ

Take your time and try to complete each group without looking at the previous pages. Don't forget to take a break between each group.

This time, take a 10-minute break and come back to complete these.

ア ト ハ ツ ロ ク サ ム ル メ ユ モ ロ ラ

メ チ ル ム ヨ ヤ ネ モ リ ハ ラ ノ キ ヌ

ワ イ ツ カ ニ ヲ リ コ タ ウ ア ン レ ロ

After a much longer break, add the romaji for each symbol below.

ヲ マ ン ミ メ ユ ホ ヨ エ マ シ レ ム コ

イ ワ マ カ タ ハ ネ マ ツ ヨ チ ニ ヌ ロ

ル ウ ノ レ モ メ ヤ ム ラ ヲ ル キ ア リ

Some of the sample words in katakana may sound familiar when pronounced.

ヘリ — helicopter

メモ — memo

ヒレ — fillet

ミルク — milk

カヌー — canoe

ワニス — varnish

ローン — loan

ナイフ — knife

フレー — Hooray!

ノート — note, Notebook

タイヤ — tire

カメラ — camera

ネーム — name/reputation

ユーモア — humor

サラリー — salary

ハンマー — hammer

ヨーヨー — yo-yo

ハンカチ — handkerchief

ユニーク — unique

ネクタイ — necktie

////////////////////////////////// **PART 4**

Additional Sounds

The basic kana characters cover a lot of the syllable sounds that we need to pronounce Japanese, but not all of them. Both sets of letters that you have just learned can be adapted with some extra annotation, to show when the sound that is normally used will need to be altered. When one of these different sounds is required the existing sets of letters are accompanied by either small marks or even extra kana. The next few pages will show you what these differences are, and how the sounds can be adapted.

Voiced Consonants

An additional set of *'voiced'* sounds are created by altering how we pronounce certain consonant sounds. The modified sounds are similar to their original, except that they require vibration in your vocal cords. Essentially, one of the basic consonant sounds is replaced by another, illustrated with a different *Romaji* letter.

Basic consonant sounds, such as *t-*, *s-*, and *k-*, are produced without your voice box, as the movement of air creates these sounds. You can check this by making a *'t-'* sound once or twice - *remember, it's not the letter 'T' or "tee,"* but a short 't-' sound. These are 'voiceless' consonants, and we refer to kana such as か/カ *(ka)* and た/タ *(ta)* in the same way. The modified, 'voiced' versions are made with the same mouth shapes but also by adding *your voice*. For example, the *'k-'* in か *(ka)* becomes a *'g-,'* and *'t-'* changes into *'d-.'*

In written Japanese, existing kana characters with different pronunciations have extra **diacritic marks**. In this case, they are also referred to as *'voicing marks'* as the new, modified consonant sounds are *'voiced'* versions of their initial form. **Dakuten** are two extra lines that we draw in the upper right, similar to quotation marks, and a small circle in the same position is called **handakuten**.

Dakuten are attached to symbols that begin with *k*, *t*, *s*, and *h-* sounds, while only those starting with *h-* sounds have *handakuten*. Diacritic marks are written after all other strokes have been drawn.

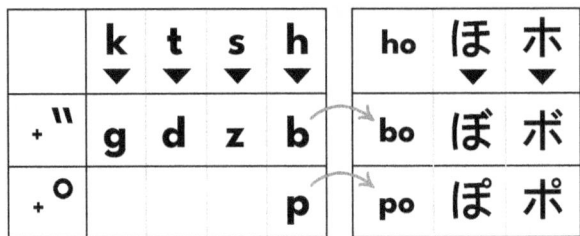

Voicing marks have been added to the basic kana - displayed to the right.

Romaji does not accurately illustrate Japanese sounds, so some characters are marked with an asterisk* to show variation from overall patterns. A 'French' 'j-' sound is better suited to 'chi' and 'shi,' while 'z-' or 'dz-' sounds are closer matches for 'tsu' and 'su.'

Katakana

	a	i	u	e	o
k / g	ガ ga	ギ gi	グ gu	ゲ ge	ゴ go
s / z	ザ za	ジ ji*	ズ zu	ゼ ze	ゾ zo
t / d	ダ da	ヂ ji (di)*	ヅ zu (du)*	デ de	ド do
h / b	バ ba	ビ bi	ブ bu	ベ be	ボ bo
h / p	パ pa	ピ pi	プ pu	ペ pe	ポ po

Hiragana

	a	i	u	e	o
k / g	が ga	ぎ gi	ぐ gu	げ ge	ご go
s / z	ざ za	じ ji*	ず zu	ぜ ze	ぞ zo
t / d	だ da	ぢ ji (di)*	づ zu (du)*	で de	ど do
h / b	ば ba	び bi	ぶ bu	べ be	ぼ bo
h / p	ぱ pa	ぴ pi	ぷ pu	ぺ pe	ぽ po

Combination Kana

Also referred to as **compound kana**, these are the written representations of hybrid sounds made by combining two others. Essentially, an extra consonant sound is added to the front of another character. The most important thing to remember is that while we write them with two kana, they take **one mora** to say.

The rules for writing *compound kana* are the same for both hiragana and katakana scripts, including the new characters for *'voiced'* sounds from the previous pages.

The written form consists of one regular-sized character that usually ends with an *'-i'* sound, such as し/シ *(shi)*, き/キ *(ki)*, ち/チ *(chi)*, etc., and a second, small character, typically や *(ya)*, ゆ *(yu)*, or よ *(yo)*:

Compound kana are used in writing completely different words to their equivalent, normal-sized counterparts. The difference in character size is more apparent when comparing words that are written using the same characters:

A single mora can change the meaning of a word, but they are relatively easy to recognize with practice. A mispronounced or misheard compound sound can have a significant impact on the meaning of what is said:

Regular ゆ
じゆう *ji-ya-u* "freedom"

Small ゅ
じゅう *jya-u* "gun"

The chart on the next page shows the most common hybrid sounds, combining an initial character ending in an *'-i'* sound with a small symbol from the *'y-'* sounds. There is no need to memorize these characters if you can remember how to read and write a hybrid sound.

Compound kana with '-i' + 'y-' sounds tend to be associated with native Japanese words (kun'yomi). You will encounter some other, less common combination sounds, especially in words of foreign origin, but they can be considered exceptions to the rules above, and it is best to learn about those if and when you see them.

	ya	**yu**	**yo**
k	きゃ キャ kya	きゅ キュ kyu	きょ キョ kyo
s	しゃ シャ sha	しゅ シュ shu	しょ ショ sho
t	ちゃ チャ cha	ちゅ チュ chu	ちょ チョ cho
h	ひゃ ヒャ hya	ひゅ ヒュ hyu	ひょ ヒョ hyo
m	みゃ ミャ mya	みゅ ミュ myu	みょ ミョ myo
n	にゃ ニャ nya	にゅ ニュ nyu	にょ ニョ nyo
r	りゃ リャ rya	りゅ リュ ryu	りょ リョ ryo
g	ぎゃ ギャ gya	ぎゅ ギュ gyu	ぎょ ギョ gyo
j	じゃ ジャ ja/jya	じゅ ジュ ju/jyu	じょ ジョ jo/jyo
b	びゃ ビャ bya	びゅ ビュ byu	びょ ビョ byo
p	ぴゃ ピャ pya	ぴゅ ピュ pyu	ぴょ ピョ pyo

Long Vowels

Extended vowel sounds, such as *'-oo'* or *'-ee,'* are shown by adding a character or mark to the kana with the sound we need to double. They are called 長音 *(chouon)* in Japanese, and they are represented in different ways in each of the kana scripts. We can easily pronounce a long sound when talking, and the rules for writing them are not too difficult either.

When writing **hiragana**, we add one of three vowel characters for long vowel sounds *(writing them at normal size)*:

> For *'a'* sounds, it's an extra あ *(a)*
> For *'i'* **and** *'e'* sounds, add い *(i)*
> For *'u'* **and** *'o'* sounds, add う *(u)*

So, to extend the *'a'* part of か *(ka)*, you add あ and write かあ *(ka-a)*. Similarly, to double the *'i'* in き *(ki)*, you write きい *(ki-i)*. く becomes くう *(ku-u)*, and so on:

The popular examples showing the importance of correct pronunciation for long vowel sounds are to compare the Japanese spellings of 'grandfather' and 'uncle,' or 'aunt' and 'grandmother.' (*Your uncle or aunt may be offended if you refer to them as a grandparent!*)

おじさん — *ojisan* — "uncle"
おじいさん — *ojiisan* — "grandfather"

(the honorific title *'-san'* is added when using the respectful *Sonkeigo* speech)

Extended vowel sounds are far easier to write in **katakana**, consisting of a simple line called the 長音符 *(chōonpu)*, or *'long sound mark,'* that follows the kana. Text in a vertical orientation has an upright line (|) which is located below the kana. Horizontal writing features a line that we draw horizontally, looking similar to a hyphen (ー):

Here, the symbols キ *(ku)* + ユ *(yu)* make combination-kana *'kyo,'* and the *'o'* sound is extended with ー before writing the final ト *(to)*. For *'cake,'* you extend the *'e'* in ケ *(ke)*:

キュート — *kyuu to* — "cute"
ケーキ — *kee ki* — "cake"

In Romaji, long vowel sounds can be represented by either writing the vowels out in full or using a *macron* (a diacritic mark) A macron is just a line above a vowel that shows its sound is longer when pronounced, e.g., *'Tōkyō,'* pronounced as *'Toukyou.'*

Long Consonants

Also referred to as **double consonants**, we can write these sounds by adding a *'small tsu'* (also called Sokuon) between two kana. The consonant sound from a character that follows a small tsu should be heard twice when reading. It's the same in both hiragana and katakana, using the small つ and ツ symbols.

For example, a small ツ between ロ (ro) and ク (ku) makes the word ロック pronounced as *"rokku,"* not *'ro-tsu-ku'* or *'ro-ku.'* It means 'rock (music)' as in ロックンロール *(rokkunrooru)*, or 'rock 'n' roll':

While words with a *small tsu* may look very similar to others, and pronunciation might not seem to vary much, they are entirely different words.

Adding a small つ between the characters い and た of the word いた makes the word いった. Pronunciation of this word is neither いつた (*'i-tsu-ta'*) or いた (*'i-ta'*) but, instead, いった is pronounced as *"i-t-ta."* The small tsu inherits a *'t-'* sound from the character た (ta):

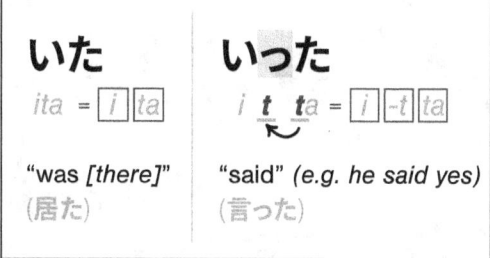

Small つ or ツ take one *mora* to pronounce, as though they were any other kana character, but they don't add an extra syllable sound. It can almost seem like you are stuttering when pronouncing words with double consonants. *The example above,* いった *might be spelled phonetically as "eet-ta." The extra 't' sound must be heard and squeezed into the same two morae as* いた *(i-ta)*.

Long consonants are *'unvoiced'* in pronunciation, including those that are usually modified by *dakuten and handakuten*. In other words, *'voiced'* consonants that follow a *small tsu* are pronounced as if they do not have dakuten.

We write the word for 'bed' as ベド *(beddo)*, but the ド *(do)* keeps its original ト *(to)* sound, as though written ベット. It's pronounced as *'be-t-to,'* not *'be-d-do.'* This word takes three *morae* to say:

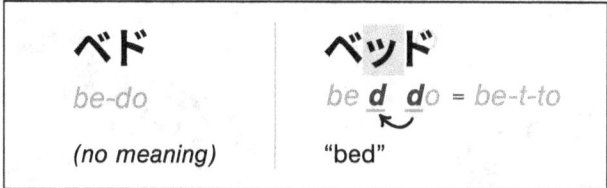

There are few words where double consonant sounds have dakuten, and they tend to be limited to foreign loanwords, so usually shown in katakana.

育 校 柱
軸 間 車 森 氏 離 全 魚
食
門 近 桜 根 逮 昼
酪 包 三 農 乃 牛 天
市 図
石 七 軽 享
祭 応 止 電 参 悪 士 詠
於 千 戒 智
交
旅
架 耳 鼓 珍 町
万 又 栈
祝 申 気 弟 月 東 成
相 久 週 刀 残
左
震 丁 枯 想 元
株 時
集
話 格 西 寸 弱 答
主
神
皮 梅 友
玉
破 虫
手 太 回 契
桂
肺
柊
安 問 誼
山 大 過 宜
胞 評
壇 駐 番
朋 亡
匹
屋
獲 万 八 歓
目
音

////////////////////////////////// **PART 5**

Introduction to Kanji

Kanji, literally meaning *'Chinese characters,'* are considered to be the most challenging part of Japanese to learn, but this book aims de-mystify them as a topic. They represent words and vocabulary, forming a significant amount of everyday language - so it's hard to get by without them.

Compared to the kana scripts, they are numerous and complex. While it's highly possible to memorize the kana in less than a day, kanji study takes far longer. Even an average native speaker probably comprehends just a fraction of the many thousands of kanji that exist. It's best not to approach kanji as a subject that can be *'learned,'* as few people truly master this writing system.

However, the good news for beginners is that knowledge of just a few hundred can enable you to start reading lots of real Japanese, especially if you also learn to use a Japanese character dictionary.

The first step for all beginners wanting to *'learn kanji'* should be to understand how they function - that's what this chapter is all about. Once you appreciate how they work, kanji will seem more accessible, and you can study them more effectively. In other words, you first need to *'learn HOW to kanji'*.

Due to the vast number of characters involved, this part of the workbook shifts its focus away from teaching about individual characters, as it did for the kana. Instead, it provides readers with information about the important, *if occasionally confusing,* aspects of Japanese kanji characters. The following pages contain more information than the earlier chapters and, by the end, you should understand *'how to kanji'* efficiently.

Kanji Origins

Deep knowledge of kanji history is not a prerequisite for study, but certain aspects of this script are easier to understand if you have just a little background information. For example, there's a reason that most kanji have multiple ways to be said...

Japanese kanji characters look like the symbols you find in the Chinese language because that is where they originate. The writing system was imported from China in phases over hundreds of years, beginning sometime in the 5th century, when Japanese traders encountered the symbols on the Korean mainland. Japan had a spoken language but no universal writing system, so they assigned written Chinese *'hanzi'* characters to words with a corresponding meaning in spoken Japanese. They also decided to keep the Chinese pronunciation of the characters.

Spoken Chinese has a much broader range of sounds, so the new writing system arrived in Japan with strange pronunciations that would be rarely understood in China.

China

Korea   **Japan**

As time went by, the traders from across China, speaking different dialects of Chinese, would import increasing numbers of alternate pronunciations for each written character alongside their wares. The Japanese would re-create every new version of a word, using their limited range of sounds, and use it alongside others. The kanji pronunciations that came from spoken Chinese are called **On'yomi readings**.

If that didn't seem complicated enough, when Japan adopted the written characters and their various semi-Chinese pronunciations, they kept their existing native words, too, which meant that the Japanese language now had more than one word for everything! Half of those were foreign-sounding *(but not understood by the Chinese)*, and the other half was the original Japanese pronunciations, known as **Kun'yomi readings**.

Chinese *'hanzi'* symbols were initially designed to resemble the meaning of words and were, for the most part, logically assigned to equivalent spoken Japanese words. The system has its fair share of exceptions, so you should be prepared to encounter occasional confusing details as you begin building your kanji knowledge.

Why Learn Kanji?

It is possible to learn how to speak conversational Japanese without ever learning how to read the language. Still, you will find written kanji almost everywhere - usage of the most complex language system in the world is increasing every day. With an array of smartphone apps and websites to help you learn, including some that enable you to type kanji more quickly, there has never been a better time to study these characters.

If you only ever learn to speak in Japanese, you will miss out on a lot of what makes the Japan culture what it is. You would be unable to read helpful touristic signage or food menus, or understand the subtitles when streaming animé cartoons - you can appreciate all of these things even more by learning how to read Japanese, even just a little bit.

Just a little knowledge can go a long way too. It's possible to skim texts and deduce meaning without learning every character. Simple kanji are combined to create additional words, so you may also be able to decipher unfamiliar symbols with knowledge of the easier ones.

If you knew that 大 *(dai)* means *'big/great'* and 好き *(suki)* means *'like,'* for example, you could understand that 大好き *(daisuki)* means *'love'* (i.e. 'a great like') without too many leaps in imagination. Kana-only texts lack punctuation and word spacing, so they are not a practical shortcut.

Work Smarter...

...not harder. That's how the saying goes. This simple idea can save you considerable time and effort when approaching kanji study. Beginners are inundated with dizzying levels of detail, and it is easy to waste time learning less practical information simply because the information is available. Before you proceed any further, the following FAQs may offer some helpful insight:

How many kanji do you need to learn?
A structured list of 2,136 Joyo Kanji is taught in the Japanese school curriculum, and up to 3000 are used with any frequency if you read Japanese newspapers - probably more! Try not to set a particular target number to be learned, as only a fraction of those 2136 are needed to start reading Japanese. You will naturally encounter the most useful kanji when you start and practice reading.

Do I need to memorize every reading?
Most kanji can have multiple pronunciations *(or 'readings')* called On'yomi and Kun'yomi, which, in simple terms, means that a single character could be said in as many as eight different ways. A lot of the time, it's likely that only one or two are even relevant or practical. You could save time by simply leaving the rest out. *(You will learn more about 'readings' soon.)*

What makes up a kanji?
Kanji characters do not consist of randomly arranged lines or pen strokes, and stroke order diagrams only show how we write characters. They are all made with one or more parts and, in turn, are combined to create even more. Those parts are mostly taken from a defined set of 214 historical *KangXi* radicals - the shapes adopted from the Chinese writing system - and they are assembled in a broadly logical way.

Can you learn kanji by writing them?
In theory, you could repeatedly write out kanji, stroke by stroke, and recognize individual characters by their shapes. This strategy works for the kana because they have simple shapes and represent just one sound. When you learn about a kanji, you also memorize its various meanings and pronunciations simultaneously. The sheer number of kanji, many with 10 or more pen strokes and highly complex stroke orders, it may be a time-consuming and potentially ineffective method on its own.

In what order should I learn kanji?
One consideration when choosing where to start might be the frequency of use. You make progress when you can practice your Japanese, either by reading, listening, or speaking the language. Each requires a vocabulary of practical words *(kanji)*.

The 'unofficial lists', curated for JLPT *(Japanese Language Proficiency Test)* preparation, would not be a bad choice, and neither would the '100 most frequently used characters.' Another alternative might be the so-called *'radicals first'* approach. Not all radicals are kanji, but all kanji have radicals. Recognizing the possible parts could make learning other lists more efficient.

What is the best way to learn kanji?
The best advice would be to develop a strategy or combination of study methods that you can stick to in the long run. Consistency is often crucial and having a routine or system that accommodates both acquisition and revision goes a long way. Use study tools that suit your style of learning; reading, writing, speaking, creative mnemonics, spaced repetition with flashcards, etc. They all work for kana and will work on kanji.

About Kanji

Kanji show larger chunks of information and are used to write vocabulary words with core meanings in sentences, like nouns, verbs, and adjectives. Once you recognize some kanji with some basic definitions, you can learn how to use grammar.

We learn hiragana and katakana by rote memorization, but kanji are significantly more numerous. Committing shapes to memory one by one is unlikely to work, especially when you must also try to learn more than one meaning and pronunciation. Kanji are not as easily memorized as a whole shape, like the kana, and are easier to recognize by the parts used to create them.

The building blocks of kanji are called radicals, and there is at least one in every kanji. Each has a primary component *(or Bushu)* that we use to categorize or index kanji in most Japanese character dictionaries. Sometimes, the pieces or combination of their parts can even show or hint at the underlying meaning.

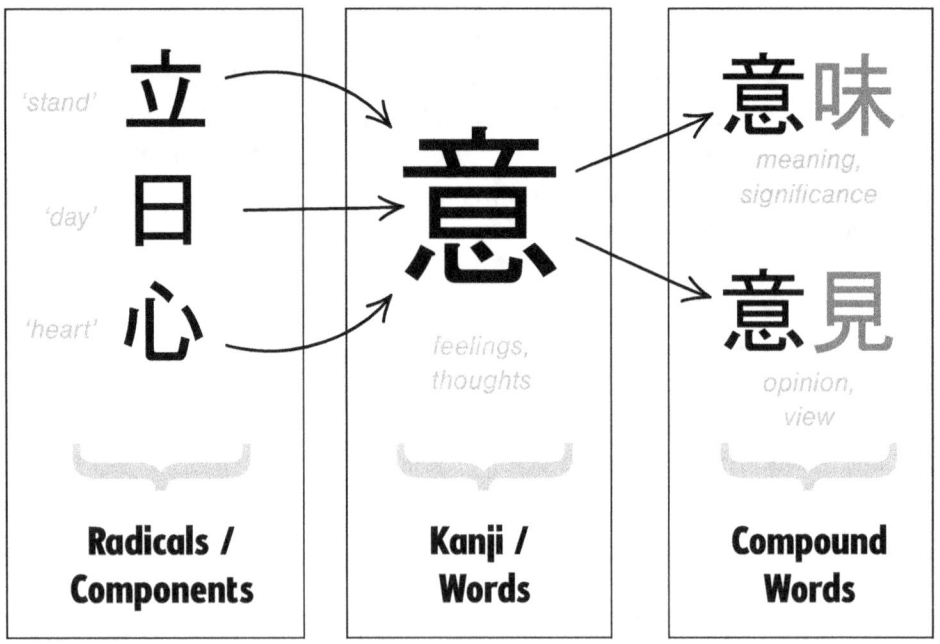

The way radicals and additional components are combined to create kanji is similar to spelling a word with letters. The individual radicals have no meaning, except those that can also be kanji in their own right, just as *Roman* letters make no sense in isolation. Some, such as *'I'* and *'a,'* can be English words in and of themselves, but most are essentially just components. While they do not work precisely the same way, the idea that radicals are a sort of alphabet may be one way for beginners to frame them.

About Radicals

Ancient written Chinese consisted of thousands of *pictographs* - essentially, these were small drawings designed to resemble whatever the meaning of the word was. Writing with *pictographs* took a long time, so the Chinese eventually simplified the system. Graphic elements with similar appearances were grouped together and effectively replaced with a single, standardized shape. After a significant overhaul, old pictographs were re-designed so that they could all be constructed from the same set of standard shapes. Those new standardized shapes are called radicals, and the updated pictographs are the kanji.

The *original* set of standardized radicals is named after the first Chinese dictionary to use them. Consisting of some 214 symbols, the *KangXi Radicals* are organized by the number of strokes needed to write them, and they are used to classify and index kanji in Japanese character dictionaries. There are a variety of 'radical lists' but the *KangXi* set remains the most commonly used.

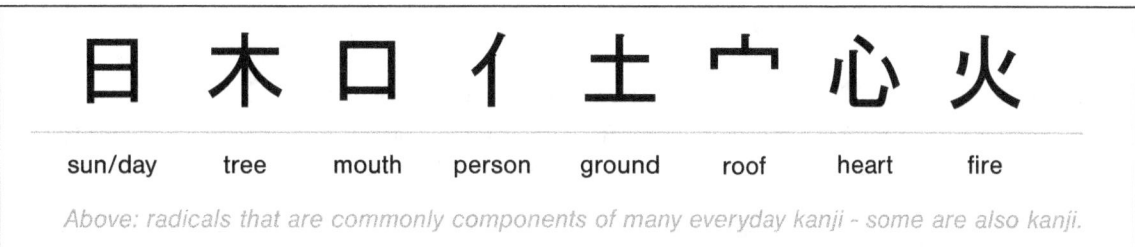

Above: radicals that are commonly components of many everyday kanji - some are also kanji.

Each radical has a sort of *nickname* that tends to describe their shape, making them easier to teach and learn about. These nicknames can sometimes cause confusion because certain radicals shapes are also used as standalone kanji, and often resemble their kanji meanings. Try to remember that, on their own, **radicals have no meaning** - they are simply components with *nicknames* that, sometimes, just happen to match their meaning as a kanji.

Every kanji has one primary radical, or **Bushu**, which generally offers insight into the kanji's meaning. Usually, this applies to objects and concepts with more 'primitive' origins, as those connotations are diluted in newer kanji:

Above: the 'fire' radical 火 could show 'primitive' meanings related to fire.

Note: the term *'radical'* usually refers to kanji components that features in the *KangXi* list, but it often serves as a name for any shape that we find in multiple kanji. Whole characters that are themselves made from radicals could be considered as radicals too - whether they are on the *Kangxi* list or not!

Where to Start

Foreign languages that you can already read will always be easier to learn. French, German, or Spanish vocabulary is collected with relative ease because of the familiar roman lettering, despite slight pronunciation differences.

When you begin learning about kanji, you might consider starting in the same place that Japanese schoolchildren do - learning similar 'first words' that kids across the world tend to learn. They have simple, everyday meanings that are useful at a young age, such as *'me,' 'face,' 'nose,'* etc.

When you examine the kanji with many of those *'first word'* meanings, they are pretty complex in appearance, taking upwards of ten pen strokes to write, making them less than ideal for the beginner who seeks simple shapes:

'First Words'

The opposite is often true for kanji that may seem *'easier to learn,'* with fewer lines and shapes. A simple form may seem quicker to memorize, but those kanji can represent advanced or specialist vocabulary that is simply useless to beginners.

In other words, there is virtually no correlation between how complicated a kanji looks and how useful the meaning of the word will be:

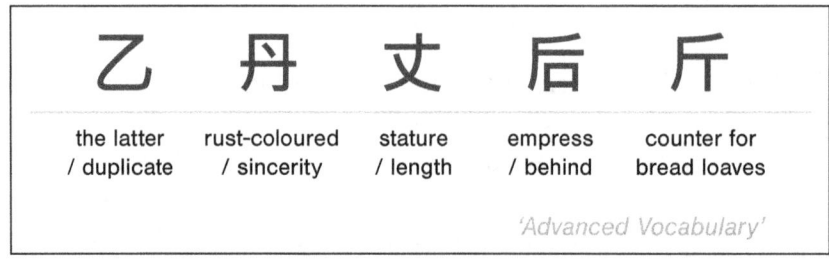

'Advanced Vocabulary'

If the complexity of shape and simplicity of meaning are not related, it all begs the question: **"What is the best order to learn kanji?"** Unfortunately, there is no right or wrong answer and it depends largely on what your goals are.

One of the common paths tends to be the 'unofficial' lists of kanji required for passing the first level in the Japanese Language Proficiency Test (JLPT), N5. The kanji on those lists are probably similar to those amongst the *'100 most frequently used kanji.'* Both options are relatively reasonable if you just want to start learning everyday kanji.

However, starting with relatively unordered kanji lists may present you with problems. You will find that characters can begin to look similar to one another, and memorizing kanji by overall shape or visual appearance becomes tricky. Just part of the way into a list of *'JLPT N5 kanji'*, you would meet kanji such as 話 & 語 , and then also 諒 / 誥...

Which was "talk" and which means "language" again?
Wait a minute. I'm sure the square with a cross means "fact."
Or is that "give instructions?"

The kanji may all have useful meanings, but you need a strategy or system to minimize the amount of time and effort that is spent checking how new and learned characters differ. With so many characters to learn, *"what is the most efficient way to learn kanji?"*

Components First

An alternative method, called **"radicals first,"** is to give priority to learning the kanji that require the fewest strokes. Although memorizing the *214 historical KangXi radicals* would probably be very useful, the word "radical" is used to describe any form *(including kanji characters)* that in turn becomes part of many more kanji.

As you work upwards through the kanji by stroke count, symbols begin to repeat as parts of others. In other words, you begin recognizing characters you have already learned as larger and larger components. Instead of seeing a kanji made up of 15+ seemingly random pen strokes, you see them as being made from just a few larger parts.

Your studies can be accelerated when you combine an ability to recognize kanji faster with memory aids like mnemonics and stories.

To illustrate:

The relatively complex-looking kanji 霜 *(frost)* is written with 17 pen strokes, but is easier to remember when you recognize it's made from 3 other kanji components:

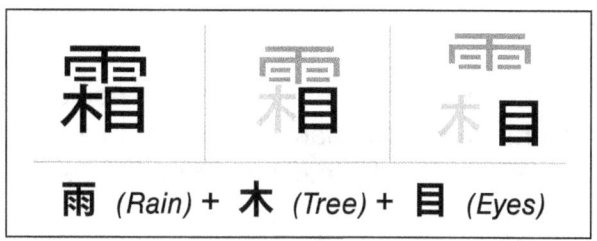

雨 *(Rain)* + 木 *(Tree)* + 目 *(Eyes)*

If you already know what the three kanji components mean, you can create a story or mnemonic to remind of what the more complicated kanji stands for:

*"When **RAIN** is above, a **TREE** provides shelter, but keep your **EYES** peeled and watch out for **FROST**!*

Those parts feature in lots of common kanji:

雨 is used to make 雲 *(cloud),* 雪 *(snow),* 電 *(electricity),* 雷 *(lightning)* etc.
木 is used to make 本 *(book),* 新 *(new),* 床 *(bed),* 暦 *(calendar)* and more.
目 is used to make 息 *(breath),* 値 *(price),* 助 *(help),* 見 *(see/view)* etc.

Radical Placement

To find kanji in Japanese character dictionaries, you first need to identify which of its parts is the primary radical *(Bushu)*. Unless the kanji is made from a single shape *(therefore, it's also the radical)*, it will be in one of seven positions:

#	Name	Placement	Position	Examples
1	Hen 偏	Left side		言(言) in 記, 扌(手) in 指
2	Tsukuri 旁	Right side		刂(刀) in 利, 力 in 助, 欠 in 歌
3	Kanmuri 冠	Upper		⺿(艸) in 花, 雨 in 雪, 穴 in 空
4	Ashi 脚	Lower		心 in 恋, 灬(火) in 点, 儿 in 兎
5	Tare 垂	Northwest		厂 in 原, 尸 in 局, 广 in 店
6	Nyō 繞	Southwest		辶(辵) in 近, 走 in 起, 廴 in 建
7	Kamae 構	Enclosures (Various)		門 in 開, 囗 in 国, 勹 in 包

Most kanji contain multiple components from the KangXi radical list, making it difficult to determine where characters might be listed in a dictionary. The **twelve steps**, summarized below, will usually lead you to the correct part:

1	Whole	- Is the whole kanji a radical in and of itself? (文, 長, & 黍)
2	Single	- There may only be one radical (丿 in 乃)
3	Enclosure	- A shape covering 2-4 sides is usually the radical (匚 in 医)
4	Left	- On left side, nothing above, below, or intersecting (木 in 板)
5	Right	- As above, but on the right side (彡 in 形)
6	Top	- Is there a clear upper radical? (大 in 奈)
7	Bottom	- Top may have 2+ but possibly one at bottom (刀 in 劈)
8	Top Left	- If not obvious from steps 1-7, check the top-left (土 in 報)
9	Top Right	- Still not sure, check the upper-right for a radical (口 in 呉)
10	Lower Right	- If still no radical, check lower-right (口 in 君)
11	Lower Left	- Lower-left (虫 in 虱). Also when all corners are radicals.
12	Inside	- Last step, sometimes obvious at start (大 in 夾, or 女 in 嬲)

Common Components & Variants

These lists contain frequently used *KangXi radicals* and components. Some radicals change shape and appearance when they occupy different positions in a kanji to fit into that space. These alternate versions are called *variants* and they can sometimes look very different from their original shapes *(shown alongside)*.

Radical nicknames can vary from one list to another - remember that the names are simply tools to assist in memorization and are not necessarily meanings. *Variants share the same nickname as the regular versions of characters but could be renamed:*

Radical	Strokes	Position	Meaning/Name
亠	2		lid, top
亻 (人)	2		person
𠆢 (人)	2		person
儿	2		legs
冖	2		cover, crown
刂 (刀)	2		knife, sword
厂	2		cliff
口 (口)	3		mouth
囗	3		border
土 (土)	3		earth
女 (女)	3		woman
子 (子)	3		child, son
⺌ (小)	3		small
⺍ (小)	3		small
宀	3		roof, house
广	3		slanting roof
彳	3		step, street
艹 (艸)	3		grass
辶 (辵)	3		road, walk
阝 (邑)	3		village, country
阝 (阜)	3		hill, mound
忄 (心)	3		heart, mind
扌 (手)	3		hand
氵 (水)	3		water
犭 (犬)	3		beast
攵 (攴)	4		activity, hit
日 (日)	4		sun, day, time

Radical	Strokes	Position	Meaning/Name
月 (肉)	4		meat, flesh
木 (木)	4		tree, wood
火 (火)	4		fire
灬 (火)	4		fire (boil)
王 (玉)	4		jewel, jade
礻 (示)	4		altar, festival
疒	5		sickness
目 (目)	5		eye
禾	5		grain
穴 (穴)	5		hole, cave
衤 (衣)	5		clothing
⺮ (竹)	6		bamboo
米 (米)	6		rice
糹 (糸)	6		thread
虫 (虫)	6		worm, insect
行	6		to go
言 (言)	7		words, say
貝 (貝)	7		shell, property
走 (走)	7		to run
足 (足)	7		foot, leg
車 (車)	7		vehicle, wheel
金 (金)	8		metal, gold
門	8		gate, door
雨 (雨)	8		rain
頁	9		head, page
魚 (魚)	11		fish

Identifying Kanji

Learners of all levels will need to check the meaning of unfamiliar kanji sooner or later. No matter how advanced your studies, the way to lookup kanji remains the same.

The best method will depend on which medium you are using for study, but the most straightforward solution will usually be to search online. If you are using a computer, smartphone, or similar device, the process is simple. Many online kanji dictionaries such as *[jisho.org]* make it easy to find meanings and pronunciations, and you can simply *copy + paste* a kanji in the search bar to get started.

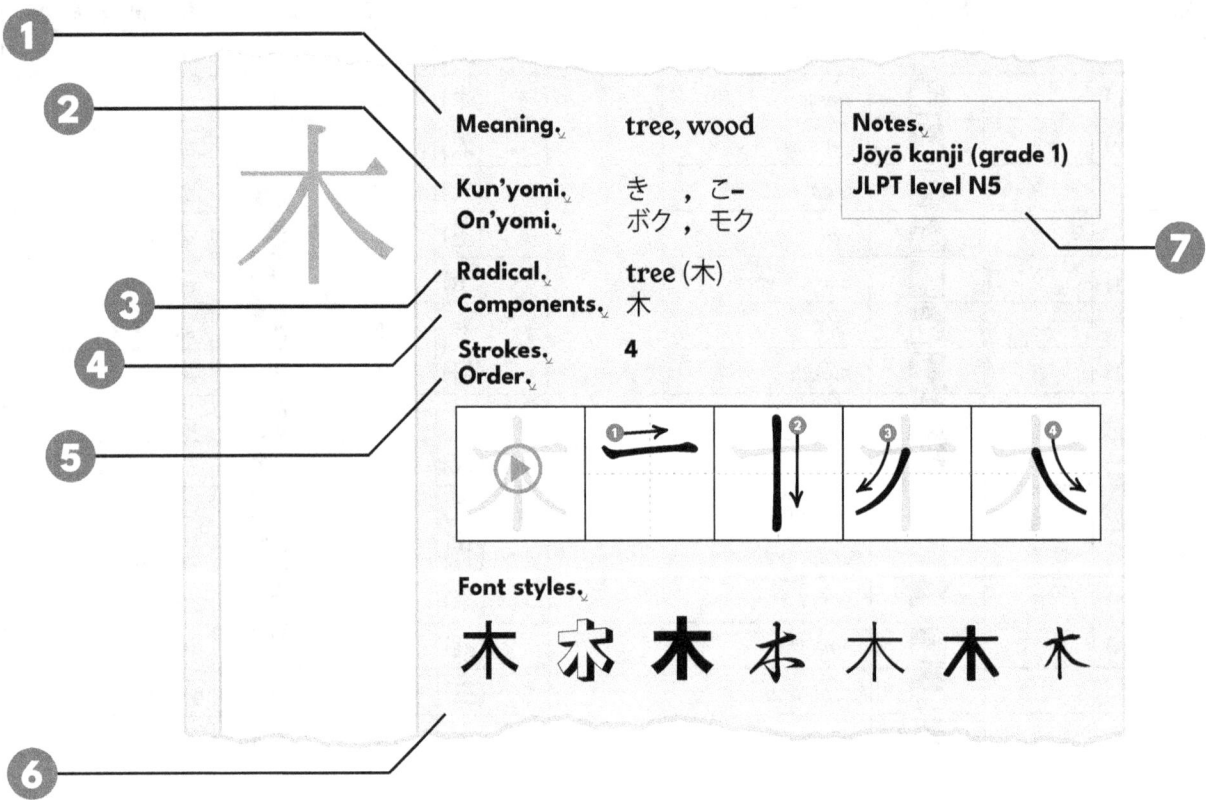

Above: the basic information typically found in online dictionaries (also see table, right)

Irrespective of the chosen method, you are usually provided with similar information upon finding the desired kanji. Some dictionaries show a bare minimum of information, while others can offer a lot more. It varies from one publication to the next, so you should consult reviews from other learners if you are unsure about the suitability of a particular dictionary for your level of knowledge. Those with extra information about using a kanji, with some example sentences or lists of compound words made with that character, are useful but contain fewer unique entries.

1	Meaning	There are many, but this will be the most common.
2	Readings	Most have multiple pronunciations, with 2 types: (a) Kun'yomi, the 'Japanese pronunciation' (b) On'yomi, so-called 'Chinese pronunciation'
3	Main Radical	The component used to index kanji in dictionaries.
4	Components	Like letters, used to make words (kanji), they are the basic building blocks of all kanji, called bushu.
5	Strokes/Order	The number of lines and the order they are written.
6	Font Styles *(sometimes)*	Variety of fonts displayed, often with a mix of both handwritten and modern, digital styles
7	Other data *(sometimes)*	Additional attributes that beginners may find useful, such as specific dictionary indices, etc.

Above: key for illustration of typical dictionary entries (see left page).

Suppose you need to look up a printed or handwritten kanji: in that case, those websites allow you to also browse and filter kanji by the components that you do recognize - even a single radical. It takes practice, especially when you are unsure which shapes are radicals, but these systems are generally intuitive, so they are worth trying next.

Another potential solution is to try software that can identify kanji written into them. You can either use a touch screen and your finger or draw the kanji with your computer mouse more crudely, and potential matches filter into view. Once again, *[jisho.org]* has this alternative function for times when you cannot *copy + paste* a character into a search engine.

Lastly, a traditional Japanese character dictionary will always be a sound investment. The most popular publications classify kanji by their primary radical, usually those in the *KangXi* list of radicals. Some may organize entries by the number of pen strokes it takes to write them. At the same time, some may use modified or alternative lists of radicals to index kanji, while others group kanji by the positions in which you find primary radicals.

Dictionaries aimed at learners with advanced kanji knowledge have longevity but can be challenging to use at earlier stages. Those aimed at beginners are easier to use but need replacing over time.

Stroke Order

All learners should try to make time for kanji writing practice in their study schedules. Stroke order plays a crucial role in forming accurate and legible characters, just as it did with kana. That said, memorizing the stroke order for so many kanji, especially as you progress to the most complex characters with *upwards of 20+ strokes,* can become very time-consuming.

Most online resources and Japanese character dictionaries will often show you the stroke order and may include animations. When that information is not available, some generalized rules can be applied to almost every kanji, saving considerable time and effort. As with all aspects of Japanese, there are exceptions to the rules, so they may not always work perfectly. They should, however, cover more than nine out of ten kanji:

Work from top to bottom, and from left to right.

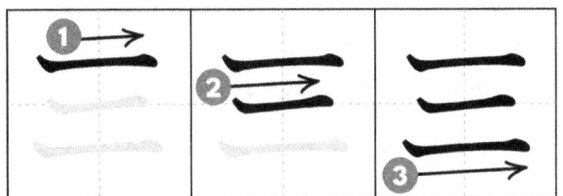 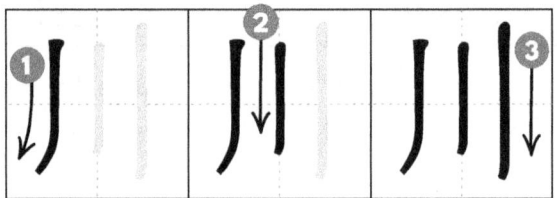

Horizontal lines first, then vertical.

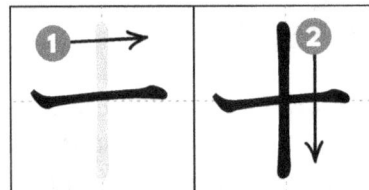 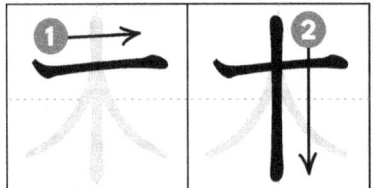

Vertical lines in the center, before strokes on the left and right.

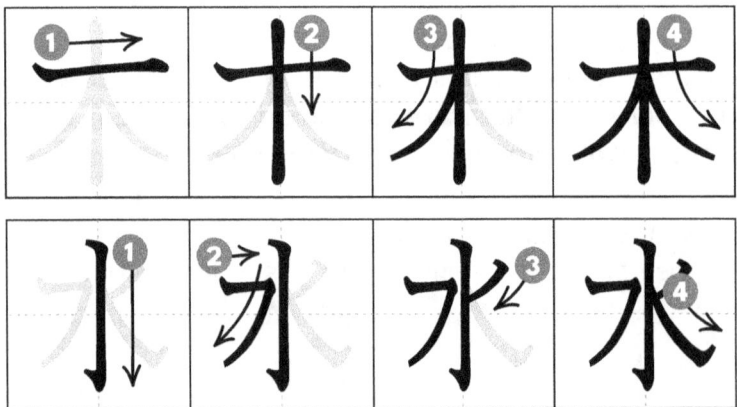

Boxes are three strokes, not four.

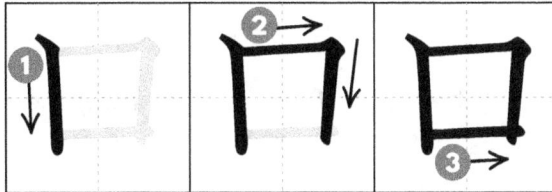

Outsides then inside (Boxes), before closing - but not C-shapes.

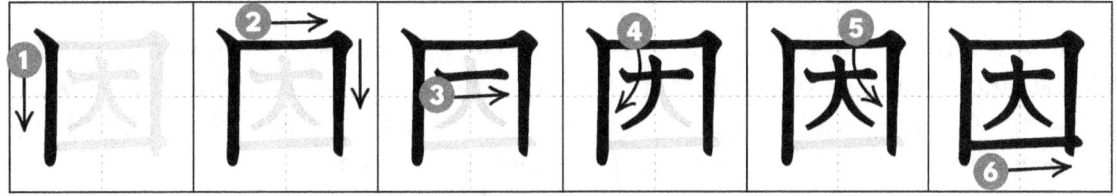

Lines overlapping lots of others come last (or later).

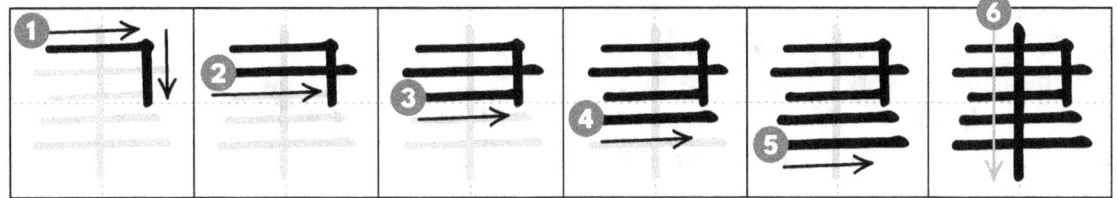

X-shapes, right > left diagonal lines before left > right (from top to bottom)

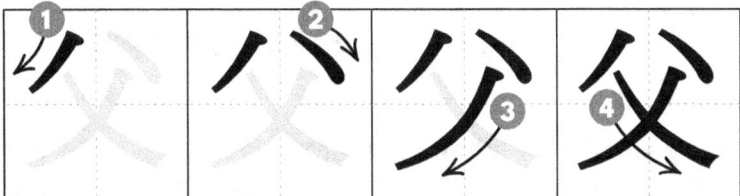

Dots/dashes on top of sections/kanji first, others at end.

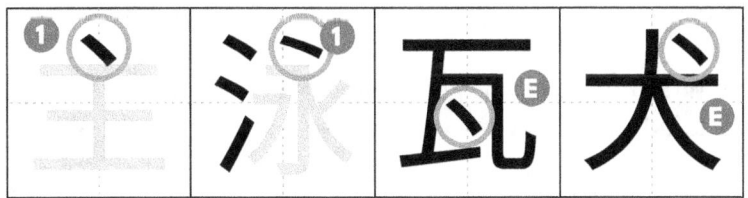

Underlining parts very last.

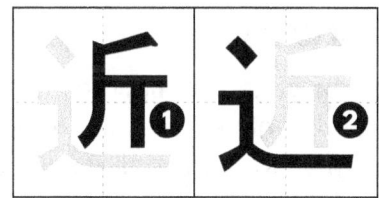

The same rules apply to even the most complex-looking kanji. Approach characters that appear to have multiple kanji using the steps above, component-by-component. Begin with the radical or kanji located in the upper-left corner or left side, and work towards the lower right corner. Muscle memory can soon take over with practice, and kanji stroke order will become an easier aspect of studying kanji.

A Few Essentials

The information in this section will not be immediately helpful to those just starting their kanji study; however, an introduction to these topics may help you determine how you study kanji.

Furigana

Japanese is notoriously difficult to read, and even those with vast kanji knowledge need a slight hint now and again. Luckily, kanji texts can come with reading aids, called **Furigana**, that describe how to interpret kanji *(or even compounds of kanji)*. They show how a kanji should be pronounced, potentially revealing the intended meaning. You commonly find furigana attached to the kanji in Japanese names, as they often contain uncommon kanji with unusual pronunciations *(Nanori)*.

Furigana (**振り仮名**) are just tiny hiragana characters that are printed beside or above the kanji they describe. Their placement depends on which direction the text is written and read.

Websites often display furigana immediately after their kanji counterparts, in parentheses *(or brackets)*, due to formatting issues:

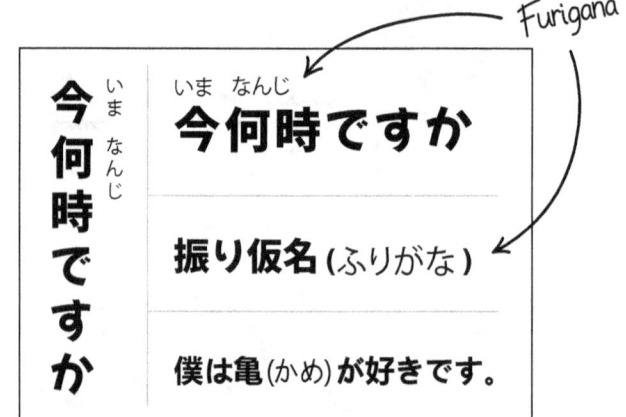

Authors, editors, and publishers usually decide whether hints are added based on the expected literacy of their audience. Kanji study materials aimed at beginners may not always have furigana as pronunciation may not be helpful without the meaning.

Okurigana

Okurigana is simply the name for the hiragana symbols that follow kanji, identifying that it represents a particular meaning from its others. It only applies to kanji, and they are almost always for kun'yomi readings.

Okurigana is suffixed to a kanji stem to inflect and conjugate verbs or adjectives. We write the present and past tense versions of a verb with the same kanji character, but different hiragana endings follow each to differentiate one from the other.

Jukugo

Jukugo is the name given to compound words made with at least two kanji, stuck together to create new words. The meaning of each kanji in a jukugo tends to contribute to the new, overall meaning and pronunciation, making it easier to work out what the vocabulary is or how to pronounce it:

Jukugo	Meaning + Meaning	Overall Meaning
子犬	Child + Dog	= Puppy
不良	Not + Good	= Bad
旅行者	Trip + Go + Someone	= Tourist, Traveller
歯医者	Tooth + Medicine + Someone	= Dentist

As a 'rule of thumb,' a kanji without okurigana is usually a noun. A jukugo with okurigana is typically a verb.

Verbs

You can spot which kanji are **verb words** by inspecting the kana that follow. Verbs end with either る *(ru)*, or hiragana that represent う *(u)* sounds, e.g., く *(ku)*, す *(su)*, or ぬ *(nu)*, etc.

Kanji Verbs	Meaning + 'u' Sound	New Meaning
言う	say + 'u' sound	= to say
学ぶ	study + 'bu' sound	= to study, to learn
目覚める	eye + awake + 'ru' sound	= to wake up, to awake

Which Reading?

It's relatively easy to determine **which reading** to use for a kanji based on word types. We can form some basic *'rules'* from general patterns that we see in everyday terms. They will not always apply in every case but should help get you started, or if you are stuck and not sure which to use:

Word Type	Reading Type	Examples
Kanji on its own	Kun'yomi	猫 (cat), 力 (power)
Jukugo (only Kanji)	On'yomi	記者 (journalist)
Kanji with Okurigana	Kun'yomi	辛い (spicy)
Jukugo with Okurigana	Kun'yomi	落ち着き (calm down)

The following pages will look at 'readings' in more detail, with sections describing irregular types of reading and how each is used.

About Readings

Most of the time, kanji associated with multiple readings will have just one or two that will be useful with any frequency. In the long run, you can save lots of time by learning only one good reading for each new character that you choose to study.

It will be a lot easier if you're only associating the meaning (and shapes) of a kanji with a single, valuable reading. You can always collect another when (and if) it shows up later. After having learned more kanji in less time, you can begin studying vocabulary sooner - where you eventually come across those other, slightly less helpful readings naturally.

This approach might not suit the preferred study methods of every student, but perhaps the concept could be adapted to suit your aims and goals.

How & When (-ish)

More detail for use of each reading:

Many words with standalone kanji use Kun'yomi readings, but not 100%. Single-kanji terms include nouns, and, for simplicity, they are usually some of the first characters that we learn. There are plenty of words that require On'yomi, including single-digit kanji numbers:

Word	Type	Reading	Meaning
人	(Kun)	ひと	person
手	(Kun)	て	hand
心	(Kun)	こころ	heart
一	(On)	いち	one
本	(On)	ほん	book
文	(On)	ぶん	sentence

A jukugo usually takes an On- reading, remembered for closely resembling the Chinese language *(with only kanji, one after another)*. Sometimes, they can take Kun- readings, but these are far less common, tending to be related to nature themes or the cardinal directions:

Word	Type	Reading	Meaning
東京	(On)	とうきょう	Tokyo
先生	(On)	せんせい	teacher
最高	(On)	さいこう	best
場合	(Kun)	ばあい	case
虫歯	(Kun)	むしば	cavity
朝日	(Kun)	あさひ	morning sun

Virtually all kanji that have okurigana use Kun- readings. The presence of okurigana can often signal that a word is a verb or an adjective, but some can also be nouns.

Word	Type	Reading	Meaning
食べる	(Kun)	たべる	to eat
行く	(Kun)	いく	to go
大きい	(Kun)	おおきい	big

Mixed Origin Readings

Compound words may have kanji with both On- and Kun- readings. We pronounce one part of the word with an On'yomi, and the other will take a Kun- reading. Some of the vocabulary represented by these types of jukugo are not uncommon, so you could encounter one sooner than you think. There are two types, with *On/Kun* and *Kun/On* readings:

The name of each type is taken from an example of each word:

Yutō-yomi (湯桶読み) compound words are those where the first kanji takes a Kun- reading and the second takes On-:

Jūbako-yomi (重箱読み) work the other way, where the first kanji takes On- and the second takes a Kun'yomi:

Word	Readings		Meaning
湯桶	ゆ + トウ =	ゆとう	hot water bucket
夕刊	ゆう + カン =	ゆうかん	evening newspaper
手帳	て + チョウ =	てちょう	notebook
重箱	ジュウ + ばこ =	じゅうばこ	nested boxes
役場	ヤク + ば =	やくば	town hall
金色	キン + いろ =	きんいろ	gold (color)

Ateji – Borrowing Kanji

Ateji are typically foreign words represented *(spelled)* using kanji. The characters were selected for their sounds *(readings)* and combined to create an equivalent phonetic word. There was rarely any correlation between the underlying kanji meanings and the word they spelled. In other words, we cannot usually decipher the meaning of *ateji* by inspecting their parts.

The Japanese eventually started using katakana to write foreign words during the Meiji Period *(1868-1912)*, but you will still encounter ateji today. They will usually be older, archaic words and sometimes preferred for the *'traditional'* appearance in specific applications, *e.g., signage.* Ateji were often used for foreign place names or countries, later simplified, and then spelled with katakana:

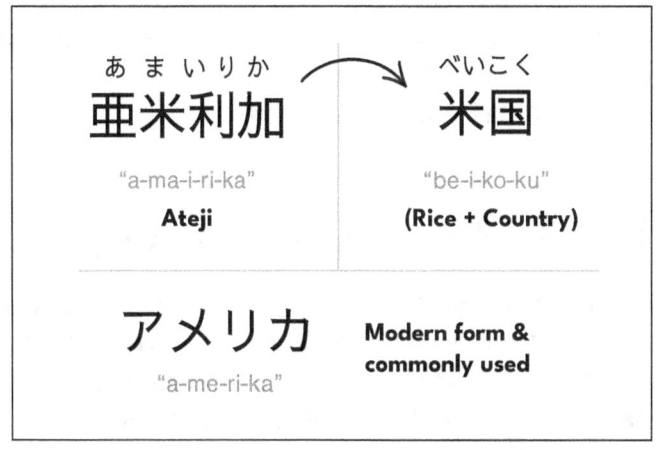

Gairaigo - Loanwords

Gairaigo is the Japanese word to describe foreign *'loanwords.'* Literally meaning *'words that came from outside' (or thereabouts),* gairaigo are representations of ideas and objects that might not have an equivalent in Japanese. They will be written with katakana and often sound similar to the original word - they have a distinctly Japanese twist, phonetically speaking:

Gairaigo deriving from the English language may be easy to understand and spell, even when heard or read for the first time. The gairaigo word for 'dry cleaning' is an excellent example, as is the more recently crafted word for *'fake news'*:

ドライクリーニング
(dorai kuriiningu)

フェイクニュース
(feiku-nyuusu)

While the majority are, not all gairaigo come from English words. They do still have a familiar sound when spoken, just to those who speak languages like German, Italian, and Portuguese:

アルバイト
(arubaito)
Meaning: Part-time work
from German 'Arbeit' (work)

Some loanwords may also express an existing idea differently. There are many words to say the same meaning, but we will use some in more or less formal situations. In another example (right), each of the terms will express a similar idea; the top one is the *Sino-Japanese (Chinese)* version that we use in formal contexts; and the *gairaigo* word at the bottom is better suited to a more casual setting:

会議
(kaigi) conference

打ち合わせ
(uchiawase)
business meeting

ミーティング
(miitingu) meeting

Certain gairaigo can be assigned a kanji character and added to the list of its Kun'yomi. They take neither a reading nor meaning from their assigned kanji, so they are not considered ateji. They tend to be common words (*e.g., metric measurement units*), so they probably need to be easier and quicker to write:

米 (メートル)
(meetoru)
Meaning: meter, metre
from French 'mètre' (meter)

Gikun - Contextual Readings

Gikun is the name given to irregular readings we assign to kanji by adding them in the space generally used for furigana. Typically, they associate a kanji word with a different meaning that probably isn't attached to that kanji. They only apply in the context of the particular publication in which you find them and often feature in graphic novels *(or comics)* to add fictional readings for made-up terms or sound effects.

Nanori - Name Readings

Nanori describes irregular readings for kanji characters only used when they are part of a name. Many names use common kanji with regular readings, but plenty of names have non-standard readings, or contain rare characters that you simply don't come across in everyday Japanese.

Family names come before your given name in Japan, and they frequently consist of kanji associated with 'nature themes.' One of the most common examples is probably 鈴木 (すずき) or *'Suzuki,'* where 鈴 means *'bell'* and 木 is *'tree'* or *'wood.'* It's common for a given name to have kanji that convey positive or beneficial traits in Japanese culture, such as 歩美 (あゆみ) or *'Ayumi,'* where 歩 means *'progress,'* and 美 will express the idea of *'beauty,'* for example.

Nanori may occasionally be the same as a kanji's On- or Kun- but they are a very particular type of reading that you cannot always find in dictionaries.

To illustrate how confusing nanori can be, you can try checking kanji readings of a famous Japanese person's name: the 124th Emperor of Japan, who ruled from 1926 to 1989, was known by his personal name 裕仁 (ひろひと), read as *Hirohito*.

裕仁
(ひろひと)
Hirohito

裕 ユウ (yu-u)
rich, abundant

仁 ジン, ニ, ニン (ji-n, ni, ni-n)
humanity, virtue, benevolence

(Emperor Hirohito is referred to as Emperor Shōwa posthumously)

Name readings can be associated with dozens of different kanji. In other words, different people with the same name will write their name with an altogether different kanji. The unisex name 'Akira' (あきら), meaning *'bright'* or *'clear,'* is one of many examples. The list of spellings for 'Akira' (right) is not exhaustive:

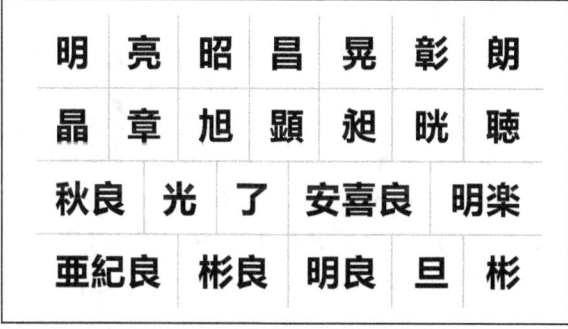

In the context of learning how to read, write, and speak Japanese, there is no need to try and memorize any nanori, as they are so numerous that you could probably spend a lifetime doing only that. Nanori can be learned naturally by simply asking the people you meet to explain how they pronounce their names.

Kokuji - Native Kanji

Even though Japan originally imported their writing system from China, the Japanese still created hundreds of native kanji using the same components. These are known as **kokuji**, or 'national characters,' describing kanji that the Japanese made in Japan.

Interestingly, kanji cannot be classified as kokuji if there happens to be an earlier Chinese kanji that looks the same - even if the two are not related, and their visual design is pure coincidence. *Kokuji* must be both made, and appear, in Japan first.

	Reading		Meaning
鴫	しぎ	shigi	snipe (fish)
鯒	こち	kochi	flat-head (fish)
鯰	なまず	namazu	catfish (fish)
鰰	はたはた	hatahata	sand-fish (fish)
鰯	いわし	iwashi	sardine (fish)
鱈	たら	tara	cod (fish)
鯱	しゃち	shachi	orca (fish)
笹	ささ	sasa	bamboo grass
榊	さかき	sakaki	cleyera japonica (tree)
樫	かし	kashi	oak (tree)

	Reading		Meaning
凧	たこ	tako	kite
俥	くるま	kuruma	rickshaw
饂	うどん	udon	udon noodles
橡	とち	tochi	horse chestnut
辻	つじ	tsuji	crossroads
垈	ぬた	nuta	swamp, wetlands
籾	もみ	momi	unhulled rice
蓙	ござ	goza	mat, matting
鑓	やり	yari	spear, javelin
叺	かます	kamasu	straw bag

Above: Kokuji were created for objects and concepts for which there was no equivalent in Chinese at the time - most kokuji represent native Japanese flora and fauna.

You probably won't need to learn about most kokuji, but there are just under ten on the official list of Jōyō Kanji. The Jōyō Kanji are some 2136 kanji that you need to know to be considered 'literate,' taught to the Japanese throughout their time in the national education system:

	Reading		Meaning
畑	はたけ	hatake	cultivated field of crops
腺	せん	sen	gland
峠	とうげ	tōge	mountain pass
枠	わく	waku	frame
塀	へい	hei	a fence or wall
搾(る)	しぼ(る)	shibo(ru)	to squeeze
働(く)	はたら(く)	hatara(ku)	work
込(む)	こ(む)	ko(mu)	to be crowded
匂(う)	にお(う)	nio(u)	to smell, to be fragrant

As you would expect, kokuji usually have only native kun'yomi readings, but some have both, and, in a few cases, there are kokuji that only have On'yomi.

Punctuation Marks

Punctuation is a relatively new addition to the Japanese language. Aside from the period *(full stop)* that came from China, Japan didn't use much punctuation until the Ministry of Education made it compulsory in 1946. Punctuation is now a crucial part of our modern language and is used extensively in digital messaging formats.

Japanese punctuation, **約物 (やくもの)** *or Yakumono,* consists of all the written marks not classified as kana, kanji, or numerals. Some will look familiar, but there are several unique marks that Western languages do not have. This overview of the characters may assist when you begin reading and writing the language more:

Width & Spacing

First, a note about typography width and spacing: Japanese characters are classed as 'full-width,' meaning they typically occupy a space equal in height and width *(a square)*. On the other hand, English *(Roman)* letters are 'half-width,' which, as you can probably guess, means that each character is half as wide as it is tall.

This spacing also applies to punctuation marks and 'spaces,' as both take up twice the width in Japanese. A 'space' will be double the width as in English, and while the marks do not look much different in appearance or size, commas and periods have extra space built into the character. The appearance will vary a little from one device to another, between different books, and in handwriting:

Period/Full Stop 。

Japanese uses a small circle instead of a dot (。 not .) placed at the end of a word when ending sentences. Its primary function in Japanese is to separate sentences, making it easier to see where one sentence ends, and another begins. An isolated sentence would not need one. The symbol is called **句点 (くてん)** *Kuten,* or **丸 (まる)** *Maru.* This character includes a half-space "。" so, when typing, you do not press 'space' between words.

Comma 、

The Japanese comma has the same function as English, providing sentence breaks, and is used for lists. They occupy the same position but point to the right instead. The Japanese name is **読点 (とうてん)** or, *Touten.* This character includes an additional half-space when typed "、" so no spaces need to be input.

Exclamation Mark ！

Otherwise known as 感嘆符 (かんたんふ), or *Kantanfu*, it is used as a way to provide emphasis, volume, and emotion. They are not common in formal texts but are used very frequently in casual messaging and social media. The typed character sits in the center of a 'full-width' space, so it looks to float between words.

Question Mark ？

In Japanese, 疑問符 (ぎもんふ), or *Gimonfu*, still shows when a question is asked, but it's almost redundant because of the interrogative particle か - used to mark an inquiry through grammar. That said, you will find it used in less formal writing.

Wave Mark 〜

This wavy dash or tilde is known as 波ダッシュー (なみだっしゅ), or *Namidashu*. It's often used in the same way that you would use a straight dash in English, likely to avoid being mistaken for the 'vowel extender' (as in the name above).

We can use a wavy dash to show a number range, like opening times or office hours (e.g., 9時〜5時). It's also used to draw out and alter vowel sounds for effect, such as the phrase おはよ〜！ *(ohaiyooo!)* meaning *"good mooorning!" (also see chōonpu, page 194)*

Interpunct ・

A uniquely Japanese punctuation mark typically used to split up words written in katakana - this applies commonly to foreign names:

The interpunct, or 中黒 (なかぐろ) *Nakaguro*, is a general separation mark that you can use to split any words requiring disambiguation, such as items in a list or titles from names. It also works as a slash between words and as a decimal point in numbers:

アンジェリーナ・ジョリー
(anjerīna・jorī)
Angelina Jolie

中学・高校
(ちゅうがく・こうこう)
Middle / High School

Ellipsis ⋯

The Japanese ellipsis, 点線 (てんせん), or *Tensen*, sits nearer the middle than the bottom of a line... This mark is typically seen with three dots, as in English, but can have anywhere between two and six at one time...... Usually used to show omissions or hesitance, and occasionally they may even be pronounced *"tenten."*

Brackets 【 】 + { } + 〈 〉 + [ ]

There are lots of different brackets or *Kakko*:

Lenticular brackets, known as 角付き括弧 (すみつきかっこ), or *Sumitsukikakko*, 【 】, are another uniquely Japanese punctuation mark. They highlight or emphasize most things and are generally used to draw attention to key phrases or points.

角括弧 (かくがっこ) or *Kakukakko* are the so-called 'cornered' brackets [ ]. They will feature in formulae and equations in the more academic areas of science or mathematics.

Wavy brackets or braces like { } are called 波括弧 (なみかっこ), or *Namikakko,* and have no particular function in general language. They have uses in mathematics and may appear inside a pair of square brackets (above).

〈 〉 are 山括弧 (やまがっこ), or *Yamakakko*, literally meaning *'mountain' brackets*. They provide emphasis to text but should not be confused with the < > symbols in English.

Parentheses ( )

丸括弧 (まるかっこ), or *Marukakko*, are commonly used for displaying kanji readings as 'in-line' furigana *(just as it is on the line above)*. These regular-looking, rounded *kakko* are just like the parentheses you already use.

Quotation Marks 「 」 + 『 』

The first pair, 「 」, are called 鈎括弧 (かぎかっこ), or *Kagikakko*, and they are known as single quotation marks. These function like the main English quotation mark, used for dialogue or quoting, and probably the type you will see most commonly.

Double quotation marks 『 』 are 二重鈎括弧 (にじゅうかぎかっこ), or *Nijukagikakko*. They are used far less frequently and usually for quotes within another quote, where you might arrange them like 「 『 』 」.

The Colon ：

This punctuation mark is not Japanese, so we write its common name in katakana as コロン *(koron)*. You are likely to see it used to write the time, as in the West, e.g., **5:04**, in place of **5時4分** *(where* 時 *is hours and* 分 *is minutes)*. We can also use it similarly to English to indicate that something written after the colon will explain or expand on what comes before it. However, this usage is usually limited to more academic texts.

Vowel Extender ー

The 'stretching bar' elongates vowel sounds written in the katakana script. The proper name is 長音符 (ちょうおんぷ), or *Chōonpu*, which means *'long sound symbol'*. It is not to be confused as a dash or hyphen; both are represented in Japanese by the 'wavy dash' though, sometimes, you may see chōonpu used at the end of non-katakana words, where it adds enthusiasm and excitement to expressions.

Diacritic Marks ゛+ ゜

Although not technically classed as punctuation, they do look like it, so worth a quick recap in this section. You learned about Dakuten (゛) and Handakuten (゜), or *Tenten* and *Maru*, in the 'Additional Sounds' section. These small marks are added to some basic kana to indicate when their pronunciation is changed *(voiced)*.

Small Tsu っ + ッ

Not punctuation, so just a quick recap! When a small *'tsu'* symbol is between regular-sized kana characters, the consonant sound from the syllable that follows it is doubled *(e.g., ろっく, pronounced as 'ro-k-ku', not 'ro-tsu-ku')*.

The Small ヶ

It looks the same as katakana ケ *(ke)*, but small ヶ is unrelated. It's an abbreviation for kanji 箇 *(か, or 'ka')*, which is a counter word. The small ヶ gets its shape from part of the kanji's radical *(bamboo, 竹)* in its variant form ⺮. Small ヶ is also a shortened version of particle が *(ga)*. It is never pronounced as the katakana ケ *(ke)* - instead, it's か *(ka)* as a counter or が *(ga)* as a particle.

The 々 Symbol

Referred to as the 'noma' mark, as it looks like the katakana for *'no'* and *'ma'* have been combined (ノ + マ = 々), this is the kanji iteration mark. This mark is not classified as a kanji and does not appear in dictionaries, so it's closer to a punctuation mark.

Essentially, the 々 symbol is only used with kanji and re-duplicates a single character that precedes it. The reading does not always duplicate, so the duplicate (second) kanji may have a slightly different pronunciation.

The summary above should prevent readers from mistaking the 'noma' as a kanji or kana symbol as teaching how and when it is used (or not) would make this book overly complex for kanji beginners.

Kanji	Readings	Meaning
山	やま *(yama)*	mountain
山山 = 山々	やまやま *(yamayama)*	mountains
人	ひと *(hito)*	person
人人 = 人々	ひとびと *(hitobito)*	people

Yen Symbol ¥

This mark is not a punctuation mark but worth highlighting, so you don't mistake it as kana or kanji. The Japanese 'Yen', or 円 (えん), is the currency of Japan. When writing, the yen sign sits in front of the numbers, but, in kanji, it would go after (e.g., ¥ 123 *or* 123 円). Both formats are acceptable - choose either the ¥ symbol or the kanji 円, never both. Use the ¥ symbol the same way as other currencies *e.g., US Dollar sign $*.

Postal Marks 〒 + ㊦

You will find these symbols on letters, postcards, and mailboxes or used to show where a post office is. The first version, without a circle, shows the particular part of the address containing the postal or ZIP code, *e.g.,* 〒105-0011 *(the postal code of Tokyo Tower)*. The second, inside a circle, is the icon used to locate post offices on maps.

Musical Note ♪

Occasionally, you may find text with musical notes. They show a reader that specific phrases are song lyrics or somebody is singing those words *(e.g.,* うさぎおひし♪ かのやま♪*)*

Alternation Mark 〽

Speaking of music, this musical punctuation mark 庵点 (いおりてん), or *Ioriten*, is used in professional songwriting and composition. It indicates the start of a song, or when a particular instrument or singer's part begins. You are unlikely to encounter this symbol in everyday texts - at least you will know what it is if and when you do.

Kaomoji

Kaomoji is the name for a particular style of 'Japanese emoticon,' where pictures are drawn by assembling a variety of lettering, characters, and punctuation marks. 顔文字 (かおもじ), or *Kaomoji*, meaning *'face letters,'* is almost an art form in itself. The familiar equivalent to kaomoji consists of simple smiley faces, e.g. :-) :(:D etc.

As a fun way to round off the section about punctuation, here is a small selection of kaomoji from a a few common categories:

Positive Emotions	Negative Emotions	Actions	Animals
(●﹏●)	(」°口°)」	ε=ε=ε= ┌(; ・_・)┘	/\/\ʕ◔ฺ益◔ฺʔ/\/\
ヽ(o^▽^o)ノ	℮((#Φ益Φ#))9	(つ ◔ฺ ς)	U•ﻌ•U
(―﹏―)	(つ ∩ ˘)つ	(∪｡∪)｡｡｡zzZ	ヽ(` (I)´)/
(*^﹏^*)	ψ(▼ヘ▼メ)~→	┌|≧∇≦|┘	／(^×^)＼
(´・ω・`)♡	(πωπ)	(￣▽￣)/♫･*:.｡. ♪	＜・)))><<
(/●ヮ●)/*:･ﾟ✧	▓▓(°︿°)▓▓	┌┐･ω･)/	ヾ(￣◇￣)ノ 〃
ヽ(^∀^)メ(^∀^)ノ	ᗢ(ಠ_ಠ ᗢ)	(/>ω<)/ :｡･:*:･ﾟ'★	(^=●ﻌ●=^)

////////////////////// **PART 6**

About the JLPT

The Japanese Language Proficiency Test, known as 日本語の能力試験 in Japanese, or *Nihongo no nouryoku shiken*, is a system of standardized exams that are used to determine a person's linguistic ability with Japanese.

Formal certification is helpful for those who seek to study or work in Japan. Potential employers and universities may require a person to obtain a qualification at a basic level before allowing them to make an application. It's also popular amongst learners simply as a means of acknowledgment or checking personal progress with the language. Exams take place in July and December twice a year, either in Japan or overseas, at special test centers in certain countries.

JLPT is the non-Japanese speaker's equivalent to the 'TOEFL' *(Test of English as a Foreign Language)* or 'IELTS' *(International English Language Testing System)* for those who do not speak English. It consists of five levels of certification, beginning at N5 (the easiest level), certifying a basic understanding and use of the language, progressing up to N1 (the most difficult) aimed at those with fluency:

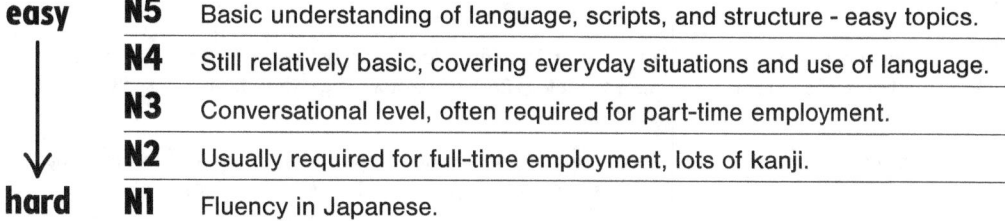

easy	**N5**	Basic understanding of language, scripts, and structure - easy topics.
	N4	Still relatively basic, covering everyday situations and use of language.
↓	**N3**	Conversational level, often required for part-time employment.
	N2	Usually required for full-time employment, lots of kanji.
hard	**N1**	Fluency in Japanese.

It's worth noting that the *Ministry of Education* and the *Japan Educational Exchanges and Services (JEES)* stopped publishing any *'Test Content Specifications'* in 2010 and learning from lists of vocabulary or kanji is discouraged. Instead, the JLPT website hosts a general summary of the competence needed for each level:

N5	The ability to understand some basic Japanese.
Reading	One is able to read and understand typical expressions and sentences written in hiragana, katakana, and basic kanji.
Listening	One is able to listen and comprehend conversations about topics regularly encountered in daily life and classroom situations, and is able to pick up necessary information from short conversations spoken slowly.

(Source: http://www.jlpt.jp/e/about/levelsummary.html - April 2022)

It may be useful and interesting to understand the requirements and assessment methods for the JLPT N5 level, whether you intend to study towards a formal qualification or not.

Although the summary table does not specify, a general knowledge of vocabulary and grammar is needed to satisfy the reading and listening requirements. The JLPT term for this is *'Language Knowledge,'* as shown in the N5 *'Composition of Test Items'* table below. This shows how the N5 examination is structured, highlighting the areas of knowledge required and how the exam will assess each:

Section + *(time)*		Test items	Purpose
Language Knowledge *(20 min.)**	Vocabulary	Kanji reading	Test reading of words written in kanji
		Orthography	Test kanji and katakana for words written in hiragana
		Contextually-defined expressions	Test words whose meaning is defined by context
		Paraphrases	Test words and expressions with similar meaning
Language Knowledge **Reading** *(40 min.)**	Grammar	Sentential grammar 1 (selecting grammar form)	Test judgment on grammar formats that suit sentences
		Sentential grammar 2 (sentence composition)	Test sentence composition that is syntactically accurate and makes sense
		Text grammar	Test judgment on suitability of sentences for text flow
	Reading	Comprehension (short passages)	Test understanding of contents by reading easy original text of approximately 80 characters regarding topics and situations involving study, everyday life and work
		Comprehension (mid-size passages)	Test understanding of contents by reading easy original text of approximately 250 characters regarding topics and situations in everyday life
		Information retrieval	Test ability to retrieve necessary information from original materials such as notices (approximately 250 characters)
Listening *(30 min.)*		Task-based comprehension	Test understanding of contents by listening to coherent text (test ability to extract necessary information to resolve specific issues and understand appropriate action to take)
		Comprehension of key points	Test understanding of contents by listening to coherent text (test ability to narrow down points based on necessary information presented in advance)
		Verbal expressions	Test ability to select appropriate verbal expressions by listening to circumstances while looking at illustrations
		Quick response	Test ability to select appropriate responses by listening to short utterances such as questions

(Source: https://www.jlpt.jp/e/guideline/testsections.html - April 2022)

The examination has three main parts: the first looks at your knowledge of vocabulary, including kanji words; the second explores your understanding of grammar rules, and then tests your ability to read and understand Japanese; and the third, final section tests the combination of all knowledge areas using audio recordings, in place of text.

*Before December 2020, test times for the first and second sections were 25 and 40 minutes, respectively.

Obtaining JLPT N5 certification requires an overall score of **80 points or more**, from a maximum available 180 marks. The *'reading'* section is worth twice as many points as the *'Listening'* section.

In addition, each of the two main sections now have a minimum score requirement, meaning low scores in either will result in failure, no matter how high a participant's final total is.

	Pts. Available for Section	Minimum Req. for Section
Language Knowledge (Vocabulary/Grammar) - Reading	0 - 120	38 / 120
Listening Section	0 - 60	19 / 120
Total Available	0 - 180	
N5 Pass (Minimum)	80 / 180	

(Source: http://www.jlpt.jp/e/guideline/results.html - April 2022)

JLPT N5 Requirements

The organizers of the JLPT no longer publish the specific vocabulary, grammar, and kanji knowledge requirements, so *'unofficial'* lists are all that you can find online. They suggest that all JLPT N5 questions and answers come from a pool of **800 vocabulary words** and **approximately 100 different kanji.** These figures cover more than a single exam requires but represent a **'safe' minimum level of knowledge.**

Fortunately, these vocabulary lists and kanji consist of simple, everyday, conversational Japanese, representing some of the most commonly used words. Topics include; numbers, dates, days, and time; family and friends; and common verb words *(such as walk, talk, read, write, and so on).*

The grammar requirements can also vary but include understanding and usage of common particles, *such as* は *(wa),* が *(ga), and* を *(wo),* and conjugation of the past and present tense - in both polite and informal speech.

Beginners with no knowledge may need to study for *up to 500 hours* before passing level N5 which equates to *less than 3 hours a day*, over a six-month period. When you consider that the JLPT exams consist of multiple-choice questions and answers, you *could* save a little time by learning only to *read* the kana scripts. However, unless you are in a rush for certification, an ability to write with kana is far too beneficial to skip. The recommended, longer-term strategy includes writing practice.

The examination process does not currently require a spoken test, making it possible to pass without talking at all - but conversations are a great way to learn and practice your Japanese, so they should not be overlooked entirely.

Learning the Kanji

The following section of the workbook contains pages dedicated to each of the kanji in those N5 groups. An example of their layout and important features can be found below:

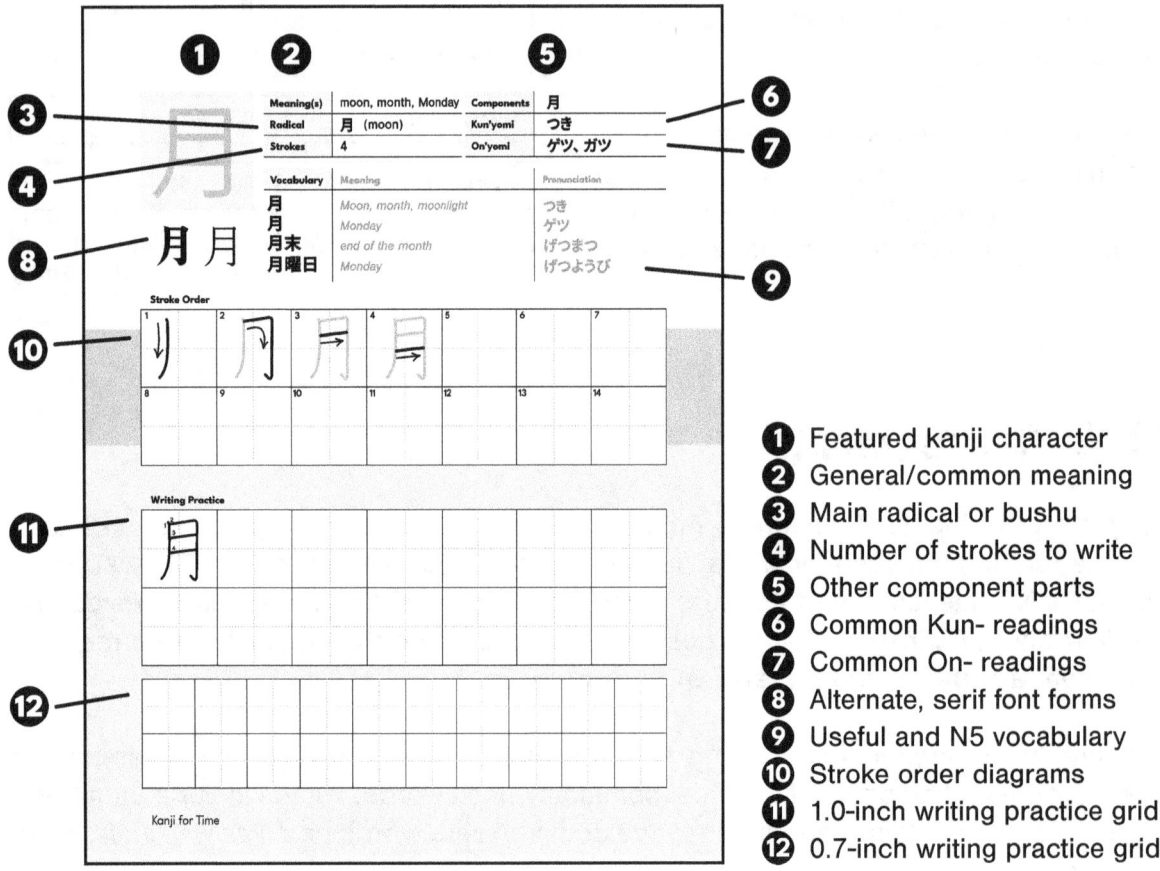

1. Featured kanji character
2. General/common meaning
3. Main radical or bushu
4. Number of strokes to write
5. Other component parts
6. Common Kun- readings
7. Common On- readings
8. Alternate, serif font forms
9. Useful and N5 vocabulary
10. Stroke order diagrams
11. 1.0-inch writing practice grid
12. 0.7-inch writing practice grid

Approaching each new kanji, take care to practice pronunciation of the readings and look at the type of vocabulary it represents. As your knowledge increases, new kanji can be associated with those you are learning now, and you will begin to see repeated shapes and patterns. Building kanji knowledge takes longer than memorizing the kana - there is simply more to remember for each one.

Each group of kanji ends with a revision section, testing your knowledge of the kanji you will have learned by that stage. The questions on these revision pages will become more difficult as you get further along in the workbook. If they become challenging, take a step back and have a break. It will take time and practice to absorb all of the information, and it's important that you can memorize basic information before moving on. You may find it useful to dip in and out of the kanji study pages periodically. You could try jumping ahead to the following chapter and begin to learn how grammar works too.

One study tactic that can work well is to re-write or transfer kanji information to a separate, blank study book. I created the *Kanji Study Companion* for exactly this purpose but almost any notebook will work - structured, organized studies are more effective!

The N5 Kanji

It makes sense to learn these N5 kanji first as they are amongst the most common you will encounter when learning vocabulary or starting to read Japanese texts. Lots of them are radicals and must be learned or memorized independently from one another. *Radicals are the fundamental parts, often with more simple shapes, from which all kanji are made.*

Learning radicals may seem difficult when starting with little or zero knowledge but, as mentioned earlier in the workbook, learning the radicals first should make it easier to learn more advanced or complex kanji later on.

Over the next few pages, the kanji that you are about to learn have been loosely grouped by general topic, e.g. numbers, time, things, places, etc. It can be easier to memorize and learn about a character when associated with another, related word.

Numbers

The romaji numbers from 1 through 10 are used very commonly in Japan, but the kanji still need learning. Fortunately, they have some of the most simple shapes! Take care not to confuse the kanji 千 with katakana チ (chi) as it has a reading that sounds the same:

N5 Kanji	Basic Meaning	N5 Vocabulary	
一	one, 1	一人	one person, alone
二	two, 2	二人	two people, pair
三	three, 3	三日	3rd day of the month
四	four, 4	四日	4th day of the month
五	five, 5	五日	5th day of the month
六	six, 6	六日	6th day of the month
七	seven, 7	七日	7th day of the month
八	eight, 8	八日	8th day of the month
九	nine, 9	九日	9th day of the month
十	ten, 10	十日	10th day of the month
百	hundred	百万円	1 million Yen
千	thousand	千万円	10 million Yen
万	ten thousand	万年筆	fountain pen
円	Yen, circle, round	円い	round

People & Things

In this group, pay particular attention to kanji that represent natural elements, such as earth, fire, and water. Japanese culture has long-placed importance on nature and these primitive concepts have been lending their meaning to lots of vocabulary over time. As a result, these kanji appear in a wide range of vocabulary and have more readings than most.

Certain kanji in this group take alternate readings for the same meaning in varied situations too, such as 母 and 父. You would pronounce these as *'ha-ha'* and *'chi-chi'* when *referring to* your parents, but as *'kaa'* (like in お母さん) and *'tou'* (like in お母さん) when addressing your parents. Pronunciations change again for the vocabulary representing the names of other relatives and, unfortunately, each must be learned individually.

N5 Kanji	Basic Meaning	N5 Vocabulary	
人	person	人々	*people*
男	man, boy, male	男の子	*boy*
女	woman, girl, female	女の子	*girl*
子	child	子供	*child*
母	mother	母	*mother*
父	father	父	*father*
友	friend	友達	*friend*
火	fire	火曜日	*Tuesday*
水	water	水曜日	*Wednesday*
木	tree, wood	木曜日	*Thursday*
土	earth, ground	土曜日	*Saturday*
金	money, gold	金曜日	*Friday*
本	book, source	日本語	*Japanese*
川	river	川	*river*
花	flower	花火	*fireworks*
気	spirit	元気	*healthy, spirit, fine*
生	life, to live, to be born, to grow	生徒	*pupil*
魚	fish	魚	*fish*
天	heaven	天気	*weather*

N5 Kanji	Basic Meaning	N5 Vocabulary	
空	sky, empty	空	sky
山	mountain	山	mountain
雨	rain	雨	rain
電	electricity	電気	electricity
車	car, vehicle	電車	electric train
語	language, word, to chat	英語	English
耳	ear	耳	ear
手	hand	手紙	letter
足	foot, to add	足	foot
目	eye	目	eye
口	mouth	出口	exit
名	name	名前	name

Adjectives

The kanji in this group are usually used for descriptions as adjectives at N5 level, and often take the Kun'yomi. On- readings are combined with other kanji to make a descriptive noun.

N5 Kanji	Basic Meaning	N5 Vocabulary	
多	a lot, many	多い	many
少	a little, few	少ない	few
古	old	古い	old
新	new	新しい	new
大	big, a lot	大きい	big
小	little, small	小さい	little
安	cheap, safety, peace	安い	cheap
高	expensive, high	高い	expensive
長	long, leader	長い	long
白	white	白い	white

Time

Japanese kanji that represent number words are frequently combined with those used for time and date vocabulary, so it makes sense to look at those in this second group.

The name for each lunar calendar month (January, February, etc.) is created by adding a number in front of the kanji 月 which represents *'month'* in Japanese. For example, the word 六月 *('6' + 'month')* means *'6th month of the lunar calendar'*, or *'June'*.

N5 Kanji	Basic Meaning	N5 Vocabulary	
日	day, sun	明日	*tomorrow*
週	week	毎週	*every week*
月	month, moon	月曜日	*Monday*
年	year	今年	*this year*
時	time, hour	時計	*clock, watch*
間	time frame, span of time	時間	*time, hours*
分	minute, part, to understand	三十分	*thirty minutes*
午	noon	午前	*morning, A.M.*
前	before	名前	*name*
後	after, later, behind	午後	*afternoon, P.M.*
今	now	今晩	*this evening*
先	before, ahead, future	先週	*last week*
来	to come	来月	*next month*
半	half, middle	半分	*half*
毎	every, each	毎日	*every day*
何	what, which, how many	何曜日	*what day of the week*

Combining the kanji 来 with another time character creates vocabulary such as 'next month' (来月, or *'future' + 'month'*). This kanji is also part of the irregular verb 来る, meaning 'to come' or 'to arrive' which, despite being one of the most commonly used (and first-learned) verbs, it does not follow basic patterns of conjugation.

You will learn more about verb conjugation patterns in a later chapter.

Verbs

The JLPT N5 will require knowledge of the kanji that represent common verb vocabulary, such as *'to eat'* or *'to drink'*. While these kanji have multiple pronunciations, they only require their Kun- reading when used as a verb word.

N5 Kanji	Basic Meaning	N5 Vocabulary	
見	to see, to be visible, to show	見せる	to show
聞	to hear, to listen, to ask	聞く	to listen, to hear
書	to write	辞書	dictionary
読	to read	読む	to read
話	to talk, conversation	電話	telephone
買	to buy	買い物	shopping
行	to go, to carry out	銀行	bank
出	to go out, to leave	出かける	to go out
入	to enter, to put in	入口	entrance
休	to rest, break, vacation	休む	to take a day off
食	to eat, food	食堂	dining room
飲	to drink, a drink	飲み物	beverage
言	to say, word or remark	言う	to say
立	to stand	立つ	to stand
会	to meet, society	会社	company

While the exam will test your command of kanji verbs and their Kun- readings, the kanji 読 (read), 書 (write), and 聞 (hear) are used with On- readings within parts of the paperwork. Each is used to describe the different sections of the test itself, and you would want to make sure you understand which part of the test you are currently undertaking.

Some other characters in this group with very common On- readings include 食 (food) and 会 (company).

Directions & Places

More common kanji with multiple uses, taking both On- and Kun- readings. There are some patterns to their usage, such as 店 usually taking the On- reading in conjunction with other kanji, but Kun- when used on its own. These patterns usually become clear over time.

N5 Kanji	Basic Meaning	N5 Vocabulary	
店	shop	喫茶店	coffee shop
駅	station	駅前	in front of the station
道	street, path, way	道具	tool
社	shrine, society	社長	president of a company
国	country	外国人	foreigner
外	outside	外国	foreign country
学	school, learning	大学	university
校	school	学校	school
上	up, above	上着	jacket
下	down, below	靴下	socks
中	middle, center, inner, between	日中	during the day, midday
北	north	北	north
西	west	西	west
東	east	東京	Tokyo
南	south	南	south
右	right	右	right
左	left	左	left

Many of the kanji in these lists have lots of different readings attached to them but the JLPT N5 doesn't require you to know every last detail about each kanji. Most of the time, the extra readings are not that common and will not be used in everyday Japanese. For this reason, each kanji study page features just a small selection of the most widely used or useful ones, with particular attention paid to those for N5-level vocabulary.

It's far easier and faster to learn a few of the more important details, allowing you to make more progress, sooner. This practice works well for most characters in these lists. With a strong foundation of kanji knowledge, based on the basics, you can easily collect more readings and vocabulary later.

Kana Quick Reference Charts

Hiragana

	w	r	y	m	h	n	t	s	k	
	わ wa	ら ra	や ya	ま ma	は ha	な na	た ta	さ sa	か ka	あ a	**a**
		り ri		み mi	ひ hi	に ni	ち chi	し shi	き ki	い i	**i**
*ん n	る ru	ゆ yu	む mu	ふ fu	ぬ nu	つ tsu	す su	く ku	う u	**u**
		れ re		め me	へ he	ね ne	て te	せ se	け ke	え e	**e**
	を wo	ろ ro	よ yo	も mo	ほ ho	の no	と to	そ so	こ ko	お o	**o**

Katakana

	w	r	y	m	h	n	t	s	k	
	ワ wa	ラ ra	ヤ ya	マ ma	ハ ha	ナ na	タ ta	サ sa	カ ka	ア a	**a**
		リ ri		ミ mi	ヒ hi	ニ ni	チ chi	シ shi	キ ki	イ i	**i**
*ン n	ル ru	ユ yu	ム mu	フ fu	ヌ nu	ツ tsu	ス su	ク ku	ウ u	**u**
		レ re		メ me	ヘ he	ネ ne	テ te	セ se	ケ ke	エ e	**e**
	ヲ wo	ロ ro	ヨ yo	モ mo	ホ ho	ノ no	ト to	ソ so	コ ko	オ o	**o**

Meaning(s)	one, 1, best, first		**Components**	一
Radical	一 (one)		**Kun'yomi**	ひと-、ひと.つ
Strokes	1		**On'yomi**	イチ、イツ

Vocabulary	Meaning	Pronunciation
一	one, for one thing, only, (not) even,	ひとつ
一	one, 1, best, first, beginning, start	いち / イチ
一寸	a little, a bit, slightly, briefly, quite,	ちょっと
一人	one person	ひとり

Stroke Order

Writing Practice

Kanji for Numbers

Meaning(s)	two, 2	Components	二
Radical	二 (two)	Kun'yomi	ふた、ふた.つ
Strokes	2	On'yomi	ニ、ジ

Vocabulary	Meaning	Pronunciation
二	two, 2	ニ / に
二日	2nd day of the month, 2 days	ふつか
二月	February, 2nd month of the calendar	にがつ
二人	two people, two persons, pair, couple	ふたり

Stroke Order

Writing Practice

JLPT N5

三

Meaning(s)	three, 3	Components	一 二
Radical	一 (one)	Kun'yomi	み、み.つ、みっ.つ
Strokes	3	On'yomi	サン、ゾウ

Vocabulary	Meaning	Pronunciation
三	three, 3	サン / さん
三日	3rd day of the month	みっか
三月	March, 3rd month of the calendar	さんがつ
三十日	last day of the month	みそか

Stroke Order

Writing Practice

Kanji for Numbers

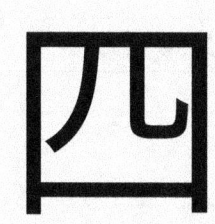

Meaning(s)	four, 4	Components	⼉ 口
Radical	口 (enclosure)	Kun'yomi	よ、よ.つ、よっ.つ
Strokes	5	On'yomi	シ

Vocabulary	Meaning		Pronunciation
四	four, 4		シ / し / よん
四日	4th day of the month		よっか
四月	April, 4th month of the calendar		シガツ
四つ	four, four years of age		よん / よっつ

Stroke Order

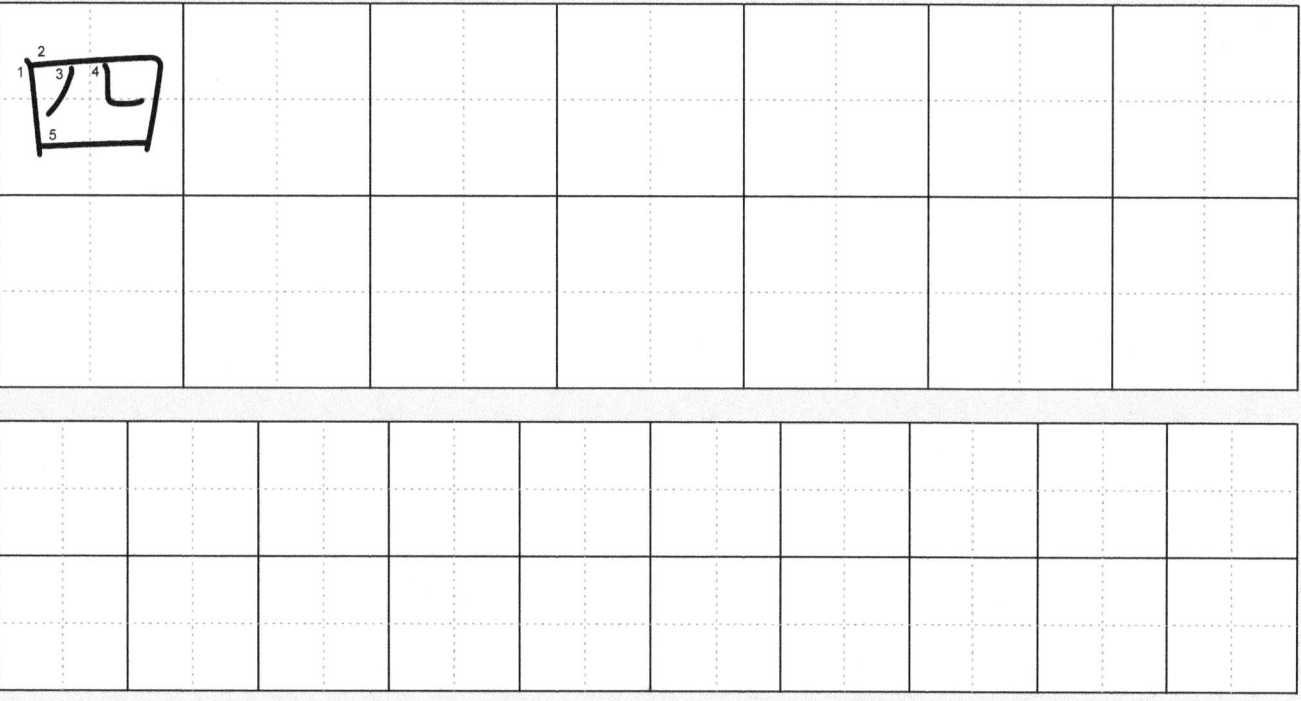

Writing Practice

JLPT N5

Meaning(s)	five, 5		Components	五
Radical	二 (two)		Kun'yomi	いつ、いつ.つ
Strokes	4		On'yomi	ゴ

Vocabulary	Meaning	Pronunciation
五	five, 5	ゴ / ご
五日	5th day of the month	いつか
五月	May, 5th month of the calendar	ゴガツ
五つ	five, five years of age	いつつ

Stroke Order

Writing Practice

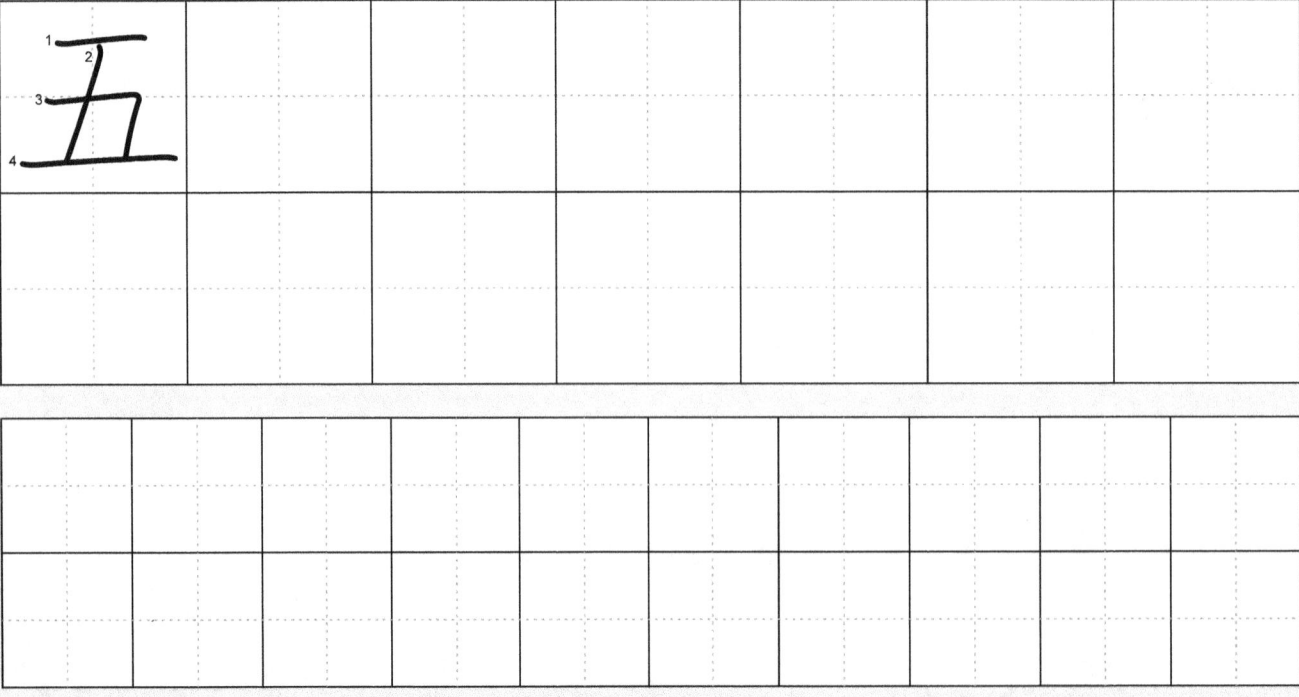

Kanji for Numbers

Meaning(s)	six, 6	Components	亠 八
Radical	八 (eight)	Kun'yomi	む、む.つ、むっ.つ
Strokes	4	On'yomi	ロク、リク

Vocabulary	Meaning	Pronunciation
六	six, 6	ロク / ろく
六日	6th day of the month	むいか
六月	June, 6th month of the calendar	ロクガツ
六つ	six, six years of age	むっつ

Stroke Order

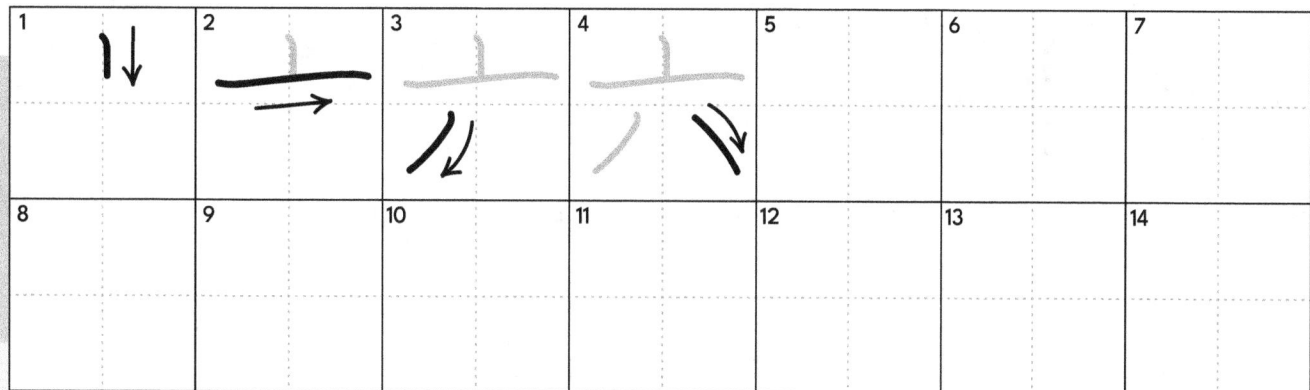

Writing Practice

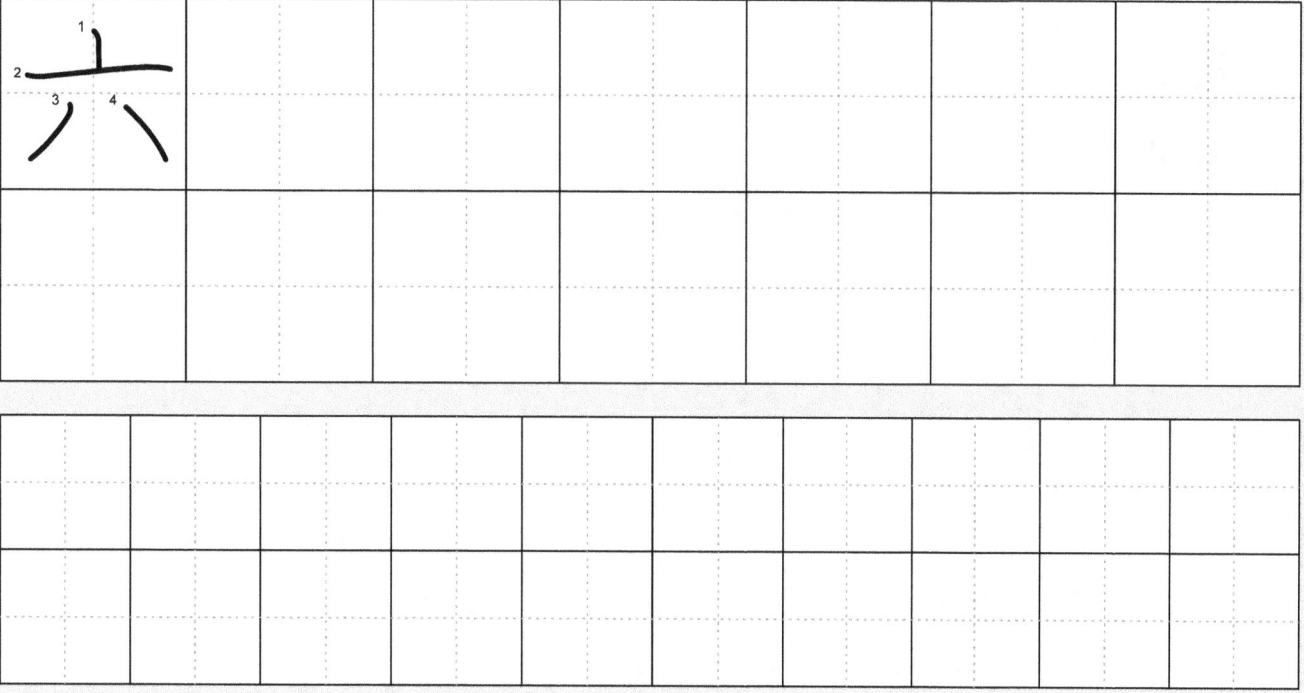

JLPT N5

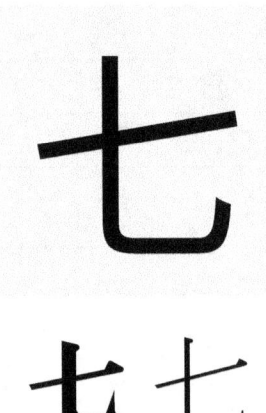

Meaning(s)	seven, 7		**Components**	乙ノヒ
Radical	一 (one)		**Kun'yomi**	なな、なな.つ、なの
Strokes	2		**On'yomi**	シチ

Vocabulary	Meaning	Pronunciation
七	seven, 7	シチ / しち / なな
七日	7th day of the month	なのか
七月	July, 7th month of the calendar	シチガツ
七つ	seven, seven years of age	ななつ

Stroke Order

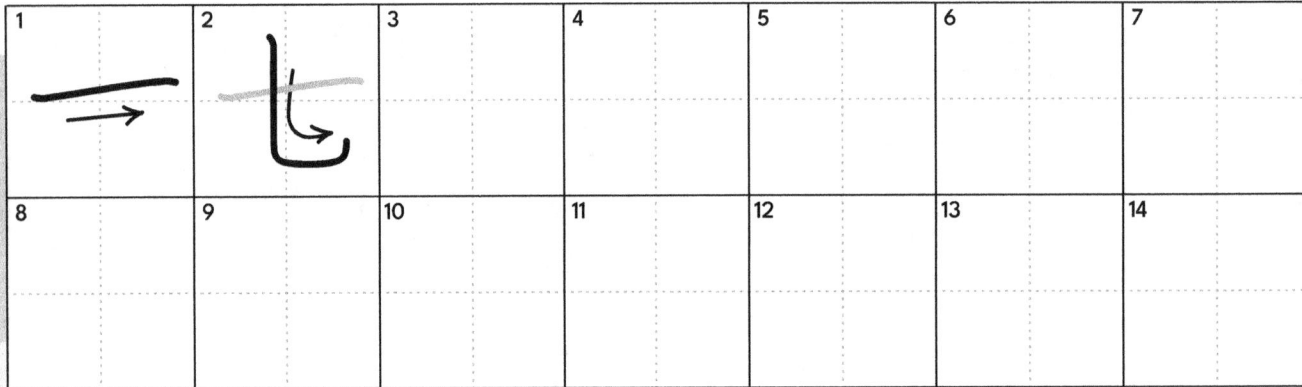

Writing Practice

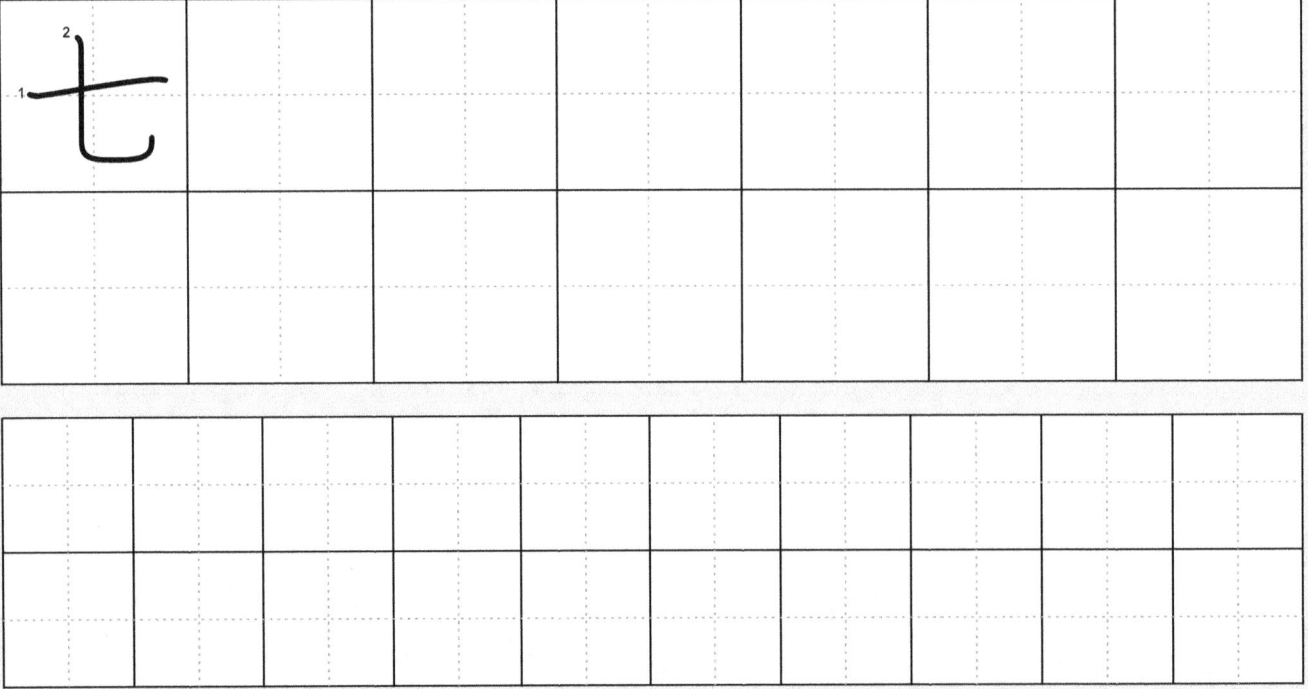

Kanji for Numbers

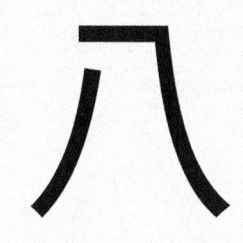

Meaning(s)	eight, 8	**Components**	八
Radical	八 (eight)	**Kun'yomi**	や、や.つ、やっ.つ
Strokes	2	**On'yomi**	ハチ、ハツ

Vocabulary	Meaning	Pronunciation
八	*eight, 8*	ハチ / はち
八日	*8th day of the month*	ようか
八月	*August, 8th month of the calendar*	だす
八つ	*eight, eight years of age*	やっつ

Stroke Order

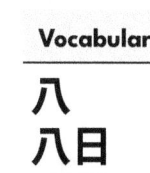

Writing Practice

JLPT N5

Meaning(s)	nine, 9	Components	九
Radical	乛 (second)	Kun'yomi	ここの、ここの.つ
Strokes	2	On'yomi	キュウ、ク

Vocabulary	Meaning	Pronunciation
九	nine, 9	キュウ / きゅう
九日	9th day of the month	ここのか
九月	September, 9th month of the calendar	クガツ
九つ	nine, nine years of age	ここのつ

Stroke Order

Writing Practice

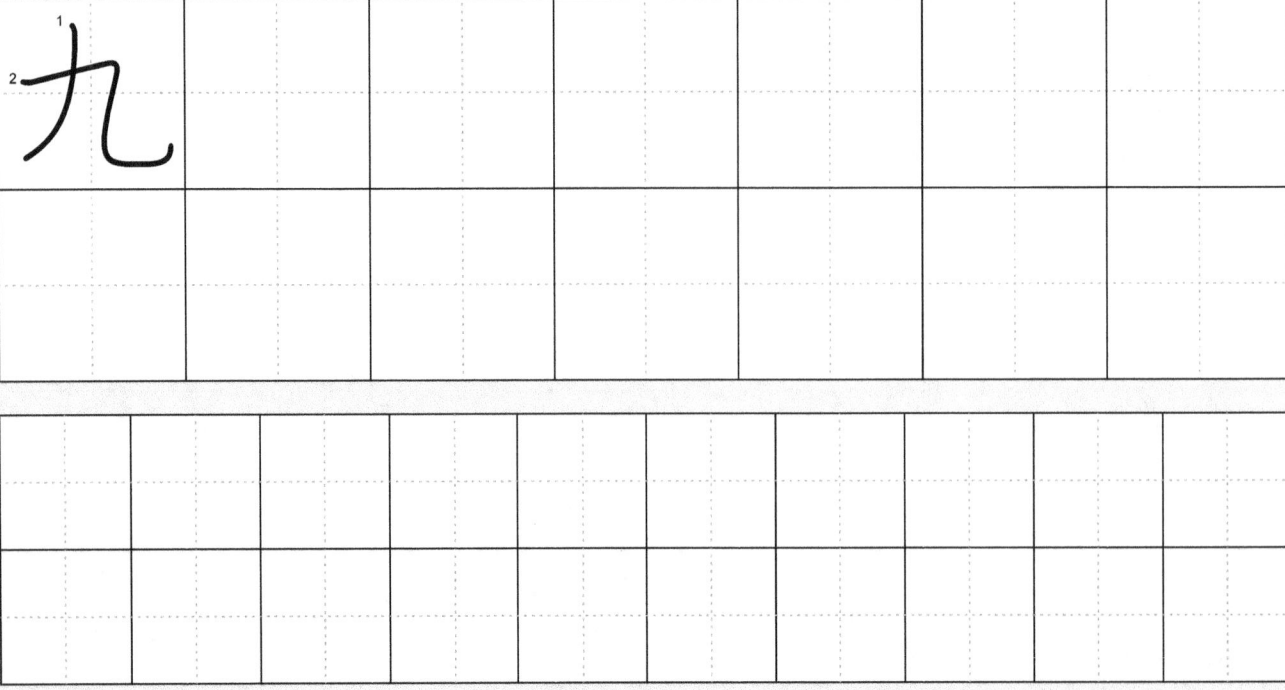

Kanji for Numbers

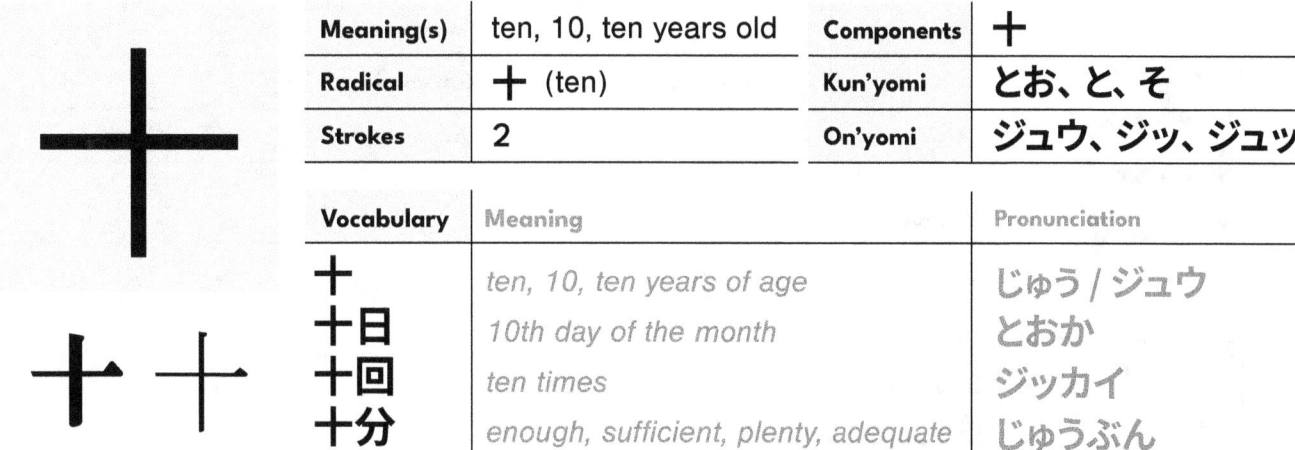

Vocabulary	Meaning	Pronunciation
十	ten, 10, ten years of age	じゅう / ジュウ
十日	10th day of the month	とおか
十回	ten times	ジッカイ
十分	enough, sufficient, plenty, adequate	じゅうぶん

Stroke Order

Writing Practice

JLPT N5

Meaning(s)	hundred, 100		**Components**	一 白
Radical	白 (white)		**Kun'yomi**	もも
Strokes	6		**On'yomi**	ヒャク、ビャク

Vocabulary	Meaning	Pronunciation
百	hundred, 100	ヒャク
百	hundred, 100, (a great) many	もも
百貨店	department store	ひゃっかてん
百万円	1 million yen (100万円)	ひゃく まんえん

Stroke Order

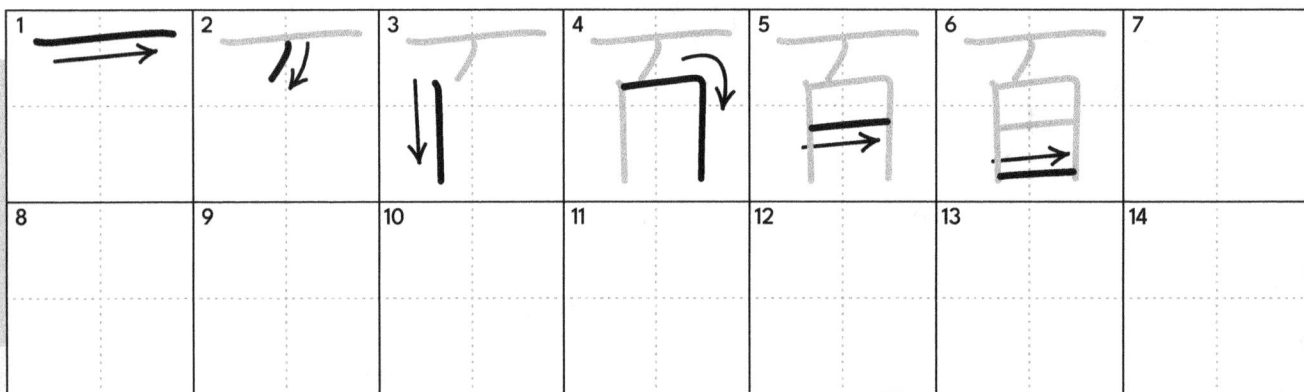

Writing Practice

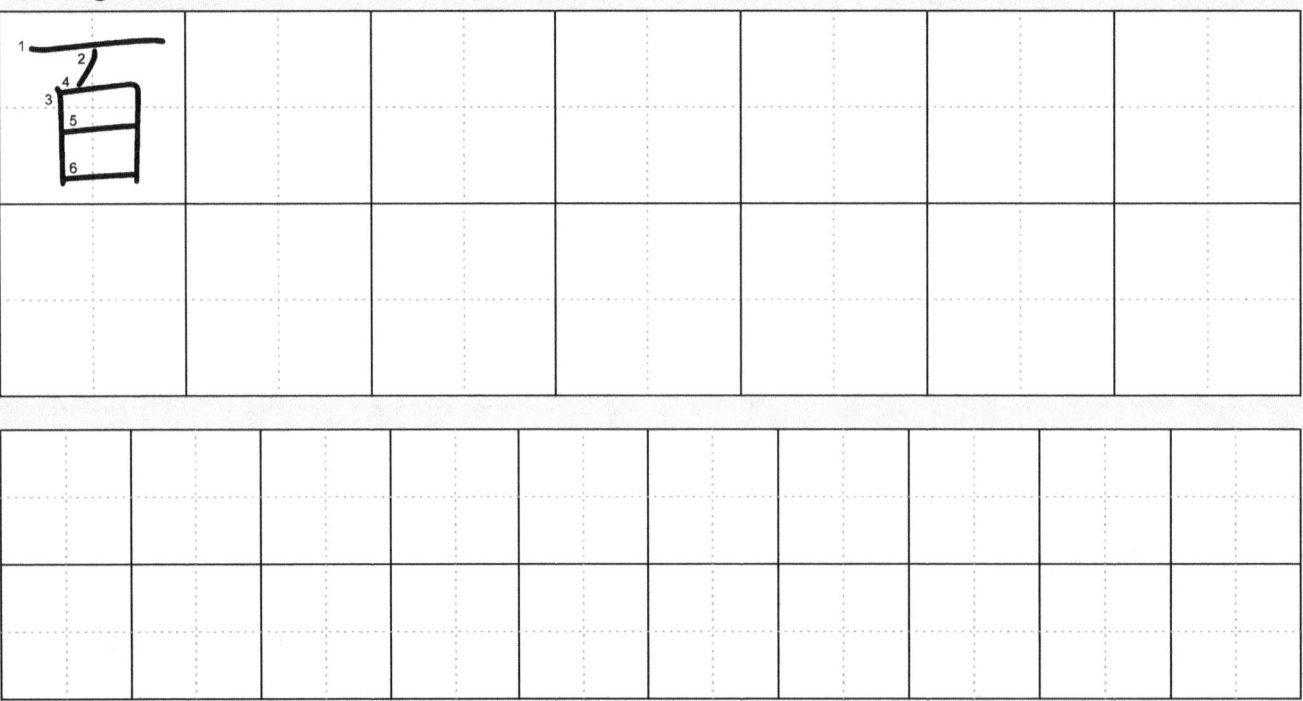

Kanji for Numbers

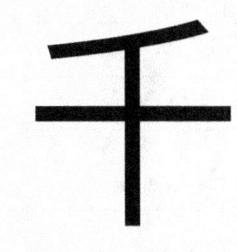

Meaning(s)	1,000, thousand	Components	ノ十
Radical	十 (ten)	Kun'yomi	ち
Strokes	3	On'yomi	セン

Vocabulary	Meaning	Pronunciation
千	1,000, thousand	セン
千	1,000, thousand	せん
百千	large number, all sorts	ひゃくせん
千万円	10 million yen (1000 万円)	いっせん まんえん

Stroke Order

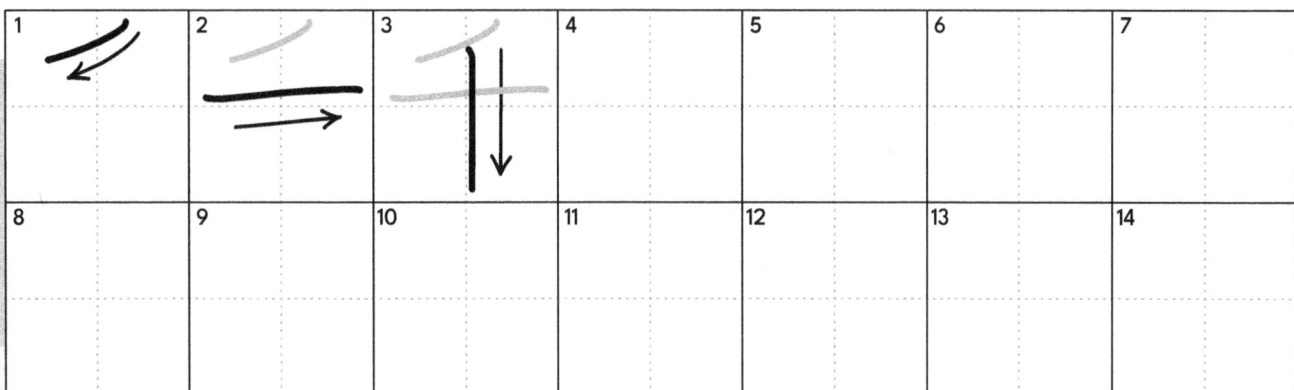

Writing Practice

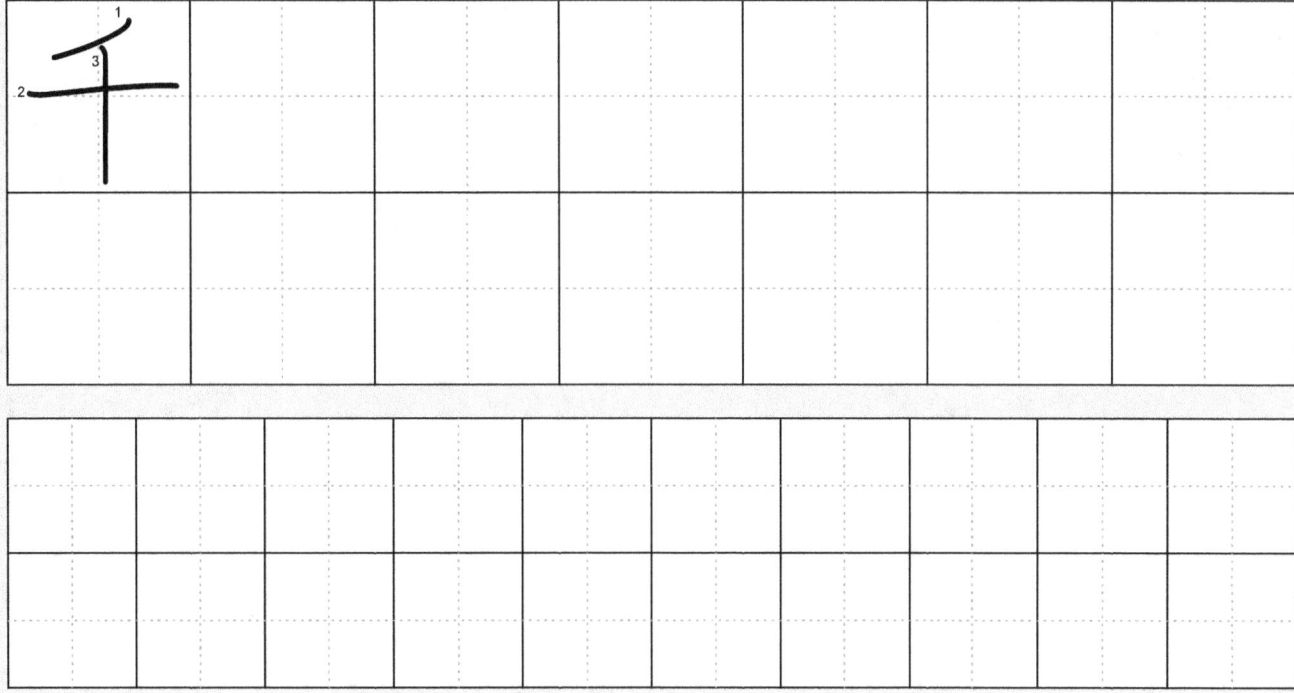

JLPT N5

万

Meaning(s)	10,000, ten thousand	**Components**	一 ｜ ノ
Radical	一 (one)	**Kun'yomi**	よろず
Strokes	3	**On'yomi**	マン、バン

Vocabulary	Meaning	Pronunciation
万	10,000, myriad, everything, all, various	マン
万	10,000, myriad, everything, all, various	いく
万能	all-purpose, utility, universal	ばんのう
万年筆	fountain pen	まんねんひつ

Stroke Order

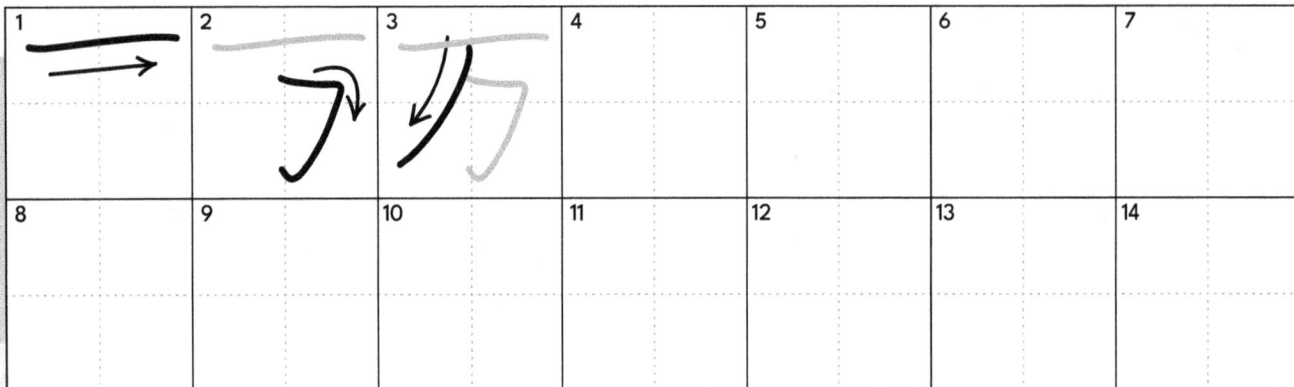

Writing Practice

Kanji for Numbers

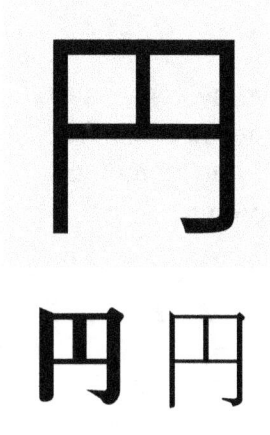

Meaning(s)	yen, circle, round	Components	一 丨 亠 冂
Radical	冂 (open)	Kun'yomi	まる.い、まる、まど
Strokes	4	On'yomi	エン

Vocabulary	Meaning	Pronunciation
円い	round, circular, spherical	まるい
円	yen (Japanese monetary unit), circle	エン
円滑	smooth, undisturbed, uninterrupted	エンカツ
円か	round, tranquil, contentedly at ease	まどか

Stroke Order

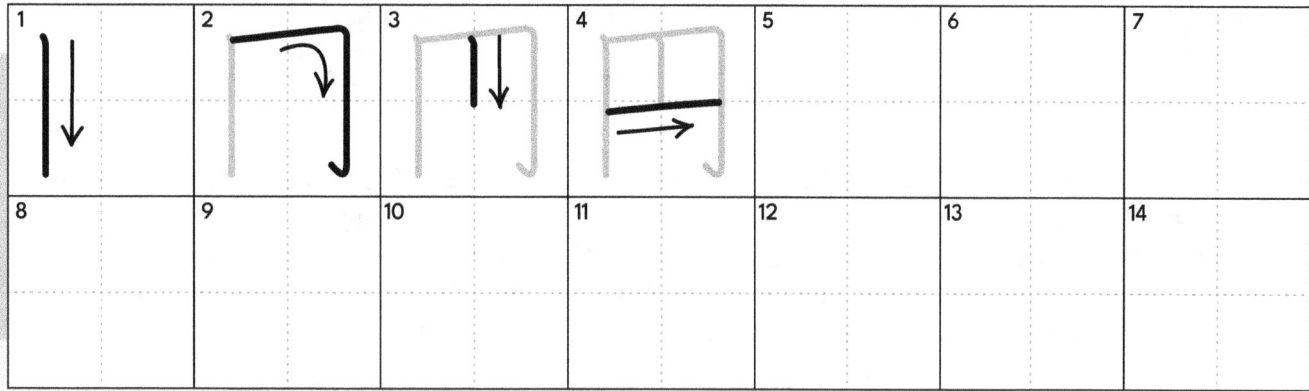

Writing Practice

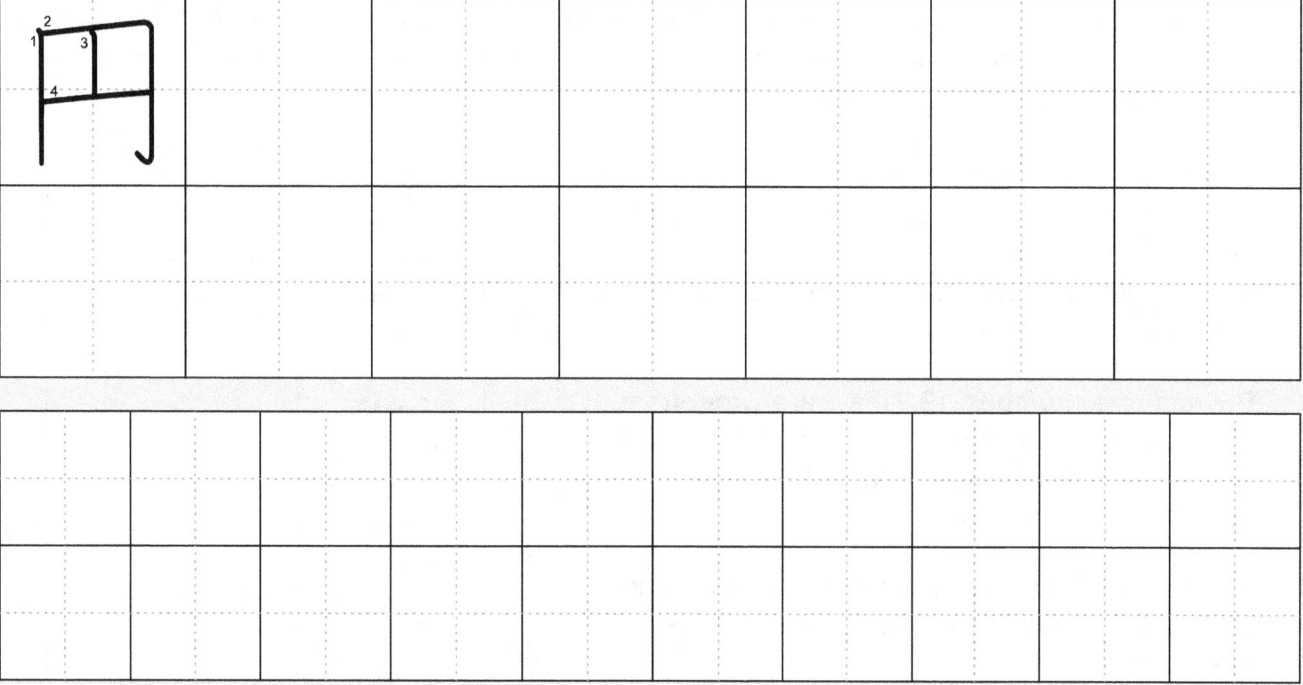

JLPT N5

More Numbers

The Japanese language uses two number systems - the first is their native system, used mainly for small numbers and special dates, and the second is Chinese in origin (or Sino-Japanese). Sino-Japanese numbers are used for most things and often combined with *counter* vocabulary, or 助数詞 *(josūshi)* to count objects, events, or actions.

#	Sino Japanese		Native		#	Sino Japanese		Native	
1	一	いち *ichi*	一つ	ひとつ *hitotsu*	6	六	ろく *roku*	一つ	むっつ *muttsu*
2	二	に *ni*	二つ	ふたつ *futatsu*	7	七	なな *nana*	二つ	ななつ *nanatsu*
3	三	さん *san*	三つ	みっつ *mittsu*	8	八	はち *hachi*	三つ	やっつ *yattsu*
4	四	よん *yon*	四つ	よっつ *yottsu*	9	九	きゅう *kyuu*	四つ	ここのつ *kokonotsu*
5	五	ご *go*	五つ	いつつ *itsutsu*	10	十	じゅう *juu*	五つ	とう *tou*

With pronunciations that sound close to negative words, 4 and 9 are considered unlucky in Japan. Pronounced as し/*shi*, number 4 sounds close to the kanji 死 *(meaning death)*, and as く/*ku*, number 9 is similar to 苦 *(meaning suffering)*. They are usually pronounced as よん/*yon* and きゅう/*kyu* instead. The number 7 is lucky but often pronounced as なな/*nana* because the other reading, しち/*shi-chi*, contains a し (死 /*death*) too!

We tend to use the Western/Romaji characters instead of kanji *(e.g., 1, 2, 10, 100, etc.)*, but still have Japanese pronunciations that need memorizing. Knowing the kanji numbers in this first chapter means you can read and pronounce most other numbers. As with many parts of the Japanese language, numbers follow distinct patterns that repeat and make them easier to see and understand.

There are no '-teen' expressions for numbers between 11-20, so numbers are made by writing and pronouncing the number 10 and another number straight after. As a *formula* it would look something like: **(10) + n**

Beyond the number 19, they are written and pronounced as multiples of ten and followed by any *'spares.'* Expressing it as a *formula*, it would look like: **(N x 10) + n**

You can apply the same pattern to every number up to 99. The multiples of 10, plus any spare right after, just as above:

11	十一 (10) + 1	じゅう いち jū i-chi
20	二十 (2 x 10)	にじゅう ni jū
22	二十二 (2 x 10) + 2	にじゅう に ni jū ni
30	三十 (3 x 10)	さんじゅう san jū
33	三十三 (3 x 10) + 3	さんじゅう さん san jū san

At 100, the pattern develops but continues to work similarly, except for occasional changes to the pronunciation here and there. The numbers from 101 to 110 are like those in the 11-19 range, with the formula: **(100) + n**

From 111 and upwards, you start with multiples of 100, followed by multiples of 10 and any *spares*.

Numbers beyond 9,999 are divided into units of ten thousand *(instead of thousands, like the West)*.

101	百一 (100) + 1	ひゃく いち hyaku i-chi
110	百十 (100)+10	ひゃく じゅう hyaku jū
120	百二十 (100)+(2x10)	ひゃく に じゅう hyaku ni jū
122	百二十二 (100)+(2x10)+2	ひゃく に じゅう に hyaku ni jū ni

For example, 1,000,000 (one million) would be *one-hundred ten-thousands*. In kanji, that would be 百万 (or 百萬) and pronounced as ひゃくまん *(hyaku man)*.

Bonus Kanji

This extra kanji is not usually in lists of JLPT N5 characters or vocabulary, but it's a number and may come in useful. It's a bit of a step up in difficulty compared to the previous group, so come back to this later. *Practice writing this kanji in the study tools section at the back.*

Meaning(s)	zero, spill, overflow	Components	一 个 卩 雨
Radical	雨 (rain)	Kun'yomi	ぜろ、こぼ.す、こぼ.れる
Strokes	13	On'yomi	レイ

Vocabulary	Meaning		Pronunciation
零	zero, nought		レイ
0	zero, 0, nought, nil, nothing, zilch		ゼロ
零す	to drop, to shed (tears), to complain		こぼす
零れる	to spill, to fall out of, to overflow		こぼれる

Stroke Order

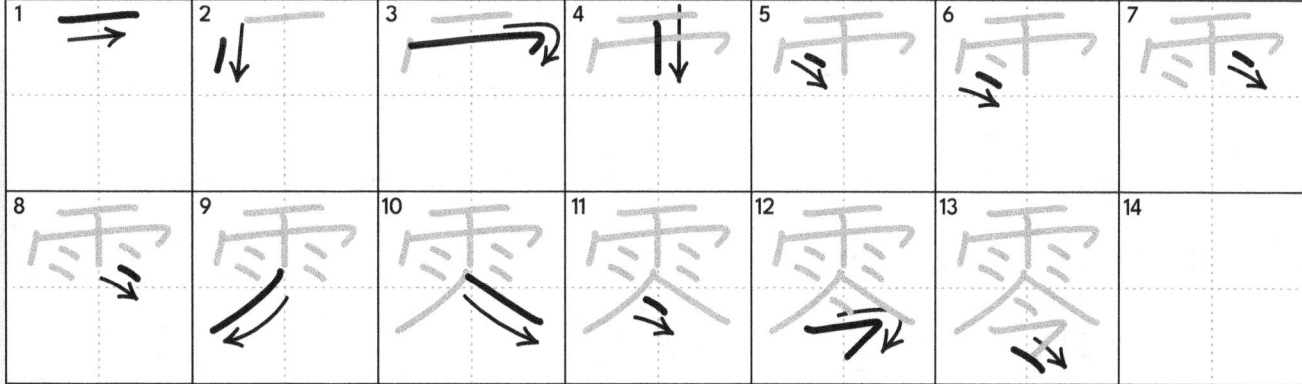

Revision: Numbers

You have just learned about your first kanji characters! Now it's time to check how much you remember and see where further revision is required. This first revision section may seem easy, but the later ones will become more difficult as you cover more kanji.

Q.01 Which of these kanji represents the *number 4*?

A. 五　B. 六　C. 四　D. 七　E. 万

Q.02 Which of these kanji represents the *number 8*?

A. 四　B. 八　C. 十　D. 九　E. 百

Q.03 Which of these kanji represents the *number 5*?

A. 百　B. 万　C. 円　D. 五　E. 千

Q.04 Which of these kanji represents the *number 6*?

A. 六　B. 十　C. 八　D. 千　E. 七

Q.05 Which of these kanji represents the *number 2*?

A. 八　B. 二　C. 千　D. 三　E. 万

Q.06 Which number is missing from the sequence 一二三四五六七八十?

A. 5　B. 8　C. 7　D. 9　E. 4

Q.07 Which of these is the correct *pronunciation* for *number 1*?

A. san　B. ni　C. go　D. ichi　E. shi

Q.08 How do you write *1,000* in Japanese kanji?

A. 九　B. 百　C. 万　D. 円　E. 千

Q.09 Which of these kanji is pronounced はち?

A. 六　　B. 七　　C. 八　　D. 九　　E. 十

Q.10 Which of these kanji is pronounced さん?

A. 一　　B. 二　　C. 三　　D. 四　　E. 五

Q.11 How do you *pronounce* the number *1000*?

A. sen　　B. shi　　C. san　　D. ni　　E. yon

Q.12 What is the number 100 in Japanese?

A. 万　　B. 百　　C. 円　　D. 九　　E. 十

Q.13 How many strokes are taken to write the *number* 四?

A. 2　　B. 3　　C. 4　　D. 5　　E. 6

Q.14 Which month of the year is written 七月?

A. March　　B. April　　C. May　　D. June　　E. July

Q.15 Which kanji word has the meaning of *enough* or *plenty*?

A. 分十　　B. 九日　　C. 円か　　D. 十分　　E. 十回

Q.16 How many strokes are taken to write the *number* 百?

A. 7　　B. 6　　C. 8　　D. 5　　E. 4

Q.17 Which of these is the correct *pronunciation* for *number 6*?

A. ku　　B. kyu　　C. roku　　D. go　　E. juu

Q.18 Which of these kanji represents the *currency of Japan*?

A. 九　　B. 百　　C. 万　　D. 円　　E. 千

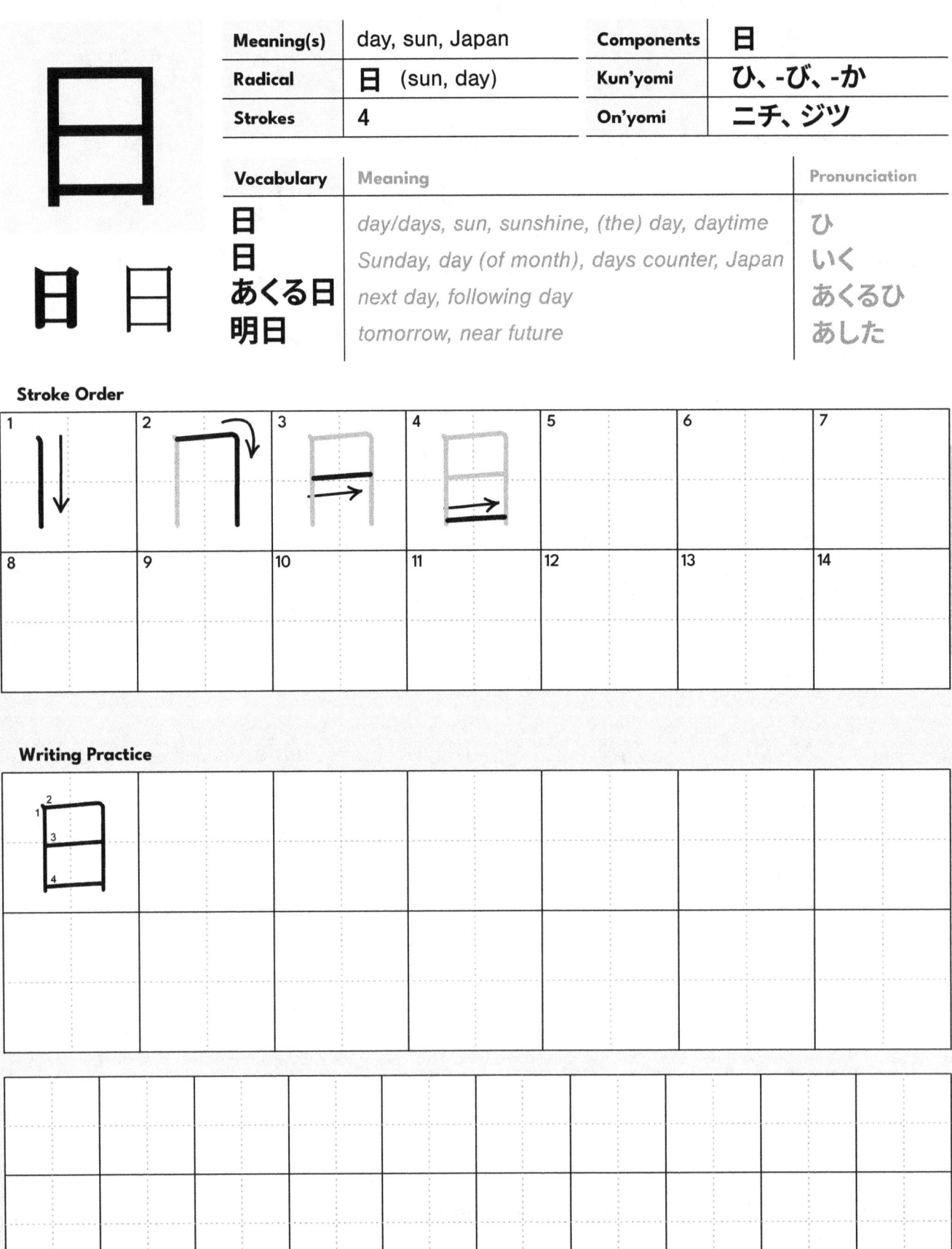

Meaning(s)	day, sun, Japan	Components	日
Radical	日 (sun, day)	Kun'yomi	ひ、-び、-か
Strokes	4	On'yomi	ニチ、ジツ

Vocabulary	Meaning	Pronunciation
日	day/days, sun, sunshine, (the) day, daytime	ひ
日	Sunday, day (of month), days counter, Japan	いく
あくる日	next day, following day	あくるひ
明日	tomorrow, near future	あした

Stroke Order

Writing Practice

Kanji for Time

Meaning(s)	week	Components	冂込口土
Radical	辶 (walk)	Kun'yomi	(none)
Strokes	11	On'yomi	シュウ

Vocabulary	Meaning		Pronunciation
週	week		シュウ
前週	last week, the week before		ゼンシュウ
毎週	every week		マイシュウ
隔週	every other week, every two weeks		カクシュウ

Stroke Order

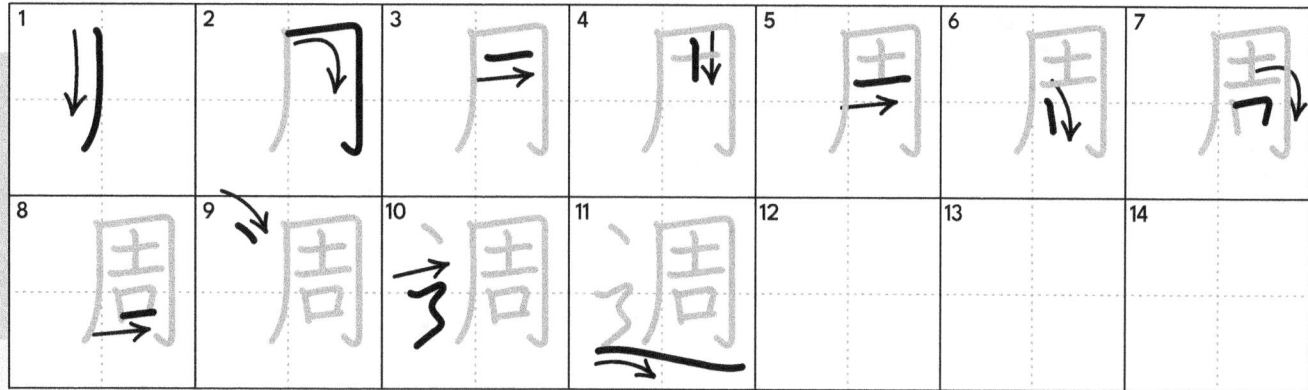

Writing Practice

JLPT N5

月　月　月

Meaning(s)	moon, month, Monday	Components	月
Radical	月 (moon)	Kun'yomi	つき
Strokes	4	On'yomi	ゲツ、ガツ

Vocabulary	Meaning		Pronunciation
月	Moon, month, moonlight		つき
月	Monday		ゲツ
月末	end of the month		げつまつ
月曜日	Monday		げつようび

Stroke Order

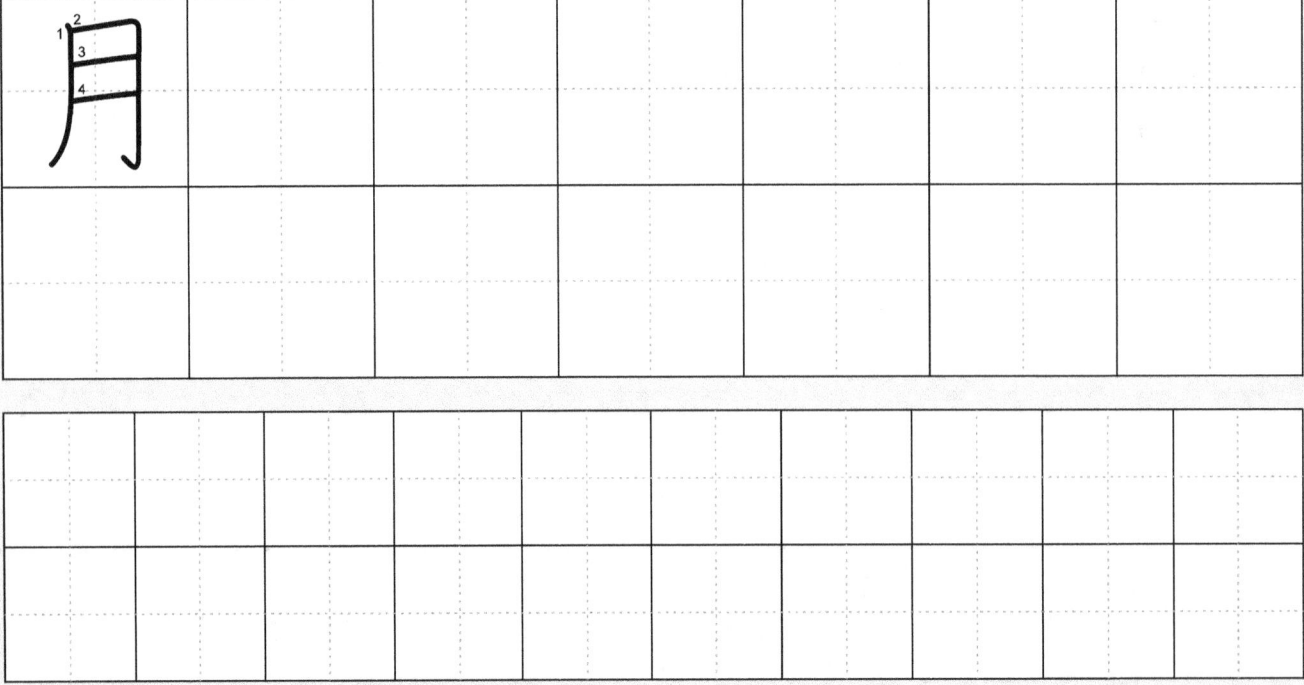

Writing Practice

Kanji for Time

年

Meaning(s)	year, counter for years	**Components**	一ノ干乞
Radical	干 (pestle)	**Kun'yomi**	とし
Strokes	6	**On'yomi**	ネン

Vocabulary	Meaning	Pronunciation
年	year, age, years	とし
年	counter for years	ネン
今年	this year	ことし
去年	last year	きょねん

Stroke Order

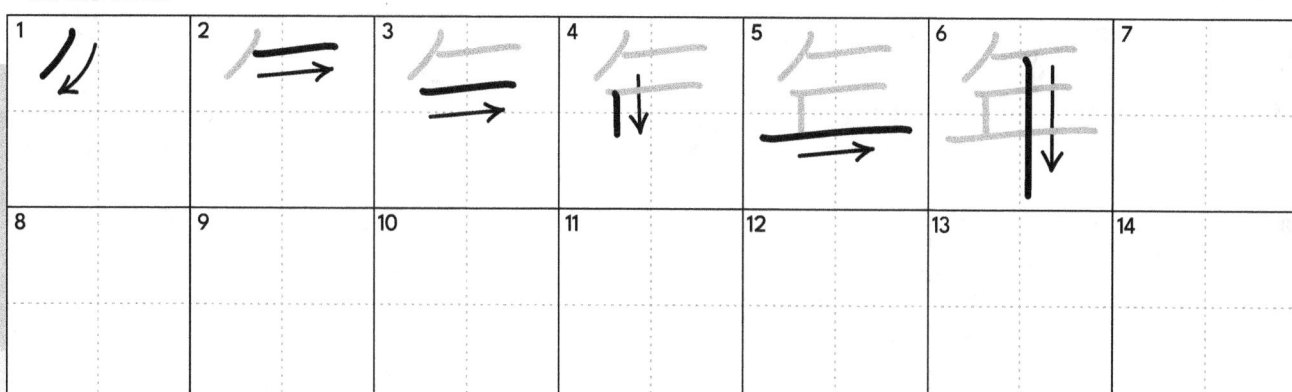

Writing Practice

JLPT N5

Meaning(s)	time, hour	Components	土 寸 日
Radical	日 (sun, day)	Kun'yomi	とき、-どき
Strokes	10	On'yomi	ジ

Vocabulary	Meaning	Pronunciation
時	time, hour, moment, occasion	とき
時	hour, o'clock, (specified) time, when ...	ジ
時計	clock, watch, timepiece	とけい
時刻表	timetable, schedule (public transport)	じこくひょう

Stroke Order

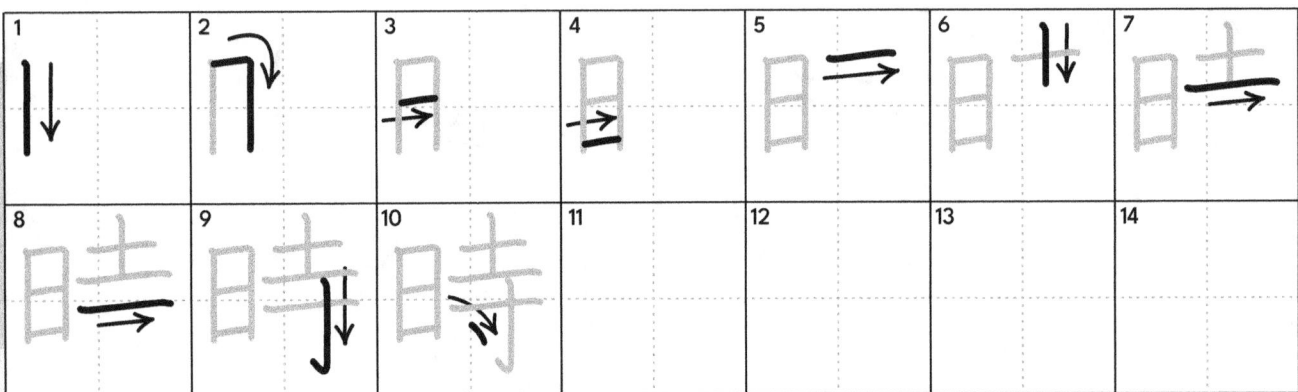

Writing Practice

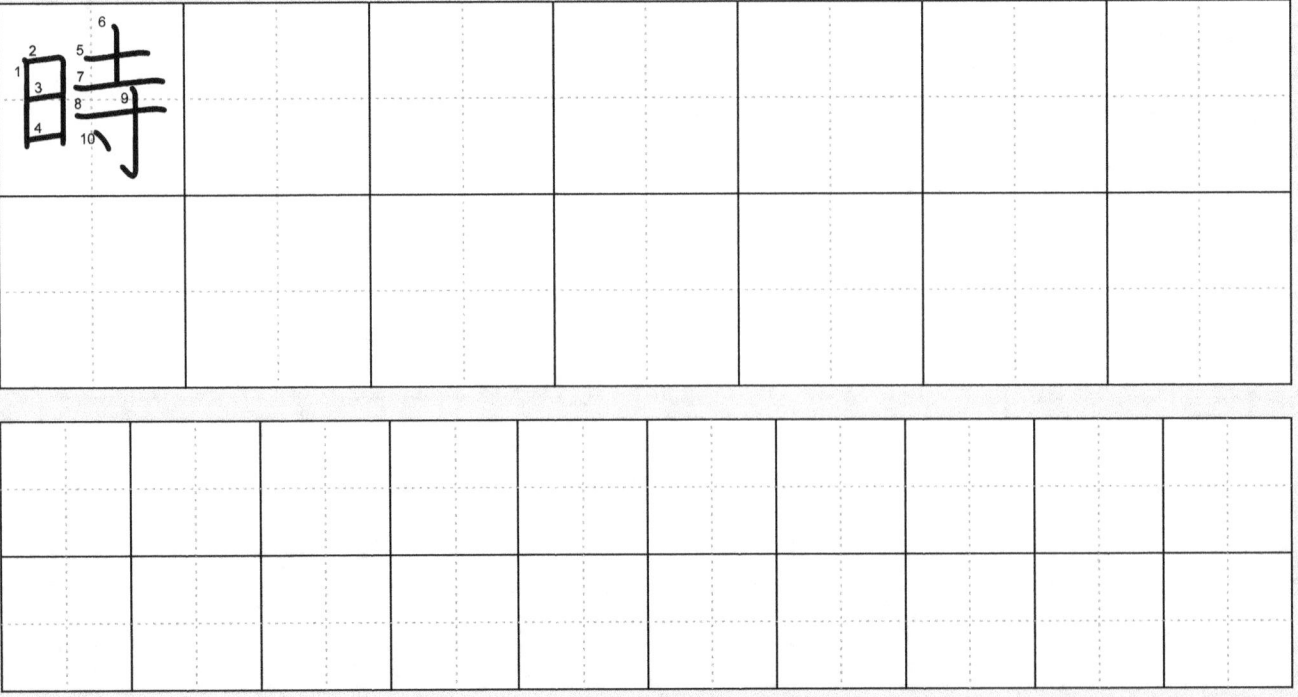

Kanji for Time

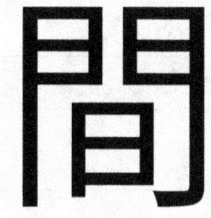

Meaning(s)	interval, space	Components	日 門
Radical	門 (gate)	Kun'yomi	あいだ、ま、あい
Strokes	12	On'yomi	カン、ケン

Vocabulary	Meaning	Pronunciation
間	space (between), gap, distance	あいだ
間	interval, period of time, among, between	カン
時間	time, hour	じかん
間違い	mistake, error, accident, mishap	まちがい

Stroke Order

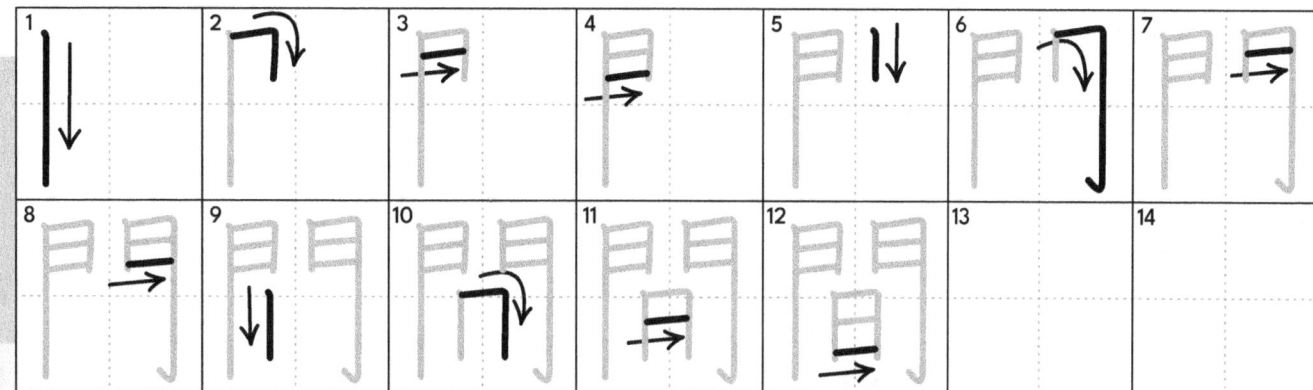

Writing Practice

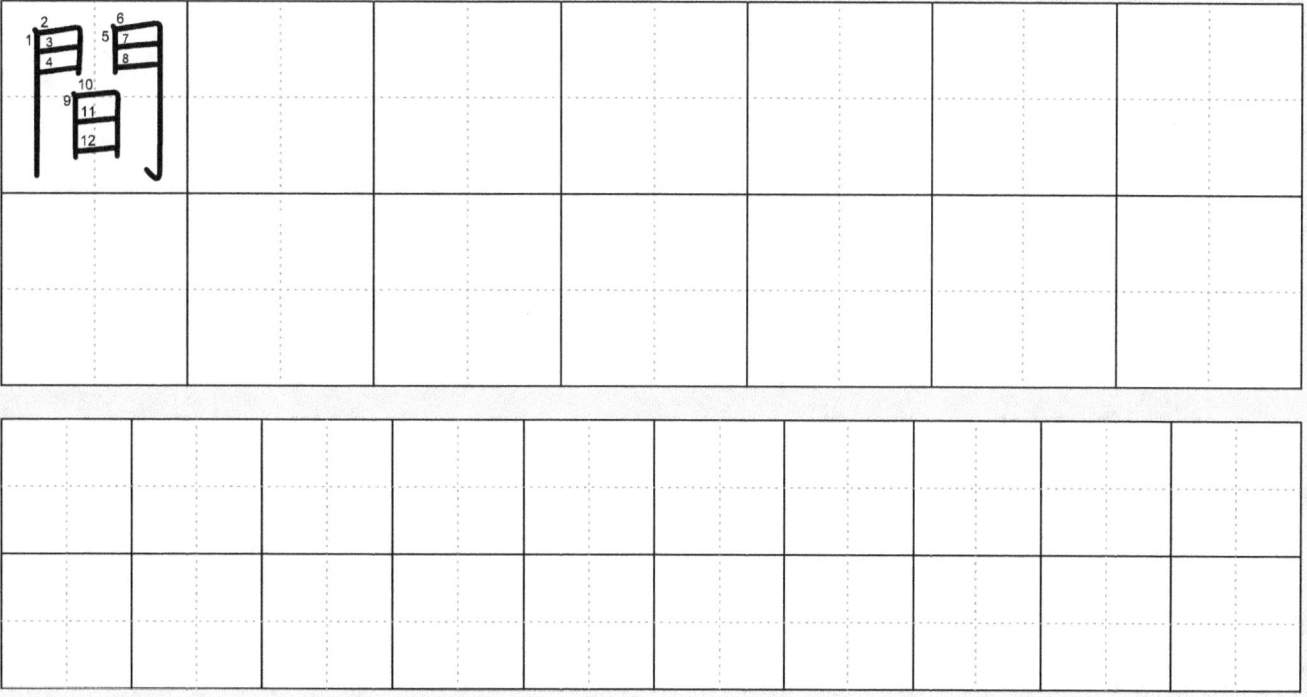

JLPT N5

Meaning(s)	part, minute, duty	Components	ハ 刀
Radical	刀 (sword, knife)	Kun'yomi	わ.ける、わ.け
Strokes	4	On'yomi	ブン、フン、ブ

Vocabulary	Meaning		Pronunciation
分	part, portion, share, enough for...		ブン
分ける	to divide (into), split (into), to separate		わける
分別	discretion, prudence, good sense		フンベツ
三十分	30 minutes (30分)		さんじゅっぷん

Stroke Order

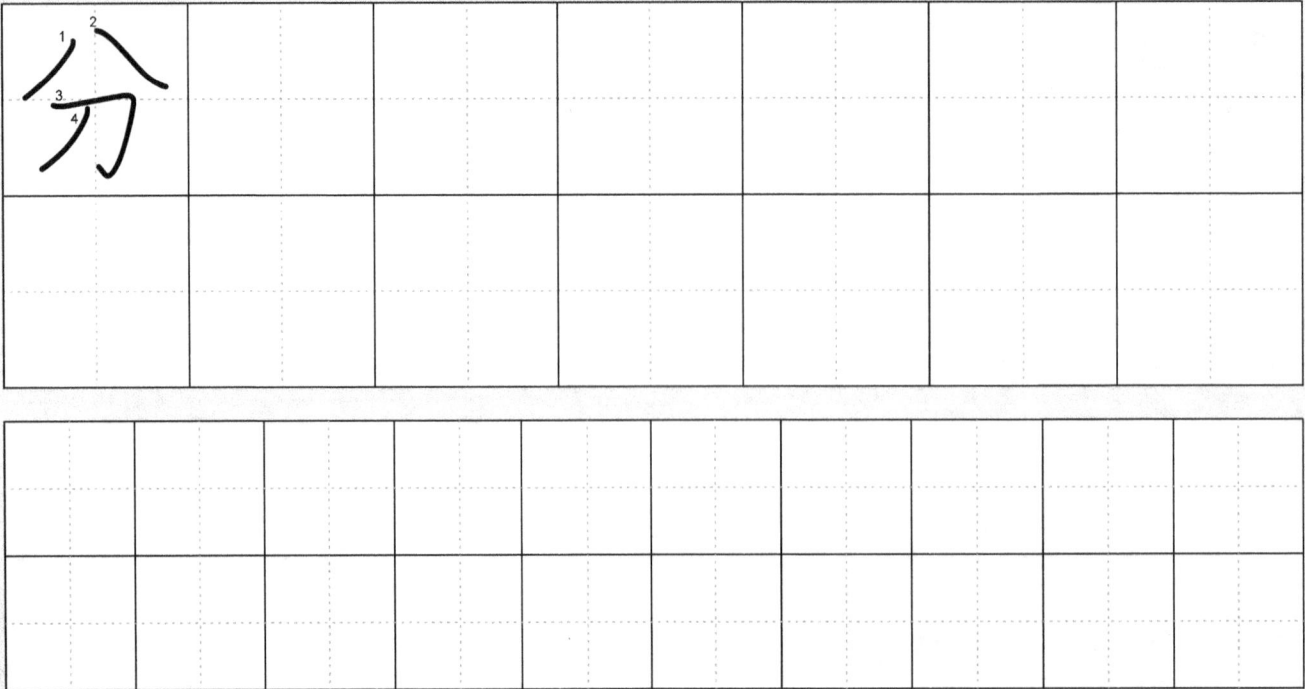

Writing Practice

Kanji for Time

午

Meaning(s)	noon, sign of Horse	**Components**	ノ十干乞
Radical	十 (ten)	**Kun'yomi**	うま
Strokes	4	**On'yomi**	ゴ

Vocabulary	Meaning	Pronunciation
午後	afternoon, PM	ゴゴ
午前	morning, AM	ゴゼン
亭午	noon	テイゴ
午	sign of the Horse, fifth calendar month	うま

Stroke Order

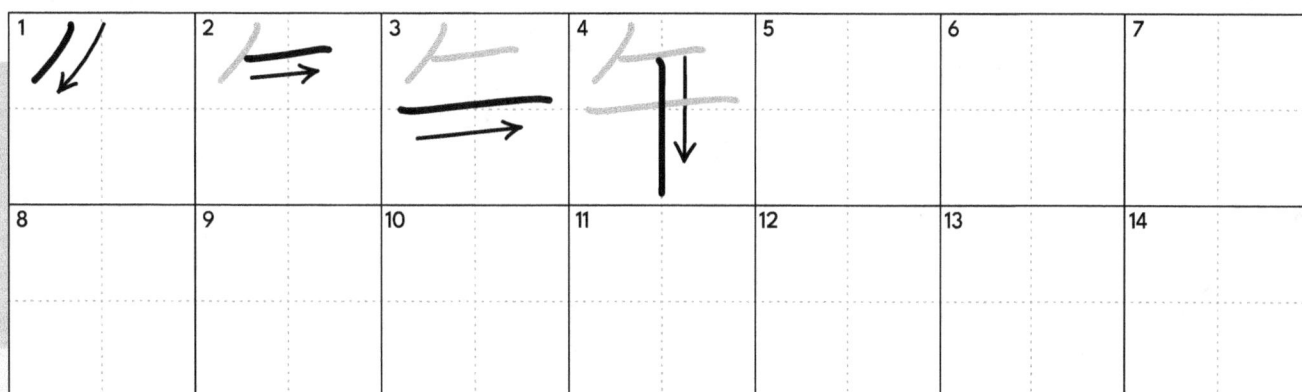

Writing Practice

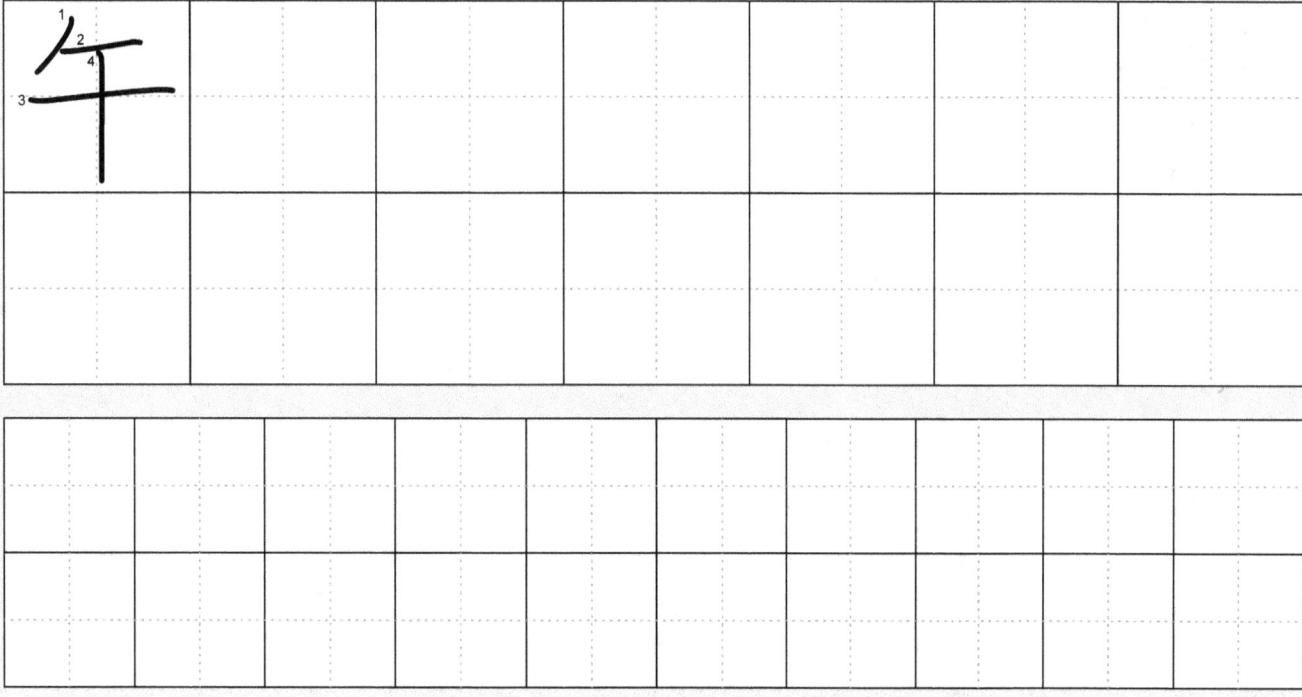

JLPT N5

Meaning(s)	in front, before	Components	一 丷 刈 月
Radical	刀 (sword, knife)	Kun'yomi	まえ、-まえ
Strokes	9	On'yomi	ゼン

Vocabulary	Meaning		Pronunciation
前	in front (of), before, earlier, ago		まえ
名前	name, given name, first name		なまえ
前	last..., previous, ex-, former, pre-		ゼン
前売り	advanced sale, booking		まえうり

Stroke Order

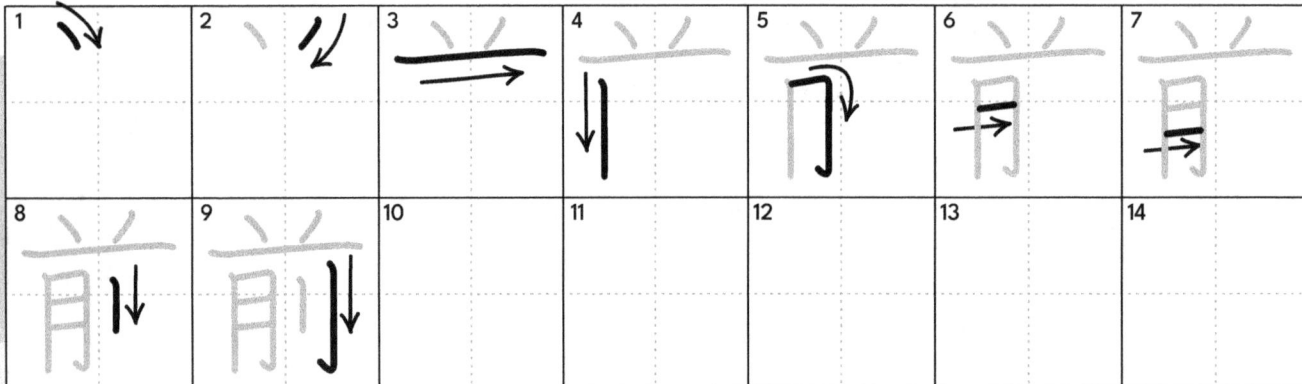

Writing Practice

Kanji for Time

Meaning(s)	behind, back, later	**Components**	夂 幺 彳
Radical	彳 (step)	**Kun'yomi**	のち、うし.ろ、うしろ
Strokes	9	**On'yomi**	ゴ、コウ

Vocabulary	Meaning	Pronunciation
後	later, afterwards, future, descendant	のち
後後 (後々)	future, distant future	のちのち
午後	afternoon, PM	ごご
後日	in the future, another day, later	ゴジツ

Stroke Order

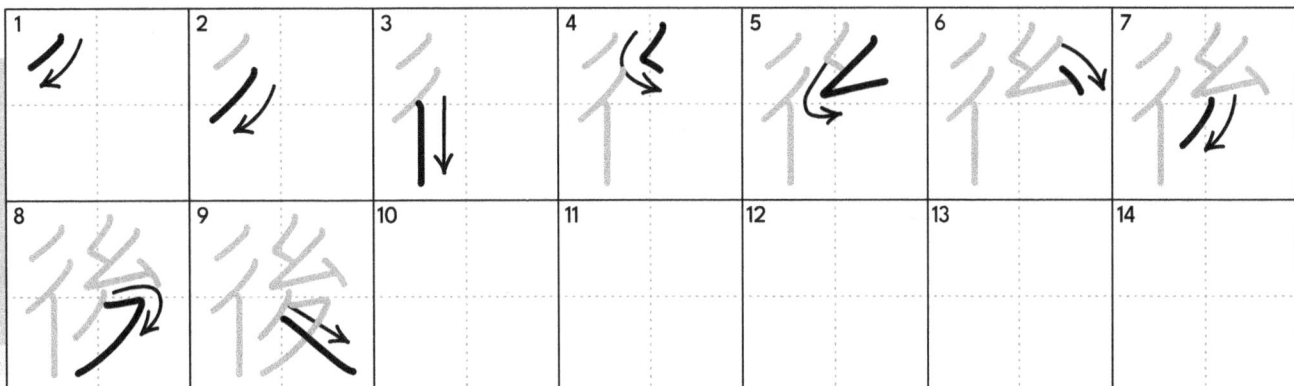

Writing Practice

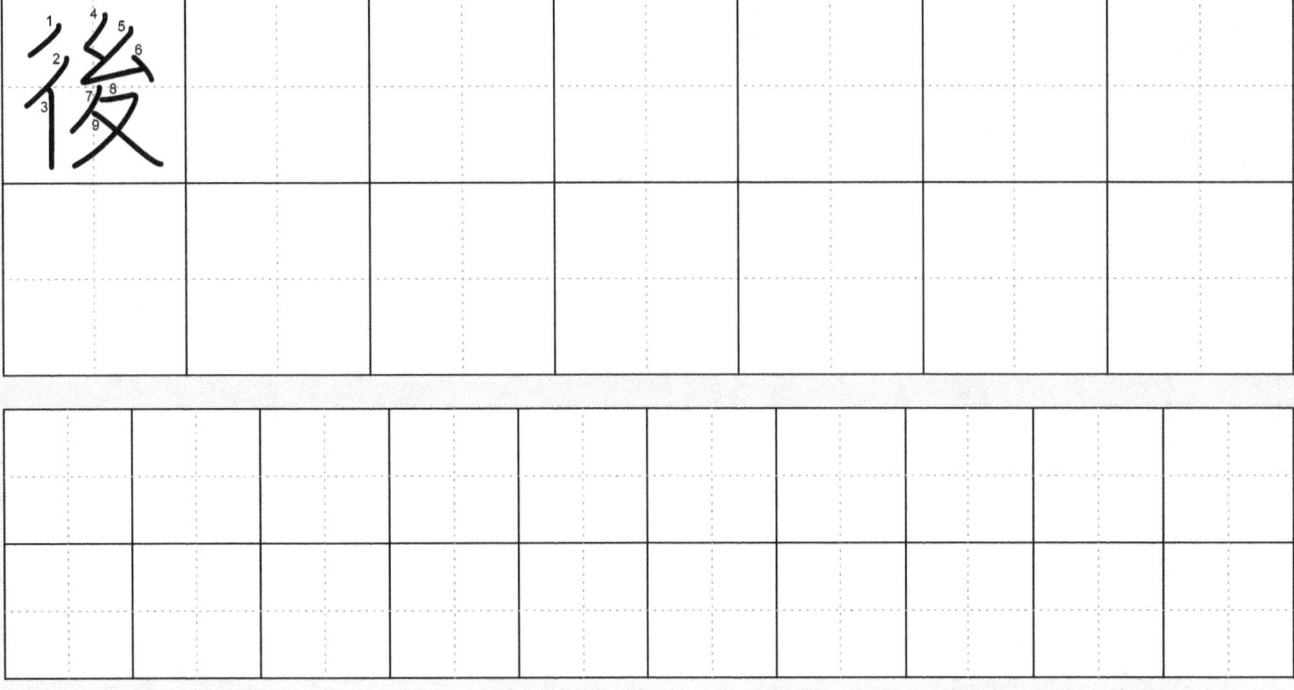

JLPT N5

Meaning(s)	now, this, the current...	Components	一 个
Radical	人 (イ) (man, human)	Kun'yomi	いま
Strokes	4	On'yomi	コン、キン

Vocabulary	Meaning		Pronunciation
今	the current ..., this, today's ...		コン
今	now, present time, soon, immediately		いま
今晩	tonight, this evening		こんばん
今朝	this morning		こんちょう

Stroke Order

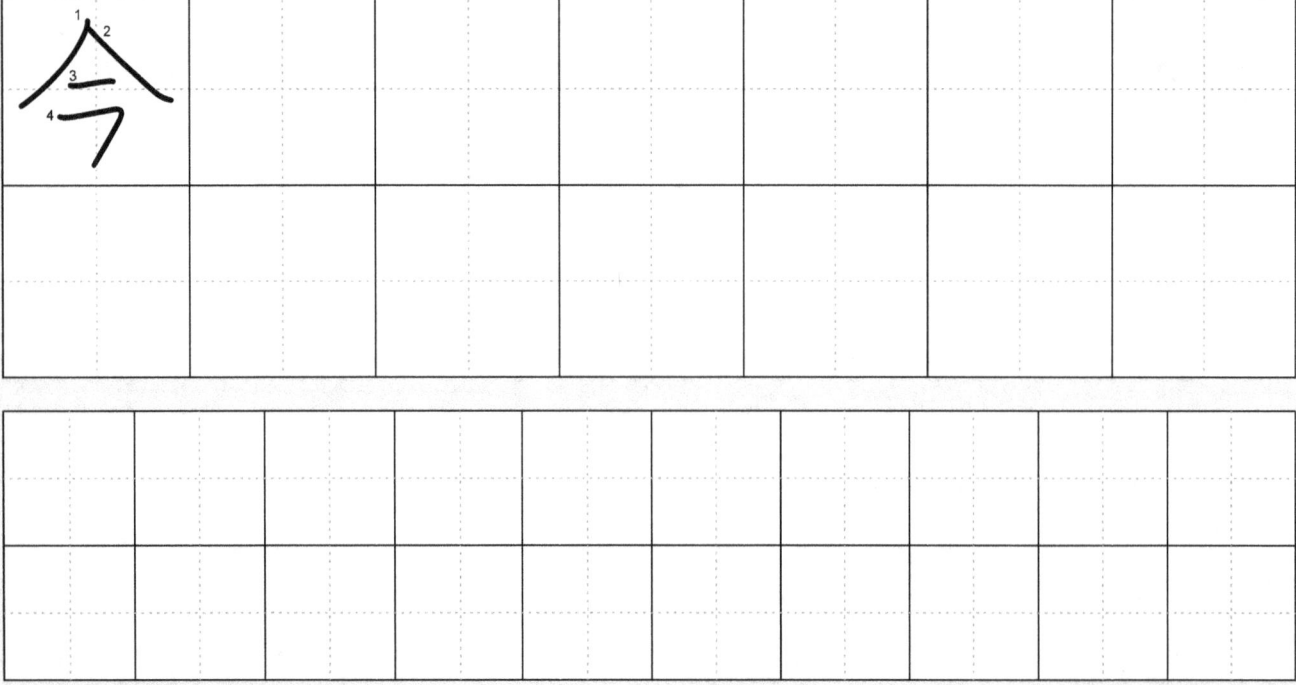

Writing Practice

Kanji for Time

先

Meaning(s)	before, previous, future	**Components**	ノ儿土
Radical	儿 (legs)	**Kun'yomi**	さき、ま.ず
Strokes	6	**On'yomi**	セン

Vocabulary	Meaning	Pronunciation
先	former, previous, old	セン
先	point, tip, end, front, first, before	さき
先週	last week, the week before	せんしゅう
先生	teacher, instructor, master	せんせい

Stroke Order

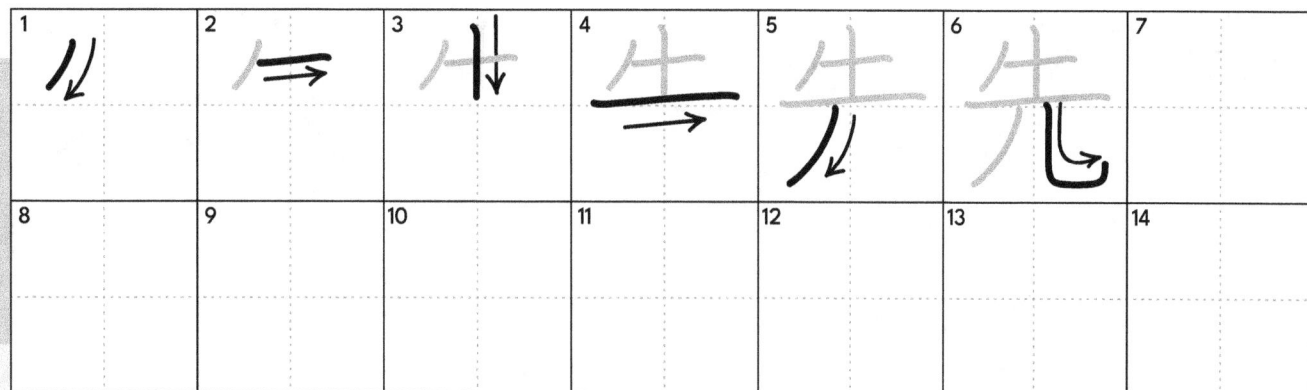

Writing Practice

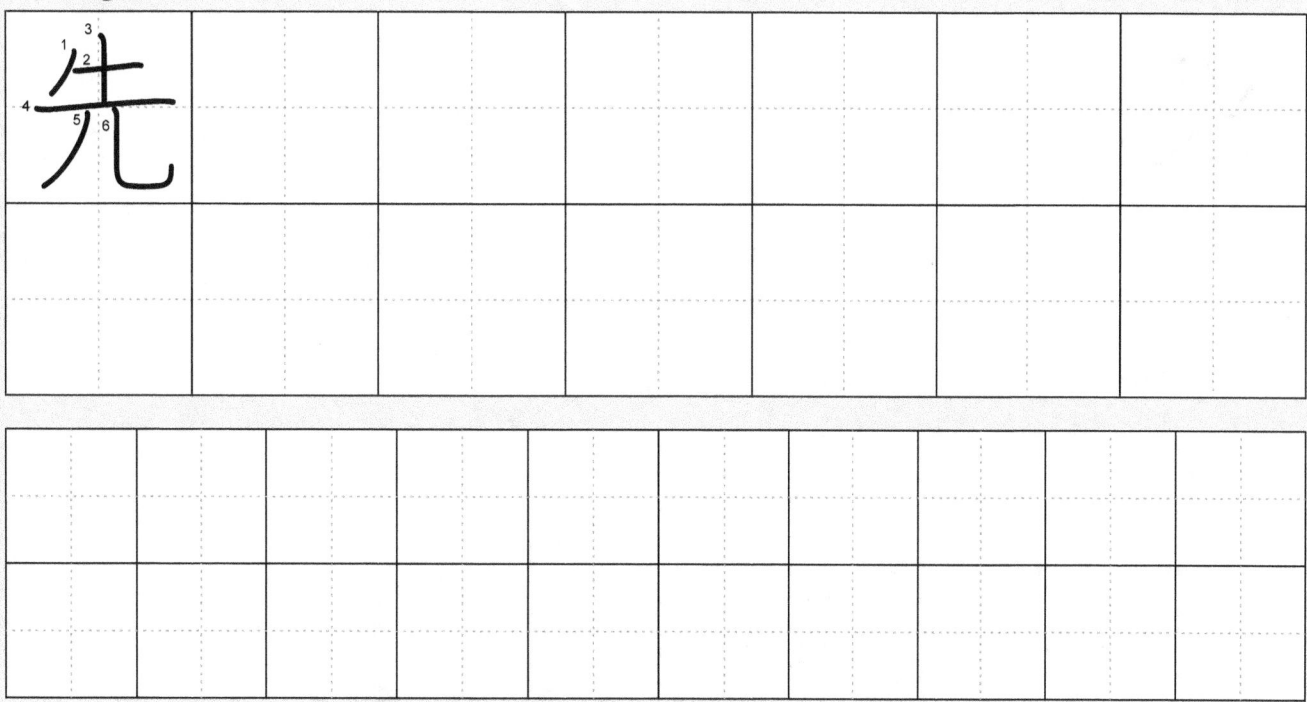

JLPT N5

Meaning(s)	come, due, next, cause	Components	丨 二 十 木 米
Radical	木 (tree)	Kun'yomi	く.る、きた.る
Strokes	7	On'yomi	ライ、タイ

Vocabulary	Meaning		Pronunciation
来	next (year, spring), coming, since		ライ
来月	next month		らいげつ
来る	to come (place, time), to approach, to arrive		くる
出来る	to be able to do, to be ready, to be made		できる

Stroke Order

Writing Practice

Kanji for Time

Meaning(s)	half, middle, odd no.	Components	丨 二 丷 十
Radical	十 (ten)	Kun'yomi	なか.ば
Strokes	5	On'yomi	ハン

Vocabulary	Meaning	Pronunciation
半	half, semi-, half-past, odd number	ハン
半分	half	はんぶん
半ば	middle, halfway, half (of), one half	なかば
大半	majority, more than half, most (of)	たいはん

Stroke Order

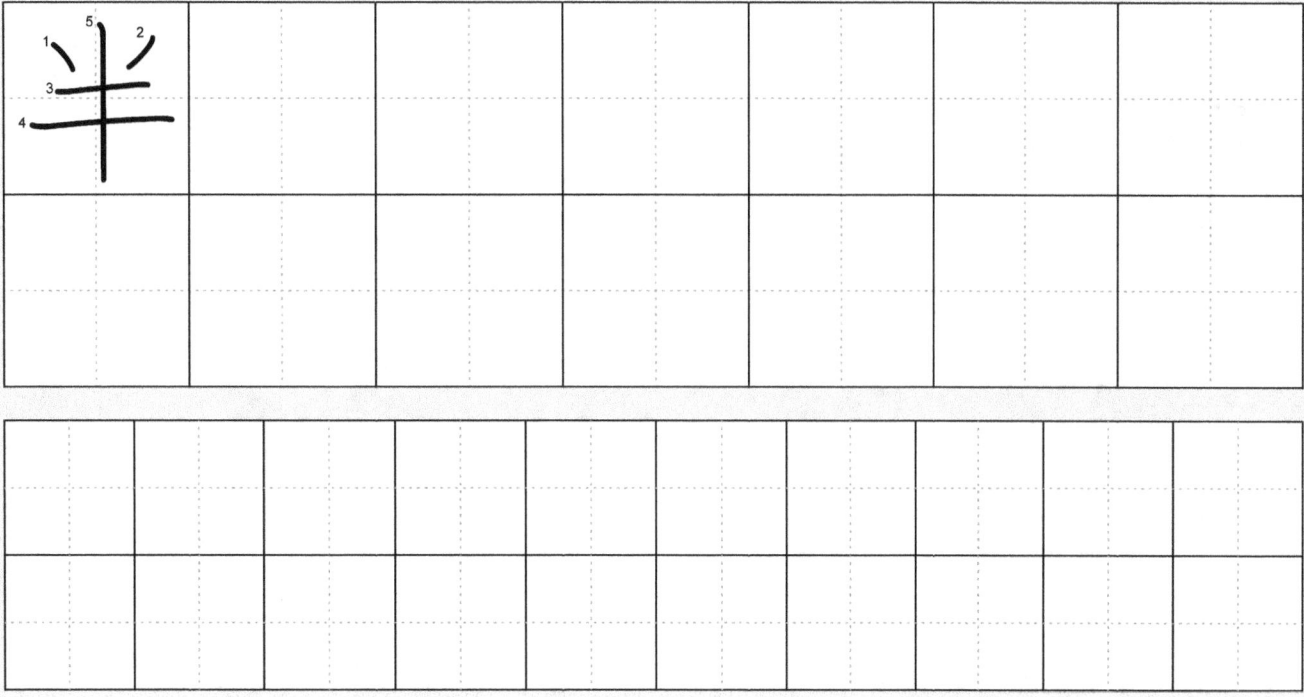

Writing Practice

JLPT N5

Meaning(s)	every	Components	毋 母 乞
Radical	毋 (母, 母) (mother)	Kun'yomi	ごと、-ごと.に
Strokes	6	On'yomi	マイ

Vocabulary	Meaning	Pronunciation
毎	each, every	ごと
毎	every (events, e.g. weekend), each	マイ
毎日	every day	まいにち
毎朝	every morning	マイアサ

Stroke Order

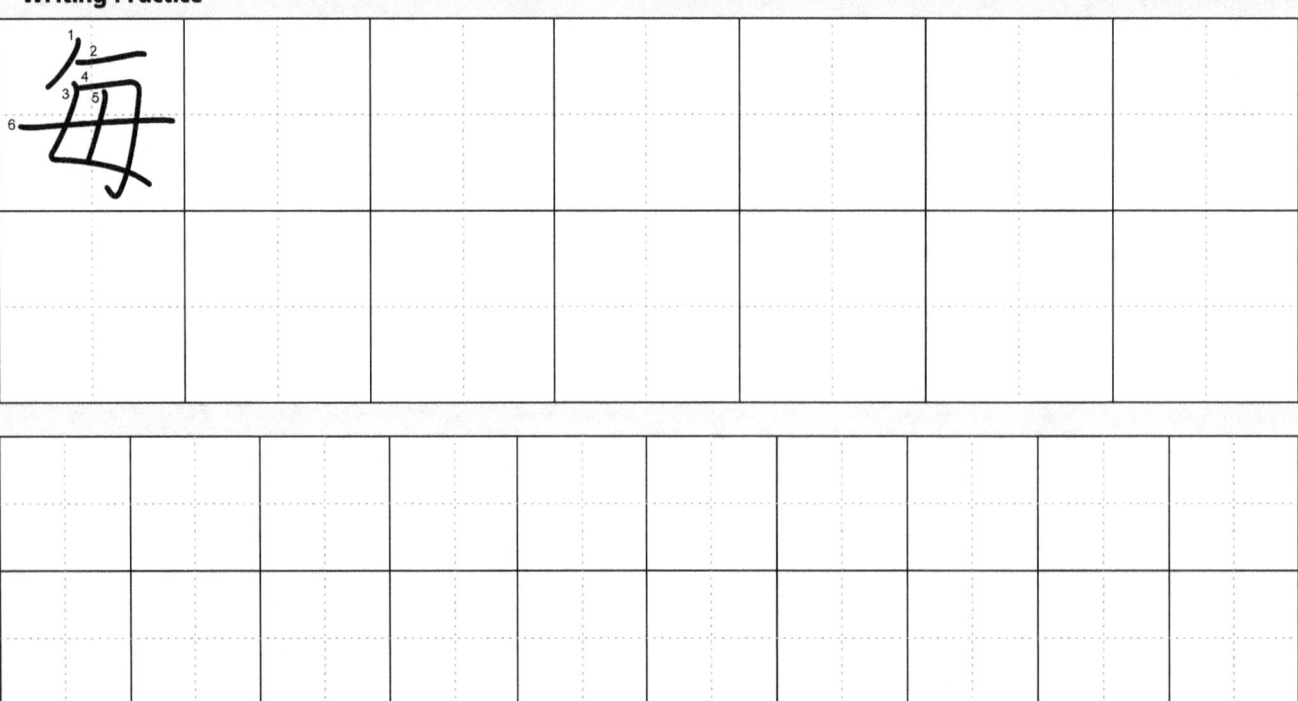

Writing Practice

Kanji for Time

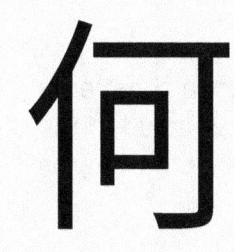

Meaning(s)	what, which, how many	Components	一 亅 化 口
Radical	人 (イ) (man, human)	Kun'yomi	なに、なん、なに-
Strokes	7	On'yomi	カ

Vocabulary	Meaning	Pronunciation
何	what, you-know-what, that thing	なに
何	what, how many, many, a lot of	なん
何か	something, some, any, somehow	なにか
何曜日	what day? what day of the week?	なんようび

Stroke Order

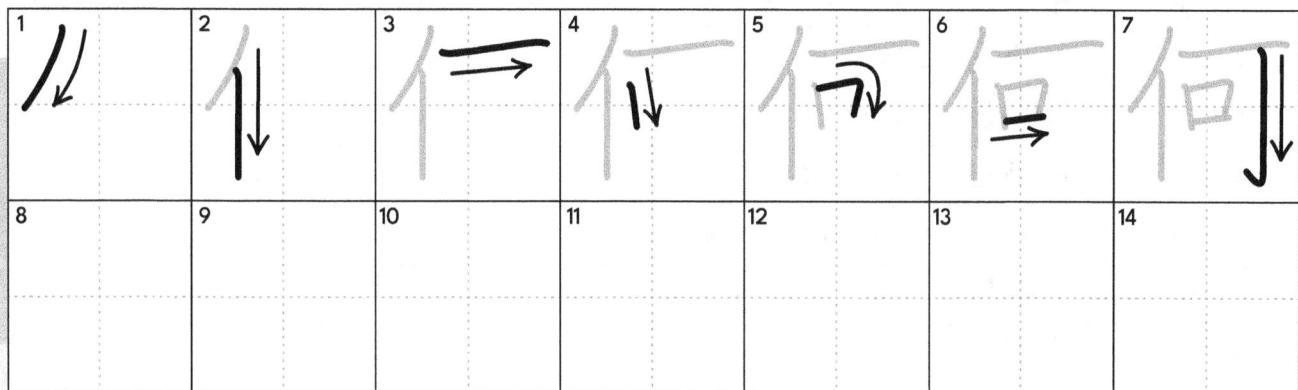

Writing Practice

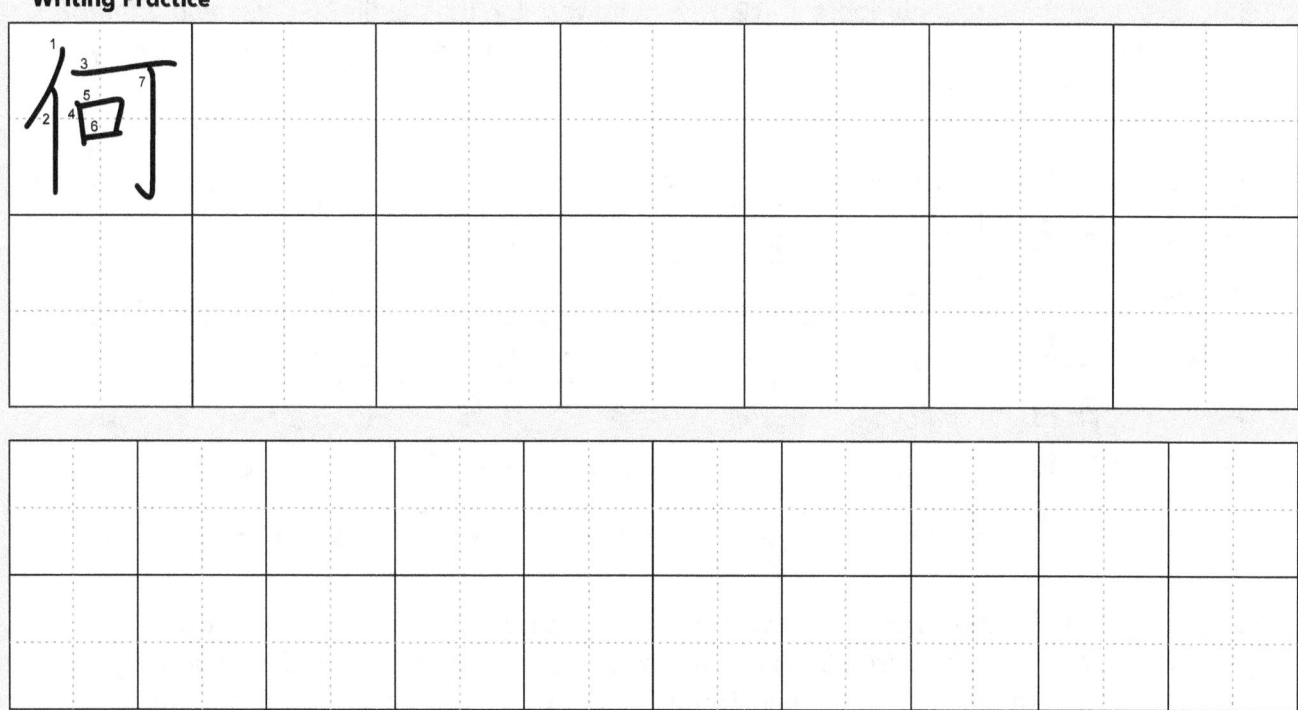

JLPT N5

Date and Time

Many common words and phrases used for times and dates follow straightforward patterns that are easy to learn. The vocabulary sections for kanji in this second group included the occasional name for days of the week and months of the year - they follow simple patterns that are easy to understand and remember when viewed together:

The days of the week have names inspired by celestial bodies, including the sun, the moon, and the five visible planets - at the time, Mercury, Venus, Mars, Jupiter, and Saturn were the only ones known to exist.

Days	Kanji Name	Pronunciation	Kanji Meaning	Planet/Origin
Monday	月曜日	げつようび　getsuyōbi	月 moon	the moon (tsuki 月)
Tuesday	火曜日	かようび　kayōbi	火 fire	mars (kasei 火星)
Wednesday	水曜日	すいようび　suiyōbi	水 water	mercury (suisei 水星)
Thursday	木曜日	もくようび　mokuyōbi	木 wood/tree	jupiter (mokusei 木星)
Friday	金曜日	きんようび　kin'yōbi	金 metal/gold	venus (kinsei 金星)
Saturday	土曜日	どようび　doyōbi	土 earth/soil	saturn (dosei 土星)
Sunday	日曜日	にちようび　nichiyōbi	日 sun	the sun (hi 日, taiyō 太陽)

Each month of the year has a name that follows a numerical system - starting from January, they are assigned the numbers 1-12 and followed by the kanji 月 *(meaning month)*, pronounced げつ *("gatsu")*. With the kanji numbers from the first group memorized, you effectively know the names of all the months of the year.

Months	Kanji	Pronunciation	Months	Kanji	Pronunciation
January	一月	いちがつ　ichigatsu	**July**	七月	しちがつ　shichigatsu
February	二月	にがつ　nigatsu	**August**	八月	はちがつ　hachigatsu
March	三月	さんがつ　sangatsu	**September**	九月	くがつ　kugatsu
April	四月	よんがつ　shigatsu	**October**	十月	じゅうがつ　jūgatsu
May	五月	ごがつ　gogatsu	**November**	十一月	じゅういちがつ　jūichigatsu
June	六月	ろくがつ　rokugatsu	**December**	十二月	じゅうにがつ　jūnigatsu

Note: Japan has other names for the months with seasonal associations, such as 霜月 *(November, the 'month of frost')*, but they are not common in use. Before adopting the modern Gregorian calendar in the late 1800s, lunar cycles determined when months began and ended, and a year was only 354 days long!

By combining a knowledge of the earlier kanji numbers with the characters in this second group, you can begin to read, write, and say the time in Japanese.

It's simpler than you think - you can add the kanji 時 to a whole number to tell somebody the time.

Used this way, 時 takes On- reading ジ (じ) and pronounced 'ji'. To say "2 o'clock," it's 二時 or 2時 which you would say as にじ (ni ji). In the same way, "12 o'clock" is 十二時 or 12時, pronounced じゅうにじ (juu ni ji).

Time	Kanji	Pronunciation	
1 o'clock	一時	いちじ	ichi ji
2 o'clock	二時	にじ	ni ji
3 o'clock	三時	さんじ	san ji
5 o'clock	五時	ごじ	go ji
10 o'clock	十時	じゅうじ	juu ji

Use the kanji 分 similarly to quantify minutes for more specific times. The On- reading is フン (ふん) and pronounced as either 'fun' or 'pun'.

To say "40 minutes" it's 四十分 or 40分 and pronounced as よんじゅっぷん (yon juppun).

Time	Kanji	Pronunciation
2 minutes	二分	にふん
5 minutes	五分	ごふん
10 minutes	十分	じゅっぷん
30 minutes	五十分	さんじゅっぷん

When asked 今何時ですか (or いま なんじ - ima nan-ji desu ka), meaning "what time is it now?", you could combine the two previous examples and say 二時四十分 or 2時40分. You would put the two phrases together to say にじ よんじゅっぷん (ni-ji yon-juppun).

Unlike the English language, Japanese does not have as many additional expressions for specific times. The equivalent to "half-past [hour]" uses the kanji 半 (はん) after any '**number** + 時.' To say "thirty minutes past 2 o'clock", it's 2時半 or にじ はん (ni-ji han).

Some of the kanji in this section are part of other time-related terminology that may be useful in everyday conversation:

Kanji	Meaning	Pronunciation	
午前	morning, a.m.	ごぜん	gozen
午后	afternoon, p.m.	ごご	gogo
朝	morning, breakfast	あさ	asa
早朝	early morning	そうちょう	sō chō
日中	daytime	にっちゅう	nitchyuu

Kanji	Meaning	Pronunciation	
夜	evening, night	よる	yoru
日の出	sunrise	ひので	hinode
夕方	evening, dusk	ゆうがた	yū gata
深夜	midnight	しんや	shin'ya

Revision: Time

It's that *time* again! Try to answer these questions without looking back at the previous pages. The questions will show you which kanji may need more attention and practice, and you may also encounter some of the number kanji from the prior group.

Q.19 Which of these kanji means *day*?

A. 何　B. 月　C. 週　D. 時　E. 日

Q.20 Which of these kanji means *week*?

A. 毎　B. 週　C. 時　D. 月　E. 日

Q.21 Which of these kanji means *month*?

A. 午　B. 日　C. 年　D. 月　E. 何

Q.22 Which of these kanji means *year*?

A. 月　B. 間　C. 年　D. 午　E. 今

Q.23 How do you write *half* or *middle* in Japanese?

A. 半　B. 来　C. 今　D. 毎　E. 年

Q.24 Which of these kanji means *minute*?

A. 九　B. 分　C. 先　D. 円　E. 千

Q.25 Which of these kanji means *hour* or *time*?

A. 時　B. 前　C. 後　D. 間　E. 何

Q.26 Which month is written 十一月?

A. December　B. October　C. November　D. September　E. August

Q.27 How would you *pronounce* the kanji 時 when giving the time?

- A. go
- B. gi
- C. ju
- D. ji
- E. gu

Q.28 Which of these kanji means *every* or *each*?

- A. 百
- B. 何
- C. 毎
- D. 五
- E. 円

Q.29 How would you pronounce *3 o'clock* in Japanese?

- A. いちじ
- B. にじ
- C. さんじ
- D. ごじ
- E. じゅうじ

Q.30 Which day of the week is 金曜日?

- A. Monday
- B. Friday
- C. Sunday
- D. Tuesday
- E. Thursday

Q.31 How many minutes does 三十分 represent?

- A. 10
- B. 13
- C. 20
- D. 23
- E. 30

Q.32 Which day of the week is 木曜日?

- A. Sunday
- B. Tuesday
- C. Friday
- D. Thursday
- E. Monday

Q.33 Which of these kanji words means *last year* or *the year before*?

- A. 前年
- B. 前午
- C. 午前
- D. 年前
- E. 前前

Q.34 Which kanji can you use to ask *what, which,* or *how many*?

- A. 何
- B. 間
- C. 先
- D. 円
- E. 来

Q.35 週 How many strokes are required to write this character?

- A. 10
- B. 11
- C. 12
- D. 13

Meaning(s)	person	Components	人
Radical	人 (亻) (man, human)	Kun'yomi	ひと、-り、-と
Strokes	2	On'yomi	ジン、ニン

Vocabulary	Meaning	Pronunciation
人	people	ひと
人	-ian, -ite, -er (e.g. Italian, performer)	ジン
人人 (人々)	people, men and women	ひとびと
人	counter for people	ニン

Stroke Order

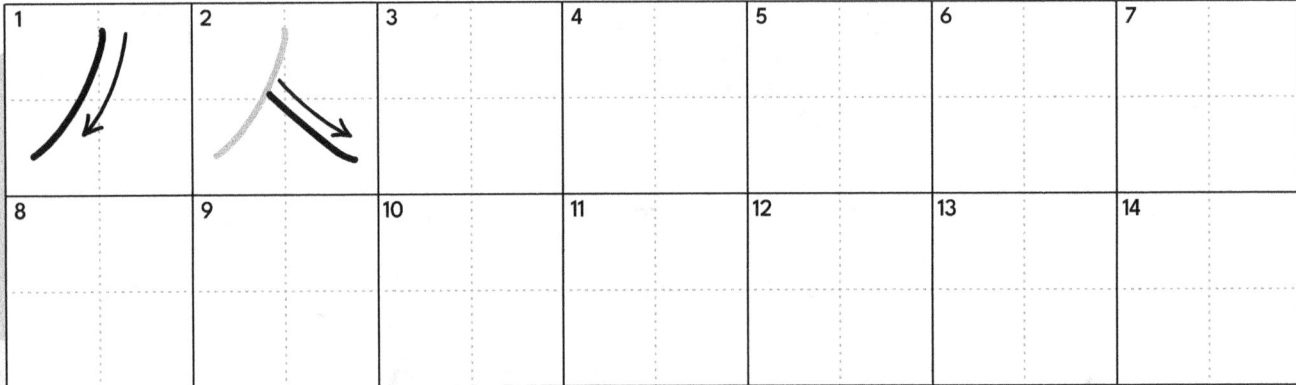

Writing Practice

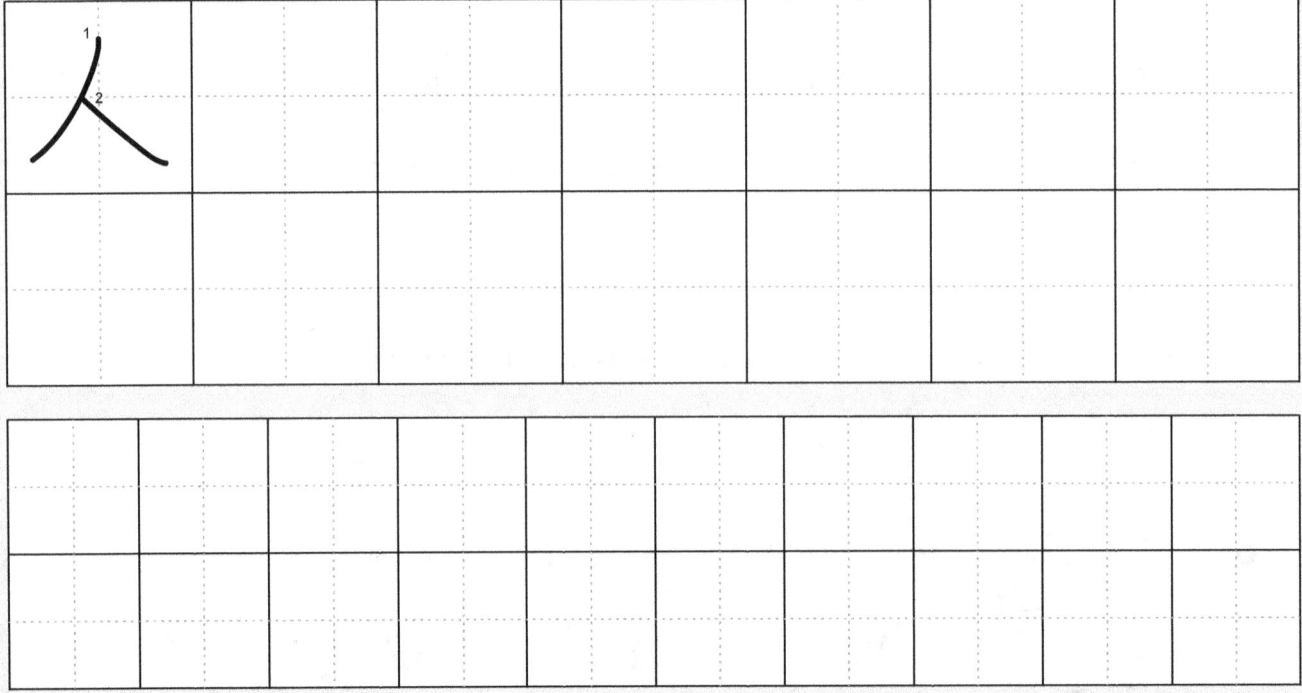

Kanji for People & Things

Meaning(s)	male	Components	力田
Radical	田 (field)	Kun'yomi	おとこ、お
Strokes	7	On'yomi	ダン、ナン

Vocabulary	Meaning		Pronunciation
男	man, male, fellow, guy, boyfriend		おとこ
男女	man (men) and woman (women)		ダンジョ
美男	handsome man		びなん
男の子	boy, son, baby boy, young man		おとこのこ

Stroke Order

Writing Practice

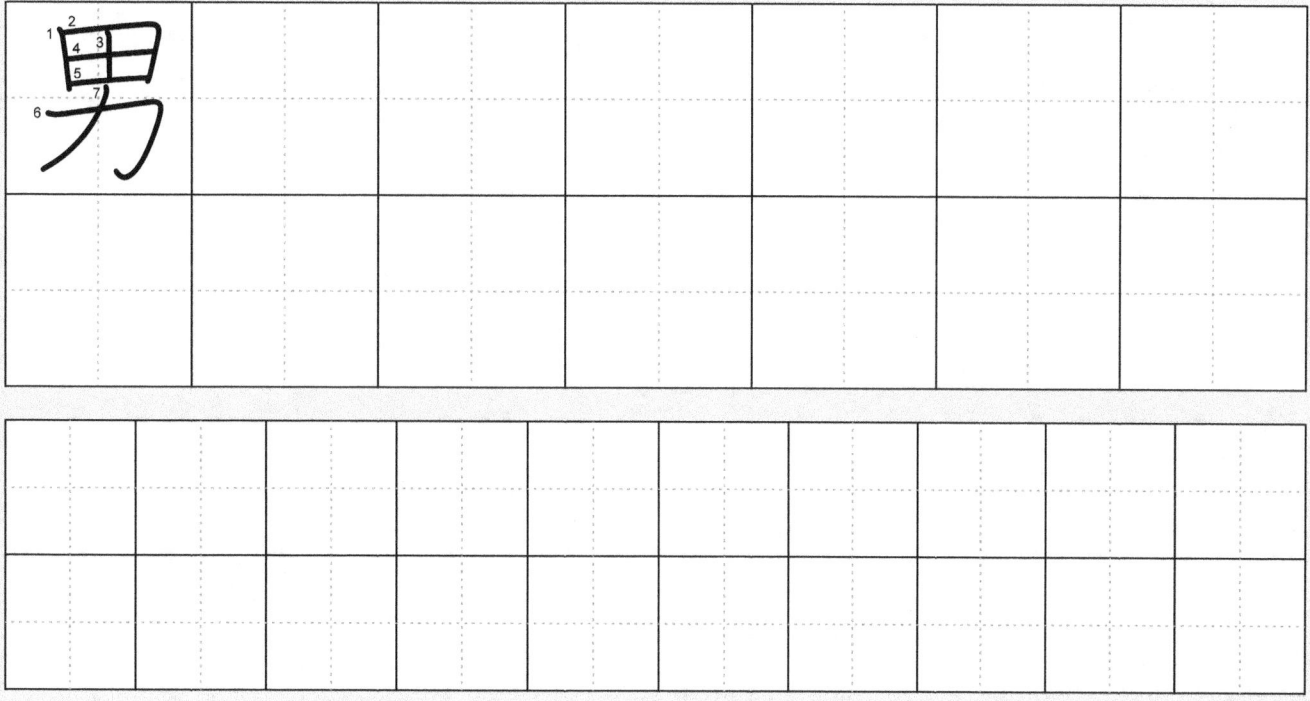

JLPT N5

Meaning(s)	woman, female	Components	女
Radical	女 (woman)	Kun'yomi	おんな、め
Strokes	3	On'yomi	ジョ、ニョ、ニョウ

Vocabulary	Meaning	Pronunciation
女	female, woman, female sex, girlfriend	おんな
女王	queen, female champion	ジョオウ
女神	goddess, female deity	めがみ
女の子	girl, daughter, baby girl	おんなのこ

Stroke Order

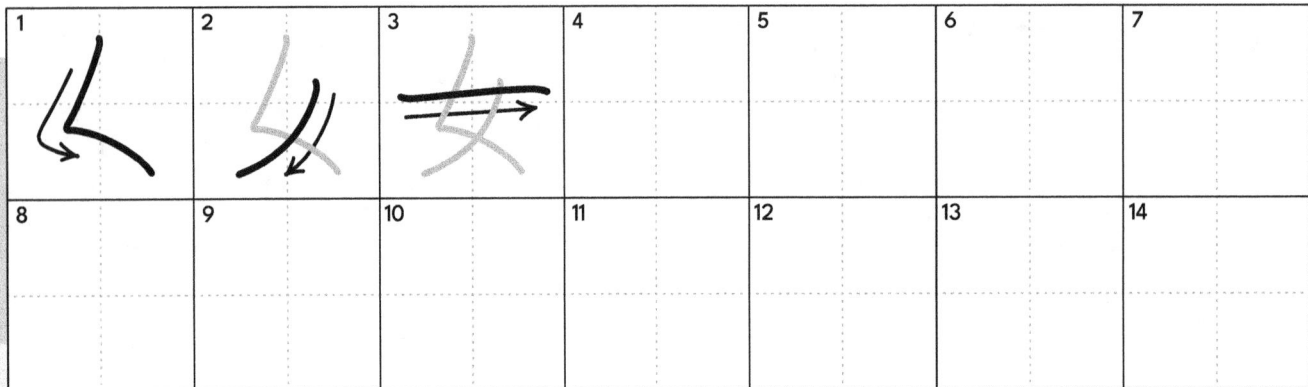

Writing Practice

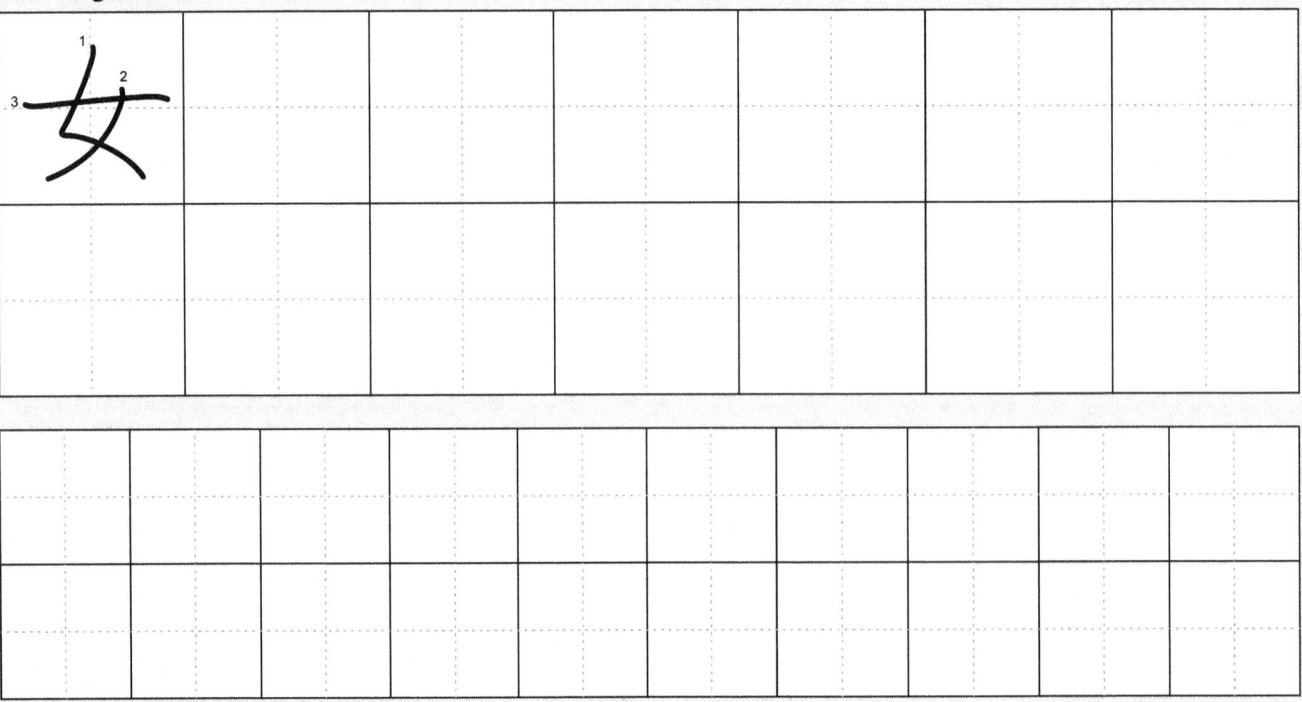

Kanji for People & Things

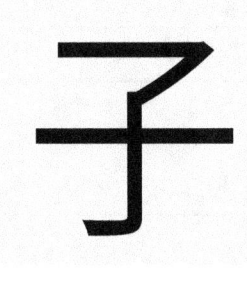

Meaning(s)	child, sign of rat	**Components**	子
Radical	子 (child, seed)	**Kun'yomi**	こ、-こ、ね
Strokes	3	**On'yomi**	シ、ス、ツ

Vocabulary	Meaning	Pronunciation
子	child, kid, teenager, youngster	こ
息子	son	むすこ
子供	child	こども
帽子	hat, cap	ぼうし

Stroke Order

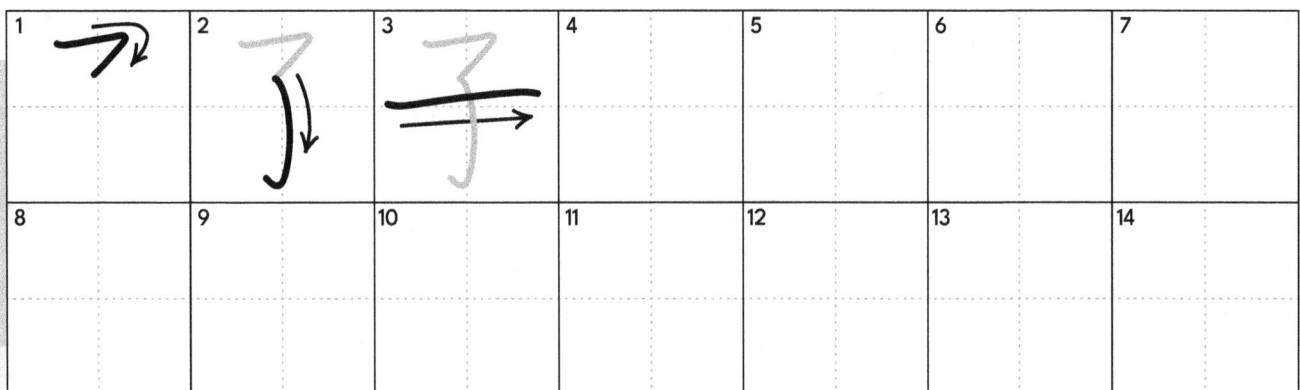

Writing Practice

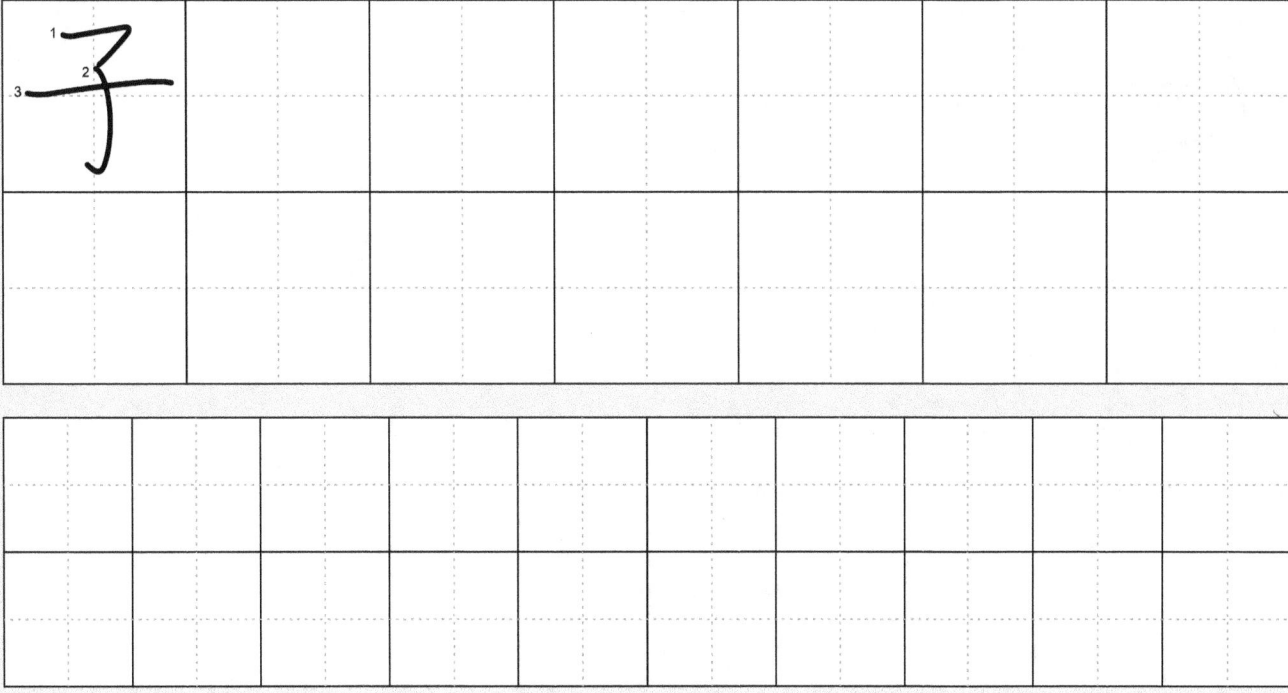

JLPT N5

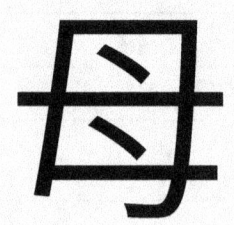

Meaning(s)	mother	Components	毋 母
Radical	毋 (母) (mother)	Kun'yomi	はは、も
Strokes	5	On'yomi	ボ

Vocabulary	Meaning	Pronunciation
母	mother	はは
父母	parents, father and mother	フボ
伯母さん	aunt	おばさん
お祖母さん	grandmother	おばあさん

Stroke Order

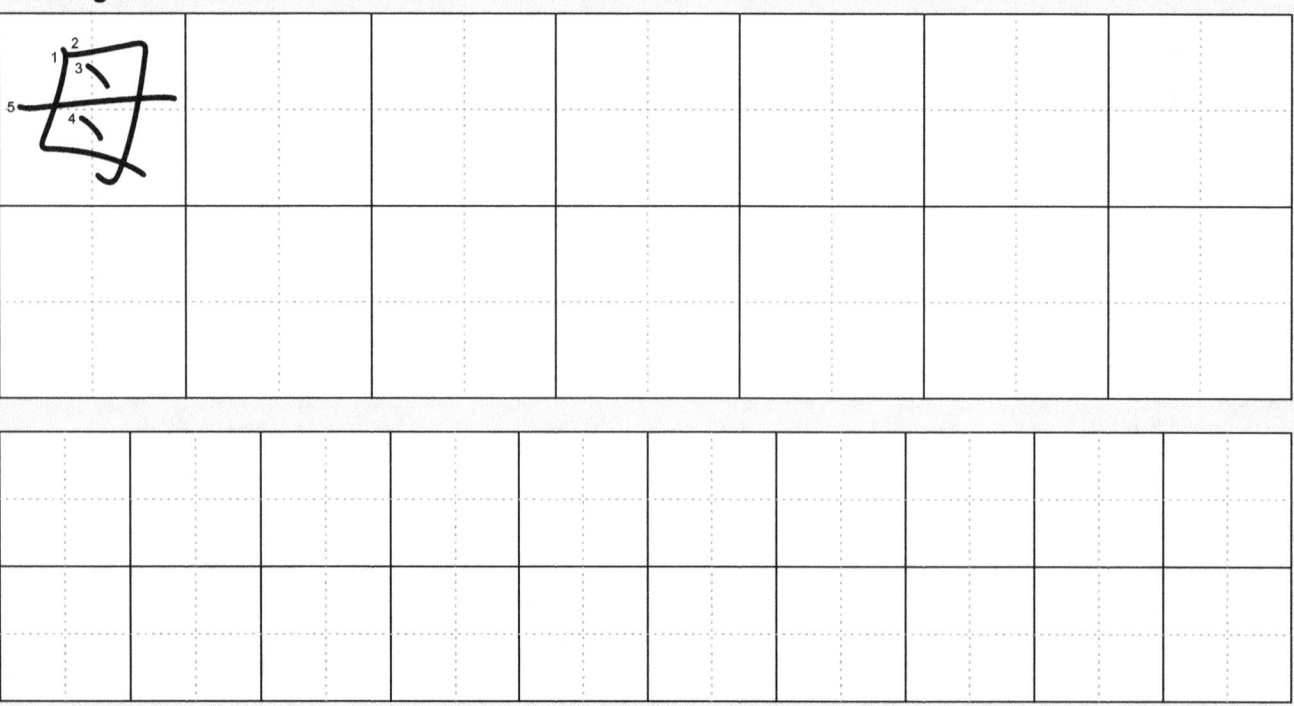

Writing Practice

Kanji for People & Things

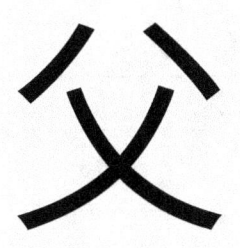

Meaning(s)	father	Components	父
Radical	父 (father)	Kun'yomi	ちち
Strokes	4	On'yomi	フ

Vocabulary	Meaning	Pronunciation
父	father	ちち
父母	parents, father and mother	フボ
祖父	grandfather, old man	そふ
祖父母	grandparents	そふぼ

Stroke Order

Writing Practice

JLPT N5

Meaning(s)	friend		Components	一ノ又
Radical	又 (right hand)		Kun'yomi	とも
Strokes	4		On'yomi	ユウ

Vocabulary	Meaning	Pronunciation
友	friend	とも
友達	friend, companion, comrade, pal	ともだち
友情	friendship, fellowship	ゆうじょう
友好的	friendly, amicable	ゆうこうてき

Stroke Order

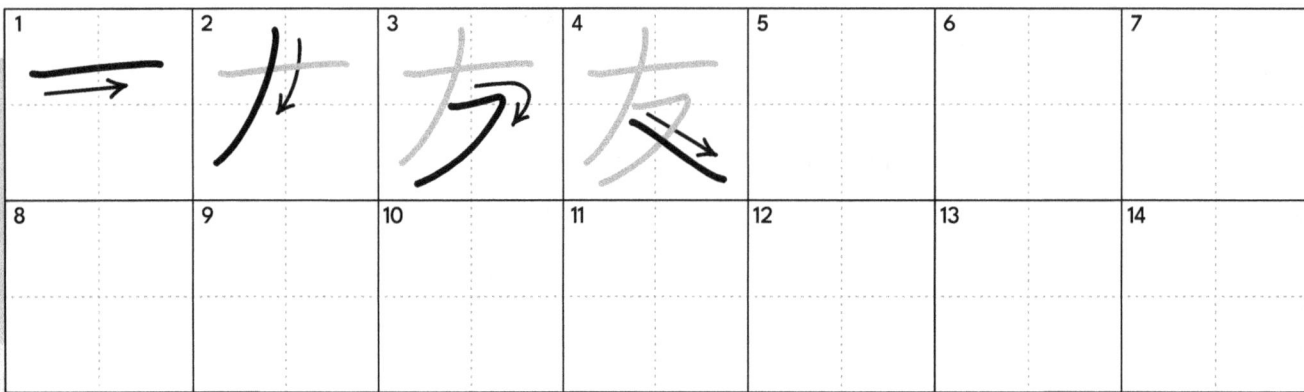

Writing Practice

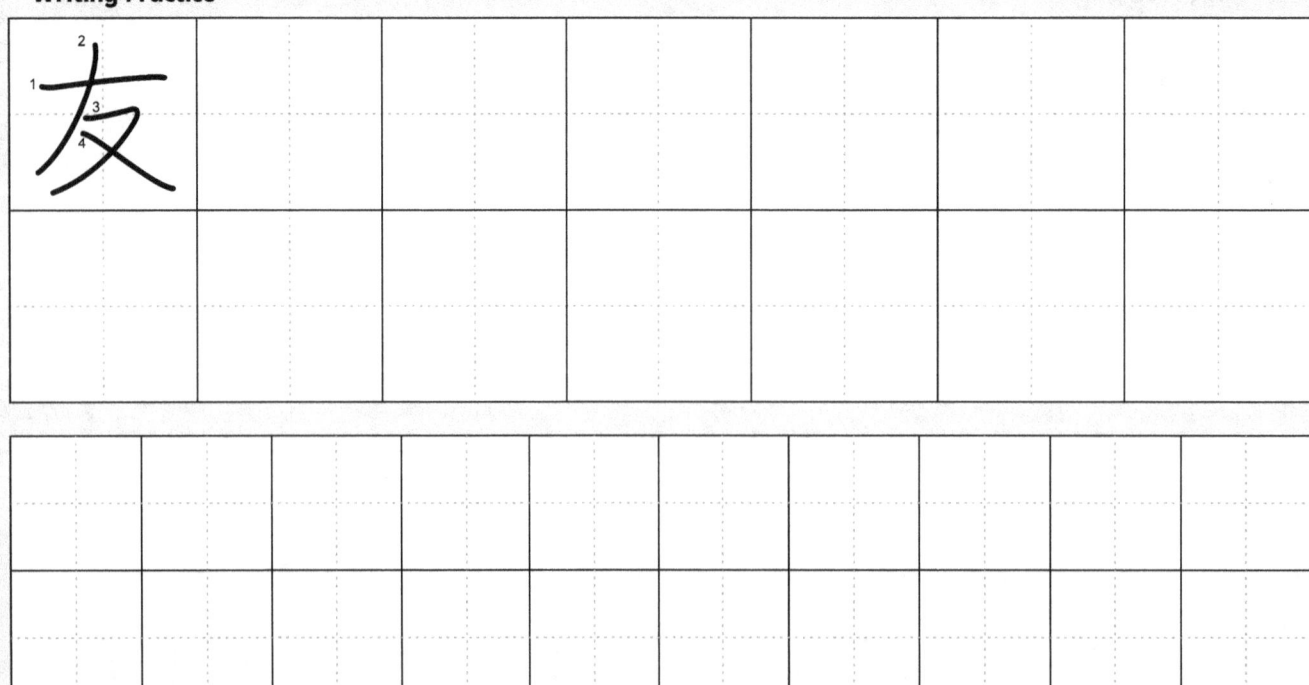

Kanji for People & Things

Meaning(s)	fire	Components	火
Radical	火 (灬) (fire)	Kun'yomi	ひ、-び、ほ-
Strokes	4	On'yomi	カ

Vocabulary	Meaning	Pronunciation
火	fire, flame, blaze	ひ
小火	small fire	ボヤ
花火	fireworks	はなび
火曜日	Tuesday	かようび

Stroke Order

Writing Practice

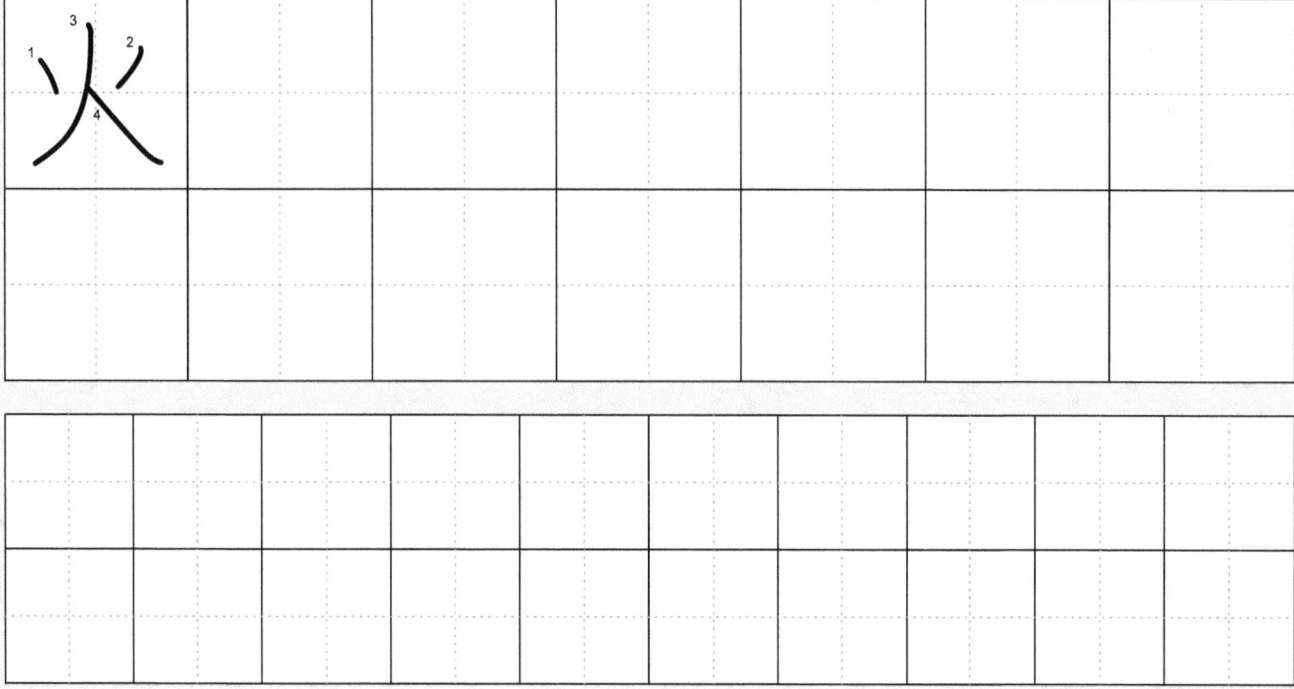

JLPT N5

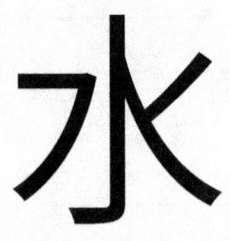

Meaning(s)	water	Components	水
Radical	水 (氵, 氺) (water)	Kun'yomi	みず、みず-
Strokes	4	On'yomi	スイ

Vocabulary	Meaning		Pronunciation
水	water (drinking), liquid, flood		みず
浄水	clean water, purified water		ジョウスイ
水泳	swimming		すいえい
水曜日	Wednesday		すいようび

Stroke Order

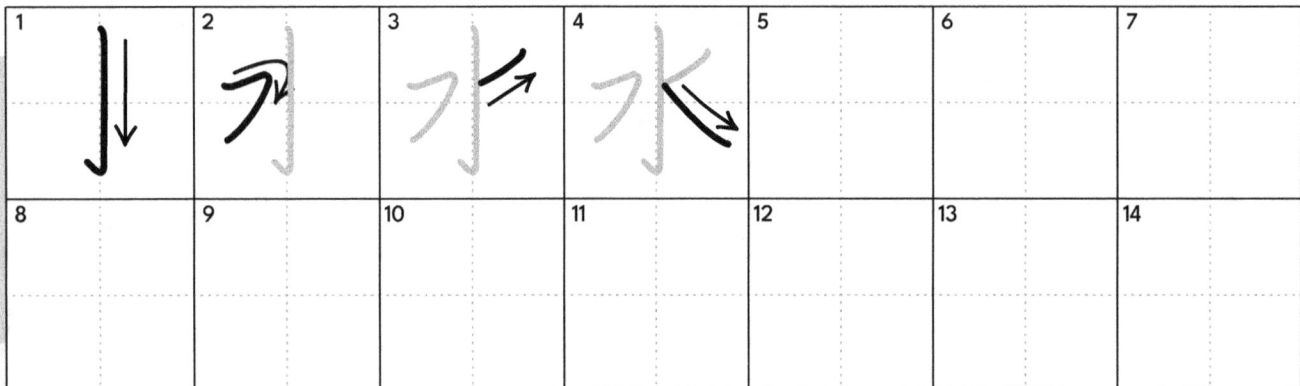

Writing Practice

Meaning(s)	tree, wood	Components	木
Radical	木 (tree)	Kun'yomi	き、こ-
Strokes	4	On'yomi	ボク、モク

Vocabulary	Meaning	Pronunciation
木	tree, shrub, bush, wood, timber	き
木木 (木々)	to be able to	きぎ
木材	lumber, timber, wood	モクザイ
木曜日	Thursday	もくようび

Stroke Order

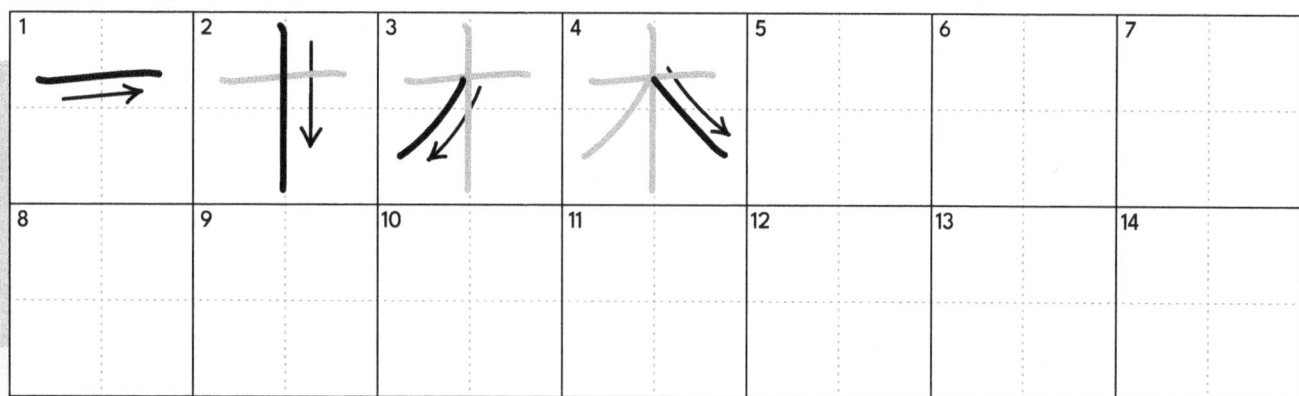

Writing Practice

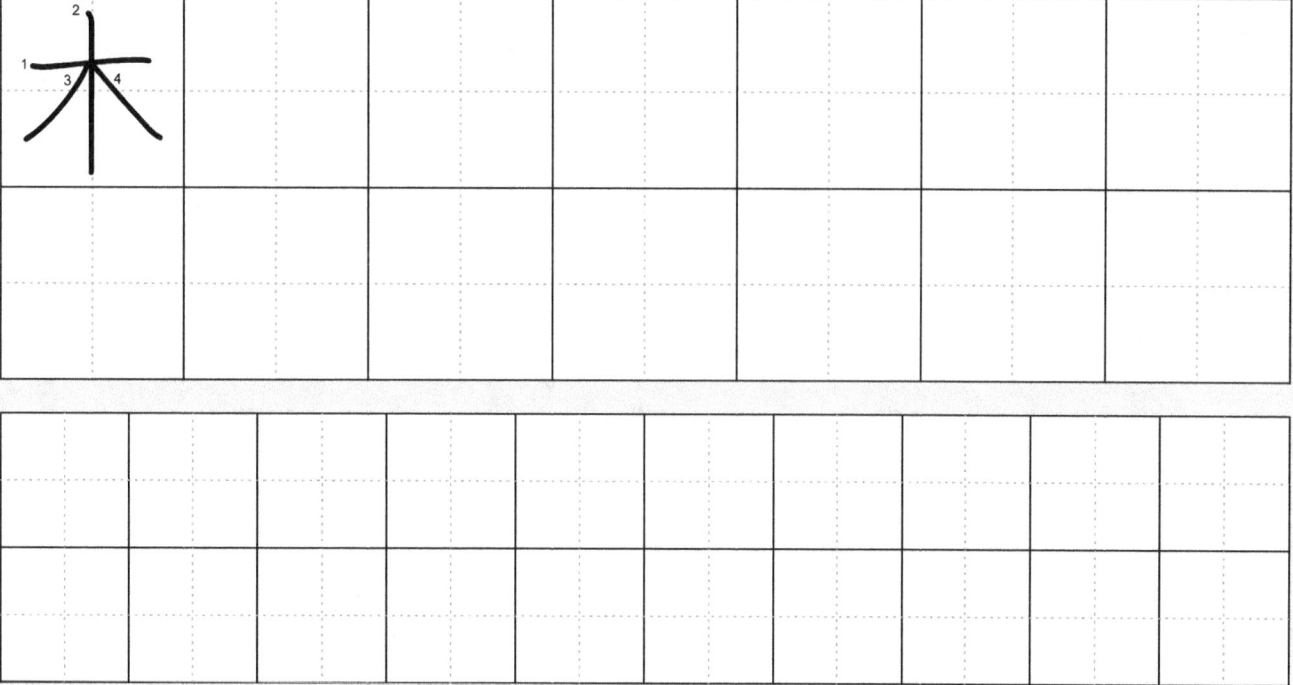

JLPT N5

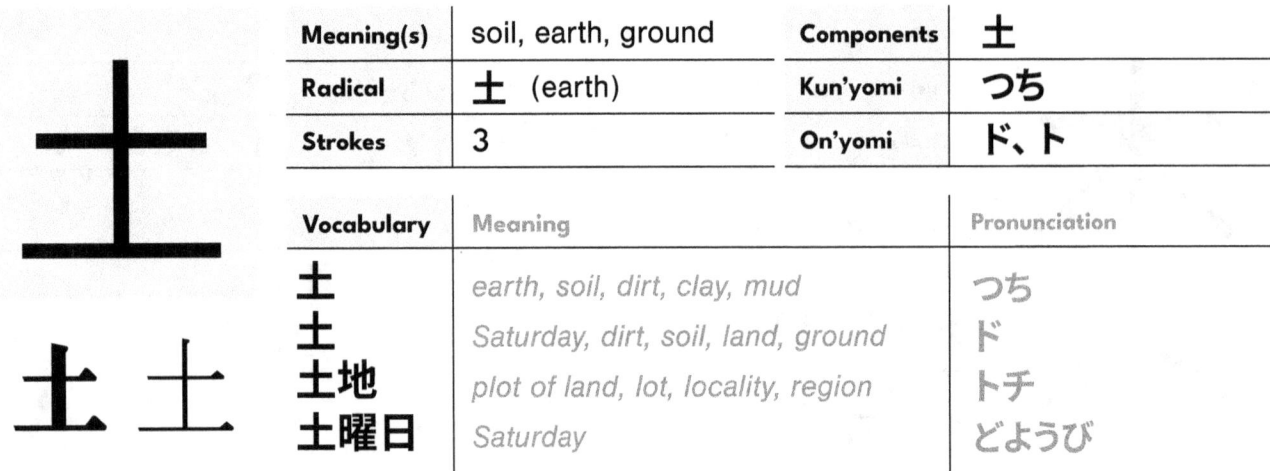

Meaning(s)	soil, earth, ground	Components	土
Radical	土 (earth)	Kun'yomi	つち
Strokes	3	On'yomi	ド、ト

Vocabulary	Meaning	Pronunciation
土	earth, soil, dirt, clay, mud	つち
土	Saturday, dirt, soil, land, ground	ド
土地	plot of land, lot, locality, region	トチ
土曜日	Saturday	どようび

Stroke Order

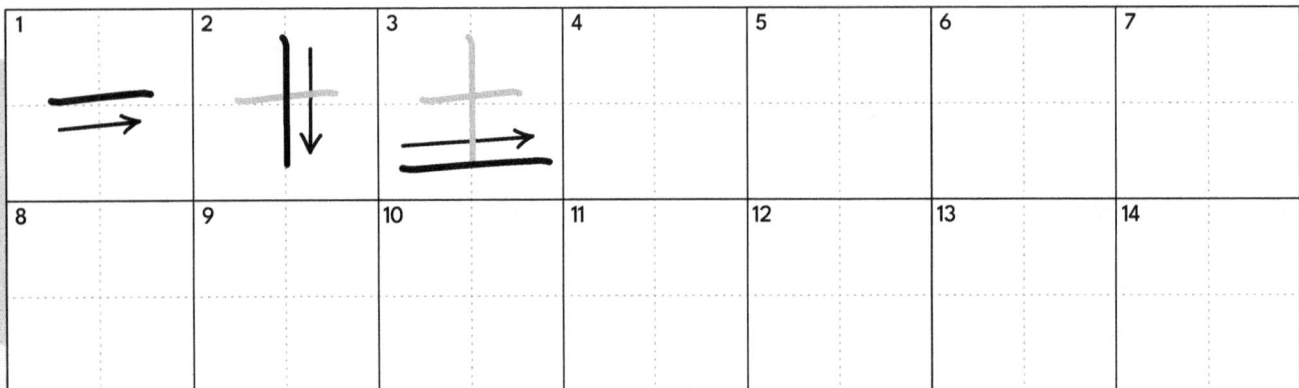

Writing Practice

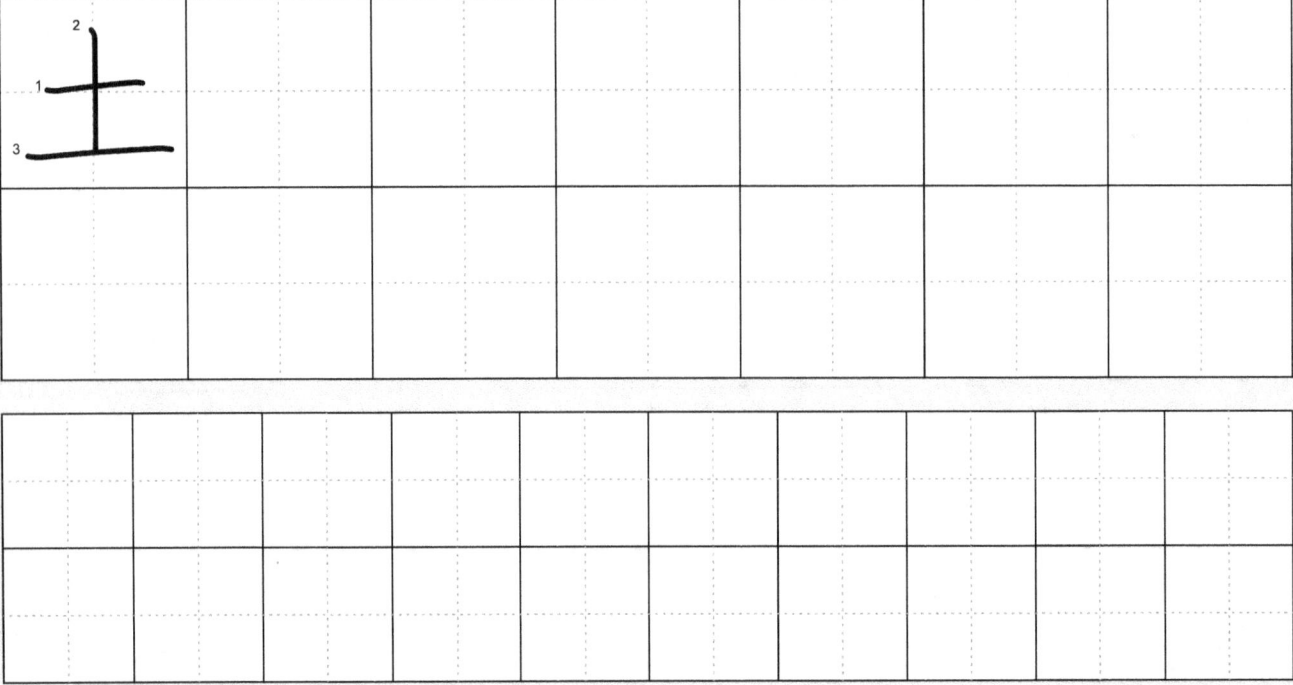

Kanji for People & Things

Meaning(s)	gold, money, metal	Components	个 ハ 幷 王 金
Radical	金 (金) (gold, metal)	Kun'yomi	かね、かな-、-がね
Strokes	8	On'yomi	キン、コン、ゴン

Vocabulary	Meaning	Pronunciation
金	money, metal	かね
金	gold (metal, color, medal), money	キン
納金	payment	ノウキン
金曜日	Friday	きんようび

Stroke Order

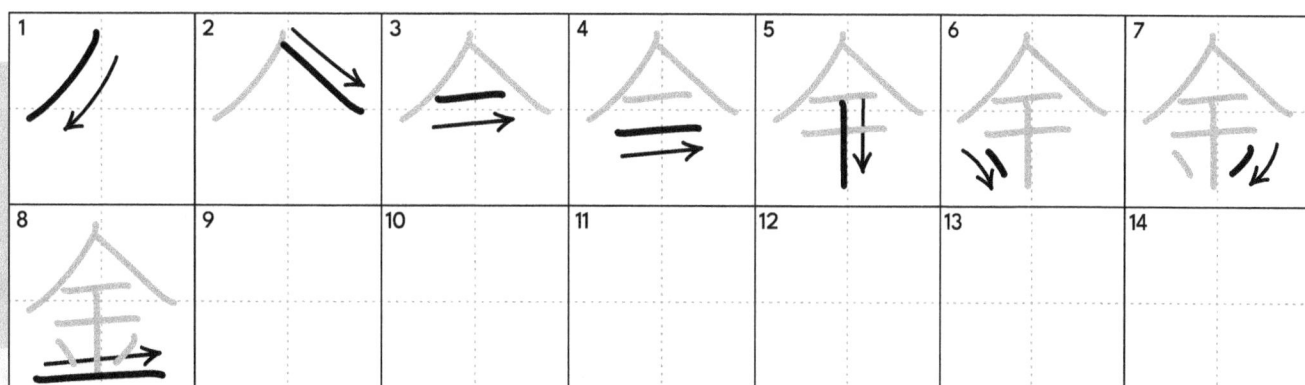

Writing Practice

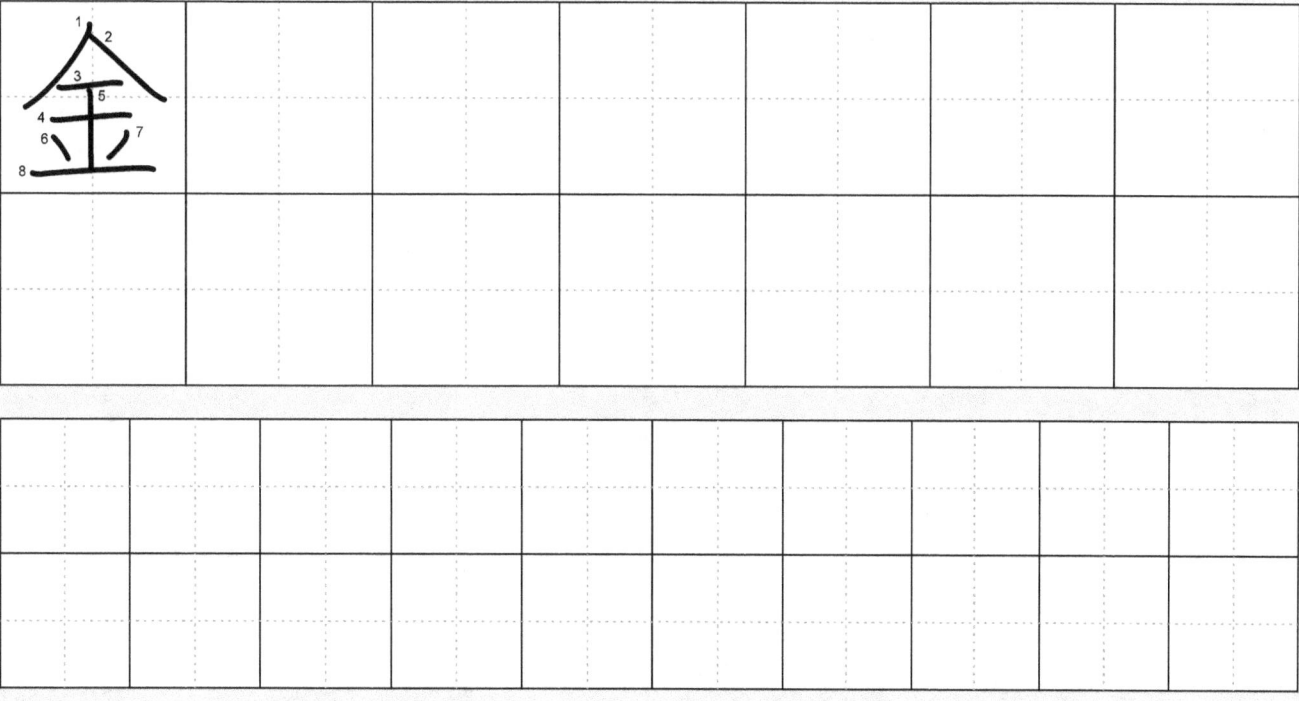

JLPT N5

Meaning(s)	book, true, main, real	**Components**	一 木
Radical	木 (tree)	**Kun'yomi**	もと
Strokes	5	**On'yomi**	ホン

Vocabulary	**Meaning**		**Pronunciation**
本	book, volume, script, this, present		ホン
本棚	bookshelf, bookcase, bookshelves		ほんだな
大本 (元)	root, origin, source, cause, basis		おおもと
日本語	Japanese (language)		にほんご

Stroke Order

Writing Practice

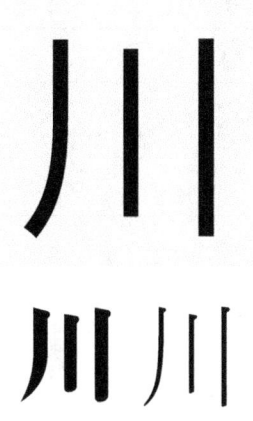

Meaning(s)	stream, river	Components	川
Radical	巛 (川、巜) (river)	Kun'yomi	かわ
Strokes	3	On'yomi	セン

Vocabulary	Meaning	Pronunciation
川	river, stream	かわ
山川	mountains and rivers	サンセン / さんせん
川岸	riverbank, riverside	かわぎし
堀川	canal	ほりかわ

Stroke Order

Writing Practice

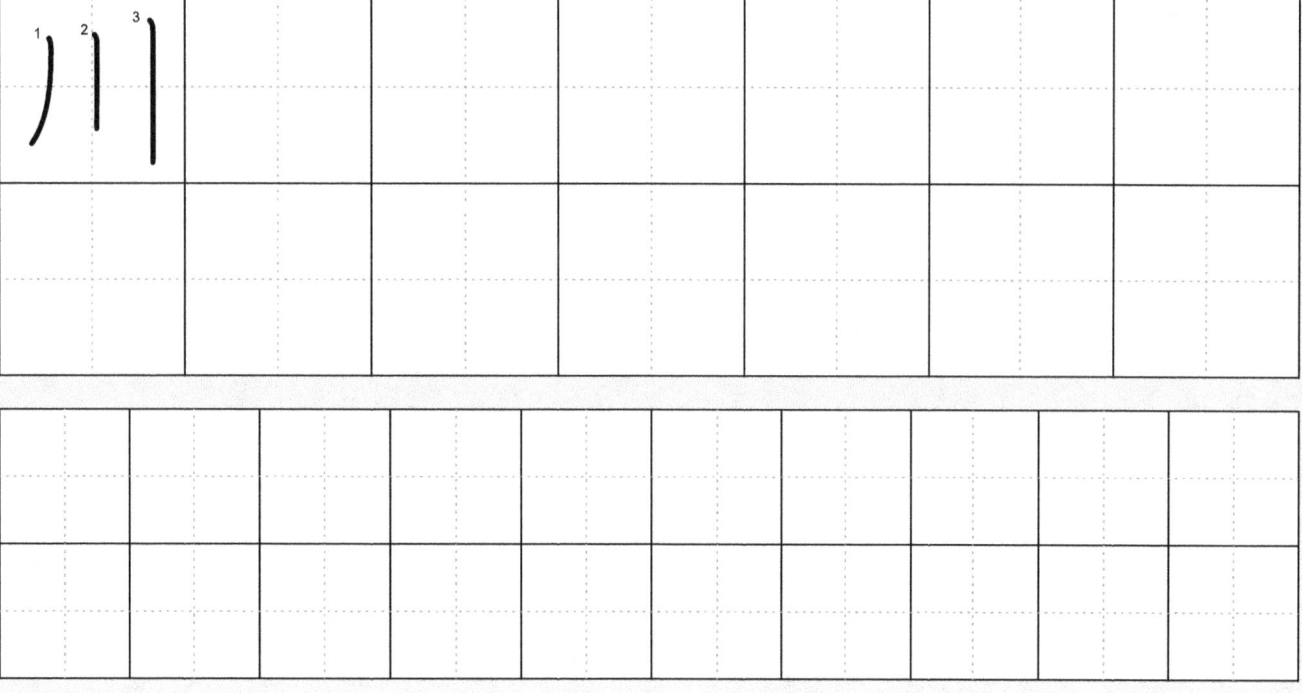

JLPT N5

Meaning(s)	flower, blossom	**Components**	化 ヒ 艾
Radical	艸 (艹) (grass)	**Kun'yomi**	はな
Strokes	7	**On'yomi**	カ、ケ

Vocabulary	Meaning	Pronunciation
花	flower, blossom, bloom, petal	はな
花見	flower/cherry blossom viewing	はなみ
花形	loral pattern, flourish, ornament	ハナガタ / はながた
花火	fireworks	はなび

Stroke Order

Writing Practice

Kanji for People & Things

Meaning(s)	spirit, mind, air,	Components	丶ノ气乞
Radical	气 (steam, breath)	Kun'yomi	き
Strokes	6	On'yomi	キ、ケ

Vocabulary	Meaning		Pronunciation
気	spirit, mind, heart, nature, motivation		き / キ
元気	lively, full of spirit, energetic, vigorous		げんき
病気	illness, disease, sickness		びょうき
気合	(fighting) spirit, motivation, effort		きあい / キアイ

Stroke Order

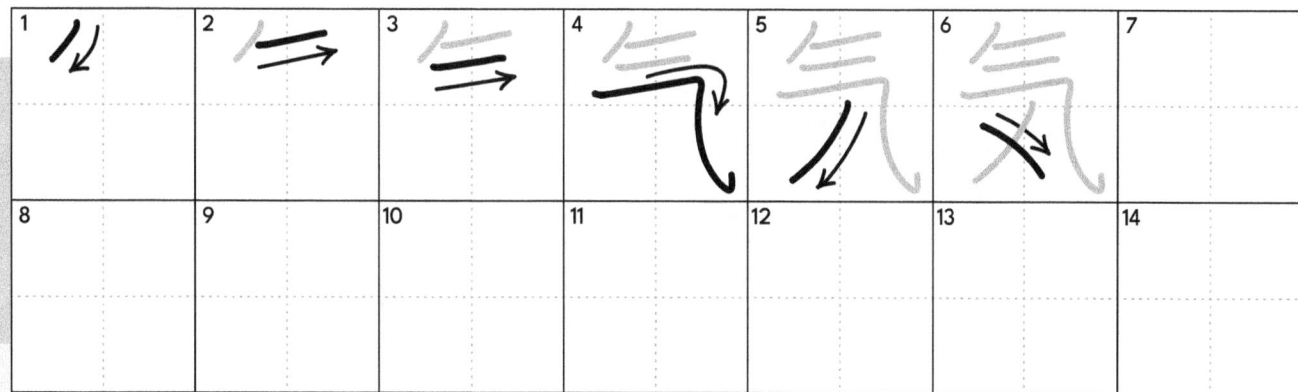

Writing Practice

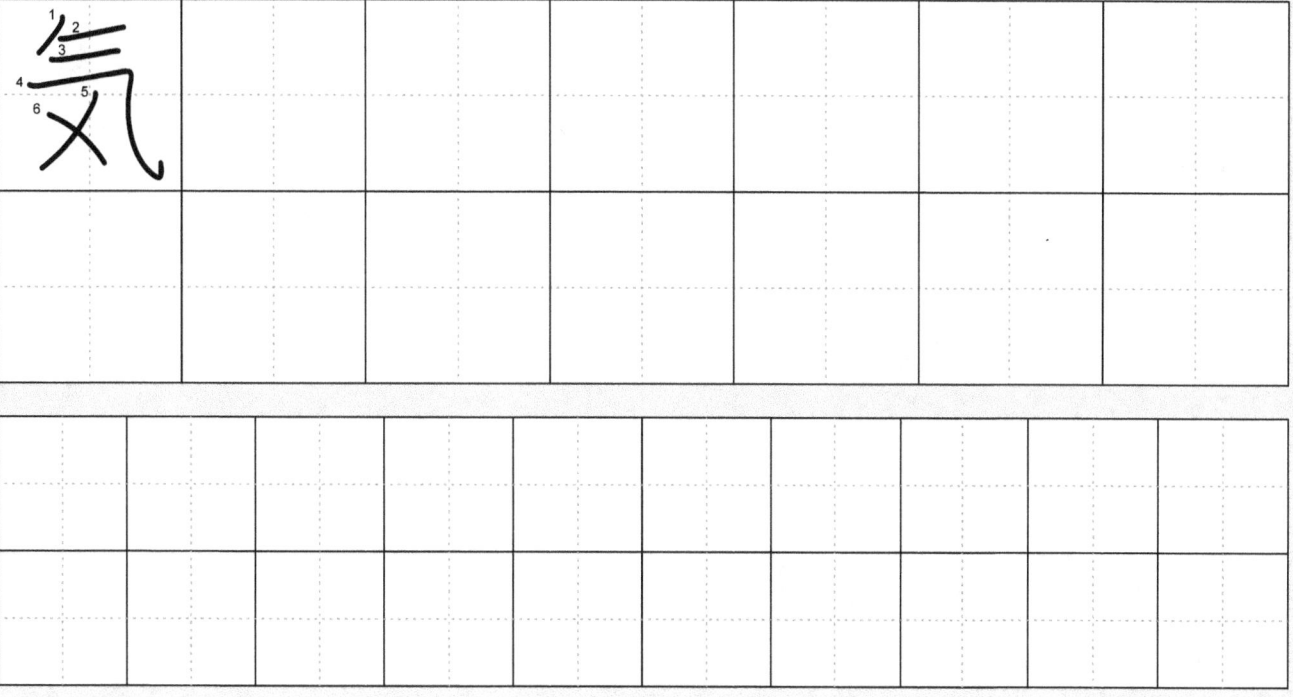

JLPT N5

Meaning(s)	life, to live, birth	Components	生
Radical	生 (life)	Kun'yomi	い.きる、い.かす
Strokes	5	On'yomi	セイ、ショウ

Vocabulary	Meaning	Pronunciation
生きる	to live, to exist, to make a living	いきる
生徒	pupil, student	せいと
生	life, living, I, me, myself, student	セイ
先生	sensei, teacher, instructor, master	せんせい

Stroke Order

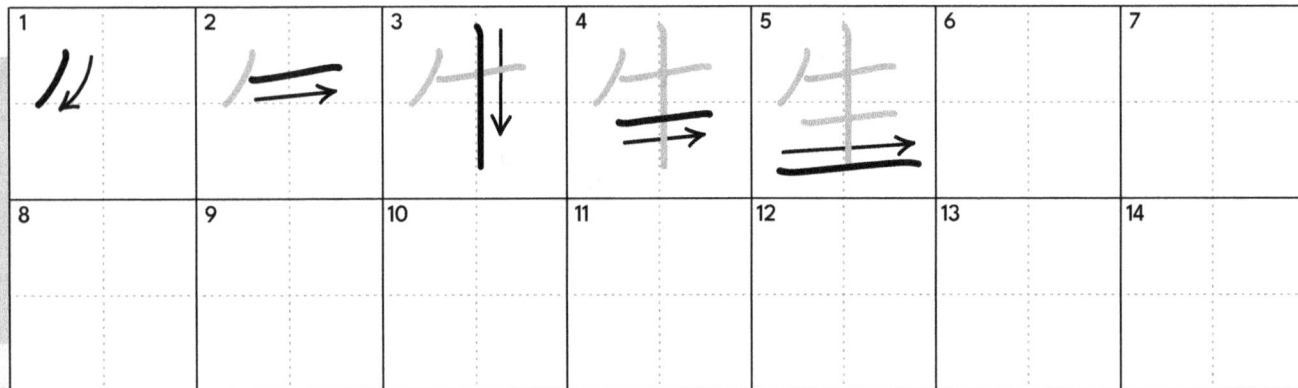

Writing Practice

Kanji for People & Things

Meaning(s)	fish	Components	杰田魚
Radical	魚 (fish)	Kun'yomi	うお、さかな、-ざかな
Strokes	11	On'yomi	ブン、モン

Vocabulary	Meaning	Pronunciation
魚	fish	さかな
魚市場	fish market	うおいちば
魚類	fish, fishes	ギョルイ
鮮魚	fresh fish	センギョ

Stroke Order

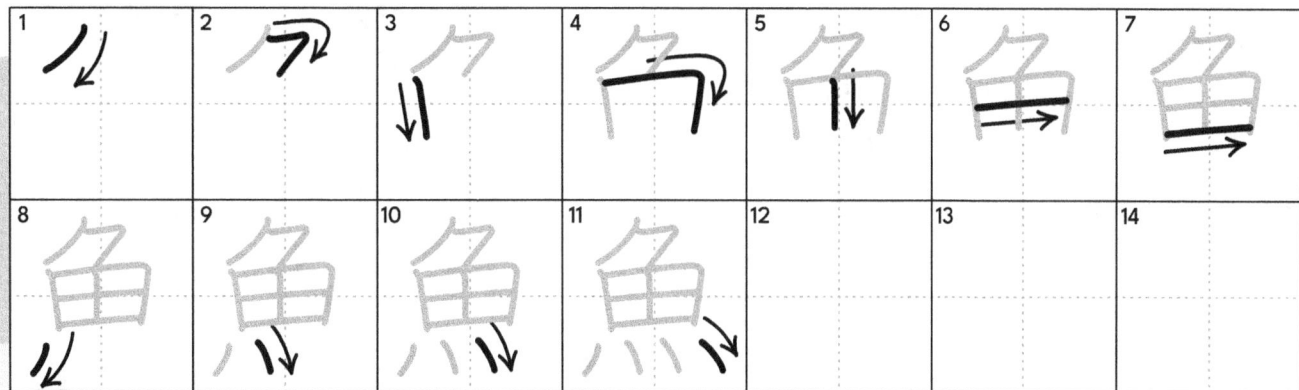

Writing Practice

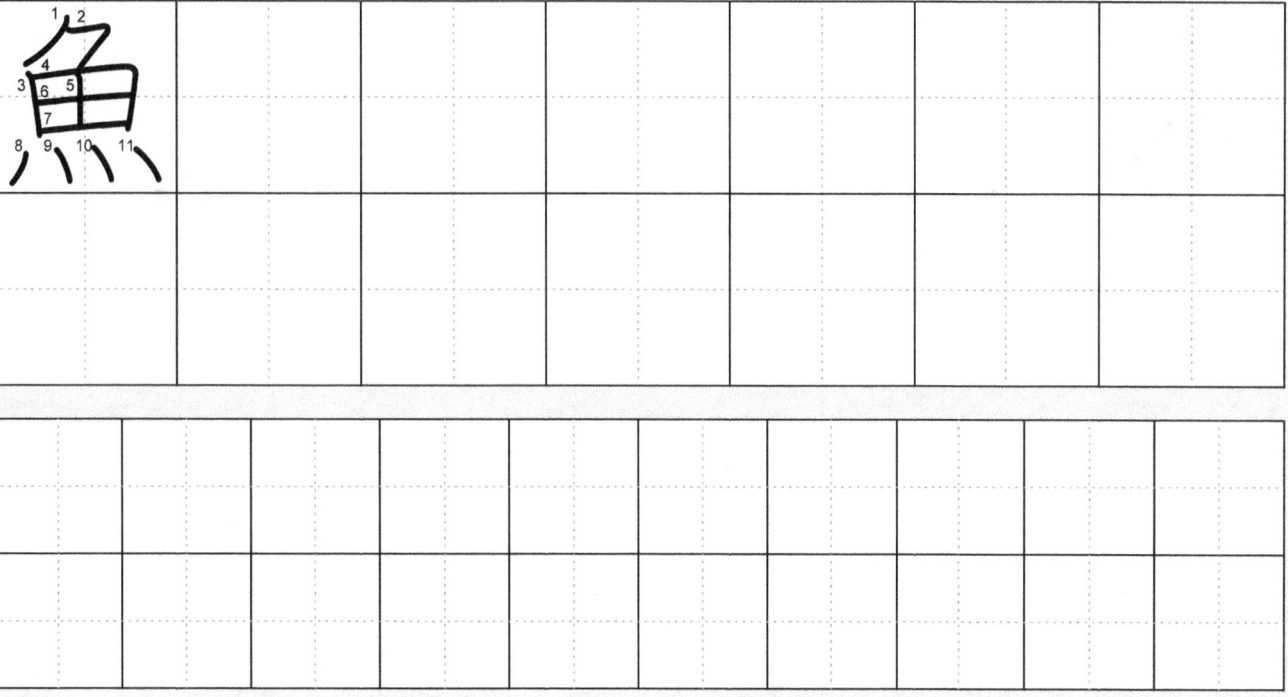

JLPT N5

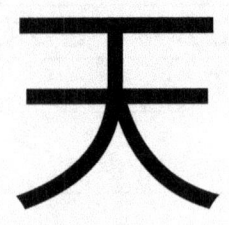

Meaning(s)	heavens, sky, imperial	**Components**	一 二 大	
Radical	大 (big)	**Kun'yomi**	あまつ、あめ、あま-	
Strokes	4	**On'yomi**	テン	

Vocabulary	Meaning	Pronunciation
天気	weather, the elements	てんき
天	sky, heaven, God	テン
天津	heavenly, imperial	あまつ
天	sky	あめ

Stroke Order

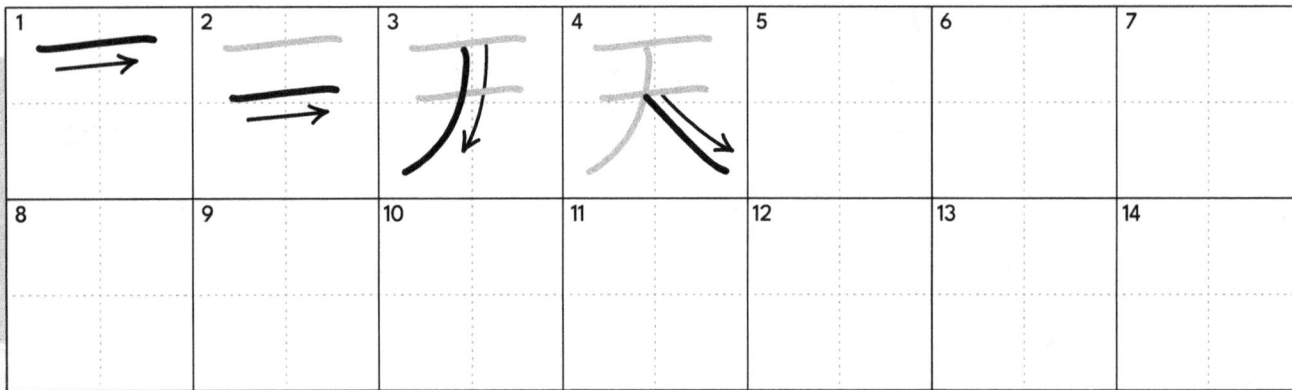

Writing Practice

Kanji for People & Things

Meaning(s)	empty, sky, void	Components	儿宀工穴
Radical	穴 (cave)	Kun'yomi	そら、あ.く、あ.き
Strokes	8	On'yomi	クウ

Vocabulary	Meaning		Pronunciation
空	sky, the air, the heavens, weather		そら
空	empty air, sky		クウ
空き	space, room, gap, vacancy		あき
空港	airport		くうこう

Stroke Order

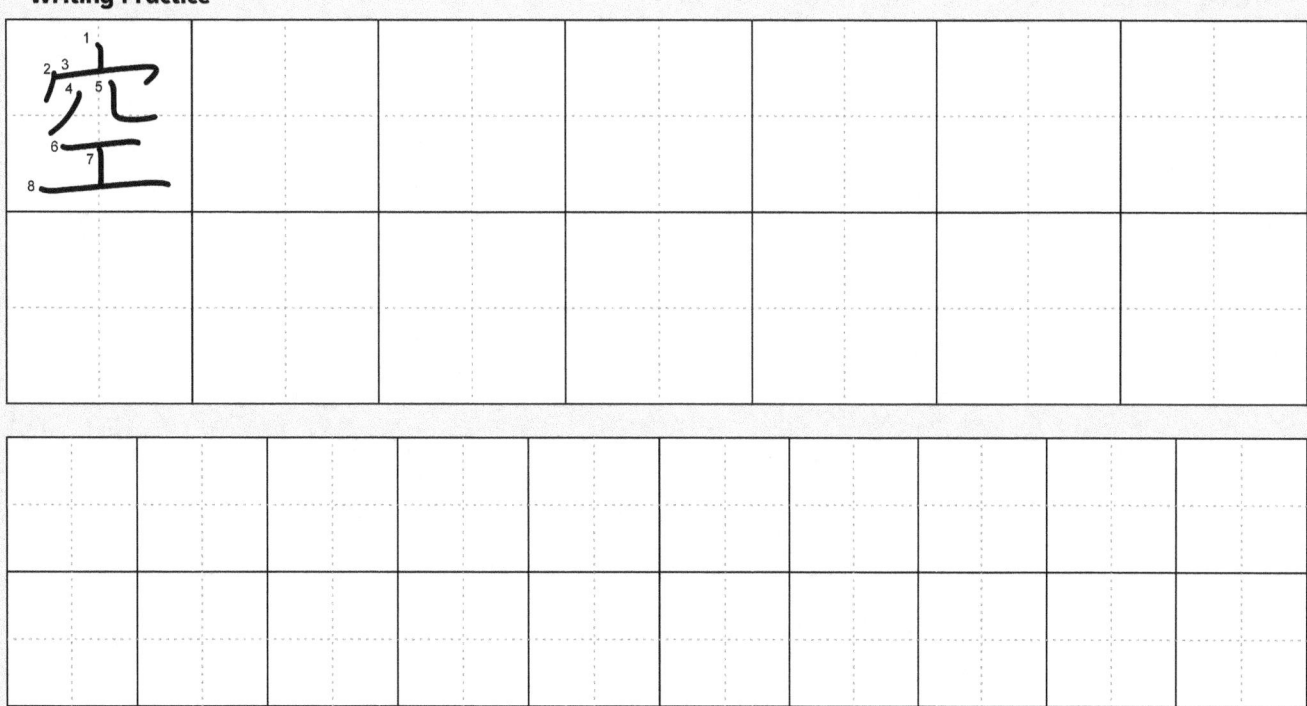

Writing Practice

JLPT N5

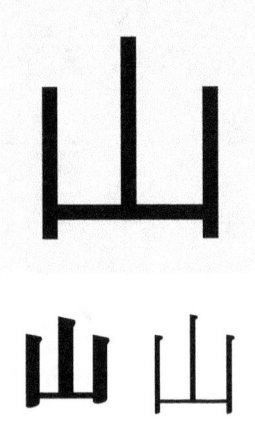

Meaning(s)	mountain	**Components**	山
Radical	山 (mountain)	**Kun'yomi**	やま
Strokes	3	**On'yomi**	サン、セン

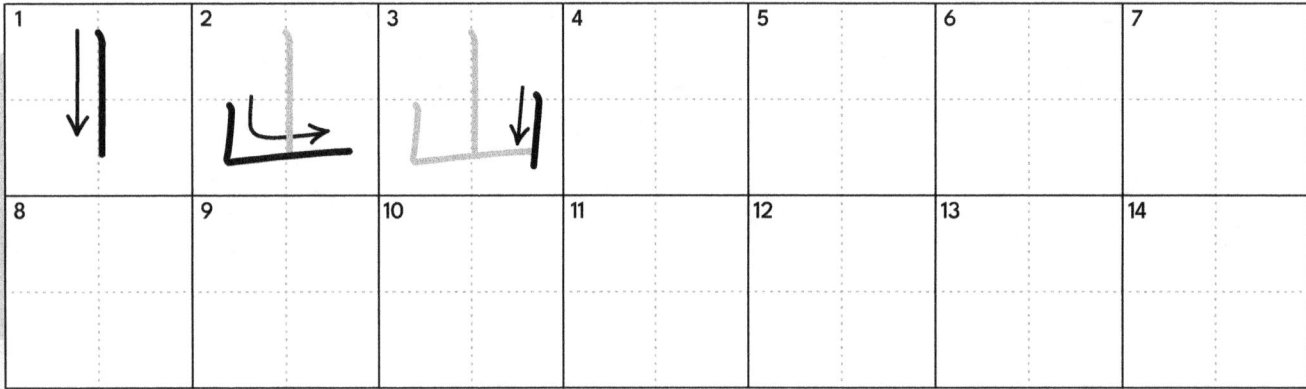

Vocabulary	Meaning	Pronunciation
山	mountain, hill, mine	やま
山	Mt., Mount	サン
火山	volcano	さんみゃく
雪山	snowy mountain	セツザン

Stroke Order

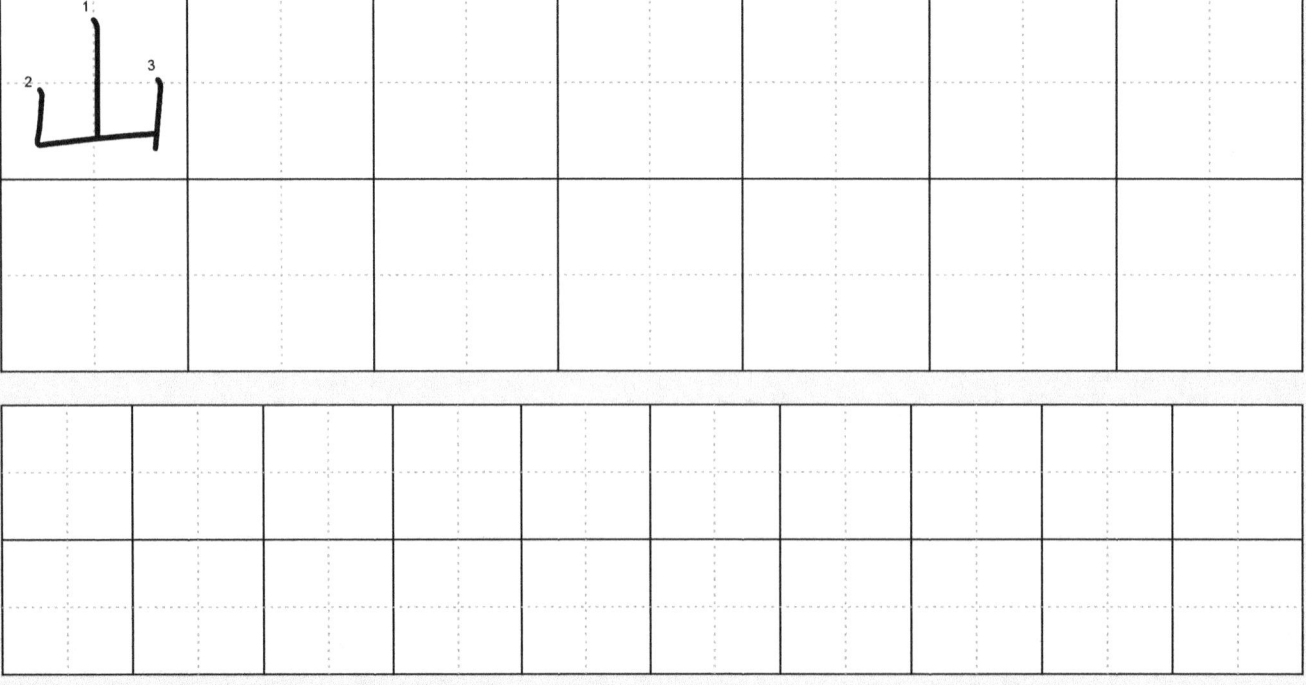

Writing Practice

Kanji for People & Things

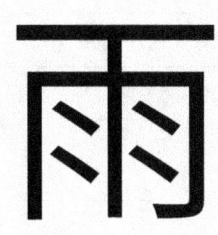

Meaning(s)	rain	Components	雨
Radical	雨 (rain)	Kun'yomi	あめ、あま-、-さめ
Strokes	8	On'yomi	ウ

Vocabulary	Meaning	Pronunciation
雨	rain, rainy day, rainy weather	あめ
雨降り	rainfall, rainy weather, rainy, wet	あめふり
雨季	rainy season	ウキ
雷雨	thunderstorm	らいう

Stroke Order

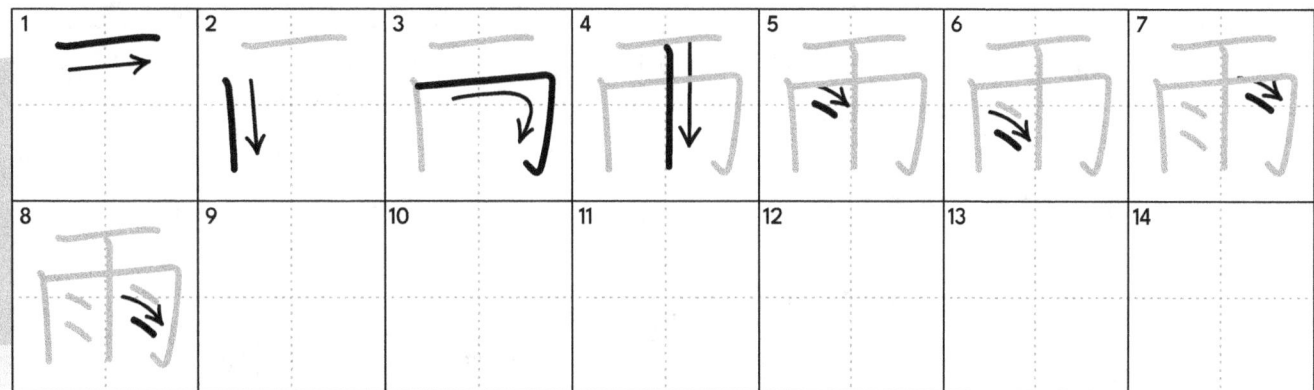

Writing Practice

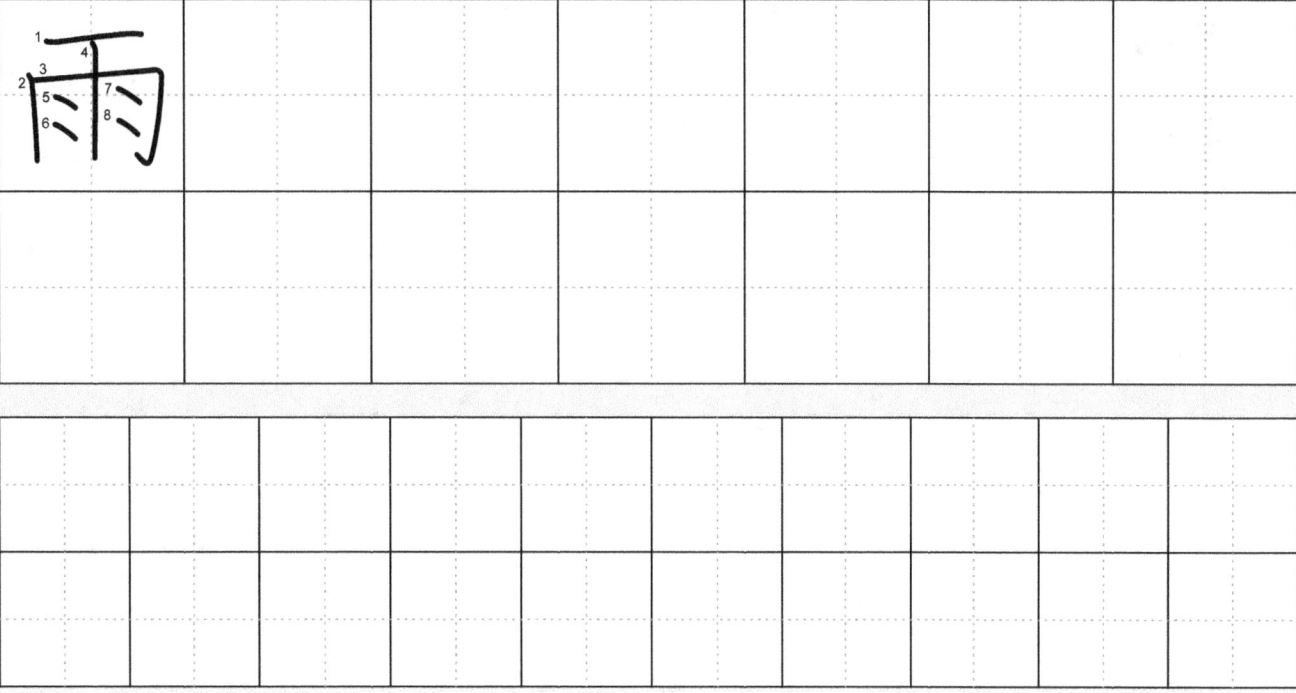

JLPT N5

Meaning(s)	electricity	Components	乙 田 雨
Radical	雨 (rain)	Kun'yomi	(none)
Strokes	13	On'yomi	デン

Vocabulary	Meaning	Pronunciation
電話	phone call	でんわ
電池	battery, cell	でんち
電化	elctrification	デンカ
電気	electricity	でんき

Stroke Order

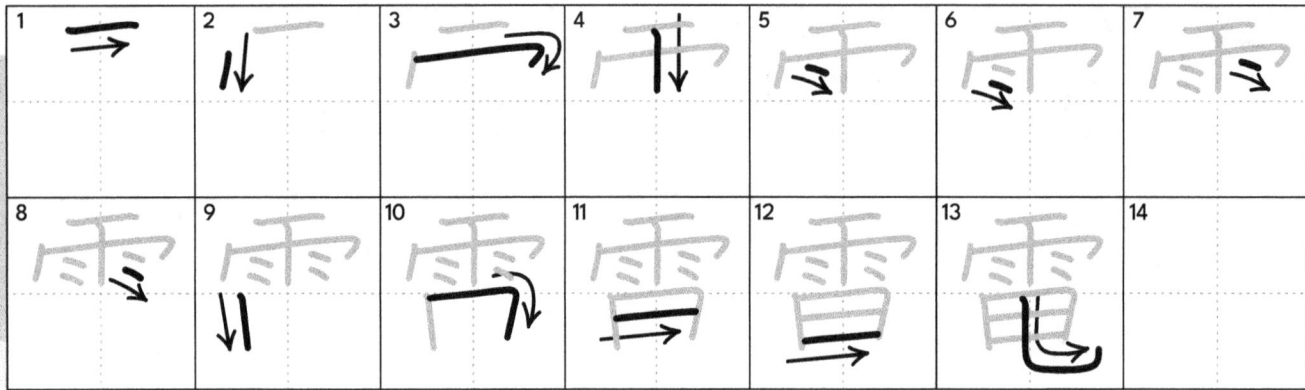

Writing Practice

Kanji for People & Things

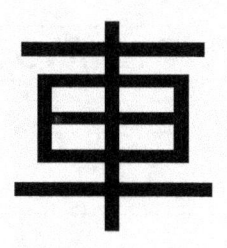

Meaning(s)	car, vehicle	Components	車
Radical	車 (car, cart)	Kun'yomi	くるま
Strokes	7	On'yomi	シャ

Vocabulary	Meaning	Pronunciation
車	car, automobile, vehicle	くるま
車	car, vehicle	シャ
車椅子	wheelchair	くるまいす
電車	electric train, train	でんしゃ

Stroke Order

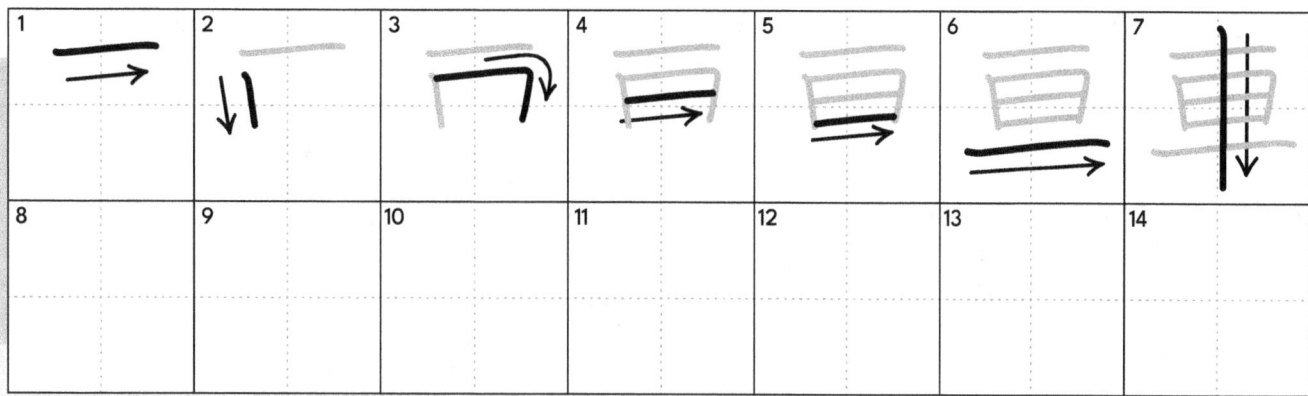

Writing Practice

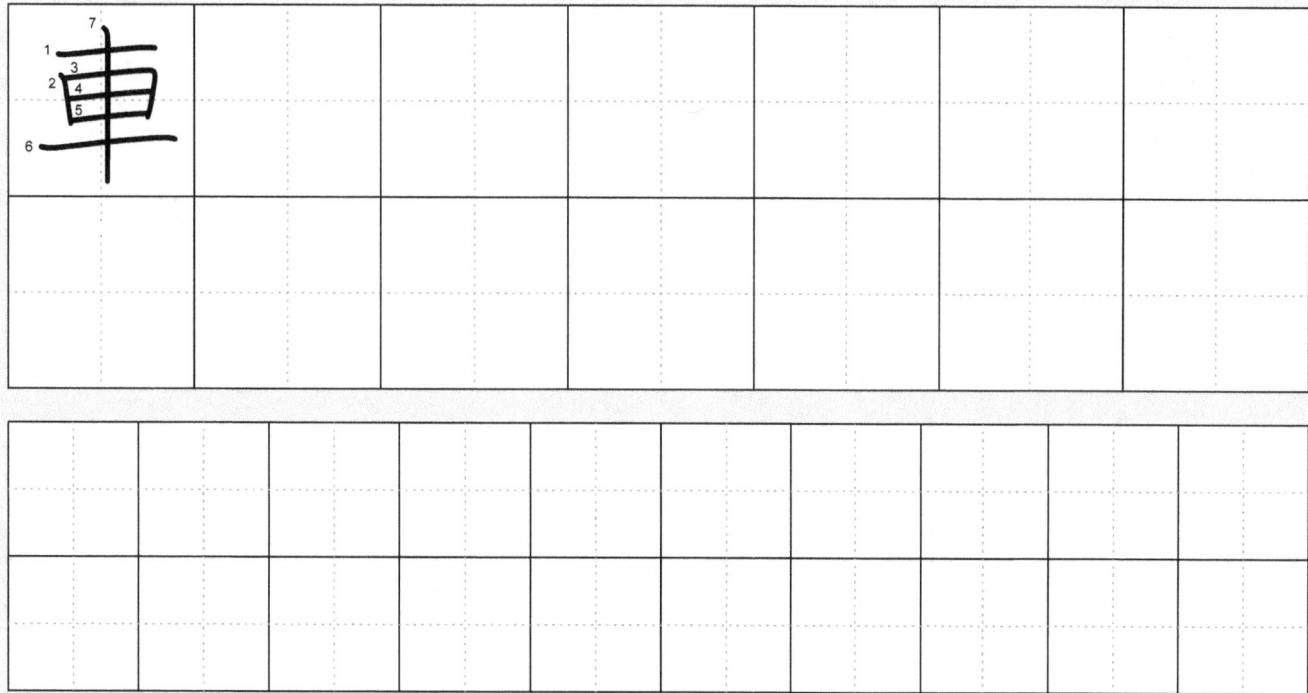

JLPT N5

Meaning(s)	word, language, speech	**Components**	耳、
Radical	言 (訁) (speech)	**Kun'yomi**	かた.る、かた.らう
Strokes	14	**On'yomi**	ゴ

Vocabulary	Meaning	Pronunciation
語	word, language, speech	ゴ
英語	English (language)	えいご
語る	to talk about, to speak of, to tell	かたる
語学	study of foreign languages	ゴガク

Stroke Order

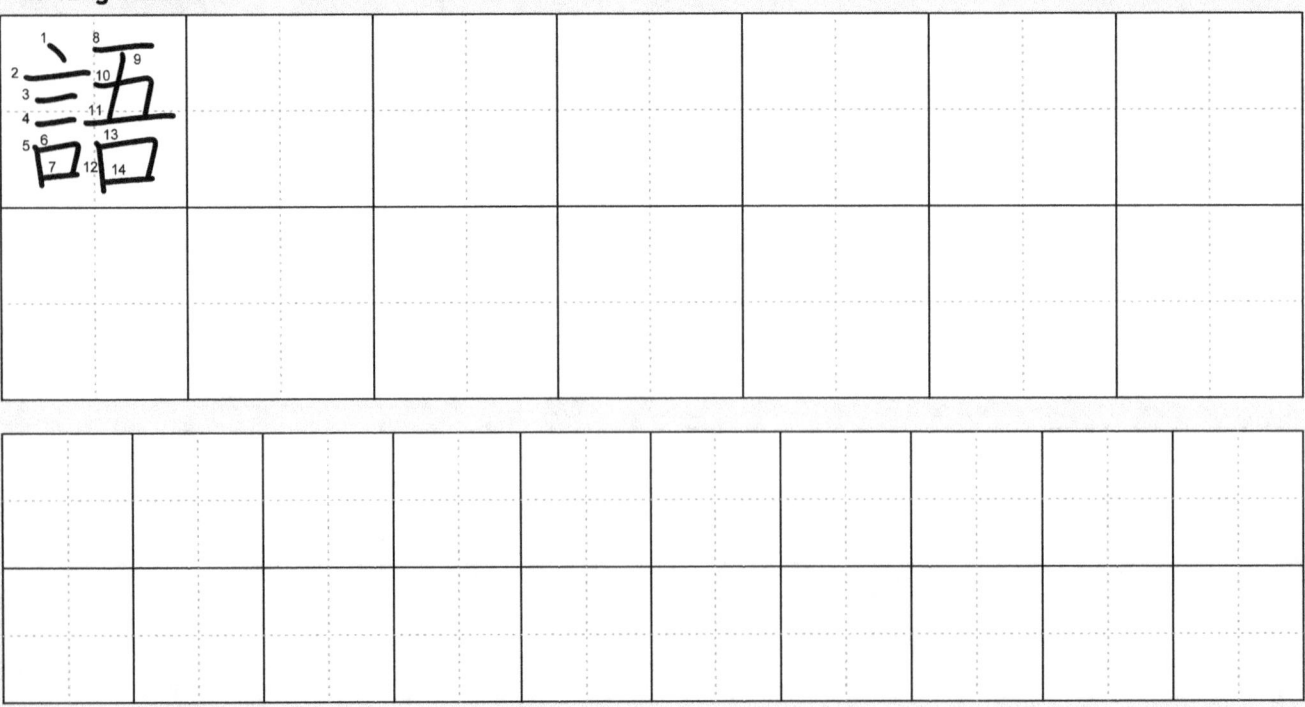

Writing Practice

Kanji for People & Things

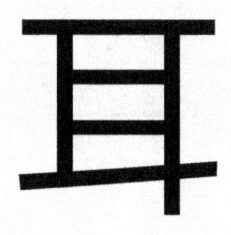

Meaning(s)	ear	Components	耳
Radical	耳 (ear)	Kun'yomi	みみ
Strokes	6	On'yomi	ジ

Vocabulary	Meaning	Pronunciation
耳	ear	みみ
左耳	left ear	ひだりみみ
遠耳	sharp hearing	とおみみ
耳障り	offensive (to the ear)	みみざわり

Stroke Order

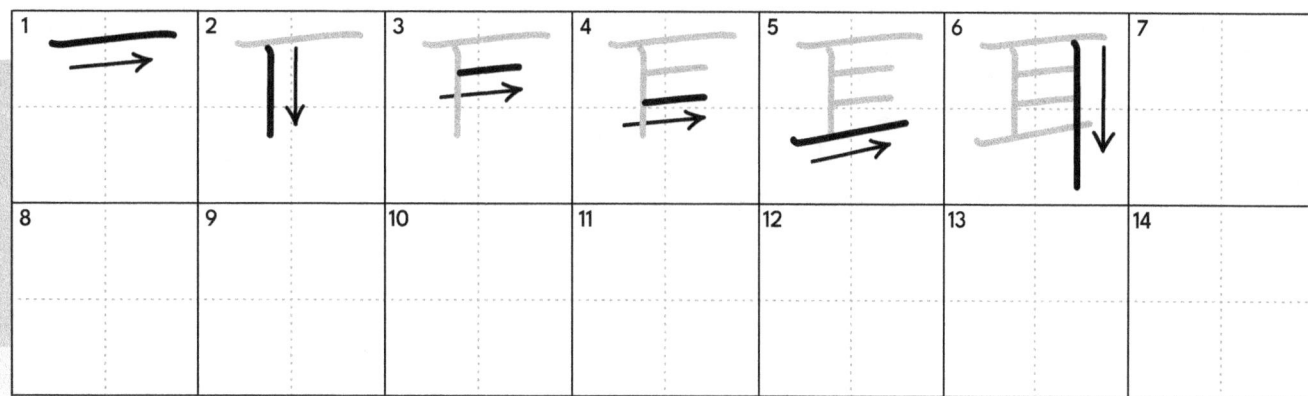

Writing Practice

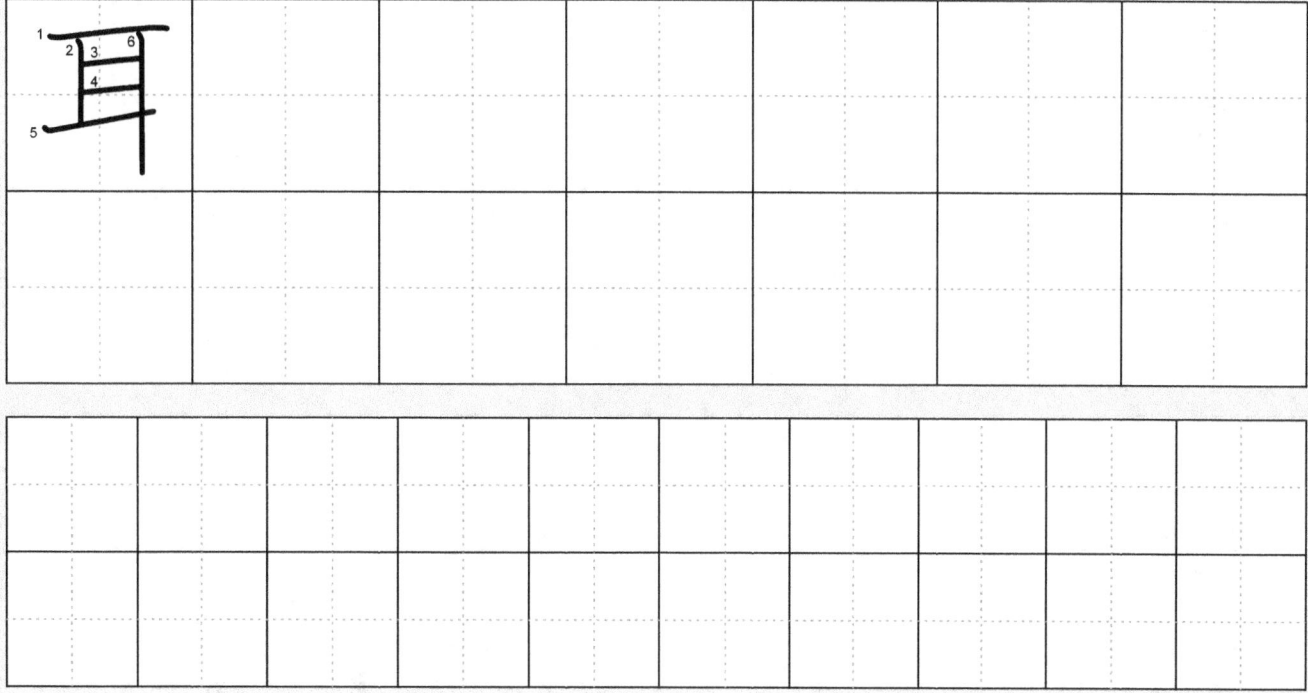

JLPT N5

Meaning(s)	hand		Components	手
Radical	手 (扌㐅) (hand)		Kun'yomi	て、て-、-て、た-
Strokes	4		On'yomi	シュ、ズ

Vocabulary	Meaning	Pronunciation
手	hand, arm, handle	て
手紙	letter, note, mail	てがみ
手記	note, memorandum	シュキ
切手	stamp (postage)	きって

Stroke Order

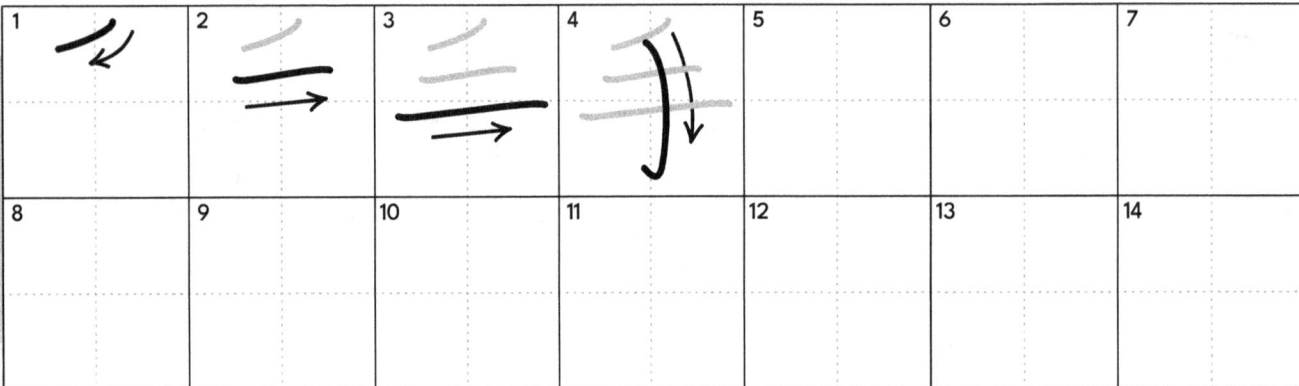

Writing Practice

Kanji for People & Things

Meaning(s)	leg, foot	Components	口止足
Radical	足 (⻊) (foot)	Kun'yomi	あし、た.りる、た.る
Strokes	7	On'yomi	ソク

Vocabulary	Meaning	Pronunciation
足	foot, paw, leg	あし
足す	to add (numbers, something)	たす
足跡	footprints	あしあと
足りる	to be sufficient, enough	たりる

Stroke Order

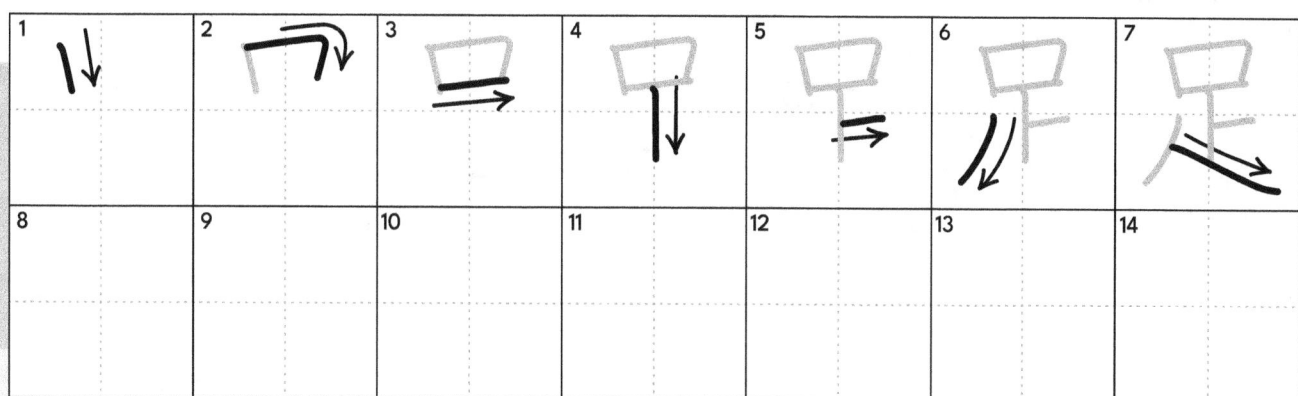

Writing Practice

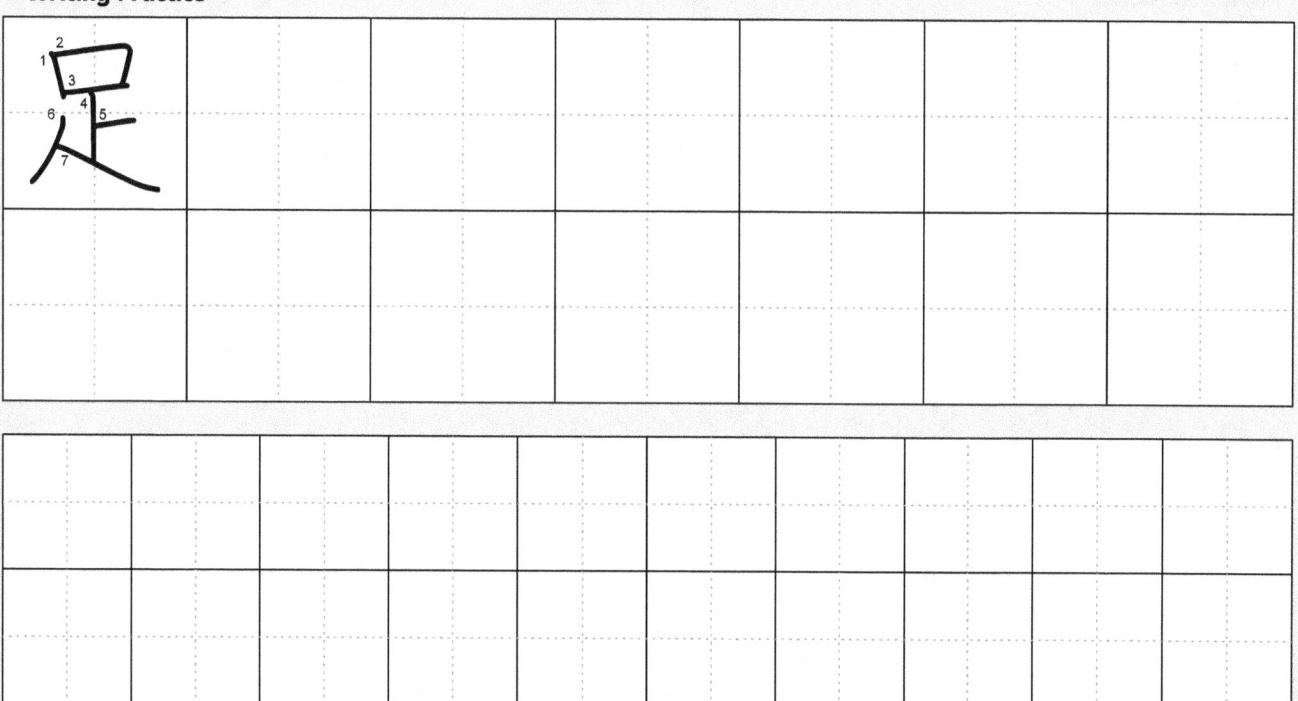

JLPT N5

Meaning(s)	eye, class, look, vision	Components	目
Radical	目 (eye)	Kun'yomi	め、-め、ま-
Strokes	5	On'yomi	モク、ボク

Vocabulary	Meaning	Pronunciation
目	eye, eyeball, eyesight, sight	め
駄目	no good, useless, broken	だめ
目的	purpose, goal, aim, objective	もくてき
細目	particulars, details, specified items	サイモク

Stroke Order

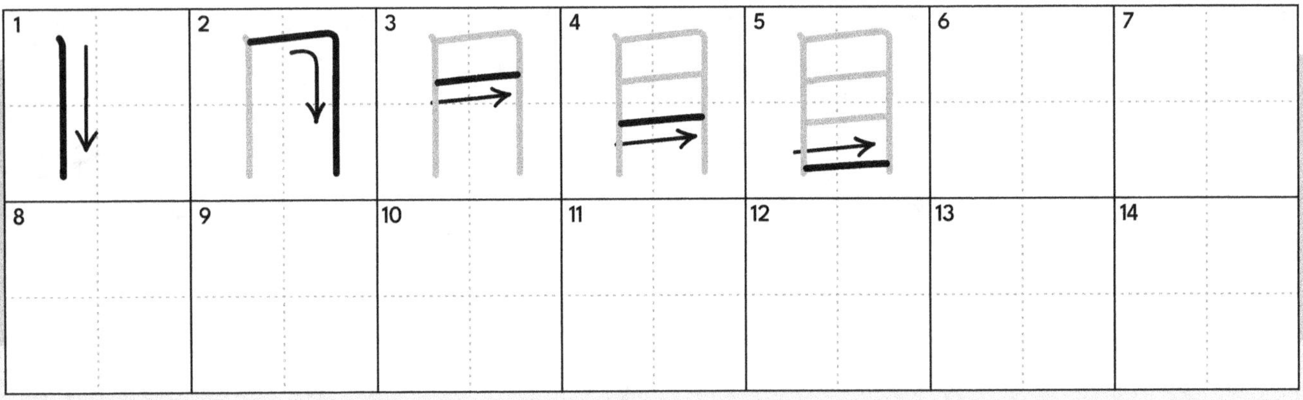

Writing Practice

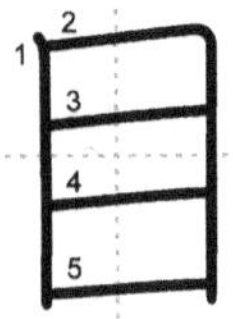

Kanji for People & Things

Meaning(s)	mouth, speech	Components	口 口
Radical	口 (mouth)	Kun'yomi	くち
Strokes	3	On'yomi	コウ、ク

Vocabulary	Meaning	Pronunciation
口	mouth, opening, hole, gap, door	くち
出口	exit, gateway, way out, outlet	でぐち
人口	population, common talk	じんこう
大口	big mouth, boastful speech, bragging	おおぐち

Stroke Order

Writing Practice

JLPT N5

Meaning(s)	name, noted, reputation	**Components**	口 夕
Radical	口 (mouth, opening)	**Kun'yomi**	な、-な
Strokes	6	**On'yomi**	メイ、ミョウ

Vocabulary	Meaning	Pronunciation
名	people counter, famous, great, noun	メイ
名前	name, given name, title	なまえ
名画	famous picture, masterpiece (painting)	メイガ
仮名	alias, pseudonym, pen name	かめい

Stroke Order

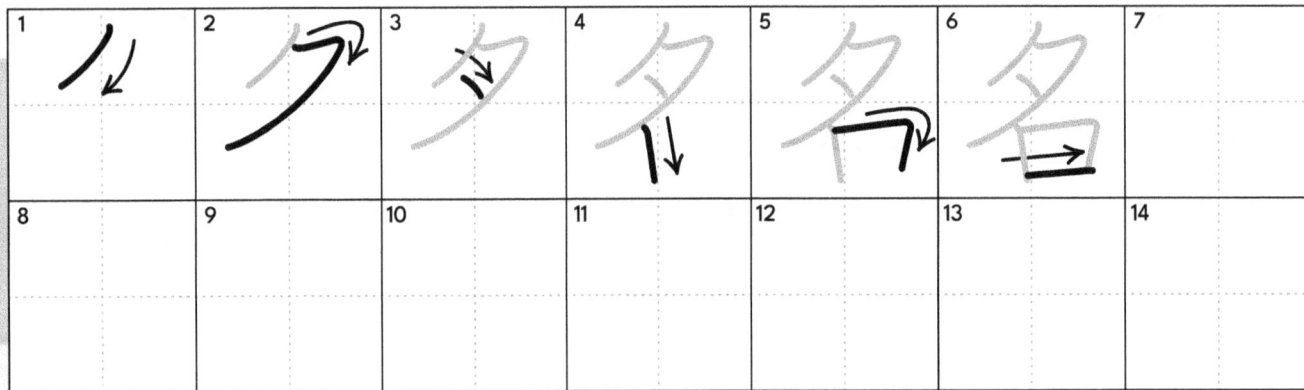

Writing Practice

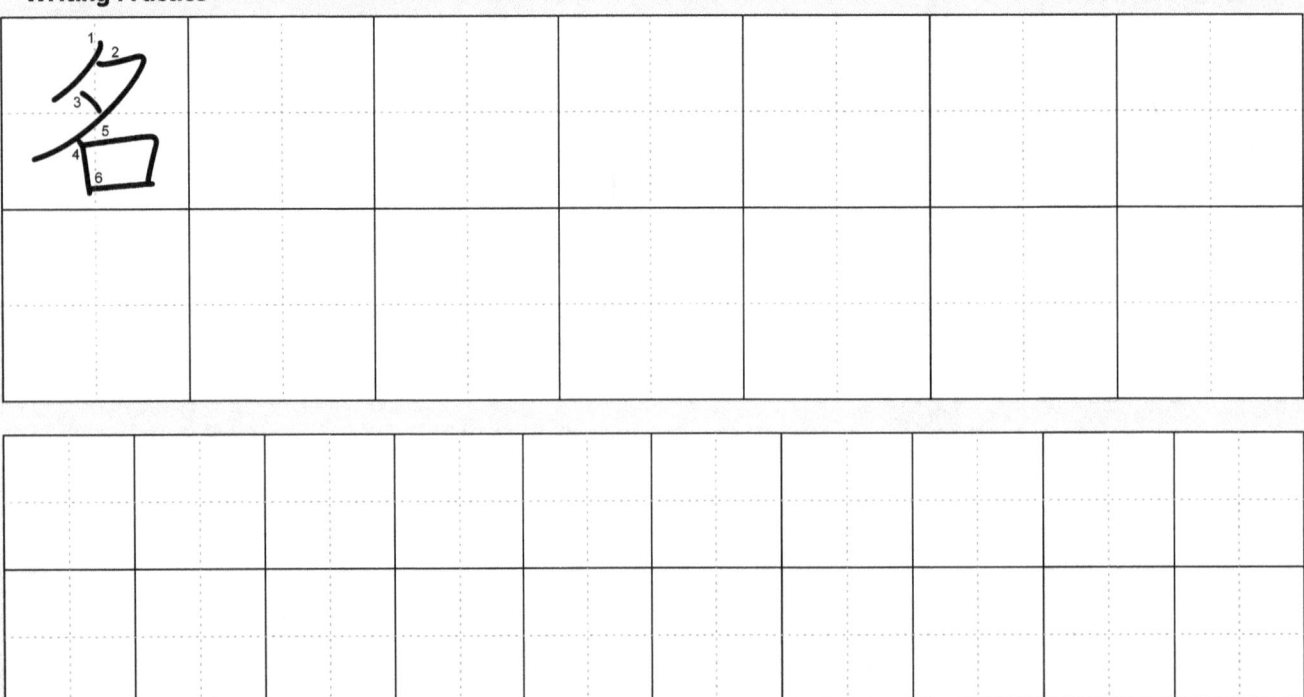

Kanji for People & Things

Family Vocabulary

While this group of kanji contained some basic terms for people and family members, the vocabulary used for addressing relatives is extensive and complicated. There are different names for relatives, depending on who we talk about and with whom we discuss them.

In Japanese culture, we refer to our family members with humble language but use more respectful terms for those of another person *(see p.330 - 'Language of Respect')*. It gets more complex when you consider that we use different words to directly address our family members, with separate terms that differentiate older siblings from younger ones. The correct name varies based on the formality of the situation too.

This chart shows some of the variations, but it is far from exhaustive:

	① Address your family (Polite)	② Refer to another's family (Polite)	③ Refer to your family (Humble)	Refer to your family (Polite)
Mother	お母さん おかあさん *okāsan*	お母さん おかあさん *okāsan*	母 はは *haha*	Column ① or ②
Father	お父さん おとうさん *otōsan*	お父さん おとうさん *otōsan*	父 ちち *chichi*	Column ① or ②
Grandmother	お婆ちゃん おばあちゃん *obāchan*	お祖母さん おばあさん *obāsan*	祖母 そぼ *sobo*	Column ① or ②
Grandfather	お祖父ちゃん おじいちゃん *ojīchan*	お祖父さん おじいさん *ojīsan*	祖父 そふ *sofu*	Column ① or ②
Younger Brother	Use given/first name	弟さん おとうとさん *otōtosan*	弟 おとうと *otōto*	Column ③
Older Brother	お兄ちゃん おにいちゃん *onīchan*	お兄さん おにいさん *onīsan*	兄 あに *ani*	Column ① or ②
Younger Sister	Use given/first name	妹さん いもうとさん *imōtosan*	妹 いもうと *imōto*	Column ③
Older Sister	お姉ちゃん おねえちゃん *onēchan*	お姉さん おねえさん *onēsan*	姉 あね *ane*	Column ① or ②

Polite and respectful terms for other people have the **honorific** suffix -さん *(-san)* at the end and are suited to more formal situations. This suffix is interchangeable with -さま *(-sama)* and shows a higher level of respect for more serious settings.

When in doubt, polite forms are the safest option. It's important to understand that misusing specific terms could be considered disrespectful and rude - referring to another person's mother using the humble term 母 or はは *(ha-ha)*, for example.

Revision: People & Things

Kanji from this group are components of many common words, so you should memorize them thoroughly. Without looking back through your study pages, complete the following quiz to see if any characters need more practice.

Q.36 Which of these kanji represents a *woman* and *female* gender?

A. 天 B. 女 C. 万 D. 土 E. 友

Q.37 Which of these kanji represents a *man* and *male* gender?

A. 山 B. 名 C. 気 D. 男 E. 母

Q.38 Which of these kanji means *mother*?

A. 金 B. 土 C. 天 D. 母 E. 車

Q.39 Which of these kanji means *father*?

A. 父 B. 火 C. 天 D. 友 E. 千

Q.40 How is the kanji 子, meaning *'child'*, pronounced?

A. ど B. こ C. の D. き E. か

Q.41 Which of these kanji represents the natural element *water*?

A. 父 B. 火 C. 水 D. 木 E. 天

Q.42 Which of these kanji means *rain* or *rainy weather*?

A. 気 B. 川 C. 雨 D. 魚 E. 電

Q.43 Which of these kanji means *eye, eyesight, or vision*?

A. 母 B. 日 C. 耳 D. 口 E. 目

Q.44 Which of these kanji means *car* or *vehicle*?

A. 車　B. 名　C. 足　D. 女　E. 語

Q.45 Which word means Japanese Language?

A. 英語　B. 三十日　C. 日月　D. 日時　E. 日本語

Q.46 Which kanji represent a *part of the body*?

A. 花　B. 名　C. 手　D. 山　E. 生

Q.47 Which of the kanji might you *order in a restaurant*?

A. 足　B. 火　C. 人　D. 魚　E. 友

Q.48 Which of these words is something you would *watch at night*?

A. 木材　B. 空港　C. 川岸　D. 花火　E. 名前

Q.49 How would you pronounce the word 名前, meaning *first* or *given name*?

A. ままえ　B. なまえ　C. なまう　D. まなえ　E. まなう

Q.50 Which of these kanji means *tree* or *wood*?

A. 木　B. 六　C. 土　D. 天　E. 人

Q.51 The character 灬 is a variant of which kanji?

A. 川　B. 火　C. 空　D. 花　E. 金

Q.52 How do you pronounce the kanji 山, meaning *mountain* or *hill*?

A. くや　B. まか　C. せい　D. くま　E. やま

Q.53 What is a common meaning of the kanji 口?

A. Hand　B. Mouth　C. Arm　D. Nose　E. Foot

Meaning(s)	store, shop	**Components**	ト ロ 广
Radical	广 (house on cliff)	**Kun'yomi**	みせ、たな
Strokes	8	**On'yomi**	テン

Vocabulary	Meaning	Pronunciation
店	store, establishment, restaurant	みせ
店	store, shop, restaurant	テン
店先	storefront, shopfront	みせさき
書店	bookshop, bookstore	しょてん

Stroke Order

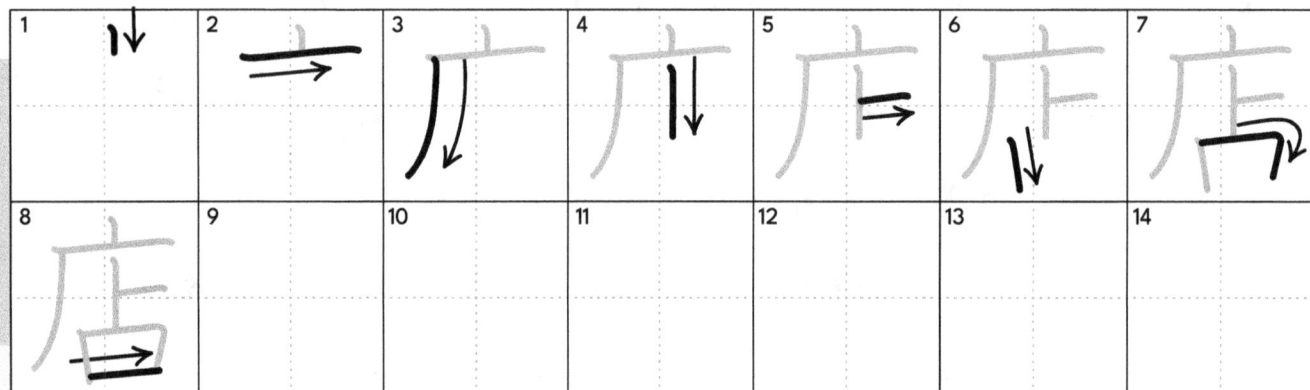

Writing Practice

Kanji for Places & Directions

Meaning(s)	station	Components	丶 尸 杰 馬	
Radical	馬 (horse)	Kun'yomi	(none)	
Strokes	14	On'yomi	エキ	

Vocabulary	Meaning	Pronunciation
駅	railway station, train station	エキ
駅員	(train) station attendant, employee	エキイン
駅前	in front of a station	えきまえ
終着駅	to go out, to leave	シュウチャクエキ

Stroke Order

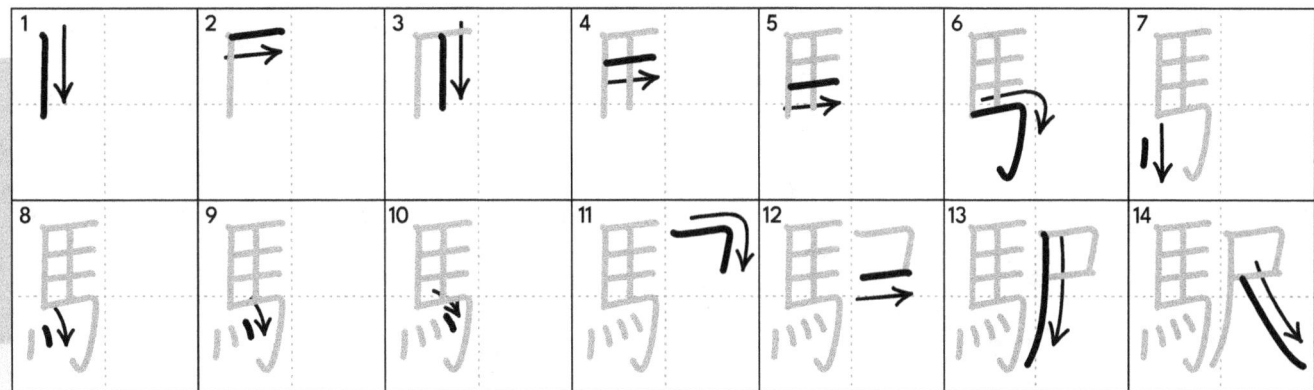

Writing Practice

JLPT N5

	Meaning(s)	street, path, way	Components	并込自首
	Radical	辵 (辶, 辶, 辶)(walk)	Kun'yomi	みち、いう
	Strokes	12	On'yomi	ドウ、トウ

Vocabulary	Meaning	Pronunciation
道	road, path, street, lane, passage	みち
道具	tool, implement, device, instrument	どうぐ
道筋	path, route, itinerary	みちすじ
道	road, path, street, route, way	ドウ

Stroke Order

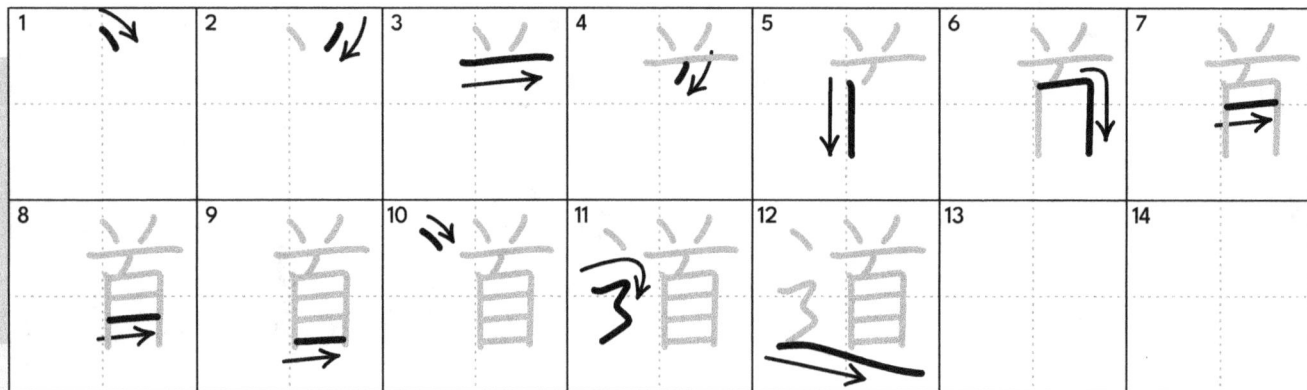

Writing Practice

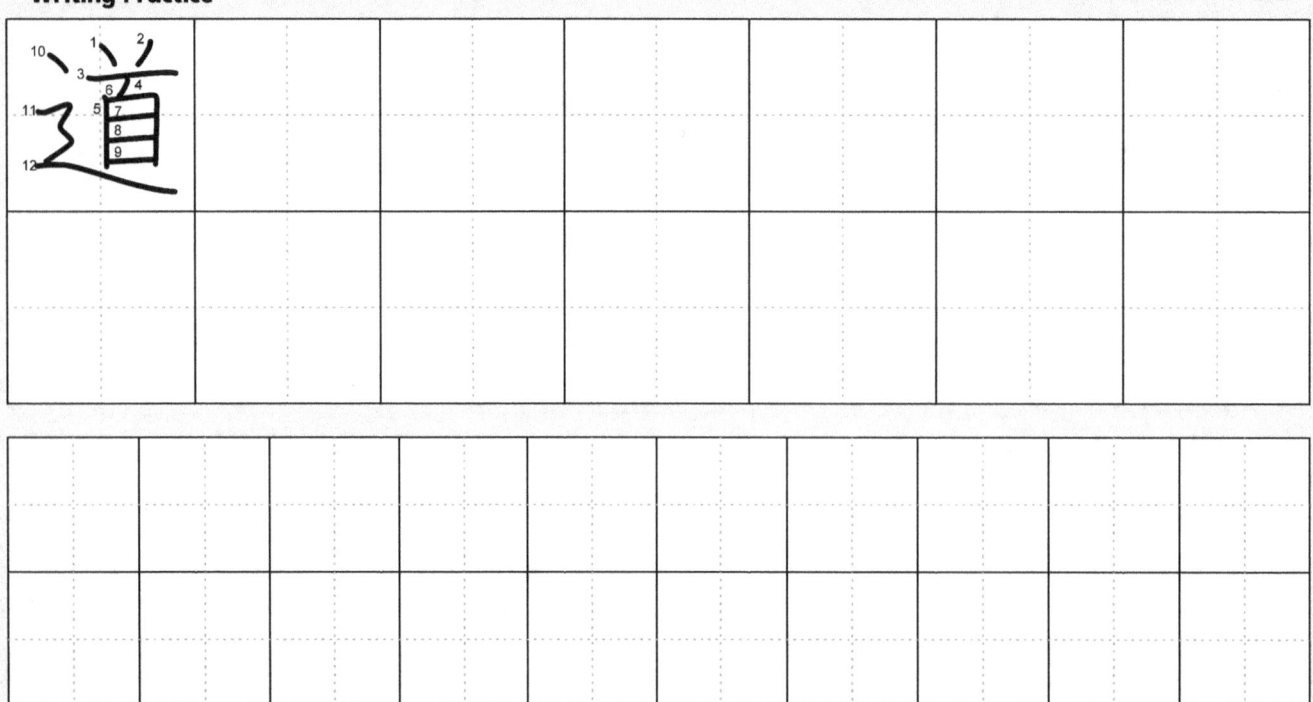

Kanji for Places & Directions

Meaning(s)	company, shrine, office	**Components**	土 礼
Radical	示 (ネ) (sign)	**Kun'yomi**	やしろ
Strokes	7	**On'yomi**	シャ

Vocabulary	Meaning	Pronunciation
社	(shinto) shrine,	やしろ
社	company, association, society	シャ
社長	company president, manager	しゃちょう
社会	society, public, community, the world	しゃかい

Stroke Order

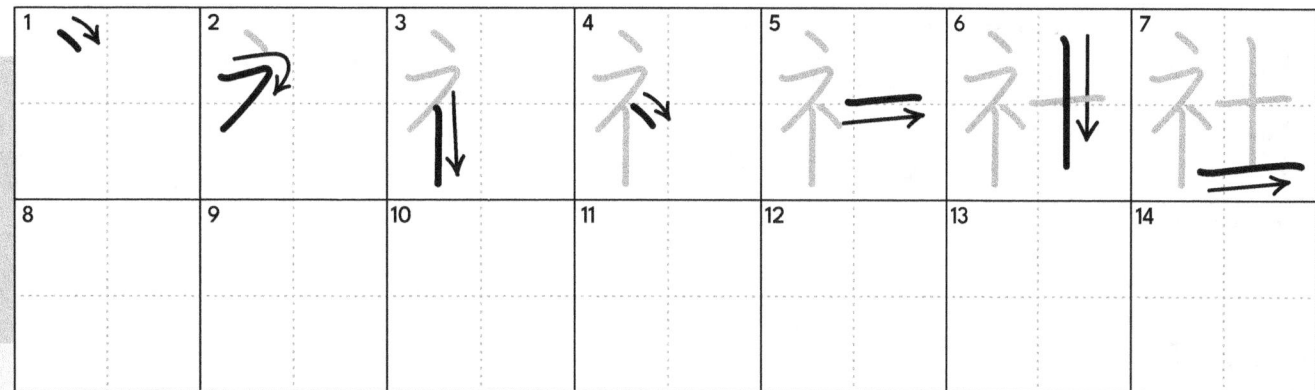

Writing Practice

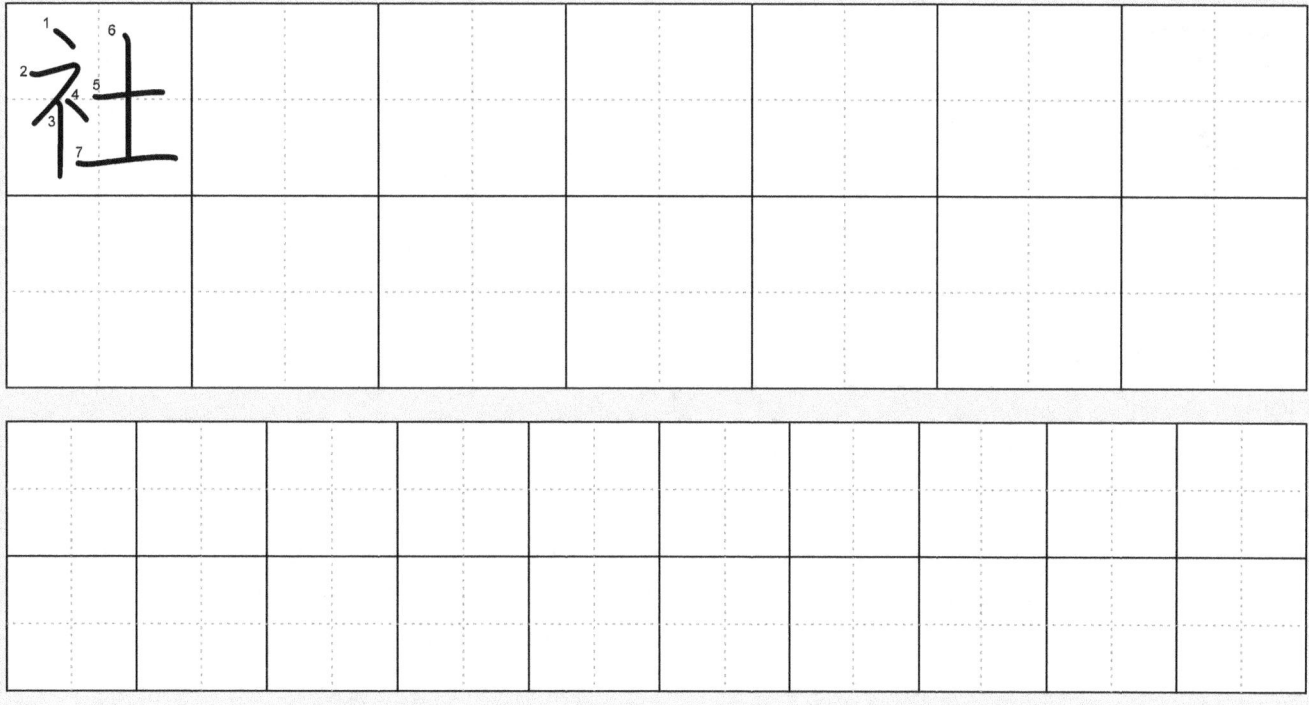

JLPT N5

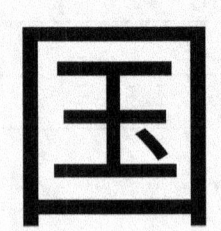

Meaning(s)	country, state, region	Components	丶 口 王
Radical	囗 (enclosure)	Kun'yomi	くに
Strokes	8	On'yomi	コク

Vocabulary	Meaning	Pronunciation
国	country, state, region	くに
国語	Japanese, national language	こくご
国益	national interest	コクエキ
外国人	foreigner, foreign citizen	がいこくじん

Stroke Order

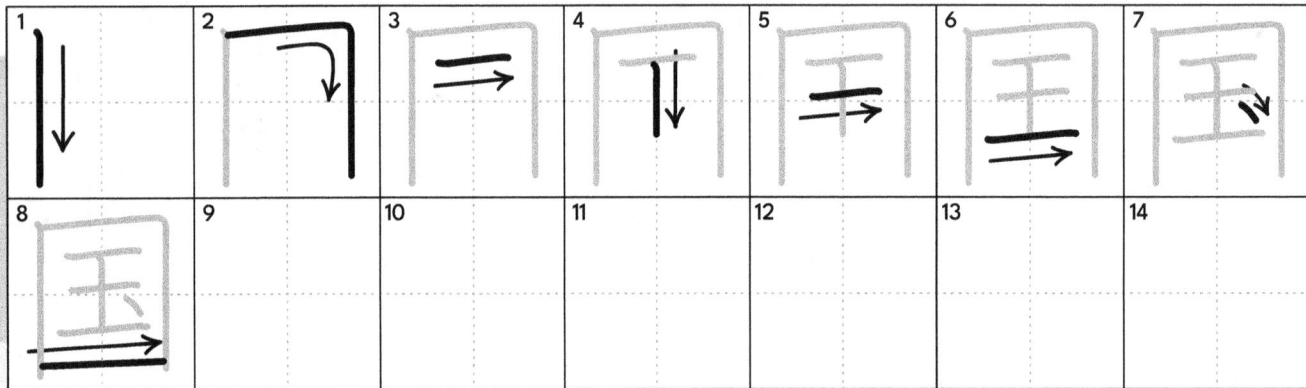

Writing Practice

Kanji for Places & Directions

Meaning(s)	outside	Components	ト 夕
Radical	夕 (sunset, evening)	Kun'yomi	そと、ほか、はず.す
Strokes	5	On'yomi	ガイ、ゲ

Vocabulary	Meaning	Pronunciation
外	outside, exterior, outside your group	そと
外	outside of, not covered by	ガイ
外国	foreign country	がいこく
海外	foreign, abroad, overseas	かいがい

Stroke Order

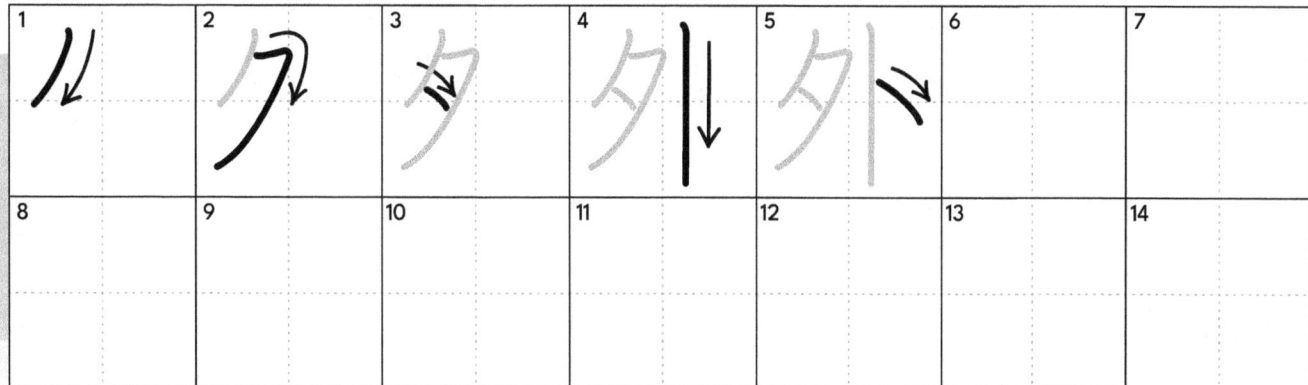

Writing Practice

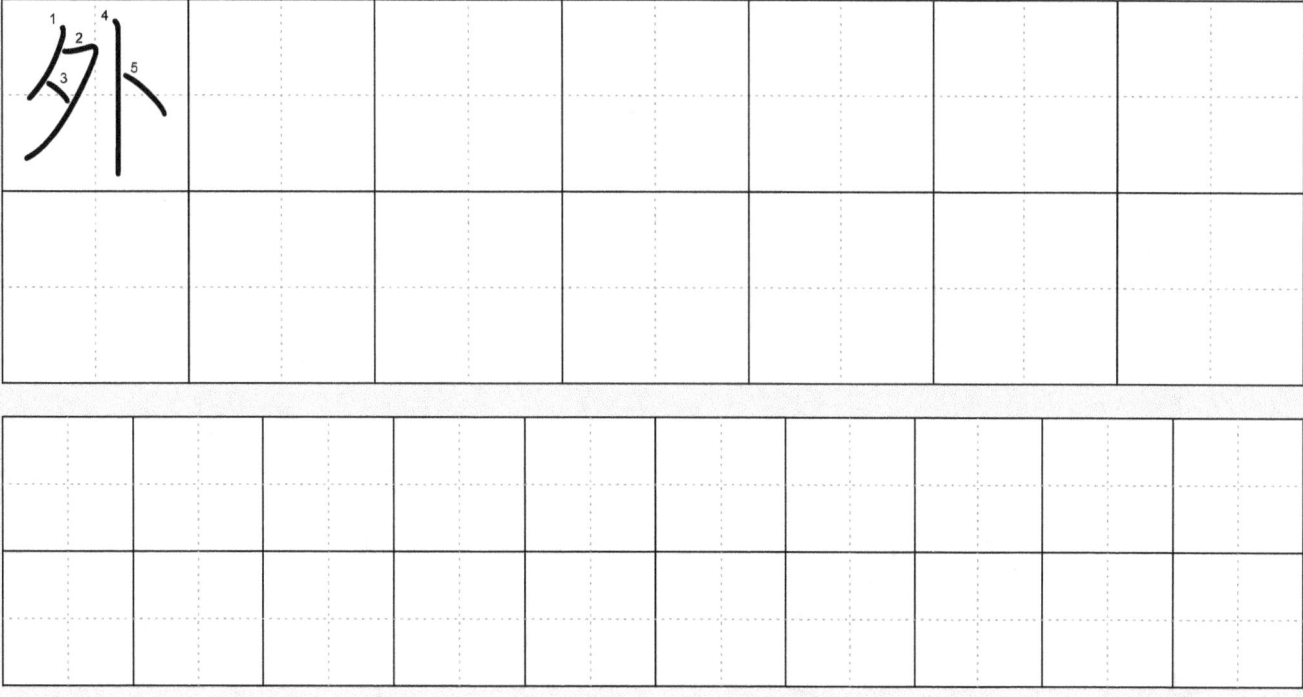

JLPT N5

Meaning(s)	study, learning, science	**Components**	冖 子 尚
Radical	子 (child, seed)	**Kun'yomi**	まな.ぶ
Strokes	8	**On'yomi**	ガク

Vocabulary	**Meaning**	**Pronunciation**
学ぶ	to study, to learn	まなぶ
大学	university, college	だいがく
学	learning, scholarship	ガク
学位	(academic) degree	ガクイ

Stroke Order

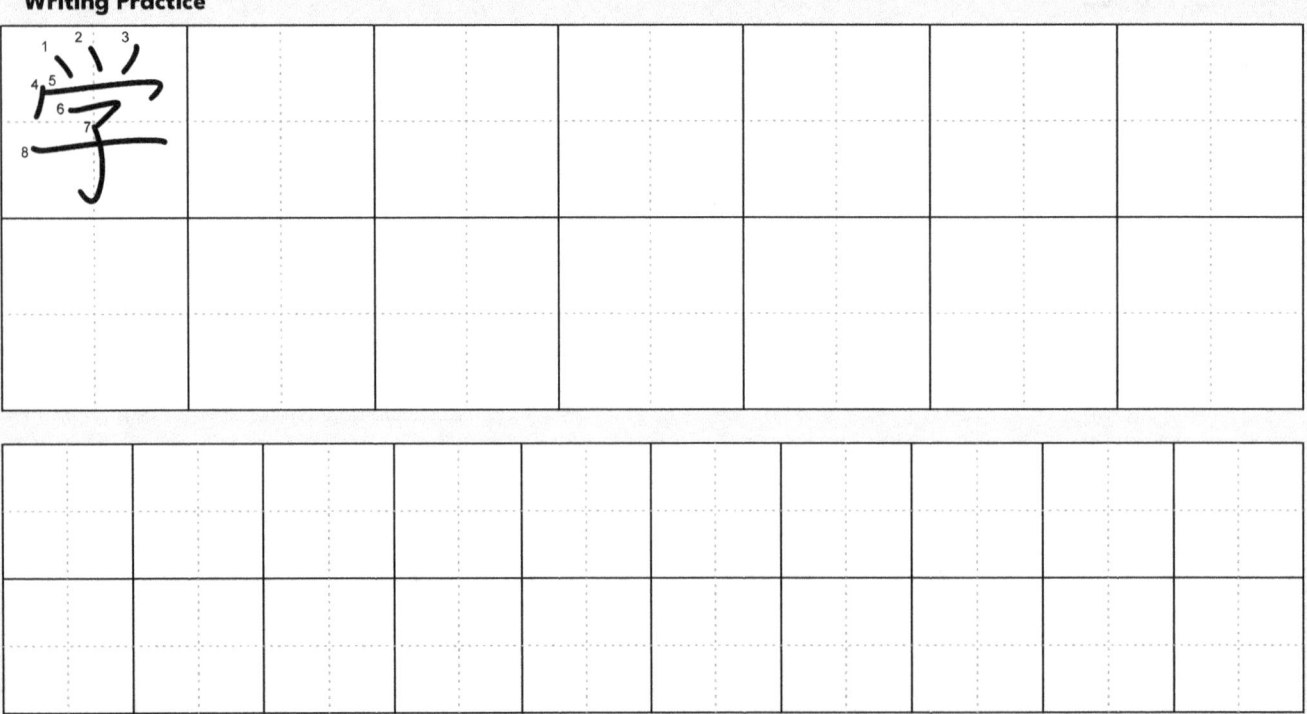

Writing Practice

Kanji for Places & Directions

Meaning(s)	exam, school	Components	亠 木 父
Radical	木 (tree)	Kun'yomi	(none)
Strokes	10	On'yomi	コウ、キョウ

Vocabulary	Meaning	Pronunciation
校	school	コウ
学校	school	がっこう
高校	senior/high school	こうこう
校長	principal, headteacher	こうちょう

Stroke Order

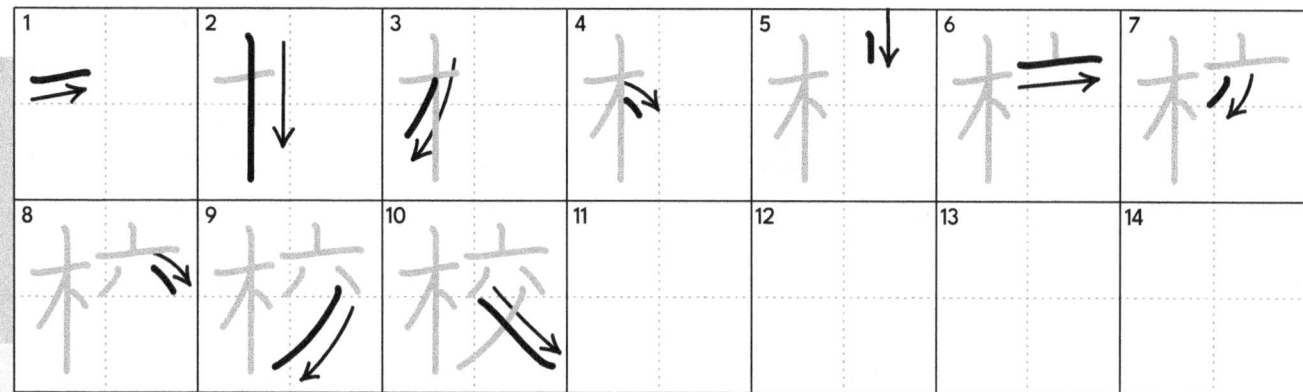

Writing Practice

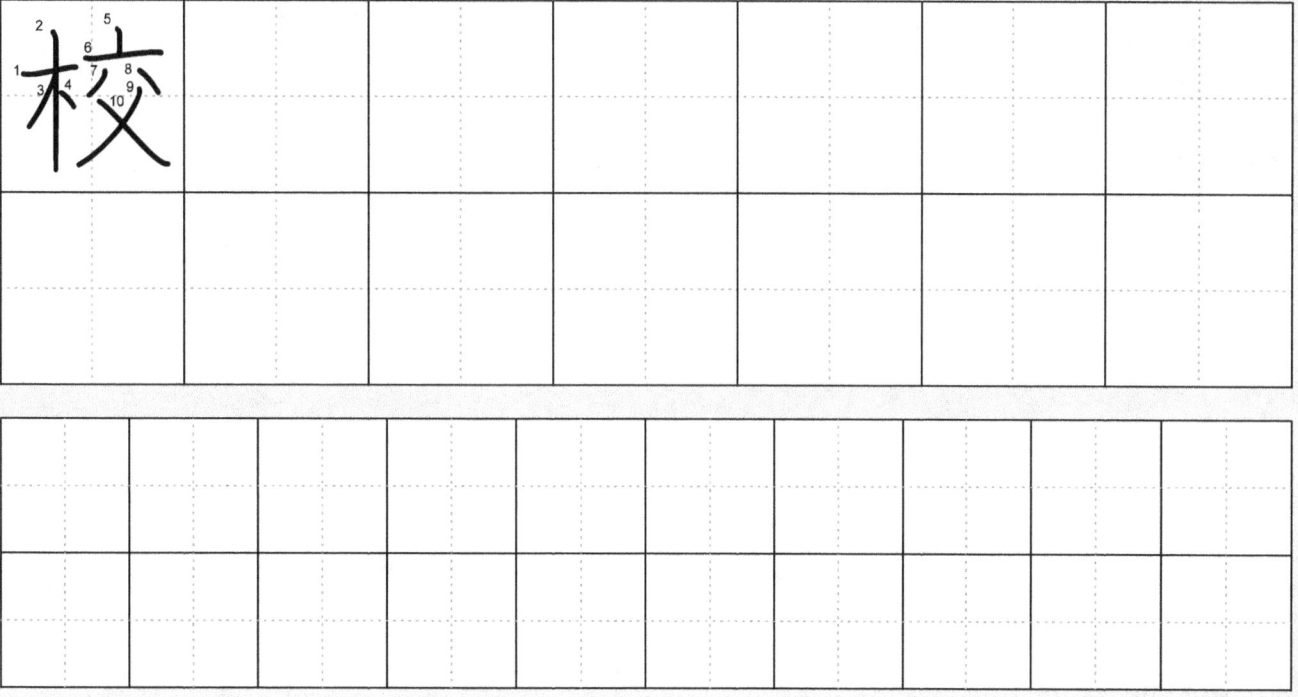

JLPT N5

Meaning(s)	above, up	Components	一 ト
Radical	一 (one)	Kun'yomi	うえ、-うえ、うわ-
Strokes	3	On'yomi	ジョウ、ショウ、シャン

Vocabulary	Meaning	Pronunciation
上	above, up, over, elder (daughter), top	うえ
上	as a matter of (fact), on top of, on, best	ジョウ
上げる	to raise, to elevate	あげる
上着	coat, jacket, outer garment	うわぎ

Stroke Order

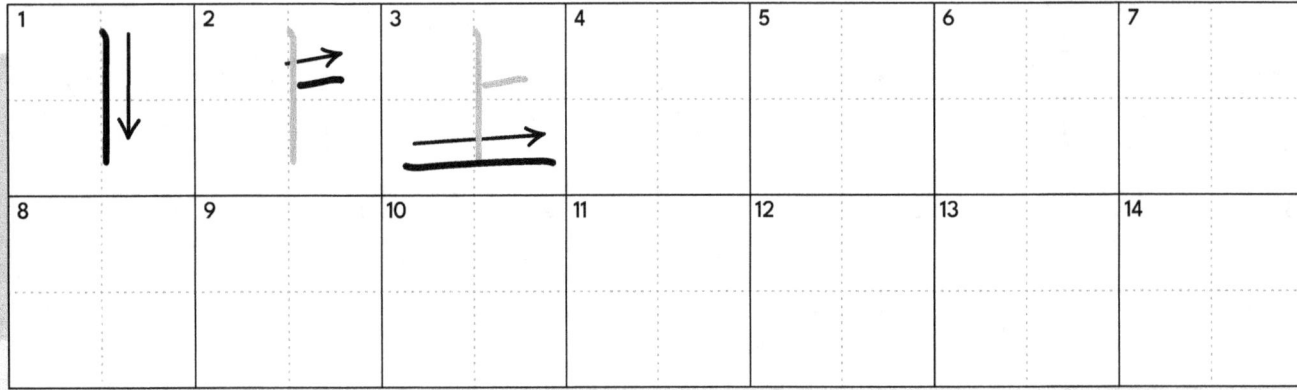

Writing Practice

Kanji for Places & Directions

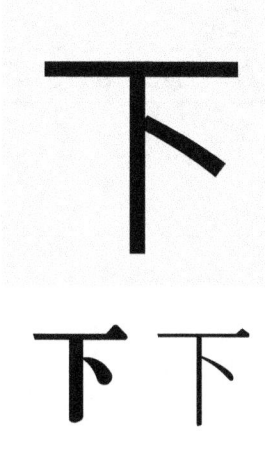

Meaning(s)	down, below	Components	一 丨 卜
Radical	一 (one)	Kun'yomi	した、しも、もと、くだ.さる
Strokes	3	On'yomi	カ、ゲ

Vocabulary	Meaning	Pronunciation
下	below, down, under, younger	した
靴下	socks, stockings	くつした
下る	to descend, go down, come down	くだる
地下鉄	subway, underground train	ちかてつ

Stroke Order

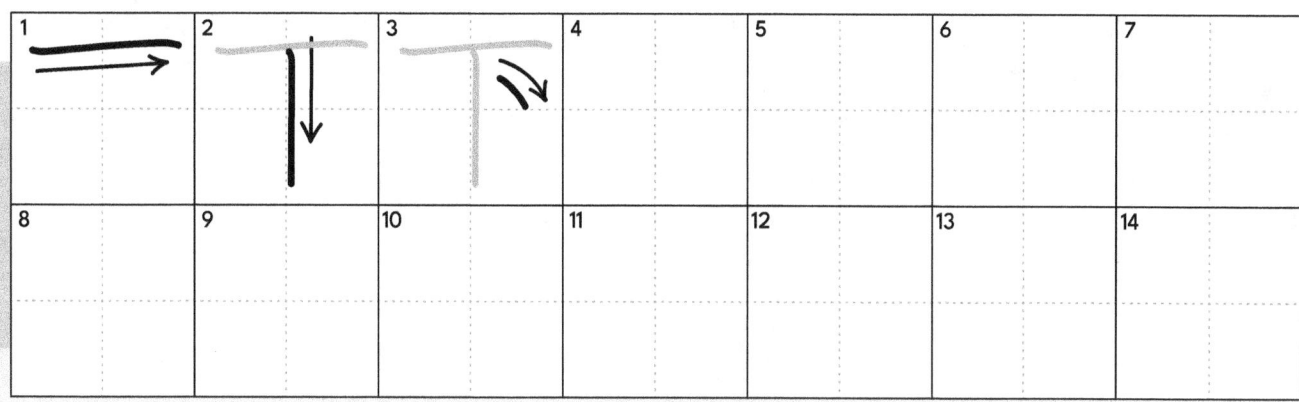

Writing Practice

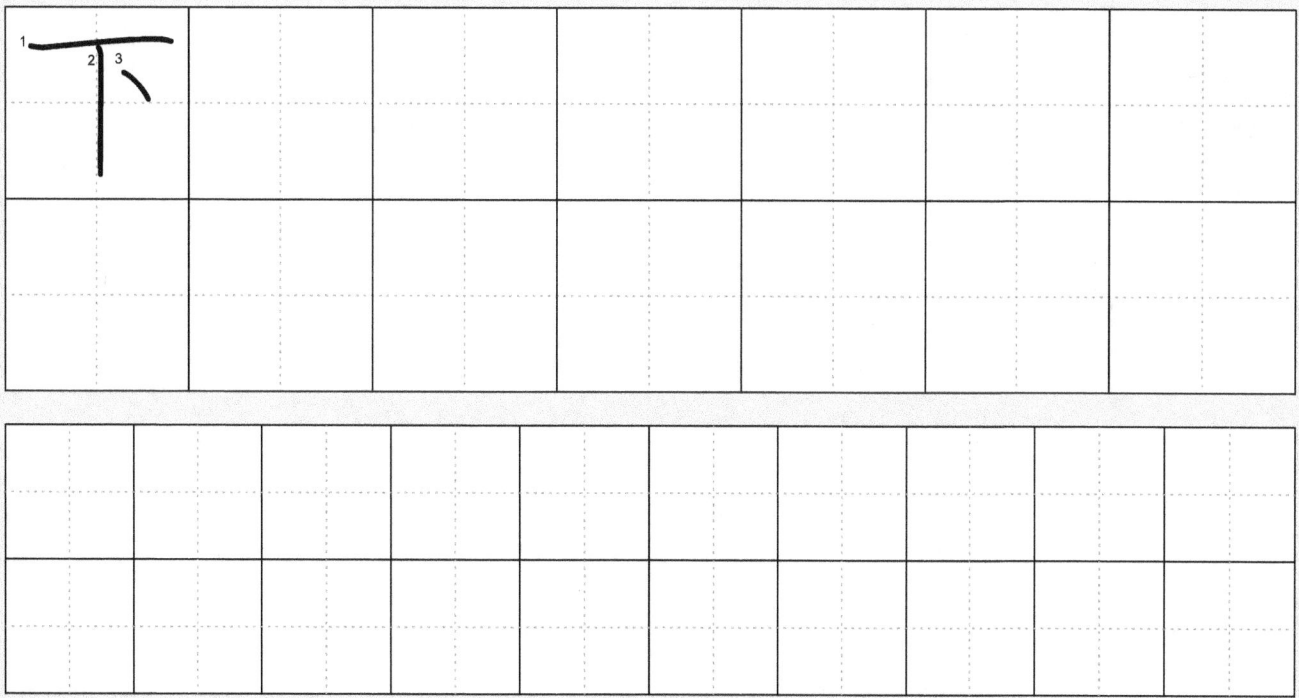

JLPT N5

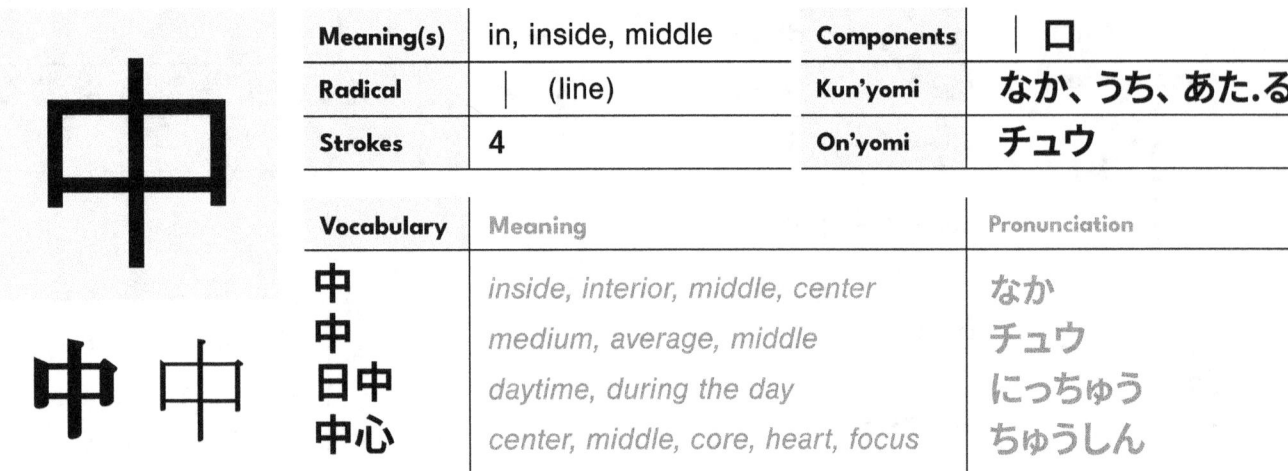

Meaning(s)	in, inside, middle	Components	丨 口
Radical	丨 (line)	Kun'yomi	なか、うち、あた.る
Strokes	4	On'yomi	チュウ

Vocabulary	Meaning	Pronunciation
中	inside, interior, middle, center	なか
中	medium, average, middle	チュウ
日中	daytime, during the day	にっちゅう
中心	center, middle, core, heart, focus	ちゅうしん

Stroke Order

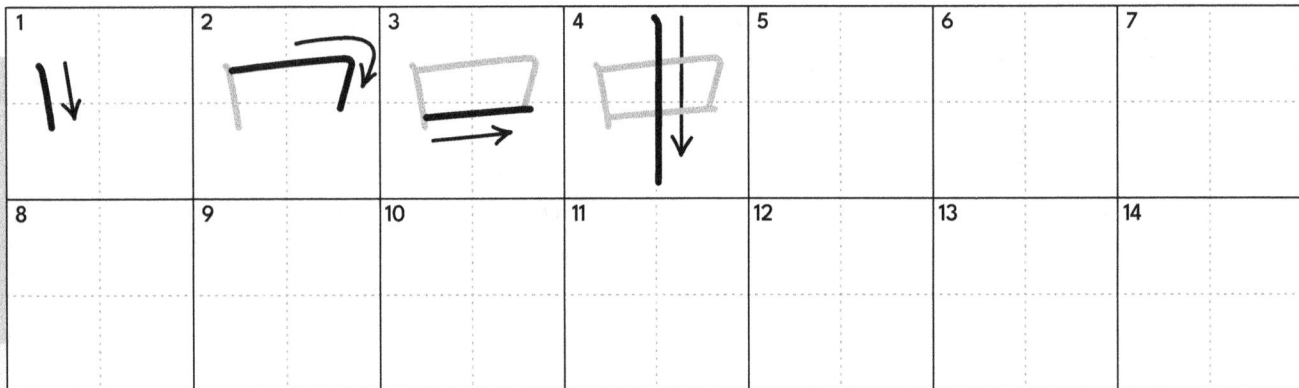

Writing Practice

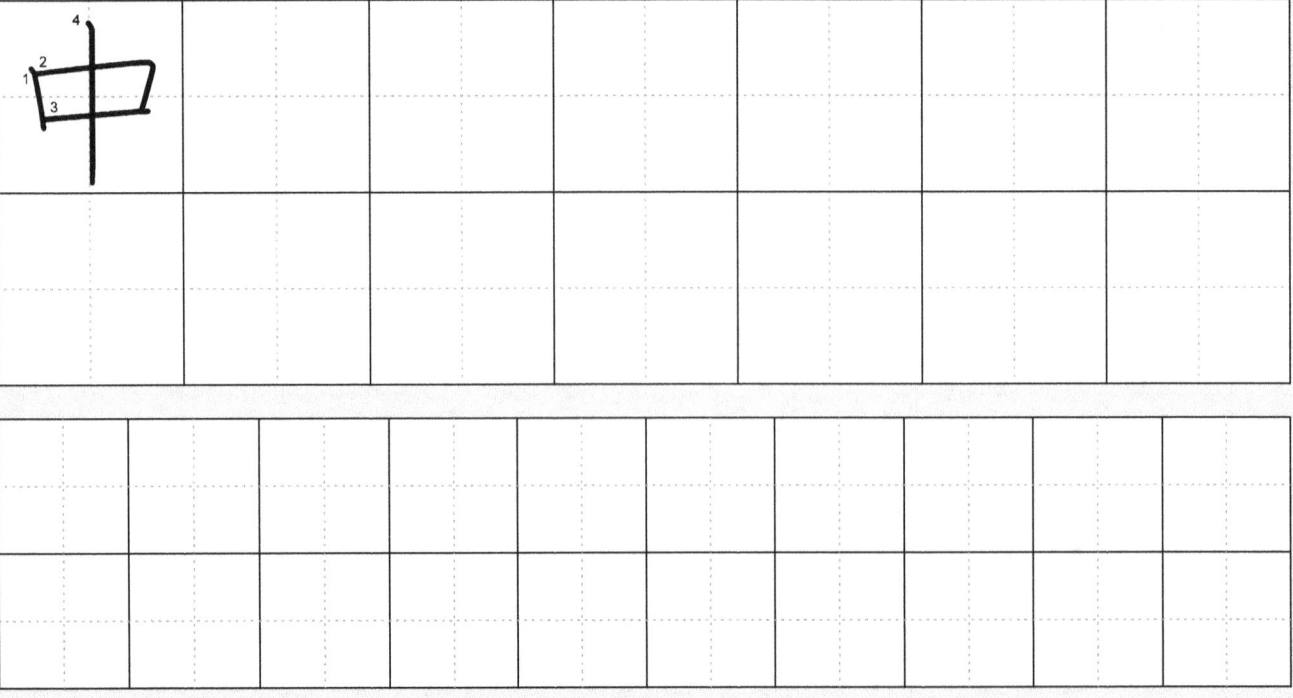

Kanji for Places & Directions

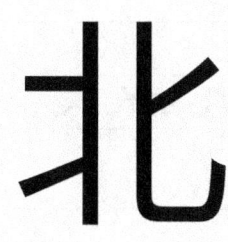

Meaning(s)	north	**Components**	ヒ 爿
Radical	ヒ (spoon)	**Kun'yomi**	きた
Strokes	5	**On'yomi**	ホク

Vocabulary	Meaning	Pronunciation
北	north, the North	きた
西北	north-west	せいほく / セイホク
北欧	Northern Europe, Nordic countries	ホクオウ
北海道	Hokkaidou (island prefecture)	ほっかいどう

Stroke Order

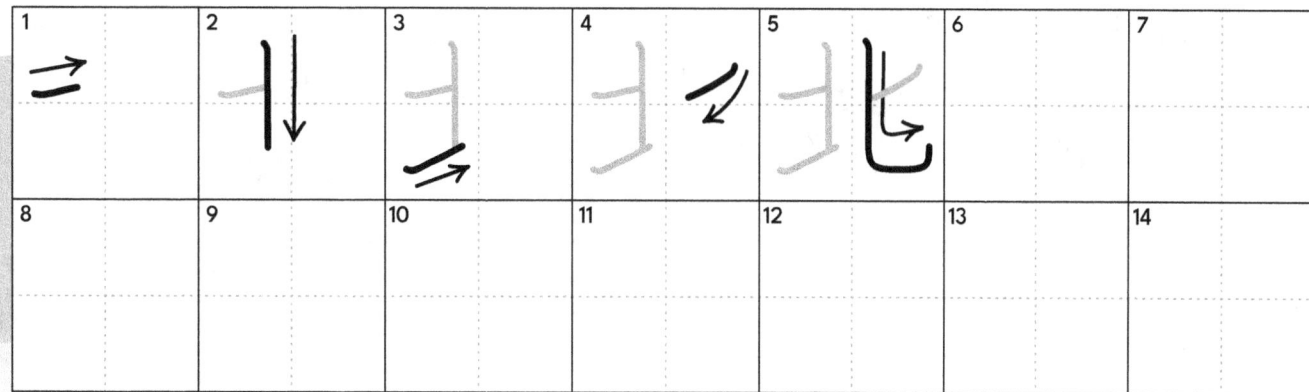

Writing Practice

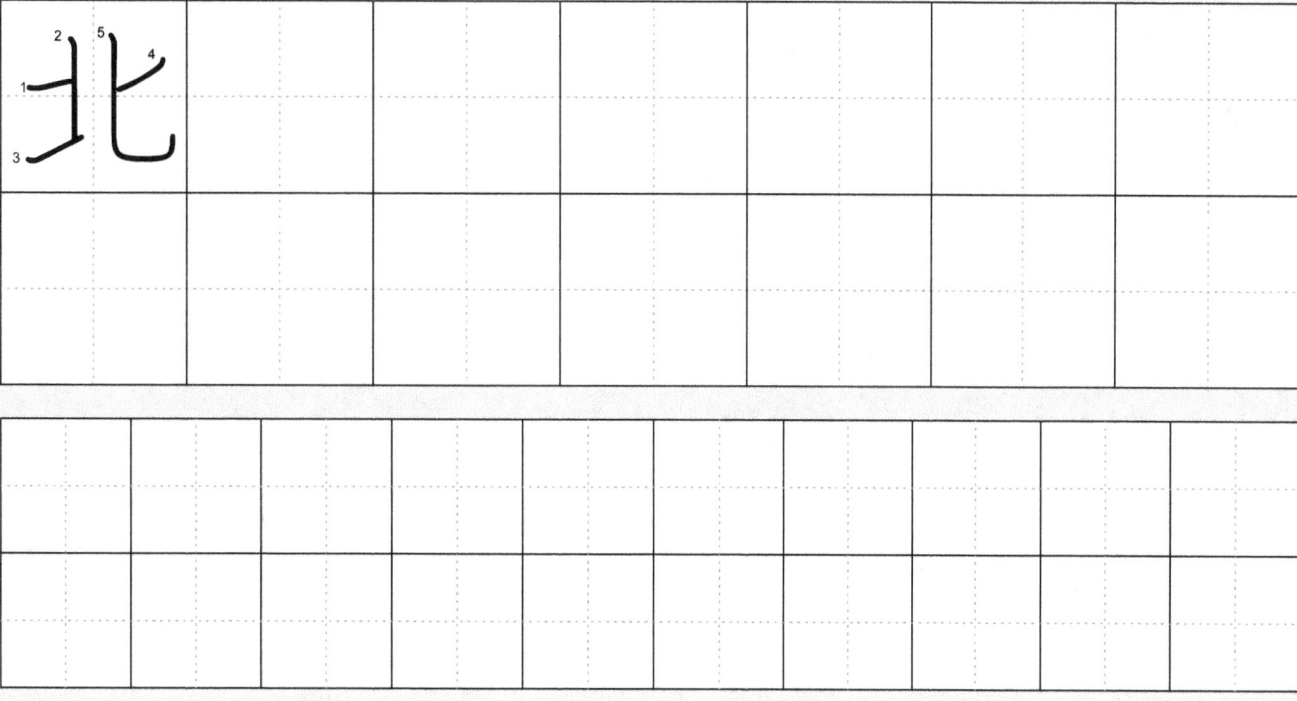

JLPT N5

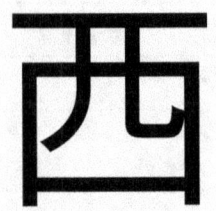

Meaning(s)	west, Spain	Components	西
Radical	西 (襾, 覀) (west)	Kun'yomi	にし
Strokes	6	On'yomi	セイ、サイ、ス

Vocabulary	Meaning		Pronunciation
西	west		にし
西方	western direction		せいほう
西	Spain, Spanish (language)		セイ
西洋	the West, Western countries		せいよう

Stroke Order

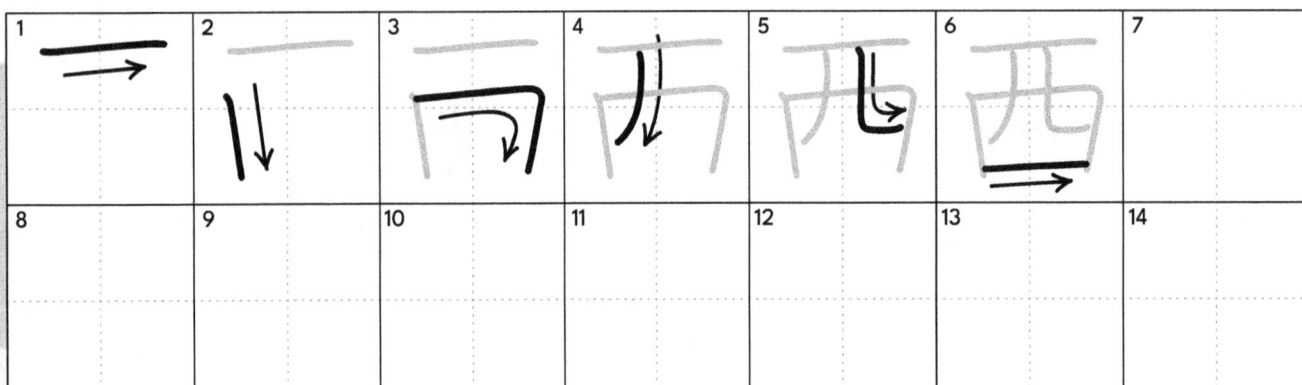

Writing Practice

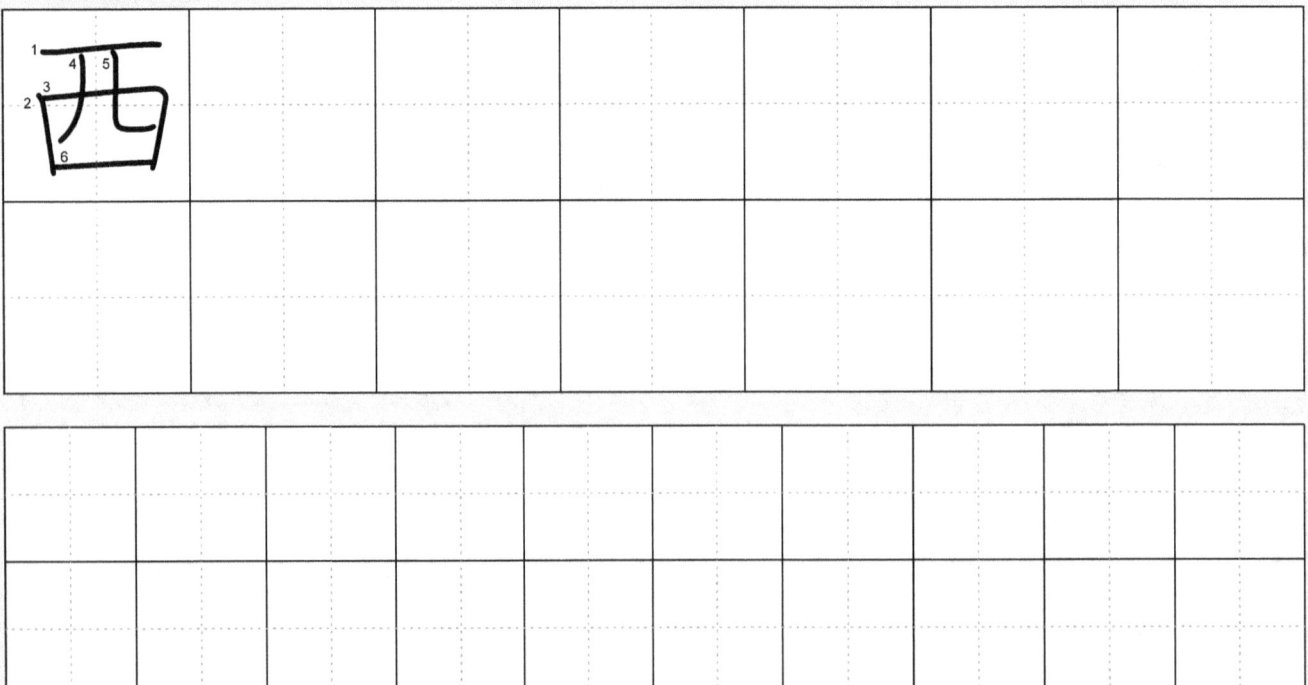

Kanji for Places & Directions

Meaning(s)	east	Components	一 丨 日 木 田
Radical	木 (tree)	Kun'yomi	ひがし
Strokes	9	On'yomi	トウ

Vocabulary	Meaning	Pronunciation
東	east	ひがし
東京	Tokyo	とうきょう
東方	eastern direction, the Orient	とうほう
東欧	Eastern Europe	トウオウ

Stroke Order

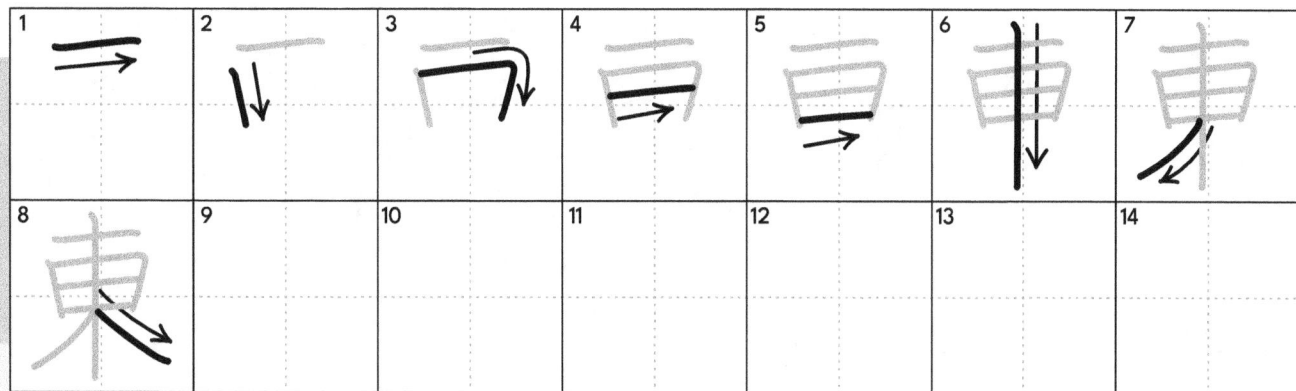

Writing Practice

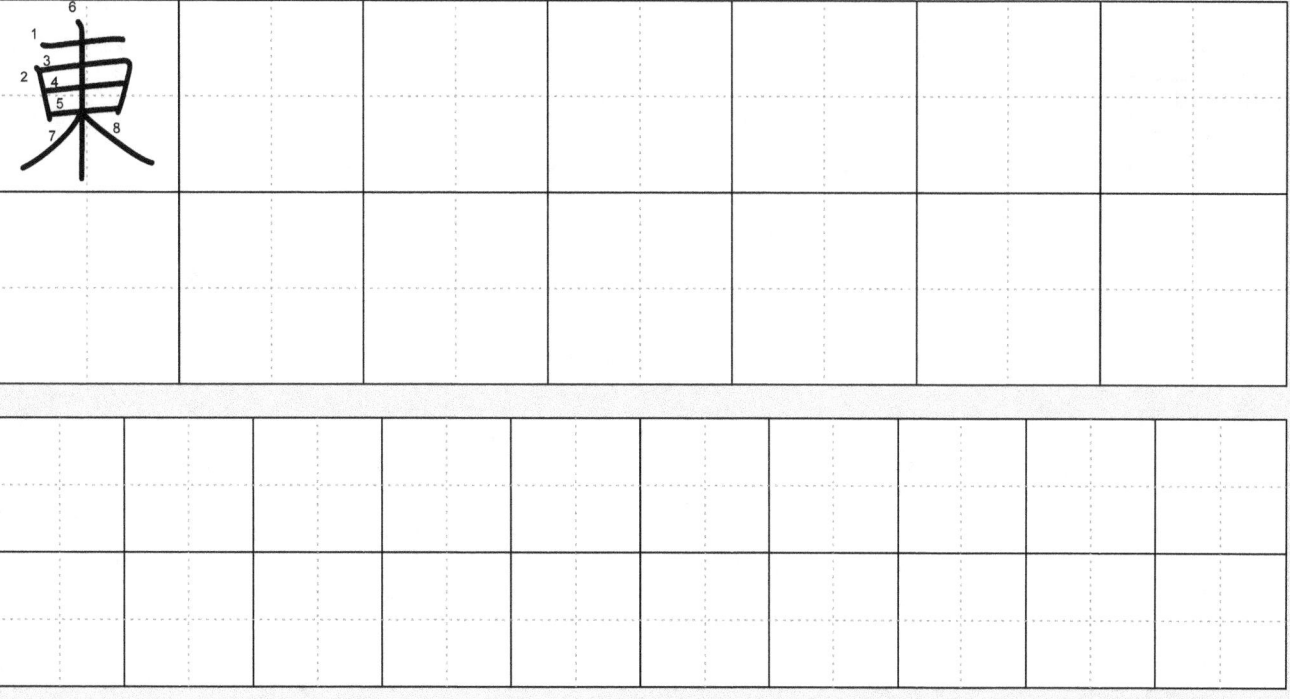

JLPT N5

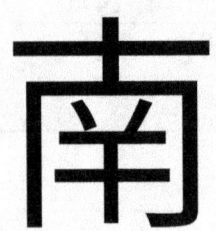

Meaning(s)	south	**Components**	丷冂十干
Radical	十 (ten)	**Kun'yomi**	みなみ
Strokes	9	**On'yomi**	ナン、ナ

Vocabulary	Meaning	Pronunciation
南	south	みなみ
東南	south-east	とうなん / トウナン
西南	south-west	せいなん / セイナン
南海	southern sea	ナンカイ

Stroke Order

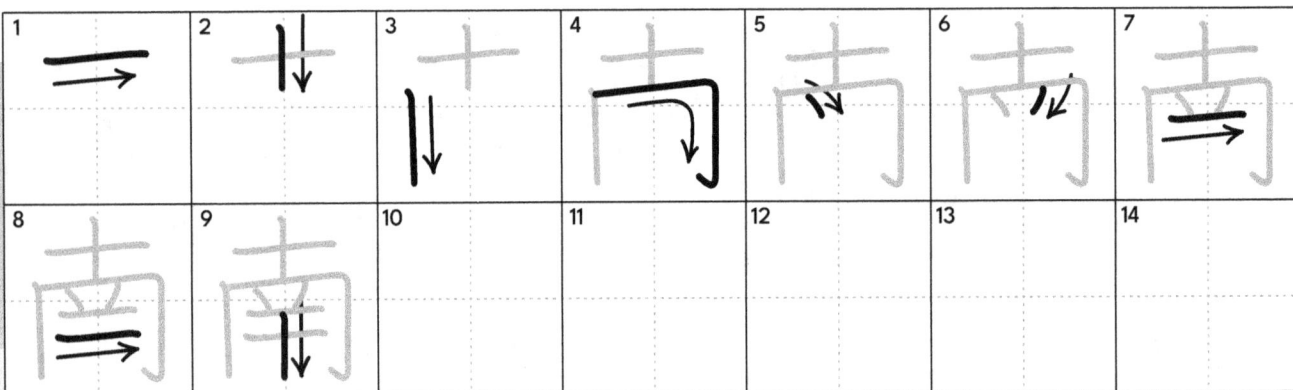

Writing Practice

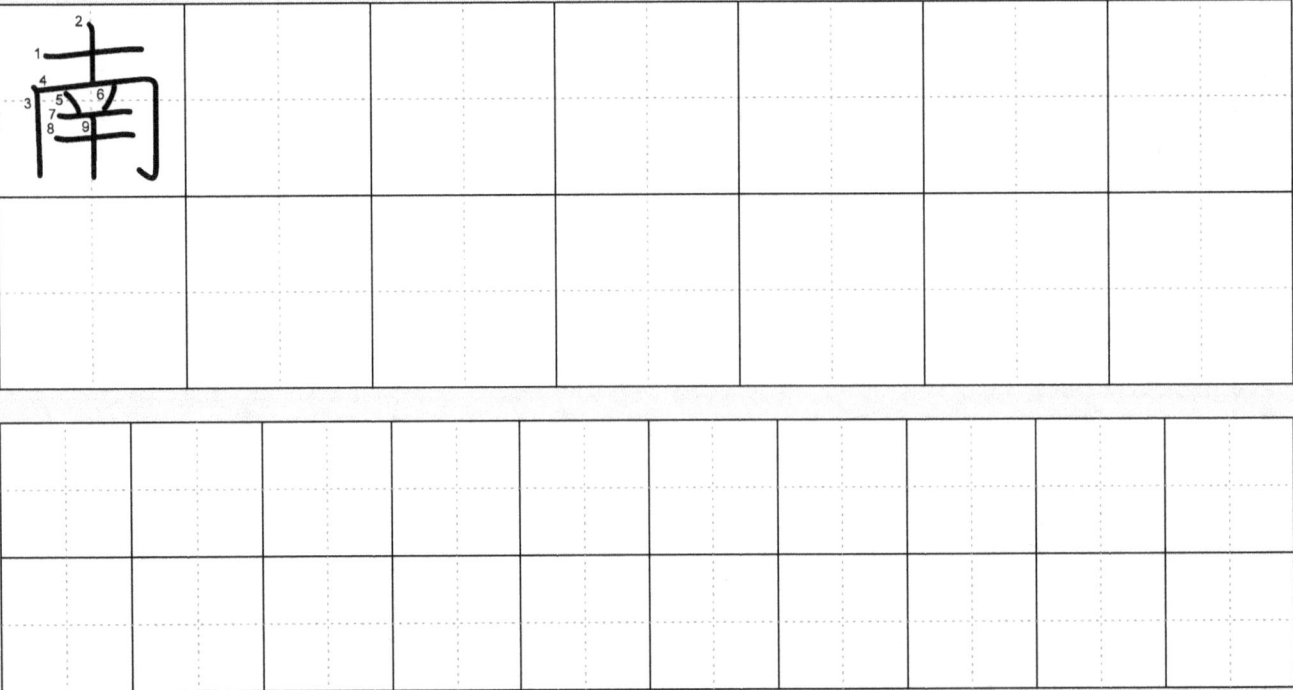

右

Meaning(s)	right, right-hand side	Components	一ノ口
Radical	口 (mouth, opening)	Kun'yomi	みぎ
Strokes	5	On'yomi	ウ、ユウ

Vocabulary	Meaning	Pronunciation
右	right, right-hand side	みぎ
右腕	right arm, right-handed person	みぎうで
最右	rightmost, right-most	サイウ
左右	left and right	サユウ

Stroke Order

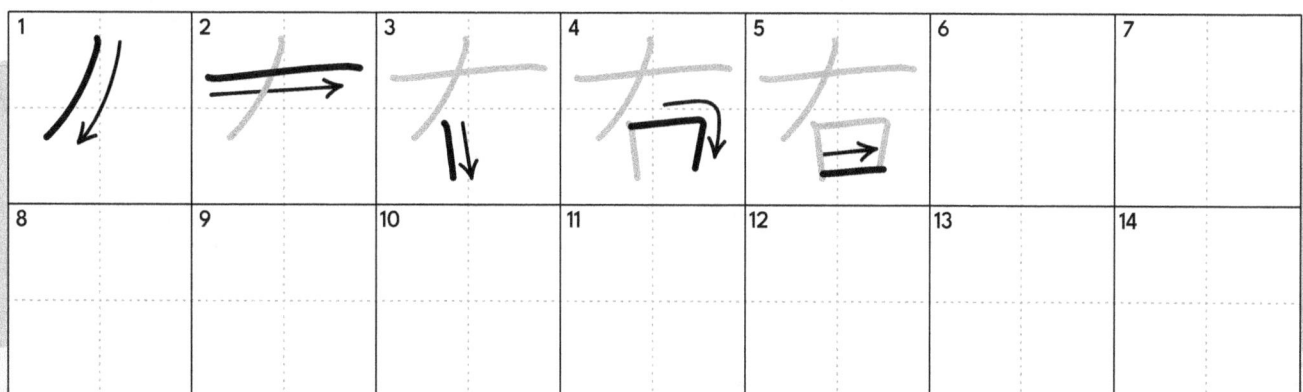

Writing Practice

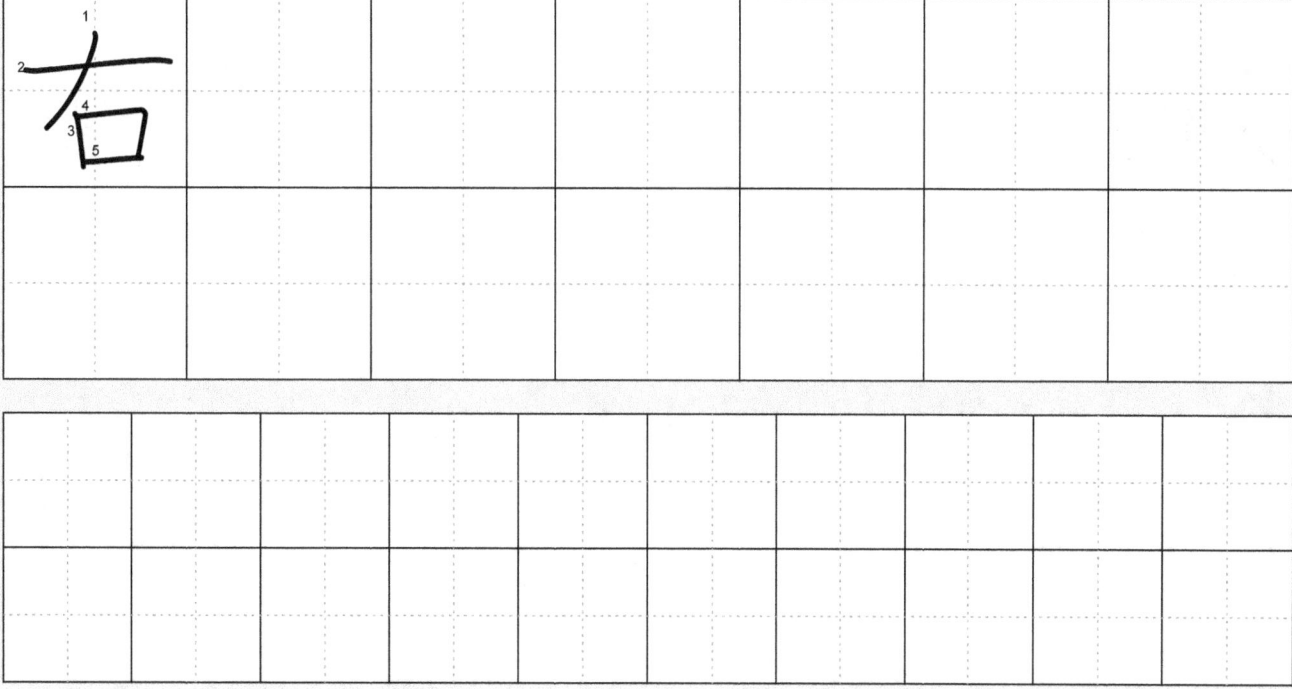

JLPT N5

左

Meaning(s)	left, left-hand side	Components	一ノエ
Radical	エ (work)	Kun'yomi	ひだり
Strokes	5	On'yomi	サ、シャ

Vocabulary	Meaning	Pronunciation
左	left, left-hand side	ひだり
左利き	left-handed person	ひだりき
左右	left and right	サユウ
左手	left hand	ひだりて

Stroke Order

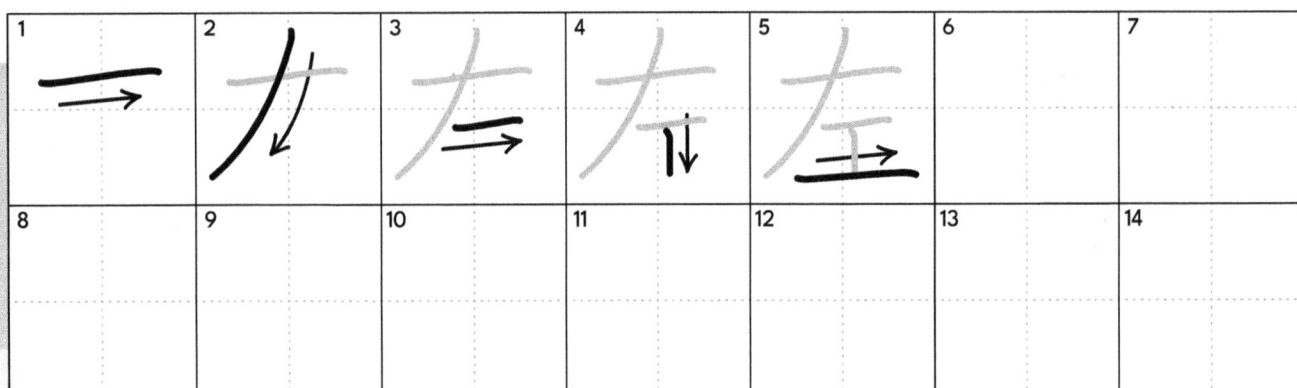

Writing Practice

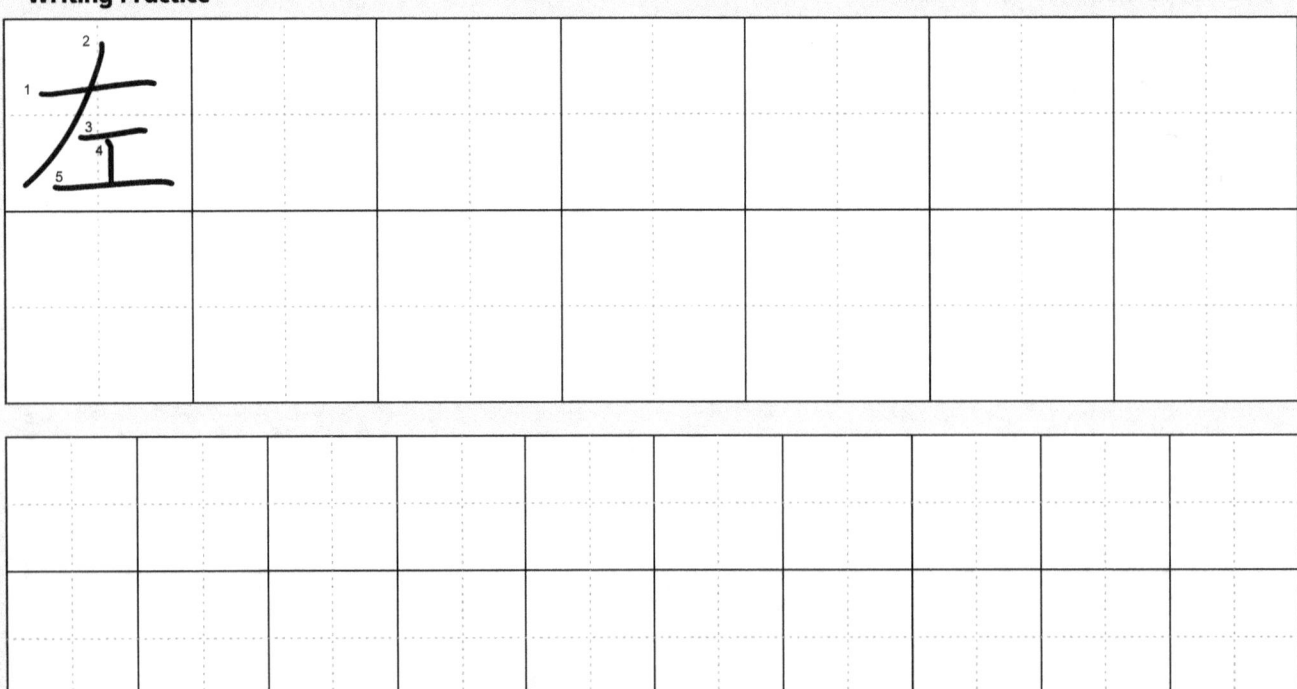

Kanji for Places & Directions

Meaning(s)	meeting, meet, party	Components	二 个 ム
Radical	人 (亻) (man, human)	Kun'yomi	あ.う、あ.わせる
Strokes	6	On'yomi	カイ、エ

Vocabulary	Meaning	Pronunciation
会社	company, workplace	かいしゃ
会う	to meet, to encounter	あう
会釈	slight bow, nod	エシャク
会	meeting / gathering	カイ / エ

Stroke Order

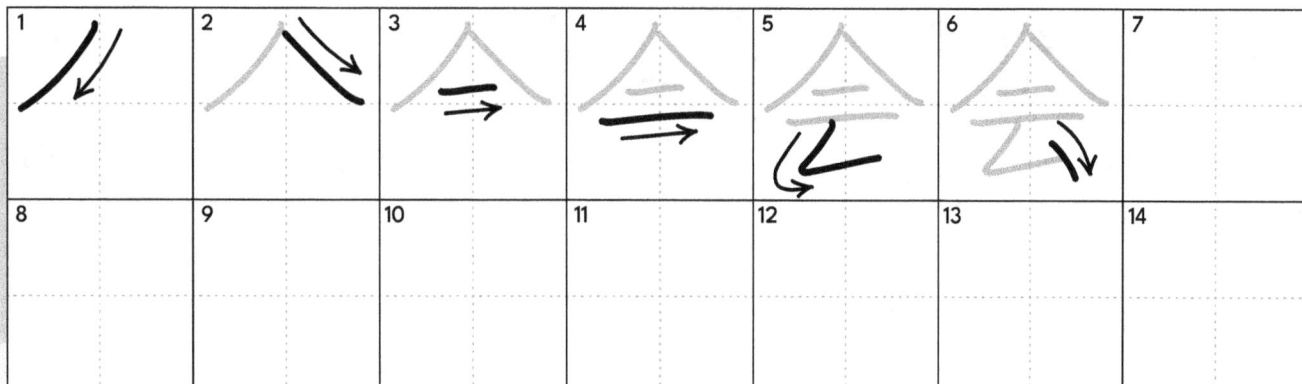

Writing Practice

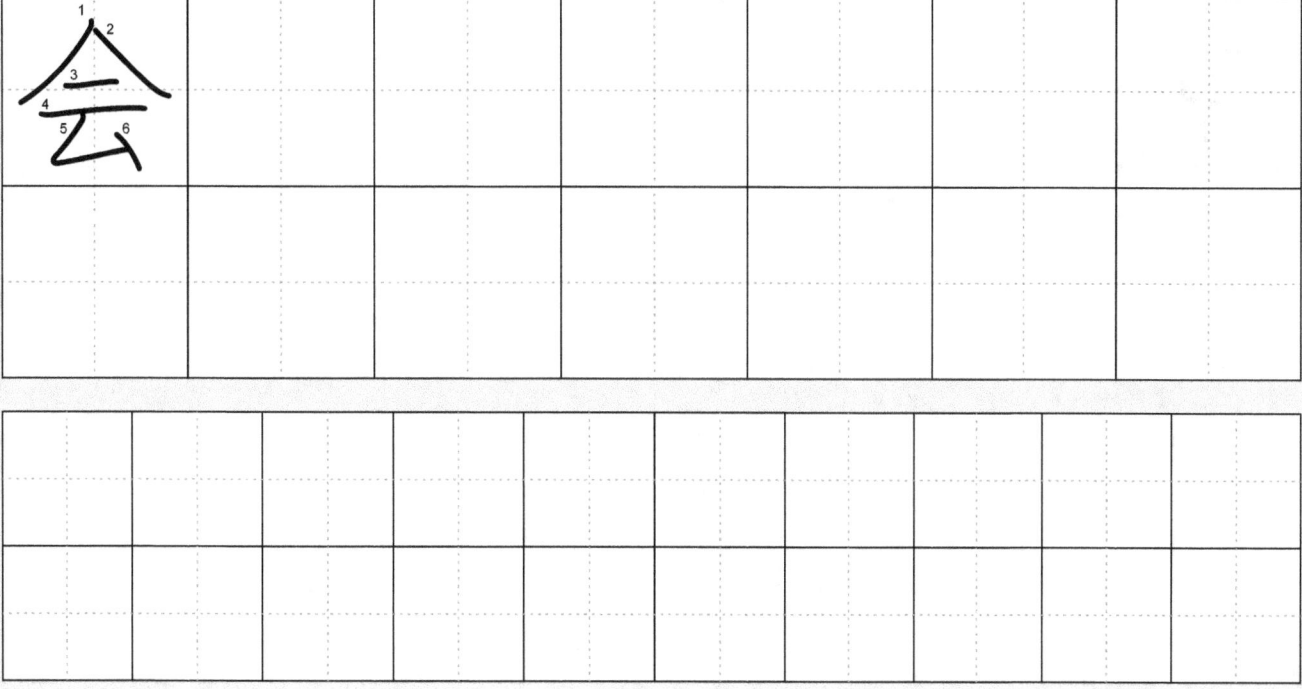

Kanji for Verbs

Meaning(s)	see, hopes, idea	**Components**	儿 目 見
Radical	見 (see)	**Kun'yomi**	み.る、み.える、み.せる
Strokes	7	**On'yomi**	ケン

Vocabulary	Meaning	Pronunciation
見せる	to show, to display	みせる
見る	to see	みる
見解	opinion, point of view	ケンカイ
花見	cherry blossom viewing	はなみ

Stroke Order

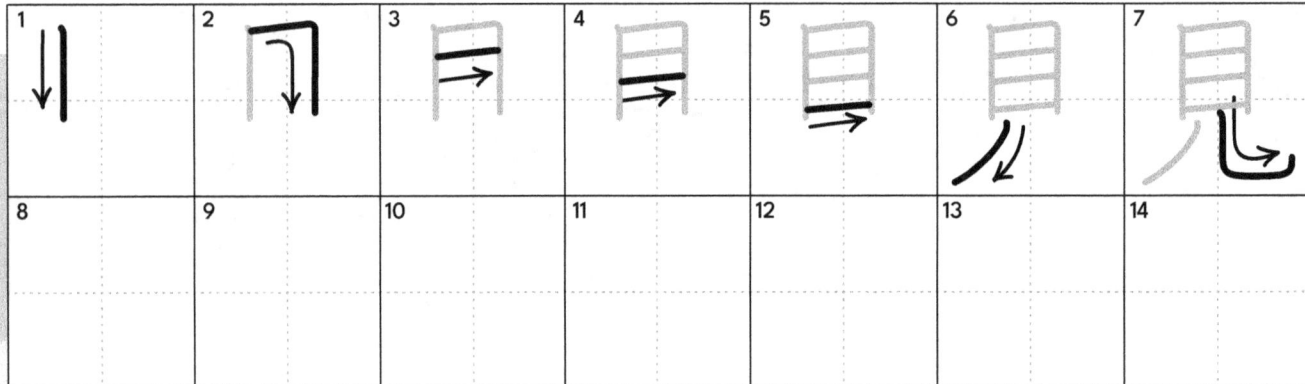

Writing Practice

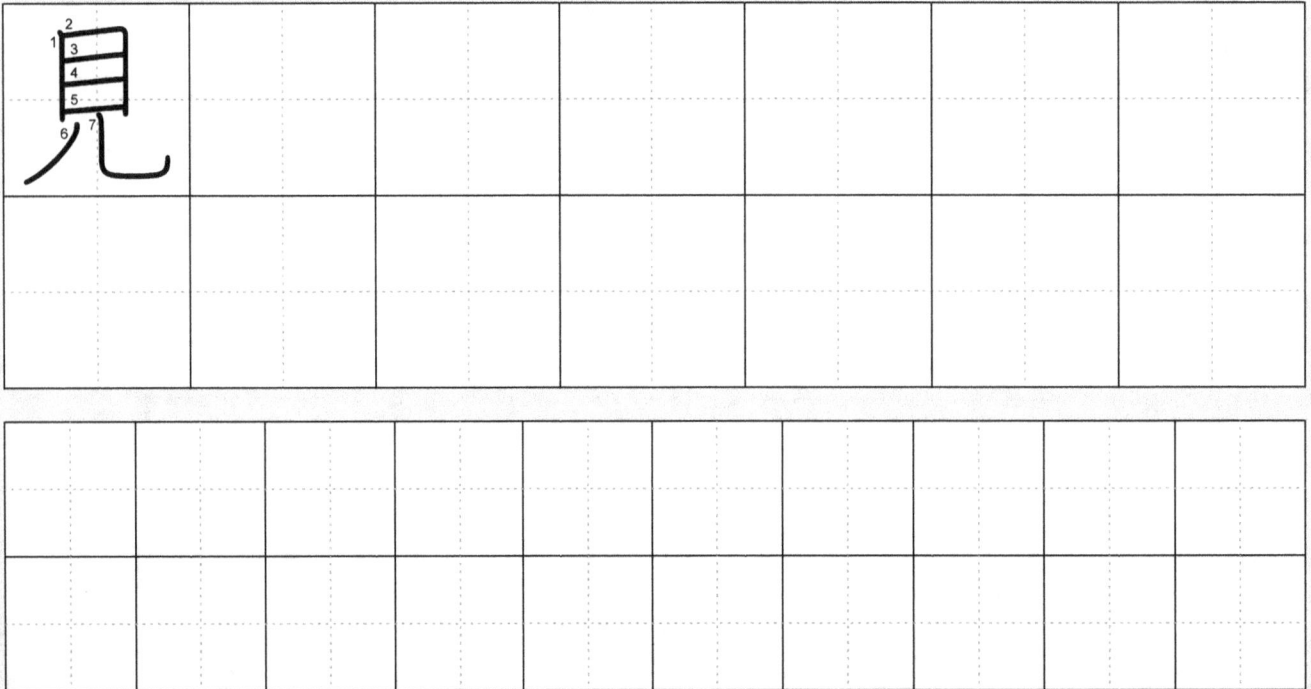

Kanji for Verbs

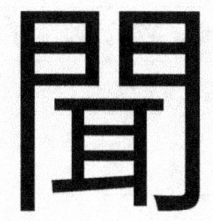

Meaning(s)	listen, hear, ask	Components	耳門
Radical	耳 (ear)	Kun'yomi	き.く、き.こえる
Strokes	14	On'yomi	ブン、モン

Vocabulary	Meaning		Pronunciation
新聞	newspaper		しんぶん
見聞	information, experience, observation		けんぶん
聞く	to hear, listen (to music)		きく
聞こえる	to be heard		きこえる

Stroke Order

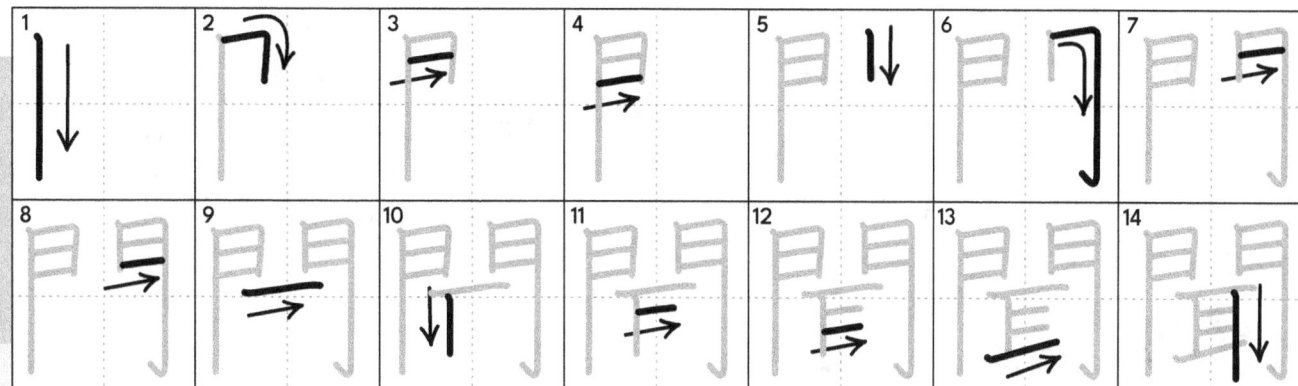

Writing Practice

JLPT N5

Meaning(s)	to write	Components	日 聿	
Radical	日 (say)	Kun'yomi	か.く、-が.き、-がき	
Strokes	10	On'yomi	ショ	

Vocabulary	Meaning	Pronunciation
辞書	dictionary	じしょ
書く	to write, draw, compose	かく
書	book, document	ショ
図書館	library	としょかん

Stroke Order

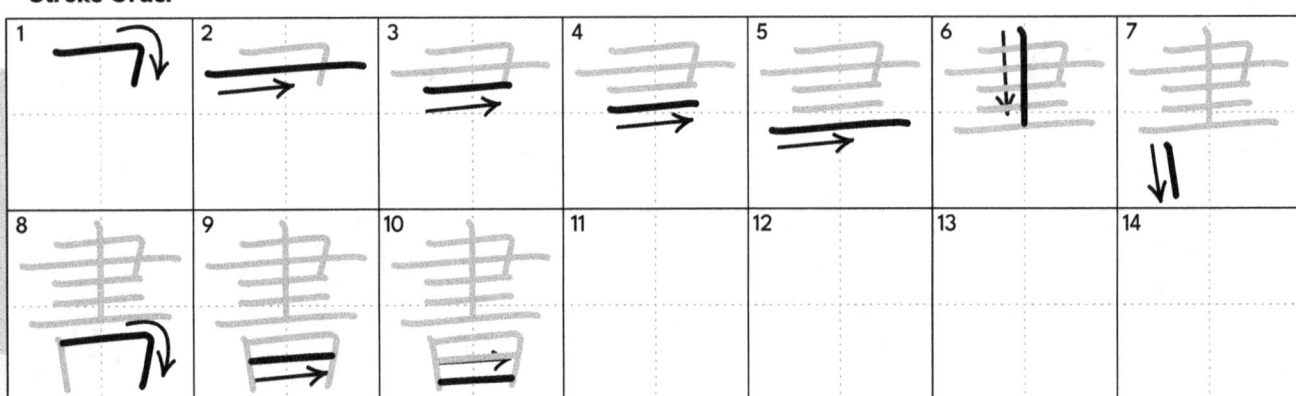

Writing Practice

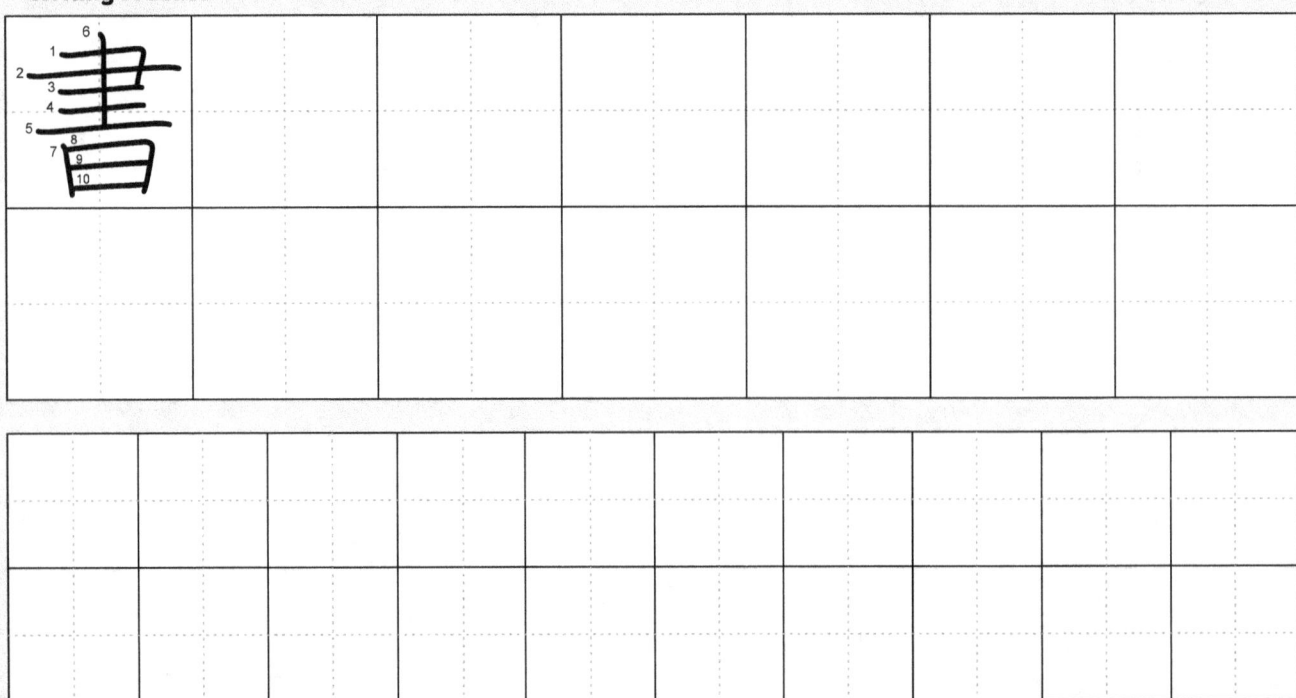

Kanji for Verbs

読

Meaning(s)	to read	**Components**	ル 亠 士 言
Radical	言 (言) (speech)	**Kun'yomi**	よ.む、-よ.み
Strokes	14	**On'yomi**	ドク、トク、トウ

Vocabulary	Meaning	Pronunciation
読む	to read, to guess	よむ
読者	reader	ドクシャ
読書	reading (a book)	ドクショ
読み方	pronunciation, reading	よみかた

Stroke Order

Writing Practice

JLPT N5

Meaning(s)	to talk	Components	口 舌 言
Radical	言（言）(speech)	Kun'yomi	はな.す、はなし
Strokes	13	On'yomi	ワ

Vocabulary	Meaning	Pronunciation
話す	to talk	はなす
会話	conversaton, chat	かいわ
電話機	telephone	でんわき
電話	telephone call	でんわ

Stroke Order

Writing Practice

Kanji for Verbs

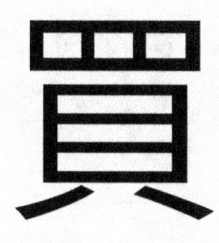

Meaning(s)	to buy	Components	八 目 買 貝
Radical	貝 (shell)	Kun'yomi	か.う
Strokes	12	On'yomi	バイ

Vocabulary	Meaning	Pronunciation
買い物	shopping	かいもの
買う	to buy, to purchase	かう
不買	not buying	フバイ
買収	acquisition, buy-out	バイシュウ

Stroke Order

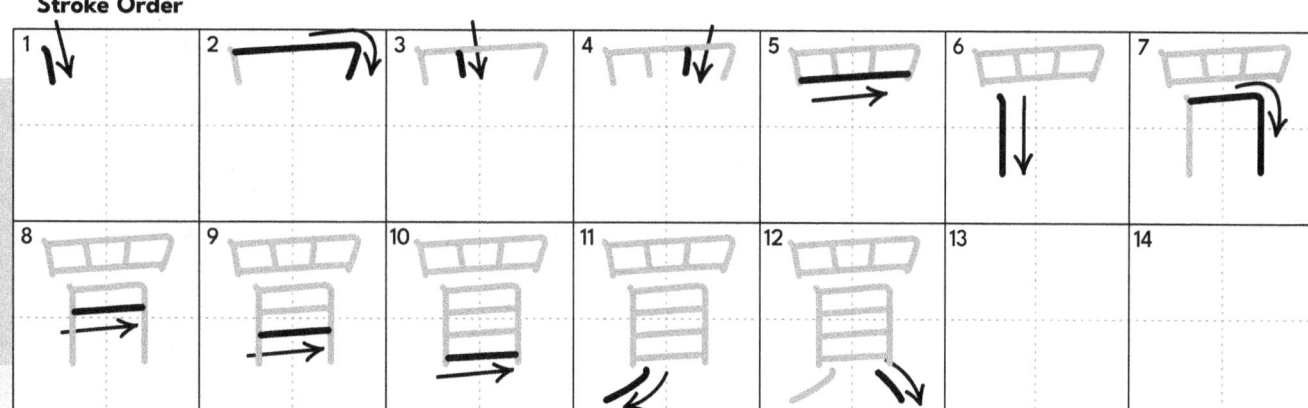

Writing Practice

JLPT N5

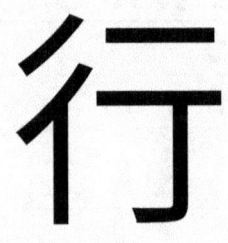

Meaning(s)	going, journey, carry out	**Components**	彳 行
Radical	行 (go, do)	**Kun'yomi**	い.く、ゆ.く、-ゆ.き
Strokes	6	**On'yomi**	コウ、ギョウ、アン

Vocabulary	Meaning	Pronunciation
銀行	bank	ぎんこう
行く	to go, to move (towards)	いく
旅行	travel, trip, journey	りょこう
飛行機	aeroplane, aircraft	ひこうき

Stroke Order

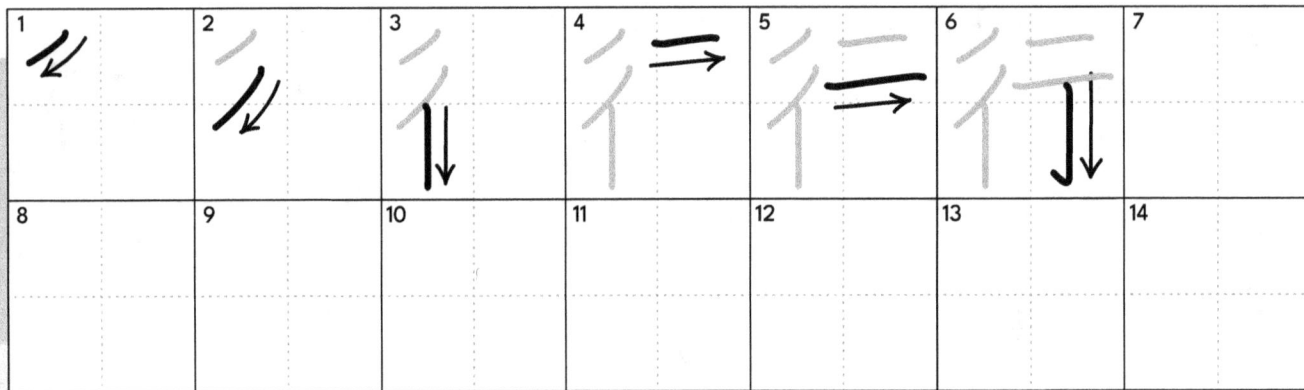

Writing Practice

Kanji for Verbs

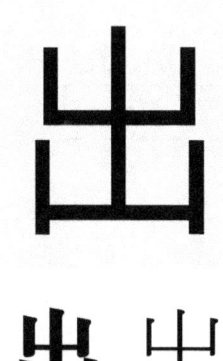

Meaning(s)	exit, leave, go out	**Components**	丨 山 凵
Radical	凵 (open mouth)	**Kun'yomi**	で.る、-で、だ.す
Strokes	5	**On'yomi**	シュツ、スイ

Vocabulary	Meaning	Pronunciation
出る	to leave, exit, go out	でる
出来る	to be able to, ready to	できる
出す	to take out	だす
出かける	to go out, to leave	でかける

Stroke Order

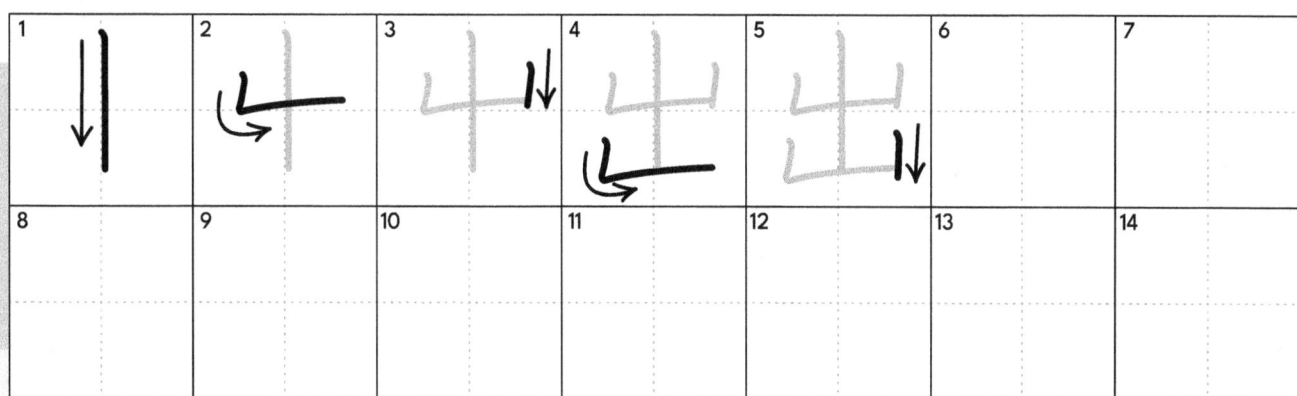

Writing Practice

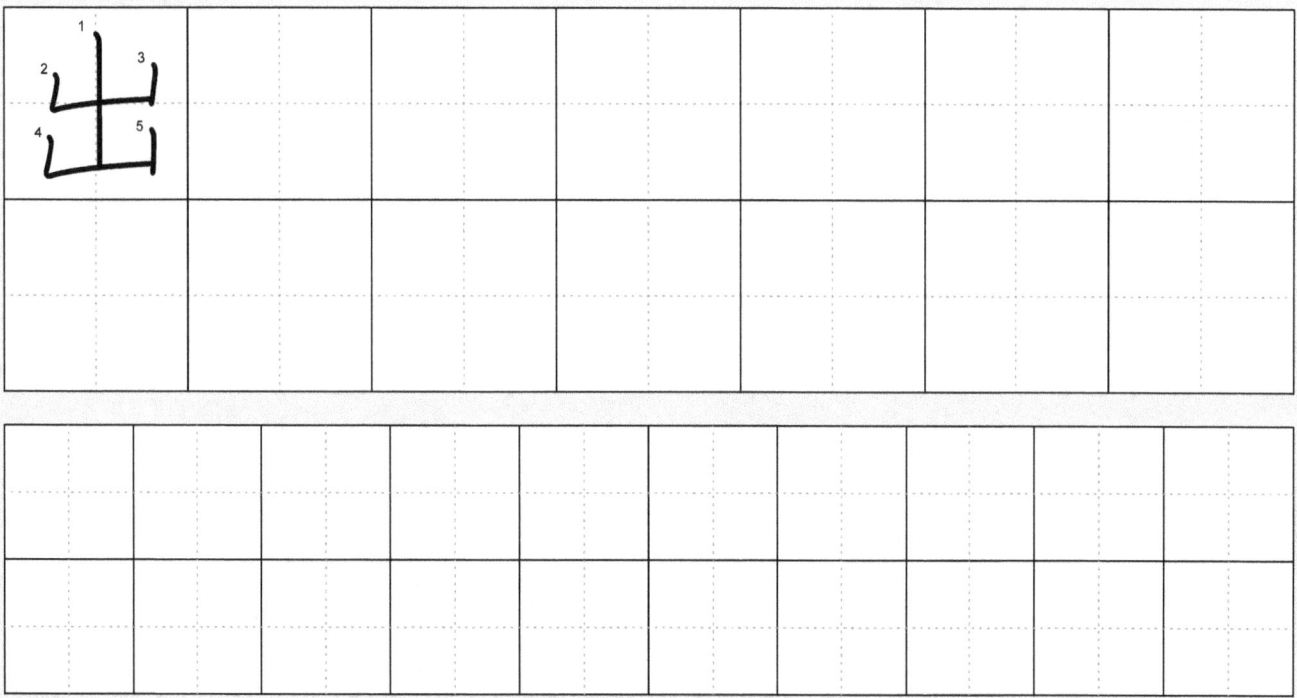

JLPT N5

Meaning(s)	to go in, to enter, insert	Components	入
Radical	入 (enter)	Kun'yomi	い.る、-い.る、-い.り
Strokes	2	On'yomi	ニュウ、ジュ

Vocabulary	Meaning	Pronunciation
入口	entrance, entry, gate	いりぐち
入る	to get in, to go in	いる
押入れ	(built in) wardrobe, closet	おしいれ
入学	admission (school), enrolment	にゅうがく

Stroke Order

Writing Practice

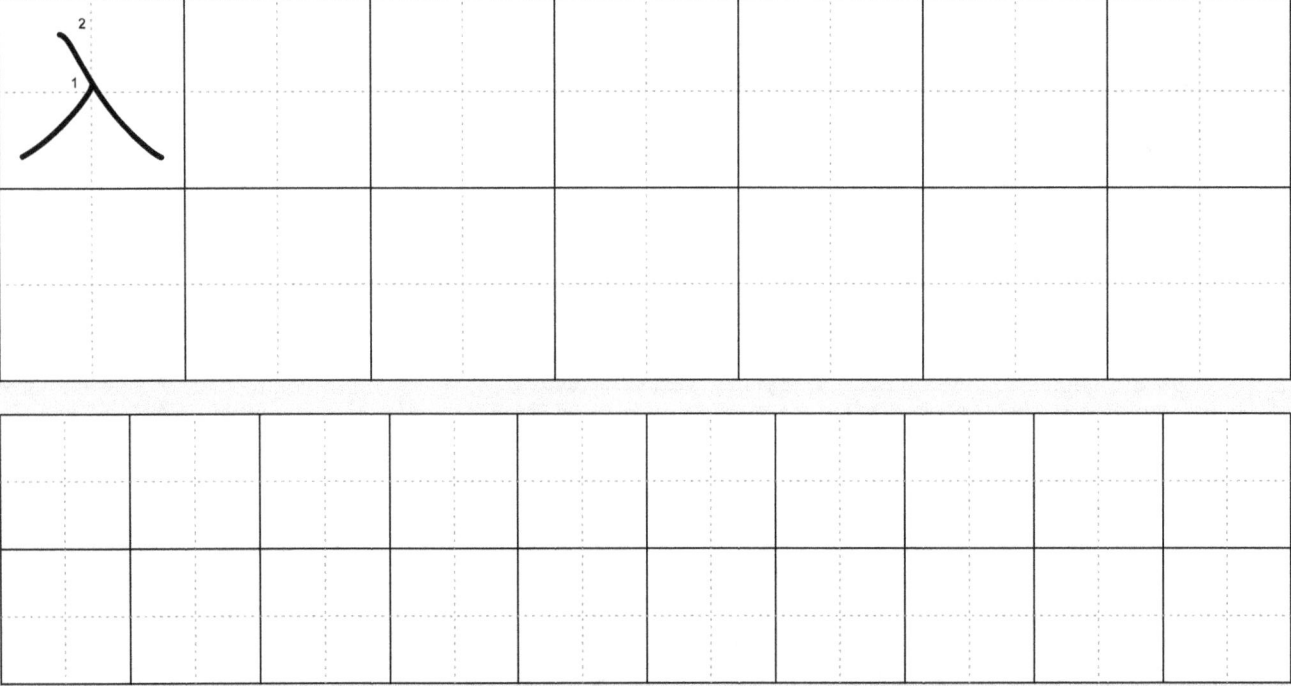

Kanji for Verbs

Meaning(s)	rest, day off, sleep	**Components**	化 木
Radical	人 (亻) (man, human)	**Kun'yomi**	やす.む、やす.まる
Strokes	6	**On'yomi**	キュウ

Vocabulary	Meaning	Pronunciation
休む	to take a day off	やすむ
休暇	day off, holiday	キュウカ
休み	rest, recess, respite	やすみ
休める	to rest, to suspend	やすめる

Stroke Order

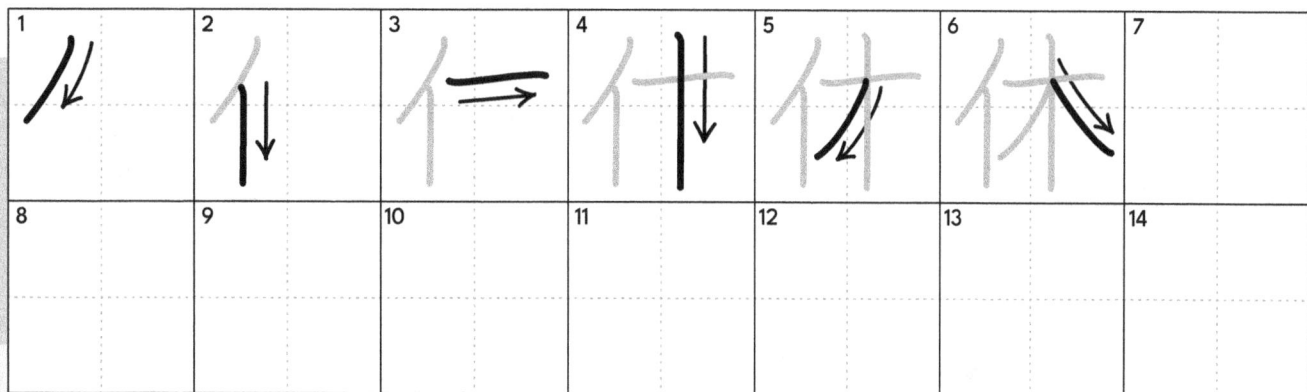

Writing Practice

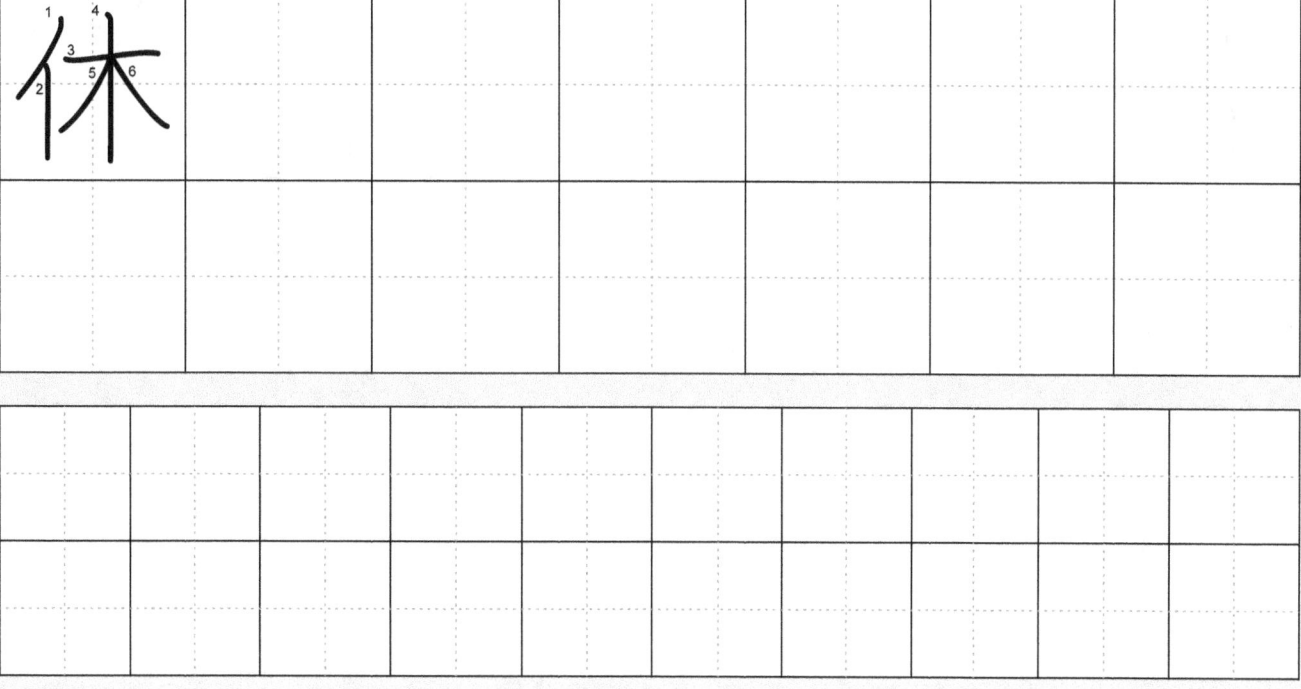

JLPT N5

Meaning(s)	to eat, food	Components	食
Radical	食 (飠) (eat, food)	Kun'yomi	く.う、く.らう、た.べる
Strokes	9	On'yomi	ショク、ジキ

Vocabulary	Meaning	Pronunciation
食べる	to eat	たべる
食堂	dining room	しょくどう
食事	meal, dinner	しょくじ
食	food	ショク

Stroke Order

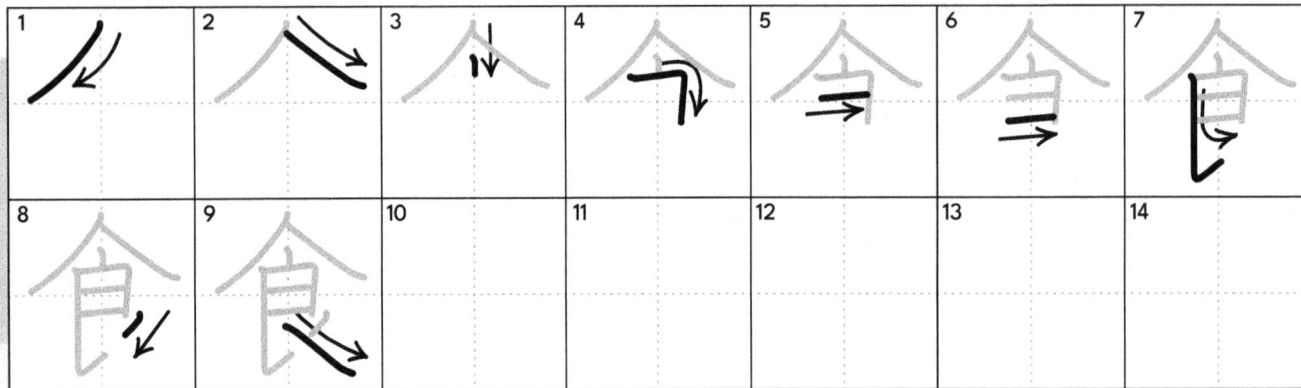

Writing Practice

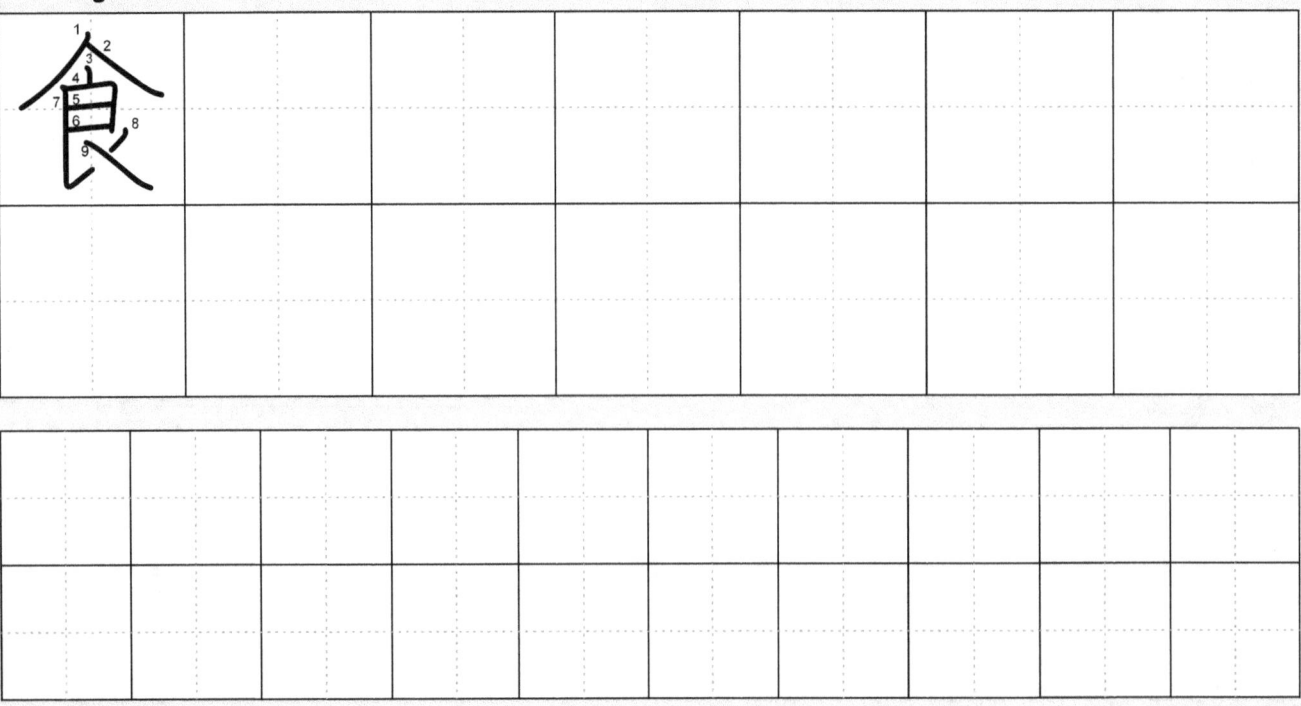

Kanji for Verbs

Meaning(s)	drink, smoke, take	Components	欠 食
Radical	食 (𩙿) (eat, food)	Kun'yomi	の.む、-の.み
Strokes	12	On'yomi	イン、オン

Vocabulary	Meaning	Pronunciation
飲み物	beverage, drink	のみもの
飲む	to drink	のむ
飲食	food and drink	インショク
飲み屋	bar, pub, tavern	のみや

Stroke Order

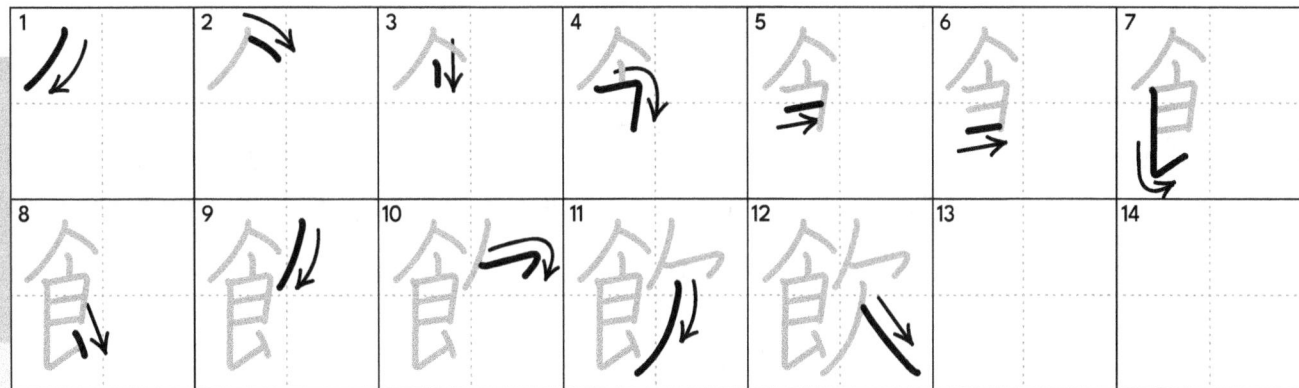

Writing Practice

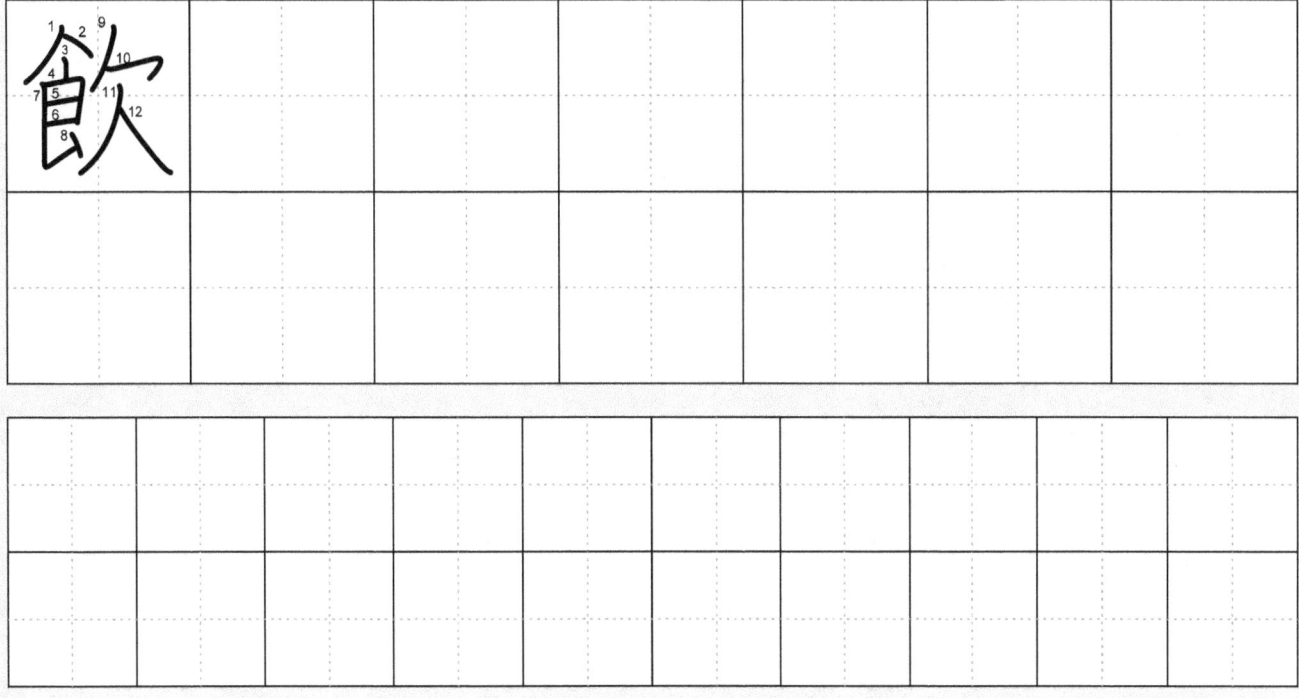

JLPT N5

言

Meaning(s)	to say, word	**Components**	言
Radical	言 (speech)	**Kun'yomi**	い.う、こと
Strokes	7	**On'yomi**	ゲン、ゴン

Vocabulary	Meaning	Pronunciation
言う	to say	いう
言葉	language, dialect	ことば
過言	exaggeration	カゴン
助言	advice, counsel	じょげん

Stroke Order

Writing Practice

Kanji for Verbs

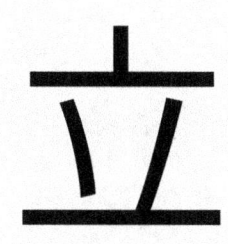

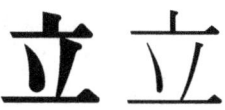

Meaning(s)	stand, rise, set up	Components	立
Radical	立 (stand, erect)	Kun'yomi	た.つ、-た.つ、た.ち-
Strokes	5	On'yomi	リツ、リュウ、リットル

Vocabulary	Meaning	Pronunciation
立つ	to stand (up), to rise	たつ
独立	independence	どくりつ
立派	splendid, fine	りっぱ
役に立つ	to be helpful/useful	やくにたつ

Stroke Order

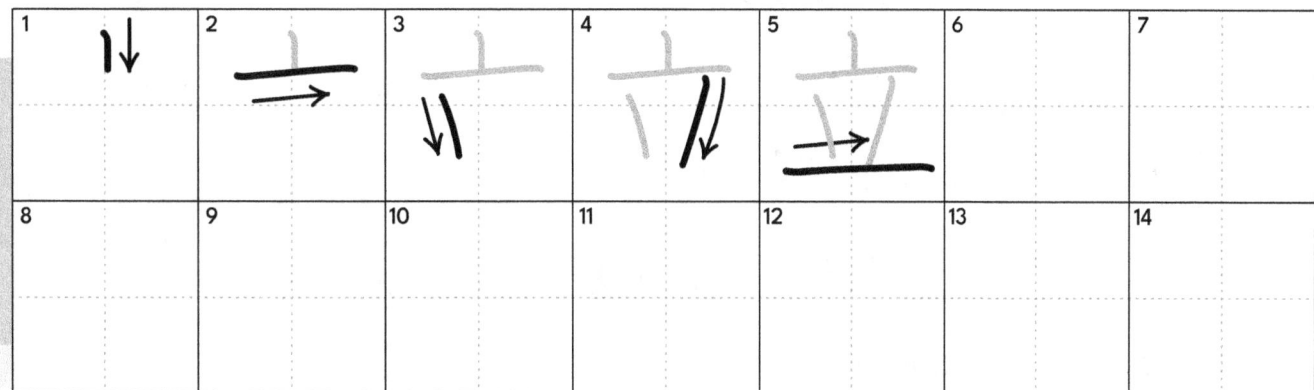

Writing Practice

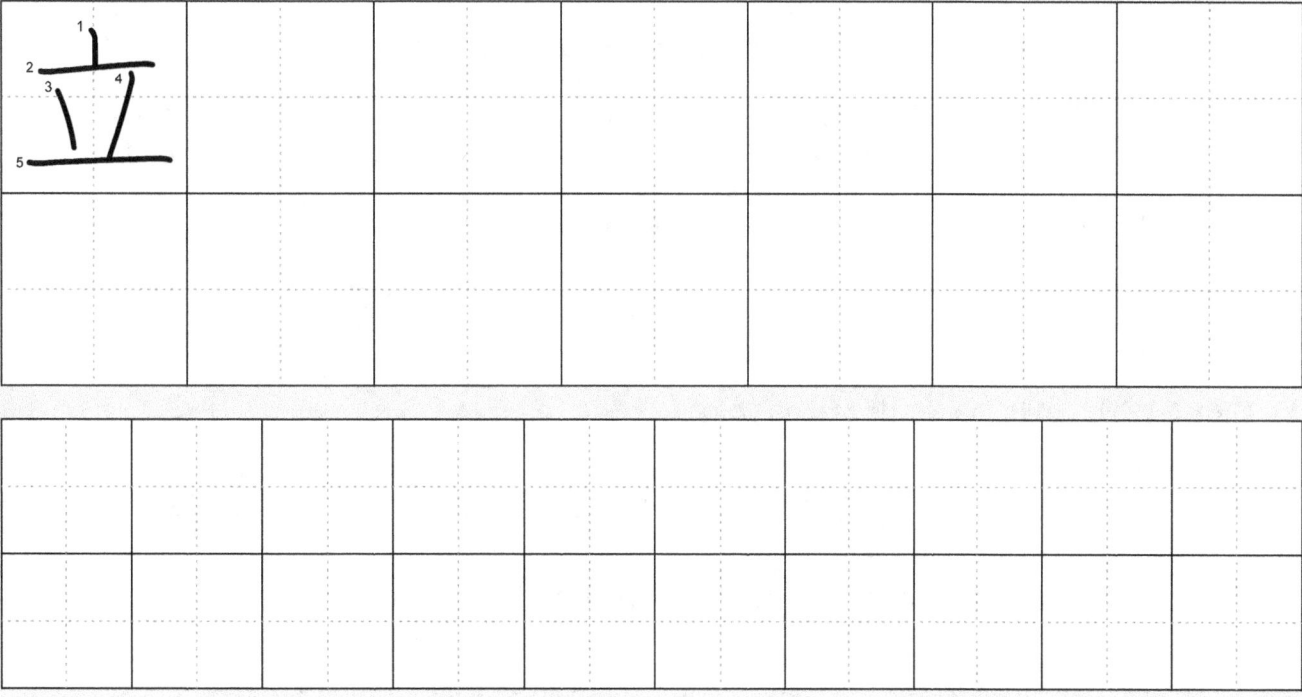

JLPT N5

Revision: Places & Directions

Q.54 Which of these kanji means *north*?

A. 下　　B. 上　　C. 南　　D. 東　　E. 北

Q.55 Which of these kanji means *south*?

A. 下　　B. 上　　C. 南　　D. 東　　E. 北

Q.56 Which of these kanji means *east*?

A. 国　　B. 西　　C. 道　　D. 南　　E. 東

Q.57 Which of these kanji means *west*?

A. 国　　B. 西　　C. 道　　D. 南　　E. 東

Q.58 Which of these kanji means *left* or *left-hand side*?

A. 右　　B. 北　　C. 左　　D. 社　　E. 外

Q.59 Which of these kanji means *right* or *right-hand side*?

A. 右　　B. 北　　C. 左　　D. 社　　E. 外

Q.60 At which of these places would you *buy groceries*?

A. 社　　B. 店　　C. 校　　D. 駅　　E. 学

Q.61 Which of these words means *Tokyo*?

A. 大阪　　B. 東京　　C. 神戸　　D. 京都　　E. 岡山

Q.62 How would you *pronounce Tokyo* in Japanese?

A. こうべ　　B. なごや　　C. おおさか　　D. とうきょう

Revision: Verbs

Q.63 Which of these kanji means *to read*?

A. 飲　　B. 話　　C. 聞　　D. 読　　E. 食

Q.64 Which of these kanji means *to write*?

A. 書　　B. 読　　C. 食　　D. 話　　E. 飲

Q.65 Which of these kanji means *to talk*?

A. 白　　B. 話　　C. 聞　　D. 書　　E. 食

Q.66 Which of these kanji means *to eat*?

A. 食　　B. 聞　　C. 読　　D. 長　　E. 言

Q.67 Which of these kanji means *to drink*?

A. 言　　B. 見　　C. 立　　D. 聞　　E. 飲

Q.68 Which of these kanji means *to meet*?

A. 立　　B. 会　　C. 入　　D. 出　　E. 行

Q.69 Which of these kanji means *to enter*?

A. 人　　B. 行　　C. 会　　D. 見　　E. 入

Q.70 Which of these kanji means *to buy*?

A. 飲　　B. 食　　C. 買　　D. 休　　E. 立

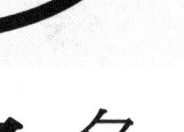

Meaning(s)	many, frequent, much	**Components**	夕
Radical	夕 (sunset, evening)	**Kun'yomi**	おお.い、まさ.に
Strokes	6	**On'yomi**	タ

Vocabulary	Meaning	Pronunciation
多い	many	おおい
多分	perhaps, probably	たぶん
滅多に	rarely, seldom	めったに
多彩	colorful, multicolored	たさい

Stroke Order

Writing Practice

Kanji for Adjectives

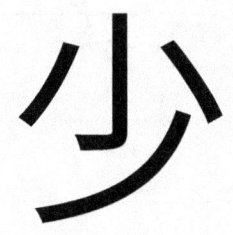

Meaning(s)	few, little	Components	ノ 小
Radical	小 (small)	Kun'yomi	すく.ない、すこ.し
Strokes	4	On'yomi	ショウ

Vocabulary	Meaning	Pronunciation
少ない	few, a little	すくない
少年	boy, lad, youth, juvenile	しょうねん
少女	girl (7-17yrs), young lady	しょうじょ
最小限	minimum, lowest, least	さいしょうげん

Stroke Order

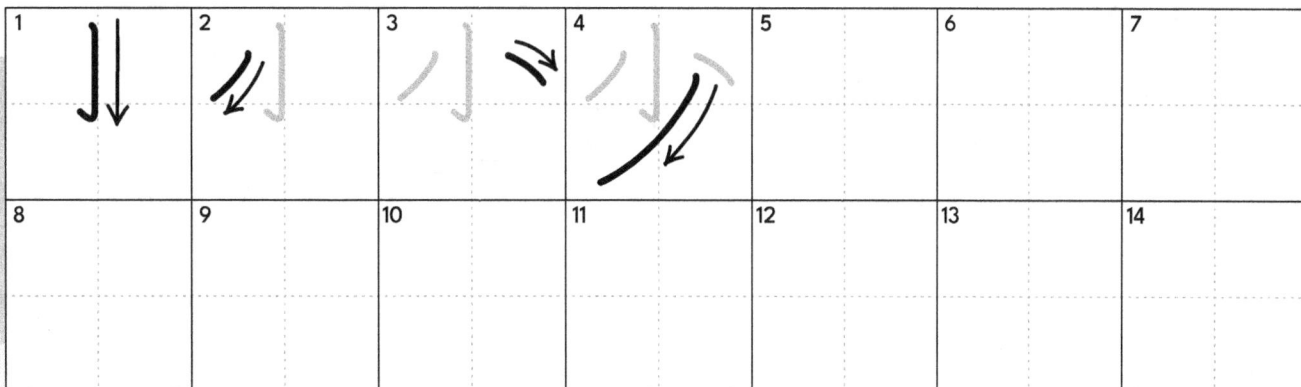

Writing Practice

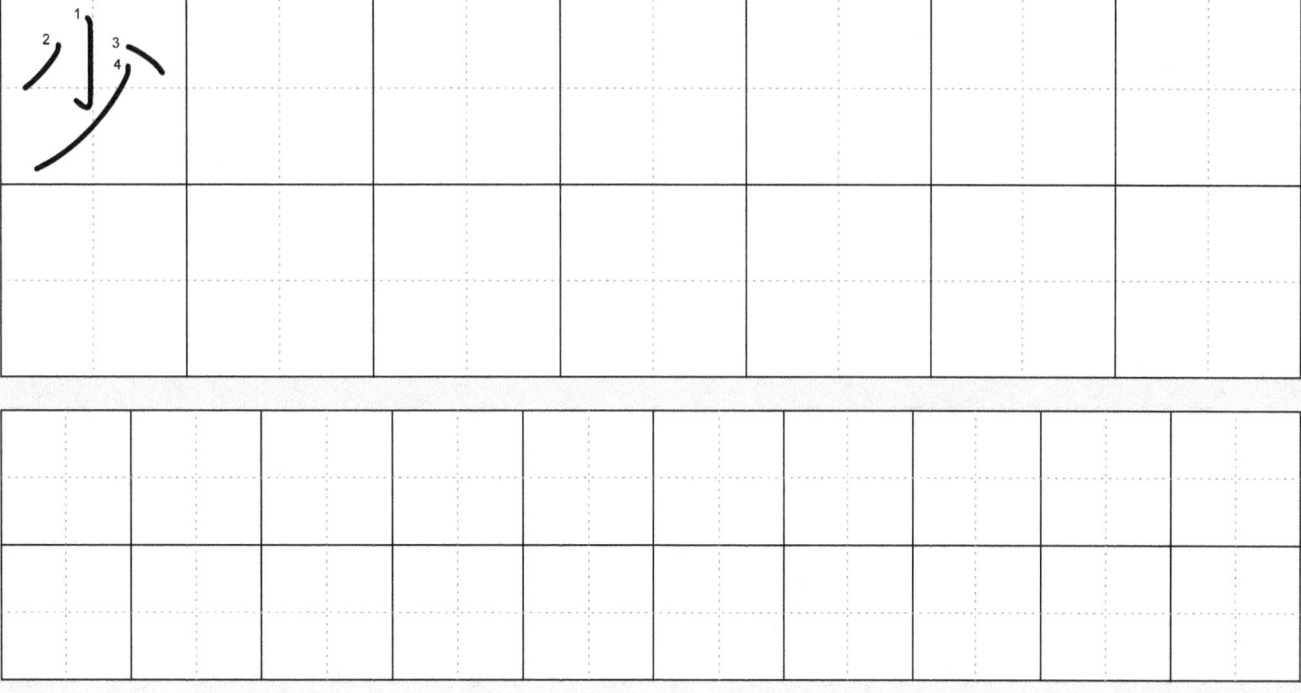

JLPT N5

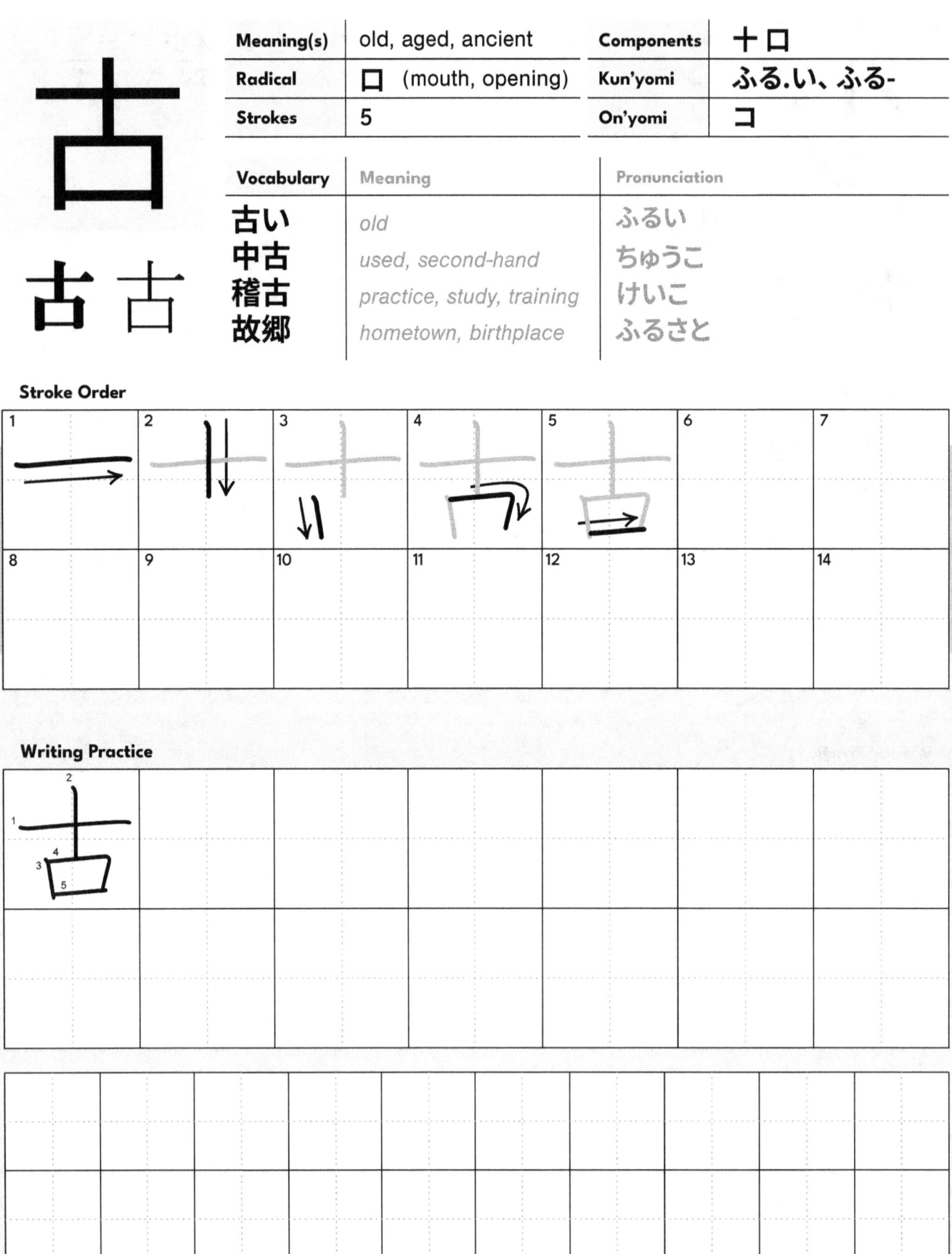

新

Meaning(s)	new, fresh, recent	Components	亠 井 斤 木 立 辛
Radical	斤 (axe)	Kun'yomi	あたら.しい、あら.た
Strokes	13	On'yomi	シン

Vocabulary	Meaning	Pronunciation
新聞	newspaper	しんぶん
新しい	new	あたらしい
新人	new face, rookie, new recruit	しんじん
新幹線	Shinkansen (bullet train)	しんかんせん

Stroke Order

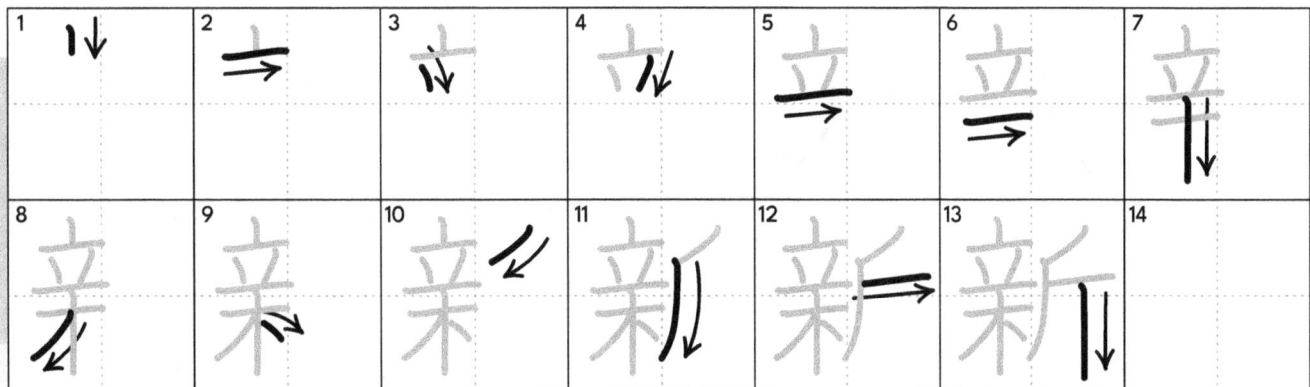

Writing Practice

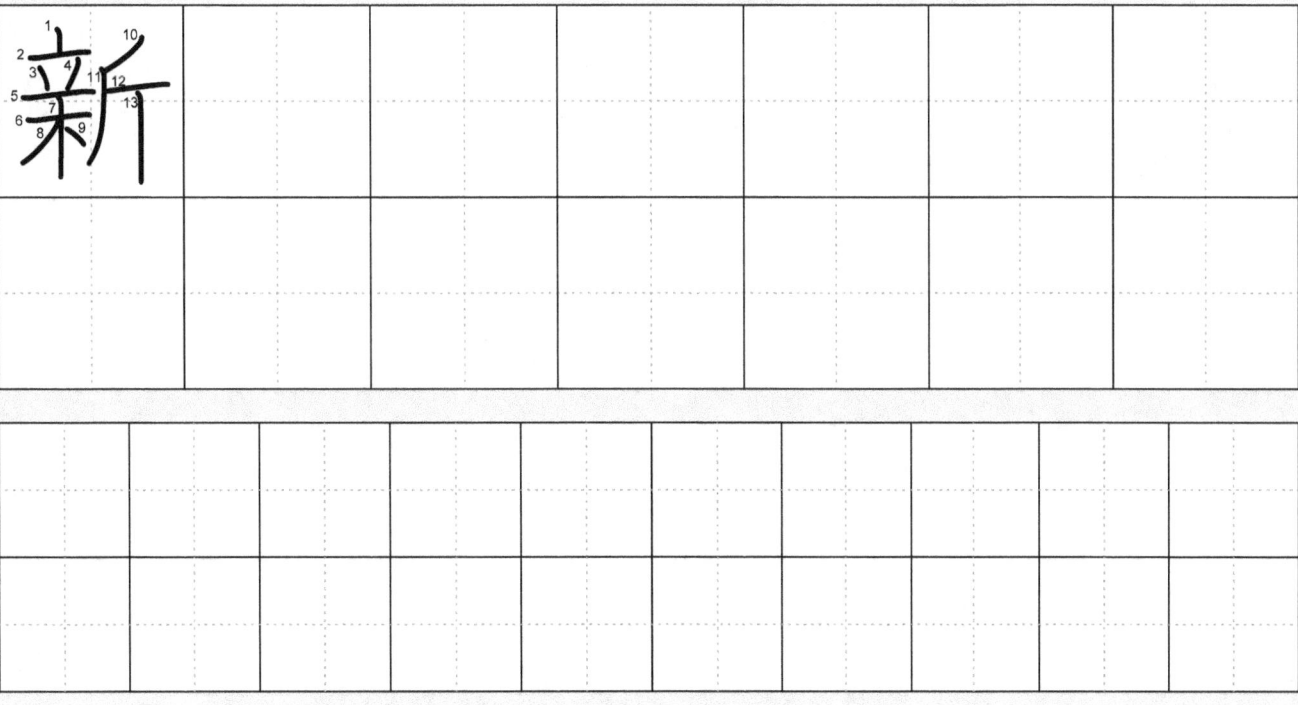

JLPT N5

Meaning(s)	large, big, important		Components	大
Radical	大 (big, very)		Kun'yomi	おお-、おお.きい
Strokes	3		On'yomi	ダイ、タイ

Vocabulary	Meaning	Pronunciation
大きい	big, large, loud	おおきい
大変	very, awfully, immense	たいへん
大学	university, college	だいがく
大事	important, serious	だいじ

Stroke Order

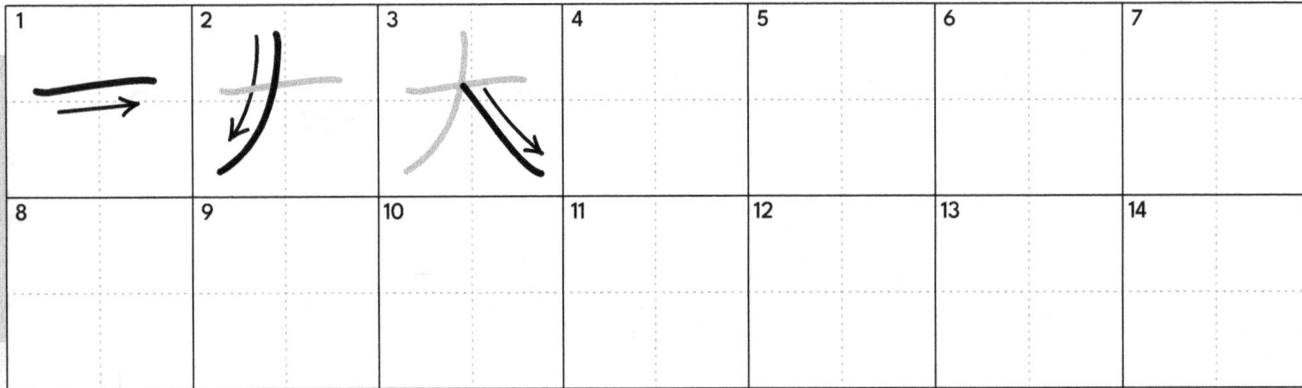

Writing Practice

Kanji for Adjectives

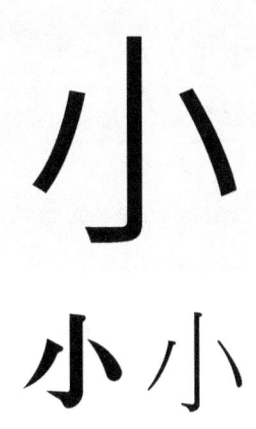

Meaning(s)	little, small, tiny	**Components**	小
Radical	小 (small)	**Kun'yomi**	ちい.さい、こ-、お-
Strokes	3	**On'yomi**	ショウ

Vocabulary	Meaning	Pronunciation
小さい	little	ちいさい
小屋	hut, cabin	こや
小指	pinky/little finger	こゆび
小学校	elementary school	しょうがっこう

Stroke Order

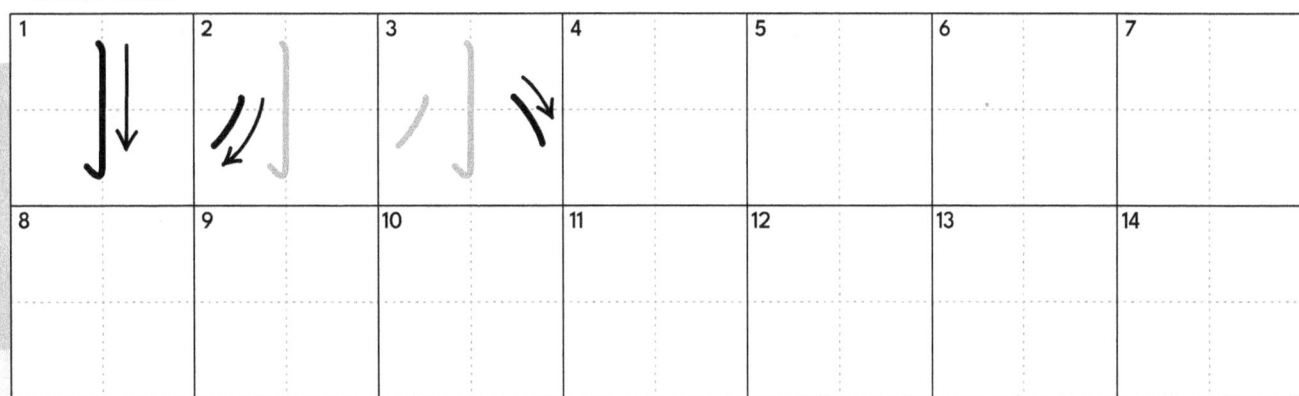

Writing Practice

JLPT N5

Meaning(s)	relax, cheap, low		**Components**	女 宀
Radical	宀 (roof)		**Kun'yomi**	やす.い、やす.まる
Strokes	6		**On'yomi**	アン

Vocabulary	Meaning	Pronunciation
安い	cheap	やすい
安全	safety, security	あんぜん
安易	easy, simple	あんい
安らか	peaceful, calm	やすらか

Stroke Order

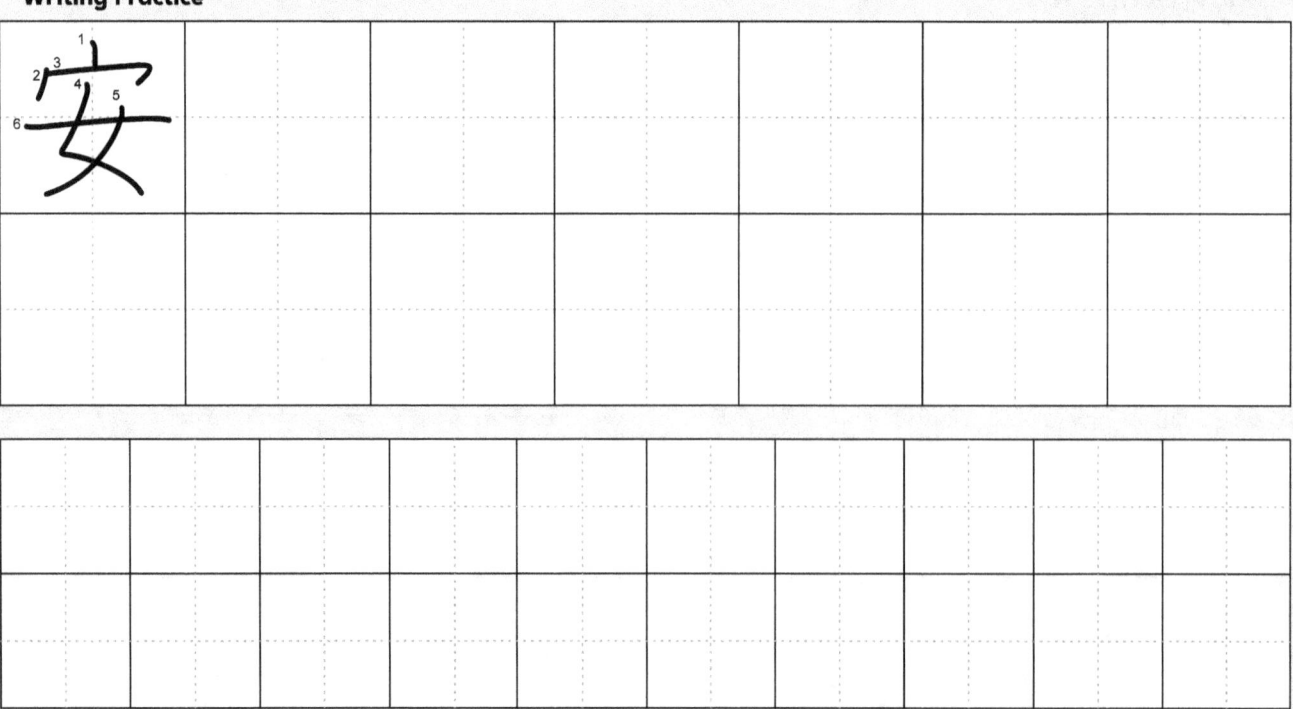

Writing Practice

Kanji for Adjectives

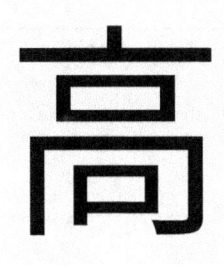

Meaning(s)	tall, high, expensive	Components	亠冂口高
Radical	高 (髙) (tall)	Kun'yomi	たか.い、たか、-だか
Strokes	10	On'yomi	コウ

Vocabulary	Meaning	Pronunciation
高い	expensive	たかい
高校	senior, high school	こうこう
高める	to raise, to lift	たかめる
名高い	famous, well-known	なだかい

Stroke Order

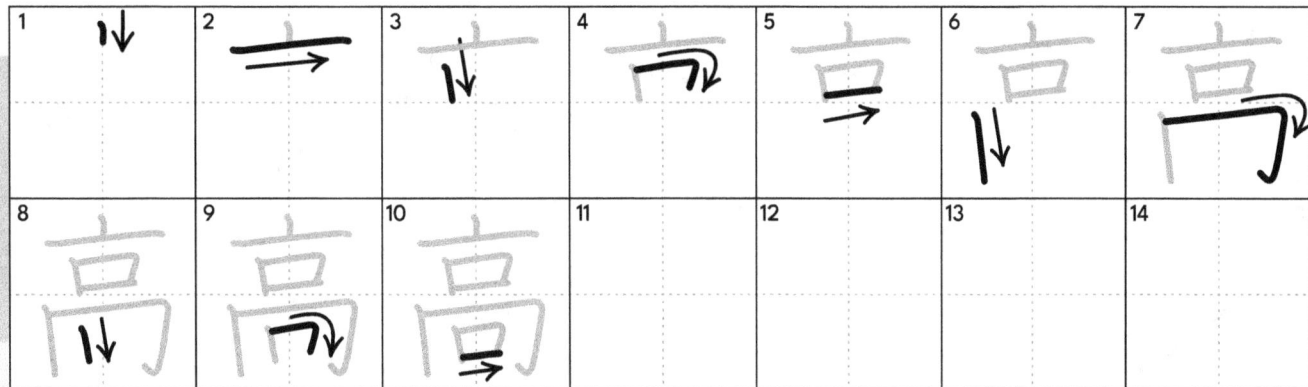

Writing Practice

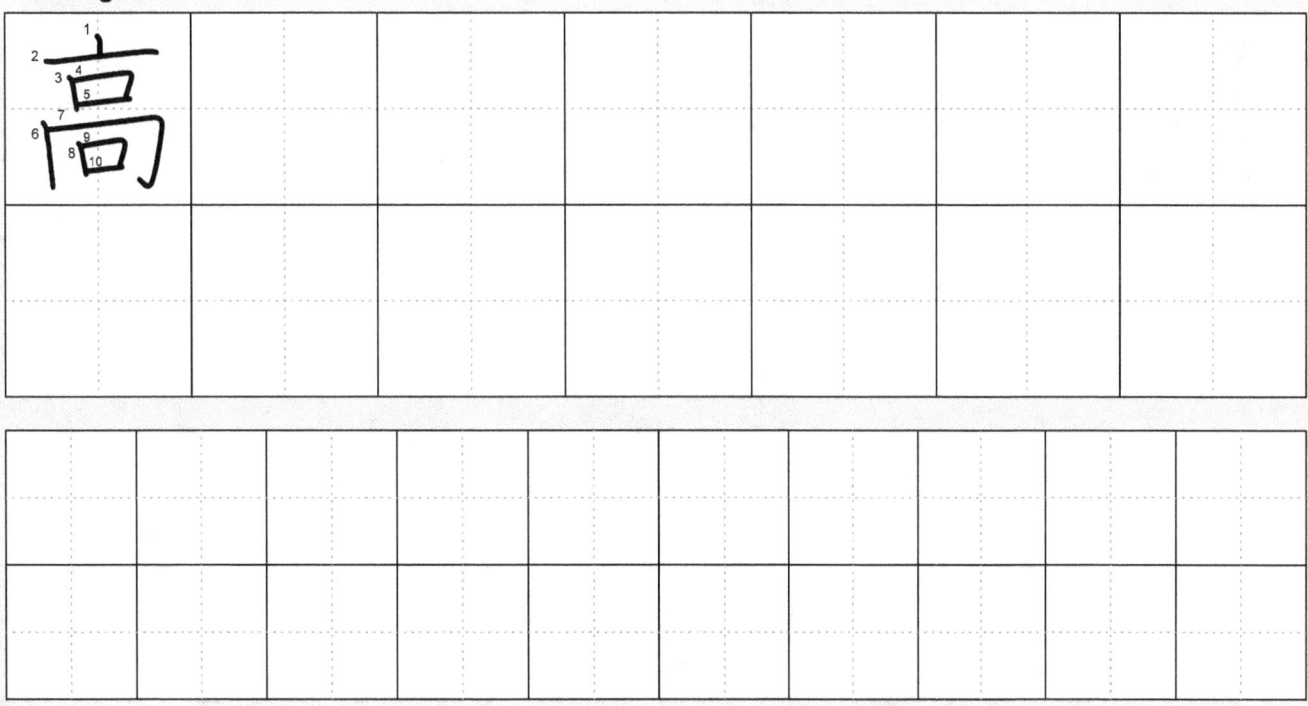

JLPT N5

Meaning(s)	long, leader, superior	Components	長
Radical	長 (镸) (grow, long)	Kun'yomi	なが.い、おさ
Strokes	8	On'yomi	チョウ

Vocabulary	Meaning	Pronunciation
長い	long (distance, length)	ながい
部長	manager	ぶちょう
校長	principal, headteacher	こうちょう
長方形	rectangle, oblong	ちょうほうけい

Stroke Order

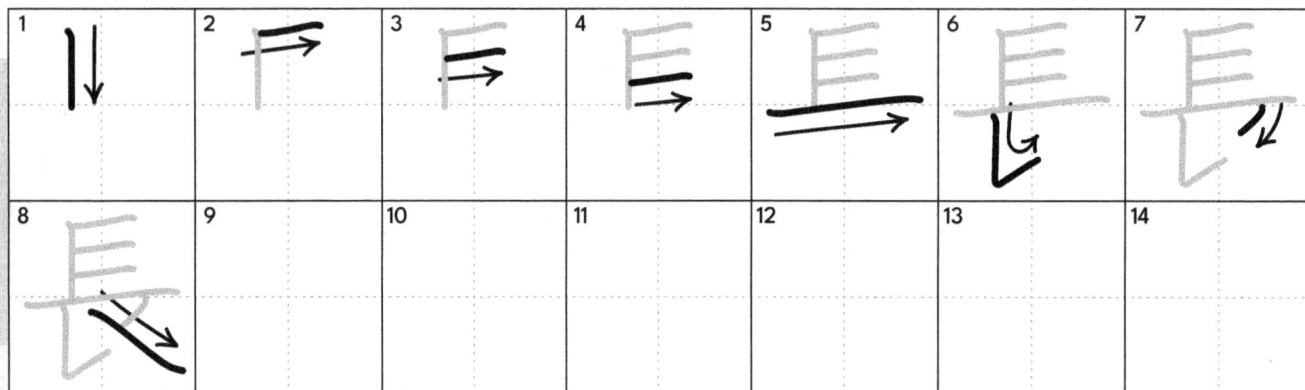

Writing Practice

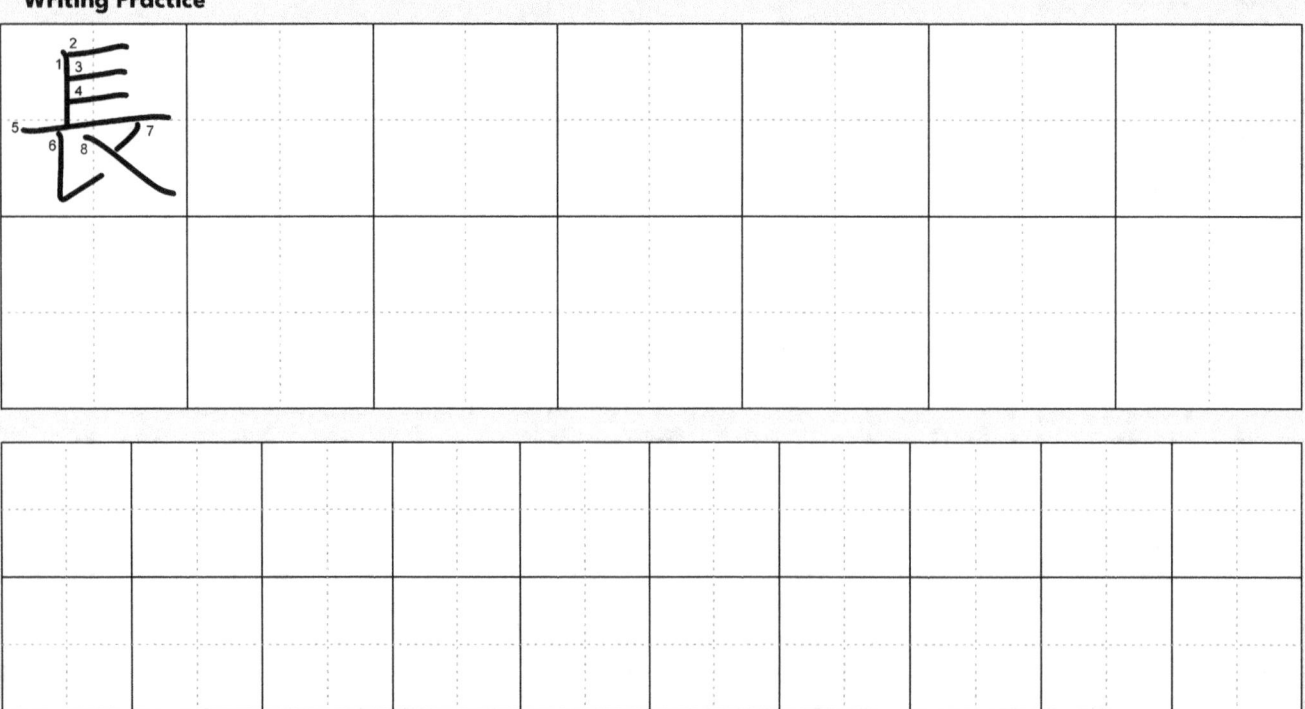

Kanji for Adjectives

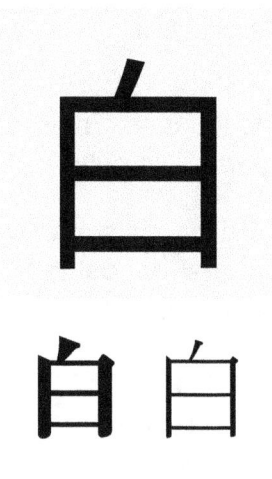

Meaning(s)	white, innocence	Components	白
Radical	白 (white)	Kun'yomi	しろ、しら-、しろ.い
Strokes	5	On'yomi	ハク、ビャク

Vocabulary	Meaning	Pronunciation
白い	white	しろい
面白い	interesting	おもしろい
青白い	pale	あおじろい
告白	admission, statement	こくはく

Stroke Order

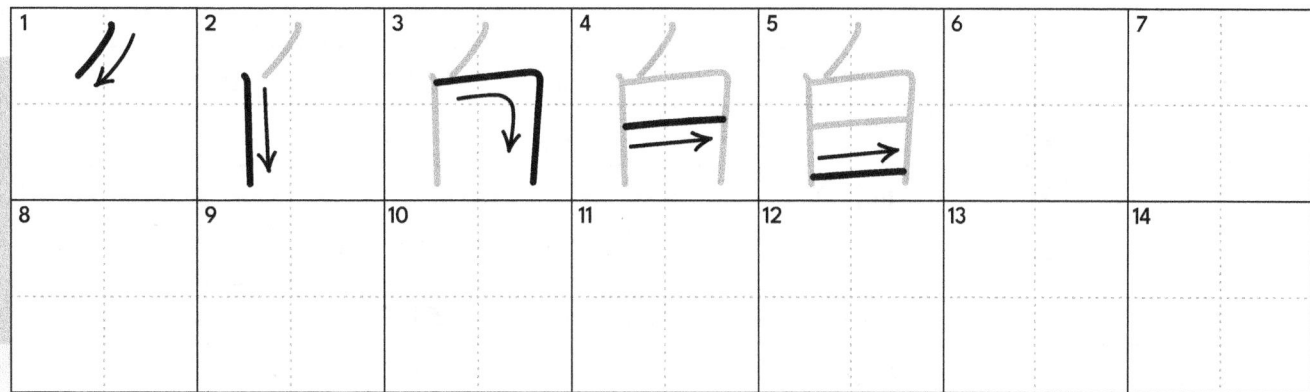

Writing Practice

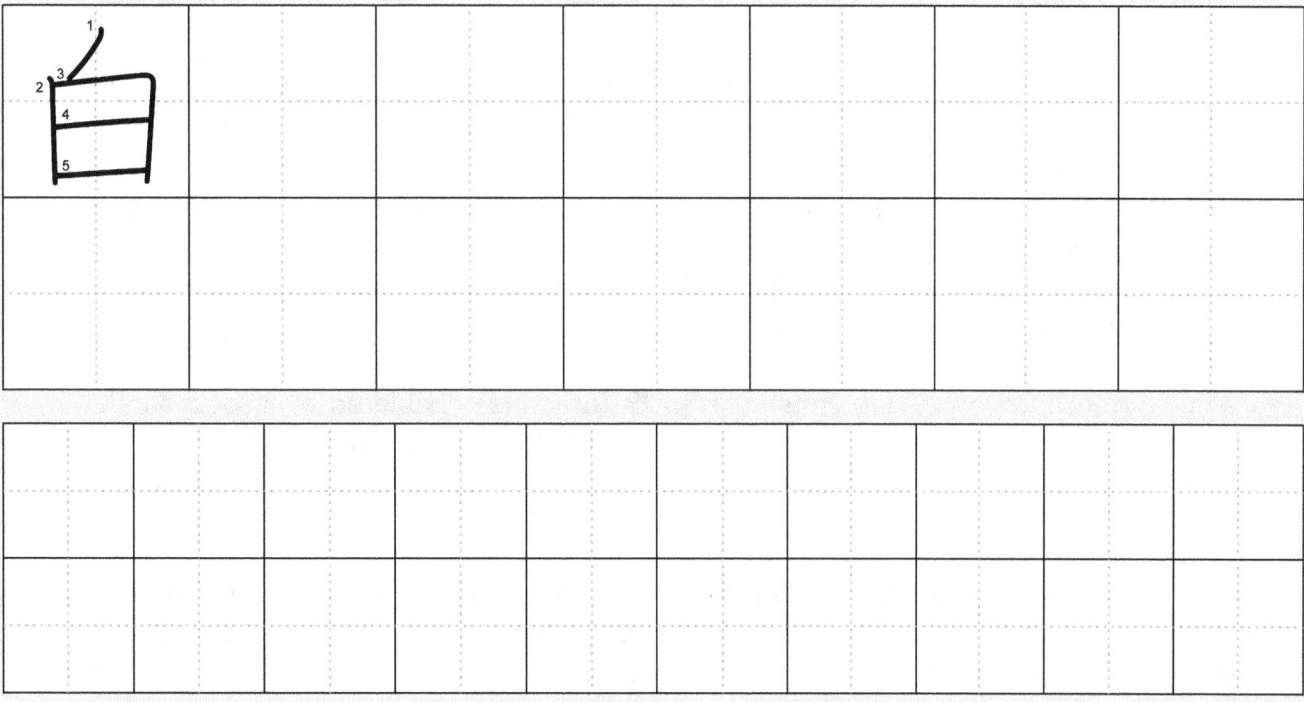

JLPT N5

Color Vocabulary

Colors are fundamental vocabulary that beginners learn in all new foreign languages. They hold additional, important meanings or associations that are important in Japanese culture.

Red, blue, black, and white are considered Japan's four *'traditional'* colors. Existing in some of the earliest historical texts, some believe these kanji represent broad visual concepts rather than specific colors, as they do today: 黒 dark *(black)*, 白 light *(white)*, 赤 clear *(red)*, and 青 vague *(blue)*.

Each color has a different kanji vocabulary to learn, but they become easy to recognize - lots of color words end with -色 (いろ, or 'iro'), meaning *"color, hue, tint, or shade."*

Color	Kanji Name	Pronunciation		Alternative (loan word)	
Red	赤	あか	aka	レッド	reddo
Yellow	黄色	きいろ	kīro	イエロー	iero-
Pink	桃色	ももいろ	momoiro	ピンク	pinku
Green	緑	みどり	midori	グリーン	guri-n
Orange	橙色	だいだいいろ	daidai iro	オレンジ	orenji
Purple	紫	むらさき	murasaki	パープル	pa-puru
Blue	青	あお	ao	ブルー	buru-
Brown	茶色	ちゃいろ	chairo	ブラウン	buraun
Black	黒	くろ	kuro	ブラック	burakku
White	白	しろ	shiro	ホワイト	howaito

赤 *(red)* is a popular color in Japan and features prominently on the national flag, where it represents the sun. It has associations with spirituality, religion, peace, and prosperity. The *Torii gates* at Shinto shrines, or 鳥居 *(とりい) in Japanese*, are painted a bright red color called 赤丹 (あかに/*akani*), as red is also symbolic of protection, power, and strength.

Samurai traditionally wore dark garments, so 黒 *(black)* is considered a masculine color. It is symbolic of formality too, and men often wear black tuxedos when they get married. There is an association with death and mourning, but this is more recent, influenced by cultures outside Japan.

Originally, 白 *(white)* was the color of mourning and is considered a sacred and blessed color in Japanese society. Historically, white garments were only worn by those attending funerals or by samurai performing ritual seppuku, but due to Western influence, it's now quite common in casual clothing. White is symbolic of peace, truth, purity, and cleanliness.

青 was once the kanji used for describing both *blue* and *green* colors. The separate kanji 緑 *(green)* was not widely adopted until the mid-1900s, explaining why lots of everyday vocabulary for *green things* still feature the *blue* kanji 青. For example, the word 青信号 means 'green (traffic) light,' but literally, it is あおしんごう *"blue (traffic) light."*

Blue symbolizes calmness or stability and is typically considered feminine. The materials used in making traditional indigo blue clothing dyes were ubiquitous, and blue came to have associations with ordinary people and being humble. Traditionally, it is a mystical color, has ancient connections with royalty, and is considered a lucky color.

The kanji colors in the table *(left)* are not automatically adjectives. They become descriptive words by adding extra characters or grammar - *just as with* 白い *on the previous page.*

The four *traditional* colors have adjective forms, made by simply adding kana い *(i)* after the kanji:

(赤 + い) + 車 = 赤い車
red   car
(akai kuruma)

Kanji colors ending -色 (いろ / *iro*) can work similarly, except that kana い *(i)* must be applied after the 色 (not the color word):

(黄色 + い) + 車 = 黄色い車
yellow   car
(kīroi kuruma)

All other kanji colors are made descriptive of an object using the **particle*** の, applying the same simple formula to bind the color word to the thing it describes:

[color] + の + [thing]

(緑 + の) + 車 = 緑 の 車
green   car
(midori no kuruma)

This formula also works for the two types of color words mentioned above, having the same overall effect. There is no need to add kana い *(i)* if using the の particle, however:

(赤 + の) + 車 = 赤 の 車
red   car
(aka no kuruma)

These descriptive nouns use the の *particle but have the same meaning as the first two examples above.*

(黄色 + の) + 車 = 黄色の車
yellow   car
(kīro no kuruma)

Alternatively, using additional sentence structure *(particles)*, you could describe an object's color by saying "[*something*] is [*a color*], e.g., この車は赤です。meaning *"that car is red"* (pronounced *ko no kuruma wa aka desu.*)

*Particles will be covered in much more detail during the grammar section of the book.

Here are some more relatively common color words that might be useful to know:

Color	Kanji Name	Pronunciation	Alternative (loan word)
Light / Sky Blue	水色	みずいろ　mizuiro	
Navy Blue	紺青	こんじょう　konjō	
Indigo 'Japan' Blue	藍	あい　ai	インディゴブルー　indigoburū
Emerald Green	碧色	へきしょく　hekiiro	
Teal / Turquoise	鴨の羽色	かものはいろ　kamonohairo	ターコイズ　ta-koizu
Peach / Skin Color	肌色	はだいろ　hadairo	
Gray	灰色	はいいろ　haiiro	グレー　gure-
Pure White	真白	まっしろ　mashiro	
Pitch Black	真黒	まっくろ　makkuro	
Bronze	青銅色	せいどういろ　seidou iro	
Silver	銀色	ぎんいろ　kiniro	シルバー　shiruba-
Gold	金色	きんいろ　giniro	ゴールド　go-rudo
Rainbow	虹色	にじいろ　nijiiro	

To complete this group, some less-frequently-used terms related to color vocabulary:

Color	Kanji Name	Pronunciation	Alternative (loan word)
Colorful	色鮮やか	いろあざやか　iro azayaka	カラフル　karafuru
Bright	明るい	あかるい　akarui	
Pale / Light	淡い	あわい　awai	
Vibrant / Vivid	鮮やか	あざやか　azayaka	
Light / Faint	薄い	うすい　usui	
Deep / Dark Color	濃い	こい　koi	
Transparent	透明	とうめい　tōmei	
Colorless	無色	むしょく　mushoku	
Milky White / Opal	乳白色	にゅうはくしょく　nyūhakushoku	オパール　opa-ru
Iridescent	玉虫色	たまむしいろ　tamamushiiro	
Holographic	-	-　horogurafikku	ホログラフィック

Revision: Adjectives

Q.71 Which of these kanji means *expensive* ?

A. 高   B. 買   C. 食   D. 長   E. 言

Q.72 Which of these kanji means *cheap* ?

A. 安   B. 九   C. 気   D. 万   E. 女

Q.73 Which of these kanji means *white* ?

A. 百   B. 目   C. 耳   D. 日   E. 白

Q.74 Which of these kanji means *big* ?

A. 人   B. 小   C. 少   D. 大   E. 八

Q.75 Which of these kanji means *small* ?

A. 八   B. 小   C. 六   D. 大   E. 木

Q.76 Which of these kanji means *many* ?

A. 右   B. 名   C. 多   D. 外   E. 女

Q.77 Which of these kanji means *old*?

A. 中   B. 古   C. 土   D. 生   E. 中

Q.78 Which of these kanji means *new* ?

A. 休   B. 社   C. 新   D. 校   E. 後

Q.79 Welches dieser Kanji bedeutet **"few"**?

A. 右   B. 小   C. 名   D. 女   E. 少

PART 7

Using Japanese

After having memorized the kana syllabaries and making a start on building your kanji knowledge, it's time to start looking at how grammar is applied. The content in this chapter is more advanced but should be simple to follow, and I will present concepts in a way that should make them easy to understand, irrespective of how far you have progressed.

Learners of all levels will benefit from a better understanding of how kana and kanji become actual Japanese sentences and texts. Even a little knowledge of some of the concepts here will give you a headstart. While those with more knowledge may be able to implement some of this information sooner, this chapter will help anybody looking to start reading Japanese.

This chapter will cover how you can bring the various written characters together and will include: particles and their role in structuring sentences, some helpful grammar patterns that you can implement with ease, how to conjugate different verb forms, and also how the language is adapted to suit more, or less, formal speech - amongst many other things.

Grammar is never the most exciting of topics, and progression naturally becomes slower at this stage in Japanese. There is a lot of information to absorb, so if the level of detail starts to overwhelm you, take a break and return. It may be good to repeat some of the earlier kana exercises or learn some new kanji if it feels overwhelming.

Language of Respect

The Japanese culture is one of respect, mindfulness, and politeness, or *Teinei*, which extends to how we use the language. As status and hierarchy are essential to everyday life in modern Japan, the language has a mandatory code of conduct that determines how you address and speak to people of different ranks. Two types of expression characterize the 'respectful language': elevating and speaking highly of people outside your immediate circle or above your position; and expressing yourself with humility and communicating in a humble, modest manner.

Anybody learning to read, write, and speak Japanese must also understand the extensive system of Honorific Speech, or 敬語 *(Keigo)*. You must first address people with the correct **Honorific Title** to show respect and politeness. Secondly, you should use an appropriate level of **Honorific Speech**.

The system of honorific speech is quite extensive and has its own unique rules for grammar and vocabulary. The following pages may save you from potentially awkward conversations or accidental expressions of disrespect. There are a variety of honorific suffixes that you must add to names and titles based on social rank and hierarchy. Additionally, different levels of polite speech affect how we say certain words when talking to other people.

Honorific Titles

Honorific titles are referred to in Japanese as 敬称 (けいしょう), or *Keisho*, and they are especially characteristic of Japan's respectful language. We respect the person we are addressing by adding small words, such as -san, -chan, or -sama, to the end of a person's family name (e.g., *Suzuki-sama*). Japanese people may add it to a foreigner's given name instead, out of respect, since that is what they would typically use (e.g., *Chris-san*).

The correct honorific suffix to add will depend on the setting, your relative social rank, and the nature of your relationship with that person. The honorific will often determine which level of polite speech the conversation will use.

A person's rank in Japan's hierarchy is determined by various criteria, such as their age, profession, a field of work, and their general social status. Some of the other factors that affect which honorific is used could be their background, education, or even gender.

Addressing somebody without an honorific title would set a highly informal tone, suggesting that your relationship is intimate or very close. It's essential, therefore, that you have an understanding of what each honorific title means. If you are unsure which is suitable, there are one or two relatively 'safe' options.

One *strict* rule to be aware of: you should **never** use an honorific when referring to yourself.

Some of the most common honorific titles include:

San さん	A neutral term, equivalent to Mr., Ms., Mrs., or Ms., typically used to address adults of equal rank/status. Versatile enough for both formal and informal speech, it's a safe option if you are unsure which other honorific is correct. It also applies to pets, stuff, company names, etc.	
Sama 様 さま	The most formal honorific and a formal version of '-*san*,' for addressing your superiors, those of higher rank, or anybody deserving of your respect. Equivalent to Sir/Madam and appropriate for addressing your customers or guests. Shows respect to elders and also for deities.	
Kun 君 くん	A masculine title that is used to address young men, boys, and male friends. Also generally applied when speaking to those with relatively junior status, younger people, and where the level of polite speech is lower. Could use at work to address somebody who started after you.	
Chan ちゃん	An endearing title, typically for addressing small children, especially girls. You can generally use it towards somebody or something that you consider 'cute.' Also used to address close friends, or a person with whom you are intimate - has particular use as a title for women by men.	
Senpai 先輩 せんぱい	Use this honorific when addressing a senior colleague or co-worker at the office or school. At college, for example, a freshman would use Senpai to refer to a sophomore this way. Generally, used for somebody of a similar social rank who is also more experienced than yourself.	
Sensei 先生 せんせい	Possibly familiar to those who watch TV or films with a Japanese theme. This honorific is suited to authority figures or persons who are experts in their field. It can be used on its own and is commonly used for teachers, doctors, lawyers, scientists, writers, politicians, etc.	
N/A よびすて	*Yobisute* is the term for an intential lack of honorific title use, and could be considered similar to 'first name basis' in the West. It's usually reserved for close friends or family or situations where the other party makes a specific request for it. Otherwise, it may be considered rude and informal.	

Other useful but less-frequently used honorifics include special titles in a business setting, such as *Buchou* (部長 / ぶちょう), for addressing your boss or manager at work, and also *Shachou* (部長 / ぶちょう) for company presidents or chief executives. Even less commonly, *Shi* (氏, し) which addresses a reader in formal writing, journals, and news.

Honorific Speech

Respectful language, 敬語 *(Keigo)* features multiple tiers of honorific speech to show increasing levels of respect when addressing people outside of your inner circle. Each level has its own special rules and grammatical features, such as alternate word forms and endings, that make it a complex topic for learners. However, it will be useful to understand what each level is and how they are used.

Keigo generally has three levels of speech:

- 丁寧語 (ていねいご), or *Teineigo*, is the **polite** form of Japanese that most foreign people tend to learn first. It is suitable for speaking to people you don't already know and for those of higher rank than yourself, making it the **safest option to use** if you are unsure.

Teineigo is characterized by sentences ending with '*-desu,*' and by verbs that end with '*-masu*' (see p.204). On the other hand, casual speech uses the 'dictionary form' of verbs, and sentences often end in だよ *(da yo)* or just よ. Another notable feature is the use of the *'honorific prefixes'* お〜 (*'o-'*) and ご〜 (*'go-'*), discussed in more detail shortly.

- 尊敬語 (そんけいご), or *Sonkeigo*, is the **respectful** Japanese that is used when you refer to others. It's for talking of senior people at work professionally and showing respect when speaking of somebody older. You can also use it to refer to those in a position of power. *Sonkeigo* is reserved for those of higher social rank, but it is also suited for use with customers or guests. The one way you should **never** use it is when referring to yourself.

Sonkeigo is characterized by exceptionally polite phrases, often longer and more rambling than usual. It's also tricky to conjugate verbs in this speech because it features many unique versions of common verb words. A quick and easy formula that usually works could be [お〜 or ご〜] + [verb stem] + になります - but, realistically, you would need to learn and memorize each of the various alternatives.

- 謙譲語 (けんじょうご), or *Kenjōgo*, is the **humble** form of Japanese speech that you may use when talking about yourself or your actions and also potentially those of people in your 'inner circle.' It would be best if you did not use this speech style to speak of strangers or anybody of a higher social rank. Humble language is used in expressions of assistance to others, apologetic phrases, and generally courteous statements.

Kenjōgo also features many different verb forms and alternative words for specific nouns. For example, instead of referring to yourself as 人 (ひと), or *hito*, meaning person, you would say 者 (もの), or *mono*.

Elegant Speech

In Japanese, 美化語 (びかご), or *Bikago*, means 'beautified speech.' It describes how you can make certain words sound more elegant, giving an added sense of politeness to your manner of speaking. We typically add the *'honorific prefix'* 御 in front of terms representing the relatives or belongings of the person we address.

This prefix is usually written in kana, as pronunciation will depend on the word it precedes. Most of the time, the prefix is お〜 *('o-')* for Kun'yomi vocabulary, and for On'yomi, it's ご〜 *('go-')*. It has an equivalent meaning to *"Your dear [acquaintance]"* or *"Honorable [object],"* but there is not a direct translation in English.

There are certain objects that only ever use お〜, such as お茶 (おちゃ) *'tea,'* or お金 (おかね) *'money,'* but you learn about these things over time. Don't be too concerned about using honorific prefixes until you can speak Japanese at a good, conversational level. Eventually, flourishes like these will allow you to convey yourself politely and likely impress those you talk to.

For now, it may be useful to recognize the sorts of words that are given an honorific prefix in written Japanese, so that they don't cause confusion during reading practice:

	Casual			Polite		
mother	母	はは	*haha*	お母さん	おかあさん	*okaasan*
father	父	ちち	*chichi*	お父さん	おとうさん	*otousan*
day off	休み	やすみ	*yasumi*	お休み	おやすみ	*oyasumi*
name	名前	なまえ	*namae*	お名前	おなまえ	*onamae*
tea	茶	ちゃ	*cha*	お茶	おちゃ	*ocha*

We add お〜 to Kun- readings, and words with native Japanese origins. Lots of these words tend to be single-kanji vocabulary, words in and of themselves, but they can be accompanied by hiragana. お〜 is commonly used for people and relatives.

	Casual			Polite		
guide	案内	あんない	*annai*	ご案内	ごあんない	*goannai*
mood	期限	きげん	*kigen*	ご機嫌	ごきげん	*gokigen*
husband	主人	しゅじん	*shujin*	ご主人	ごしゅじん	*goshujin*
plan	計画	けいかく	*keikaku*	ご計画	ごけいかく	*gokeikaku*
question	質問	しつもん	*shitsumon*	ご質問	ごしつもん	*goshitsumon*

ご〜 is added in front of On- readings and Sino-Japanese words (Chinese origin).

Basics of Grammar

To put your newfound Japanese knowledge to good use, you will have to first learn about some of the rules surrounding grammar. With lots of other dedicated resources available to learn more in-depth about this topic, this small part of our book seeks to provide you with a step-by-step guide to some of the basics.

Just as the alphabet became easier to learn with some basic background knowledge, the grammar rules in Japanese will too. The following pages will explain a more streamlined series of rules in simple terms that should make it feel easier to learn and apply grammar to your Japanese.

Sentence Structure

First of all, Japanese sentences are arranged differently from those in English. When you compare the two languages, we see the following patterns:

English word order = **S V O** / Subject > **Verb** > Object *(E.g. I eat oranges)*
Japanese word order = **S O V** / Subject > Object > **Verb** *(E.g. I oranges eat)*

The specific order of words in English sentences tells us **who** *(the subject)* is **doing** *(a verb)* **what** *(the object)*. Fixed word order matters to the meaning.

Japanese is less rigid, and the order in which we words write words has less impact on the fundamental meaning. *Except for verbs,* the order of the other words is flexible. Sentences are structured using '*particles*' instead. In simple terms, particles are merely markers that tell us how one word relates to another - especially to verbs.

In this example, the 'direct object' *(oranges)* is marked with を and would have the same meaning, regardless of location. Particles follow a word to tell us what that word does - the word can move, with its particle, while keeping its function.

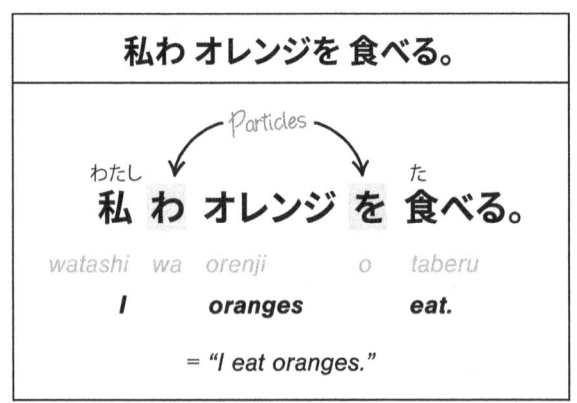

So, while Japanese sentences tend to follow patterns *like SOV,* the important detail to understand is that **particles determine the meaning**, **not the word order.**

As 'rules' tend to make life easier for beginners, and because Japanese sentence structure is governed by particles, just remember - **verbs always come at the end of sentences.**

Introduction to Verbs

- There is no future tense in Japanese. What it does have is a basic past tense (e.g., *to have eaten, "I ate"*) and also a 'not past' tense *(e.g., to eat, "I eat")*. 'Not past' is effectively the present tense but has this name because we use the same versions of words to create an equivalent to the future tense.

You force sentences to infer present or future tense by ruling out other interpretations. We achieve this by specifying a time frame, adding words referencing the present or future *(e.g., now, tomorrow, next year, etc.)*, or through context and expressions of future intent.

This example shows how adding a time word means we can only understand the sentence as being about a future event. In other words, the future tense is implied, and no other meaning, past or present, is drawn from it:

"I will eat oranges tomorrow."

- **Japanese verbs do not change for different people** carrying out that action. These alternate verb forms are more prevalent in languages like French, Spanish, or Italian, where words vary, depending on who is 'doing' the activity *(e.g. 'Parlo,' Italian for "I speak," becomes 'Parla' for "he speaks" or 'Parlano' for "they speak," etc.)* In Japanese, 話す (はな).

- **Japanese words are not gendered** like they are in other foreign languages, which means you have less to remember or learn. In French, for example, feminine and masculine words are referred to with different word forms for 'the' or 'a' - e.g. **'la/une** chat' *('the/a cat,'* feminine) or **'le/un** chien' *('the/a dog,' masculine)*. You must memorize which gender each word has and which rules/words apply.

While it's not quite the same thing, men and women can use different versions of the same word, here and there. The most common is the word for 'cool,' where women may say すごいね *(sugoi ne)*, but men often shorten it to すげー *(suge-)*. The short version may sound more masculine when pronounced.

- **We use the same words for singular and plural nouns**. Whether talking about one *'orange'* or 2 *'oranges,'* it's always オレンジ. There are no irregularities to memorize either, where plural words don't follow the *[noun + 's']* pattern, such as *'mouse/*mice.' Japanese uses the same word, 鼠 (ねずみ), whether there are one, two, or twenty mice. Where the number of *nouns* is important, you add context with other words.

Masu & Desu, for Politeness

Japanese has different word forms to suit the differing levels of politeness in speech. The **polite,** *formal* **option should be your 'default' mode**, used when talking to a stranger or somebody of a superior rank *(see Honorifics, page 330)*.

Meaning 'polite language,' 丁寧語(ていねいご), or *Teineigo*, is acceptable for use with most anybody and means you will avoid any danger of accidentally being disrespectful or rude. It's not too tricky to change casual speech to suit polite speech. Essentially, polite speech is characterized by sentences ending with **'-masu'** and **'desu.'**

When sentences end with a verb, the verb should take its *'-masu' form*. To create this, we need to find the verb stem by stripping any existing grammatical suffixes first. *It's not as complicated as it sounds:*

Dictionaries show verbs with a plain, present tense ending. We extract the stem *(or root)* from that word before adding the *'-masu' suffix*.

• For any verb that ends with る *('ru')*, you simply drop the 'る' part and add ます *('-masu')*:

* *-ru verbs are known as 'Ichidan' verbs*

• It's slightly different for verbs that end with other *'-u'* sounds - *i.e., characters from Row* う *in the hiragana tables (u, ku, gu, tsu, mu, etc.)*

First, you change the *'-u'* sounding symbol into its corresponding *'-i'* sound *(ku > ki, gu > gi, su > shi, etc.)*, and *then* you can add ます *(masu)* to the end:

** *-u verbs are known as 'Godan' verbs.*

• There are two *irregular* verbs, する *(suru)* and 来る *(kuru)*, that work a little differently.

Each ends with a る *('ru')* that you will replace with the '-masu' suffix, but both *begin* with a *'-u'* sound that we switch out for their *'-i'* sound counterpart. す becomes し, & く becomes き :

Incidentally, **you have just learned how to retrieve verb stems**, also referred to as the *'masu stem,'* which you can also use to conjugate for other grammatical forms.

*/** *Verbs, their categories, and verb conjugations are covered in the next few pages.*

Informal speech is easy, as the plain, *'dictionary'* form doesn't need altering for the present tense. For casual speech, you can use the regular '-ru' and '-u' versions of a verb: 食べる (たべる) *taberu,* 'to eat,' 飲む (のむ) *nomu,* 'to drink,' and so on.

The second aspect of polite speech is the use of です or *'desu.'* The quick and easy 'rule' is: to **add *'desu'* to the end of sentences that don't end in *'-ru'* or *'-u'* verbs** *(as they would otherwise end '-masu').*

The most fundamental role of です *(desu)* is marking politeness. You can add it to the end of your sentences without necessarily changing the underlying meaning. *Unless it ends with a verb already - then it needs to be '-masu.'*

です *(desu)* adds the politeness you need for formal speech:

However, *'desu'* has other uses too. Typically meaning *'is,' 'it is,'* or *'to be,'* です *(desu)* is a verb in and of itself. It's commonly translated as the polite, present tense form of だ *(da),* but technically, they are both connecting words called a *copula.*

A *copula* brings the subject of a sentence and its description together - "oranges **are** fruits" or "the ocean **is** blue." They are almost a *sort of suffix* that makes another word work as a verb. We use *'desu'* as this is already its polite form:

です *(desu)* is a valuable word to know when creating your first sentences. It will show [one thing] equals [another thing], that A = B, or something *'is'* something:

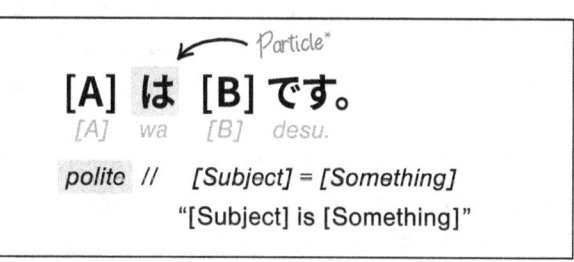

です can also highlight the properties of something/somebody. It will show identity or can describe a particular state (of being):

*Note: は *(wa)* is a particle that marks nouns as the topic of the sentence [A], but without emphasizing that part important information. It does not mean ' = / equals'.

Inside & Outside

Understanding the uniquely Japanese concept of **Uchi** and **Soto** can help you learn when and why you should use honorific language. In Japanese, 内 (うち), or *Uchi*, means "inside," and 外 (そと), or *Soto*, means "outside." This pair of words play a fundamental role in many aspects of everyday life. The core idea is to separate things between **Uchi**, also translated as 'home,' or 'house,' and **Soto**, the 'outside,' particularly for people and social interactions.

At a basic level, the way that we remove outdoor footwear before entering the home is an excellent example of *Uchi* and *Soto* in practice. Your outdoor shoes are considered *Soto* and so only used outside, but your indoor slippers are considered *Uchi*. To wear outdoor shoes in any house would be considered disrespectful. Similar principles apply to people, and acquaintances are divided into two distinct groups and treated differently - your 'in-group' and the 'out-group.' Behaviour and language will differ in the company of people from either group.

Your 'in-group,' or 'inner circle' typically consists of the people with whom you are most comfortable being yourself. This group usually includes your closest friends and family but may extend to the colleagues in your team at work. Staff outside your team would not be in your *Uchi*. Formal speech, *Keigo*, is not usually needed when speaking to those in *Uchi*, as you have a robust and familiar relationship with these people. *Doing so could make things very awkward, as if you are deliberately putting distance between you.*

The 'out-group,' or *Soto,* is the opposite, and it includes all other people from 'outside' of your immediate circle. You could be somewhat familiar with people in this group, but they are not people with whom you could be your true self - as you would amongst your *Uchi*. This group is where those of senior rank would fit - your elders, people above you at work, and generally anybody with status or authority over you. *Soto people* should be treated with respect and politeness, and you would address these people in the correct manner with a suitable level of *Keigo*, or honorific language.

Unless referring to yourself or members of your 'in-group' during a conversation, you would always use a respectful level of language when talking to somebody from your 'out-group.' You should always speak humbly of yourself and 'in-group.' You would not refer to people in your Uchi with honorific titles when talking to people in your Soto.

Another interesting difference between conversations with your *Uchi* or *Soto* is the practice of 'Honne' and 'Tatemae.' Briefly, 本音 (ほんね), or *Honne*, is where you can refer to your true feelings amongst your *Uchi*. Your *Honne* might be an opinion that doesn't conform to the expectations held by broader society or even expected to be held by somebody in your circumstance or position. In contrast, your 建前 (たてまえ), or *Tatemae*, is a front, or façade, that you present to fit in amongst your *Soto*.

Verb Categories

Conjugating verbs in Japanese is not as complex as it sometimes appears. A certain level of consistency means that we can usually apply rules in lots of cases. Most of the time, you take the [verb stem] and add the appropriate ending for the meaning you want the verb to have. As briefly mentioned on the page that talks about '-masu' and 'desu,' Japanese verbs fall into one of **three categories**, each of which tells you how you should conjugate the verb:

1. '-u verbs' - **Godan** verbs, or 五段動詞 (ごだんどうし) *godan-doushi*
2. '-ru verbs' - **Ichidan** verbs, or 一段動詞 (いちだんどうし) *ichidan-doushi*
3. ...and two - **Irregular** verbs, or 不規則動詞 (ふきそくどうし) *fukisoku-doushi*

• **Godan** verbs end with '-u' sounds - the characters from the う-row in hiragana charts. The name translates to '5-level verbs,' where 五 *(go)* means "five" and 段 *(dan)* means "level," because the '-u' at the end of these verbs can change into any of the other vowel sounds when conjugated - meaning five possibilities, or 'levels.'

話す	*hanasu*	'to speak'	聞く	*kiku*	'to hear'	
飲む	*nomu*	'to drink'	遊ぶ	*asobu*	'to play'	*(Examples of*
死ぬ	*shinu*	'to die'	買う	*kau*	'to buy'	*Godan verbs)*

• **Ichidan** verbs end in '-ru' る but, more specifically, those that end with '-iru' or 'eru' (in dictionary form). Their name translates to '1-level verbs,' where 一 *(ichi)* means "one." They are far easier to conjugate because, as their name suggests, they act in the opposite way to *Godan* verbs. *Ichidan* verb stems keep to just one vowel sound, no matter which kind of ending is applied.

Verbs ending in either [a/o/u] + る are categorized as *Godan* verbs, including certain '-iru' and 'eru' verbs. Unfortunately, the only way to determine which category a verb falls into is to check in a dictionary.

食べる	*taberu*	'to eat'	要る	*iru*	'to need'	
見る	*miru*	'to see'	切る	*kiru*	'to cut'	
出る	*deru*	'to leave'	知る	*shiru*	'to know'	
寝る	*neru*	'to sleep'	入る	*hairu*	'to enter'	
起きる	*okiru*	'to get up/wake up'	喋る	*shaberu*	'to chat'	
調べる	*shiraberu*	'to investigate'	走る	*hashiru*	'to run'	

(Ichidan verbs ending '-iru' & 'eru')　　　*(Godan verbs ending '-iru' & 'eru')*

• **Irregular** verbs are just the two words mentioned previously, する *(suru)* and 来る *(kuru)*. Both are common and tend to be memorized quite naturally.

Common Conjugations

The following pages provide an overview of each category of verb rules. You don't need to memorize these right away - you can use them for reference later.

Overall it's a little easier to conjugate verbs for the polite *'-masu'* speech, so that is where we will begin. You may recognize the first set of rules for the present tense form, as they were explained a few pages back. As you will see, the rules are consistent between the different verb forms:

● Polite — Present Tense *'-Masu' Form*

Just as you learned a few pages back, the polite, present tense *'-masu'* form is easy to create. You find the stem and simply add ~ます *(-masu)* to the end:

Category	Conjugation Rule	Example			
る verbs	Remove る, add ~ます	食べる	*taberu* ↝ 食べます	*tabemasu*
う verbs	う to い-row, add ~ます	飲む	*nomu* ↝ 飲みます	*nomimasu*
Irregular	Stem becomes し	する	*suru* ↝ します	*shimasu*
	Stem is **k-** *(or ki, or ko)*	来る	*kuru* ↝ 来ます	*kimasu*

For う-verbs, with readings that end with characters in the う-row of your hiragana charts, all う sounds *(e.g., ku, mu, nu, etc.)* change to their counterpart in the い-row - their *'-i'* sound equivalents *(e.g., ki, mi, ni, etc.)*.

● Polite — Past Tense *'-Mashita' Form*

We create the polite, past tense version in a very similar way. This time, we find the verb stem and add ~ました *(-mashita)* to the end:

Category	Conjugation Rule	Example			
る verbs	Remove る, add ~ました	食べる	*taberu* ↝ 食べました	*tabemashita*
う verbs	う to い-row, add ~ました	飲む	*nomu* ↝ 飲みました	*nomimashita*
Irregular	Stem becomes し	する	*suru* ↝ しました	*shimashita*
	Stem is **k-** *(or ki, or ko)*	来る	*kuru* ↝ 来ました	*kimashita*

● Polite — *Negative* Present Tense *'-Masen' Form*

The polite form of negative, present-tense verbs is straightforward too. Take the same *'-masu'* stem and add ~ません *(-masen)* to the end:

Category	Conjugation Rule	Example		
る verbs	Remove る, add ~ません	食べる *taberu*	→	食べません *tabemasen*
う verbs	う to い-row, add ~ません	飲む *nomu*	→	飲みません *nomimasen*
Irregular	Stem し, add ~ません	する *suru*	→	しません *shimasen*
	Stem '*k-*', add ~ません	来る *kuru*	→	来ません *kimasen*

● Polite — *Negative* Past Tense *'-Masen Deshita' Form*

Conjugation for the polite, negative, past-tense is similar to above, but you add a little more this time. Take the *'masu'* stem and add ~せんでした *(-masen deshita)* to the end:

Category	Conjugation Rule	Example
る verbs	Remove る, add ~ませんでした	食べませんでした *tabemasen deshita*
う verbs	う to い-row, add ~ませんでした	飲みませんでした *nomimasen deshita*
Irregular	Stem し, add ~ませんでした	しませんでした *shimasen deshita*
	Stem '*k-*', add ~ませんでした	来ませんでした *kimasen deshita*

This conjugation combines the regular past-tense version of the verb ('-masen' form) with the negative conjugation of です *('desu,' meaning 'to be').*

More often than not, beginners automatically learn only the polite language, with the polite '-masu' verb conjugations. This strategy will help you avoid having a potentially awkward or rude manner in early conversations. However, the tone of your initial practice conversations is likely to be less formal, so learning the 'plain' or 'dictionary form' is a better, long-term option. If you can only use and practice the polite forms of speech, it could become difficult to understand real, conversational Japanese - the sort that you might commonly have with friends, family, or even colleagues, in practice.

● Plain — Present Tense *'Dictionary Form'*

This version is really simple. The plain, present-tense version of verbs is the same as the version that you will find displayed in dictionaries - no conjugation is necessary:

Category	Conjugation Rule	Example		
る verbs	n/a	食べる	*taberu*	"to eat"
う verbs	n/a	飲む	*nomu*	"to drink"
Irregular	n/a	する	*suru*	"to do"
	n/a	来る	*kuru*	"to come"

● Plain — Past Tense *'-Ta' Form*

The plain, past-tense conjugations of う-verbs depend on which '-u' sounds their dictionary form *(otherwise known as the 'infinitive')* ends with:

Category	Conjugation Rule	Example			
る verbs	Remove る, add ~ました	食べる *taberu*	→	食べた	*tabeta*
う verbs	Ending う/つ/る, remove then add ~った	買う *kau*	→	買った	*katta*
	Ending く, remove then add ~いた	聞く *kiku*	→	聞いた	*kiita*
	Ending ぐ, remove then add ~いだ	泳ぐ *oyogu*	→	泳いだ	*oyoida*
	Ending す, remove then add ~した	話す *hanasu*	→	話した	*hanashita*
	Ending ぬ/ぶ/む, remove then add ~んだ	飲む *nomu*	→	飲んだ	*nonda*
Irregular	Stem becomes し	する *suru*	→	しました	*shita*
	Stem is **k-** *(or ki, or ko)*	来る *kuru*	→	来ました	*kita*

An example of one common exception to these rules is 行く *(iku), meaning 'to go,' which has a different conjugation that makes it easier to pronounce. It becomes* 行った *or 'itta,' not 'iita.'*

● Plain — *Negative* Present Tense *'-Nai' Form*

For verbs ending with characters in the う-row of your hiragana charts, all う sounds *(e.g., ku, mu, gu, etc.)* change to their counterpart in the あ-row - their equivalent *'-a'* sound *(e.g., ka, ma, ga, etc.)*. There is just one exception - for those with a reading that ends in う / *'u'* itself, change the う into わ / *'wa' (not just あ / 'a')*:

Category	Conjugation Rule	Example			
る verbs	Remove る, add ~ない	食べる *taberu*	→	食べない	*tabenai*
う verbs	う to あ-row, add ~ない	飲む *nomu*	→	飲まない	*nomanai*
	Ends う, change う to わ, then add ~ない	買う *kau*	→	買わない	*kawanai*
Irregular	Stem し, add ~ない	する *suru*	→	しない	*shinai*
	Stem *ko*, add ~ない	来る *kuru*	→	来ない	*konai*

The exceptions sound more natural with わ *('wa')*. Otherwise, words such as 買う *(kau)*, meaning *'to buy,'* or 歌う *(utau)*, *'to sing,'* would become awkward to pronounce. It's also worth noting that the stem for 来る *(kuru)* is こ *(ko)* and not き *(ki)* here.

● Plain — *Negative* Past Tense *'-Nakatta' Form*

This conjugation is similar to the negative present tense, with the same changes to vowel sounds and same exceptions, only it ends with ~なかった *(nakatta)* instead:

Category	Conjugation Rule	Example			
る verbs	Remove る, add ~なかった	食べる *taberu*	→	食べなかった	*tabenakatta*
う verbs	う to あ-row, add ~なかった	飲む *nomu*	→	飲まなかった	*nomanakatta*
	Ends う, change う to わ, then add ~なかった	買う *kau*	→	買わない	*kawanakatta*
Irregular	Stem し, add ~なかった	する *suru*	→	しなかった	*shinakatta*
	Stem *ko*, add ~なかった	来る *kuru*	→	来なかった	*konakatta*

As Japanese has no future tense versions of words, you have now covered the major verb conjugations! There is just one more significant form to learn about - the '-te' form.

Te- Form て

The '-te' form is a common conjugation with many practical uses. We use it when describing ongoing actions or an activity that we are currently doing. When doing two things at once, it can combine two verbs and is used to ask somebody to do something.

● **Continuous** **Present Progressive** *'-Te' Form*

The *'-te' form* is the conjugation used to create verbs that end with **"-ing"** in Japanese. The rules are similar to those for the plain *'-ta'* form, but changing た for て *('-te')*:

Category	Conjugation Rule	Example			
る verbs	Remove る, add ~て	食べる	taberu	食べて	tabete
う verbs	Ending う/つ/る, remove then add ~って	買う	kau	買って	katte
	Ending く, remove then add ~いて	聞く	kiku	聞いて	kiite
	Ending ぐ, remove then add ~いで	泳ぐ	oyogu	泳いで	oyoide
	Ending す, remove then add ~して	話す	hanasu	話して	hanashite
	Ending ぬ/ぶ/む, remove then add ~んで	飲む	nomu	飲んで	nonde
Irregular	Stem し, add ~て	する	suru	して	shite
	Stem '*k-*', add ~て	来る	kuru	来て	kite

Combine て *('-te')* form with ください *('kudasai')*, meaning *"please (do for me),"* to ask someone to do something for you:

Use て *('-te')* form to express doing two things simultaneously. You usually apply it to the first verb, but it can depend on the tense:

You can also use *'-te'* form to politely ask if it's alright to carry out an action by adding the phrase て + もいいですか *(-te mo iidesu ka)*:

さら あら
お皿を 洗って ください。
o sara o aratte   kudasai
"Please wash the dishes."

さら あら うた
お皿を 洗って 歌っています。
o sara o aratte   utatte   imasu.
"I wash the the dishes and sing"

うた
歌ってもいいですか?
utatte mo iidesu   ka?
"Please can I sing?"

Useful Grammar Patterns

With some kanji knowledge and vocabulary, you can use these common grammar patterns to extend the range of your reading ability, improve conversation skills, and practice using the language in more everyday situations:

Because...

The particle から (kara) is equivalent to the English word *"because,"* used to connect clauses where we give a reason, explaining that *"[something] because [something]"* in one long sentence. It makes the sentence sound more natural, and, although the first example would make perfect sense, the reason would usually come first in these sentences:

> のどが渇いた、飲みます。
> nodo ga kawaita, nomimasu.
> *"I am thirsty. I'll drink."*
>
> のどが渇いたから、飲みます。
> nodo ga kawaita kara, nomimasu.
> *"Because I am thirsty, I will drink"*

Want & Desire

You can change any verb to mean that you *"want to [do something]"* by simply adding the characters 〜たい (*'-tai'*) to the verb stem. So, 食べる (taberu) becomes 食べたい (tabetai), & 飲む (nomu) becomes 飲みたい (nomitai) etc.:

> ケーキが食べたいです。
> kēki ga tabetai desu.
> *"I want to eat cake."*
>
> ケーキが欲しいです。
> kēki ga hoshī desu.
> *"I want a cake."*

It's different for nouns but easy to learn - apply the formula *[noun]* + が欲しい (ga hoshī):

There is/was... (& not)

There are two verbs for expressing that *[something]* exists or existed. Phrases such as *"there is"* and *"there is not..."* are made with the *Ichidan* verb いる (iru) for living things or people *(except for plant life), e.g., a man, a dog, and so on*. We create the same phrases using the Godan verb ある (aru) for non-living objects, *e.g., a car, a book, etc.*

Remember, it's the same word for one of something or plurals, and to make the polite forms negative, change '-masu' to '-masen':

> 猫がいる
> neko ga iru
>
> 猫がいます
> neko ga imasu
>
> *"There is a cat"*

> 車がある
> kuruma ga aru
>
> 車があります
> kuruma ga arimasu
>
> *"There is a car"*

> 猫がいません
> neko ga imasen
>
> *"There are no cats"*

> 車がありません
> kuruma ga arimasen
>
> *"There are no cars"*

Intention & Planning

The plain verb form shows when we *"will do [something]"* but gives listeners a sense that it's a fairly casual plan:

When your intentions are stronger, you can add つもり (tsumori) to the *'dictionary form'* of a verb to express to a listener that you have a firm resolve to do something:

If your plans are firm, however, you can add the word 予定 (よてい), or yotei, which means 'plan,' to verbs, implying absolute certainty that the activity will happen:

Suggestions/Offers

You can turn statements into offers or suggestions by adding ましょう ('-mashou') to a verb stem. This easy grammar pattern has a meaning similar to *"let's [do something]"* and can become a question if you add the 'questioning particle' か (ka) to the end of the phrase, meaning *"shall we [something]?"*

That kind of suggestive question has a casual and potentially presumptuous tone, possibly putting the listener on the spot and feeling unable to decline. A better way to ask would be to use the *polite, negative verb form* and the particle か, creating a question similar to *"Why don't we [do something]?"*:

Questions

The sentence ending ですか ('-desu' + 'ka') is a great way to turn almost any phrase into a question. Asking a question in Japanese is often as simple as adding the particle か (ka) at the end of your sentences *(see Particles, p.348), especially in writing*. It is even easier to ask questions in speech, as raising the tone of your voice at the end of a phrase is enough to imply a question, just as in English. *(imagine saying "Lunch?")*

The question mark ' ? ' is not typically used in writing; however, it is not uncommon to see it in casual writing, such as instant messaging or social media.

Uncertainty

There are a couple of ways to say *"maybe"* or *"probably"* in Japanese. It depends on the level of politeness, the situation, and your level of certainty. The context will usually play a role in how these words are used and understood.

We add the polite presumptive でしょう *(deshou)* to the end of sentences when speculating, replacing the sentence ender *'-desu.'* This term adds a general sense that something *"is probably"* going to happen, or seems like it *"will probably"* happen. You can also use it to mean *"I assume"* or *"I think,"* telling the listener that what you are saying is judgment, based on your interpretation of some information.

Deshou is commonly heard in weather reports, giving speakers an authoritative tone and asserting a higher level of certainty - *but still less than 100%:*

The plain form, だろう *(darou)* has a similar meaning, such as *"I believe," "I assume,"* or *"I guess,"* and is used when you're fairly sure of what you are saying:

The same grammar can form questions, in context, as a way to seek confirmation or agreement from a listener. You can simply change the tone of your voice:

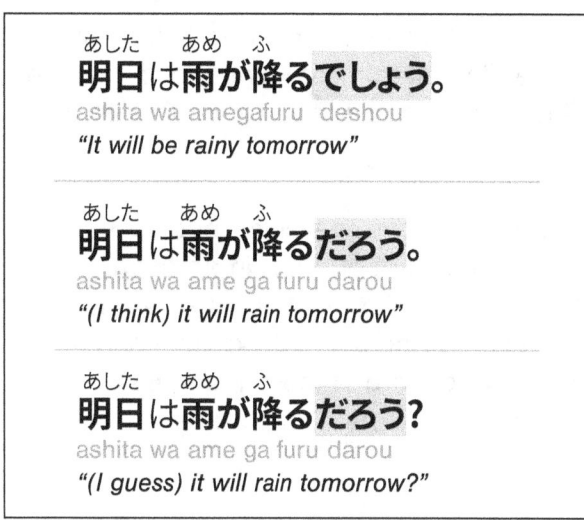

(relatively high certainty)

When describing something that you think *"might"* happen, the term かもしれません, or *kamoshiremasen*, could be used instead. The grammar pattern is the same, but this expression shows lower certainty:

(less certainty than *deshou*)

• Both forms of *deshou* may be accompanied by the word 多分 (たぶん), *tabun*, reducing certainty and adding a sense of *"maybe," "perhaps,"* or *"probably."*

Mainly for informal speech, *tabun* can help answer a question when you are not sure if something will happen or not. i.e., when the outcome could go either way, or you are 50% certain:

(uncertain / informal, not certain either way)

Introduction to Particles

Japanese does not rely on word order to convey the meaning of a sentence in the way that English does. Instead, sentence structure is determined by the use of **particles**. These are additional characters placed immediately after each part of a sentence or clause, showing us what function words have. In simple terms, they show us how words are connected.

Often referred to as *'postpositions,'* particles are small, linking words that are similar to *'prepositions'* in English. As the name suggests, they just come after the word they relate to in Japanese. Instead of saying *"to Japan,"* you say *"Nihon ni,"* (日本に), for example, where に *(ni)* is the particle equivalent of *"to."*

The most frequently used particles are probably は, が, and を, but there are many others. While difficult to master, the basic mechanics of most particles are relatively easy to grasp. This section provides an overview of the most prominent particles and their fundamental roles.

In a lot of ways, particles should make Japanese grammar easier to learn as they are almost like a set of rules, in and of themself. The trick is working out which equivalents they cover in English *(if any)*. There are entire textbooks dedicated to the discussion of particles, so the following list and explanations are relatively concise. They will get easier as you are exposed to more of the language, and, unfortunately, it simply takes time to get accustomed to certain aspects of Japanese.

Subject & Topic Markers

The usage of particles は *(wa)* and が *(ga)* can be a grey area, even for Japanese people, so it's often difficult to fully explain them to those who learn the language.

The main obstacle faced by native English speakers learning about particles は and が is how the English language does not separate the subject and topic of a sentence, at least in the way that Japanese does.

Considering how sentences will usually describe a person or thing (subject) carrying out an action (verb), the subject and topic of most sentences will usually be the same thing in English. It has a strict word order where sentences have a precise *[Subject + Object + Verb]* (SOV) structure. Japanese, however, is more flexible and, generally, less direct. Lots of information will tend to be implied or inferred through context.

Essentially, the *topic* is extra context and not connected to the other words by grammar. The *Subject* will usually connect to verbs, and have a distinct grammatical role.

At a glance, は and が seem to do a similar job, but their functions are quite different:

The Topic Marker は (as a particle, pronounced 'wa', not 'ha')

Unlike most particles, including が (ga), the so-called *topic marker* は (wa) does not directly relate to the verb in a sentence. Instead, it highlights a part of a sentence or clause as background information or context for the discussion:

"Chris ate a cake."

クリス は ケーキ を 食べました。
kurisu wa kēki o tabemashita

クリス が ケーキ を 食べました。
kurisu ga kēki o tabemashita

Here, *"Chris"* is the subject of the action/verb, as he has eaten the cake. The sentence is generally about Chris and what he has done, so he would also be the sentence's topic in Japanese. Therefore, either は or が could be used and grammatically correct.

However, each version conveys a different meaning and has a different interpretation...

The *topic marker* は (wa) reduces the importance of the word it marks so that the listener would focus more on the following information. In other words, は (wa) would emphasize what happened, and *"Chris"* is added for clarification. Effectively, it's like saying, "*Speaking of Chris, [he] ate a cake,*" or "*As for Chris...*"

The particle は (wa) is used to contrast 'something' with 'other things' by emphasizing a particular part of a sentence; and also for elaboration, where a listener would already know something about what is discussed.

The Subject Marker が (pronounced 'ga')

The so-called *subject particle* が (ga) has a more well-defined role, marking the subject of a clause or sentence through a direct, grammatical relationship. When we mark a person, animal or thing with が (in the example above, *"Chris"*), it's very much about '*what Chris did.*' Generally speaking, it draws attention to '*who, did what.*'

This example, right, features both particles:

The subject in this sentence is "cake," marked by the particle が. Emphasis is placed on the fact that '*cake is liked.*' The *"I"* is a reminder that the speaker is talking about themself:

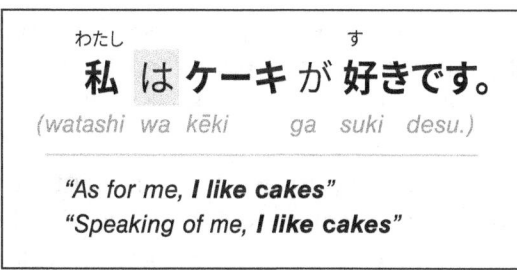

私 は ケーキ が 好きです。
(*watashi wa kēki ga suki desu.*)

"As for me, **I like cakes**"
"Speaking of me, **I like cakes**"

Other uses for this particle include; distinguishing one option or thing from some others; introducing new information to a conversation that is not already in the context; describing something in particular with an adjective; and also to connect sentences or clauses, like the word "but," or the phrase "even though...," for example.

'Question' Marker か *(pronounced 'ka')*

More accurately, this particle marks the unknown. It is referred to as the *'question marker'* because we use it in a similar way. It effectively replaces the usual punctuation mark that you would use to end a question in English (**?**). You can turn any sentence or statement into a question using the particle か at the end.

The particle か comes at the end of questions in more formal speech, and you would raise the tone of your voice at the end of the sentence, just as you would when asking a question in English. The written, formal version of a question would finish with か。

You don't need to pronounce this in more casual conversations, as raising the tone of your voice at the end is enough. Nowadays, you can end sentences with a question mark symbol (**?**) when writing in casual situations.

The か particle is also used when listing options and alternatives and each is separated by a か. Here, the meaning is equivalent to the word *"or"* in English:

> ケーキか オレンジか、どちらが 好きですか?
> *(kēki ka orenji ka, dochira ka suki desu ka?)*
> "Do you like cakes or oranges?"
> *(Cakes or oranges, which one is preferred?)*

You may have noticed that the example question also features the *subject marker* が *('ga')*. It always follows words that form a question, such as *"which,"* *"what,"* and *"who."* A regular か particle comes at the end as it's a question.

The Object Marker を *('wo', pronounced as 'o')*

The を particle simply marks the direct object of a sentence or clause and immediately follows nouns or phrases directly linked to the verb. When a verb describes a motion, the particle を highlights where the motion is or what is affected.

This example sentence shows that breakfast is the object, marked by the particle を, and it's directly linked to the verb *(to eat)*:

> 私は朝ご飯を食べました。
> *(watashi wa asagohan o tabemashita)*
> *polite* // "I ate breakfast"
>   As for me, ate breakfast.

It's reasonable to assume this sentence would be part of a conversation where it's clear from the context that the speaker is referring to themselves. Speaker and listener would likely be acquainted, so the polite verb is replaced with the plain version. The initial 私は can also be left out.

> 朝ご飯を食べた。
> *(asa gohan o tabeta)*
> *plain* // "I ate breakfast"
>   (I) ate breakfast.

(Changes made for variety amongst examples)

Possession & Modification の
(pronounced 'no')

The の particle has several functions relating to possession and labeling. To create the correct possessive form in Japanese, you can simply add the particle の *(no)* to pronouns. Showing possession in English is far more complicated, with different words depending on who or what something 'belongs to,' or where words sit in a sentence *(i.e., me=my/mine, she=her/hers, and they=their/theirs, etc.)* In Japanese, there is just の + noun.

So, 私のケーキ is *"my cake"* or *"a cake that I made,"* depending on the context. You could say 私の or *"mine"* if the context allows. It shows ownership of something when placed after a person/people:

You can also use this particle to combine two nouns, creating a kind of *'compound noun.'* Here, the first noun 猫 ("cat") + の *(no)* becomes a sort of *'label'* that applies to the second thing, showing it is *cat-related*. The second noun is the *'main'* thing or meaning:

That newly *'labeled'* noun can also become a *label* itself - just add another の and noun to show that something is *'cat toy -related'* :

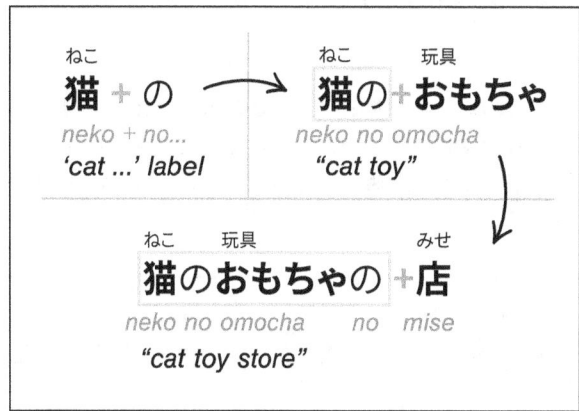

- の can turn non-noun words, such as adjectives, verbs, and clauses, into nouns so that they can become a sentence's subject, grammatically speaking. This process is called *nominalization*, and の acts as the *nominalizer*.

When saying *"I like eating,"* for example, the word that functions as the verb is "like," and the word *"eating"* is the *thing* that is 'being liked.' The particle の changes the verb *'to eat'* into *[the act of eating]*, a noun:

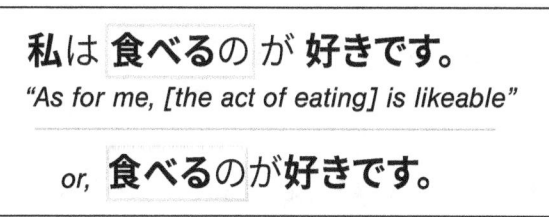

- Another everyday use is replacing nouns with a more generic word, equivalent to *"one," "it,"* or *"this"* in English. The name of something understood from context can be referred to with a simple の instead:

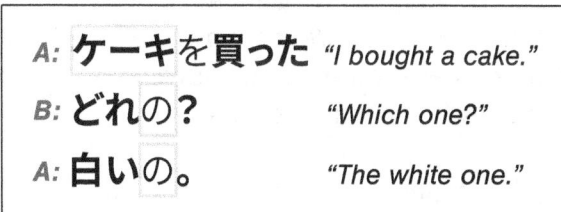

Other uses for this particle include: making types of adjectives and asserting an order or statement *(when placed at the end of a sentence)*.

Time, Movement, & Aim　に (pronounced 'ni')

The fundamental role of particle に (ni) is to mark a location where something exists. This particle has many uses, primarily highlighting a fixed destination or exact position. Some of the equivalent words in English include "at," "to," "on," "in," and "into," etc.

By simply adding に (ni) to the end of a word, you can define it as a fixed place where something or somebody either currently is, was, or will be in the future:

(私は)大学 に 行く。
watashi wa daigaku ni iku
"(As for me) I'm going to college."

In sentences with a motion verb, particle に marks the place that something/somebody moves to (i.e., where it/they eventually end up):

ケーキをテーブルに置く。
kēki o teeberu ni oku
"to place the cake on the table"

We can also mark **specific** times, dates, and even intervals where an action repeats with に (e.g., 'twice a year' or 'once a month,' etc.):

七時に起きます。
shichi-ji ni okimasu.
"I get up at 7 o'clock"

(私は)クリスにケーキを上げました
(watashi wa) kurisu ni kēki wo agemashita
"(As for me) I gave Chris a cake"

に is used less commonly for marking *indirect objects* to show when an action is aimed at a person, place, or thing:

昨日どこに行ったのですか？
kinō doko ni itta no desu ka?
Where did you go yesterday?

You can also use this particle when forming questions:

Direction & Destination　へ (as a particle, pronounced 'e')

As a particle, へ pronounced 'e' *(not 'he')* can also mark direction or destination. We use it with verbs that express directional movement, as へ gives phrases a less 'final' sense.

日本へ 行きます
nihon e ikimasu
"heading towards Japan"

In the example using particle に, Japan is an intended, final destination, or target. When we use へ instead, interpretations will be more akin to *'setting out towards Japan,'* or *'in the direction of Japan,'* and not a destination:

日本に 行きます
nihon ni ikimasu
"going to Japan"

How & Where Particle で (pronounced 'de')

Another particle with location-based functions but for describing *how and where something happens,* instead of movement. Words marked with で show **how** an activity is carried out and the **means** needed to do the action.

It may mark any tools, vehicles, or materials required for an action to take place, and also any particular method involved:

> えんぴつ　しゅくだい　か
> 鉛筆で 宿題を 書きました。
> *enpiitsu de shukudai o kakimashita.*
>
> "I wrote my homework using a pencil."
> 'with a' or 'in' [pencil]

で marks a location where an action takes place, whereas に marks the exact spot that activity happens:

> つくえ　しゅくだい　か
> 机で 宿題を 書いた。
> *tsukue de shukudai o kakimashita.*
>
> "I wrote my homework **at** my desk"

Both these examples are grammatically correct, but the one with に *means that the speaker wrote the homework onto the very surface of the desk itself:*

> つくえ　しゅくだい　か
> 机に 宿題を 書いた。
> *tsukue ni shukudai o kakimashita.*
>
> "I wrote my homework **on** my desk"

で is used to describe *why* an event happens, but not usually when the reason is a choice. In other words, when something **causes** the action:

> びょうき　だいがく　い
> (私は) 病気で大学に 行けなかった。
> *byōki de daigaku ni ikenakatta*
>
> "Due to sickness, (I) couldn't go to college"
> "(I) was too sick to go to college"

We can also use で to mark words showing how much time is required to **complete** or **finish** an activity - *for time limits and deadlines:*

> じかん　お
> 1時間で起きます
> *1-jikan de okimasu*
>
> "(I will) get up in 1 hour"
> "(I'll) get up in an hour"

Other uses include; marking quantity, time, and money to show extent; requirement of cost; and also when you need to describe range or scope (e.g., "within," or "among").

If you have any difficulty remembering how to use any of the different location marking particles, this may help:

> に *(ni)* fi**ni**shing destination or a time
> へ *(e)* **he**ading this *points towards*
> で *(de)* **de**scribes how & where

Connecting & Listing Particle   と   (pronounced 'to')

Particle と (to) can sometimes be referred to as the *'glue particle,'* since its primary function is creating connections between nouns - it is equivalent to *"and,"* or *"or"* in English. When listing items, it indicates that a list is concise or **complete**, and nothing else can be added.

• As an equivalent to the word *"and"* in English, you can connect things by adding a と particle to each word. The crucial aspect to remember is that this particle implies that everything you mention would make up the complete list of things:

猫と犬
"cats and dogs"

君と僕
"You and I"

ひらがなとカタカナは簡単
"Hiragana and Katakana are easy"

• We can use と as an equivalent to the English word *"with"* and shows who is with us when we carry out an action:

彼とケーキを食べた。
"I ate cake with him"

• You can keep adding people or things to a list, as long as と follows each - and together, they form a complete list:

彼と彼女とケーキを食べた。
"I ate cake with him and her"

This particle has a few other uses, including marking the end of a quote or thought. It also highlights words with onomatopoeia and connects clauses in *'if [this], then [that]'* types of sentences - where a condition is set out, followed by a result.

Incomplete List Particle   や   (pronounced 'ya')

Grammatically similar to と (to), you also use particle や (ya) for listing things in parallel, except that you use や when the stuff you're listing forms part of a longer list.

や implies that your list is not exhaustive or **incomplete** and that you could add other things, *e.g.,* *"A and B (and so on),"* *"X and Y (etc.),"* or *"A and B (among others)"*:

店でペンや鉛筆を買いました。
mise de pen ya enpitsu o kaimashita
*"I bought pens and pencils
(and something else) at the store"*

For lists with three or more items *(using two or more や particles)*, it is perfectly acceptable and natural to replace the second や *(& third, etc.)* with commas:

パンやケーキ、クッキーを焼きます。
pan ya kēki   ya kukkī   o yakimasu
"I bake bread, cakes, cookies (and so on)"

The more formal way to stress that some other things have not been listed is to add など *(nado)* to the last noun:

パンやケーキなどを焼きます。
pan ya kēki   nado o yakimasu
"I bake bread, cakes, and more"

Also, Too, & Both - Particle　も　　　(pronounced 'mo')

Particle も *(mo)* has an equivalent meaning to *"also"* or *"too"* in English. It marks words to show when they belong to a set of other things. Effectively, whatever applies to one thing *(a group of things or imaginary list of things)*, also applies to this other thing. It will often replace the particles は *(wa)*, が *(ga)*, and を *(o)*, but not any other particles.

In this example, も *(mo)* marks *"dogs"* because the speaker likes them in addition to *"cats."* They are adding dogs to a '*set*' of '*animals they like*':

(私は)猫が好きです、犬も 好きです。
neko ga suki   desu、inu mo suki desu.
"I like cats, I also like dogs"

Here, the particle も *(mo)* is affixed to the word *"me/I,"* so the speaker is adding themselves to a '*list*' of '*people who love cats*' - perhaps responding to somebody who has said the same:

私も 猫が大好き です。
watashi mo neko ga daisuki desu.
"I also love cats" (or, "I love cats, too")

It can also mean *"both"* and *"all."* When asked, *"Do you like cats or dogs?"* the speaker might respond:

(私は)猫も犬も大好きだ。
neko mo inu mo daisuki da.
"I love cats **and** dogs."

Lastly, it's also used as equivalent to the word "even," for emphasis when the thing added to the *imaginary list* seems excessive or 'beyond normal':

...蛇も大好きです！
...hebu mo daisuki   desu!
"...I even love snakes."

Sentence Ending Particles　よ & ね　　　(pronounced 'yo' and 'ne')

Ending a sentence with ね *(ne)* adds a question like *"isn't it?"* or *"right?"*, marking information as received and agreed with, or simply for confirmation:

ケーキ は 美味しいですね。
kēki wa oishīdesu   ne
"The cake is delicious, right?"

If you end a sentence with particle よ *(yo)*, it gives the sense that what you say is new or informative to the listener, like saying *"you know"* in English:

彼は美味しいケーキを焼きますよ。
kare wa oishī   kēki   o yakimasu   yo
"His cakes are delicious, you know"

Even More Particles

Particles are a vast topic and you will discover many more over time. This additional list summarizes a small selection of other, less frequently-used terms, but it is not exhaustive. Lots of particles have too many uses to fit on this page!

よね	**'yone'** - When よ+ね combine to end a sentence, the function is similar to that of both particles alone. What's said is believed to be new, but it's not certain or obvious if it is. ケーキを食べますよね？ *(kēki o tabemasu yo ne?)* "You'll eat the cake, right?"
だけ	**'dake'** - Similar in meaning to *"just,"* *"only,"* or *"not more than,"* this particle marks the extent or limit of something. It can be used in phrases like *"as [something] as possible."* 百円だけあげる *(hyaku-en dake ageru)* "I will give you just 100 yen."
しか	**'shika'** - Also marks extents or limits, typically if they cause problems for the speaker, so it has a meaning equivalent to *"only [something] and no more,"* or *"nothing but..."* ケーキしか焼けない *(kēki shika yakenai)* "I can only bake cakes."
ばかり	**'bakari'** - Uses include: following numbers to mark estimates; for phrases such as "not only ... but"; and also means "only" or "nothing but...". *It usually requires context.* ケーキばかり焼いています *(kēki bakari yaite imasu)* "(I do) nothing but bake cakes."
より	**'yori'** - Used in comparisons with a meaning similar to *"than."* Marks words to express *"more than"* (with a positive spin). Also, for saying *"from"* when writing to someone. 彼は彼女より背が高い *(kare wa kanojo yori segatakai)* "He's taller than she is."
でも	**'demo'** - Another particle for "but," depending on the situation, it can emphasize the following clause. Often marks words describing possibility or suggestion. でもこのケーキは美味しい *(demo kono kēki wa oishī)* "...but, this cake is delicious!"
ほど	**'hodo'** - *"About"* or *"approximately"* with numbers. For degrees equivalent to a limit, e.g., *"to the extent of,"* and marks 'greater' in comparisons: *"She is not as tall as he is."* 彼女は彼ほど背が高くない *(Kanojo wa kare hodo se ga takakunai)*
から	**'kara'** - Marks a place or time *"from"* where something begins, a point of origin, or a source of information. Works with particle まで in phrases like *"from [X], to [Y]."* 大学から戻ります *(daigaku kara modorimasu)* "I will return from college"
まで	**'made'** - Opposite of から (above) and marks an endpoint. Used for space, distance, time, and numbers. Typically *"until."* When followed by に, it becomes *"by"* or *"before."* 家に着くまで走った *(Ie ni tsuku made hashitta)* "I ran until I got home"

//////////////////////////////// **PART 8**

Study Tools

This section provides some additional tools to aid in your studies. You could write directly in the book but feel free to cut out and copy the pages for personal use. I always try to keep the number of *empty* pages to a minimum, making room for more useful information in the earlier chapters.

The following double-sided sheets contain additional grid templates that are intended for character writing practice, with combinations of 1-inch or 0.7-inch squares, both with and without dotted center guidelines - each version should cater to a variety of purposes and preference.

Also included in this section are some basic, kanji-specific templates for any other kanji you want to practice. Space is made for recording important kanji knowledge, such as readings, individual stroke order, and so on.

Pages 379-416 contain double-sided templates that readers can cut out or copy to create a mini *flashcard* deck - helpful for revision and testing your memory. While they may not be as durable as purpose-made cards, I wanted to include them to save you from additional expense. The *cards* show individual characters and their crucial learning points, such as pronunciation, stroke order, or sound change rules. Kanji cards feature essential readings, identifying information, and useful vocabulary, too. Some blank, *spare* flashcard templates in this section may be useful for creating custom cards *or replacing any that go missing!*

For those who prefer to write directly in a workbook, I have published additional companion writing practice books to use in conjunction with this publication. They each contain the different template types in this chapter. *The Kana and Kanji Companion* books are similar to writing refill pads but with Japanese writing grids. *The Kanji Study Companion* book works as a ledger, with an index area for organizing new kanji and the knowledge you collect.

My companion books are available on Amazon's global marketplaces.

Writing Practice Template

(1-inch grid with guides) Japanese Made Simple - by Dan Akiyama

Writing Practice Template

Japanese Made Simple - by Dan Akiyama *(1-inch grid with guides)*

Writing Practice Template

(1-inch grid with guides)   Japanese Made Simple - by Dan Akiyama

Writing Practice Template

Japanese Made Simple - by Dan Akiyama   *(1-inch grid without guides)*

(1-inch grid without guides)   *Japanese Made Simple - by Dan Akiyama*

Writing Practice Template

(1-inch grid without guides)   *Writing Practice Template* — *Japanese Made Simple - by Dan Akiyama*

Writing Practice Template

Japanese Made Simple - by Dan Akiyama *(0.7-inch grid with guides)*

Writing Practice Template

Japanese Made Simple - by Dan Akiyama   *(0.7-inch grid with guides)*

Writing Practice Template

Japanese Made Simple - by Dan Akiyama   (0.7-inch grid without guides)

Writing Practice Template

N5 N4 N3 N2 N1

KANJI DETAILS

ON'YOMI KUN'YOMI

RADICAL(S) VOCAB VOCAB

SENTENCE / MNEMONIC / NOTES

KANJI STROKE ORDER

KANJI WRITING PRACTICE

N5 N4 N3 N2 N1

Kanji Study Template - by Dan Akiyama

N5 **N4** **N3** **N2** **N1**

KANJI DETAILS

ON'YOMI

KUN'YOMI

RADICAL(S) | VOCAB | VOCAB

SENTENCE / MNEMONIC / NOTES

KANJI STROKE ORDER

KANJI WRITING PRACTICE

Kanji Study Template - by Dan Akiyama

N5 N4 N3 N2 N1

KANJI DETAILS

ON'YOMI

KUN'YOMI

RADICAL(S) | VOCAB | VOCAB

SENTENCE / MNEMONIC / NOTES

KANJI STROKE ORDER

KANJI WRITING PRACTICE

N5 N4 N3 N2 N1

Kanji Study Template - by Dan Akiyama

N5 N4 N3 N2 N1

ON'YOMI KUN'YOMI

RADICAL(S) VOCAB VOCAB

SENTENCE / MNEMONIC / NOTES

KANJI DETAILS

KANJI STROKE ORDER

KANJI WRITING PRACTICE

Kanji Study Template - by Dan Akiyama

N5　N4　N3　N2　N1

KANJI DETAILS

ON'YOMI　　　　　　KUN'YOMI

RADICAL(S)　VOCAB　　　　VOCAB

SENTENCE / MNEMONIC / NOTES

KANJI STROKE ORDER

KANJI WRITING PRACTICE

N5　N4　N3　N2　N1

Kanji Study Template - by Dan Akiyama

N5 N4 N3 N2 N1

KANJI DETAILS

ON'YOMI

KUN'YOMI

RADICAL(S) | VOCAB

VOCAB

SENTENCE / MNEMONIC / NOTES

KANJI STROKE ORDER

KANJI WRITING PRACTICE

Kanji Study Template - by Dan Akiyama

a
Pronounce as 'ah' like the 'a' in car.

あ

ka
Pronounce like the 'kha' in khakis.

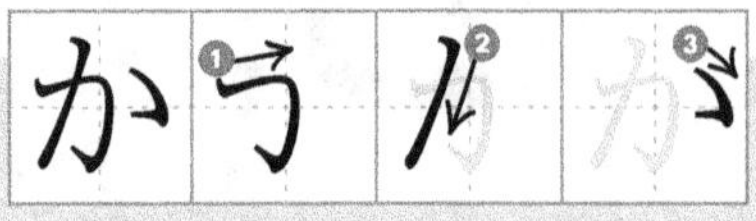

か

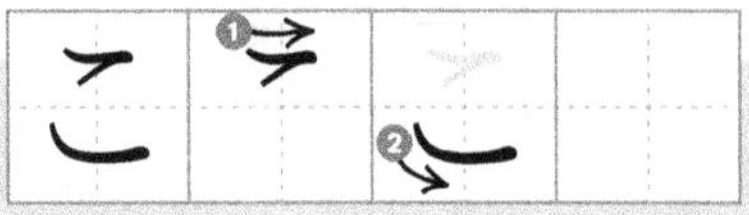

sa
Sounds like the 'sa-' in sarcasm.

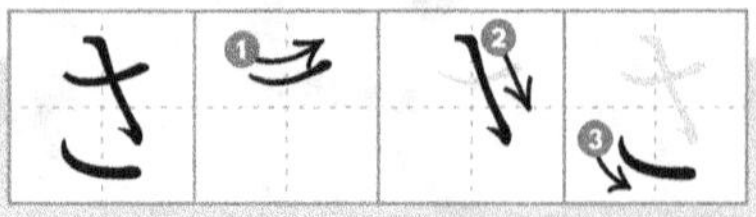

さ

i
Sounds like 'i' in king, or 'ee' in cheek.

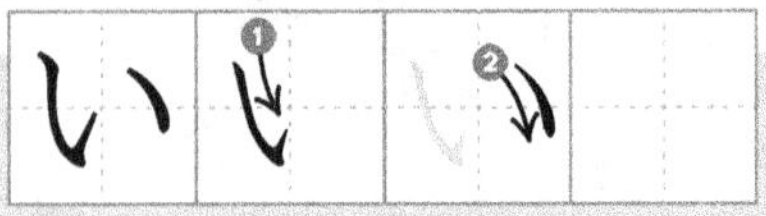

い

ki
This kana looks and sounds like a 'key'.

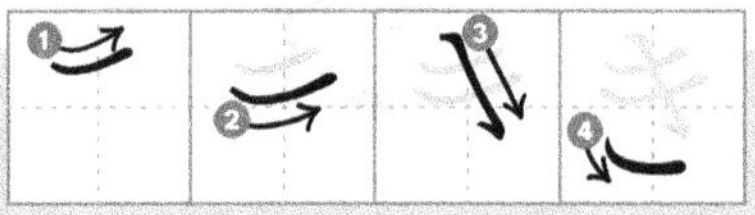

き

shi
Sounds exactly like the 'shi' in sashimi.

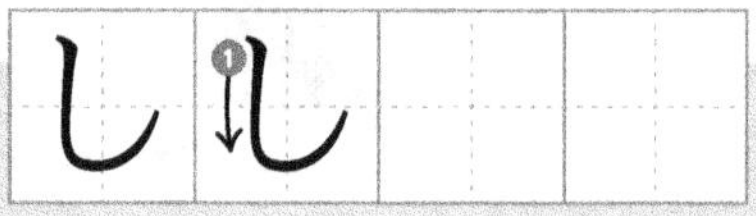

し

u
Similar to 'oo' but like the 'ue' in true.

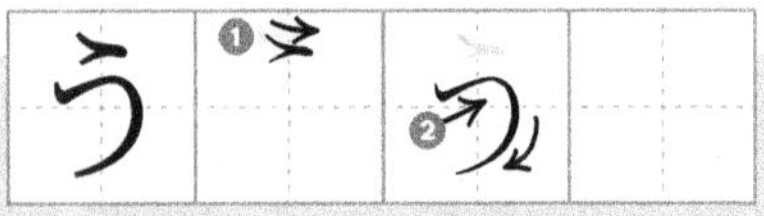

う

ku
Pronounced like the 'coo' in cool.

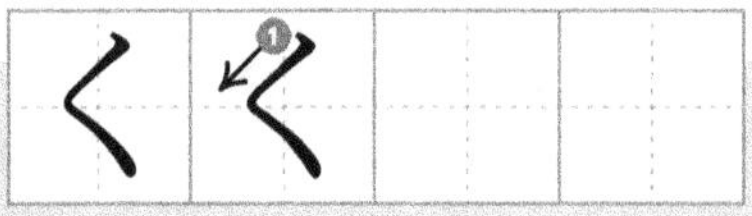

く

su
Sounds similar to the 'sou' in soup.

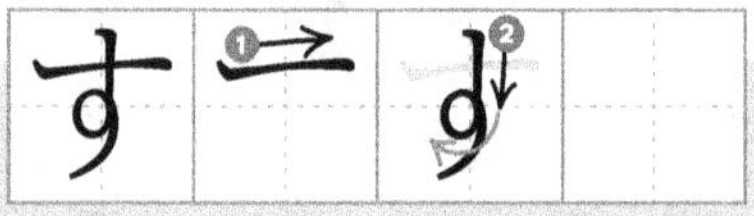

す

e
Pronounced as 'eh' like the 'e' in bed.

え

ke
Sounds like the 'ke' in kettle.

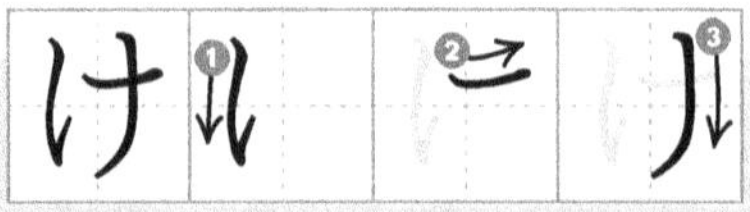

け

se
Pronounced 'seh' (almost like say).

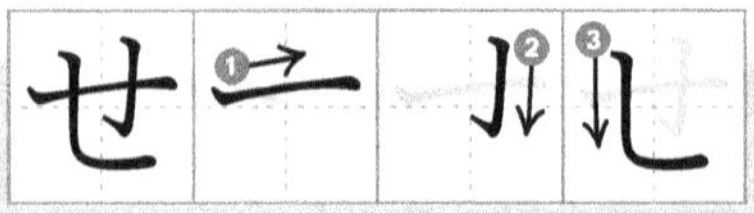

せ

o
Sounds like the 'o' in box.

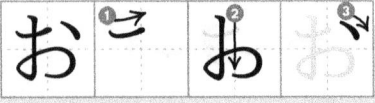

ko
Sounds like the 'co' in comb.

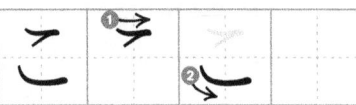

so
Sounds like the 'so-' in soccer or sorry.

は	な	た
ひ	に	ち
ふ	ぬ	つ
へ	ね	て
ほ	の	と

ta
Sounds like the '-ta' in Santa.

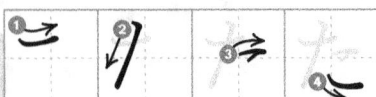

na
Sounds just like the '-na's in banana

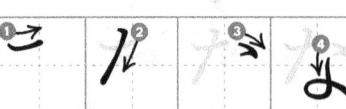

ha
Pronounce as 'ha' like in hand.

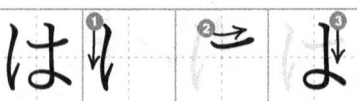

chi
Sounds just like the 'chee' in cheeks.

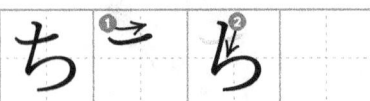

ni
Sounds similar to the word 'knee'.

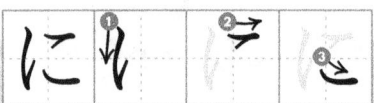

hi
Pronounced like the 'hee' in heel.

tsu
Sounds like 'two' and the name 'Sue'.

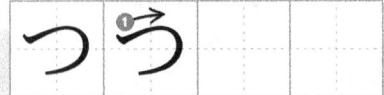

nu
Sounds like the 'noo' in the word noon.

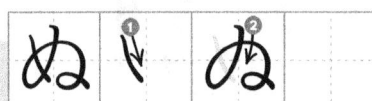

fu
Sounds like both 'fu' and 'hu' - or 'hfu'.

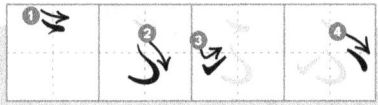

te
Sounds like the 'te-' in teddy bear.

ne
Sounds similar to 'nay' or 'neigh'.

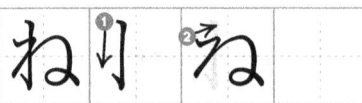

he
Pronounce as 'heh', almost like 'hey'.

to
Sounds like the 'to-' in tonic.

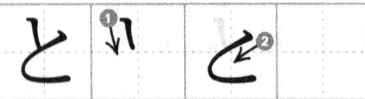

no
Sounds very similar to the word 'No'.

ho
Pronounce like the 'ho-' in horse.

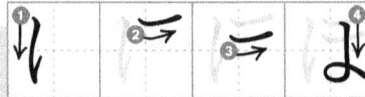

ma
Sounds like the 'ma-' in the word man.

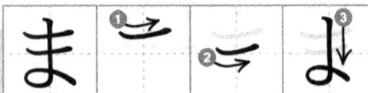

ya
Sounds much like the 'ya-' in yak.

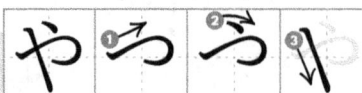

ra
Sounds a lot like the 'ra-' in rabbit.

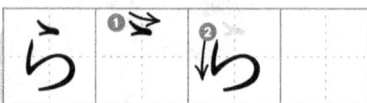

mi
Sounds exactly like the word 'Me'.

yu
Sounds just like the word 'You'.

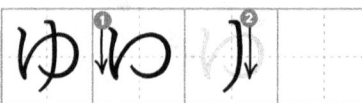

ri
Sounds a lot like the 'rea-' in reach.

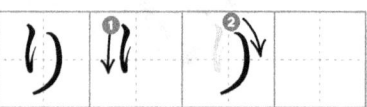

mu
Similar to the 'moo' in moon.

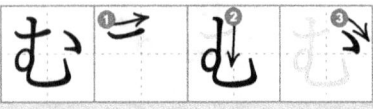

yo
Sounds like the informal greeting 'Yo'.

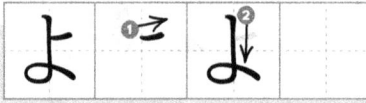

ru
Sounds like the '-ru' in guru.

me
Sounds like the 'me-' in men.

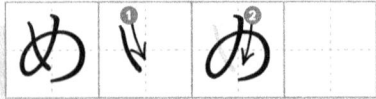

wa
Sounds like the 'wa-' in wacky or wax.

re
Sounds like the 'ra-' in race, like 'ray'.

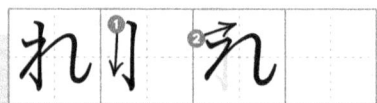

mo
Sounds similar to the 'mo-' in monsoon.

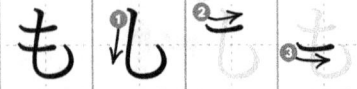

n
Similar to the '-n' in plane, or 'nnn'.

ro
Sounds like the '-rro' in churro.

 サ katakana	 カ katakana	 ア katakana
 シ katakana	 キ katakana	 イ katakana
 ス katakana	 ク katakana	 ウ katakana
 セ katakana	 ケ katakana	 エ katakana
 ソ katakana	 コ katakana	 オ katakana

a
Pronounce as 'ah' like the 'a' in car.

ka
Pronounce like the 'kha' in khakis.

sa
Sounds like the 'sa-' in sarcasm.

i
Sounds like 'i' in king, or 'ee' in cheek.

ki
This kana looks and sounds like a 'key'.

shi
Sounds exactly like the 'shi' in sashimi.

u
Similar to 'oo' but like the 'ue' in true.

ku
Pronounced like the 'coo' in cool.

su
Sounds similar to the 'sou' in soup.

e
Pronounced as 'eh' like the 'e' in bed.

ke
Sounds like the 'ke' in kettle.

se
Pronounced 'seh' (almost like say).

o
Sounds like the 'o' in box.

ko
Sounds like the 'co' in comb.

so
Sounds like the 'so-' in soccer or sorry.

 ハ katakana	 ナ katakana	 タ katakana
 ヒ katakana	 ニ katakana	 チ katakana
 フ katakana	 ヌ katakana	 ツ katakana
 ヘ katakana	 ネ katakana	 テ katakana
 ホ katakana	 ノ katakana	 ト katakana

ta
Sounds like the '-ta' in Santa.
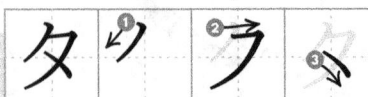

na
Sounds just like the '-na's in banana
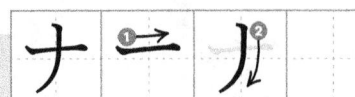

ha
Pronounce as 'ha' like in hand.

chi
Sounds just like the 'chee' in cheeks.
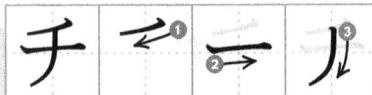

ni
Sounds similar to the word 'knee'.
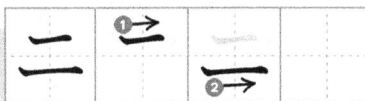

hi
Pronounced like the 'hee' in heel.
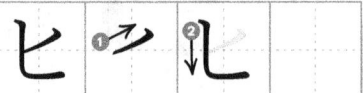

tsu
Sounds like 'two' and the name 'Sue'.
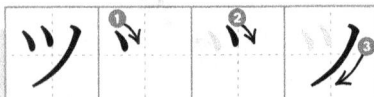

nu
Sounds like the 'noo' in the word noon.
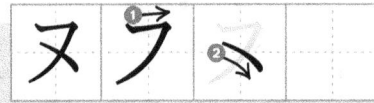

fu
Sounds like both 'fu' and 'hu' - or 'hfu'.
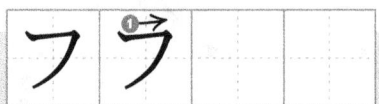

te
Sounds like the 'te-' in teddy bear.
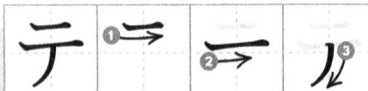

ne
Sounds similar to 'nay' or 'neigh'.

he
Pronounce as 'heh', almost like 'hey'.

to
Sounds like the 'to-' in tonic.
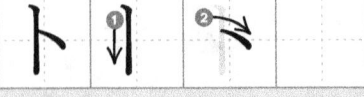

no
Sounds very similar to the word 'No'.

ho
Pronounce like the 'ho-' in horse.
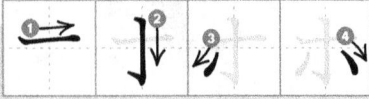

 katakana	 katakana	 katakana
 katakana	 katakana	 katakana
 katakana	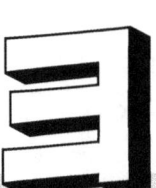 katakana	 katakana
 katakana	 katakana	 katakana
 katakana	 katakana	 katakana

ma
Sounds like the 'ma-' in the word man.

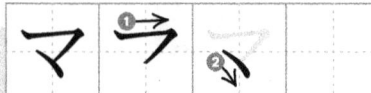

ya
Sounds much like the 'ya-' in yak.

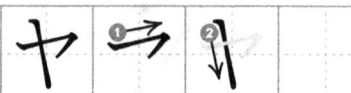

ra
Sounds a lot like the 'ra-' in rabbit.

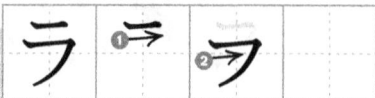

mi
Sounds exactly like the word 'Me'.

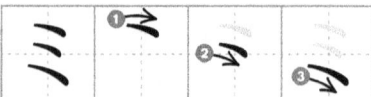

yu
Sounds just like the word 'You'.

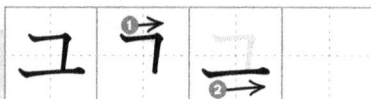

ri
Sounds a lot like the 'rea-' in reach.

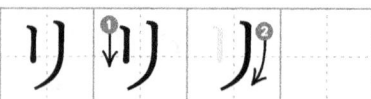

mu
Similar to the 'moo' in moon.

yo
Sounds like the informal greeting 'Yo'.

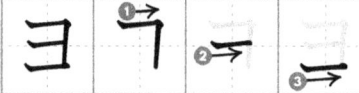

ru
Sounds like the '-ru' in guru.

me
Sounds like the 'me-' in men.

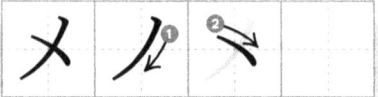

wa
Sounds like the 'wa-' in wacky or wax.

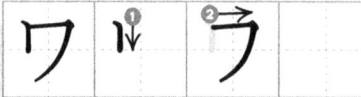

re
Sounds like the 'ra-' in race, like 'ray'.

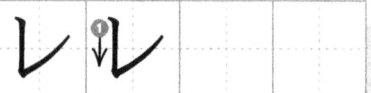

mo
Sounds similar to the 'mo-' in monsoon.

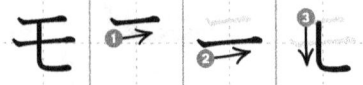

n
Similar to the '-n' in plane, or 'nnn'.

ro
Sounds like the '-rro' in churro.

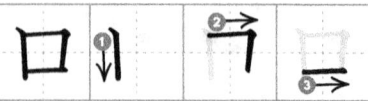

spare	つツ small tsu	を hiragana
spare	ああ long vowels	ヲ katakana
spare	ぽぽ dakuten	しゃ compound kana

w	r	y	m	h	n	t	s	k	H
わ wa	ら ra	や ya	ま ma	は ha	な na	た ta	さ sa	か ka	あ a	a
	り ri		み mi	ひ hi	に ni	ち chi	し shi	き ki	い i	i
*ん n	る ru	ゆ yu	む mu	ふ fu	ぬ nu	つ tsu	す su	く ku	う u	u
	れ re		め me	へ he	ね ne	て te	せ se	け ke	え e	e
を wo	ろ ro	よ yo	も mo	ほ ho	の no	と to	そ so	こ ko	お o	o

WO
Pronounced as お
(like the O in "box")

を

(を is a Particle)

WO
Pronounced as オ
(like the O in "box")

ヲ

(ヲ is a Particle)

Small tsu っ and ッ
= double consonant sound
(adds one mora)

ロク ロック
roku   ro +k ku

Katakana + extender

ケーキ | キュート
kee ki | kyuu to

Hiragana + extra vowel

for [a] sounds   + あ (a)
for [i] / [e] sounds + い (i)
for [u] / [o] sounds + う (u)

Regular kana '-i' + small kana 'y-'
e.g. し/き/ち + や/ゆ/よ

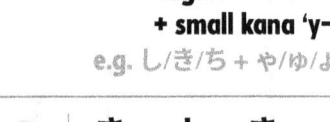

H: き + よ = きょ
   ki   yo   kyo

K: キ + ヨ = キョ

Kana with diacritic marks
= 'voiced' consonants
dakuten ゛ / handakuten ゜

	k	t	s	h	ho ほ ホ
゛	g	d	z	b	bo ぼ ボ
゜				p	po ぽ ポ

一

N5 Kanji	**Numbers**

Kun	ひと-、ひと.つ
On	イチ、イツ
Radical	一
Strokes	1
Parts	一

二

N5 Kanji	**Numbers**

Kun	ふた、ふた.つ
On	ニ、ジ
Radical	二
Strokes	2
Parts	二

三

N5 Kanji	**Numbers**

Kun	み、み.つ、みっ.つ
On	サン、ゾウ
Radical	一
Strokes	3
Parts	一 二

四

N5 Kanji	**Numbers**

Kun	よ、よ.つ、よん
On	シ
Radical	口
Strokes	5
Parts	儿 口

五

N5 Kanji	**Numbers**

Kun	いつ、いつ.つ
On	ゴ
Radical	二
Strokes	4
Parts	五

六

N5 Kanji	**Numbers**

Kun	む、む.つ、むっ.つ
On	ロク、リク
Radical	八
Strokes	4
Parts	亠 八

七

N5 Kanji	**Numbers**

Kun	なな、なな.つ、なの
On	シチ
Radical	一
Strokes	2
Parts	乙 ノ 匕

八

N5 Kanji	**Numbers**

Kun	や、や.つ、やっ.つ
On	ハチ、ハツ
Radical	八
Strokes	2
Parts	八

九

N5 Kanji	**Numbers**

Kun	ここの、ここの.つ
On	キュウ、ク
Radical	乛
Strokes	2
Parts	九

Meaning(s)	**three, 3**		Meaning(s)	**two, 2**		Meaning(s)	**one, 1, best, first**
三	サン / さん *three, 3*		二	ニ / に *two, 2*		一	ひとつ *one, only*
三日	みっか *3rd of month*		二日	ふつか *2nd of month*		一	イチ *1, best, first, start*
三月	さんがつ *March, 3rd month*		二月	にがつ *February*		一寸	ちょっと *a little/bit, slightly*
三十日	みそか *last day of month*		二人	ふたり *two people, pair*		一人	ひとり *one person*

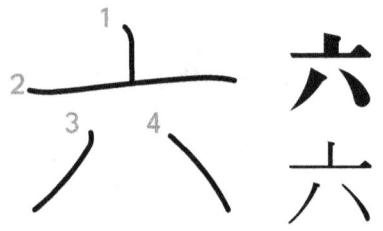

Meaning(s)	**six, 6**		Meaning(s)	**five, 5**		Meaning(s)	**four, 4**
六	ロク / ろく *six, 6*		五	ゴ / ご *five, 5*		四	シ / し *four, 4*
六日	むいか *6th of month*		五日	いつか *5th of month*		四日	よっか *4th of month*
六月	ロクガツ *June, 6th month*		五月	ゴガツ *May, 5th month*		四月	シガツ *April, 4th month*
六つ	むっつ *6, 6 years of age*		五つ	いつつ *5, 5 years of age*		四つ	よっつ *4, 4 years of age*

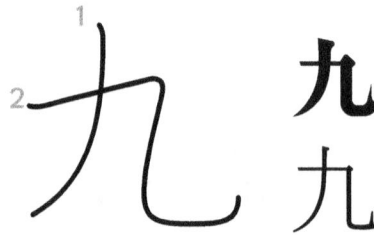

Meaning(s)	**nine, 9**		Meaning(s)	**eight, 8**		Meaning(s)	**seven, 7**
九	キュウ / きゅう *nine, 9*		八	ハチ / はち *eight, 8*		七	シチ / しち *seven, 7*
九日	ここのか *9th of month*		八日	ようか *8th of month*		七日	なのか *7th of month*
九月	クガツ *September*		八月	ハツ *August, 8th month*		七月	シチガツ *July, 7th month*
九つ	ここのつ *9, 9 years of age*		八つ	やっつ *8, 8 years of age*		七つ	ななつ *7, 7 years of age*

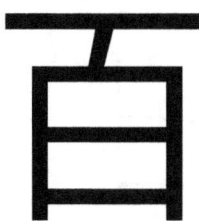
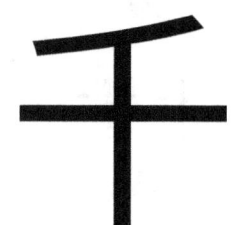

N5 Kanji **Numbers**

Kun	とお、と、そ
On	ジュウ、ジッ
Radical	十
Strokes	2
Parts	十

N5 Kanji **Numbers**

Kun	もも
On	ヒャク、ビャク
Radical	白
Strokes	6
Parts	一 白

N5 Kanji **Numbers**

Kun	ち
On	セン
Radical	十
Strokes	3
Parts	ノ 十

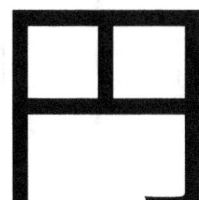
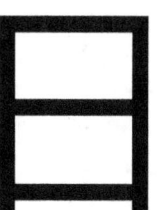

N5 Kanji **Numbers**

Kun	よろず
On	マン、バン
Radical	一
Strokes	3
Parts	一 丨 ノ

N5 Kanji **Numbers**

Kun	まる.い、まど
On	エン
Radical	冂
Strokes	4
Parts	一 丨 ⼇ 冂

N5 Kanji **Time**

Kun	ひ、-び、-か
On	ニチ、ジツ
Radical	日
Strokes	4
Parts	日

N5 Kanji **Time**

Kun	(none)
On	シュウ
Radical	辵
Strokes	11
Parts	冂 込 口 土

N5 Kanji **Time**

Kun	つき
On	ゲツ、ガツ
Radical	月
Strokes	4
Parts	月

N5 Kanji **Time**

Kun	とし
On	ネン
Radical	干
Strokes	6
Parts	一 ノ 干 乞

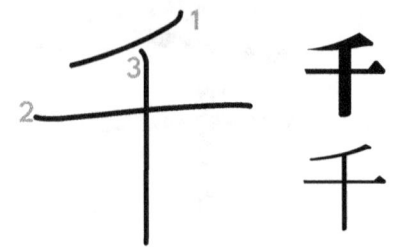 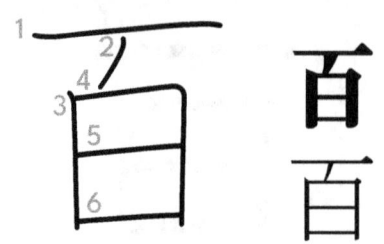 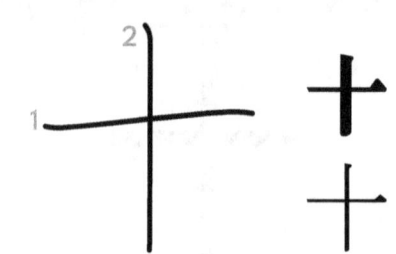

		Meaning(s): 1,000, thousand			**Meaning(s):** hundred, 100		**Meaning(s):** ten, 10, ten years old

千	セン 1,000, thousand	百	ヒャク hundred, 100	十	じゅう / ジュウ ten, 10
千	せん 1,000, thousand	百	もも hundred, many	十日	とおか 10th of month
百千	ひゃくせん large number	百貨店	ひゃっかてん department store	十回	ジッカイ ten times
千万円	いっせん まんえん 10 million yen	百万円	ひゃく まんえん 1 million yen	十分	じゅうぶん enough, sufficient

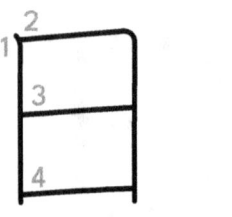 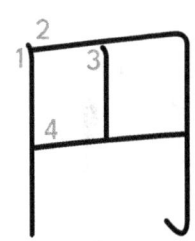 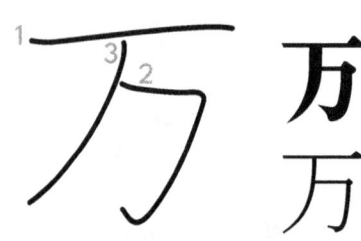

Meaning(s): day, sun, Japan   **Meaning(s):** yen, circle, round   **Meaning(s):** 10,000, ten thousand

日	ひ day/s, sun, daytime	円い	まるい round, circular	万	マン 10,000, everything
日	いく Sunday, Japan	円	エン yen, circle	万	いく 10,000, various
あくる日	あくるひ next day	円滑	エンカツ smooth	万能	ばんのう all-purpose
明日	あした tomorrow	円か	まどか round, tranquil	万年筆	まんねんひつ fountain pen

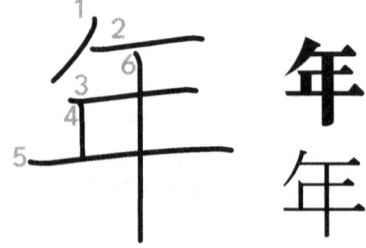 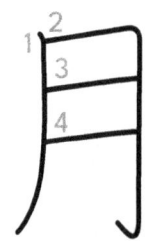 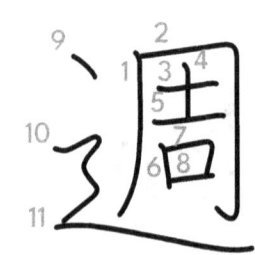

Meaning(s): year, year counter   **Meaning(s):** month, Monday   **Meaning(s):** week

年	とし year, age, years	月	つき Moon, month	週	シュウ week
年	ネン counter for years	月	ゲツ Monday	前週	ゼンシュウ last week
今年	ことし this year	月末	げつまつ end of the month	毎週	マイシュウ every week
去年	きょねん last year	月曜日	げつようび Monday	隔週	カクシュウ every other week

時

N5 Kanji **Time**

Kun	とき、-どき
On	ジ
Radical	日
Strokes	10
Parts	土寸日

間

N5 Kanji **Time**

Kun	あいだ、ま、あい
On	カン、ケン
Radical	門
Strokes	12
Parts	日門

分

N5 Kanji **Time**

Kun	わ.ける、わ.け
On	ブン、フン、ブ
Radical	刀
Strokes	4
Parts	ハ刀

午

N5 Kanji **Time**

Kun	うま
On	ゴ
Radical	十
Strokes	4
Parts	ノ十千乞

前

N5 Kanji **Time**

Kun	まえ、-まえ
On	ゼン
Radical	刀
Strokes	9
Parts	一并刈月

後

N5 Kanji **Time**

Kun	のち、うし.ろ
On	ゴ、コウ
Radical	彳
Strokes	9
Parts	夂幺彳

今

N5 Kanji **Time**

Kun	いま
On	コン、キン
Radical	人(亻)
Strokes	4
Parts	一个

先

N5 Kanji **Time**

Kun	さき、ま.ず
On	セン
Radical	儿
Strokes	6
Parts	ノ儿土

来

N5 Kanji **Time**

Kun	く.る、きた.る
On	ライ、タイ
Radical	木
Strokes	7
Parts	丨二十木米

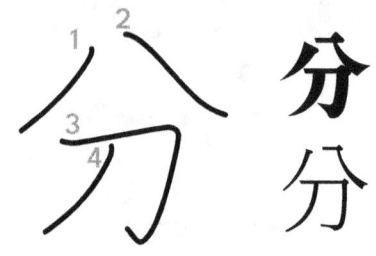

Meaning(s): **part, minute, duty**

分	ブン *portion, share*
分ける	わける *to separate*
分別	フンベツ *discretion*
三十分	さんじゅっぷん *30 minutes*

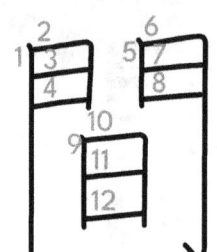

Meaning(s): **interval, space**

間	あいだ *space, distance*
間	カン *interval*
時間	じかん *time, hour*
間違い	まちがい *mistake, error*

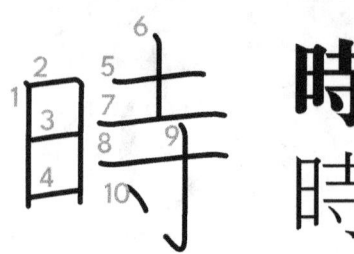

Meaning(s): **time, hour**

時	とき *time, moment*
時	ジ *hour, o'clock*
時計	とけい *clock, timepiece*
時刻表	じこくひょう *timetable*

Meaning(s): **behind, back, later**

後	のち *later, future*
後々	のちのち *distant future*
午後	ごご *afternoon, PM*
後日	ゴジツ *in the future, later*

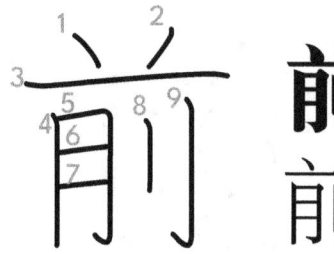

Meaning(s): **in front, before**

前	まえ *in front (of), before*
名前	なまえ *name, given name*
前	ゼン *last..., previous*
前売り	まえうり *adv. sale, booking*

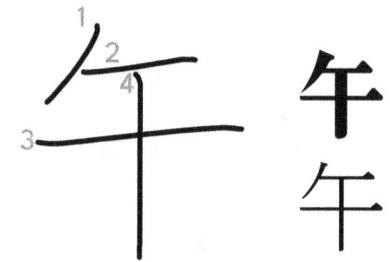

Meaning(s): **noon, sign of Horse**

午後	ゴゴ *afternoon, PM*
午前	ゴゼン *morning, AM*
亭午	テイゴ *noon*
午	うま *sign of the Horse*

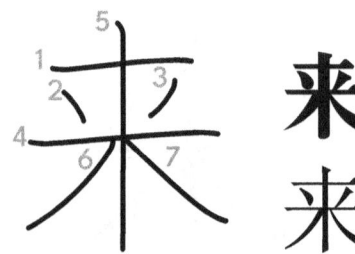

Meaning(s): **come, next, cause**

来	ライ *coming (yr), since*
来月	らいげつ *next month*
来る	くる *to come, to arrive*
出来る	できる *to be able to do*

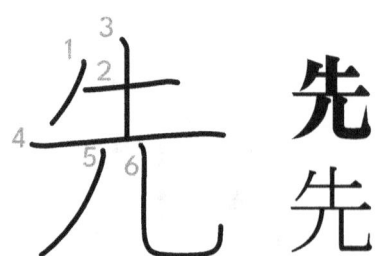

Meaning(s): **before, future**

先	セン *previous, old*
先	さき *point, end, front*
先週	せんしゅう *last week*
先生	せんせい *teacher, master*

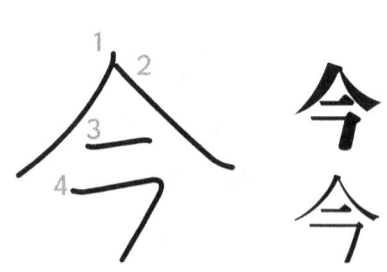

Meaning(s): **now, this, current...**

今	コン *the current..., this,*
今	いま *now, soon*
今晩	こんばん *tonight, this evening*
今朝	こんちょう *this morning*

N5 Kanji **Time**

Kun	なか.ば
On	ハン
Radical	十
Strokes	5
Parts	丨 二 丼 十

N5 Kanji **Time**

Kun	ごと、-ごと.に
On	マイ
Radical	毋 (母, 母)
Strokes	6
Parts	毋 母 乞

N5 Kanji **Time**

Kun	なに、なん、なに-
On	カ
Radical	人 (亻)
Strokes	7
Parts	一 亅 化 口

N5 Kanji **People & Things**

Kun	ひと、-り、-と
On	ジン、ニン
Radical	人 (亻)
Strokes	2
Parts	人

N5 Kanji **People & Things**

Kun	おとこ、お
On	ダン、ナン
Radical	田
Strokes	7
Parts	力 田

N5 Kanji **People & Things**

Kun	おんな、め
On	ジョ、ニョ、ニョウ
Radical	女
Strokes	3
Parts	女

N5 Kanji **People & Things**

Kun	こ、-こ、ね
On	シ、ス、ツ
Radical	子
Strokes	3
Parts	子

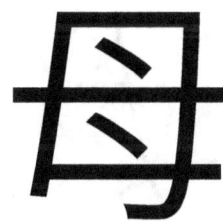

N5 Kanji **People & Things**

Kun	はは、も
On	ボ
Radical	毋 (母)
Strokes	5
Parts	毋 母

N5 Kanji **People & Things**

Kun	ちち
On	フ
Radical	父
Strokes	4
Parts	父

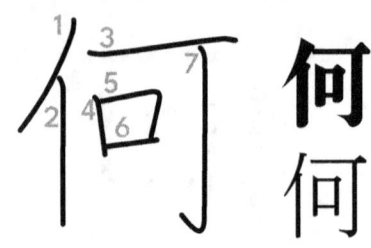 何

Meaning(s): **which, how many**

何	なに *what, that thing*
何	なん *what, how many*
何か	なにか *something, some*
何曜日	なんようび *what day?*

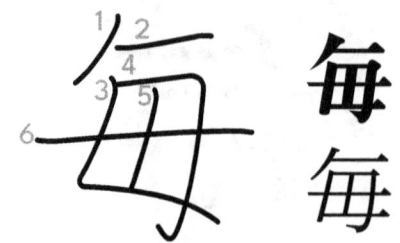 毎

Meaning(s): **every**

毎	ごと *each, every*
毎	マイ *every..., each*
毎日	まいにち *every day*
毎朝	マイアサ *every morning*

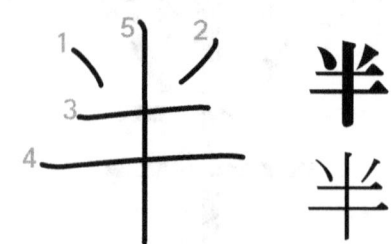 半

Meaning(s): **half, middle, odd no.**

半	ハン *half, odd number*
半分	はんぶん *half*
半ば	なかば *middle, one half*
大半	たいはん *majority, most (of)*

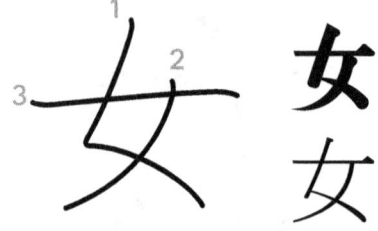 女

Meaning(s): **woman, female**

女	おんな *female, girlfriend*
女王	ジョオウ *queen*
女神	めがみ *female deity*
女の子	おんなのこ *girl, daughter*

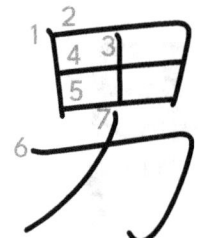 男

Meaning(s): **man, male**

男	おとこ *male, boyfriend*
男女	ダンジョ *men & women*
美男	びなん *handsome man*
男の子	おとこのこ *boy, young man*

 人

Meaning(s): **person**

人	ひと *people*
人	ジン *-ian, -ite, -er*
人々	ひとびと *people*
人	ニン *people counter*

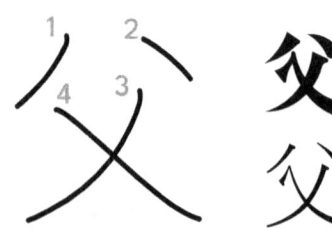 父

Meaning(s): **father**

父	ちち *father*
父母	フボ *parents*
祖父	そふ *grandfather, old man*
祖父母	そふぼ *grandparents*

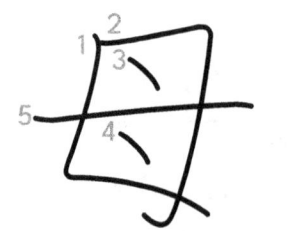 母

Meaning(s): **mother**

母	はは *mother*
父母	フボ *parents*
伯母さん	おばさん *aunt*
お祖母さん	おばあさん *grandmother*

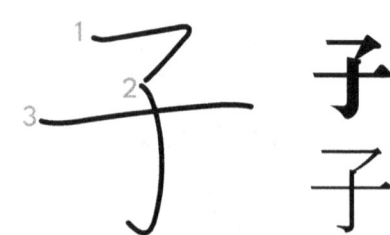 子

Meaning(s): **child, sign of rat**

子	こ *child, kid, teen*
息子	むすこ *son*
子供	こども *child*
帽子	ぼうし *hat, cap*

友

N5 Kanji People & Things

Kun	とも
On	ユウ
Radical	又
Strokes	4
Parts	一ノ又

N5 Kanji People & Things

Kun	ひ、-び、ほ-
On	カ
Radical	火 (灬)
Strokes	4
Parts	火

N5 Kanji People & Things

Kun	みず、みず-
On	スイ
Radical	水 (氵, 氺)
Strokes	4
Parts	水

N5 Kanji People & Things

Kun	き、こ-
On	ボク、モク
Radical	木
Strokes	4
Parts	木

N5 Kanji People & Things

Kun	つち
On	ド、ト
Radical	土
Strokes	3
Parts	土

N5 Kanji People & Things

Kun	かね、かな-、-がね
On	キン、コン、ゴン
Radical	金 (釒)
Strokes	8
Parts	个八并王金

N5 Kanji People & Things

Kun	もと
On	ホン
Radical	木
Strokes	5
Parts	一木

N5 Kanji People & Things

Kun	かわ
On	セン
Radical	巛 (川、巜)
Strokes	3
Parts	川

N5 Kanji People & Things

Kun	はな
On	カ、ケ
Radical	艸 (艹)
Strokes	7
Parts	化匕艾

Meaning(s): **water**

水	みず water, liquid
浄水	ジョウスイ clean water
水泳	すいえい swimming
水曜日	すいようび Wednesday

Meaning(s): **fire**

火	ひ fire, flame
小火	ボヤ small fire
花火	はなび fireworks
火曜日	かようび Tuesday

Meaning(s): **friend**

友	とも friend
友達	ともだち friend, companion
友情	ゆうじょう friendship
友好的	ゆうこうてき friendly, amicable

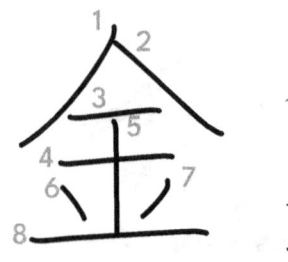

Meaning(s): **gold, money, metal**

金	かね money, metal
金	キン gold, money
納金	ノウキン payment
金曜日	きんようび Friday

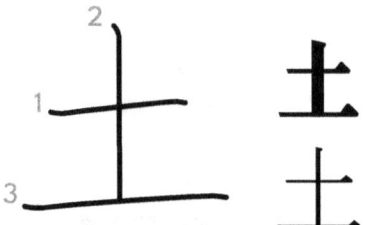

Meaning(s): **soil, earth, ground**

土	つち earth, soil, dirt
土	ド Saturday, ground
土地	トチ plot of land, region
土曜日	どようび Saturday

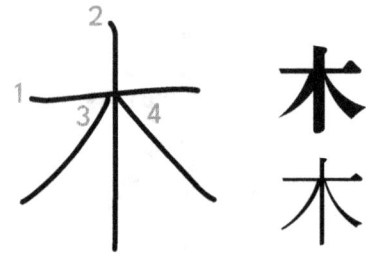

Meaning(s): **tree, wood**

木	き tree, wood, timber
木々	きぎ to be able to
木材	モクザイ lumber, timber
木曜日	もくようび Thursday

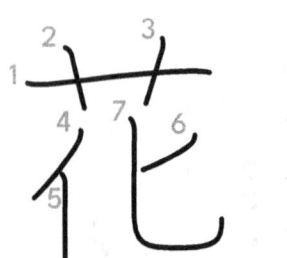

Meaning(s): **flower, blossom**

花	はな flower, blossom
花見	はなみ blossom viewing
花形	ハナガタ flourish
花火	はなび fireworks

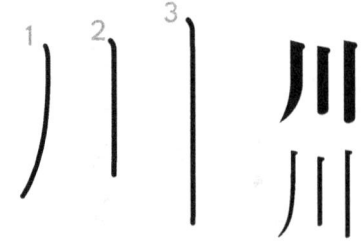

Meaning(s): **stream, river**

川	かわ river, stream
山川	サンセン mountains & rivers
川岸	かわぎし riverbank, riverside
堀川	ほりかわ canal

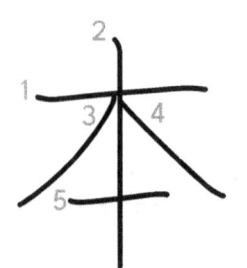

Meaning(s): **book, true, main, real**

本	ホン book, volume, this
本棚	ほんだな bookshelf/case
大本 (元)	おおもと root, origin, cause
日本語	にほんご Japanese (lang.)

気

N5 Kanji — **People & Things**

Kun	き
On	キ、ケ
Radical	气
Strokes	6
Parts	丶ノ气乞

生

N5 Kanji — **People & Things**

Kun	い.きる、い.かす
On	セイ、ショウ
Radical	生
Strokes	5
Parts	生

魚

N5 Kanji — **People & Things**

Kun	うお、さかな
On	ブン、モン
Radical	魚
Strokes	11
Parts	杰田魚

天

N5 Kanji — **People & Things**

Kun	あまつ、あめ
On	テン
Radical	大
Strokes	4
Parts	一二大

空

N5 Kanji — **People & Things**

Kun	そら、あ.く、あ.き
On	クウ
Radical	穴
Strokes	8
Parts	儿宀工穴

山

N5 Kanji — **People & Things**

Kun	やま
On	サン、セン
Radical	山
Strokes	3
Parts	山

雨

N5 Kanji — **People & Things**

Kun	あめ、あま-、-さめ
On	ウ
Radical	雨
Strokes	8
Parts	雨

電

N5 Kanji — **People & Things**

Kun	(none)
On	デン
Radical	雨
Strokes	13
Parts	乙田雨

車

N5 Kanji — **People & Things**

Kun	くるま
On	シャ
Radical	車
Strokes	7
Parts	車

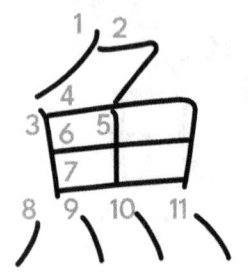
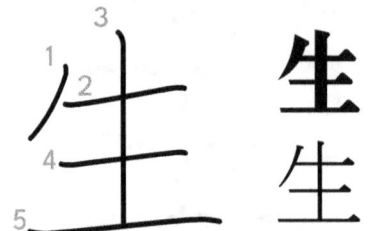

		Meaning(s)	**fish**
魚	さかな *fish*		
魚市場	うおいちば *fish market*		
魚類	ギョルイ *fish, fishes*		
鮮魚	センギョ *fresh fish*		

		Meaning(s)	**life, to live, birth**
生きる	いきる *to live, make living*		
生徒	せいと *pupil, student*		
生	セイ *life, living, me, I*		
先生	せんせい *sensei, teacher*		

		Meaning(s)	**spirit, mind, air,**
気	き / キ *spirit, mind, heart*		
元気	げんき *lively, energetic*		
病気	びょうき *illness, sickness*		
気合	きあい / キアイ *(fighting) spirit*		

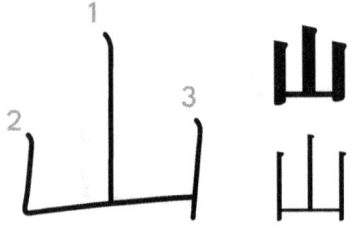
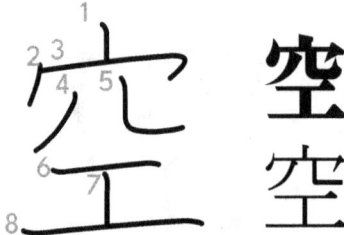
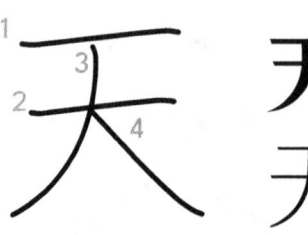

		Meaning(s)	**mountain**
山	やま *mountain, hill*		
山	サン *Mt., Mount*		
火山	さんみゃく *volcano*		
雪山	セツザン *snowy mountain*		

		Meaning(s)	**empty, sky, void**
空	そら *sky, air, weather*		
空	クウ *empty air, sky*		
空き	あき *space, vacancy*		
空港	くうこう *airport*		

		Meaning(s)	**sky, imperial**
天	てんき *weather elements*		
天気	テン *sky, heaven, God*		
天津	あまつ *heavenly, imperial*		
天	あめ *sky*		

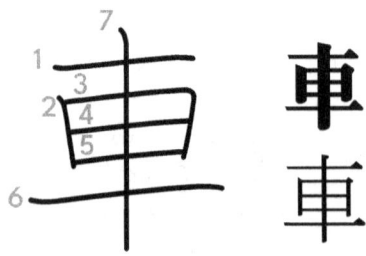
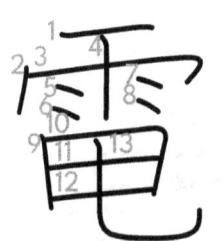
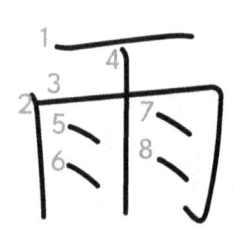

		Meaning(s)	**car, vehicle**
車	くるま *car, vehicle*		
車	シャ *car, vehicle*		
車椅子	くるまいす *wheelchair*		
電車	でんしゃ *electric train*		

		Meaning(s)	**electricity**
電話	でんわ *phone call*		
電池	でんち *battery, cell*		
電化	デンカ *elctrification*		
電気	でんき *electricity*		

		Meaning(s)	**rain**
雨	あめ *rain, rainy weather*		
雨降り	あめふり *rainfall, rainy, wet*		
雨季	ウキ *rainy season*		
雷雨	らいう *thunderstorm*		

語

N5 Kanji — People & Things

Kun	かた.る、かた.らう
On	ゴ
Radical	言 (言)
Strokes	14
Parts	吾

耳

N5 Kanji — People & Things

Kun	みみ
On	ジ
Radical	耳
Strokes	6
Parts	耳

手

N5 Kanji — People & Things

Kun	て、て-、-て、た-
On	シュ、ズ
Radical	手 (扌 、龵)
Strokes	4
Parts	手

足

N5 Kanji — People & Things

Kun	あし、た.りる
On	ソク
Radical	足 (𧾷)
Strokes	7
Parts	口 止 足

目

N5 Kanji — People & Things

Kun	め、-め、ま-
On	モク、ボク
Radical	目
Strokes	5
Parts	目

口

N5 Kanji — People & Things

Kun	くち
On	コウ、ク
Radical	口
Strokes	3
Parts	口 口

名

N5 Kanji — People & Things

Kun	な、-な
On	メイ、ミョウ
Radical	口
Strokes	6
Parts	口 夕

店

N5 Kanji — Direction & Places

Kun	みせ、たな
On	テン
Radical	广
Strokes	8
Parts	卜 口 广

駅

N5 Kanji — Direction & Places

Kun	(none)
On	エキ
Radical	馬
Strokes	14
Parts	丶 尸 杰 馬

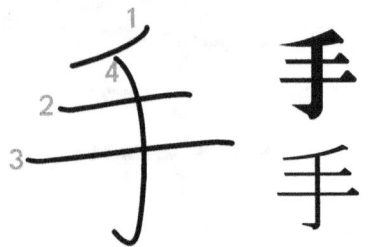

Meaning(s)   **hand**

手	て hand, arm, handle
手紙	てがみ letter, note, mail
手記	シュキ note, memo
切手	きって stamp (postage)

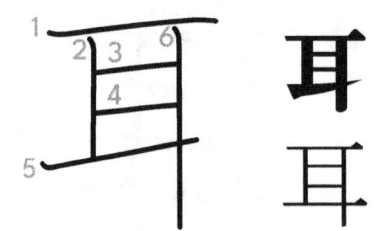

Meaning(s)   **ear**

耳	みみ ear
左耳	ひだりみみ left ear
遠耳	とおみみ sharp hearing
耳障り	みみざわり offensive (to ear)

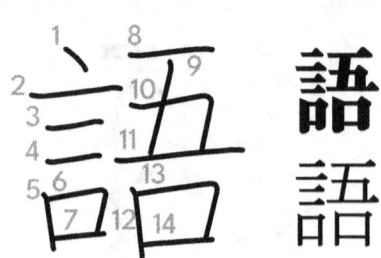

Meaning(s)   **word, language**

語	ゴ word, language
英語	えいご English (language)
語る	かたる to talk about, to tell
語学	ゴガク study of languages

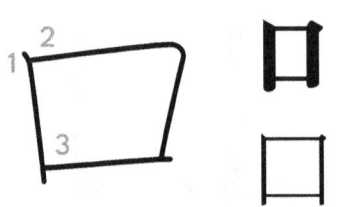

Meaning(s)   **mouth, speech**

口	くち mouth, opening
出口	でぐち exit, way out
人口	じんこう population
大口	おおぐち bragging

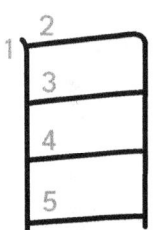

Meaning(s)   **eye, class, look**

目	め eye, eyeball, sight
駄目	だめ useless, broken
目的	もくてき purpose, goal
細目	サイモク particulars, details

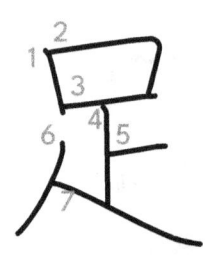

Meaning(s)   **leg, foot**

足	あし foot, paw, leg
足す	たす to add (numbers, things)
足跡	あしあと footprints
足りる	たりる to be enough

Meaning(s)   **station**

駅	エキ train station
駅員	エキイン station attendant
駅前	えきまえ in front of station
終着駅	シュウチャクエキ to go out, leave

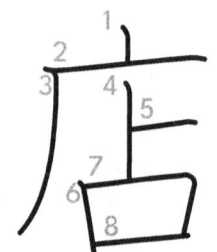

Meaning(s)   **store, shop**

店	みせ store, restaurant
店	テン shop, restaurant
店先	みせさき storefront, shopfront
書店	しょてん bookshop/store

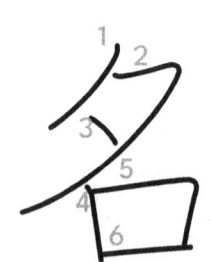

Meaning(s)   **name, reputation**

名	メイ people counter, noun
名前	なまえ given name, title
名画	メイガ famous picture
仮名	かめい alias, pseudonym

道

N5 Kanji — **Direction & Places**

Kun	みち、いう
On	ドウ、トウ
Radical	辵 (辶, 辶, 辶)
Strokes	12
Parts	并込自首

社

N5 Kanji — **Direction & Places**

Kun	やしろ
On	シャ
Radical	示 (ネ)
Strokes	7
Parts	土礼

国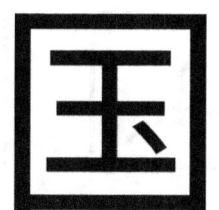

N5 Kanji — **Direction & Places**

Kun	くに
On	コク
Radical	囗
Strokes	8
Parts	丶口王

外

N5 Kanji — **Direction & Places**

Kun	そと、ほか、はず.す
On	ガイ、ゲ
Radical	夕
Strokes	5
Parts	ト夕

学

N5 Kanji — **Direction & Places**

Kun	まな.ぶ
On	ガク
Radical	子
Strokes	8
Parts	冖子尚

校

N5 Kanji — **Direction & Places**

Kun	(none)
On	コウ、キョウ
Radical	木
Strokes	10
Parts	亠木父

上

N5 Kanji — **Direction & Places**

Kun	うえ、-うえ、うわ-
On	ジョウ、シャン
Radical	一
Strokes	3
Parts	一ト

下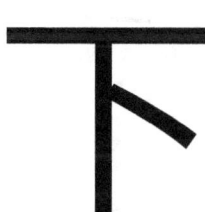

N5 Kanji — **Direction & Places**

Kun	した、しも、もと
On	カ、ゲ
Radical	一
Strokes	3
Parts	一丨ト

中

N5 Kanji — **Direction & Places**

Kun	なか、うち、あた.る
On	チュウ
Radical	丨
Strokes	4
Parts	丨口

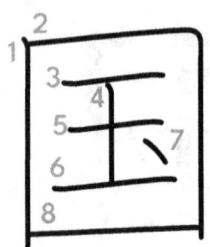 国
Meaning(s): **country, state**

国	くに country, region
国語	こくご national language
国益	コクエキ national interest
外国人	がいこくじん foreigner

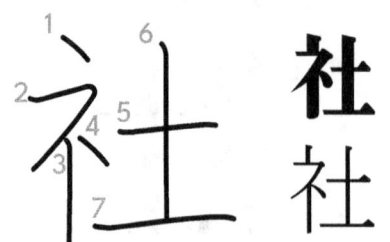 社
Meaning(s): **company, office**

社	やしろ (shinto) shrine,
社	シャ company, society
社長	しゃちょう company president
社会	しゃかい public, the world

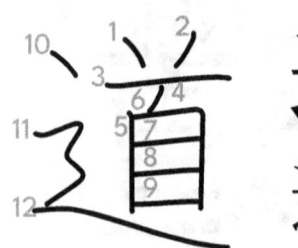 道
Meaning(s): **street, path, way**

道	みち road, path, street
道具	どうぐ tool, instrument
道筋	みちすじ route, itinerary
道	ドウ road, route, way

 校
Meaning(s): **exam, school**

校	コウ school
学校	がっこう school
高校	こうこう senior/high school
校長	こうちょう principal, head

 学
Meaning(s): **study, learning**

学ぶ	まなぶ to study, to learn
大学	だいがく university, college
学	ガク learning, scholarship
学位	ガクイ (academic) degree

 外
Meaning(s): **outside**

外	そと outside, exterior
外	ガイ outside of
外国	がいこく foreign country
海外	かいがい abroad, overseas

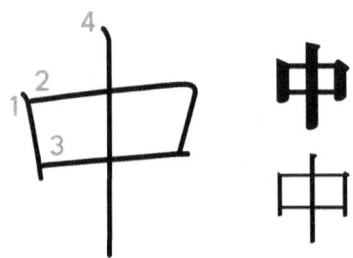 中
Meaning(s): **in, inside, middle**

中	なか inside, center
中	チュウ medium, average
日中	にっちゅう daytime
中心	ちゅうしん middle, core, focus

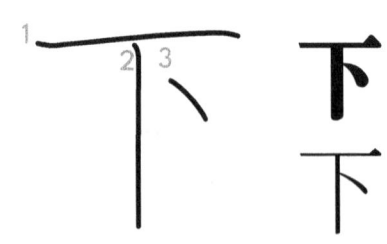 下
Meaning(s): **down, below**

下	した below, down, under
靴下	くつした socks, stockings
下る	くだる descend, go down
地下鉄	ちかてつ underground train

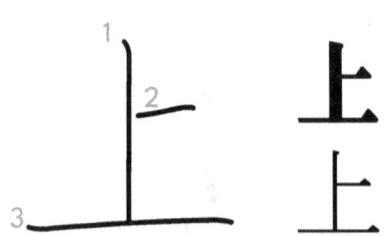 上
Meaning(s): **above, up**

上	うえ above, up, over, top
上	ジョウ as a matter of (fact)
上げる	あげる to raise, to elevate
上着	うわぎ coat, jacket

北

N5 Kanji **Direction & Places**

Kun	きた
On	ホク
Radical	匕
Strokes	5
Parts	匕 爿

西

N5 Kanji **Direction & Places**

Kun	にし
On	セイ、サイ、ス
Radical	西 (襾, 覀)
Strokes	6
Parts	西

東

N5 Kanji **Direction & Places**

Kun	ひがし
On	トウ
Radical	木
Strokes	9
Parts	一 丨 日 木 田

南

N5 Kanji **Direction & Places**

Kun	みなみ
On	ナン、ナ
Radical	十
Strokes	9
Parts	丼 冂 十 干

右

N5 Kanji **Direction & Places**

Kun	みぎ
On	ウ、ユウ
Radical	口
Strokes	5
Parts	一 ノ 口

左

N5 Kanji **Direction & Places**

Kun	ひだり
On	サ、シャ
Radical	工
Strokes	5
Parts	一 ノ 工

見

N5 Kanji **Verbs**

Kun	み.る、み.える
On	ケン
Radical	見
Strokes	7
Parts	儿 目 見

聞

N5 Kanji **Verbs**

Kun	き.く、き.こえる
On	ブン、モン
Radical	耳
Strokes	14
Parts	耳 門

書

N5 Kanji **Verbs**

Kun	か.く、-が.き、-がき
On	ショ
Radical	日
Strokes	10
Parts	日 聿

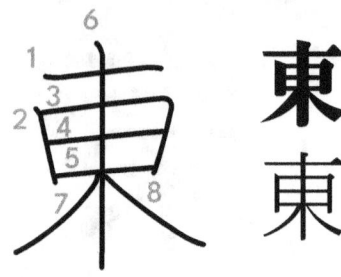

Meaning(s): **east**

東	ひがし *east*
東京	とうきょう *Tokyo*
東方	とうほう *eastern direction*
東欧	トウオウ *Eastern Europe*

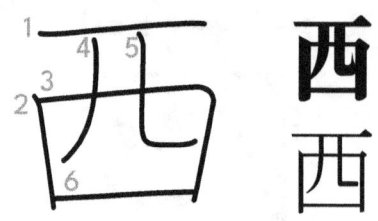

Meaning(s): **west, Spain**

西	にし *west*
西方	せいほう *western direction*
西	セイ *Spain, Spanish*
西洋	せいよう *the West*

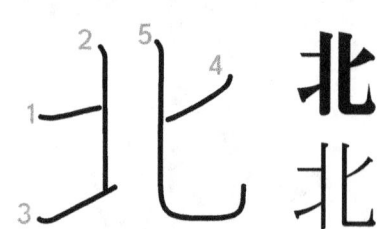

Meaning(s): **north**

北	きた *north, the North*
西北	せいほく / セイホク *north-west*
北欧	ホクオウ *Northern Europe*
北海道	ほっかいどう *Hokkaidou*

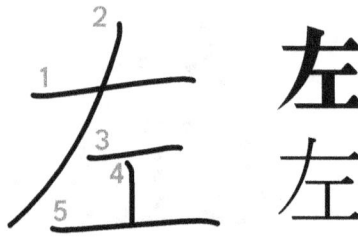

Meaning(s): **left (hand side)**

左	ひだり *left*
左利き	ひだりき *left-handed person*
左右	サユウ *left and right*
左手	ひだりて *left hand*

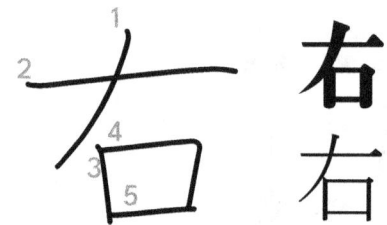

Meaning(s): **right (hand side)**

右	みぎ *right*
右腕	みぎうで *right arm/handed*
最右	サイウ *right-most*
左右	サユウ *left and right*

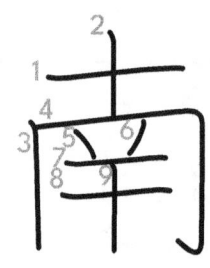

Meaning(s): **south**

南	みなみ *south-east*
東南	とうなん / トウナン *south-west*
西南	せいなん / セイナン *southern sea*
南海	ナンカイ *south*

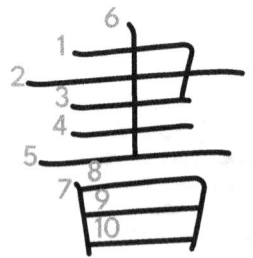

Meaning(s): **to write**

辞書	じしょ *dictionary*
書く	かく *to write, draw*
書	ショ *book, document*
図書館	としょかん *library*

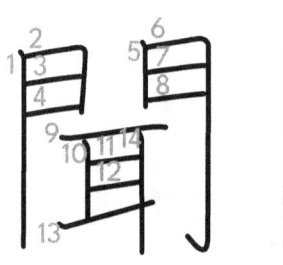

Meaning(s): **listen, hear, ask**

新聞	しんぶん *newspaper*
見聞	けんぶん *information*
聞く	きく *to hear/listen*
聞こえる	きこえる *to be heard*

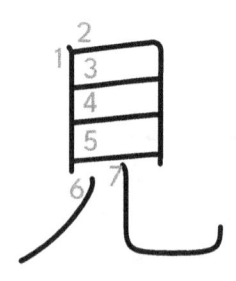

Meaning(s): **see, hopes, idea**

見せる	みせる *to show, to display*
見る	みる *to see*
見解	ケンカイ *point of view*
花見	はなみ *blossom viewing*

読

N5 Kanji **Verbs**

Kun	よ.む、-よ.み
On	ドク、トク、トウ
Radical	言 (言)
Strokes	14
Parts	儿 亠 士 言

話

N5 Kanji **Verbs**

Kun	はな.す、はなし
On	ワ
Radical	言 (言)
Strokes	13
Parts	口 舌 言

買

N5 Kanji **Verbs**

Kun	か.う
On	バイ
Radical	貝
Strokes	12
Parts	八 目 買 貝

行

N5 Kanji **Verbs**

Kun	い.く、ゆ.く、-ゆ.き
On	コウ、ギョウ、アン
Radical	行
Strokes	6
Parts	彳 行

出

N5 Kanji **Verbs**

Kun	で.る、-で、だ.す
On	シュツ、スイ
Radical	凵
Strokes	5
Parts	丨 山 凵

入

N5 Kanji **Verbs**

Kun	い.る、-い.る、-い.り
On	ニュウ、ジュ
Radical	入
Strokes	2
Parts	入

休

N5 Kanji **Verbs**

Kun	やす.む、やす.まる
On	キュウ
Radical	人 (亻)
Strokes	6
Parts	化 木

食

N5 Kanji **Verbs**

Kun	く.う、た.べる
On	ショク、ジキ
Radical	食 (飠)
Strokes	9
Parts	食

飲

N5 Kanji **Verbs**

Kun	の.む、-の.み
On	イン、オン
Radical	食 (飠)
Strokes	12
Parts	欠 食

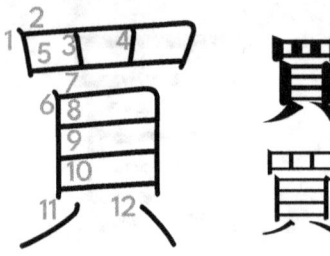

Meaning(s): **to buy**

買い物	かいもの shopping
買う	かう to buy/purchase
不買	フバイ not buying
買収	バイシュウ acquisition

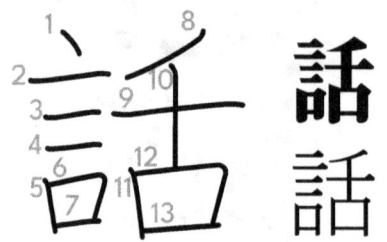

Meaning(s): **to talk**

話す	はなす to talk
会話	かいわ conversaton, chat
電話機	でんわき telephone
電話	でんわ telephone call

Meaning(s): **to read**

読む	よむ to read, to guess
読者	ドクシャ reader
読書	ドクショ reading (a book)
読み方	よみかた pronunciation

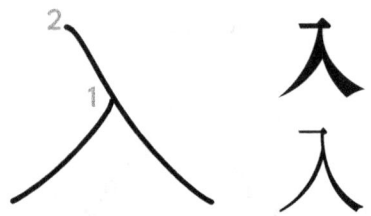

Meaning(s): **to go in, to enter**

入口	いりぐち entrance, entry
入る	いる to get in, to go in
押入れ	おしいれ wardrobe, closet
入学	にゅうがく admission (school)

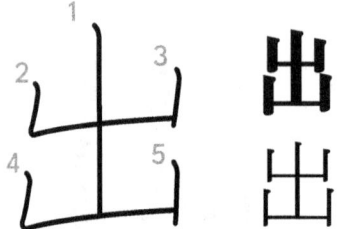

Meaning(s): **exit, leave, go out**

出る	でる to leave, exit
出来る	できる to be able to
出す	だす to take out
出かける	でかける to leave

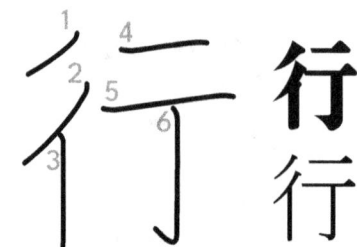

Meaning(s): **going, carry out**

銀行	ぎんこう bank
行く	いく go/move (toward)
旅行	りょこう travel, trip, journey
飛行機	ひこうき aeroplane, aircraft

Meaning(s): **drink, take**

飲み物	のみもの beverage, drink
飲む	のむ to drink
飲食	インショク food and drink
飲み屋	のみや bar, pub, tavern

Meaning(s): **to eat, food**

食べる	たべる to eat
食堂	しょくどう dining room
食事	しょくじ meal, dinner
食	ショク food

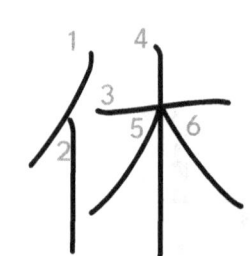

Meaning(s): **rest, day off, sleep**

休む	やすむ to take a day off
休暇	キュウカ day off, holiday
休み	やすみ rest, recess
休める	やすめる to rest, to suspend

N5 Kanji **Verbs**

Kun	い.う、こと
On	ゲン、ゴン
Radical	言
Strokes	7
Parts	言

N5 Kanji **Verbs**

Kun	た.つ、-た.つ、た.ち-
On	リツ、リュウ
Radical	立
Strokes	5
Parts	立

N5 Kanji **Verbs**

Kun	あ.う、あ.わせる
On	カイ、エ
Radical	人(亻)
Strokes	6
Parts	二亇厶

N5 Kanji **Adjectives**

Kun	おお.い、まさ.に
On	タ
Radical	夕
Strokes	6
Parts	夕

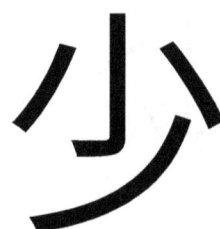

N5 Kanji **Adjectives**

Kun	すく.ない、/こ.し
On	ショウ
Radical	小
Strokes	4
Parts	ノ小

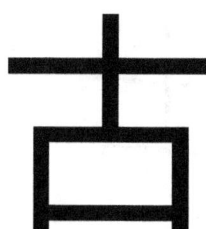

N5 Kanji **Adjectives**

Kun	ふる.い、ふる-
On	コ
Radical	口
Strokes	5
Parts	十口

新

N5 Kanji **Adjectives**

Kun	あたら.しい、あら.た
On	シン
Radical	斤
Strokes	13
Parts	一井斤木立辛

N5 Kanji **Adjectives**

Kun	おお-、おお.きい
On	ダイ、タイ
Radical	大
Strokes	3
Parts	大

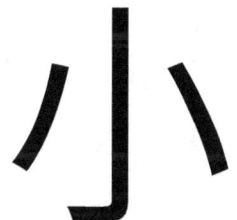

N5 Kanji **Adjectives**

Kun	ちい.さい、こ-、お-
On	ショウ
Radical	小
Strokes	3
Parts	小

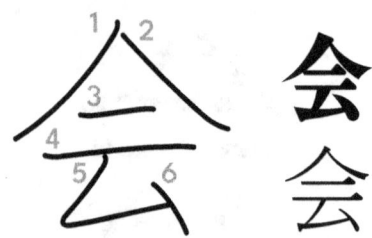

Meaning(s): **meeting, party**

会社	かいしゃ company, workplace
会う	あう to meet, encounter
会釈	エシャク slight bow, nod
会	カイ / エ meeting/gathering

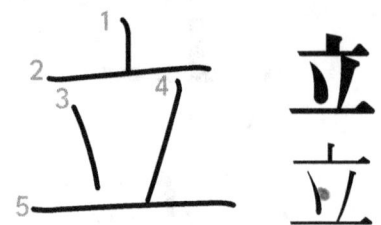

Meaning(s): **stand, rise, set up**

立つ	たつ to stand (up)
独立	どくりつ independence
立派	りっぱ splendid, fine
役に立つ	やくにたつ to be useful

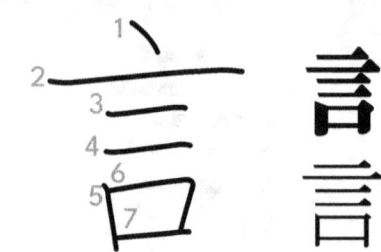

Meaning(s): **to say, word**

言う	いう to say
言葉	ことば language, dialect
過言	カゴン exaggeration
助言	じょげん advice, counsel

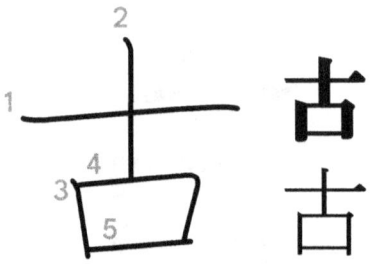

Meaning(s): **old, aged, ancient**

古い	ふるい old, ancient
中古	ちゅうこ used, second-hand
稽古	けいこ practice, study
故郷	ふるさと birthplace

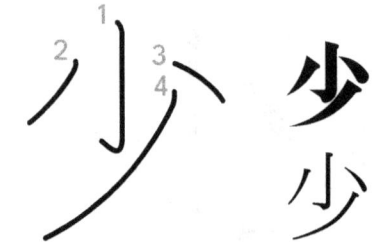

Meaning(s): **few, little**

少ない	すくない few, a little
少年	しょうねん boy, lad, youth
少女	しょうじょ girl, young lady
最小限	さいしょうげん minimum, lowest

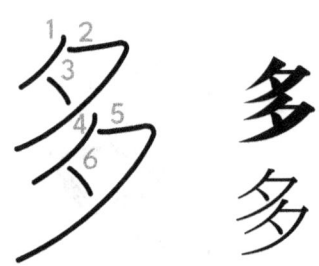

Meaning(s): **many, frequent, much**

多い	おおい many
多分	たぶん perhaps, probably
滅多に	めったに rarely, seldom
多彩	たさい colorful

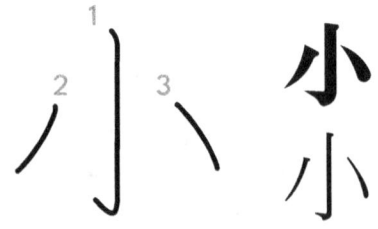

Meaning(s): **little, small, tiny**

小さい	ちいさい little, small
小屋	こや hut, cabin
小指	こゆび pinky/little finger
小学校	しょうがっこう elementary school

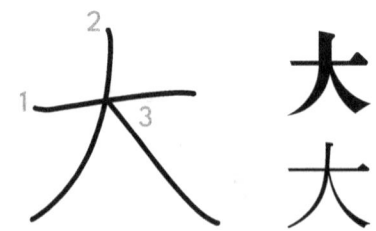

Meaning(s): **big, important**

大きい	おおきい big, large, loud
大変	たいへん very, immense
大学	だいがく university, college
大事	だいじ important, serious

Meaning(s): **new, fresh, recent**

新聞	しんぶん newspaper
新しい	あたらしい new, recent
新人	しんじん new face, recruit
新幹線	しんかんせん bullet train

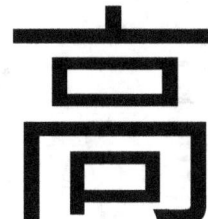

N5 Kanji **Adjectives**

Kun	やす.い、やす.まる
On	アン
Radical	宀
Strokes	6
Parts	女 宀

N5 Kanji **Adjectives**

Kun	たか.い、たか
On	コウ
Radical	高 (髙)
Strokes	10
Parts	亠 冂 口 高

N5 Kanji **Adjectives**

Kun	なが.い、おさ
On	チョウ
Radical	長 (镸)
Strokes	8
Parts	長

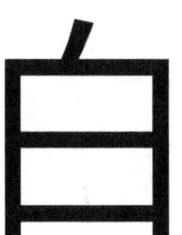

N5 Kanji **Adjectives**

Kun	しろ、しら-、しろ.い
On	ハク、ビャク
Radical	白
Strokes	5
Parts	白

JLPT Level

Kun	
On	
Radical	
Strokes	
Parts	

JLPT Level

Kun	
On	
Radical	
Strokes	
Parts	

JLPT Level

Kun	
On	
Radical	
Strokes	
Parts	

JLPT Level

Kun	
On	
Radical	
Strokes	
Parts	

JLPT Level

Kun	
On	
Radical	
Strokes	
Parts	

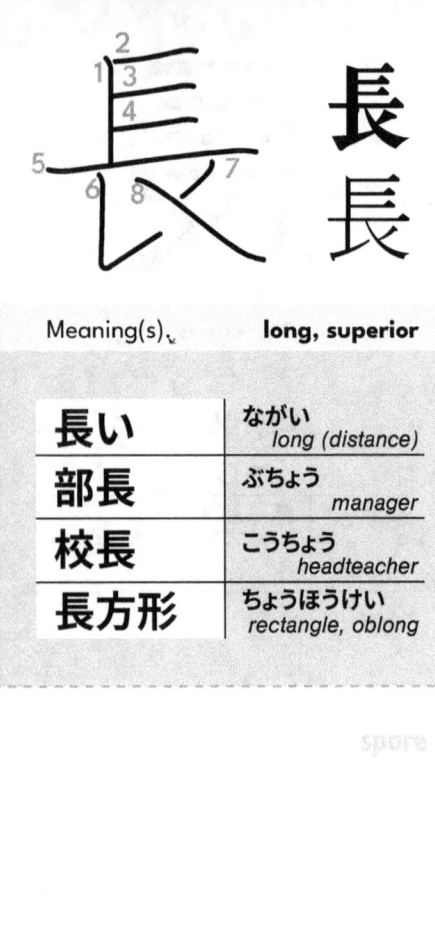
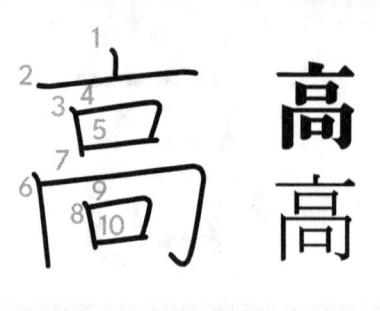

Meaning(s): **long, superior**

長い	ながい *long (distance)*
部長	ぶちょう *manager*
校長	こうちょう *headteacher*
長方形	ちょうほうけい *rectangle, oblong*

Meaning(s): **tall, high, expensive**

高い	たかい *expensive*
高校	こうこう *senior, high school*
高める	たかめる *to raise, to lift*
名高い	なだかい *famous*

Meaning(s): **relax, cheap, low**

安い	やすい *cheap*
安全	あんぜん *safety, security*
安易	あんい *easy, simple*
安らか	やすらか *peaceful, calm*

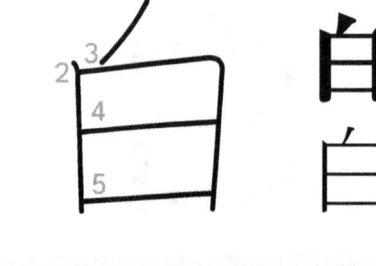

Meaning(s):

Meaning(s):

Meaning(s): **white, innocence**

白い	しろい *white*
面白い	おもしろい *interesting*
青白い	あおじろい *pale*
告白	こくはく *admission*

Meaning(s):

Meaning(s):

Meaning(s):

spare	spare	spare

JLPT Level		JLPT Level		JLPT Level	
Kun		**Kun**		**Kun**	
On		**On**		**On**	
Radical		**Radical**		**Radical**	
Strokes		**Strokes**		**Strokes**	
Parts		**Parts**		**Parts**	

spare	spare	spare

JLPT Level		JLPT Level		JLPT Level	
Kun		**Kun**		**Kun**	
On		**On**		**On**	
Radical		**Radical**		**Radical**	
Strokes		**Strokes**		**Strokes**	
Parts		**Parts**		**Parts**	

spare	spare	spare

JLPT Level		JLPT Level		JLPT Level	
Kun		**Kun**		**Kun**	
On		**On**		**On**	
Radical		**Radical**		**Radical**	
Strokes		**Strokes**		**Strokes**	
Parts		**Parts**		**Parts**	

Meaning(s)

Meaning(s)

Meaning(s)

Meaning(s)

Meaning(s)

Meaning(s)

Meaning(s)

Meaning(s)

Meaning(s)

Answer Key

Check your responses to the kana revision quizzes here:

Page					Page				
029	あう	au	あい	ai	037	あい	oi	あう	au
	いえ	ie	あお	ao		うえ	ue	こえ	koe
	おい	oi	ああ	aa		お	o	かく	kaku
	うえ	ue	いい	ii		きく	kiku	おけ	oke
	いう	iu	おう	ou		こけ	koke	かお	kao
						いけ	ike	あき	aki
						かう	kau	いう	iu
						えき	eki	あかい	akai
						いく	iku	あおい	aoi
						ここ	koko	きおく	kioku
Page					Page				
054	すし	sushi	とち	tochi	068	なに	nani	きぬ	kinu
	つち	tsuchi	うた	uta		ほね	hone	ほし	hoshi
	そと	soto	かた	kata		ぬの	nuno	ひと	hito
	さけ	sake	しち	shichi		ひふ	hifu	のき	noki
	こと	koto	さす	sasu		へた	heta	にし	nishi
	くつ	kutsu	あした	ashita		はな	wana	はいく	waiku
	かこ	kako	とおい	tooi		ふね	fune	かたな	katana
	てつ	tetsu	きせつ	kisetsu		かに	kani	せいふ	seifu
	せき	sato	さとい	satoi		ひな	hina	いのしし	inoshishi
	たつ	tatsu	ちかてつ	chikatetsu		はし	washi	へいそつ	heisotsu
Page					Page				
080	やま	yama	むね	mune	093	わん	wan	さくら	sakura
	ゆめ	yume	きもの	kimono		てら	tera	うちわ	uchiwa
	よむ	yomu	さしみ	sashimi		つる	tsuru	まつり	matsuri
	もも	momo	ゆかた	yukata		これ	kore	ほたる	hotaru
	みや	miya	えまき	emaki		ふろ	furo	ふとん	futon
	こめ	kome	みこし	mikoshi		のり	nori	れきし	rekishi
	つゆ	tsuyu	うきよえ	ukiyoe		はる	haru	わふく	wafuku
	むし	mushi	せともの	setomono		れい	rei	りろん	riron
	まつ	matsu	すきやき	sukiyaki		しろ	shiro	ひのまる	hinomaru
	うめ	ume				にほん	nihon	さむらい	samurai
Page					Page				
124	カツ	katsu	コーチ	kōchi	160	ヘリ	heri	タイヤ	taiya
	アイス	aisu	ソース	sōsu		メモ	memo	カメラ	kamera
	ケーキ	kēki	スキー	sukī		ヒレ	hire	ネーム	nēmu
	アウト	auto	タクシー	takushī		ミルク	miruku	ユーモア	yūmoa
	サーチ	sāchi	ステーキ	sutēki		カヌー	kanū	サラリー	sararī
	コート	kōto	セーター	sētā		ワニス	wanisu	ハンマー	hanmā
	ツアー	tsuā	サーカス	sākasu		ローン	rōn	ヨーヨー	yōyō
	テスト	tesuto	オーケー	ōkē		ナイフ	naifu	ハンカチ	hankachi
	シーツ	shītsu	エーカー	ēkā		フレー	furē	ユニーク	yunīku
						ノート	nōto	ネクタイ	nekutai

Compare your kanji revision performance against the answers below:

Numbers
Page 224

01	c	10	c
02	b	11	a
03	d	12	b
04	a	13	d
05	b	14	e
06	d	15	d
07	d	16	b
08	e	17	c
09	c	18	d

Time
Page 244

19	e	28	c
20	b	29	c
21	d	30	b
22	c	31	e
23	a	32	d
24	b	33	a
25	a	34	a
26	c	35	b
27	d		

People & Things
Page 278

36	b	45	e
37	d	46	c
38	d	47	d
39	a	48	d
40	b	49	b
41	c	50	a
42	c	51	b
43	e	52	e
44	a	53	b

Places & Directions
Page 312

54	e
55	c
56	e
57	b
58	c
59	a
60	b
61	b
62	d

Verbs
Page 313

63	d
64	a
65	b
66	a
67	e
68	b
69	e
70	c

Adjectives
Page 327

71	a
72	a
73	e
74	d
75	b
76	c
77	b
78	c
79	e

Thank you

Congratulations on your progress with the Japanese language! I really appreciate your choosing it from the selection of other available titles and hope that you found this four-in-one version of the *Japanese Made Simple* series both valuable and enjoyable. I have always aimed to pack my books with lots of practical information that is easy to follow, providing readers with excellent value for money.

This series continues to be a labor of love, but the process of writing and independently publishing books is challenging. While I try to produce accurate language guides, little details are easy to overlook - I would be grateful if you could alert me to any problems or mistakes so that I can promptly fix them for future readers.

Lastly, I need to ask you for a favor.

Nothing would make me happier than for more people to learn Japanese with my books, and it would be really helpful if you could spare a moment to leave your review or feedback on *Amazon*. The hard truth is that we all rely on reviews to guide purchasing decisions, and your positive feedback can make a huge difference to 'the little guys' and writers like me.

Be sure to let me know how I might improve the content or what you would like to see in future follow-up books. *I'll look forward to hearing your thoughts.*

Until next time, *arigatōgozaimasu!*

ありがとうございます!!

Dan.

Learning Japanese Made Simple

Complete Series Workbook Edition (4-in-1 Book)

Learn how to Read, Write, and Speak Japanese with Hiragana, Katakana, & Kanji

Beginner's Guide & Integrated Workbook

Dan Akiyama